D1265709

Oceania
a regional study

Foreign Area Studies
The American University
Edited by
Frederica M. Bunge
and Melinda W. Cooke
Research completed
June 1984

On the cover: Tahitian double war canoe

Second Edition, 1984; First Printing, 1985

Library of Congress Cataloging in Publication Data

Main entry under title:

Oceania, a regional study.

    (Area handbook series) (DA pam ; 550—94)
    "Research completed June 1984."
    Bibliography: p.
    Includes index.
    1. Islands of the Pacific. I. Bunge, Frederica M.
II. Cooke, Melinda W. III. American University
(Washington, D.C.). Foreign Area Studies.
IV. Series. V. Series: DA pam ; 550—94.
DU17.026   1985   990   85–6043

Headquarters, Department of the Army
DA Pam 550–94

Foreword

This volume is one of a continuing series of books prepared by Foreign Area Studies, The American University, under the Country Studies/Area Handbook Program. The last page of this book provides a listing of other published studies. Each book in the series deals with a particular foreign country, describing and analyzing its economic, national security, political, and social systems and institutions and examining the interrelationships of those systems and institutions and the ways that they are shaped by cultural factors. Each study is written by a multidisciplinary team of social scientists. The authors seek to provide a basic insight and understanding of the society under observation, striving for a dynamic rather than a static portrayal of it. The study focuses on historical antecedents and on the cultural, political, and socioeconomic characteristics that contribute to cohesion and cleavage within the society. Particular attention is given to the origins and traditions of the people who make up the society, their dominant beliefs and values, their community of interests and the issues on which they are divided, the nature and extent of their involvement with the national institutions, and their attitudes toward each other and toward the social system and political order within which they live.

The contents of the book represent the views, opinions, and findings of Foreign Area Studies and should not be construed as an official Department of the Army position, policy, or decision, unless so designated by other official documentation. The authors have sought to adhere to accepted standards of scholarly objectivity. Such corrections, additions, and suggestions for factual or other changes that readers may have will be welcomed for use in future new editions.

William Evans-Smith
Director, Foreign Area Studies
The American University
Washington, D.C. 20016

Acknowledgments

The authors are grateful to numerous individuals in various agencies of the United States government and in international, diplomatic, and private organizations in Washington, D.C., who gave of their time, research materials, and special knowledge to provide data and perspective.

The authors also wish to express their gratitude to members of the Foreign Area Studies staff who contributed directly to the preparation of the manuscript. These include Dorothy M. Lohmann, Andrea T. Merrill, Denise Ryan, and Lenny Granger, who edited the manuscript and the accompanying figures and tables; Harriett R. Blood and Gustavo Adolfo Mendoza, who prepared the graphics; Charlotte Benton Pochel, who typed the manuscript; and Margaret Quinn, photocomposer. The authors appreciate as well the assistance provided by Gilda V. Nimer, staff librarian; Ernest A. Will, publications manager; and Eloise W. Brandt and Wayne W. Olsen, administrative assistants, and Rachel Johnson, indexer.

Special thanks are owed to Reiko I. Seekins, who designed the cover and the illustrations for the title page of each chapter. The inclusion of photographs in this study was made possible by the generosity of various individuals and public and private organizations. The authors acknowledge their indebtedness to those who provided original work not previously published, in particular Patricia Luce Chapman, chairperson of the Micronesia Institute in Washington D.C., who shared many photographs of Micronesia.

Contents

Chapter 5. Strategic Perspective ....

Melinda W. Cooke

HISTORICAL BACKGROUND—World War II—The Post-war Era: 1945–75—SECURITY SETTING SINCE 1976—THE ANZUS TREATY AND OTHER SECURITY ARRANGEMENTS—OCEANIA IN STRATEGIC TERMS—The United States—Australia and New Zealand—France—The Soviet Union—THE NUCLEAR ISSUE

Appendix A. Selected Events of World War II Involving the Pacific Ocean ....

Melinda W. Cooke

Appendix B. Regional Organizations ....

Rinn-Sup Shinn

Appendix C. Security Treaty Between Australia, New Zealand, and the United States of America ....

List of Figures

List of Tables

Preface

Oceania: A Regional Study replaces the *Area Handbook for Oceania*, which was researched and written in mid-1970 and published in 1971. At the time of publication of the earlier work, only four of the 19 political entities studied were independent, and the others were associated in varying forms of dependency with Australia, Britain, France, New Zealand, and the United States. In contrast, as of mid-1984 nine of the 20 political entities studied were independent states, and two were self-governing states in free association with New Zealand. The remaining nine were associated in varying degrees of dependency with Britain, Chile, France, New Zealand, and the United States; of these the United States-administered Trust Territory of the Pacific Islands were undergoing political transition to four separate political entities— three self-governing states in free association with the United States and one commonwealth of the United States. In light of these developments, as well as major social and economic changes throughout the region, a new examination of Oceania is warranted.

Oceania has several meanings, but for this study it is defined as an island area bordered by, and including, the island of New Guinea and the United States trust territories on the west; Hawaii and Easter Island on the north and east, respectively; and Australia and New Zealand on the south. This study, however, does not include topical treatment of Australia and its dependencies, New Zealand proper, Hawaii, various uninhabited United States Pacific islands, and the western half of the island of New Guinea, which forms part of Indonesia. These territories may nevertheless be mentioned in the context of overall historical development or strategic interests in the region. It should be noted that although certain areas having special relationships with the United States, such as Guam and American Samoa, might be sensitive about being examined as "foreign," they have been included because it was not possible to look at the whole of Oceania without reference to their important role in the region.

The opening and closing chapters of the study pertain to the region as a whole—the first giving a broad cultural and historical overview of Oceania and the last treating the region from a strategic perspective. The three intervening chapters deal with geographical, historical, social, economic, political, and security aspects of particular contemporary societies. For convenience of organization the study arranges each of the 20 states and territories of Oceania into the appropriate cultural divisions of Melanesia, Micronesia, and Polynesia. This has involved making several choices, resulting for instance in the outlying Polynesian islands of some Melanesian states being treated in the chapter on Melanesia. Appendix A chronicles events involving Oceania during World War II. The organization, aims, and activities of the two major regional groups are addressed in Appendix B. The text of the 1951 Security Treaty Between Australia, New Zealand, and the United States of America (the ANZUS treaty) is found in Appendix C.

After the manuscript for this study was completed, political violence in New Caledonia captured headlines around the world. In the summer of 1984 most of the parties of the Independence Front dissociated themselves from the territory's autonomy statute and formed the Kanaka and Socialist National Liberation Front (Front de la Libération Nationale Kanak et Socialiste—FLNKS). The FLNKS boycotted and seriously disrupted territorial elections held on November 18 and created a provisional government, under the leadership of Jean-Marie Tjibaou, for what it planned to be an independent country called Kanaky. Despite pleas for order from High Commissioner Edgard Pisani, who arrived in early December to renegotiate the autonomy statute, French settlers ambushed and killed two of Tjibaou's brothers and eight other Kanakas on December 5. On January 11, 1985, Kanaka activists killed a white teenager, touching off riots in Nouméa. One day later police shot and killed two important leaders of the provisional government's so-called security forces. The violence prompted French president François Mitterrand to send an additional 1,000 security troops to the area and, unexpectedly, to make a personal visit to the distant territory on January 19. He was met in Nouméa by angry crowds demonstrating their support for French rule. Acts of sabotage and other violence continued in February, and negotiations intensified. Although it seemed that some sort of referendum on limited "independence" would be held by the end of the year, it was less certain that the political violence could be quelled.

Compared with the dramatic events in New Caledonia, developments elsewhere in Oceania were mere ripples of change. In September 1984 France quietly promulgated French Polynesia's autonomy statute, which gave the elected leadership (henceforth headed by a president) control over local government but which failed to mollify the pro-independence opposition groups. During the same month, the people of Palau failed yet again to obtain the three-fourths majority required to approve its

Compact of Free Association with the United States. In October the Solomon Islands electorate continued its tradition of replacing about half of its parliamentary representatives, who in turn voted to replace Prime Minister Solomon Mamaloni with former Prime Minister Peter Tali Kenilorea; almost immediately the new government set about undoing Mamaloni's decentralization of public administration. In American Samoa Governor Peter Coleman gave up his legal battle to run for a third consecutive term, allowing the election of lawyer A.P. Lutali in November. Nearby in Western Samoa the electorate overwhelmingly returned Prime Minister Tofilau Eti Alesana's Human Rights Protection Party to power in February 1985.

The strategic environment in Oceania became somewhat unsettled after David Lange's Labour Party came to power in New Zealand in July 1984. The government refused to allow nuclear-powered vessels or those carrying nuclear weapons to land in the country, forcing a showdown with the United States in February 1985. The United States pulled out of naval exercises scheduled for March, threatened economic reprisals, and curtailed some forms of defense cooperation. Neither side, however, expressed a desire to abrogate the trilateral security agreement known as the ANZUS treaty. Australia, the third member of the alliance, played a middle role between the feuding allies, announcing that it would continue bilateral cooperation with both. The ANZUS countries were agreed in their distrust of the Soviet Union, which was making inroads in the Pacific in 1985 by offering lucrative fisheries agreements to Kiribati and Tuvalu.

Like its predecessor, this study seeks to provide a compact and objective exposition of dominant social, economic, political, and national security aspects of contemporary societies in Oceania. In presenting this new work the authors have relied primarily on official reports of United States government agencies and international organizations and journals, newspapers, and materials reflecting recent field research by indepedent scholarly authorities. Detailed data on many aspects of the societies under study were not always readily available, however. Full references to sources consulted are included in the detailed chapter bibliographies at the end of this book.

Spellings of place-names in this book generally conform to official standard names approved by the United States Board on Geographic Names. For several of the newly independent states, however, these were checked for current usage against the *Atlas of the South Pacific*, published by the External Intelligence Bureau of the Prime Minister's Department of New Zealand, and the list of "Obsolete and Alternative Names for the Pacific Islands" included in the *Pacific Islands Yearbook, 1981*. An effort has been made to limit the use of foreign and technical words in the text, but where this has not been appropriate, such terms have been defined briefly where they first appear in any chapter or reference has been made to the Glossary, which is included for the reader's convenience. English usage follows *Webster's Ninth New Collegiate Dictionary*.

All measurements are in metric terms. The following conversion table will assist those who may not be familiar with metric equivalents.

Table 1. Metric Conversion Coefficients

When you know	Multiply by	To find
Millimeters	0.04	inches
Centimeters	0.39	inches
Meters	3.3	feet
Kilometers	0.62	miles
Hectares (10,000 m)	2.47	acres
Square kilometers	0.39	square miles
Cubic meters	35.3	cubic feet
Liters	0.26	gallons
Kilograms	2.2	pounds
Metric tons	0.98	long tons
	1.1	short tons
	2,204	pounds
Degrees Celsius	9	degrees Fahrenheit
(Centigrade)	divide by 5 and add 32	

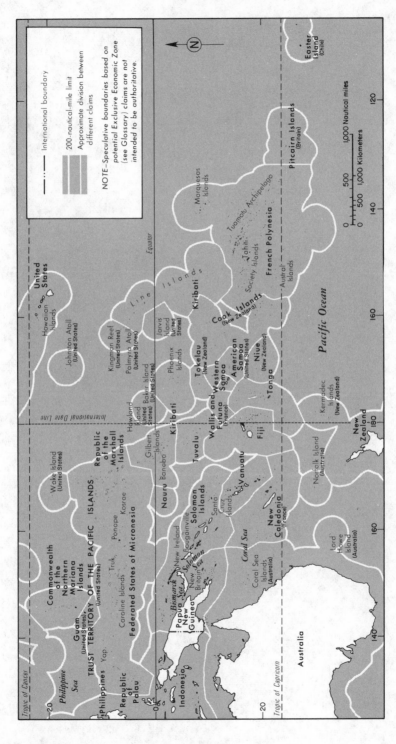

Figure 1. Oceania as an Aquatic Continent, Showing 200-Nautical-Mile Exclusive Economic Zone Claims, 1984

Chapter 1.   Overview

*Outrigger canoe from the Caroline Islands, taken from an 1815
drawing by Louis Choris*

THE SHEER SIZE of Oceania is impressive, as is the scope of the region's contrasts. The Pacific is the biggest and deepest of the world's oceans and is the earth's largest single geographic feature. It occupies more than one-third of the globe's surface, an area greater than all of the world's landmasses lumped together. Within the Pacific region there are about 25,000 islands, more than one-half of the world's total. The discrepancy between land and sea, however, is great. Collectively, the islands comprise somewhat more than 1.6 million square kilometers, but those islands are set in a sea area of more than 88 million square kilometers. The Pacific stretches approximately 16,000 kilometers along the equator, and the north-to-south expanse from the Bering Strait to the Antarctic Circle is about 15,000 kilometers (see fig. 1).

When discussing the cultures and languages of Oceania, anthropologists and linguists usually think of the "insular Pacific" or the "island Pacific" as opposed to the "Pacific rim" or "Pacific basin." The Pacific rim usually refers to the large continental masses and the large nations (or at least their coastlines) that define the ocean's perimeters. The Pacific islands have very few cultural or linguistic connections with the rim as defined in this sense. The term *Pacific basin* is vague and may or may not include both rim and insular land areas.

Most commonly, Western scholars have divided the insular Pacific into three main cultural areas: Melanesia, Micronesia, and Polynesia (see fig. 2). These divisions are somewhat arbitrary and tend to obscure the fact that there are no clear-cut boundaries. Nonetheless, Melanesia, meaning the "black islands," derives from the word *melanin,* which is the chemical in the skin that accounts for dark pigmentation—a characteristic shared by Melanesians. The islands that are clearly Melanesian are, from west to east: the entire island of New Guinea and its outliers to the east; the Solomon Islands; New Caledonia; and the islands that make up Vanuatu (formerly the New Hebrides). Fiji is usually included as part of Melanesia, but in reality it is more of a transition area. The Fijians are primarily of Melanesian racial stock but share much in common culturally with Polynesians. Today Fiji uses this somewhat borderline status to its own political advantage and can align with either Melanesian or Polynesian interests. In brief, Melanesia can be considered to have five components that extend from New Guinea to Fiji, all lying south of the equa-

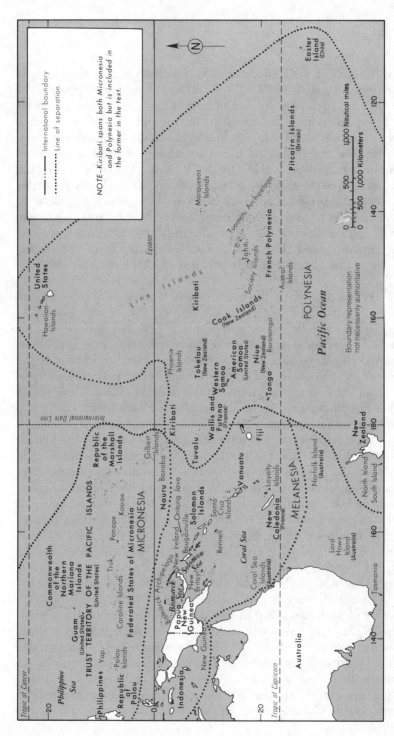

Figure 2.   Melanesia, Micronesia, and Polynesia

tor and west of the international date line (with the exception of a few of Fiji's smaller eastern islands).

Micronesia, meaning the "little islands," lies north of Melanesia and, with a few exceptions, north of the equator. The label "little islands" is appropriate because a majority of Micronesia's more than 2,000 islands are atoll formations. A band known as the Caroline Islands is situated above New Guinea and the Solomons. It includes at least five culturally distinct groups— Palau and Yap in the west and, moving eastwards through the Carolinian atolls, Truk, Ponape, and Kosrae. To the north of the Carolines are the Mariana Islands, the people, language, and culture of which are referred to as Chamorro. The double chain of atolls known as the Marshall Islands forms part of Micronesia's eastern boundary. Another atoll archipelago, the Gilbert Islands (now part of Kiribati), lies to the south and east and extends a few degrees south of the equator. Lastly, the single island of Nauru is southwest of the main body of the Marshalls, also slightly below the equator.

Polynesia ("many islands") is geographically the largest of the Pacific's cultural areas, and distances between island groups are by far the greatest. Polynesia is defined as a triangle drawn from Hawaii in the north, Easter Island in the southeast, and New Zealand in the southwest. However, the western leg of the triangle between New Zealand and Hawaii cannot be a straight line. Using a bit of license, the cartographer must make the line bulge to the west to include Tuvalu (formerly the Ellice Islands) with the rest of Polynesia.

The boundaries between the cultural areas are convenient oversimplifications for the purposes of study. Fiji is one problematic example, and there are others. Although Kiribati, for instance, is always classified as Micronesian, many of its inhabitants exhibit Polynesian cultural traits derived from their Polynesian neighbors of Tuvalu and the Samoa Islands, and many Polynesian words have found their way into the local language, which is without question Micronesian. The elaborate chieftaincies of traditional Ponape and Kosrae in the eastern Carolines of Micronesia have traits that suggest Polynesian influence. At the western end of the Pacific, Palau and Yap appear to have been influenced by Melanesians, and the inhabitants of a few small islands off the north coast of extreme Western New Guinea appear very much like Carolinian atoll dwellers in physical type and material culture; in fact, they have been referred to as para-Micronesians.

All of the above suggests that once the Pacific had been peopled, its inhabitants did not remain in place for the convenience of future observers. After the major movement of peoples into the region, some restless Polynesians moved back in a westerly direction to inhabit islands in Micronesia and Melanesia that are now referred to as Polynesian outliers. The atoll communities of Kapingamarangi and Nukuoro south of Ponape in the eastern Carolines are two such examples in Micronesia. A larger number of Polynesian outliers are found directly south and southwest of Kapingamarangi and Nukuoro between the Solomons and New Caledonia in Melanesia. Numbering over one dozen, the most well-known are Ontong Java, Tikopia, Bellona, and Rennell.

The place of New Zealand and Australia in the insular Pacific deserves special treatment. When considering the pre-European era, all observers agree that the indigenous Maori people of New Zealand were Polynesians who had modified their culture in ways that were adaptive to their homeland's temperate climate. In fact, there is little doubt that the Maori had their origins in the area of the Cook and Society islands. Aborigines of Australia illustrate a different story. Although the ancient ancestors of the Aborigines and the very first settlers of New Guinea appear to have had some connections, the Aborigines became quite isolated from developments in the insular Pacific and pursued their own course of cultural evolution. They remained adamantly attached to a hunting and gathering way of life, while peoples of the insular Pacific became agriculturists. Most Pacific anthropologists do not categorize the Aborigines among the peoples of the Pacific. In the colonial period, the period of decolonization, and the present, however, both Australia and New Zealand must be viewed as major actors in the region. In this context they are modern nation-states located in the Pacific and deeply involved in regional affairs.

Physical Environment

The islands of the insular Pacific are unequally distributed within the vast expanse of ocean, and large portions of it are indeed quite empty. Portuguese explorer Ferdinand Magellan, the first European known to transit the Pacific, discovered this basic fact of geography the hard way. He sighted only a few uninhabited reefs on his journey across the Pacific from South America to the Philippines before he sighted Guam in 1521. Had he missed Guam, he would have thought that the ocean was without human inhabitants.

A discontinuity of underlying rock formations, known as the

Andesite Line, separates the continental islands of the western Pacific from the volcanic basalt islands of the central and eastern Pacific. The Andesite Line runs along the eastern side of the two Polynesian groups of New Zealand and Tonga, to the east and north of Melanesia, and then to the east of the three westernmost groups of Micronesia (Palau, Yap, and the Marianas). The islands lying to the west of the line are composed of mixed rock types characteristic of continental masses. They are markedly deformed by folding and faulting, and they contain ancient metamorphic rocks, such as schist, gneiss, and slate; sediments, such as clay, coal, and sandstone; and intrusive granite and siliceous eruptive rocks, such as andesite. Some geologists believe that the line is the easternmost limit of a continental landmass that once extended from Asia into the Pacific.

The discontinuous line proceeds northward, running east of Japan. It then runs south of the Aleutian Islands and down the western side of the islands that lie off the west coast of the Americas. The area within the loop of the line has been called the "real Pacific basin" and has deep troughs and oceanic volcanic peaks composed primarily of heavy dark basalt. The peaks may be high volcanic islands above the ocean's surface or they may be partially or completely submerged. Upon submerged platforms coral reefs and atolls are found. The average depth of the Pacific Ocean is about 4,200 meters; the extreme depth is about 10,700 meters between Guam and Mindanao.

Island Types

Geographer William Thomas has distinguished four major kinds of islands in the region. There are two kinds of "high" islands: continental and volcanic. The best examples of the former are the large islands of Melanesia, which are characterized by extremely rugged interior mountain ranges, divided plateaus, and precipitous interior valleys. Lower and coastal areas tend to be divided by twisting rivers, alternating swampy areas and coastal plains, or narrow coastal shelves. Significantly, the topography creates barriers that function to keep human populations separated and divided into small linguistic and political communities.

Of the high volcanic islands, those of Hawaii are the most familiar. Steep cliffs and mountain ranges are divided by deep valleys, the floors of the latter usually opening to coastal flat zones of varying widths. Erosion of older islands, especially on their exposed windward sides, has produced gentle slopes. Tahiti and many other islands in the Society and Marquesas islands, as well as Rarotonga in the Cook Islands, are examples of high volcanic islands. Ponape and Kosrae are examples of high volcanic islands in Micronesia. Most islands of this kind have freshwater sources, but volcanic soils are generally poor for agriculture.

Volcanic islands are often surrounded by fringing reefs that may lie at distances anywhere from a relatively few to several hundred meters from the shoreline. The water areas between shore and reef often provide good fishing grounds. Significantly, however, fringing reefs form another major kind of island—atolls.

There are two kinds of "low" islands. First, there is the atoll, a series of islands that are built upward from a coral reef and that typically enclose a central lagoon of varying shape. Charles Darwin first suggested, and most marine biologists today remain convinced, that atolls were once fringing reefs around volcanic islands that have become submerged. The lagoon is situated where the volcanic peak once stood above the water.

The reefs are built by coral and calcareous algae, which thrive in warm, relatively shallow, clear saline water. Coral is the skeleton of a fleshy polyp, a marine creature that secretes lime from seawater. Such polyps live in large colonies, their interconnected skeletons adhering to the calcareous remains of their ancestors. As the volcanic substructures sink, the polyps continue their reefbuilding and eventually become all that remains above the surface. The coral structures lie at extreme depths. Drillings at Eniwetok in the northern Marshalls reached depths of 1,300 to 1,400 meters before the volcanic basalt bedrock was struck.

Atolls can vary in size, from Kwajalein in the Marshalls, which has a lagoon about 145 kilometers long and 32 kilometers wide, to the smallest, which may be no more than two or three kilometers in diameter. The islets of an atoll are seldom more than three to five meters above high-tide level, and land areas are almost dwarfed by lagoon areas. Soil covers are poor and extremely thin, and the only fresh water that is available is rainwater that is either collected or, on some of the larger islands, floats as a thin lens beneath the soil and the denser salt water that permeates the porous coral rock below sea level. The atolls are extremely vulnerable to severe weather disturbances, such as typhoons, unusually high seas, or droughts.

Not all Pacific islands are in the process of subsiding. To the contrary, numerous raised coral atolls are scattered over the region, and they represent the second kind of low island. In such cases the central lagoon has partially or totally disappeared, and the atoll's border has been elevated above the surrounding sea. Examples of raised coral islands are Nauru, Banaba (formerly

*Rabaul on New Britain in Papua New Guinea
is located in the caldera of a collapsed volcano.
In mid-1984 geologists continued
to detect expansion of the floor of the bay,
usually an indication of impending volcanic activity.*
Courtesy Steven R. Pruett

Ocean Island), and Niue.

Truk in the central Carolines is an interesting formation. Its fringing reef is quite extensive, and a number of islets are dispersed over it. The volcanic basalt formation at the center appears still to be in the process of sinking, and well over a dozen small and relatively low islets still dot the lagoon. Thomas describes Truk as an "almost atoll" and lists at least eight different combinations of atolls and reef formations.

Atolls occur in most areas of the Pacific, but some archipelagoes are composed solely of the low islands. As noted, most of the Micronesian islands are atolls. The Marshalls and Kiribati consist exclusively of atolls. In the long stretch from the high islands of Palau and Yap in the west and Ponape in the east, "the almost atoll" of Truk is the only exception to a string of atolls that extends for over 3,200 kilometers. In Polynesia all the islands of Tuvalu, Tokelau, and the Tuamotu Archipelago are low islands, as are most of the Cooks.

Climate

With the major exceptions of New Zealand and Easter Island, the Pacific islands lie within the tropics, and humiditdy is relatively high. Most of the islands have rather uniform and warm year-round temperatures, ranging between nighttime lows near 20°C and highs in the mid- to high twenties. Other variables are quite important. On atolls and the windward side of the higher islands, the warm temperatures and high humidities are somewhat offset by the cooling properties of trade winds. The leeward sides of the high islands and the jungle interiors of the continental islands can be extremely uncomfortable. In contrast, the highlands of the Melanesian islands, particularly New Guinea, can be quite cool, and frost is an occasional threat to crops.

Again, with the exception of New Zealand and Easter Island, there are no abrupt seasonal changes that compare with those in temperate zones. Rather, the year is divided into rainy and dry seasons. North of the equator the heaviest rainfall occurs from June to October and, south of the equator, from November to March. The rainy and dry seasons are directly related to the intensity of the prevailing trade winds. Above the equator the trades come out of the northeast and blow toward the west. Below the equator they come from the southeast, also blowing toward the west.

The trade winds give way to the monsoon winds in the westernmost Pacific, where the alternate cooling and heating of continental Asia produces a seasonal reversal of winds. From November to March the northwest monsoon from Asia brings rain to the western Carolines, New Guinea, and the Solomons. In the summer the southeast monsoon reverses the process.

There are also horizontal zones of wet and dry areas. Some of the heaviest rainfall occurs in a belt that lies between 1°38' and 8°30' north latitude. Rainfall in that region may be as much as 4,500 millimeters annually. North and south of that wet zone is a relatively dry belt that often receives one-third the rainfall of that of the wet zone. Farther north and south of the dry zones, wetter zones are again encountered. Dry spells do occur locally and sometimes across large portions of the area. For example, the atolls south of Ponape in the eastern Carolines experience occasional annual droughts.

The atolls are always more vulnerable to the vagaries of weather because their landmasses are too small to affect meteorological conditions. In contrast, high islands intervene to help shape their own weather system. Hot and humid air rises from the larger landmasses, mixing with the cooler air of higher elevations to form clouds and rainfall. As a consequence, the windward sides of high islands are the first to interact with the incoming trade winds to produce rain. Windward sides receive the most rainfall, have the greatest amount of erosion, and often have the richest and deepest soil covers. The leeward side is generally dry.

The most serious storms in the region are cyclonic storms known as typhoons or hurricanes. Their causes are only partially understood, but they are usually generated in the east and move westward. The winds that spiral around the center of these storms have velocities commonly ranging from about 25 to more than 115 kilometers per hour. Those that cause great destruction and often denude and reshape the configuration of entire atolls have been clocked at over 250 kilometers per hour. Typhoons can occur at any time of the year, but they are most frequent during the rainy season.

Resources

Mineral deposits occur only on the larger continental islands. It has long been known that New Caledonia possesses large amounts of nickel and some chrome and cobalt. Nickel has been the mainstay of that island's economy for years. Fiji has had a gold-mining operation of modest scale. Otherwise, and until quite recently, the mineral resources of the Pacific have been described as extremely limited. It now appears, however, that such a conclusion was premature. The picture began to change in the 1960s and 1970s with the development of an open-pit copper mine on Bougainville in Papua New Guinea. In mid-1984 the Bougainville mine was one of the largest in the world. Copper has also been found in several other areas of mainland Papua New Guinea, but these deposits had yet to be developed as of the mid-1980s.

Major gold deposits have recently been found in Papua New Guinea, and the Ok Tedi mine in the western part of the nation promised to be a major gold producer throughout the 1980s. After 1990 it is projected that Ok Tedi will be mined for copper as well as gold; the lode contains lesser quantities of other metals as well. Smaller gold deposits have been found elsewhere, and it was possible that Papua New Guinea was on the brink of a gold rush in the mid-1980s.

Explorations in Fiji in 1983 produced a major new gold find. This, as well as the recent discoveries in Papua New Guinea, suggests that there may be room for considerable optimism for similar finds throughout the rest of Melanesia, whose islands share a common geological history. Attempts were under way in 1984 to launch a program to train local geologists to conduct more thorough searches of their home islands.

In 1983 oil was struck in the southern Highlands of Papua New Guinea. The oil is of extraordinarily high quality, and the field is estimated to hold 100 million barrels. Elsewhere, explorations for oil have occurred mainly off the coastal areas of Papua New Guinea, Fiji, and Tonga. As of 1984 none had yielded positive results, but further exploration was focused off the north coast of Papua New Guinea.

Although a brighter picture was developing in Melanesia, there was no reason for such optimism elsewhere. The relatively new volcanic islands rarely contain workable mineral deposits. The only valuable mineral deposits sometimes found on coral islands are phosphate rock. The raised atolls of Banaba and Nauru have been major producers, but the supplies of the former were exhausted, and it was predicted that those of the latter would be depleted within a decade or less.

The flora and fauna of the region are derived from Southeast Asian sources, and the number of species rapidly declines eastward across the Pacific. Prior to human occupation, birds helped to vegetate islands by carrying plant seeds and depositing their droppings on barren landscapes. Other seeds were carried by winds and ocean currents. Humans facilitated the process when they migrated into the area, bringing with them most plants needed for subsistence. Coconuts, breadfruit, pandani (screw pines), bananas, papayas, and tuberous crops, such as taro and yams, were brought from insular Southeast Asia. The full inventory of subsistence crops is usually found only on high islands, and some dry atolls support only coconuts, pandani, and arrowroot— all in all an extremely limited fare.

Such atolls could not have supported human habitation had it not been for the abundant marine life found in lagoons and the surrounding ocean. Lagoons and reef areas provide fish, lobsters, shrimps, eels, octopuses, bivalves, and other sea creatures. Tuna, bonito, and other large fish are caught at sea.

Terrestrial fauna is relatively limited. Bats, rats, and, in New Guinea, a variety of marsupials were the only mammals to precede humans into the western Pacific. Early human migrations helped carry the rat eastward, as well as to introduce pigs, dogs, and chickens. Snakes and lizards are found on most islands, but crocodiles are limited to New Guinea and Palau in the west. Many seabirds provide a minor part of the diet.

The introduction of different species of plants and animals since European times brought further alterations to island ecologies. Cash crops, such as cacao, coffee, vanilla, sugar, pineapple, and citrus fruits were added to the plant inventory. Goats, deer, horses, and cattle are now at home on many high islands.

Prehistory

The Pacific region is distinguished by being "last" in several important respects. It was the last major world area to be occupied by human beings. Hundreds of years after the ancestors of today's Pacific islanders had reached almost every landmass in the vast ocean, it became the last major area of the world to be probed by representatives of the Western world. The Pacific was also the last major world area to experience colonization at the hands of Western powers and the last major area of the globe to achieve independence and/or self-government. The process began when Western Samoa gained its independence in 1962, and it was almost complete as of the mid-1980s.

The region was also one of the last to be investigated by archaeologists. With the exception of New Zealand, there were no scientific archaeological excavations until after World War II, and well into the 1960s knowledge of Pacific prehistory was still in its infancy. In the last two decades, however, research in archaeology and linguistics has accumulated to the extent that the early movements of Pacific peoples can be outlined with a reasonable degree of confidence. Such confidence is warranted in that the data from archaeological and linguistic research complement each other and point to the same general conclusions.

By 40,000 years ago and perhaps as early as 50,000 years ago, populations of hunters and gatherers had managed to reach Australia and New Guinea from regions in insular Southeast Asia. Distances of open water separating Australia and New Guinea from island Southeast Asia at the time were less than today because of the lower sea levels associated with the Ice Ages of the Pleistocene era. Nonetheless, it appears that the immigrants still had a minimum of 70 kilometers of open water to cross before they could colonize the virgin territories. (As a point of comparison, human populations were not established on Crete and Cyprus in the Mediterranean until about 8,000 years ago, and Cyprus is about 80 kilometers from the mainland.)

Oceania: A Regional Study

It appears that the first people who entered the area were the
direct ancestors of modern Australoids. The latter are the
Aborigines of Australia, the Highlands peoples of New Guinea,
and almost certainly the Negritos found in the interiors of
Malaysia and the Philippines. The Melanesians of today are basically Australoid, but some reveal a genetic complexity that resulted from mixtures with later arrivals in the region.

By 6,000 years ago the Australoids had reached the nearby islands of New Britain and New Ireland and perhaps the Solomons.
By 4,000 years ago they had probably reached New Caledonia and
Vanuatu. Reflecting the great length of time they were in the islands, their languages became widely diversified. It has proved
impossible to trace or demonstrate past relationships that may
have existed with many of today's languages. Collectively, they
are referred to as Papuan languages, but this is a catchall category
and should not be mistaken for a language family as such.

Somewhere around 5,000 years ago, a second movement of
people in insular Southeast Asia began. These people were of a
Mongoloid racial stock and were speakers of related languages
that form the Austronesian (formerly known as the Malayo-
Polynesian) language family. Linguists' reconstruction of proto-
Austronesian vocabulary indicates that the early Austronesian
speakers made pottery, built seagoing outrigger canoes, and practiced a variety of fishing techniques. Eventually, the Austronesians came to dominate all of insular Southeast Asia, pushing
westward through the Indian Ocean as far as Madagascar off the
coast of Africa and crossing the entire Pacific to become the ancestors of Micronesians and Polynesians.

It appears that the movement of Austronesians into the
Pacific first began with settlement along the northern coast of
New Guinea. Later, it seems that they moved directly from insular Southeast Asia into the three westernmost archipelagoes of
Micronesia—Palau, Yap, and the Marianas, which lie due north
of New Guinea. Between 3,500 and 3,000 years ago, the Lapita
culture (named after a site in New Caledonia) appeared in the archaeological record all across Melanesia. Distinct forms of pottery
were part of the culture, and evidence shows that its people possessed the navigating skills necessary to move easily back and
forth across Melanesia. Their agricultural system was based almost entirely on tubers and fruits (taro, yams, breadfruit,
bananas, coconuts, and sago palms).

Linguistic evidence indicates that eastern Micronesia was
settled by a northward movement from eastern Melanesia in the
vicinity of Vanuatu. By about 3,000 years ago, Fiji, Tonga, and

14

Samoa had been settled by Lapita people, and thus Polynesia had been penetrated by human beings. During the next thousand years the early forms of Polynesian culture evolved in Tonga and the Samoa Islands. Sometime around the birth of Christ the early Polynesians began their own voyages in large double canoes that could carry the food plants and domestic animals required to found new settlements. The Marquesas Islands in eastern Polynesia were reached by about 300 A.D. Easter Island, one of the most isolated spots on earth, was probably reached a century later. By the end of another 500 years, central Polynesia and the northernmost islands of Hawaii were settled. New Zealand was colonized by around 900 A.D.

Thus, the body of archaeological, botanical, linguistic, and zoological evidence points to insular Southeast Asia as the original homeland for Pacific peoples. There is some evidence that Polynesians had contact with the Pacific coast of South America after the islands were settled, and it appears that they brought the sweet potato back from the area of Peru and Ecuador. Contrary to some popular and fanciful accounts, it is quite certain that Polynesians are not of American Indian ancestry.

Languages

All Pacific languages may be classified either as a member of the Austronesian language family or as one of the Papuan languages, the catchall category that essentially lumps all the non-Austronesian languages. With its distribution from Madagascar to Easter Island, the Austronesian language family is the most widespread in the world. Reflecting the prehistoric migrations of people into the Pacific, all Micronesian languages, all Polynesian languages, and the newer languages in Melanesia (those that are not Papuan) belong to the Austronesian family.

Linguistic diversity in the Pacific is directly related to the length of time that migrants stayed in a particular area. Polynesia, the last to be settled, is linguistically the most homogeneous. Linguists do not agree on the total number of Polynesian languages, however. The languages of each major archipelago and some isolated small islands, such as Niue and Easter, are mutually unintelligible. However, the languages are quite closely related, and Polynesians moving about the area are quick to learn languages other than their own. Bruce Biggs, a linguist and an authority on Polynesian languages, identifies 17 languages within the Polynesian triangle and 11 others among the outliers.

Micronesia is ranked second in its degree of linguistic diversity. The languages of the three westernmost groups, which were settled first and directly out of insular Southeast Asia (Palau, Yap, and the Marianas), form a subgrouping. They reveal a greater antiquity in the area and are quite different from one another. With the exception of the two Polynesian outliers, all other Micronesian languages are classified as "nuclear Micronesian." They share many grammatical and lexical features and appear to reflect their common origin in eastern Melanesia. Again, linguists disagree about the exact number of separate and mutually unintelligible languages. The languages of the Gilberts, the Marshalls, Nauru, Ponape, and Kosrae are distinct. Trukese is a separate language, but disagreement surrounds the languages from Truk and across the Carolinian atolls. Ulithi and Woleai are distinct from Trukese, but whether the languages of the other atolls should be considered separate languages or simply dialects of the same language is disputed.

With its mixture of Austronesian and Papuan languages and greater length of human settlement, Melanesia is linguistically the most complex. The total number of languages may be conservatively estimated to be in the neighborhood of 1,200. Many of the languages are spoken by only a few hundred people at best, and, not surprisingly, language problems have beset all governments in the cultural area. Variations of a Pidgin English, also known as neo-Melanesian, are spoken in Papua New Guinea, the Solomons, and Vanuatu, where it is known as Bislama. It serves as a lingua franca and provides a common bond and identity for the inhabitants of the countries. In Papua New Guinea another lingua franca, known as Motu or Police Motu, was in use in the southern part of the country, but it is less common than the pidgin and may be declining in popularity.

Traditional Societies

The cultures that had evolved in the Pacific by the time of European contact exhibited considerable variability. Generalizations are risky at best when describing so large an area and so many different societies. However, many of the societies in Polynesia and Micronesia had developed certain features that distinguished them from the majority of those in Melanesia. In both Polynesia and Micronesia there was a high degree of social stratification, and social status and rank were associated with control over land, a resource that is relatively scarce on volcanic islands and atolls. In the larger continental islands of Melanesia, the same ruggedness of terrain that kept people separated into many linguistic groups also helped keep groups small; thus, land played a less important role in determining social position.

Polynesia

In the Western world Polynesia has always been the best known or, perhaps more correctly, the most famous region of the Pacific. The reports of such early explorers as James Cook, William Bligh, George Vancouver, and Louis Antoine de Bougainville inflamed the imaginations of Europeans and Americans. The kingdoms of Polynesian chiefs and the trappings of their courts were colorful and impressive. The relative ease of life, the seemingly endless bounty of tropical islands, and the accounts of casual sexuality had a tremendous impact upon those who were laboring in the sweatshops of the newly industrialized nations and perhaps all who were caught up in the moral climate of the Victorian era.

Most Polynesian societies were organized around two basic principles: bilateral descent and primogeniture. The basic descent groups have been called ramages to denote their branching characteristics. That is, descent in a ramage was traced to a founding ancestor. That ancestor had a number of children. The firstborn child, whether boy or girl, had the highest rank within the family. Each child in turn became the founder of a branch of the ramage, and the branches were ranked according to the birth order of the founders. This was repeated with succeeding generations, thus adding new branches to the ramage in an ever continuing process of expansion. In recounting genealogies, the line was usually traced through the ancestor of highest rank in each generation, whether male or female. Thus, descent was neither matrilineal nor patrilineal but was bilateral. The system allowed for considerable flexibility. This very flexibility has been viewed as an adaptation to land scarcity because choices of descent group affiliation would tend to establish a balance between available land and population density.

The ramage system has often been misunderstood, however, and has been described as a patrilineal system because of its definite preference for descent through males and for the rule of primogeniture. There was a strong belief in the innate superiority of the firstborn, particularly the firstborn son. Ideally, succession to a chieftaincy was from a male to his eldest son, and a line of senior-ranking males was traced to the founding ancestor.

Close relatives, such as cousins, did not marry, but marriage

17

within the ramage was common. Thus, a ramage was a group of people related to one another in a complicated variety of ways through either their fathers, their mothers, or sometimes both. Each ramage member could be ranked according to his or her relative position within the ramage genealogy. The oldest male of the senior line, i.e., a long line of firstborn males, had the highest rank. He held the title of chief (variously known as *ariki, alii,* and other names). Males of lesser seniority were chiefs of a lower order and perhaps had authority over subdivisions of the ramage. The junior lines of the ramage were commoners, but the distinctions between aristocrats and commoners were often vague; everyone could claim some relationship to those of chiefly status. Genealogies, especially those of chiefs, were extremely important, and they were recalled for scores of generations.

Chiefs, especially those of senior ranking, possessed mana. It was "power for accomplishment" and could reside in people or inanimate objects. Thus, any person or object capable of more than ordinary performance had mana by definition. A chief skilled in diplomacy, leadership, and warfare or a hook that caught exceptional quantities of fish had mana, and the fact was self-evident by performance. In some places mana was thought to be inherited so that each successive generation had more than previous generations had.

Mana commanded great respect. Its bearer was both sacred and dangerous. Charged with such invisible power, a chief had to be separated from others by rites of avoidance or *tabu* (taboo). Powerful chiefs could not come into direct contact with commoners, and objects they touched had to be avoided. Chiefs could declare sections of their domain off-limits or *tabu,* and the collection of resources was forbidden until the *tabu* was lifted.

Chiefs had authority and commanded respect and deference. They exercised political and economic leadership, but with certain exceptions they were not "despots," and those of lesser rank were in no way their serfs. All people had rights to land. Although chiefs had some control over basic decisions regarding the use and exploitation of land, lagoons, and reef areas and received symbolic tribute during first fruit and harvest ceremonies, they did not live off the labor of others. Rather, they cultivated food of their own and fished from the sea as did their fellows.

In his monumental book *Ancient Polynesian Society,* anthropologist Irving Goldman classified the kind of Polynesian society described above as "traditional." Most Polynesian societies were of this type. They included the Maori, who had settled New Zealand relatively late, and smaller scale societies found on atolls and the smaller volcanic islands, such as Tikopia. In these societies seniority of descent provided mana and sanctity, established rank, and allocated authority and power in an orderly manner. The traditional society was essentially a religious system headed by a sacred chief and given stability by a religiously sanctioned gradation of worth.

Goldman distinguished two other kinds of Polynesian societies: "open" and "stratified." The open societies appear to be transitional societies between the traditional and the stratified. In the open system the importance of seniority had become downplayed to allow military and political effectiveness to govern status and political control. It was more strongly military and political than religious, and stability was maintained more directly by the exercise of secular power. Status differences were no longer graded but tended to be sharply defined. Examples of the more open societies were those of Easter Island, the Marquesas, the Samoa Islands, and Niue.

The Marquesas Islands may have been the most fully evolved example of an open society. Genealogical and achieved statuses were of about equal importance. Genealogical status was not adequate in itself, and the ultimate test of political power was the ability of a chief to attract and hold followers. If a chief could not build a following, if he could not control kin and allies alike, he had little to show for his title. He was either a political chief or, for all practical purposes, none at all. In the Samoa Islands descent and seniority of line were of even less importance. Leaders known as *matai* were, and continue to be, selected by their kinsmen to lead extended kin groupings by reason of their abilities and accomplishments.

Stratified societies developed where populations and resources were the largest. Hawaii, Tahiti, and Tonga were the best examples. Clearly defined and hierarchically ordered social classes were well developed. Because the chiefs ruled thousands of people, genealogical connections could no longer be traced between all segments of society. The chiefs formed a class unto themselves and married within that class. The highest ranking chief possessed all land; commoners were landless subjects. The administration was impersonal and totalitarian.

Hawaii represented the greatest development of a stratified system. There were 11 grades of *alii*. Entire islands or major divisions of the largest islands were held by an *alii nui*, or single chief, and his rule was often despotic. His domain was subdivided among lesser chiefs in return for tribute and service. Actual administration of government was often turned over to a *kalaimoku*, or land manager. Lesser chiefs could be removed when they displeased the *alii nui*. When the latter died or was overthrown, the lands of the domain were reallocated by his successor. The chiefs had great sanctity, and it was believed that they were descended from gods. In addition to the chiefly and commoner classes, there was a slave or outcast class.

Shortly after European contact, all of the Hawaiian Islands were unified under a single *alii*, who came to be known as King Kamehameha. Although he used Europeans to solidify his rule over all the islands, it appears that the process was already well under way and would have occurred without foreign assistance. There were similar developments in Tahiti and Tonga; the latter remains a monarchy to this very day (see Tonga, ch. 4).

Throughout most of Polynesia there was a pantheon of gods that varied only slightly from one archipelago to another. In Hawaii, Kane was the creator, Lono was the god of rain and agriculture, and Ku was the god of war and warriors. There were a variety of other nature deities, and at all levels of society ancestral gods were important. The proper worship of major gods was conducted by priests drawn from the ranks of the junior *alii* lines, and at the level of commoners, heads of extended families looked after the ancestors. The society of the Samoa Islands was an exception to the general Polynesian pattern, for it was more secular, less attention was paid to the supernatural, and the concept of mana was weak.

Warfare was almost universal. At stake were the power and reputation of rival chiefs. Indeed, status rivalry was particularly acute in Polynesian societies, and this concern made intelligible much of Polynesian behavior. Most of Polynesia has undergone fundamental transformations since European contact, but vestiges of the past have remained. Samoans have proven to be remarkably resilient, and the organization of this society has retained much of its traditional form. On many islands—particularly those that are remote—the ramage organization still defines the relations among kin and rights to land. Chiefly powers have been greatly diminished everywhere, and they no longer exist at all in highly Westernized Hawaii.

Micronesia

With two major exceptions, Micronesia remained a cultural area in which matrilineal institutions dominated. At birth, individuals, regardless of gender, became members of their mothers' matrilineage. The lineage was usually three to five generations deep, and in most places the corporate group held the land. As in Polynesia, siblings were ranked by their birth order, the head of each lineage being its senior ranking male. Succession to lineage headship was matrilineal, i.e., a male was succeeded by his younger brothers in the order of their birth and then by their eldest sister's eldest son.

Aggregations of lineages shared a common name and formed a social category that anthropologists refer to as matriclans. The lineages belonging to the same clan were dispersed among several islands or an entire archipelago; usually no genealogical connections were known between them. Nonetheless, clan members had a feeling of common kinship, and the clan was exogamous, i.e., one had to marry outside the clan. The clan was a vehicle for the provision of hospitality, for one was obligated to protect and provide food and shelter for one's fellow clan members, whether strangers or friends. The exogamous and dispersed clans functioned as a security net; one could rely on clan members when in need or when traveling between islands.

The social organization of the Carolinian atolls was quite egalitarian. Within Truk itself, each island within the lagoon was divided into two or more districts, and each was occupied by a politically autonomous community. The landholding matrilineages of the community were ranked according to the order in which they were settled in the district. The highest ranking lineage was the first to have settled in the district; its head is also the community's chief. Most of the Carolinian atolls were organized like the communities of Truk.

The Carolinian atolls from Ulithi in the west to those as far east as Namonuito (immediately west of Truk) belonged to a supra-atoll network that has misleadingly been called the Yapese Empire. Until recent times an annual expedition was organized to render tribute to Gatchepan village on the high island of Yap. The atoll communities were progressively ranked from highest to lowest from west to east. Ulithi was ranked the highest; Namonuito, Pulap, Puluwat, and Pulusuk in the east were ranked the lowest. The expedition began with canoes from the eastern atolls sailing west to Lamotrek. There, the higher ranking Lamotrek chief took charge, and the expedition moved farther west to the next stop. The same process was repeated until Ulithi was reached, whereupon the Ulithi chief took command and the canoes proceeded to Yap, where tribute was rendered. The priests of Gatchepan purportedly protected the atolls from disaster and could send typhoons and/or drought if tribute was not rendered.

Conquest was never involved, and thus it is a misnomer to

refer to this interatoll network as an empire. Rather, the relations between the actors in the network appear to have developed as an effective means of adapting to the ecology of the far-flung atolls. The atoll dwellers received food and commodities not available on the atolls, and they could look to Yap for assistance in times of disaster. It should be noted that the annual expedition moved from east to west, the same direction as the dependable trade winds. Like the system of clans, the empire was essentially a social security system for the coral islanders.

Paramount chieftaincy and distinct social classes characterized the traditional organization of the high islands and the Marshallese atolls. On the high islands of Palau, the Marianas, Ponape, Kosrae, and the Marshalls, certain clans or lineages were of paramount chiefly status, and their members constituted a privileged ruling class. Each of the islands or island groups was divided among the chiefs, who had ultimate control of the land within their respective domains. Their powers were substantial and in most cases included the ability to render judgments of life or death upon members of the commoner class.

The most centralized political regimes occurred on Ponape and Kosrae. In both instances a single chiefly line ruled the entire island. In Ponape the ruling dynasty oversaw the construction of Nan Madol, the largest archaeological site in all of Oceania. It is composed of some 90 artificial islands linked by canals over a complex of more than 36 hectares. Its monumental architecture was constructed from log-shaped basalt crystals each weighing several tons. For reasons that are not clear, the Ponape Dynasty collapsed shortly before the arrival of Europeans, and only Kosrae had a centralized political structure at the time of contact. Ponape was divided into the five separate paramount chiefdoms that are found on the island today.

In the Marshalls the several paramount chiefs were headquartered in ecologically favored areas, for the southern atolls lie within the relatively wet climatic zone above the equator and possess the best soils, largest resource bases, and greatest populations. The chiefs' domains extended into and embraced the northern atolls, which are dry and resource poor and have small populations.

Like the Marshalls, the Gilbert Islands are composed of atolls. The northern atolls also fall within the wet zone. Ecologically, they are very much like the southern Marshalls. Paramount chiefdoms also existed in the northern atolls. Their authority did not, however, extend southward to include the southern atolls, which like the northern Marshalls are dry, resource poor, and

*Nan Mandol, the largest
archaeological site in Oceania
stretches across 90 artificial
islands.The monumental
construction of
log-shaped basalt crystals
is located in Ponape State
of the Federated States
of Micronesia
Courtesy Patricia
Luce Chapman*

lightly populated. The people of the Gilberts lacked the system of dispersed matriclans that served to link the residents of different atolls. The Gilberts were influenced greatly by their Polynesian neighbors to the south, and the social organization of the archipelago was a variant of the Polynesian system of bilateral descent. Because the chiefly realms were restricted to the north, the poorly endowed southern atolls had community councils and were more egalitarian.

Yap was unique not only in Micronesia but also in the Pacific as a whole. The exogamous matriclans of Yapese society were like those found elsewhere in Micronesia but in contrast to the others contained no corporate matrilineages as subunits. Rather, land was held by patrilineages. Each Yapese village was composed of a number of patrilineages that were corporate landholding groups. Within the villages the land parcels, not the social groups, were ranked. The patrilineage that held the highest ranked land was for that reason the highest ranking lineage, and its head was the village chief. A Yapese saying indicates the importance of land on Yap as well as in the entire region: "The man is not chief, the land is chief." Yap was complex in other ways. Villages were divided into higher and lower castes, i.e., the land of the villages was so ranked. The high caste was further divided into five classes; the lower caste was divided into four. Nowhere in the Pacific have distinctions of social class been so pronounced.

With a few exceptions, religious systems in Micronesia were not as complex as those in Polynesia; there was no overall and widespread pantheon of deities. Cosmologies tended to be simple. Ancestral spirits and supernatural beings that resided in objects of nature were important in some areas.

As in Polynesia, warfare was endemic. In an egalitarian society such as Truk, the small political entities engaged in regular conflict. Elsewhere, the paramount chiefs warred among themselves in efforts to extend their respective domains.

The social organization and culture of the Chamorro people of the Marianas were virtually destroyed shortly after European contact, and Kosrae lost its centralized chiefly organization. As have the Samoa Islands in Polynesia, Yap has maintained much of its traditional culture and social organization. The Carolinian atolls have also tended to be culturally conservative. Although their power and authority have been substantially decreased, the paramount chiefs of Palau, Ponape, and the Marshalls continue to be quite influential personages. The paramount chiefs of the Gilberts have largely been eclipsed, but the bilateral organization of the society has changed little.

Melanesia

With the exception of New Caledonia, which has been radically altered by colonial rule, a majority of Melanesian societies have retained much of their traditional culture and social organizations. This is certainly the case for the Solomon Islands, Vanuatu, and Papua New Guinea, where as much as 90 percent of the populations are still self-sufficient subsistence agriculturists.

Every anthropologist who has attempted to generalize about Melanesia has emphasized its great diversity. After writing a general survey of the area, Anne Chowning concluded that Melanesia is best regarded as a geographical region in which some culture traits occur with greater frequency than they do in some of the surrounding areas. It contains what might be called smaller cultural areas similar to those that have been defined for parts of Africa.

Ian Hogbin, a long-term observer of the area, has described some of those traits and has commented that Melanesians usually impress Europeans as being hardworking agriculturists, preoccupied with trade, the accumulation of wealth, the ramifications of kinship, ancestor worship, and secret societies. At the same time, they are motivated by deep-seated fears and insecurities that find outlet in an extreme development of malevolent magic and in constant warfare. It may be added that other very prominent features of Melanesia are the widespread absence of complex and permanent forms of political organization and the small size of political entities. The area is also unhealthy compared with the rest of the Pacific. Malaria, probably the most serious scourge, takes a heavy toll on lowland dwellers.

Groups no larger than a few hundred people were common in the lowlands, the exceptions being in the Sepik River region of New Guinea, where groups could contain a thousand people. The largest groups are found in the Highlands of New Guinea; these may reach several thousand, but numbers of around a thousand are more typical.

Political units were most commonly headed by a man or several men, who were literally called "big men." The position of a big man was largely achieved; he had to create his own following, although it has recently been realized that the sons of big men do have an advantage over others. A big man must be ambitious and energetic, possess the ability to manipulate others and get them in his debt, organize large-scale activities, be successful in the accumulation of wealth (pigs, valuables, and garden produce), and show generosity in distributing that wealth. In the past and in many areas, a big man also had to prove himself as a warrior and show special magical knowledge. It was common for a big man to have several wives in order to serve as the work force necessary to cultivate adequate gardens and nurture pigs.

There are exceptions to the big-man kind of polity. One such exception is found in the Trobriand (Kiriwina) Islands, which lie off the east coast of New Guinea. (Its people are among the most well-known in Melanesia; volumes have been written about them by Bronislaw Malinowski, a scholar who helped shape modern anthropology.) The Trobriands have ranked matriclans and paramount chiefs who exert extensive authority. Paramount chiefs in New Caledonia are similar to some chiefs in Polynesia, and a hereditary two-class system with chiefly offices exists in a number of Melanesian societies, mostly on smaller islands. In addition to the Trobriands, other exceptions to the big-man typology are found in the Schouten Islands, the Arawe Islands, Buka, the Buin area of Bougainville, and other parts of the easternmost islands.

Settlement patterns range from elaborately laid out villages, such as those in the Trobriands, to the much more common and very dispersed homesteads found in the New Guinea Highlands. Land tenure systems vary greatly but are often tied to descent groups, and almost every possible variety of the latter is found in the region. In very broad terms matrilineal descent systems are limited and are mostly found in eastern Melanesia: the New Hebrides, the Solomons, New Ireland, the eastern half of New Britain, most of the Massim (the eastern tip of New Guinea out into the Trobriands and other offshore islands), and a few locations along the north coast of New Guinea. Many of the societies of the New Guinea Highlands are patrilineal in ideology but in practice exhibit great flexibility and numerous exceptions to a patrilineal system.

Two forms of wealth are ubiquitous in the area: pigs and small portable valuables. Pig exchanges are an integral part of ceremonial life and are usually involved in the payment of brideprice, a practice common in Melanesia. The small valuables take a variety of forms, depending upon locale, and include dogs' teeth, curved boars' tusks, porpoise teeth, pierced stone disks, red feather belts, and packets of salt—a scarce commodity in the New Guinea Highlands.

Trade and exchange networks are also a common feature. In many instances food and utilitarian items are exchanged along well-established networks that apparently are of considerable antiquity. Fish and shells are traded inland from coastal areas. Some villages specialize in the manufacture of pottery and exchange their products for food and other items. The exchange of valuables also follows long-established routes. The most well-known of these are great ceremonial trading expeditions known as the *kula* ring in the Trobriands. Two types of heirloom jewelry are circulated among the islands. Red shell necklaces move along a clockwise route, and white shell armbands are exchanged in a counterclockwise direction. Pieces of the jewelry that have made many complete circuits around the ring and have been owned by men of great prestige are especially valuable. Utilitarian items are also exchanged during the *kula* transactions.

Nowhere in Oceania are the differences between the sexes as marked as in Melanesia. Women suffer an inferior status, and yet they are commonly feared by men. Women are viewed as sexually, physically, and spiritually draining. Too much sex and contact with women is to be avoided. Especially during menstruation and after childbirth, women are considered to be dangerous and contaminating, not just to men but to everything with which they might come into contact. In many places men and women sleep apart in separate houses, and men, as if to emphasize their separateness, may belong to secret societies whose centers are huge, elaborately decorated clubhouses.

More than anywhere else in the Pacific, the Melanesian concern with magic and sorcery amounts almost to an obsession. Practically every facet of life has its associated rituals. There are magical spells to ensure the growth of crops, bring success in fishing, guarantee victory in war, and cure sickness. Certain rites bring harm and failure to personal and community enemies. The writings of Malinowski on Trobriand magic and anthropologist Reo Fortune's account of sorcery on Dobu in the D'Entrecasteaux Islands reflect the Melanesian preoccupation with these concerns and the attention they have received in the literature.

In Melanesia it is impossible to make a clear distinction between magic and religion. Experts agree that spiritual beings are usually part of the ordinary physical world and are not transcendental. Ancestor worship is almost universal, and roughly the same sorts of spiritual beings are parts of the belief systems of many different peoples. Generally, there is no great concern with the creation or origin of the world or the universe.

In the past, warfare was also a constant feature of Melanesian life; it has remained so in the New Guinea Highlands. Virtually every community continually warred with at least some of its neighbors. Revenge was the most frequent cause. Each killing or injury had to be repaid, and the process was literally endless. Head-hunting and cannibalism were common in many areas.

Melanesian creativity reached its zenith in its elaborate art forms, particularly in the lowlands. Painting, wood carving, and inlay work are lavish and are found in such ceremonial objects as masks, human and animal figures, drums, canoes, and innumerable other items. In some areas of New Guinea and the Solomons, almost every object, no matter how utilitarian, is decorated. In other areas, particularly the New Guinea Highlands, decoration is focused on the human body, taking the form of facial and body paint, elaborate headdresses, and costumes. In many respects Melanesian societies tend to represent the extremes. Indeed, anthropologist Ronald Berndt used the title *Excess and Restraint* for his study of four linguistic groups in the eastern New Guinea Highlands.

Era of European Discovery

By the beginning of the sixteenth century, the Portuguese had established themselves in the East Indies, maintaining trading posts at Malacca on the Malay Peninsula, the Moluccas (Spice Islands; present-day Maluku Islands in Indonesia), and a few other locations. They arrived at these distant outposts by voyaging around the Cape of Good Hope, up the east coast of Africa, and east across the Indian Ocean, bringing them to the edge of, but not into, the insular Pacific.

Seeking to challenge Portugal's hold on the East Indies, Spain sought alternate routes to the area as well as another potential prize. As far back as the sixth century B.C., it had been posited that the world was a globe and that there was a great landmass on the southern part that gave balance to the northern landforms. Armchair geographers had come to call the unseen southern continent Terra Australis Incognita. For Christopher Columbus and others centuries later, the two Americas represented barriers to a western route from Europe to the East Indies and the southern continent.

Like Columbus, Magellan was convinced that there was a route around the Americas, and, finding only skepticism at home, he eventually led an expedition from Spain. He sailed around the southern tip of South America and through the strait that now bears his name. He proceeded from southeast to northwest across the Pacific and reached Guam in 1521. Magellan pushed on farther westward and discovered the Philippines, where he was killed in an encounter with the indigenous people. His voyage demonstrated the immense size of the Pacific, and his crew continued homeward to complete the first circumnavigation of the earth.

The Spanish failed to dislodge the Portuguese in the East Indies, but they eventually took possession of the Philippines in 1565. To link the Philippines to the motherland, a trans-Pacific route was established from Manila to Acapulco, Mexico, overland to the Caribbean, and on to Spain.

During the remainder of the sixteenth century, the Spanish and Portuguese were the dominant explorers in the region. Representatives of both countries sighted and claimed the large landmass of New Guinea. Sailing to the Peruvian port of Callao, the Spaniard Álvaro de Mendaña de Neira discovered the Solomon Islands in the late 1560s. Attempting to retrace his voyage, he sailed again from Callao in 1595. He discovered the Marquesas Islands—the first inhabited Polynesian islands seen by Europeans.

Mendaña did not live to see the end of his voyage, and his command passed to his chief pilot, Pedro Fernández de Quirós, who became obsessed with finding the southern continent. Setting sail in 1605, he traveled through the Tuamotus, which were of little interest to him, and went on to discover the New Hebrides Islands, which he wrongly identified as the sought-after continent. Quirós returned to Mexico, but his own chief pilot, Luis Váez de Torres, sailed from Manila after passing along the southern coast of New Guinea through what is now called the Torres Strait. His voyage demonstrated that New Guinea is an island and not part of the undiscovered continent.

By 1602 the Dutch had replaced the Portuguese in the East Indies, and during the seventeenth century they made the major explorations in the Pacific. The Dutch United East India Company monopolized trade in the Indies, and its investors tended to be conservative. Where the Spanish and Portuguese had been adventurers seeking gold, new lands, and souls for the glory of church and state, the Dutch were primarily pragmatic entrepreneurs searching for new trade routes and new markets.

In 1606 Dutch navigators discovered northern Australia while exploring the southern coast of New Guinea. Several exploratory voyages sponsored by the company in the 1620s and 1630s helped to map the northern and western coasts of Australia, which they called New Holland. They did not establish with certainty, however, that all the territory explored formed part of the long-sought-after southern continent. In 1642 Captain Abel Tasman sailed around the southern coast of Australia and encountered the island now known as Tasmania. Continuing around Australia, he discovered New Zealand, Tonga, and parts of Fiji early the next year. Tasman was the first European navigator to enter the Pacific from the west; he was also the first to make a complete circuit around Australia. After a second voyage in 1644, Tasman had contributed more knowledge about the Pacific than any other European up to his time.

During the latter part of the seventeenth century, the Dutch concentrated on their business concerns, and although voyages to New Guinea and western Australia occurred, no vigorous exploratory effort was pursued. After Tasman's voyages, no major discoveries were made in the South Pacific until the voyage of another Dutchman, Admiral Jacob Roggeveen, about 80 years later. Roggeveen, who was not affiliated with the Dutch United East India Company, discovered exotic Easter Island, part of the Tuamotus, and the Samoa Islands in 1722. His efforts were not appreciated by the Dutch; instead, Roggeveen was accused of having trespassed on the company's monopoly. His discoveries rekindled interest in Pacific geography and exploration elsewhere.

Much of that interest, however, was carried on by armchair geographers in Europe. The reports and maps from previous expeditions were subjected to scrutiny and debate in academia. The Dutch had not freely shared the results of their explorations, and for others the uncertainty about Terra Australis Incognita remained.

Beginning in 1764 the tempo of actual exploration in the Pacific gained momentum, and within a relatively short time a series of voyages by four Englishmen and one Frenchman occurred. Douglas L. Oliver, a dean of Pacific anthropology, has described the period as one in which Oceania geography was transformed from a speculative into an exact science. Between 1764 and 1769 the three English captains John Byron, Samuel Wallis, and Philip Carteret made significant voyages of exploration. Wallis discovered Tahiti; Carteret sailed over much unexplored but vacant ocean, thereby eliminating many of the areas where the southern continent might possibly have been located.

In an effort to challenge the British and restore prestige that had been damaged by events in Europe, the Frenchman Louis Antoine de Bougainville was instructed to circumnavigate the globe. Bougainville followed Wallis to Tahiti. Thereafter, he proceeded to the Samoa Islands. His next landfalls were the islands of the New Hebrides, New Guinea, and the Solomons.

Although Bougainville's accomplishments were considerable, the eighteenth-century voyages of exploration in the Pacific were dominated by the British, Captain James Cook proving to be the most formidable of them all. Cook made three voyages—the first in 1768–71 and the others in 1772–75 and 1776–79. Although all of Cook's accomplishments cannot be recounted here, he further explored the Society Islands during his first voyage and surveyed the coasts of New Zealand and most of the eastern coast of Australia. During the second voyage he came close to Antarctica, discovered Niue, New Caledonia, and Norfolk Island, and charted new islands in the Tuamotus, Cooks, and Marquesas. His third voyage took Cook along the American northwest coast and Alaska in search of the hoped-for northwest passage. Among other discoveries, Cook came upon the Hawaiian Islands; it was there that he met his death in 1779.

The era of major exploration and new discoveries essentially ended by 1780 after the voyages of Cook. One observer reportedly commented that "he left his successors with little to do but admire." Certainly the major archipelagoes had been located and mapped, and Cook's observations and charts later proved to be remarkably accurate.

The explorers not only made a significant impact on the people of the Pacific but their accounts also captured the imagination of Westerners. Both sides had learned that there were new and unfamiliar peoples in the world. Trade for food and water supplies had taken place, and islanders had come to appreciate the value of iron and other Western goods. Romantic myths about the south sea islands were launched in Europe and America, and philosophers took island peoples to be examples of humans in a pristine state of nature. After their long voyages sailors had found island women especially attractive; thus, the mixture of races had begun. Cook lamented that venereal disease was already evident by the time of his last voyage.

In the initial contacts with islanders, misunderstanding and violence occurred often. In fact, violence accompanied the beginning and the end of the era. During his call at Guam in 1521, Magellan was angered when some Chamorros made away with his vessel's skiff. He took 40 men ashore, burned 40 or 50 houses and several canoes, killed seven men, and recovered the skiff. A stolen vessel was also the immediate cause of Captain Cook's death at Kealekekua Bay in Hawaii in 1779. On this occasion a cutter was stolen, and when Cook went ashore to demand its return, he lost his life at the hands of the Hawaiians.

The Interlopers

From the 1790s until about the 1860s, the first interlopers who actually established residence in the Pacific appeared. Polynesia and Micronesia received the most attention. Melanesia was initially avoided because of the hostility of the inhabitants and the inhospitable environment. Further, the widespread absence of chiefs made it more difficult to deal with the Melanesians.

The outsiders may be divided into two categories: the sacred and the profane. Usually the latter arrived first. They have been variously labeled as beachcombers, sealers, whalers, and traders, and some individuals changed labels as they shifted from one enterprise to another. Engaged in the affairs of the sacred, the missionaries usually appeared after the beachcomber communities had been established. The two groups were often at loggerheads with each other.

Beachcombers, who first began to appear with the explorers, were men who had jumped ship or were the survivors of shipwrecks. They were later joined by escapees from British and French penal colonies in Australia, Norfolk Island, and New Caledonia and by men who were malcontents at home or simply adventurers fascinated by tales of the south seas. The beachcombers have commonly been described as being overly fond of alcohol and as having unsavory characters. They came from almost every nation in Europe and the Americas.

Although it is true that many were undesirables and that most did not make a great impact on history, the importance of some cannot be denied. The beachcombers were the first foreigners to establish residence in the islands and to learn the indigenous languages. Many married or formed long-term liaisons with island women and left numerous offspring. Some were attached to chiefly families and were used by chiefs to serve as advisers and/or intermediaries in relations with Europeans. Their service as interpreters gave them some control over communication. Missionaries new to the field abhorred dependence upon the beachcombers and were usually quick to learn the local language themselves. A few gained considerable prominence and influence and remained in the islands for the rest of their lives. Some adopted trading as a profession, while others, perhaps the majority, left or died without a trace.

A few left more than a trace and became well-known. For example, Isaac Davis and John Young were detained in Hawaii by King Kamehameha and became advisers who helped him solidify his rule over the archipelago. David Whippy was left by an entrepreneur in Fiji and became a major figure in Fijian politics at the time Fiji lost its sovereignty. William Mariner, a young Englishman, was detained in Tonga by a chiefly family for four years (1806–10); he was a keen observer and provided an excellent account of Tongan society and language. Herman Melville spent time in the Marquesas as a beachcomber, later incorporating his experiences in two novels, *Typee* and *Omoo*. James O'Connell, a colorful Irishman and somewhat of a rogue, left a valuable account of several years on Ponape in the late 1820s and early 1830s.

Beginning in the late 1790s, commercial ships began to carry sealers and fur traders between the northwest coast of America and China. Trade in salt pork was established between Tahiti, where it was produced, and Sydney. The sealers and fur traders visited the islands as they plied their vessels across the Pacific, trading primarily to obtain food and freshwater supplies. For them, as well as for the whalers who followed them, the islands were well liked as recreation spots.

Sandalwood, which had long been valued in China, caused considerable excitement when it was discovered in Polynesia and Melanesia. Although the sandalwood trade did not last long, it brought violence and bad relations almost everywhere. Generally, the sandalwooders had a very bad reputation; they often attempted to shortchange islanders, sometimes bullying them into participating in the trade. Chiefs, especially those in Hawaii, used the trade to enhance their own welfare at the expense of the commoners. It was a blessing that the trade ran its course in relatively short order. The three main areas first affected were Fiji (1804–16), Hawaii (1811–28), and the Marquesas (1813–17). Trade was first established in the 1820s in Melanesia—primarily among the New Hebrides, the Loyalty Islands, and New Caledonia—and lasted until about 1865. Other Pacific products also found markets in China, and traders promoted the collection of bêche-de-mer (or trepang—a sea cucumber used for soups), mother of pearl, and tortoiseshell.

More importantly, the Pacific was found to have rich whaling grounds. By the 1820s whalers were operating all over the region. The enterprise began with both British and American whalers, but it soon became dominated by New England interests out of Nantucket and New Bedford. The crews, however, were a mixed bag composed of not only New Englanders but also American Indians, runaway slaves, renegade British sailors, Europeans of several nationalities, and Pacific islanders, especially Hawaiians.

The whaling industry grew rapidly; many more than 700 American vessels worked the Pacific during the peak decade of the 1850s. Through the 1860s and 1870s the industry declined as whaling grounds were depleted and as whale oil for lamps was replaced by kerosene.

Ports of call sprang up in response to the industry. Whalers put ashore to restore and resupply vessels for what came to be known as "refreshment." The latter referred to all kinds of activities: a relief from the rigors of sea, fresh foods, the excitement of new faces, the swilling of booze, and the securing of willing sexual partners. Liquor, guns, hardware, and textiles were traded for the commodities and services required by the seafarers. Hawaii, Tahiti, and the Marquesas were the first to feel the impact in Polynesia. Ponape and Kosrae became favorite spots in Micronesia. Eventually New Zealand was very much involved. Three ports were especially famous for their refreshments: Honolulu in Hawaii, Papeete in Tahiti, and Kororareka in New Zealand. Honolulu and Papeete survived and continued to thrive after the decline of whaling; Kororareka did not. Everywhere the whalers had a deleterious impact on indigenous peoples. The incidence of venereal disease as well as other diseases increased, violence was common, alcohol ravaged people unaccustomed to strong drink, and firearms heightened the seriousness of indigenous conflicts. Depopulation began to be a serious problem in many island groups, one that would continue throughout the twentieth century.

The copra trade also had a great impact on the islands; in fact, no other Western economic activity has touched the lives of so many Pacific islanders. By the mid-nineteenth century there was a large demand for tropical vegetable oils in Europe; thus, the oil of the meat of the coconut became of value.

Germans launched the copra trade. The firm of Johann Cesar Godeffroy and Son began with an oil-processing plant in Western Samoa in 1856. It soon changed to exporting copra, which was later processed in Europe. Godeffroy acquired large plantations in the Samoa Islands and by the 1870s had agents scattered across the Pacific from Tahiti to the Marianas.

Later, other plantations were established, and other large-scale companies became involved with copra and other commerce. However, the consequences were much more widespread. The coconut palm grows almost everywhere, even thriving on coral atolls, and copra production is simple, requiring little or no capital investment. In the most basic form of production, the white meat of a mature nut is cut from its shell and dried in the sun. Consequently, copra production is suited for even the poorest and most remote spots in the Pacific. The boats of small traders as well as large trading firms can collect copra throughout an island chain, exchanging cash and goods in return. In spite of difficulties stemming from price fluctuations, copra has therefore been a natural product for the islands and has been a major income earner for the inhabitants. As increased numbers of coconut palms were planted, the copra trade altered the landscapes of entire islands, especially the atolls. A coral atoll whose islands are entirely covered with the palms is a post-copra-trade phenomenon.

It is an understatement to say that the last category of foreigners to be considered, the missionaries, also had an immeasurable impact on Pacific societies. The missions have been as successful, if not more so, in the Pacific as in any other place in the world. It all began with the Spanish and conversions to Catholicism. The Spanish sailing route between Mexico and the Philippines made Guam, the southernmost of the Marianas, a convenient port of call for reprovisioning and refreshment. In 1668 a Catholic mission and military garrison were established there. Initially, the effort seemed successful, and the priests adopted a strategy that was later to become commonplace. They first worked to bring the paramount chiefs into the fold; soon the more common folk followed.

In 1670 a few priests and catechists were killed after a misunderstanding with the Chamorros; the Spanish soldiers retaliated, and the Chamorro wars followed. The Spanish were nothing less than ruthless, and by 1694 Spain's conquest of the entire Marianas was complete. Of an estimated 100,000 Chamorros, the indigenous population was reduced to about 5,000. For administrative convenience and to provide a labor force close at hand, most of these were resettled on Guam. Spain had, in effect, established the first European colony in the Pacific. Within a short time Chamorro culture was essentially lost as the surviving Chamorros intermarried with their Spanish masters and Filipinos. The language survives, although in a much altered form.

The next round of missionization did not occur until over a century later, when the Protestants entered Polynesia. In 1797 the London Missionary Society landed its first contingent of missionaries in Tahiti. Like the earlier priests on Guam, these missionaries quickly developed the same sociological insight. If the chiefs could be converted, the process would quickly spread downward through the lower ranks of the stratified society. Within twenty years the Tahitian mission had enjoyed considerable success. By the 1830s the efforts of the London Missionary Society had spread westward, through the Society Islands to the Cook and Samoa islands.,

Other Protestant groups followed close on the heels of the London Missionary Society and, like the latter, for the most part came from Britain. The Church Missionary Society, organized in Britain, moved to New Zealand in 1814 to spread the gospel among the Maori. The British-based Wesleyan Missionary Society established a station in New Zealand in 1819; within a few years it was at work in Tonga, Fiji, and the Loyalty Islands, the latter representing intrusions into insular Melanesia. The Melanesian Mission was started in New Zealand; its initial work was with people in the Banks, Loyalty, and Solomon islands. By 1866 a mission school was established on Norfolk Island, and Melanesians were brought there for instruction.

The Americans entered the field when the Boston-based American Board of Commissioners for Foreign Missions (ABCFM) landed its first missionaries in Hawaii in 1820. The ABCFM effort, also known as the Boston Mission, followed the pattern of working through the highest chiefs. Success was relatively quick. By mid-century ABCFM missionaries, including a few Hawaiian converts, extended their work to the eastern Carolines, the Marshalls, and eventually to the Gilberts.

The first serious effort launched by Catholics in the eastern Pacific came in 1827, when a band of priests arrived in Hawaii. In an act that characterized future relations between the two branches of Christianity, the Protestants expelled the unwanted competition. The Catholics retreated for a few years and then reentered Polynesia with an adroit move, landing priests in the remote Mangareva Islands southeast of Tahiti in 1834, where they were not watched and were unopposed. After gaining a command of the language, they established missions in Tahiti in 1836 and in the Marquesas in 1838. They were also the first missionaries to reach New Caledonia, in 1843. Fiji and the Samoa Islands saw their first Catholic missions in 1844.

By the 1850s and 1860s missionaries were at work in all the island groups. Melanesia, as usual, came last and was the most difficult to penetrate. The widespread absence of chiefs, the fragmented and small political units, and the great diversity of languages made it a true nightmare. Indeed, the American and European missionaries often did not take up the challenge; they sent a good number of their recent Polynesian converts in their stead.

The Protestants and Catholics could not have been more different. The Protestants wanted to bring not only their religion but also their own New England and British habits and work ethic. They insisted on clothing the women from head to toe and urged islanders to adopt Western-style houses. They attempted to suppress sexuality and railed against the evils of demon rum and tobacco. Their message contained more hellfire and brimstone than brotherly love and compassion.

The Protestants received much encouragement but not a great amount of financial support from home, and this helped form a particular style of missionization. An emphasis was placed on training indigenous pastors and making the new congregations become economically self-supporting. The missionaries themselves sometimes engaged in farming and trading. At times their own offspring became influential in island economies. The ultimate goal for the mission effort, however, was to train the indigenous pastors and church committees to take charge of the entire operation. For the most part, the strategy worked. The missionaries also got involved often in local politics and were very influential in shaping the monarchies that developed in Hawaii, Tahiti, and Tonga.

In contrast the Catholics were French, and the same motives that caused the French to send Bougainville on his voyage around the world were evident in the mission field. France was trying to regain its global prestige; its main rival was Britain. The French government had colonial ambitions in the Pacific and gave support to the Catholic effort. The Catholic missionaries promoted French language and culture as well as the dogma of their faith. No effort was made to create an indigenous church, and the French fathers remained very much in charge. They were also as much agents of French imperialism as of their faith.

The Protestants had agreed to divide the Pacific among themselves and respected one another's bailiwicks. The Catholics did not play by the same rules, for in areas where Protestants had become established, Catholics confronted them. Eventually, the two branches of Christianity overlapped almost everywhere, but in most island groups one side was dominant. Both evidenced a considerable amount of intolerance and bigotry, and each claimed to have the legitimate faith, portraying the other's message as an untruth at best. Religious wars were fought among island people in a few places. Even today the rifts between the two are often great. As recently as a few years ago, the people of one atoll in the Marshalls could not cooperate to form a local community council to govern their affairs because of the deep antagonisms between Protestants and Catholics.

On the positive side, missions provided education and, in some cases, modest medical care before colonial governments would concern themselves with such things. More important, the missionaries developed orthographies for many of the previously unwritten languages. In order to read the Scriptures, it was necessary to be literate, and the art of reading was taught with great vigor. Today most people of the Pacific are literate in either their vernacular or, in the case of Melanesia, the local pidgin.

By the mid-nineteenth century the initial stage of pioneering in the Pacific by outsiders was over, and circumstances were in place for two major developments during the latter half of the century. First, greater commercial development was to occur for the benefit of Europeans and Americans. Second, and related to the first, the process that had begun on Guam—the partitioning of the Pacific among the colonial powers—would be completed.

With regard to commercial development in the latter part of the nineteenth century, Douglas L. Oliver, in his now classic book, *The Pacific Islands,* has identified three kinds of people as having had the greatest importance: planters, blackbirders, and merchants. Although some planters had arrived earlier, a great many more arrived during the late 1800s, most from Australia and New Zealand. As Oliver has pointed out, the planter was a new kind of man; he did not come for refreshment or in search of souls. He came to stay and make a commitment to the development of a plantation, and he wanted land. Although other tropical plants were tried, the only ones of any real significance were copra, sugar, coffee, cacao, vanilla, fruit, cotton, and rubber. The last was mainly limited to New Guinea, and cotton only enjoyed a boom on Fiji during the American Civil War, when supplies from the American South to the rest of the world were cut off. Copra plantations have been the most numerous and widespread.

Planters needed cheap labor, but they did not find what they wanted among Polynesians and Micronesians. People from both areas worked extremely hard in short spurts when some culturally valued task was at hand, but they would not tolerate the monotonous routines of daily plantation chores. There were two solutions. For the sugar plantations of Hawaii and Fiji, laborers from outside the region were imported. In Hawaii, Japanese, Chinese, and Filipinos were brought in, and they stayed to become part of the archipelago's society. In Fiji, Indians were imported as indentured laborers; they too stayed and came to comprise about one-half the population. The sugar industry produced revolutionary changes in both island groups.

For plantations elsewhere in the islands and the sugar fields of Queensland in Australia, Melanesians became the primary targets for blackbirding. In theory, blackbirding was a system of indentured labor whereby islanders obligated themselves for a few years of labor in exchange for being fed, paid a small wage, and returned home with a bonus of cash and goods or some variant thereof. In reality, islanders were often tricked or trapped into the arrangement, and their rewards were not always what they expected. Blackbirders delivered newly acquired "recruits" to their new masters and made handsome profits for themselves. Some of the laborers were treated reasonably well. Others were not, and some never saw their homes again. In the last analysis, blackbirding was a form of slavery. As the colonial powers divided the Pacific, they brought the seamy practice to an end.

Following the planters and blackbirders, several large mercantile firms emerged, including the German firm of Godeffroy, which collapsed and was succeeded for a while by other German firms. New Zealand and Australian interests became dominant, however, and several firms came to take up the major share of trade. They absorbed smaller trading operations, or smaller traders became their agents. Auckland and Sydney essentially became the financial capitals of the Pacific.

The Partitioning of the Pacific

Before the mid-nineteenth century, only two colonial powers had laid claim to territory in the insular Pacific. Guam and the rest of the Marianas were firmly under Spanish rule. Spain also claimed much of the remainder of Micronesia but had made no move to establish any real control. As a result of their involvement in the East Indies, the Dutch had been familiar with the western portion of New Guinea since the seventeenth century. In 1828 they laid formal claim to the western half of the island, but the Dutch did not establish a permanent administrative post until some 70 years later. Britain had founded its penal colony in Australia in 1788, and the continent was eventually divided into several separate colonies; unification came later.

Convicts who had served their time and free settlers from Australia and Britain soon spilled over into New Zealand. In 1840 Britain took possession of New Zealand, which in 1841 separated as a colony from Australia. Thereafter, Australia and New Zealand, particularly the former, strongly urged Britain to annex every island and reef in the Pacific. Britain's position was that it did not wish to commit itself to greater overseas expansion in the

Pacific. The Dutch did not have further ambitions outside of western New Guinea. The United States was still very much involved in whaling and the fur trade in the northern Pacific; it had no possessions in the Pacific and was not seeking territorial expansion in the area at the time.

France did have ambitions. A proposal to build the Panama Canal was being revived at the time, and it appeared that the Marquesas and Tahiti might become valuable as ports along a sailing route between the canal and Australia and New Zealand. France made its move in 1842 by declaring its sovereignty in the Marquesas and a protectorate over Tahiti. In the same year the smaller Wallis Island also came under French control. New Caledonia, a major prize, was next to come under the tricolor when France declared its sovereignty there in 1853; the French priests who had been working there unopposed were very much involved in the process. New Caledonia was used as a penal colony from 1865 to 1894, and nickel mining began in the 1870s. With Tahiti and New Caledonia in hand, France had established itself as a colonial power in the Pacific. Later, between 1881 and 1887, France annexed other islands in and around Tahiti to become dominant in eastern Polynesia and consolidate what is now French Polynesia.

After New Caledonia came under French rule, the next major territorial acquisition was made by Britain. In 1874 feuding chiefs ceded Fiji to the British, and the situation was essentially a salvage operation. On this occasion and later, the British acquired territories to satisfy Australia and New Zealand and to bring stability and law and order. In Fiji, British, American, and other planters had been pleading for protection; the warring chiefs could not bring about any stability, and blackbirding was rife. Britain was under pressure to provide a solution and did so with some reluctance.

Australia and New Zealand were pleased that Britain had finally taken action. The two had been disturbed by France's takeover of New Caledonia to their north. They were further concerned, if not alarmed, at Germany's entry into the Pacific. The German firm of Godeffroy had begun operations in the Samoa Islands in 1856 and had spread its agents out across the Pacific within a few years. Within the Samoa Islands the Americans, British, and Germans tried several schemes of governance, none of which succeeded. The United States was primarily interested in the excellent harbor at Pago Pago; the Germans were concerned with the protection of their economic investment and plantations. The British had less at stake, and the Samoans were engaged in civil war among themselves. As in Fiji, some stability was needed, but the rivalry among the three major powers did not allow for an easy solution.

In the meantime, Germany continued to expand its commercial interests and made its first territorial acquisition when it annexed northeast New Guinea and the adjacent Bismarck Archipelago in 1884. Germany declared a protectorate over the Marshalls in the following year.

Germany's action in New Guinea caused great concern in Australia; the last thing the Australians wanted was another non-English-speaking and potentially hostile foreign power to their north; New Caledonia had been quite enough. The still reluctant British moved at last and claimed the southeastern portion of New Guinea, immediately north of Australia. In 1885 the British and the Germans agreed upon the boundary between the German northeast portion (German New Guinea) and the Australian southeast portion (British New Guinea, or Papua). In 1888 Britain assumed full sovereignty over Papua. In the same year, Germany added Nauru to its empire at the insistence of German traders, who had been on the island for about two decades.

In the next few years Britain began to exercise what in Australia's view was its proper role in the area. Its next acquisitions were not impressive, however; they were mostly atolls. British protectorates were declared over the Cook, Phoenix, Tokelau, and Gilbert and Ellice islands by 1892. The Australians and New Zealanders were pleased when Britain declared a protectorate over most of the Solomon Islands on their northern flanks in 1883. The New Hebrides remained the only group in Melanesia not claimed by an outsider power.

The years 1898 and 1899 witnessed the end of Spain's presence in the Pacific, the entry of the United States, further German expansion, and the resolution of the problem in the Samoa Islands. In 1898 the United States defeated Spain in the Spanish-American War and acquired the Philippines and Guam, the latter still valued as a coaling station. For a mere pittance Germany bought the rest of Spanish Micronesia.

With the aid of the United States Marines, the Hawaiian monarchy was overthrown by a group of businessmen of American birth or descent in 1893. Although there was some initial opposition, including that of President Grover Cleveland for a few years, Hawaii was annexed by the United States in 1898. The United States had acquired its second Pacific territory, which became the fiftieth state of the union in 1959.

Tiring of the situation in the Samoa Islands, Britain, Germany, and the United States arrived at a solution. In 1899 Britain renounced its claims, and the next year Germany and the United States divided the archipelago. Germany got the lion's share, which became Western Samoa. The United States acquired the smaller eastern portion with its coveted Pago Pago harbor, and American Samoa was born. Britain also got something out of the deal, for Germany renounced potential rights or claims to Tonga and Niue in favor of Britain and gave the British undisputed claim to all of the Solomon Islands east and southeast of Bougainville and Buka. That left the New Hebrides as the only remaining sizable island group that was not an official colony. Before that was to be changed, however, several minor items were to be taken care of. In 1900 Niue was claimed as a British protectorate, and in the following year Britain turned both it and the Cook Islands over to New Zealand for annexation. In 1900 Tonga and Britain signed a treaty in which Tonga essentially agreed to turn over its foreign affairs but in reality was extensively guided and influenced by the British.

Finally came the New Hebrides. After a couple of decades of rule by a joint British and French naval commission, Britain and France, fearful of further German ambitions, established a condominium government over the archipelago in 1906. The arrangement was always awkward and never satisfactory to anyone, but it closed the islands to others. Also in 1906, Australia, whose separate colonies had been joined in a federation only five years previously, assumed the administration of Papua. What had begun on Guam in 1668 was completed: the Pacific had been partitioned by eight colonial powers. One of the eight, Spain, had been forced out, leaving Australia, Britain, France, Germany, the Netherlands, New Zealand, and the United States.

World War I and Aftermath

From the turn of the century until the outbreak of World War I, the region was a sleepy and peaceful backwater of the world. The white man was firmly in charge. Planters extended their holdings and increased the scope of their operations. Missionaries brought increased routinization to their established mission stations and continued to search out the pagan peoples. As islanders became more dependent on Western imports, they became more locked into the world economic order. Colonial governments increased the effectiveness of their rule, and in

Melanesia efforts were made to bring more of the interior and highlands people under administrative authority.

The viewpoint in the Pacific was that World War I was by and large a white man's folly fought on the other side of the world. The main consequences were the ouster of Germany from the region and the introduction of Japan as a colonial power. Germany's colonial era in the Pacific thus turned out to be brief, lasting about three decades.

When the war broke out, the Japanese navy occupied Germany's Micronesian possessions north of the equator. Germany's possessions south of the equator went to Britain or its two offshoots, Australia and New Zealand, and the Pacific became more of a "British lake" than ever before. Australia took German New Guinea, New Zealand acquired Western Samoa, and Britain, Australia, and New Zealand jointly claimed Nauru, although Australia exercised administrative responsibility. After the war all of the former German colonies were legally assigned to the new administering powers as Class C Mandates within the framework of the League of Nations. Essentially, the mandates were areas of the world judged to be not yet capable of self-government.

After the war the equator became a major dividing line, profoundly affecting events in the Pacific. In the northeast, remote Hawaii remained outside the mainstream of island affairs. Guam remained an isolated American bastion in western Micronesia. The bulk of Micronesia, however, was Japan's mandate, and Japan had a clear-cut colonial policy: establish Japanese settlers in the islands, develop the islands economically for the benefit of Japan, make the islanders conversant in the Japanese language and appreciative of Japanese culture, and restrict access to all but Japanese citizens. The policy was followed without fail, and Japan essentially integrated its mandate into its expanding empire. There was very little communication with the rest of the Pacific, and in the late 1930s Japan began to fortify the islands. By that time the estimated 50,000 Micronesians were outnumbered two to one by Japanese and their imported Okinawan and Korean laborers. The title of a book by journalist Willard Price, *Japan's Islands of Mystery*, reflected the rest of the world's view of Japanese Micronesia.

South of the equator, France had its three possessions: French Polynesia, tiny Wallis and Futuna (the latter was combined with Wallis for administrative purposes in 1909), and New Caledonia. It shared the New Hebrides condominium with Britain. The Dutch colony of West New Guinea and American Samoa were the other two exceptions to the "British lake" south of the equator, and the colonies in the area moved more and more into the economic and political spheres of Australia and New Zealand. In the 1920s Britain shed one of its unwanted responsibilities, turning the Tokelaus over to New Zealand.

The interwar years were peaceful, and the Pacific returned to its sleepy backwater status in the world. The colonial order was firmly established and largely unquestioned. *Pacific Islands Monthly,* affectionately known to its readers as PIM, was founded in 1930 by R.W. Robson in Sydney. It became quite influential and helped to give the Pacific south of the equator a regional identity. By sharing news and views each month, people began to think of the larger Pacific as a whole and not just as the smaller regions with which they had special interests. Robson was an advocate of regionalism; he believed there should be cooperation and a sharing of information among the governments of the Pacific.

Some advancements in the welfare of the indigenous peoples were made during this period. Depopulation had largely ceased, most populations had stabilized, and some were making a recovery. Also, following a worldwide trend, there was an increased concern for the welfare of dependent peoples, which had some tangible consequences in the islands, especially in the area of health and medicine—a fact reflected in population trends. Education, however, was largely left to the missions. Douglas L. Oliver has suggested that, influenced by anthropologists, some colonial administrations became somewhat more enlightened, but this would appear to have been the exception rather than the rule.

World War II and Aftermath

December 7, 1941, marked the Japanese attack on Pearl Harbor and the beginning of the war in the Pacific that forever changed the region. Micronesia and Melanesia felt the brunt of it. Shortly after Pearl Harbor, Japan invaded Nauru and the Gilberts in the east and Guam in the west, and for the first time in history, all of Micronesia was under one rule. New Guinea—especially the northeastern mandated area—experienced a massive Japanese invasion, which was repelled at great cost to all, including the indigenous peoples. The Japanese advance carried eastward into the Solomons, and Bougainville and Guadalcanal saw some of the heaviest fighting of the war (see World War II, ch. 5).

The war experience in New Caledonia and the New Hebrides was different, for there was no ground combat there.

Nouméa in New Caledonia became the headquarters of much of the United States effort in the southwest Pacific. Thousands of American troops were stationed there, and the United States military essentially ran the island and kept the mining operations going. The three major American bases in the New Hebrides were used as staging zones for operations elsewhere.

The American invasion of Micronesia began at Tarawa in the Gilberts in 1943. The Marshalls were next, and air attacks destroyed the Japanese naval fleet in the Truk lagoon in early 1944, although neither Truk nor any other islands in central Micronesia were invaded. Instead, they were bypassed when the United States went straight on to Guam and the Northern Marianas in June and July. It was from Tinian in the Northern Marianas that the nuclear attacks on Hiroshima and Nagasaki were launched in early August 1945.

Least affected by the war was Polynesia. Air, communication, and supply bases were established at one time or another on Tonga, Tahiti, the Samoa Islands, and the Cooks. Duty for service personnel in these areas was often slow, and outside the militarized islands the war had little effect other than causing shortages in imported goods and interruptions in shipping—conditions that were more or less universal in the wartime Pacific.

At the end of the war the economies of eastern New Guinea and Micronesia were in shambles. Local peoples had suffered greatly, and the physical infrastructures of both lay in ruins. In the Solomons only the localized areas affected by the war were similarly disrupted. The rest of Melanesia was in reasonably good shape; Polynesia had been the most fortunate.

It soon became apparent, however, that the war had made intangible changes in the society. Pacific islanders would never again view their colonial masters in the same light. During the early stages of the war, the Australians in New Guinea were forced to flee from the Japanese invaders, and it was quite evident to all that the help of the Americans had been required to bring about a victory. Some confidence in the white colonial rulers was lost. Further, Americans had interacted with islanders on a more egalitarian basis than the latter had ever experienced under colonial rule, and this raised questions about the older social order. It was significant—especially so in Melanesia—that islanders saw American blacks working alongside their white counterparts and in possession of the marvels of Western technology. The dependent status of darker skinned people was opened to reconsideration.

Also evident was a general postwar restlessness in which dependent peoples were demanding more political rights and a larger share of the economic pie. The old mandate system was replaced by a trusteeship within the framework of the new United Nations (UN). Part of the responsibility of the administering powers was to lead dependencies toward increased self-government. Indeed, the trusteeships were viewed only as temporary political arrangements until this goal could be achieved. This trend was a continuation of the concerns for the welfare of indigenous peoples that had emerged during the years between the wars. Given such developments, it was unrealistic for the colonial administrators, planters, and traders to expect that the clock could be turned back.

At war's end the United States replaced Japan in much of Micronesia, and the area became the Trust Territory of the Pacific Islands (TTPI). The colonial powers had been reduced to six in number: Australia, Britain, France, the Netherlands, New Zealand, and the United States.

Regionalism and Independence

Reflecting the new ideological notions in the air, Australia and New Zealand invited the other four colonial powers—or, as they were coming to be known, metropolitan powers (much more polite than "colonial")—to join them in the formation of the South Pacific Commission (SPC) in 1947. The SPC was to encourage international cooperation in promoting the economic and social welfare of the dependent peoples of the Pacific. The United States made its former military headquarters in Nouméa available for the SPC's headquarters. The SPC was to engage in research and act as an advisory body to colonial administrations. Its functions were restricted to noncontroversial matters, such as economic development, social welfare, education, and health. The metropolitan powers did not wish others to intervene in their own colonial administration, and political and military issues were explicitly ruled beyond the pale of the SPC.

The SPC functioned as planned. Results of research in the noncontroversial areas were shared, and training programs in the areas of health, pest control, education, and other practical matters were developed. In 1950 the South Pacific Conference was held for the first time. The conference, an auxiliary body of the SPC, was composed of delegates from the Pacific islands and met every third year to advise the commission. The conference was to become extremely important in ways that had not been foreseen.

For the first time, representatives of countries from all over the Pacific met on a face-to-face basis. They found the experience very much to their liking, and there began to emerge a new regional identity—that of a "Pacific islander,"—as opposed to more local identities, such as Samoan, Maori, or Tongan.

Originally, only representatives of the six colonial powers actually belonged to the SPC and held ultimate authority. Over time, Pacific islanders at the conference insisted on having a greater voice in the decisionmaking processes and lobbied for an annual conference. Such requests became difficult to delay after 1962. Western Samoa had never really accepted the yoke of colonial rule. Movements of self-rule and expressions of extreme discontent had occurred during the New Zealand administration, and in 1962 Western Samoa became the first Pacific nation to achieve political independence. In the face of some resistance it joined the colonial powers, taking a seat in the SPC in 1965. By that date, however, one of the original colonial powers had been lost to the SPC. When Indonesia occupied West New Guinea in 1962, the Netherlands was no longer involved in the Pacific, and it ceased being an SPC member. After the Dutch departed, the number of colonial powers was reduced to five: Australia, Britain, France, New Zealand, and the United States. Today former West New Guinea is known as Irian Jaya and is considered part of Indonesia.

Once begun, the momentum toward decolonization could not be stopped. Eight other island countries had joined Western Samoa as sovereign nations by mid-1984: Nauru (1968), Fiji (1970), Tonga (1970), Papua New Guinea (1975), Solomon Islands (1978), Tuvalu (1978), Kiribati (1979), and Vanuatu (1980). The name changes of the latter three occurred with independence. Five of the new states—Fiji, Papua New Guinea, Solomon Islands, Vanuatu, and Western Samoa—were members of the United Nations.

The Cook Islands and Niue, both former dependencies of New Zealand have carved out a status known as "free association" that is novel to the world political arena. The Cook Islands were the first to achieve this status, in 1965. The Cooks had neither the resources nor the personnel to move immediately toward total independence, so it was agreed that they would be self-governing in internal affairs. New Zealand would handle defense and, insofar as requested, external affairs. The Cooks received financial support from New Zealand, and either side could unilaterally terminate the understanding. The formal agreement was intentionally left somewhat vague, and the free association relationship has been allowed to evolve in its form and substance. Initially, New Zealand handled most of the external affairs of the Cooks. Subsequently, the Cooks began to represent itself in regional affairs, taking greater control of its international relations and negotiating several bilateral treaties with other countries. Niue followed suit in 1974, and to date it has been content to let New Zealand handle most of its external affairs.

As more countries achieved independence or self-government, reform of the SPC became increasingly necessary. Some change did occur during the late 1960s and 1970s. The conference became an annual affair and gained greater control over SPC programs. Eventually, the islander-dominated conference became the superior body, having ultimate decisionmaking authority, and the commission became its executive branch. The child had become the parent; the parent had become the child. At the 1983 conference in Saipan, all past voting inequities were erased; every member of the conference gained an equal vote.

The SPC, however, remained a troubled organization in the mid-1980s. It began as a metropolitan body and will probably never shed that image. The metropolitan powers contributed by far the bulk of the SPC's budget, and although they attempted to keep a low profile, it was felt that they used their financial contributions as leverage to gain undue influence. Moreover, the SPC remained an apolitical organization, as was reaffirmed in its 1983 publication, *The South Pacific Commission: History, Aims, and Activities,* which clearly stated that the SPC "does not concern itself with the politics of the states and territories within the region. . . ."

The SPC included all states, territories, and dependencies in the Pacific, which made for strange political bedfellows. The inability to engage in political debate was an irritant, for the self-governing countries wished to consider the incomplete process of the decolonization of the region as well as issues relating to the testing, storage, dumping, and deployment of nuclear weapons and the transit of nuclear-armed or nuclear-powered vessels.

Such frustrations were not new; they led to the founding of a separate regional organization, the South Pacific Forum, in 1971. The forum included the heads of governments of the newly independent and self-governing nations in addition to Australia and New Zealand. The latter two were recognized as being geographically a part of the region and integrally involved in its economies and politics. The forum met annually and exercised quite substantial influence in that it spoke for the governments that had shed their colonial masters.

In 1972 the forum established as its executive arm the South Pacific Bureau for Economic Cooperation (SPEC), headquartered in Fiji. That organization carried out the directives of the forum and as of the mid-1980s had promoted regional economic projects in areas of trade, investment, shipping, air services, telecommunications, marketing, and aid. SPEC has played a primary role in assisting in consultations between the forum and external organizations, such as the Association of South East Asian Nations (ASEAN), the UN's Economic and Social Commission for Asia and the Pacific (ESCAP), and the European Economic Community (EEC). The forum has expressed strong criticism of the slow pace of decolonization in French Oceania and the continued nuclear testing by France on Mururoa Atoll in French Polynesia. To date, the forum's major disagreements with the United States have been related to the American failure to ratify the international treaty drafted after years of negotiation by the UN Conference on the Law of the Sea, proposals to store or dump nuclear wastes in the Pacific, and deployment of nuclear ships and weapons in the region. In response to proposals put forth on the Law of the Sea, the island states claimed jurisdiction over all resources within the 200-nautical-mile Exclusive Economic Zone (EEZ—see Glossary) extending off their shores. The United States rejected the applicability of this claim over highly migratory species, such as tuna—a position the island states viewed as an attempt to invade their resources.

Some forum members were strongly of the opinion that the SPC was a vestige of colonialism. Forum members belong to both organizations, and some claimed that it was too expensive and time-consuming to maintain two major regional organizations. Since the late 1970s Papua New Guinea in particular has taken the stance that there should only be one major regional organization and that the forum and the SPC should be merged. The notion seems to be that the functions of the SPC should be absorbed by SPEC in ways that would reduce the influence of those countries geographically outside the region, i.e., Britain, France, and the United States.

The forum was very much a club of the states of the Commonwealth of Nations. In the decolonization process Australia, Britain, and New Zealand shed almost all of their Pacific dependencies. There were only two minor exceptions. Small Tokelau, which had fewer than 2,000 residents and only three atolls, desired to maintain its ties with New Zealand—a position it had made clear to the UN. The tiny and isolated Pitcairn Islands, populated by about 45 people descended from the mutineers of the H.M.S. *Bounty,* remained a British colony.

In this context, France and the United States were in somewhat of a delicate position; they were viewed in the region as the
last representatives of the old colonialism in the Pacific. As of mid-
1984 France continued to hold French Polynesia, Wallis and
Futuna, and New Caledonia. These had the status of overseas territories, were considered an integral part of France, and had
elected representation in the French government. France has
been the target of considerable criticism because it has insisted on
maintaining its presence in the Pacific, and the French feel
strongly that their language and culture should be perpetuated in
the islands. Events during 1983 and 1984 suggested, however,
that France might be softening its position and that greater autonomy and perhaps even independence might be a possibility for
New Caledonia. Any such development would surely have repercussions in French Polynesia, where pro-independence groups
have been strong in the past.

American Samoa and Guam remained United States territories; there was little likelihood of any significant change in
their political status. The United States continued to be the administering authority of the Trust Territory of the Pacific Islands
(TTPI). Negotiations on the TTPI's future political status began in
the late 1960s and lasted a long time. Initially, it was assumed that
the TTPI would remain unified while its new status was
negotiated. Instead, for a variety of complex reasons, fragmentation occurred, and four political units emerged: the Commonwealth of the Northern Mariana Islands, the Republic of the Marshall Islands, the Republic of Palau, and the Federated States of
Micronesia (FSM), the last including the former TTPI administrative districts of Yap, Truk, Ponape, and Kosrae.

In 1975 the Northern Marianas voted for commonwealth
status, which would make it a part of the United States; the
United States Congress approved the action the next year. Legally, however, the Northern Marianas would remain part of the
TTPI until the trusteeship was dissolved. After 1976, however,
both sides operated under a convenient fiction, acting as if the
Northern Marianas had already achieved commonwealth status;
it elected its own governor and legislature.

For a time it appeared that the FSM, Marshalls, and Palau
were headed toward free association arrangements initially based
on the model of the Cooks and Niue. As negotiations proceeded,
however, significant differences from that model developed. The
Compacts of Free Association in Micronesia are lengthy and very
complex legal documents. They deny strategic access to any pow-

ers other than the United States, which reserves the right to intervene in island affairs if and when it determines that such action is vital to its own national defense. The financial subsidies being offered the three countries are in the magnitude of multiples of millions annually, and they are the envy of others. In essence, it can be said that the three are granting the United States a number of rights and prerogatives that limit their own autonomy in exchange for large financial subsidies. It was clear that the United States would maintain a considerable presence and substantial influence in these island groups.

In 1979 the FSM and the Marshalls formed their own constitutional governments. Palau followed in 1981. Each polity elected a president and legislature. Plebiscites in the FSM and Marshalls approved the Compacts, and the agreements were sent to the United States Congress with the support of the administration of Ronald Reagan in mid-1984. Free association was not approved in Palau because of incompatibilities between the Palauan Constitution and the terms of the Compact in regard to nuclear concerns. Negotiations were continuing in mid-1984.

The Future

The decolonization of the Pacific, although not complete, has been peaceful and has proceeded relatively smoothly. The strains within the two major regional organizations will probably result in some reorganization or realignment in the next few years, but the process will not be rushed. Part of the new Pacific identity involves what islanders refer to as the "Pacific Way." It is said that Pacific islanders share a common heritage and have their own style, one that differs from that of the West. The people do not rush, human relations are conducted peacefully, and decisions are made through discussion and consensus. Confrontation is avoided, and social values take precedence over materialistic values.

Pacific islanders contend that they have always lived and behaved in such a manner. Considering the warfare and feuding of the past, this contention is not historically accurate, and certain elements of the Pacific Way are a myth—but a good myth that stresses that the conduct of human relations should be carried out in ways that show care and concern for the welfare of all. Perhaps the notion of the Pacific Way will assist insular peoples and their governments in approaching the problems of the future in cooperative and constructive ways.

It would seem that the greatest set of problems in the near future will be those stemming from rapidly increasing populations. Since the stabilization of populations and the end of depopulation during the period between the two wars, there has been a turnaround, and improved health and medical care since World War II has contributed to great growth rates of Pacific populations. Perhaps the most extreme example was in the TTPI, where the population almost tripled from about 50,000 during World War II to 140,000 in mid-1984. The population of French Polynesia has increased from 98,400 to 159,000 in mid-1984. Tonga has seen an increase from 77,500 to 104,000 in the same period. Fiji experienced an increase from roughly 500,000 to 680,000 in mid-1984.

The Pacific islands have only a limited capacity to accommodate increased populations, and the present rates of increase will soon strain island economies and ecosystems. To date, however, family planning and birth control programs have not proved popular anywhere. Urbanization has also occurred at a rapid pace. In part, the increased tempo of urban growth is the result of increased population sizes, but, as everywhere in the world, the urban centers draw from the rural areas those people who are in search of employment, education, health and medical care, and the diversions available there. Urban centers are placing an increased burden on local ecosystems; thus, facilities necessary for the support of urban life are often strained. The capitals of atoll nations are the most difficult of all to sustain, for the limited environment of the atoll is in no way suited for high-density and large populations. Local governments and SPC programs have attempted to make rural life more attractive, but to date the population movement continues from the countryside to the city.

With the exceptions of Papua New Guinea, nickel-rich New Caledonia, and perhaps Fiji, island economies are limited and fragile. Cash crops are few and, in the atolls, limited to copra. The islands are vulnerable to typhoons, drought, and plant infestations. A single disaster can bring damage requiring years of recovery. Indigenous commercial fishing operations are few and underdeveloped, but island governments have great hopes for the future exploitation of the ocean. With two or three exceptions, countries are heavily dependent upon economic aid from abroad, in most cases from the former colonial power. In this respect many of the old ties and linkages remain.

The challenges of the future are great, and the political stability of governments will in large part depend upon how successful they are in developing strategies to cope with the very real problems at hand. There is no doubt that external assistance will continue to be required. This very fact creates yet another problem for the island states in maintaining true sovereignty over their affairs while also depending on foreign donors.

Chapter 2.   Melanesia

*Stilt house for male adolescents and bachelors
on Malaita in the Solomon Islands*

AS DIVERSE INTERNALLY as they are different from each other, the islands of Melanesia—those in Papua New Guinea, Solomon Islands, Vanuatu, New Caledonia, and Fiji—defy convenient generalizations. Their traditional societies were fragmented into over 900 small linguistic groups that had their own forms of social and political organizations, little contact with each other, and no ambitions to develop national organizations. Only after the coming of the Europeans did these small social groups begin to merge into larger identities. This process was most rapid in Fiji, where traditional groups were more homogeneous than those in the other islands. History presented both Fiji and New Caledonia with a new source of social division; immigrant Indians in the former and French settlers in the latter soon became numerically, as well as politically and economically, important. Elsewhere, the foreigneres remained tiny minorities, in contrast to the indigenous Melanesians.

The physical differences between the islands are obvious; Papua New Guinea dwarfs the rest, having six times the population and 25 times the land area of Fiji, the next largest area in Melanesia. And yet all of the Melanesian territories are large by Pacific standards, a fact that contributes to their importance in regional and international forums. Their economies also differ in scale. In the early 1980s the per capita gross domestic product of New Caledonia was 14 times that of the poorest country, Vanuatu, some 12 times that of Solomon Islands, about nine times that of Papua New Guinea, and four times that of Fiji. The predominantly agrarian Melanesian sectors of each of these economies, however, resemble each other, and many Melanesian households live in ways fundamentally unchanged from those of their ancestors. Politically, New Caledonia is the exception; although the other Melanesian states have achieved independence, it remained a French territory in mid-1984. The other Melanesian states gave rhetorical support to the movement of its indigenous inhabitants to become the last Melanesians to obtain nationhood.

FIJI

Political Status	Independent state (1970)
Population	680,000 (1984 midyear estimate)
Land Area	18,333 square kilometers
Currency	Fiji dollar (F$)
Major Islands and Island Groups	Viti, Levu, Vanua Levu, Taveuni, Kadavu, Lomaiviti Group, Yasawa Group, Lau Group, Rotuma

Flag: British flag and Fiji shield—encompassing British lion, cross of St. George, sugarcane, coconut palm, dove of peace, and bananas—on blue field

Physical Environment

Fiji, a multiethnic society of native Melanesians—called Fijians—and immigrant Indians, encompasses some 332 islands and islets, about one-third of which are inhabited. The largest island Viti Levu, accounts for 57 percent of the land area and for over three-quarters of the population; Vanua Levu has another 30 percent of the land and 18 percent of the people. The distance from the northernmost to the southernmost islands is around 1,200 kilometers; that from the western to the eastern extremities is about 650 kilometers.

Vitu Levu has four basic kinds of terrain: plateau, mountain, upland, and coastal. In the center of the island the Nadrau Plateau rises some 900 to 1,000 meters above sea level, covering about 130 square kilometers of dense and marshy forest. Two mountain ranges running north and south of the plateau form the major divide, and the northern range contains Mount Victoria, at 1,424 meters the highest point in Fiji. Other mountain ranges above 600 meters separate the island into four upland areas that are heavily dissected by rivers. The undulating coastal hills and lowland plains contain most of the population. Numerous meandering rivers—of whhich the longest is the Rewa River—and many coastal streams create a complex drainage system and offer excellent hydroelectric potential. Reef systems intersecting with those of nearby islands form barriers around most of the island, sheltering large expanses of coastal waters and making good anchorages, especially at Suva.

Vanua Levu, having several jutting peninsulas, is less regularly shaped than its larger neighbor to the south. The main mountain range forms one plateau and two tablelands that have many peaks over 900 meters. The plains are generally lower, less undulating, and drier than those of Viti Levu, and the rivers are smaller but about as numerous.

Two other large islands, Kadavu and Taveuni, are each about the same size at just over 400 square kilometers. Like the main islands and most of the far-flung island groups, they are of volcanic origin. Most of the Lau Group, however, consists of raised limestone structures scattered across some 114,000 square kilometers of ocean and shares more characteristics with Tonga than with Fiji.

The tropical climate is controlled by southeast tradewinds, which blow from February to November. December and January have lighter, shifting winds, but storms and hurricanes also batter the islands. The temperature varies little during the year, from about 23°C to 27°C, dropping some 5°C at night and in the higher altitudes. The hottest months are from December through April, when the humidity is highest. The eastern and southeastern portions of the large islands—the windward sides—receive 2,800 to 3,500 millimeters of rainfall per year; the drier, leeward sides average about 1,800 to 2,000 millimeters.

The vegetation in Fiji is similar to that found elsewhere in Melanesia. Herbaceous plants, shrubs, grasses, and mangrove swamps along the coasts give way to trees, shrubs, and agricultural crops farther inland and on the lower slopes. The most striking contrast is between the windward and leeward sides—the former are mostly covered with tropical evergreens and other lush forest and the latter with low-lying trees and grasses. The rain forests contain some good commercial species but are not as dense as those in Southeast Asia. The limestone islands usually have tropical palms rather than montane species. About one-third of the 3,000 species of plants are indigenous, some of which are rare and beautiful.

Most of the animal life is not native, including pigs, rats, and dogs, which were introduced early in the country's history. Several species of bat, a flying squirrel, a few snakes (none of them poisonous), some lizards, and a chameleon are native, as are many of the nearly 70 species of birds. Some native ground-nesting species, however, have been killed off by the mongooses that were imported to control the rat population. Insects are abundant but do not include the malarial mosquito.

For census and administrative purposes, Fiji is divided into 15 provinces, which in turn are grouped into four divisions (see fig. 3). Rotuma Province is subsumed in Eastern Division. According to the latest decennial census, taken in 1976, some 37 percent of the population lived in urban areas—about 20 percent

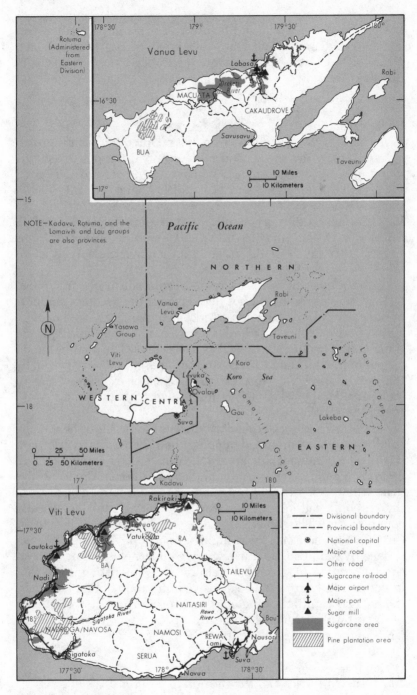

Figure 3. Fiji, 1984

towns of Labasa, Nadi, and Nausori. The rural population was concentrated in the sugar-growing areas of Ba, Macuata, and Nadroga/Navosa provinces, where the Indian ethnic group was in the majority.

Historical Setting

The Melanesian settlers who first peopled the islands probably arrived during the second millennium B.C.; pottery shards found near Sigatoka on Viti Levu have been dated to 1290 B.C. Divergent dialects and styles of pottery suggest that related groups from New Caledonia or the New Hebrides (present-day Vanuatu) joined the earlier settlers some time before the twelfth century A.D. The oral tradition and the ruins of fortifications suggest that much of the interaction among these early communities was hostile.

The importance of warfare and cannibalism in early Fijian history, however, should not detract from the accomplishments of the early culture. The subsistence economy produced enough agricultural surplus to afford some regional specialization and trade in fine handicrafts as well as necessities. The double-hulled canoes of Fiji facilitated interisland commerce and were prized by the neighboring Tongans. Large festivals of exchange *(solevu)* took place on special occasions and brought together hundreds of traders at a time.

Political and social organization was hierarchical, headed by chieftains who contended among themselves for power and status. The dominant chiefs were the war chiefs of various confederations *(vanua)* of clan groups and communities. Almost always male, the chiefs ruled in the name of the ancestral guardians of their people, although they were usually assisted by priestly counterparts. The office of chief, which became hereditary through the male line, was highly ritualized. Although characterized by cannibalistic ritual, warfare nonetheless brought about the integration of dissimilar cultural and linguistic groups into larger political entities. The decisive unification of Fiji, however, did not occur until the nineteenth century, primarily as the result of the growing influence of the Europeans, who came to the islands in the seventeenth century.

European Influence and the Cession to Britain

The early explorers who discovered Fiji for Europe were the least influential of the newcomers and did not put ashore for long.

The first was Dutch explorer Abel Tasman, who spotted the islands in 1643; the most famous was probably William Bligh, alleged tyrant of the H.M.S. *Bounty,* who passed through in his open longboat in 1789 and returned three years later in a large vessel. In the early nineteenth century, however, a few traders became more influential. They came from Australia, North America, and British India to barter first for sandalwood and then for bêche-de-mer, a sea cucumber used in Chinese cooking. Regardless of their place of origin, the white traders and settlers were identified as European by the Fijians. Periodic violence between the traders and the Fijians marred these earliest contacts.

Some of the Europeans jumped ship and stayed in Fiji to seek a lifelong adventure. They soon married Fijian women and established a mixed-blood community at Levuka, on the island of Ovalau, off Viti Levu. These so-called beachcombers were the go-betweens for the traders, who needed their linguistic and managerial talents to contract and bargain with the Fijians. Commodore Charles Wilkes of the United States Exploring Expedition, which made the first systematic survey of the islands in 1840, was able to get one of the beachcombers appointed the first American consular representative to Fiji.

Although the indigenous culture at first proved strongly resistant to their efforts, Christian missionaries had an important and revolutionary effect on Fiji. The first missionaries were native Tahitians trained by the London Missionary Society; they arived in 1830 from Tonga. In 1835 evangelists David Cross and William Cargill also arrived from Tonga, sent by the Methodist church. One of their lasting contributions was the development of a writing system for the native dialects. Fijians flocked to Christianity, however, only after the conversion of their most powerful chieftains.

In the early nineteenth century the islet of Bau had become the center of power for the western part of Fiji, and by 1850 the second of two strong leaders, Cakobau, emerged as preeminent chief. He was even addressed by the Europeans as King of Fiji. In 1851, however, a revolt against his authority spread quickly from along the Rewa River, and after several defeats Cakobau decided that a conversion to Christianity might be expedient. His new spiritual status enabled him to secure the support of an American vessel and a battlefield alliance with a Christian king from Tonga. Cakobau's victory in 1855, however, encompassed only western Fiji; he anxiously watched the growing influence of another Christian prince from Tonga, Ma'afu, in the Lau Group. The conversion of these chiefs ensured the success of the missionary effort in Fiji, one consequence of which was the cessation of cannibalistic rituals.

The political involvement of the European powers started in earnest after the arrival of William T. Pritchard (son of George Pritchard, missionary and British consul in French Polynesia), the first British consul, in 1858. He took office amid British fears that France or the United States might annex Fiji. He was able to convince Cakobau, who feared both Ma'afu and a pressing American claim against him in a case involving property damages, to cede the islands to Britain. In return, Britain would sustain and protect Cakobau and his people. Although the offer was refused by Britain and Pritchard was recalled, the move attracted settlers from Australia and New Zealand, who came to farm cotton—then at a premium price because of the Civil War in the United States. By 1870 some 2,000 European settlers were in Fiji; they brought 1,000 people from other Pacific islands to work in the new fields.

At first the political situation seemed to stabilize: Ma'afu, who had received some European support in setting up a government over the Lau Group, Taveuni, and much of Vanua Levu, reluctantly agreed to swear allegiance to Cakobau in 1871. Controversies over the level of taxation, the collapse of the international market for cotton, and the harsh treatment of plantation laborers, however, soon caused a fiscal crisis and even violence. In 1872 the new British consul, John Bates Thurston, reported the confusion to Britain and appealed for the annexation of the islands. A commission of inquiry was dispatched in March 1874, and on its advice Britain prepared to annex the country. On October 10 Cakobau, Ma'afu, and 11 other Fijian chiefs signed the formal Deed of Cession, and Fiji became a British colonial possession. The colony began on a most inauspicious note—in early 1875 a measles epidemic wiped out at least one-fifth of the Fijian population.

Colonial Development and Independence

The main currents of the colonial era, which lasted until 1970, were the rapid immigration of indentured Indian laborers to build a plantation economy based on sugarcane, the maintenance of special land and political rights for the Fijians, and the gradual opening of the unrepresentative colonial administration to participation by the various ethnic groups. Political independence from Britain came to hinge on the development of a formula for sharing political power among these ethnic communities.

The priority of the first governor, Sir Arthur Gordon, was above all to restore the confidence of the Fijians after the tragic epidemic; only secondarily did he see to the concerns of the European settlers, many of whom were bankrupt. The Europeans received no elected representation for 30 years while the colonial administration attempted to transform the traditional administrative structure to suit its rule. Government revenue was collected in kind from the Fijian chiefs, who acted as representatives of the government. The ready assistance of the chiefs in putting down a rebellion in the interior of Viti Levu in 1876—the last organized violence of major consequence—verified the wisdom of Gordon and his adviser, Thurston, who eventually became governor himself.

The government was averse to having Fijians work on European plantations and strictly regulated blackbirding, the virtual kidnapping of people from some areas of the Pacific to work on plantations. Instead, to promote its idea of an economy based on sugarcane, the government sanctioned the indenture of laborers from the Indian subcontient, who began arriving in 1879. Nine years later there were 6,000 Indians residing in Fiji; by 1916, when the official immigration ended, there were more than 50,000. At the time of the first census, in 1936, there were 85,000 Indians, of whom 72 percent had been born in the colony. Fewer than half of the immigrants ever returned to India, although their status and lot were extremely low, often verging on slavery.

Revenue from the sugar industry, which became the near monopoly of one Australian processing company, the Colonial Sugar Refining Company, enabled the government to expand its construction program, particularly in the new capital and port of Suva. While exports suffered long periods of low prices, substantial booms and steady growth in the other periods ensured prosperity at least for the European community. The Fijians participated only marginally in this economic activity, selling little more than coconuts or bananas to supplement their subsistence farming.

The political development of the colony took a decisive turn in 1904, when six elected Europeans and two Fijians nominated from the Council of Chiefs were admitted into the Legislative Council, an advisory body to the governor. In 1916 the governor appointed one Indian member, and in 1929 the first Indian representatives were elected. The governor ignored a campaign on the part of some Indians to establish an electoral system based on the principal of "one man, one vote," in which everyone would choose from the same slate of candidates, regardless of ethnic affiliation.

The preserved system gave each community five representatives: the Europeans and the Indians each had three elected and two appointed representatives; the Fijians nominated five individuals for appointment. Throughout this period, however, the governors and their administrators held final authority over all policy. Indeed, historian Timothy Macnaught has shown that after Thurston's death in 1897 most British administrators—in their well-intentioned zeal to "modernize" the society—became highhanded in their dealings with the Fijian chiefs.

Behind this political evolution lay economic and social tensions that revolved primarily around the question of land. Except for the 1905–09 period, when 8,000 hectares of property were sold to the Europeans, land sales were prohibited. The government upheld reluctantly and after great delay the claims of some early settlers to about 162,000 hectares of land. After 1920, when the system of indenture was terminated, the Indians became tenant farmers on lands owned primarily by the Fijian communities, who held all unalienated land. None of the groups seemed content with this situation, but when the Council of Chiefs approved the leasing of all lands not required for their immediate needs in 1936, tensions eased. Thereafter, a complicated system of ownership and tenure developed. Essentially, the Indians worked the commercial agricultural lands, the Fijians received rents, and the Europeans supplied the capital to process and trade the sugarcane produced.

The system was supported by conservative Fijians, such as Ratu Josef Lalabalavu Vaanialialia Sukuna, an Oxford-educated descendant of the great chiefs and an equally great legislator and politician. The only populist movement, which attempted ineptly to replace the European middlemen with a Fijian company, was led by Apolosi R. Nawai, whom the government considered to be a fanatic and a threat and who spent most of his life after 1909 in prison.

After World War II, in which a number of Fijians distinguished themselves in service on behalf of the Allied forces, the pace of political reform quickened—especially in the 1960s, when indirect and colonial forms of administration seemed out of place. In 1963 the legislative council was enlarged yet again, and women of all ethnic groups participated in elections for the first time. Two political parties were born: the Alliance Party, a multiracial but predominantly Fijian organization headed by Ratu Sir Kamisese Mara, and the Federation Party, also multiethnic in appeal but dominated by the Indian community. In 1964 the Executive Council became a cabinet in all but name, and one year later a constitutional conference in London further enlarged the Legislative Council and adopted procedures to elect some members from a common voting roll. The number of representatives from each ethnic group, however, remained fixed.

The intense fighting between the two major political parties over the issue of voting procedures gradually cooled. In April 1970 another constitutional conference was held in London. The conference endorsed the complex procedures in use as the best means of selecting a proposed House of Representatives. After drafting the Constitution and approving its implementation without further election, the conference agreed that Fiji would become independent on October 10, 1970. In January 1973, a year after the first parliamentary elections held under the Constitution returned the Alliance Party to power, Ratu Sir George Cakobau, great-grandson of the chief who had sworn allegiance to Queen Victoria, replaced the colonial holdover as governor general.

The Social System

Ethnicity continued to be the primary basis for social identification in 1984. In general, racial and linguistic factors determined ethnic affiliations, but other cultural affinities, such as religion and social organization, were also associated with one or another ethnolinguistic group. Economic development and the expansion of public administration and education have cut across some of these ethnic boundaries, producing similar social and economic classes within ethnic groups. Nevertheless, relations between the ethnic communities were the main focus of public attention.

Ethnolinguistic Groups

The term *Fijian* may only refer to a member of the Fijian ethnic community and not to other inhabitants of the country. The ethnic composition of the population, according to official estimates for mid-1981, was Fijians, 44.5 percent; Indians, 50.7 percent; Part Europeans, 1.7 percent; Rotumans, 1.2 percent; other Pacific islanders, 0.9 percent; Chinese, 0.7 percent; Europeans, 0.6 percent; and others, 0.1 percent.

The indigenous Fijians are basically Melanesians but have an admixture of Polynesian physical and cultural characteristics. Their traditional systems of social organization—hierarchical, patrilineal, and elaborately ceremonial—are akin to those of Polynesia and are much more homogeneous from area to area than are those elsewhere in Melanesia. Although there are many local variants, which may be grouped into eastern and western Fijian dialect groups, the eastern dialect of Bau—into which the Bible was translated in the nineteenth century—has been deemed the official language of Fijians. Most of the chiefly families have traced their origins to the arrival ages ago of a Polynesian chieftain who landed on northwestern Viti Levu and established the first *yasuva*, sometimes translated as tribe. In the late 1970s there were some 600 *yasuva* on Viti Levu alone. Like the language dialects, the Fijian ethnic group can be divided into eastern and western factions; the easterners, dominated by the chiefs of Bau and the Lau Group, have had the most influence in government.

The *yasuva* was formed of subsidiary groups. At the bottom were extended families, which were further grouped into patrilineal subclan and clan groups. The latter, called *mataqali*, became the official landowning units in the colonial era and remained so in the 1980s, when some 6,600 *mataqali* were registered. Before the 1970s an individual's relationship to the *mataqali* was often unclear and even tenuous, but as land has become scarcer, the *mataqali* seemed to be asserting greater influence over individuals.

Fijian culture is full of ceremony, and the most popular has been the ceremonial drinking of kava, a nonalcoholic beverage extracted from a pepper plant. Although it was sold commercially for refreshment, it was used in all proper rituals for birth, marriage, death, the installment of a chief, and so forth. The practice of *solevu*, especially the exchange of precious whales teeth, has also persisted. Despite discouragement from the government since colonial times, Fijians often were obligated to share their wealth with kinfolk on demand, with the understanding that they could receive a returned favor in the future.

Although Fijians have achieved positions of power and influence in the government and public administration, many, especially in the hinterlands and the outlying islands, remained subsistence farmers, growing taro and yams as staples. More and more, however, these households have turned to the commercial economy. In 1976 over 38 percent of the technical, professional, and managerial work force was Fijian. Fijians made up 59 percent of all service workers, about 57 percent of agriculturists, some 35 percent of industrial workers, about 33 percent of clerical staff, and 19 percent of sales personnel.

Almost all of the Indians living in Fiji in 1984 had been born and raised there and were citizens. Many of the distinctions

*Fijian man offering
a half-coconut shell
full of kava,
the national drink
Courtesy Fiji
Visitors Bureau*

within the community that had been important in India had withered away or changed. As late as 1980, however, one anthropologist identified four important subgroups related to the region of origin in India—Northerners, Southerners, Punjabis, and Gujaratis—and two that depended on religious affiliation—Hindus and Muslims. The Punjabi group included the Sikhs, and together with the Gujaratis these people had immigrated freely into Fiji outside of the indenture system. Within the Hindu community, stringent codes of behavior for members of castes have disappeared along with the organizations to supervise them. Most Hindus, however, were aware of their caste and tended to marry within it. Caste affiliation also contributed somewhat to social status, which was generally determined by educational, professional, and economic achievement. Regardless of the subgroup, most Indians—especially in the rural areas—have maintained the ideal of a patrilineal extended family system and have interacted most commonly with such kin.

On the basis of language use, it seemed that the community has become more homogeneous. Whereas one-quarter of the Indians who immigrated to Fiji were from the southern areas of India and spoke the Dravidian languages of Tamil and Telegu, the 1966 census showed that only 4 percent of all Indians still used these languages in the home. Hindustani or Hindi has replaced the numerous dialects and was spoken in 90 percent of all Indian households in 1966. The same census showed that 3 percent of the households spoke Gujarati, 1.5 percent Urdu, and the rest other languages. According to one survey, however, nearly 62 percent of the Muslims preferred their children to learn Urdu as a second language to English.

As in colonial times, the Indian population has continued to dominate the sugarcane industry. In addition, they worked small farms cultivating rice and vegetables and raising livestock. According to the 1976 census, about 37 percent of the Indian community was employed in farming, forestry, and fishing, representing some 40 percent of all workers in this sector. The Indians represented 43 percent of all professional and technical workers, some 49 percent of all managers and administrators, about 53 percent of all clerical workers, some 58 percent of industrial and transportation workers, and over two-thirds of sales personnel. In 1980 they made up more than one-half of the high-level positions of the Fiji Public Service, the police force, the Ministry of Education, and the Ministry of Health. Between 1974 and 1978 the Indians constituted more than two-thirds of those who passed the New Zealand university entrance examination, the prerequisite for university study in Fiji.

The Europeans and Part Europeans were primarily the descendants of Australian and New Zealand settlers, many of whom took local spouses. The Europeans were originally the plantation owners but have moved into commerce, industry, and government service. In the 1970s, however, the opportunities for government service tended to decrease, and many Europeans left the country. The 1976 census showed them nonetheless to be greatly overrepresented in professional, technical, administrative, and managerial employment. The Part European community has continued to grow, and some have asserted their independence from the Europeans by calling themselves Part Fijians. In 1976 members of this group were disproportionately employed in managerial, administrative, clerical, and sales work.

The Rotumans were a small minority, most of whom have migrated to Viti Levu from their distant home. They are Polynesian but mix well with the Fijians. Other Pacific islanders living in Fiji include some Solomon Islanders, Tongans, Samoans, and people from Kiribati. The people of Banaba (formerly Ocean Island) in Kiribati and some Tuvaluans have purchased islands in Fiji to replace their abandoned home islands; they remained under Fiji law in 1984 but had special autonomy. All these groups were distributed evenly throughout the various categories of economic livelihood.

The Chinese first came to Fiji in the 1870s. Their numbers grew until the 1960s, when many decided to emigrate to Canada. The community included people from four southern Chinese dialect groups. The Chinese were overrepresented in the same economic areas as the Part Europeans. They maintained one Chinese-language school in Suva.

Religion and Education

Fiji is a crossroads of three of the world's great religions: Christianity, Hinduism, and Islam. The Constitution does not sanction an official religion but does invoke the name of God and guarantees the freedom of religious belief and proselytization. According to the 1976 census, only 1 percent of the population chose not to associate itself with a religion. About 51 percent of the population classified themselves as Christian, about 40 percent as Hindu, and 7.7 percent as Muslim.

Among Protestant Christian denominations, Methodists have been the most successful, building on the achievements of the early missionaries. They made up about 73 percent of the Christian community in 1976; nearly all were Fijian. The Roman Catholic church claimed about 17 percent of Christian adherents, including significant minorities of Chinese, Indians, Europeans, and Part Europeans. The Seventh-Day Adventist, Assembly of God, and Anglican churches each had 2 to 3 percent of the Christian community, while other denominations made up the rest.

Some 80 percent of the Indians identified themselves as Hindu. Each predominantly Indian community had at least one Hindu temple, and often there was a second temple representing a reformed sect. Although public and even household rituals have become infrequent, all Hindus took part in Fiji's two most important festivals, Holi and Dewah. Some of the orthodox Hindus—especially Southerners—performed rites of purification, such as puncturing their faces with metal skewers.

Muslims made up 15.4 percent of the Indian community in 1976. Over 63 percent of this group were Sunni Muslims. The largest mosque is at Lautoka, but there are numerous other mosques in other parts of Viti Levu in particular. Some 45 percent of the Muslims lilved in Ba Province.

Education has been closely associated with religion in Fiji since the Christian missions set up the first schools more than a century ago. As late as 1977, when detailed statistics were last available, Christian missions still ran 113 schools, while other religious bodies managed another 76. Local committees were in charge of 575 schools, and the government directly managed 35 others. Although school attendance was not compulsory, enrollment was universal in the 662 primary schools operating in 1981. Over 60 percent of the relevant age-group was enrolled in the 138 secondary and 36 technical and vocational schools operating that year. The number of primary students per teacher dropped from more than 30 students in 1970 to about 218 students in 1981. There were 18 students per teacher in secondary schools.

The increased enrollments and improved teacher-to-student ratio were aided by large government expenditures. In 1981 all classes through seventh grade were free, slightly behind the government target of having free education through eighth grade by 1980. Government support was in the form of full salaries for government-trained teachers, grants for privately trained teachers, free textbooks and other materials, and remittances for all student fees. The government spent approximately F$309 (for value of the Fiji dollar—see Glossary) per student in 1981, a 69-percent increase in real terms since 1971. Four teacher colleges—two of them state-run—had facilities for training some 600 teachers per year, but the number of graduates was reduced in 1981 as the nation neared its capacity for absorbing them. Fiji is the single largest contributor to and the home of the University of the South Pacific, based in Suva. The country has a small school of medicine, an agricultural college, a theological college, and a technology institute.

Throughout the history of the education system, the Indian community has urged that the government take over and transform the committee-run schools into genuinely multiethnic institutions. For its part the government has avowed that it favors desegregation, but as of 1978 more than 90 percent of the primary schools in the rural areas were under the control of a single ethnic group. By contrast nearly one-third of the primary schools in Suva were multiethnic. The secondary schools were more likely to have representatives from all ethnic groups, even in the countryside, because of their relative scarcity. The bifurcation of the school system persisted in the teachers' organizations, one of which represented Indian and the other Fijian teachers.

Through the fourth grade the language of instruction is the official Bauan dialect in the Fijian classes, Hindi in the Hindu Indian classes, Urdu in the Muslim Indian classes, and English in the European and Part European classes. Thereafter, English, which is taught as a second language from the very start, becomes the sole language of instruction. Fijian and Hindi are optional testing areas in the junior-level examinations taken at the end of the tenth grade.

The most controversial educational policy has been the preference system for Fijian students at the university level. The government's policy has been that 50 percent of all scholarships be given to Fijians, even if this has meant a lowering of entrance requirements. Indian opposition to this system was a factor in the 1977 elections and has flared up on several other occasions.

The influence of religious and educational training on the value systems of the individuals and groups within Fiji society has been a matter of conjecture. The individualism of the Christian and Muslim faiths and the disintegration of the caste system among Hindus may be causing the deterioration of family obligations in the panoply of traditional social values. The educational curriculum, which has depended on imported textbooks and ideologies, may be further stressing the importance of individual effort and profit. One education analyst decried the incursion of Western ideas of consumption and capitalism as a blow to the rich traditional cultures of Fiji. Nonetheless, even those Fijian families that have escaped to Suva remained obligated to their rural kinfolk. Another remnant of the traditional cultures has been the continued low status of women, which has been reinforced by strictures in the Muslim and Hindu faiths. Arranged marriages have also continued in many Indian households.

Changes in the standards of social behavior have not all been for the good. Pressures for educational and economic achievement have weighed heavily on some young minds, causing psychological disorders and even suicides. One report suggested that suicides committed by youths was on the rise in the 1980s. The fact that Fijian suicide appeared to be rare suggested that some of the traditional communal supports were still operative in that community in the 1980s. Marijuana use was a growing but relatively limited problem among the youth of all ethnic groups.

Population and Social Welfare

The population of Fiji grew rapidly even after the end of official Indian immigration. The highest natural growth rates occurred in the 1950s, when the average was over 3 percent per year; the rate declined dramatically during the 1970s, when it was just under 2 percent per year. Urban growth trends were higher still and resulted in the concentration of about one-fifth of the population in the greater metropolitan area around Suva. The acceptance of modern methods of birth control and family planning by some 38 percent of married women in the childbearing ages as of 1977 has helped lower the growth rate. At the same time, both the death rate and the infant mortality rate have been well below those of countries having a similar economic status.

The major concentrations of the Indian population outside the capital city were in the sugarcane districts on the western and northwestern sides of the two main islands. The heaviest concentration of Fijians was in the lower Rewa River Valley on the eastern coast of Viti Levu. Other Fijian villages were located along the coasts, rivers, and streams.

The quality of life (by international standards) for the average Fiji citizen has been good. The life expectancy was nearly 70 years in 1982, infant mortality was less than 37 deaths per thousand, and although the number of people per physician was relatively large, the number for each nurse and each hospital bed was low. Over 70 percent of the population had access to safe water supplies, and over 96 percent had the use of sanitary sewerage facilities. Housing development has been chiefly an urban problem; some 13 percent of the people living in urban Suva were classified as squatters in 1983. In general, however, the housing stock has expanded to meet the needs of the growing population—with the exception of major setbacks, such as occurred during a hurricane in 1983. Government spending on housing and social services rose nearly twice as rapidly as the population during the 1971–81 period, even after accounting for inflation.

Because of budgetary constraints, however, welfare payments did not change from the maximum of F$40 a month for a family of four during the 1975–83 period. In 1982 only 4,000 people were classified as destitute, but the number was estimated to have grown by 20 percent in 1983. Many of the squatters living in Suva, moreover, earned more monthly income than the official poverty line, thus barring them from receiving support. More and more of the individuals on the social welfare rolls have been abandoned wives and chldren—a sign, perhaps, of a deteriorating family system.

The Economy

Although the gross domestic product (GDP—see Glossary), equivalent to about US$1,134 per person in 1982, was high by comparison with some other developing countries, the economy still depended heavily on sugar exports and tourism—both of which were sensitive to fluctuations in the international economy. About one-third of the Fijian work force, moreover, was still employed in subsistence farming or fishing. Fijians produced little for sale in the commercial sector, where the other ethnic groups generated most of the wealth. The narrow basis for future economic growth, persistent unemployment, and differences in the standard of living between urban and rural households continued to disturb the government, which nonetheless has presided over a relatively prosperous economy since the nation's independence.

National income statistics for Fiji have not been completely reliable, but the available data show that during the 1960–79 period, GDP grew by between 5 and 6 percent per year in real terms. The yearly pace of economic growth has varied, and it slowed considerably in the 1980s. Economic activity and income actually shrank in 1980, 1982, and 1983 because of depressed international sugar prices, increases in the cost of imported oil, and the onslaught of a hurricane and prolonged drought.

The structure of economic demand has changed slightly. From the 1958–60 period to the 1978–80 period, exports decreased in value from over 51 percent to 45 percent of GDP. Government consumption expenditure rose from 16 to 17 percent of GDP, while private consumption declined from 65 to 62 percent of GDP. Investment changed most strikingly from 16 to 24 percent of GDP. Some of the increase, however, went to the purchase of imports, raising their value from 48 to 50 percent of GDP. The gap between exports and imports widened further in 1981 and 1982, according to preliminary statistics, averaging about 9 percent of GDP.

The level of employment and unemployment, which was a major concern to the nation's economic policymakers, was difficult to determine because of the large subsistence sector. The labor force was probably growing by 2.5 to 3 percent per year during the 1976–81 period, but formal employment expanded at best by 2.9 percent per year. The negative economic growth rates experienced since that time suggest that the employment situation has deteriorated significantly.

Economic Policy and Management

The Fiji government has favored private enterprise and initiative since colonial times but has directed the economy through consecutive five-year plans, the eighth of which spanned the period from 1981 to 1985. The plans have helped guide public investment over the long run, despite temporary changes in fiscal policy during individual years. The seventh and eighth plans concentrated on expanding investment in the rural sector, encouraging Fiji citizens to enter business ventures either on their own or jointly with foreign help, and improving the basic needs of the population through investment in public service.

Total government expenditure during the 1976–80 period averaged more than one-quarter of GDP, rising slightly during the period. Current expenditures were equivalent to 19 percent of GDP and increased more rapidly than capital expenditures. In 1981 total expenditure rose to more than 29 percent of GDP, pushed upward by capital spending, which topped 9 percent of GDP for the first time. The increased capital expenditures were devoted to a major water supply project in the Nadi and Lautoka areas and a large hydroelectric project. Budget estimates for 1982 and 1983, which were made before a major hurricane hit the islands in 1983, projected that total expenditures would remain at around 30 percent of GDP. Although capital spending was expected to fall off sharply, pressures for salary increases from the civil service and the cost of financing the national debt would boost the overall level of spending.

Expenditures on social services and welfare have made up the largest category of public spending, representing more than than 37 percent of the total in the 1976–80 period as spending on economic services and infrastructure rose. Interest payments on the outstanding government deficit also increased, from an average of about 6 percent of total expenditures during the 1976–80 period to nearly 10 percent of the total in the 1981–83 period.

The reasons for the increase in the government deficit from less than 4 percent of GDP in the 1976–80 period to nearly 6 percent in the 1981–83 period were the close link between government revenue and economic growth and the political difficulty in cutting expenditures and raising taxes. Domestic taxes were equivalent to 12 percent of GDP in the 1976–80 period, and taxes on international trade added another 6 percent. The total tax burden rose to about 20 percent of GDP in 1981. In 1982 and 1983, however, total tax revenue was estimated to have declined from 18 percent of GDP, particularly because of decreased revenues from excise and custom duties. Part of the shortfall was caused by reductions in export taxes for sugar and coconut products, which faced poor international prices until 1983.

Managing the money supply within the context of the balance of payments and inflation has been a major activity of the Ministry of Finance and the Central Monetary Authority, the nation's central bank. Much of the economy's inflation has been imported, particularly since the surge of international oil prices began in 1973. The overall average increase in the consumer price level was about 10 percent per year during the 1972–82 period, but the worst years were those immediately after major adjustments to the price of imported oil. After peaking at about 14.5 percent in 1980, however, inflation fell to around 6 to 8 percent in the 1981–83 period. The central bank has generally followed a countercyclical monetary policy that encouraged domestic credit to expand when export earnings were low and restricted growth when the balance of payments was favorable. One noteworthy trend since the late 1970s has been the tendency of the government and official agencies, such as the public utilities, to grab a larger share of the available domestic credit; their claims rose from 15 to 26 percent of domestic credit during the 1976–82 period. To prevent any additional crowding out of the private sector, the government raised as many of its financing needs as possible overseas.

The central bank strictly regulated the local banking industry by maintaining maximum deposit and lending rates in all categories of finance in addition to reserve and central bank discount requirements. Beginning in late 1981, however, the banking authorities raised interest rates significantly. In 1983 and 1984 the Ministry of Finance introduced new banking legislation drafted with the advice of the International Monetary Fund (IMF—see Glossary) to reform the system. Among the many changes that were designed to make the financial market more efficient were the creation of merchant banks and the elimination of interest rate controls on large deposits and loans. In 1980 Fiji had five commercial banks—four foreign and one government-owned—one government development bank, and numerous credit unions.

Foreign trade has been critical to the well-being of the insular economy (see table 2). Merchandise exports, excluding reexports, have fluctuated between 15 and 25 percent of the value of GDP; earnings from services, especially tourism, have been equivalent to around 30 percent of GDP. The government has actively promoted exports by sending trade missions overseas, participating in international commodity and trade agreements, and closely monitoring foreign financial and trade markets. The central bank has carefully pegged the value of the Fiji dollar to the weighted value of the currencies of its major trading partners—Australia, Britain, Japan, New Zealand, and the United States (see table 3). Imports have averaged over 50 percent of the value of GDP, and customs duties have been relatively low in comparison with other developing countries.

Capital inflows in the form of international loans and investment have offset the frequent current account deficits; Fiji has received little grant assistance. The government had long-term loans of about F$146 million outstanding in 1982; debt-service payments were expected to be equivalent to some 7 percent of the value of export earnings in 1983. Direct foreign investment, which came to a complete halt in the 1976–78 period, increased by more than 50 percent per year from 1979 to 1982, when it totaled F$32 million. The government created the Economic Development Board in 1979 to be a one-stop center for approving foreign investments. The agency was elevated to executive rather than advisory status in 1981 and seems to have been at least partially responsible for the upsurge in investment. Although the government claimed to have one of the most favorable incentive programs for foreign investors in the world, a report compiled by a British consultant suggested that the system remained complex, understaffed, and inadequate by international standards.

Table 2. Fiji. Balance of Payments, 1981–83[1]
(in millions of Fiji dollars)[2]

	1981	1982	1983
PAYMENTS			
Merchandise imports			
Chemicals	17.6	14.2	21.9
Duty-free goods	25.5	23.9	23.4
Food, beverages, and animals	62.3	59.4	58.4
Machines and equipment	50.6	36.3	38.6
Mineral fuels	88.0	108.8	103.4
Raw materials	14.6	10.8	15.7
Textiles, clothing, and footwear	28.5	25.6	29.1
Transportation equipment	36.1	18.0	23.7
Government imports	10.3	12.3	1.2
Other imports	83.7	95.4	99.0
Total merchandise imports	417.2	404.7	414.4
Other current payments			
Transportation	10.7	7.2	8.1
Travel and tourism	13.7	14.1	14.9
Overseas investment income	25.6	38.8	27.2
Unrequited transfers	15.0	12.6	14.2
Other	60.4	70.5	55.5
Total other current payments	125.4	143.2	119.9
Capital payments[3]			
Private	11.5	11.5	11.2
Official	7.6	12.4	14.1
Total capital payments	19.1	23.9	25.3
TOTAL PAYMENTS	561.7	571.8	559.6

Table 2. *(Continued)*
(in millions of Fiji dollars)[2]

	1981	1982	1983
RECEIPTS			
Merchandise exports			
Copra and copra products	6.1	3.5	7.6
Fish	19.1	11.7	16.5
Ginger	1.3	1.4	1.5
Gold	13.9	14.7	18.0
Sugar	156.8	130.6	123.2
Timber	4.2	2.9	2.7
Other exports	6.4	8.2	8.9
Reexports of fuel	16.6	22.5	22.9
Other reexports	6.7	6.9	5.2
Total merchandise exports	231.1	202.4	206.5
Other current receipts			
Transportation	22.1	28.3	16.9
Travel and tourism	113.1	125.5	108.5
Overseas investment income	19.7	14.6	13.6
Unrequited transfers	16.7	18.0	17.8
Other	68.5	76.2	127.7
Total other current receipts	240.1	262.6	284.5
Capital receipts[4]			
Private	8.3	12.4	12.9
Official	47.2	53.4	39.0
Total capital receipts	55.5	65.8	51.9
TOTAL RECEIPTS	526.7	530.8	542.9
Merchandise trade balance	-186.1	-202.3	-207.9
Current account balance	-71.4	-82.9	-43.3
Capital account balance	36.4	41.9	26.6
Overall balance	-35.0	-41.0	-16.7
Change in net foreign assets	-14.0	-13.8	1.6
Adjustment[5]	21.0	27.2	18.3
Net foreign assets	120.1	106.3	108.0
Gross foreign reserves[6]	120.1	119.8	122.7

[1]Data are from foreign exchange records and are somewhat lower in value than customs statistics.
[2]For value of the Fiji dollar—see Glossary.
[3]Chiefly long-term.
[4]Chiefly long-term; data for 1981 include an allocation from the International Monetary Fund (IMF—see Glossary).
[5]Errors and omissions and changes in the value of foreign assets.
[6]Including borrowing from the IMF.
Source: Based on information from Fiji, Central Monetary Authority, *Annual Report, 1983*, Suva, 1984, 38a–39a.

The government has also intervened in the labor market via the Tripartite Forum, established in 1976. The forum has brought together for annual wage negotiations representatives of the Fiji Trade Union Congress—the largest labor federation in the country—the Fiji Employers' Consultative Association, and the government. Although the forum has no statutory authority, the

Table 3. Fiji. Direction of Trade, 1981–83[1]
(in millions of Fiji dollars)[2]

Country	Year	Imports	Exports Domestic	Exports Reexports	Exports Total
Australia	1981	194.1	16.8	2.9	19.7
	1982	184.7	22.2	6.9	29.1
	1983	188.6	25.6	2.5	28.1
New Zealand	1981	75.1	18.8	3.0	21.8
	1982	74.5	22.6	3.1	25.7
	1983	80.8	10.3	1.9	12.2
Japan	1981	86.4	18.6	0.7	19.3
	1982	67.7	4.5	0.7	5.2
	1983	82.6	5.3	0.7	6.0
Britain	1981	29.5	64.6	2.8	67.4
	1982	19.8	58.3	1.6	59.9
	1983	24.9	59.6	1.3	60.9
United States	1981	38.7	23.9	3.8	27.7
	1982	17.5	19.0	7.5	26.5
	1983	19.1	16.8	3.9	20.7
Singapore	1981	37.7	9.0	0.1	9.1
	1982	43.8	8.8	0.7	9.5
	1983	20.7	9.3	0.3	9.6
Canada	1981	2.8	9.6	1.1	10.7
	1982	2.2	5.5	1.0	6.5
	1983	2.8	4.5	1.1	5.6
Other	1981	75.6	32.5	60.9	93.4
	1982	65.4	40.4	62.9	103.3
	1983	73.8	46.2	55.5	101.7
TOTAL	1981	539.9	193.8	75.3	269.1
	1982	475.6	181.3	84.4	265.7
	1983	493.3	177.6	67.2	244.8

[1]Imports are based on cost, insurance, and freight (c.i.f.) values and exports on free on board (f.o.b) values.
[2]For value of the Fiji dollar—see Glossary.
Source: Based on information from Fiji, Central Monetary Authority, *Annual Report, 1983*, Suva, 1984, 89.

members have generally agreed to abide by its findings. The decisions of this body have had an important effect on negotiations between the many smaller unions and employers' groups unaffiliated with the tripartite representatives. The 45 unions in existence in 1982 represented slightly more than one-half of the paid work force of 80,000.

In general, the government has steered clear of outright wage and price controls. Wages were expected to be determined by collective bargaining agreements or, in the absence of unions, by the determination of wage councils, having equal representation from both management and labor. The government has set up agencies to regulate prices for the major utilities and selected agricultural, forestry, and fishery commodities. In 1983 there were 14 nonfinancial public enterprises engaged in producing or marketing economic goods and services.

Agriculture, Forestry, and Fishing

Natural tropical forests covered some 848,000 hectares—nearly one-half the area of Fiji—in 1982. Sugarcane fields and coconut plantations stretched over some 140,000 hectares, pine tree plantations over 58,300 hectares, and mangrove swamps another 38,600 hectares. The remaining 750,000 hectares consisted of built-up areas or land used for subsistence and other types of agriculture. Sugarcane land has been the most economically useful for over a century, but the government expected the developing pine plantations to be valuable in the 1990s. The terms of land tenure and sugarcane marketing have been the most controversial issues facing the economy for decades. The nationalization of the sugar industry in 1973 went far toward placating the sugarcane farmers, but the land issues remained a sore point for the Indian community.

The basic controversy stemmed from the fact that the Fijian *mataqali* owned about 83 percent of all the land. The government had acquired title to 7 percent of the land, and another 10 percent belonged to the non-Fijians. As a result, about 30 percent of Fijian-owned land has been rented out, primarily to Indian farmers. Disputes between landlords and tenants over the payment of rent, the length of tenure, and compensation for improvements to the land have been frequent.

The Native Land Trust Board, established in 1940, determined which lands were to be reserved exclusively for Fijian use and administered the leasing of unreserved lands. The board was responsible for collecting all lease monies on behalf of the Fijians and in 1978 received F$1.7 million. In 1975 the board set up a subsidiary, the Native Land Development Corporation, to promote commercial farming among the Fijians. The Department of Land, Mines, and Surveys administered the leases for state-owned properties.

In 1967 representatives of the major ethnic groups and political parties agreed on the terms of the Agricultural Landlord and Tenant Ordinance, just in time for the nation's independence.

The legislation provided that leases be drawn up for a minimum of 10 years on a renewable basis. In 1976 the legislature lengthened the minimum lease period to 30 years, giving the Indians somewhat more security. Rents, which had not been changed since the passage of the original ordinance, were allowed to be adjusted every five years. In addition, the amendments set up special land tribunals throughout the country, which had all the powers of a court in adjudicating land disputes.

Sugarcane. For more than a century sugarcane has been the mainstay of the economy, accounting for 70 to 80 percent of export revenues and for around 16 percent of GDP, including processing. The industry has employed about one-fourth of the work force and has indirectly benefited many others. The management of production changed drastically in March of 1973, when the government bought out all of the shares of the Colonial Sugar Refining Company and set up a monopoly named the Fiji Sugar Corporation (FSC). Since then, the FSC has monopolized all sugar milling. About 21,724 farms averaging 4.5 hectares in size sold their production to the mills for conversion into raw sugar and molasses in 1983. A separate government marketing organization sold most of the milled products overseas.

Since the late 1950s the quantity of sugarcane supplied by the small farmers has more than doubled; production rose from 2.7 million tons to more than 4 million tons from 1977 to 1982 alone. The increase resulted almost exclusively from the expansion of the area cultivated; farming skills, such as the proper application of fertilizer, variety selection, and land management have been well developed for 30 years or more. The average yield per hectare harvested has increased, however, from 57 tons in the 1956–60 period to 65 tons in the 1976–80 period. Most of the variation was caused by weather conditions, the single most important factor in production. The 1982 harvest was a record 4.1 million tons of cane. In 1983 and 1984, however, the combined effects of a hurricane and a prolonged drought caused a severe hardship for most farmers. Analysts projected in late 1983 that F$12 to F$18 million of financial subsidies would be needed to get the industry up to the production of 415,000 tons of refined sugar by 1987—about 15 percent less than in 1982.

The production shortfall was making it difficult for Fiji to live up to its contractual obligations for deliveries to several international markets. Fiji had about 256,000 tons of raw sugar in 1983 to fulfill contracts for 380,000 tons worldwide. Since 1982 the government has been able to stockpile 18,000 tons of reserves previ-

Modern sugar mill (above) and
sugar transportation terminal at Lautoka (below)
Courtesy Fiji Visitors Bureau

ously committed to the International Sugar Organization (ISO), in which Fiji was an active member. The ISO was willing to let the nation retain another 26,000 tons by the end of 1984. These reserves would enable the country to keep its contracts with Britain, which paid an attractive price for Fiji sugar. The marketing authority also hoped to cancel part of the agreements with New Zealand, Malaysia, and China so that it could fulfill its contracts with the European Economic Community (EEC), which also paid a special price under the terms of the Lomé Convention (see Glossary). Fiji's EEC quota was 174,000 tons in 1983. The government also imported some white sugar from the Philippines in 1983 for domestic consumption in order to free supplies of brown sugar for export to the United States. Despite these measures, however, the timing of the shortfall with a cyclical rise in the world price for sugar was expected to cost the nation some F$80 to F$100 million of lost revenue.

The long-term prospects for Fiji sugar remained good in 1984. The farmers received an excellent incentive to produce from the pricing system, which returned some 70 to 75 percent of revenues from sugar sales to them, after deductions were made for the costs of marketing, research, and the staffing of a few management boards. The actual percentage depended on the quantity of sugar produced. Using tractors or trucks, the farmers bore the cost of transporting the cane to the nearest mill or to the nearest loading point on the FSC railroad system. Each sugar mill, moreover, maintained a field services staff that contacted the farmers and instructed them in the use of the appropriate varieties and fertilizers, which the FSC also supplied. The FSC has expanded its milling capacity at all of the mills and has been rehabilitating its aging equipment since 1982, although some of the work has been postponed because of financial constraints. Despite these improvements and the relatively high wages paid to the farmers and mill workers, the costs of sugar production in Fiji remained among the 10 lowest in the world.

Fiji has also been a leader in world research on sugarcane. Its research center in Lautoka maintained some 4,000 hybrid varieties and produced about 1,500 experimental varieties each year. Except for the possible introduction of cane in the Rewa River Valley, most of the future extension of the area planted would be in less fertile soils on sloping terrain, thus necessitating the development of hardier sugarcane varieties. The research staff has been concentrating on this problem.

Other Crops and Livestock. Although some Fijians engaged in commercial sugarcane farming in 1984, a vast majority worked subsistence farms, obtaining their cash requirements from the sale of coconuts or copra. About one-half of the copra produced, however, came from plantations owned by Europeans or Part Europeans, who often employed Fijian laborers. The other half came from native stands. About 59 percent of the 22,000 tons of copra produced in 1982 came from Northern Division, particularly from the Savusavu area of Vanua Levu and from Taveuni, where the plantations were located. Rotuma, the Lau Group, and the Lomaiviti Group produced most of the rest, chiefly from native stands. Production, however, decreased from nearly 31,000 tons in 1977. Not only had the trees become aged and unproductive but also many coconuts were being diverted to urban consumers. The government more than doubled the area planted with new coconut varieties in 1982 to 680 hectares. A new pricing proposal that would raise the average earnings of farmers some F$40 per ton of copra was opposed by the two international companies processing coconut oil in 1983 but would go a long way to improving the incentives for production. One domestic processor, however, said he was happy with the new payment formula.

The government has not been very successful in its drive to make the country self-sufficient in the production of rice, a major staple of the Indian community. Over one-half of the nearly 44,000 tons of unmilled rice consumed in 1982 was imported at a cost of about F$6.4 million. Over three-quarters of the rice produced came from about 8,500 hectares of rain-fed fields; only 1,100 hectares of irrigated fields were harvested. China and Australia were offering assistance in irrigated rice culture at Navua, on the southern coast of Viti Levu, and along the Dreketi River in Vanua Levu. Most of the rain-fed rice fields were located in the sugarcane areas.

Root crops—especially taro, cassava, and yams—have been the most important staples of the diet. Since most production took place on subsistence farms, production statistics have been available chiefly for commercial farms. According to the 1978 agricultural census, taro was produced on about 2,900 hectares of land, only 500 hectares of which were commercial. As of 1982 the area under commercial production had been increasing by over 12 percent per year and production itself by 15 percent per year. Commercial cassava production also increased by 15 percent per year to 16,150 tons from 850 hectares in 1982. Yams were mostly grown in Northern and Eastern divisions; commercial production increased by over 68 percent per year from 1976 to 1982, when 3,570 tons were harvested on 255 planted hectares.

Other crops grown primarily for export included ginger, cacao, passion fruit, oranges, pineapples, and coffee. With the exception of ginger, the production of which grew by over 11 percent per year after 1977 to 4,500 tons in 1982, farm output has been small. Abundant vegetables for the home market were produced on small farms in the Sigatoka River Valley, known as the nation's "salad bowl," and in the Rewa River Valley.

A major objective of the government has been to improve the domestic supplies of livestock products, and, except for mutton, the goal has virtually been met. In 1982 Fiji was able to produce domestically all of its poultry, some 97 percent of its pork, about 92 percent of its beef, approximately 72 percent of its goat meat, but none of its mutton requirements. Most of the cattle farms, including many under the supervision of the Fiji Development Bank, were in Central and Western divisions. Australian and New Zealand aid teams were assisting in the development of a 40,000-hectare scheme on Kadavu and on some 25,000 hectares of farms in the upper reaches of the Sigatoka River. Local dairy production was concentrated on small farms in the Rewa River area, which produced less than 15 percent of the nation's needs in 1982. In 1983 New Zealand promised Fiji some F$300,000 of assistance to build the country's first tannery. The drought in 1983 and 1984, however, seriously weakened the existing cattle herds.

Forestry. Wood products have been an important source of building materials, cash earnings, and energy. During the 1970s the country became virtually self-sufficient in the production of sawed timber and plywood and began to export small quantities. In 1981 about 220,000 cubic meters were harvested, of which some 17,000 cubic meters were exported; about 2,500 square meters of veneers and plywoods were also sold overseas. Altogether about 250,000 hectares of natural forest were considered to be of commercial value. The Forestry Department, however, has strictly regulated the harvest to maintain at least 60 percent of the forest cover in the logging areas and to prevent the extraction of undersized trees.

In an effort to maximize the rich potential for forestry, the government established the Fiji Pine Commission in 1976 to plant pine plantations on unused or denuded land. By 1982 the commission controlled some 40,000 hectares of plantations; private planters and the Forestry Department had also established some pine plantations. The commission was planting an additional 2,000 hectares a year in the early 1980s. Experience has shown that livestock could also be raised successfully among the trees. In 1982 only about 12,000 cubic meters of plantation pines were exported; by 1985 the government hoped to more than triple production. By the late 1980s the government planned to export some F$50 million of pine logs, chips, and pulp each year—more than one-third of the value of sugar exports. In one plantation area, however, the local chieftain has opposed the government's chosen joint venture partner, British Petroleum, in exploiting the pine forests.

In the 1960s and early 1970s Fiji also developed some 11,000 hectares of mahogany plantations. A tree disease attacked the plantations in 1972, halting expansion, but in 1982 an estimated 16,000 cubic meters of hardwoods were felled in these forests. Efforts to expand the area under tropical hardwoods were proceeding more slowly than for softwoods.

Fishing. Commercial fishing remained relatively underdeveloped in 1984. The government-owned Ika Corporation maintained a fleet of 13 pole-and-line tuna fishing vessels, eight of them hired from other domestic and foreign companies. Its catch in 1982, however, was only 3,830 tons, down from a modest record of 4,700 tons the year before. The director of the corporation was forced to resign in 1983 because the company had accumulated debts totaling more than F$2.2 million. The director had nevertheless taken important steps to replace the large, inefficient vessels with smaller, more fuel-efficient ones from a government shipyard in Suva. The outgoing director had advised hiring Japanese skippers to take over the helms of the company ships until the Fijian captains were better trained.

Private purse seine and longline vessels also fished for tuna from bases in Fiji, catching more than 4,000 tons in 1982. Shark fins, smoked fish, shellfish, and other fish and fish commodities totaled more than 4,700 tons in 1982. The total production for that year was down from 13,800 tons in 1981. As a result, the value of fishery exports decreased from F$18.8 to F$13 million.

The 2,800 coastal fishing vessels that produced fresh fish for local consumption have marketed more and more of their produce at centers run by the National Marketing Authority or private canneries. The government authority has expanded the amount of freezer space at its facilities and has regulated fish prices so that the fishing families could receive a profitable margin. Coastal fishing was hindered by the rapid drop-off of the continental shelf around many of the islands, which made fishing for bottom fish difficult. Coastal fishing vessels nevertheless netted about one-third of the catch in 1982. Fish farming, which had an excellent potential in Fiji, was at the experimental stage in the early 1980s and produced only a small catch.

Industry and Services

The industrial sector depended greatly on Fiji's agriculture. The most important industries were for processing sugarcane, copra, timber, and food. The production of commercial energy from the nation's hydroelectric resources has become more important than the small mining industry, which has been able to export only limited quantities of gold. Even more significant for employment and income has been the services sector, including transportation, communications, and a host of commercial activities catering to the needs of both the country's people and the many visiting tourists.

Mining and Energy. Gold has been the principle commodity produced for more than 45 years. The town of Vatukoula grew up around the Emperor Mine. Production, however, dropped steadily in the 1970s, and only 88 kilograms were produced for export in 1981. In 1982 the government renewed the mining company's contract for another 21 years, and a second Australian-based firm joined an expanded project. The new partner was helping the old company to recover from some F$3 million in losses and to prospect about 6,000 hectares of land next to the existing mine. Some 1,000 Fijian workers employed at the mine had been hard hit by layoffs in the early 1980s.

Besides a few quarrying operations, the only other mining activity has been exploratory. Some prospecting for commercial quantities of copper was being carried out near Suva in 1984. A Japanese consortium explored some bauxite reserves but abandoned the work in 1974. No significant sources of petroleum or mineral fuels have been discovered, although some 7,150 kilometers of survey work was finished during the 1969–70 period. Another 7,000 kilometers were surveyed using newer technology in the 1979–81 period, often in the areas previously explored. Despite the occurrence of favorable source rocks both onshore and offshore, the seven wells drilled have found no recoverable reserves. The pace of the drilling efforts was slowing in the 1980s, and the poor results have discouraged foreign oil companies. If discoveries were to be made, most observers believed the drilling would have to go much deeper than before, to 3,000 to 5,000 meters.

The lack of domestic supplies of hydrocarbons has made the country extremely dependent on imported energy. In 1982 oil imports for domestic use totaled 397,000 tons; this volume accounted for 43 percent of the energy produced that year. Coal imports have been a minor source of energy, but domestically produced fuelwood and bagasse (sugarcane husks) made up more than one-half of the energy supplied. The fuelwood was mostly burned in the rural areas for home cooking or copra drying; some was converted to charcoal for sale in the urban areas. The sugarcane mills burned bagasse to produce electricity for their milling operations and even sold some overflow to the public utility. The government regulated the prices of commercial energy but generally allowed increased import prices to be passed on to the consumers. As a result, oil consumption declined by about 2 percent per year during the 1975–82 period.

Oil consumption was expected to drop dramatically after the completion of new facilities for producing electricity, the major form of oil energy. The government utility, the Fiji Electricity Authority (FEA), produced about 95 percent of the nation's electricity in 1982 on the islands of Viti Levu, Vanua Levu, and Ovalau. The installed capacity was 85 megawatts, the chief load centers being Suva, Lautoka, Nadi, Labasa, Savusavu, and Levuka. In late 1983, however, the first stage in the country's most important development project ever, the Monasavu Hydroelectric Scheme, was completed. Located high in the Nadrau Plateau, the F$220 million project would eventually have an installed capacity of 80 megawatts—enough to supply the country's needs through the early 1990s. Although initially the power project would have twice the needed capacity, it would still be less expensive than importing diesel fuel and would reduce the nation's import bill by some 60 percent at a saving of about F$18 million per year. The only drawback to the successful completion of the project was the prospect of discharging the more than 7,000 workers who have built the facilities on difficult terrain. After two years of delay, the project was expected to be fully completed by 1985, when it would be able to produce 400 million kilowatt-hours of electricity, about 190 million kilowatt-hours more than projected domestic consumption. Other proved areas for hydroelectric development on Viti Levu, which were under investigation in 1984, totaled more than 1,600 megawatts of capacity.

Vanua Levu and the smaller islands required different kinds of facilities than Viti Levu. Small-scale hydroelectric sites were under investigation on Vanua Levu and Taveuni, and the FEA has programmed the construction of a dam to serve Labasa. In addition to supplies from the nearby sugar mill, the local sawmills and planned wood-processing plants might be able to burn their waste to add electricity to the system. In the outlying areas solar power generators have been installed to run the government-owned telecommunications equipment. Rural residents were poorly served by the existing system; whereas one-half of the homes in the urban and suburban areas had electrical connections in 1982, only one-fourth of those in the rural areas received electricity. The FEA, which had responsibility only for the major islands, was adding about 2,000 new connections each year. The Public Works Department was in charge of installing small generators in the outlying islands and had set up eight diesel plants serving 4,000 people during the 1978–82 period. The government estimated that 80,000 additional connections would be required to cover the entire country. The Ministry of Energy and Mineral Resources has been in charge of the country's energy plans.

Transportation and Communications. Roads have become the most important means of transportation on the main islands; a 500-kilometer highway roughly encircled Viti Levu in 1981. Altogether there were about 3,300 kilometers of roads in Fiji in 1981, of which some 1,200 had all-weather surfaces. About 400 kilometers of highway, including the resurfaced road from Nadi to Suva, had asphalt surfaces. In 1981 there were 22,000 private cars, some 16,400 trucks, about 3,500 taxis and rental cars, over 1,100 buses, some 3,400 tractors, and 2,400 motorcycles licensed for use.

Interisland shipping has been taken over by barges towed by tugs; the Marine Department has also allowed passengers to ride its ships. The main port of entry, Suva, handled more than 750 foreign and 650 local vessels in 1981. Lautoka, which opened a new wharf the year before, served 322 foreign and 126 domestic ships. The other port of entry, at Levuka, primarily served fishing fleets. In 1981 the local shipping fleets included 234 vessels totaling 19,500 gross registered tons.

Air transportation has become increasingly important for the tourist industry and for interisland traffic. Air Pacific, the official international carrier, maintained a fleet of three jet and four propeller aircraft in 1981, which flew in and out of the expanded international airport at Nadi. The government owned about three-quarters of the company, which has suffered yearly losses. Fiji Air, a private concern previously owned by Air Pacific, had a fleet of six small aircraft that served some 13 local airports.

All 725 kilometers of permanent 0.61-meter-gauge railroad track was maintained by the FSC. The company has accepted passengers on occasion but has never charged fares.

The telecommunications network has improved steadily. Automatic exchanges were in operation at most of the major towns on Viti Levu in 1984; telephone and radio-telephone facilities were in place on nearly every populated island. Fiji has been a communications center for the other Pacific countries and was linked to Australia and New Zealand via an undersea cable. There was a satellite receiving station near Suva.

The government controlled all radiobroadcasting through the services of the Fiji Broadcasting Commission, which transmitted programs in Fijian, Hindi, and English on three separate stations. There was no television station in 1984; the 6,000 television sets in use were set up for video cassettes or for expensive satellite reception. In 1983 a United States corporation offered to set up low-power facilities to broadcast in English and Fijian simultaneously using special decoders on the television receivers. The government has said it preferred to set up a cassette network first.

About one dozen newspapers and periodicals, written in Fijian, Hindi, and English, provided a vital and vociferous free press. The oldest newspaper, the *Fiji Times*, was established in 1869. More than 34 post offices and many postal agencies served even the remotest areas of the country and kept the population in written contact with one another.

Tourism and Other Commercial Enterprises. Earnings from tourism reached F$64 million in 1982 and were expected to surpass those from sugarcane exports in 1983. The government estimated, however, that some F$78 million in revenue leaked out of the country in 1982 in payments to the foreign firms and individuals who controlled much of the industry. That year 204,000 tourists visited the islands, a new record. However, the destruction of 685 of the 4,000 available hotel rooms by a hurricane in 1983 would probably interfere with the industry's growth. The boom in hotel construction since the late 1970s was slowing somewhat, and local industry specialists argued that medium-priced rather than luxury facilities were sorely needed. One-half of the tourist arrivals in 1982 were from Australia; New Zealand and Japan contributed much of the remainder.

The Ministry of Commerce and Industry and other government agencies have been attempting to get local enterprises to produce more and more of the goods and services needed by the tourists and local population. Imports of building materials and supplies for the most expensive resorts continued to consume valuable foreign exchange. Three industrial zones have, however, grown up around Suva and were spreading toward Nausori. The government has set up industrial estates at Lautoka, Nausori, Ba, Tavua, Labasa, Savusavu, Rakiraki, Levuka, and on Taveuni and was planning to open new parks in more rural areas. The major industries that have developed included those producing soaps, beer, rum, canned food, small ships, cement, cigarettes, and aluminum products. The Economic Development Board has most actively sought foreign investors to set up fruit farms for both the domestic and the export sectors.

In 1982 there were 3,340 commercial establishments registered in Fiji; 92 percent were headquartered in the country, about 4 percent in Australia, some 1 percent in Britain, and the rest in unspecified countries. Only 1 percent of the local companies sold stock openly to the public. A study conducted in 1980 showed that foreign-controlled companies accounted for anywhere from 28 to 53 percent of the nation's GDP, depending on the definitions of "control" and "GDP" used. Only 2 percent of the workers in these companies were expatriates. Cooperative enterprises have been in existence since the 1950s, and in 1979 more than 1,100 cooperative societies served some 40,000 members. About 800 of the cooperatives were consumer oriented, marketing goods in the villages. There were some 21 wholesale cooperatives, two of which collected copra from the villages. In 1978 the agency in charge of developing cooperatives was promoted to the cabinet level. In 1982 state-owned enterprises were involved in the production of timber, fish, electricity, sugar, and livestock. State enterprises also provided air transportation, broadcasting, telecommunications, banking, and marketing services.

The Political System and Security

The British-issued Fiji Independence Order of 1970, which includes the Constitution of Fiji, enshrines the principle that the Fijian community is entitled to some special privileges but establishes a British-style parliamentary system open to free and vigorous political competition for all. The rivalry between the often ethnically based political parties has been restricted only by common rules of public order and by the constitutional requirement that parliamentary representation reflect a statutory ethnic balance. The independent judiciary, autonomous commissions, free press, and political police and military forces have helped preserve the free political environment.

The Constitution guarantees to all citizens, regardless of race or creed, fundamental human rights, including life, liberty, secu-

Government offices in Suva,
the national capital of Fiji
Courtesy Fiji Visitors Bureau

rity, free conscience and expression, free assembly, and the protection of privacy and property. It grants citizenship to all persons born or registered as Commonwealth citizens in Fiji as of May 6, 1970, together with their offspring. Commonwealth citizens may become naturalized Fiji citizens after residing in the country for seven years; others must wait nine years. The Constitution does, however, contain special provisions concerning certain ethnic groups. It effectively preserves all legislation regarding the special administration of land tenure and local government for the Fijian and Rotuman communities by requiring a four-fifths vote in the House of Representatives to alter it. Immigrants from the island of Banaba in Kiribati, who live on Rabi Island, are similarly protected (see Kiribati, ch. 3).

The Constitution furthermore requires that parliamentary seats be apportioned according to ethnic quotas that do not necessarily coincide with the population census. In the House of Representatives, which originates and enacts all legislation, there must be 22 Fijians, 22 Indians, and eight others, who have come to be known as General Elector representatives. All adults over the age of 21 who wish to vote must register on two lists—the Communal Roll and the National Roll. According to the former, each voter selects one candidate from his or her ethnic group, filling 12 Fijian, 12 Indian, and three General Elector seats. The National Roll allows each individual to vote for one candidate in each of the three ethnic categories to choose the remaining seats. The Senate, which has only limited powers of legislative review, consists of eight members nominated by the Great Council of Chiefs, seven by the prime minister, six by the leader of the opposition, and one by the Council of Rotuma. Representatives, elected by universal adult suffrage, sit for terms of five years and senators for six, unless parliament is dissolved by a vote of no confidence or on the decision of the prime minister.

The titular head of state is the British sovereign, who appoints the governor general of Fiji based on the recommendation of parliament. The governor general in turn conducts the ceremonies of the head of state. Since 1973 the governor general has been a Fijian.

The prime minister is empowered to appoint a cabinet, which in 1984 consisted of 18 ministers. Each is usually backed by a department having national and local offices. The Constitution also requires that the prime minister and governor general appoint an attorney general, ombudsman, and auditor general, as well as officers to manage elections and prosecutions. It also charters commissions to oversee various public services.

The Great Council of Chiefs, the modern version of the Council of Chiefs established in the late nineteenth century, headed the Fijian administration. Its membership has become more and more representative, including some of the Fijian members of the House of Representatives, representatives of 13 elected provincial councils, and others appointed by the minister of Fijian affairs. The minister of Fijian affairs has usually been in charge of rural development and sometimes has been the deputy prime minister. The Fijian Affairs Board, subsumed in this ministerial portfolio, took care of the day-to-day affairs of Fijian administration, approving the membership and regulations of the provincial councils.

Outside of the Fijian provincial councils and special councils for Rotuma and Rabi islands, local government was managed by four appointed divisional administrations and elected city and town councils. The divisional commissioners, appointed by the prime minister, set up district offices in the main population centers; in many rural areas, however, the local officials of the Health Department were the sole representatives of the central government. In 1981 city councils served the residents of Suva and Lautoka, while town councils operated in Nadi, Ba, Sigatoka, Labasa, Nausori, Levuka, Savusavu, and Lami. The councils could raise revenues as they saw fit but also received support from the central government. The dual system of representation has left rural Indians out of local government, and many have urged that the provincial councils be expanded to include Indian representatives.

The Constitution creates a legal system consisting of the Supreme Court, the Fiji Court of Appeals, and resident magistrate's courts. Up to seven judges, in addition to the chief justice, may be appointed to the Supreme Court by the governor general, who acts on the advice of the prime minister, the leader of the opposition, and the Judicial and Legal Services Commission. The Supreme Court rules on all constitutional issues and performs functions identical to those of the High Court of Justice in Britain. It also acts as the Fiji Court of Appeals in criminal and civil cases sent from the magistrate's courts. Further appeals can be made to the Privy Council in London. In a departure from the British system of jurisprudence, court cases are decided not by a jury but by the presiding judge or judges on the advice of no fewer than two legal assessors. The Judicial and Legal Services Commission appointed 14 resident magistrates in 1980 that were responsible for convening 12 full-time and 20 part-time courts around the country. Magistrate's courts heard all criminal cases involving property and those involving personal harm below the level of manslaughter.

Politics

Political analysts, such as R. S. Milne, have identified three persistent issues in Fiji politics: the electoral process, the land tenure system, and the management of the sugarcane economy. The interest groups that vied for a voice in public policy were organized primarily along ethnic lines and channeled their influence through political parties similarly divided. In general, all parties seemed to agree on a democratic and free-market approach to the political and economic development of Fiji. The Indian community, however, felt that the constitutional system has impeded the full representation of its interests and aspirations.

The first political party in Fiji history was the Fijian Association. Founded in 1954 by Ratu Sukuna, its aims were to support the existing Fijian administration against pressures for reform. After the 1963 elections a group of students that had returned from Britain—including Ratu Kamisese Mara—transformed the association into a more modern party having specialized agencies, well-organized branches, and a mass appeal to the voters. Before and during the constitutional conference held in London in 1965, Mara forged relations with representatives of other ethnic groups—in particular, the Europeans and Part Europeans. In March 1966 the Fijian Association became the senior member of the new Alliance Party, which included the Indian-run National Congress of Fiji (later the Indian Alliance) and the General Electors' Association. The Alliance Party led the country to independence and has formed every new government since then under the leadership of Mara, who came to be known officially as Prime Minister Ratu Sir Kamisese Mara.

The Alliance Party modernized in response to the well-organized and activist National Federation Party (NFP), which emerged in 1964 out of the most militant of the sugarcane workers' unions. One analyst has concluded that the NFP won over the support of the orthodox Hindus and Muslims in these early years, while the reformists from both groups joined the Alliance Party. Whatever the case, the NFP became the party of the Indian community, advocating the abolition of the Communal Roll and increased Indian influence in the government. Allegations that the party founder's immediate successor, Siddique Koya, was cooperating too readily with Mara's government split the NFP into two factions in 1977. In 1979, however, the party reunited under the leadership of Jai Ram Reddy, who was the opposition leader in 1984.

A small but highly controversial force in Fiji politics was the Fijian Nationalist Party. Formed by Sakeasi Butadroka, who was expelled from the Alliance Party in 1972, the party's slogan was "Fiji for the Fijians." In 1975 Butadroka went so far as to introduce a bill in parliament that would have forced all of the Indians to leave Fiji. The reaction to the inflammatory bill was predictably condemnatory, but the party captured a sizable portion of the Fijian electorate in the first of two polls in 1977.

A new political party called the Western United Front (WUF) appeared on the scene in 1981. Created by a previously independent Fijian member of parliament, Ratu Osea Gavidi, the WUF represented the interests of a group of Fijian *mataqali* in the western part of Viti Levu that opposed certain provisions of the government pine forest scheme.

Four parliamentry elections have taken place since Fiji's independence, but only three have formed governments. The 1972 election resulted in 63 percent of the seats in the House of Representatives going to the Alliance Party and the rest to the opposition NFP. In the March and April elections of 1977, the NFP took 50 percent of the seats after the upstart Fijian National Party siphoned one-fourth of the Fijian vote from the Alliance Party. The NFP, however, was unable to form a government because it split into two factions, and a new election was held in September. Prime Minister Mara's party made a remarkable recovery, aided in part by Butadroka's confinement for violations of the law. The Alliance Party won 62 percent of the seats.

The July 1982 elections were much more closely contended than those in late 1977, and the campaign was marred by acrimonious allegations of foreign involvement on behalf of both major parties. The voter turnout was a record 86 percent, and the voting was almost entirely along ethnic lines. The Alliance Party took all 12 of the Fijian communal seats, capturing 86 percent of the vote, while the NFP won all 12 Indian seats with 84 percent of the vote. The Alliance Party took all the national seats in the election districts having a Fijian majority and two seats in districts having only narrow Indian majorities. The remainder of the Indian districts gave their seats to the NFP. The WUF, which ran in coalition with the NFP, won two seats in the National Roll. The Alliance Party took six of the eight General Elector seats. The poor showing of the government party caused Mara to tender his resignation, but he was coaxed back into heading a new government.

In 1983 a special Royal Commission of Inquiry investigated charges by both major parties that the other had engaged in unfair and illegal campaign practices. The opposition accused the government of smear tactics that aimed to stir up ethnic disquiet and charged that an Australian consulting firm had advised the government to buy off some of the opposition candidates. The government accused the NFP of receiving money from agents of the Soviet Union in exchange for a promise that it could open an embassy and other facilities in Suva. The government also accused the opposition of cooperating with Australian leftists who filmed a documentary critical of the Mara government. In early 1984 the commission declared that the evidence on all sides was seriously lacking and recommended that criminal charges of any kind not be pursued.

A broader coalition of national uity has been proposed on several occasions, but in 1984 its prospects seemed dim. The closest the country has come to a grand coalition was during the period leading up to and immediately following independence, when the Alliance Party and the NFP cooperated out of necessity in the negotiations with Britain and in the building of a new government structure without resort to violence. Agreement on the nationalization and management of the sugar industry, for example, was achieved by a joint committee of both parties in the House of Representatives. The rise of the Fijian National Party, however, made coalition politics impractical. Faced with the loss of a sizable part of the Fijian electorate, Mara rejected a bid from one of the factions of the NFP to form a coalition government, which would have risked the further alienation of his Fijian supporters. In 1980, one year after the former president of the Indian Alliance and minister of economic planning, Vijay Singh, defected to the NFP, Mara himself suggested a coalition. Jai Ram Reddy, however, would accept nothing short of an equal sharing of power and ultimately denounced the offer as unfair. The acrimony of the 1982 campaign and the investigation into its management in 1983 hindered the prospects for a coalition in 1984.

The major interest groups—including labor unions, business organizations, religious bodies, and educational organizations—generally divided along ethnic lines. Labor groups were perhaps less segmented into ethnic components than other groups, but individual unions within the two multiethnic labor federations were often predominantly Fijian or Indian in membership. They remained concerned about the bread-and-butter issues of wages and benefits peculiar to their industry. The business community was represented in local chambers of commerce and employers' groups. Because few Fijians had achieved entrepreneurial success, there were usually two separate chambers of commerce—one for the Indian and one for the rest of the non-Fijian community. Separate religious organizations within the Muslim and Hindu communities represented conservative and orthodox opinions on language, education, and public morality. The Methodist church has remained largely apolitical. One particularly active Indian group managed schools that catered to students from the southern Indian community.

Foreign Relations and Security

Fiji has rivaled Papua New Guinea for leadership of the island states of Oceania. Fiji has been the home of the South Pacific

Bureau for Economic Cooperation—the secretariat of the South Pacific Forum—and the University of the South Pacific since their inception (see Appendix B). Mara represented the South Pacific Forum in 1982 during negotiations with France over the status of New Caledonia. He has also led his country in active participation in the organizations of the United Nations (UN), including its peacekeeping forces.

Fiji has maintained especially close relations with Australia, New Zealand, and Tonga. Australia and New Zealand were its major trading partners, and among all Pacific nations Fiji benefited most from the South Pacific Area Regional Trade and Economic Cooperation Agreement (SPARTECA—see Glossary), effected with these countries in 1981. SPARTECA has created F$10 million to F$15 million in duty-free exports for Fiji each year. Relations with the other Melanesian countries were good but not always warm. Vanuatu, disturbed by Fiji's pro-Western stance and loose affiliation with the Polynesian countries, has even proposed creating a regional organization of Melanesian states that would exclude Fiji (see Vanuatu, this ch.).

In the rivalry between the superpowers, Fiji has avowed its neutrality. Its refusal to enter into the Nonaligned Movement has been defended on the grounds that that organization was tilting toward the Soviet Union. Fiji's own political and economic choices, however, have made it seem more sympathetic to the Western nations and Japan, a fact that neatly coincided with its traditionally warm relations with Britain and the Commonwealth of Nations. Fiji's national motto, "Fear God and serve the Queen," was not a quaint anachronism. Another sign of Fiji's accommodation toward the Western nations was its decision in 1983 to reverse its previous policy of banning from Fiji ports nuclear-powered ships or vessels carrying nuclear weapons. The government continued its support, however, for efforts to establish a nuclear-free Pacific and adamantly opposed nuclear weapons testing and the storage of radioactive materials in the region.

Fiji was not a signatory of any international security agreement. The foreign minister stated in 1983, however, that the government acted on advice from Australia and New Zealand—members of the Security Treaty Between Australia, New Zealand, and the United States of America (the ANZUS treaty)—in reversing its policy on nuclear ships (see The ANZUS Treaty and Other Security Arrangements, ch. 5; Appendix C). These countries suggested that, should Fiji change its policy, it would receive ready assistance form them in preserving its security. Since colonial times, Fiji military officers have trained in Australia and New

Zealand, and both New Zealand and British troops have used Fiji as a training ground for jungle warfare. Until 1981 the chief of staff of the Royal Fiji Military Forces (RFMF) was a New Zealander.

The all-volunteer RFMF has never seen action on Fiji territory; in 1983 there were nearly as many Fiji soldiers stationed in the Sinai and Lebanon as part of the UN forces as there were in Fiji. All told, the RFMF army had 2,500 uniformed soldiers in 1983—about 1,900 regulars and some 600 so-called territorial forces. The latter could either be former regulars or new recruits and, like the regulars, were eligible for service in the UN forces. One infantry battalion was stationed in Lebanon, another in the Sinai, and a third at home in 1983; there was also a small engineering company and a modest artillery company.

In 1974 the RFMF created a naval division to carry out the increasingly important function of patrolling the nation's 200-nautical-mile Exclusive Economic Zone (EEZ—see Glossary). Based in Suva, the navy had 26 officers and 145 sailors in 1983. It had three former United States "Redwing" coastal minesweepers, one 303-ton survey craft, an eight-ton survey launch, and an 85-ton patrol craft. The division set up a national surveillance center in 1984 that depended on radio and telephone reports from passing vessels and aircraft to report activities within the EEZ. The RFMF had no air wing and depended on visiting New Zealand aircraft, especially helicopters, for occasional training missions. In early 1984 Australia mooted the possibility of staging periodic air reconnaissance missions out of Nadi Airport that would carry RFMF soldiers patrolling the EEZ.

The Fijians have found service in the RFMF most attractive, but in the late 1970s at least one-third of the forces were Indian. Since 1981 the chief of staff of the RFMF has been a Fijian. Service in the UN forces in the Middle East, for which the RFMF soldiers received about triple the salary offered at home, was especially attractive. The RFMF has trained about 600 new soldiers each year for rotating service in the UN forces. The government, however, has had trouble collecting payments for its military services from the UN, and the political opposition advocated pulling out of the forces altogether.

Internal security was the responsibility of the Royal Fiji Police, modeled in all but dress after the British police force. Fijians made up some 53 percent of the total force of 1,316 people in 1979, while Indians constituted 42 percent. The ethnic composition was about the same at all levels, but the commissioner of police in 1982 was Indian. There were only 24 policewomen.

During the normal course of duty, the police did not carry weapons. The police were authorized to set up a special constabulary to help in day-to-day work or in times of special national need.

Fiji has avoided the ethnic violence common to many other multiethnic societies. The nation's 11 prisons, which had room for 976 persons in 1983, held an average of 14,000 crowded prisoners that year. Only one-fourth of the inmates were jailed for more than one year, and some 40 percent were locked up for failing to pay fines. From 75 to 80 percent of the prisoners were Fijian. Severe overcrowding led to small riots in the Suva and Lautoka facilities in 1980. The Fiji Law Reform Commission advocated in 1983 that alternate forms of punishment, such as community service, be instituted to reduce the number of prisoners serving light sentences. An experimental program of this kind had been started in the early 1980s.

NEW CALEDONIA

Official Name	Territory of New Caledonia and Dependencies
Political Status	Overseas Territory of France
Capital	Nouméa
Population	145,400 (early 1984 estimate)
Land Area	19,103 square kilometers
Currency	Cours du Franc Pacifique franc (CFPF)
Major Islands and Island Groups	New Caledonia (Grand Terre) Isle of Pines Loyalty Islands (Ouvéa, Lifou, Maré), Bélep Islands, Chesterfield Islands

The Territory of New Caledonia and Dependencies (New Caledonia) is located in the southwest Pacific, about 1,500 kilometers from the east coast of Australia and 5,000 kilometers west of Tahiti in the Territory of French Polynesia. It has been an overseas territory of France since 1956. Vanuatu, formerly the New Hebrides, lies to its northeast. New Caledonia is a part of the Melanesian cultural area, although its indigenous Melanesian population is outnumbered by European, Polynesian, and Asian settlers and their descendants. Most Melanesians were subsistence farmers, but mining was the most important economic sector, nickel and nickel products forming as much as 95 percent of exports by value. In mid-1984 New Caledonia's political future remained unclear. Different political parties advocated the constitutional status quo, internal autonomy, or complete independence. Negotiations between the French government and local leaders continued, but a settlement of New Caledonia's ultimate political status remained elusive in a society marked by deep ethnic, regional, and class differences.

Physical Environment

The main island of New Caledonia, also called New Caledonia, comprises almost 88 percent of the territory's total land area (see fig. 4). It is one of the largest islands in Oceania, surpassed in size only by New Guinea, New Britain, and North and South islands in New Zealand. The Loyalty Islands parallel the Grande Terre in a chain running northwest to southeast, 100 kilometers to the east. They include the three principal islands of Ouvéa (160 square kilometers), Lifou (1,115 square kilometers), and Maré (650 square kilometers) and a number of smaller islands, such as Tiga, the Astrolabe Reefs, Beautemps-Beaupré Atoll, and Walpole Island. The Isle of Pines (134 kilometers) lies to the southeast of the main island, while a number of smaller islands, including the Bélep Islands, lie to the northwest. The Chesterfield Islands are located 400 kilometers to the west of the main island in the Coral Sea.

A very well-developed line of barrier and fringing reefs surrounds the main island, the Isle of Pines, and the Bélep Islands and extends northward to join the D'Entrecasteaux Reefs, which include the Huon and Surprise islands. The reefs have a total circumference of about 1,600 kilometers. They form a lagoon along the coasts of the main island, particularly the east coast, which is ideal for fishing and coastal navigation.

The French government enforces a territorial limit of 12 nautical miles in its dependencies, including New Caledonia. Enabling legislation passed in 1976 provides for an EEZ (see Glossary) of 200 nautical miles. An unofficial estimate of New Caledonia's sea area, including the EEZ, is over 1.7 million square kilometers. In early 1984 the governments of France and Vanuatu pressed conflicting claims to Île Mathiew and Hunter Island at the southern end of the New Hebrides group.

Insular Relief and Drainage

The main island of New Caledonia is often described as "continental" in its geology because its rock formations, including metamorphic and sedimentary strata, as well as volcanic intrusions, are similar in their diversity to those of much larger continental landmasses. This contrasts with the relatively homogeneous geology of most other Pacific islands that were formed either from coral deposits or volcanic activity. (New Caledonia has no active volcanoes.) It accounts for New Caledonia's mineral wealth—nickel, chrome, cobalt, and iron—located for the most part in the southern and western parts of the island.

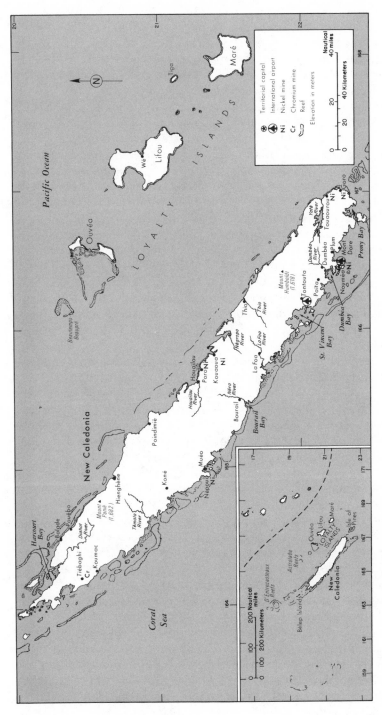

Figure 4. New Caledonia, 1984

The terrain of the main island is mountainous. The topography is characterized by a "confused series of peaks and ranges" that slope steeply to the east coast and more gradually to the west coast. The highest peaks are Mount Panié (1,682 meters) in the north and Mount Humboldt (1,618 meters) in the south. A lowland plain of lakes is found at the southern end of the main island, where the island's only sizable lakes are located.

The coastline of the main island is 800 kilometers long. Steep cliffs, having an elevation of several hundred meters, fall to the sea along the east and southeast coasts. Along the west coast, however, the cliffs are lower, and there are extensive marshes in coastal lowland areas. Good harbors are found at Prony Bay at the southeastern tip of the island, in Dumbéa Bay west of Nouméa, and at points farther to the north, such as St. Vincent Bay, Bourail Bay, and Harcourt Bay. The island is amply drained by a complex network of rivers and streams. The longest of these is the Diahot River, navigable for only 32 kilometers, while the Houaïlou, Négropo, Thio, Yaté, Dumbéa, La Foa, Néra, and Témala rivers are navigable for only about six to eight kilometers. Where rivers empty into the sea, passes form through the barrier reefs because coral cannot grow there.

Unlike the main island, the Loyalty Islands are raised coral formations. Maré and Lifou are uplifted plateaus with slight elevations along the coast, and Ouvéa is an atoll. The rock formations are limestone, and caves are plentiful. Ouvéa possesses a central lagoon, which is fringed on the west by islets. The Isle of Pines and the Bélep Islands are geological extensions of the main island.

The Climate

New Caledonia's climate is moderately tropical, lacking extremes of temperature and humidity. The average yearly temperature is about 23°C, and there is little seasonal variation. In the hottest month, February, temperatures reach 26°C, and the coolest, August, averages about 20°C. A warm, rainy season lasts from December to March, punctuated by frequent and sometimes destructive tropical storms. The cool season lasts from June to August. The prevailing winds are the trade winds, blowing from the southeast. These moderate the temperature and bring greater rainfall to the southern and southeastern regions of the main island. The west coast of the island, sheltered from the trade winds, is drier and suffers occasional drought. The Loyalty Islands enjoy essentially the same climate as the main island, although rainfall is less, owing to the lack of elevation.

Vegetation and Animal Life

The vegetation of the island of New Caledonia is diverse, especially in comparison with that of other Pacific islands. It is adapted to a relatively dry climate, resembling the vegetation of Australia more than that of neighboring Vanuatu. Because of the main island's geographical isolation, 83 percent of all plant species are unique to it. Two vegetation zones are generally recognized: the more humid east coast, where forests are concentrated, and the drier west coast, a region of savannas.

At one time forests may have covered practically all of the main island, but they have been seriously depleted by overcutting and brushfires. The most extensive remaining forests are confined to relatively inaccessible mountain areas where rainfall is plentiful. According to 1983 government statistics, 22.8 percent of the total land area of the main island is covered by dense forests and an additional 15.1 percent by other forest growth, particularly *niaouli*, a low, eucalyptus-like tree with fire-resistant wood that predominates in areas where the original forest cover has been cleared. Mangrove forests are found in the swamps of the west coast. There is very little sandalwood remaining on the island, owing to European exploitation in the nineteenth century.

There are many species of indigenous evergreen trees on the island. The most remarkable is the "column pine," found in both coastal and upland areas, that can grow to heights of 50 meters. Its pillar-like shape and symmetrical branches have impressed travelers arriving by sea since at least the time of Captain James Cook.

Savanna, or grassland, vegetation covered more than one-fifth of the main island, according to 1983 statistics, and is found largely, though not exclusively, in the drier west coast region. Savannas often include stands of *niaouli* trees. The maquis, found on more than one-fourth of the total land area, is an aggregation of scrub or brush, stunted in growth, which contains a large number of botanically interesting species capable of surviving in the red laterite soil. It is found for the most part in the southern part of the main island, at elevations below 500 meters.

The vegetation of the Isle of Pines and the Loyalty Islands is less diverse than that of the main island but contains patches of forest, savanna, and scrub. Coconuts grow along the coasts of all the islands.

New Caledonia has few indigenous species of land mammals because of its distance from continental landmasses. The seven

107

native species are all bats or flying foxes. Dogs, sheep, cattle, horses, and other domestic animals were introduced by the Europeans along with less desirable newcomers, such as rats. It is a striking fact that pigs, which played a central role in the traditional economy and social practices of other Melanesian peoples, were not known to the inhabitants of New Caledonia before Europeans introduced them. Deer, brought from the Philippines in 1962, multiplied rapidly in the absence of natural predators and caused considerable damage to fields and pastures, although their numbers have been drastically reduced by hunters.

Historical Setting

The prehistory of New Caledonia is a matter of considerable speculation, based principally on archaeological evidence. Papuan peoples may have come to New Caledonia from the Asian mainland, by way of New Guinea, the Solomon Islands, and the New Hebrides, as early as 30,000 years ago, followed by Austronesians in the third millennium B.C. (see Prehistory, ch. 1). There also appears to have been considerable migration between the second millennium B.C. and the birth of Christ. Lapita pottery, a low-fired ceramic that in some cases is quite intricately decorated, has been found at sites ranging from New Guinea to Samoa, but it is named for a site on the northwest coast of the main island of New Caledonia. It is dated as early as the second millennium B.C. Lapita artifacts on New Caledonia and elsewhere in the western Pacific were superseded by a different material culture, unique to the Melanesian cultural area, around the first millenniumn A.D. On the Isle of Pines a remarkable assembly of around 300 earth mounds has been discovered that may date as early as 6000 B.C., and rocks carved with human figures and geometrical designs are found throughout New Caledonia.

Contacts between the Loyalty Islands and the Polynesian cultural area to the east were apparently frequent in the centuries before the coming of the Europeans. Polynesian voyagers from Wallis Island, in what is now the Territory of the Wallis and Futuna islands, probably came to Ouvéa in the mid-eighteenth century. Earlier groups of Polynesians—from Wallis, the Samoa Islands, and Tonga—may have reached Maré and Lifou. From the Loyalty Islands, these migrants went farther west on to the main island, establishing communities at Balade, Hienghène, and Houaïlou on its east coast and Koumac and Bourail on its west coast. Not all migration, however, was from Polynesia. The chiefs of a powerful community on the Isle of Pines were descended from the Melanesian rulers of Anatom Island in Vanuatu.

The indigenous population of the main island may have been as high as 70,000 in the period before European colonization. Evidence for this relatively large population (in the 1976 census the number of Melanesians was given as 55,598) includes the remains of hillside irrigation terraces for the cultivation of taro (a tuber that is a staple food in Oceania), found throughout the island but now abandoned. Politically and linguistically, the people were divided into a large number of highly self-sufficient communities governed by local chiefs, and the dialects of neighboring groups were often mutually unintelligible. They were almost constantly in a state of war, and cannibalism was widely practiced.

First European Contacts

The island of New Caledonia lay at some distance from the sea routes established by Spanish and Dutch explorers and traders in the sixteenth and seventeenth centuries, and it was not until the late eighteenth century that the main island and the Loyalty Islands were discovered by Europeans.

In September 1774 Captain Cook sailed within sight of the east coast of the main island. Cook and members of his crew came ashore a little to the north of Balade. The steep cliffs and stands of pines reminded the captain of the Scottish coast, and he named the island "New Caledonia," Caledonia being Latin for Scotland. He described the inhabitants in a complimentary way as active, robust, courteous, and disinclined to engage in thievery (apparently common in other places Cook visited). Sailing south along the east coast, he reconnoitered the Isle of Pines but did not encounter the Loyalty Islands. The first recorded European sighting of the Loyalties did not occur until 1793.

French interest in the main island dates from King Louis XVI's orders to Jean-François de Galaup, Comte de La Pérouse, to explore the island's economic potential during his expedition to the Pacific, commencing in 1785. La Pérouse disappeared in the South Pacific in 1788, and three years later the French government sent Antoine de Bruni d'Entrecasteaux to discover his fate. During his voyage, which was unsuccessful in its primary aim of locating La Pérouse, d'Entrecasteaux charted the west coast of the main island. In April-May 1793 he laid over at Balade but, unlike Cook, found the inhabitants hostile, apparently because they were suffering the effects of an extended drought. La Pérouse's fate continued to intrigue the French, and as late as 1827 Jules-Sébastien-César Dumont d'Urville explored the Loyalty Islands in search of remains of his expedition.

Commerce and evangelism brought Europeans in some numbers to New Caledonia in the mid-nineteenth century. Sandalwood, a fragrant, oily wood that the Chinese burned at funerals and other ceremonies, was a highly treasured, exotic commodity, which Western merchants could exchange at Chinese ports for tea and porcelains. The Hawaiian and the Marquesas islands and Fiji were stripped of sandalwood by the 1820s, and entrepreneurs turned their attention to sandalwood groves on various islands in Melanesia. It was not until 1841, however, that they found large quantities of sandalwood on the Isle of Pines, the Loyalty Islands, and the main island. The trade was a dangerous and ultimately destructive business. Although the islanders were willing to exchange the wood for lengths of iron wire, hatchets, and other goods (Europeans soon appreciated their talents as sharp traders), they were always suspicious and unpredictably hostile. Numerous massacres of sandalwood traders occurred. In turn, the Europeans treated the islanders harshly, and they carried diseases, such as measles, that decimated island populations.

In 1840 and 1841 the London Missionary Society sent Samoa and Cook islands catechists to the Isle of Pines and to Touaourou on the main island; their mission stations did not flourish, however, and were closed down by 1845. They had more success on Maré and Lifou in the Loyalty Islands, in large part owing to the receptiveness of the local Polynesian population. Roman Catholic missionaries of the Society of Mary led by Monsignor Guillaume Douarre, who had been consecrated bishop of New Caledonia by Pope Gregory XVI, arrived at Balade on the main island in 1843. Like the ministers of the London Missionary Society, they suffered numerous reversals in their dealings with the islanders but, unlike the Protestants, benefited from France's official policy of supporting Roman Catholic missionary activity. When a French colony was established in New Caledonia in 1853, the place of the Marists was ensured.

French Colonization

France sought to rival Britain as a naval and colonial power in the Pacific and in 1842 imposed a protectorate over Tahiti (see French Polynesia, ch. 4). The French flag flew over Balade on the main island when the Marist mission was established there in 1843, but British pressure led to a French withdrawal in 1846 over the strenuous objections of Bishop Douarre, who advocated annexation. However, in 1850 the French government sent the warship *Alcmène* to New Caledonia to chart the waters and explore the coasts. When some of its crew met a grisly end at the hands of Melanesians at the northern end of the main island in December, French troops stationed on the *Alcmène* killed a large number of Melanesians and burned villages and crops in the region. The pace of French involvement quickened. British ships had been in New Caledonian waters, and there had been talk of establishing a coaling station on the southern end of the main island to serve the Sydney-Panama route. In 1851 the Marists, who had been forced off the island by the Melanesians, reestablished their mission stations at Balade and Pouébo and requested French armed protection. In 1853 the newly enthroned French emperor, Napoléon III, ordered one of his admirals, Auguste Fébvrier-Despointes, to sail to New Caledonia and establish a formal claim. On September 24, 1853, Fébvrier-Despointes arrived at Balade and raised the tricolor. Persuading local chiefs to sign agreements they most likely could not fully comprehend, he sailed on to the Isle of Pines and negotiated its annexation with another local chief on September 29, 1853.

In the words of one Australian historian, "seldom was glory acquired so cheaply" as in the annexation of New Caledonia. It was literally grabbed from underneath the noses of the British, who had their own naval forces in New Caledonian waters. London, tied to France in an alliance against Russia, was in no position at the time to protest. The islands' potential as a naval base in the southwest Pacific and their natural resources were well appreciated, but in official French eyes New Caledonia's remoteness made it particularly valuable as a penal settlement similar to the ones established in French Guyana in South America.

The Loyalty Islands remained unclaimed by France until 1866. The London Missionary Society had been established there since the 1840s and the Marists since the 1850s. Local chiefs, in a miniature reenactment of Europe's Thirty Years' War, declared themselves and their subjects either Protestant or Catholic and fought among themselves. On the imposition of French control, British naval and commercial influence was excluded decisively from New Caledonian waters, but the London Missionary Society was allowed to operate under restricted conditions in the Loyalty group.

The center of French administration on the main island was moved from Balade to Nouméa in the southwest, which offered a well-protected harbor. Nouméa became the capital of the colony of New Caledonia in 1860. (Previously it had been under the jurisdiction of a French governor stationed in Tahiti.) From the very beginning the attitude of the native peoples, known to Europeans at that time as the Kanakas (originally a Polynesian term meaning "man," used to refer to all Melanesians in the southwest Pacific), was hostile. An influx of settlers from Europe and Australia deprived them of their lands, and the Marist missionaries challenged both traditional religious beliefs and the authority of the chiefs. Good relations were maintained, however, with the Canala and Houaïlou tribes on the east coast. They accepted French suzerainty and in turn were in a better position to deal with their old neighbors and rivals.

By the late 1870s the position of the Melanesian population had seriously deteriorated. Their best lands had been seized by settlers, and beginning in 1876 they were forced onto native reserves, where land was usually of poor quality. The introduction of cattle by Europeans wrought a special hardship, for large areas of land were needed for pastures. In June 1878 a revolt was instigated by Atai, a tribal chief living in the valley of the La Foa River on the west coast. Atai succeeded in getting many of the tribes of the central region of the main island to put aside their differences and join the insurrection that reached as far south as the environs of Nouméa. He was killed, however, in an ambush in September, and the French, using troops of the Canala and Houaïlou tribes, were able to suppress the revolt by June 1879.

The 1878–79 revolt represented the strongest Melanesian challenge to French rule in New Caledonia. To prevent another insurrection, French authorities instituted the *indigénat,* an administrative system that deprived the Melanesians of the protection of law and put them under the control of officials who had great latitude in imposing fines and punishments. In 1897–98 the system of administration for Melanesians was further transformed through the incorporation of local chiefs into a rigid official framework. The native reservations were divided into 50 districts, headed by a "Great Chief" appointed by the colonial governor. Families were forcibly relocated to 150 "new villages," which were laid out in grid fashion in areas easily reached by the gendarmerie. The policy of creating native reservations continued through the early twentieth century. Given the pressures exerted by European settlers to obtain the best land, however, the government trimmed down the reservations so that by 1907 they comprised only about 20 percent of the total land area of the colony and only 10 percent of the area of the main island, most land on the Isle of Pines and the Loyalty Islands having been recognized as native reserves.

As the French forced the Melanesians into the suffocating

confines of a colonial administration in which chiefs lost their traditional prestige and clans were separated from their ancestral lands, the traditional society rapidly disintegrated. Disease and alcoholism decimated the population. Estimated at around 60,000 around the time of the 1878 revolt, the population dwindled to 42,500 in 1887 and to 27,100 in 1921. There was some increase during the 1930s, but even in 1976, when the last official ethnic breakdown of the population was recorded, there were 55,598 Melanesians—less than the number in 1878 and only 42 percent of the total population.

After the revolt the cult of *toki*, or the "red god," a deity brought from the New Hebrides and the Loyalty Islands, reached the main island. Cultists carried amulets that they believed gave them great, and usually malevolent, power. The fear and distrust engendered by the practitioners of the cult contributed to the breakdown of Melanesian society and also played a role in a revolt that occurred on the main island in 1917.

Around 20,000 convicts were brought to New Caledonia between 1864 and 1897. They were confined to penal settlements or sent out in labor gangs to built roads, string telegraph wires, or work in mines or logging camps. The better behaved convicts were "leased" to European settlers or even given their own land to farm. Most were ordinary criminals, and their presence gave the colony an unsavory reputation. After the bloody suppression of the Paris commune in May 1871, however, a large number of political exiles arrived in New Caledonia. These "Communards," many of whom were highly educated or skilled, contributed much to the development of the colony, particularly the Isle of Pines. One of the most remarkable, Louise Michel, an anarchist, taught Melanesian schoolchildren in Nouméa and took a genuine interest in Melanesian culture and ways of life—a rare thing in a European at that time. Her memoirs express great sympathy for the 1878–79 revolt, which she compared to the Communards' own struggle for liberty in France. Although all the Communards were given permission to return home by 1881, the penal regime continued for another 16 years until the colonial governor, Paul Feillet, persuaded Paris to abolish it. Thereafter, Feillet and his successors encourged the immigration of free colonists from Europe and Asia.

Interest in the main island's mineral potential goes back to the time before the establishment of French rule. In 1863 gold was discovered along the banks of the Diahot River in the northern part of the island, and in 1872 copper ore was discovered in exploitable quantities near Balade. Other commercially valuable mineral deposits uncovered around this time included lead, zinc, chrome, and silver. Cobalt ore was discovered in 1875, and from then until 1909 New Caledonia was the world's principal supplier of this metal. It was nickel, however, that transformed the economy of the colony. Although nickel was discovered on the island in 1863, it was not until 1874 that commercial exploitation was begun. An Australian, John Higginson, established the Société Le Nickel (SLN) in 1876 and earned himself the title of the "nickel king" as, largely through his efforts, New Caledonia became the world's premier supplier of this metal. The discovery of nickel in Canada in 1892 put an end to the first nickel boom, although in the early 1980s nickel continued to be New Caledonia's most important export, and the SLN maintained a dominant position in the mining sector.

The Colony to the End of World War II

Governor Feillet initiated a program to encourage European colonization in the mid-1890s, wherein French farmers possessing assets of at least 5,000 francs were offered 25 hectares of free land. Three hundred families had established themselves successfully by the first decade of the twentieth century, and they and their children soon outnumbered the remaining convict population. Opportunities in the mining sector also stimulated European and Australian immigration. Gradually, a population of New Caledonia-born Europeans emerged, the descendants of convicts, political detainees, and free settlers having roots in the colony going back several generations. Like the French colonists of North Africa, the *pieds-noirs*, these "Caldoches" were culturally French but regarded New Caledonia, rather than France, as their home. Most were concentrated around Nouméa and along the coasts, while the Melanesians remained in their reservations. Even more than other colonial capitals, Nouméa with its grid pattern of streets, cathedral, public buildings, and comfortable, European-style houses, was in structure and spirit a European town in which the indigenous people were very much out of place. Political developments involved the European population exclusively. Elective municipal governments had been established in Nouméa and other European settlements beginning in the 1870s, and a General Council for the colony was inaugurated in 1895. This council, initially elected by male French citizens, had limited powers that included responsibility for local taxation and certain categories of the colonial budget.

The abolition of the penal regime deprived European colonists of a convenient supply of workers, and the colonial administration began encouraging the immigration of laborers from Asia and other parts of Oceania in order to provide an alternative source of cheap labor. These immigrants came from localities as diverse as the New Hebrides, China, Japan, and French Indochina. The most important groups, however, were indentured laborers brought from Vietnam (at that time part of French Indochina) and the island of Java in the Netherlands East Indies (present-day Indonesia). In the words of one observer, anthropologist Douglas L. Oliver, "9,000 Javanese and 5,000 Tonkinese (Vietnamese) supplied the muscle and sweat to keep the colony solvent." They worked in the mines and ore refineries or were contracted out to European farmers as agricultural laborers. Many returned home when their contracts of indenture, which ran for three to five years, expired. Others settled permanently in the colony.

An official census taken in 1936 counted a total population for the colony of 53,245. By that time New Caledonia had clearly become a multiethnic, plural society. The largest ethnic group was still the Melanesians, some 28,800 persons. Europeans numbered 15,954 and Japanese 1,430. A final category, described in contemporary accounts as "colored immigrants," totaled 7,061. These presumably included Vietnamese, Javanese, and a sprinkling of non-New Caledonian Melanesians.

The 1936 census revealed that only 59.3 percent of the Melanesian population lived on the main island; most of the remainder lived in the Loyalty Islands. In the late 1930s only 1,500 Melanesians lived outside the reservations. At this time they remained vulnerable to disease and general demoralization and were largely neglected by the French administration. Europeans and Asian immigrants on the one hand, and Melanesians on the other, lived in separate worlds, an arrangement that functioned reasonably well in the period before World War II but had serious implications for the postwar period when the indigenous population began demanding its political and social rights.

During World War I New Caledonia contributed a contingent of 2,170 soldiers to the Pacific Battalion. More than half of these were Melanesian volunteers. The battalion saw action on the Western Front in Europe, where more than one-fourth of them died on the battlefield.

After the fall of France in June 1940 to Nazi Germany and the establishment of the collaborationist Vichy regime of Marshal Henri-Philippe Pétain, a popular movement emerged in the colony to support General Charles de Gaulle's Free French government. The pro-Vichy colonial administration was toppled in September 1940, and a new governor loyal to de Gaulle and the Allies was installed. Japanese expansion into the southwest Pacific came hard on the heels of their attack on Pearl Harbor in December 1941. Its mineral resources made New Caledonia a rich prize, but the Japanese naval advance into the Coral Sea, just west of New Caledonia, was halted in May 1942 (see World War II, ch. 5).

During the war New Caledonia served as a major strategic base for United States, Australian, and New Zealand forces. The enormous military presence caused social disruption and a high level of inflation, which continued into the postwar period. The demand for nickel and other strategic metals generated by the war effort brought riches to some and a measure of prosperity to others, including the Melanesian laborers who had been used to a subsistence standard of living. Although the boom collapsed at the end of the war (reviving during the 1950–53 Korean War), New Caledonia's traditional isolation had been permanently breached, and European colonials and Melanesians alike were to experience a revolution of rising expectations.

Political and Social Developments in the Postwar Period

After the war the French government conceded a greater measure of autonomy to the territory as a whole, also granting political rights to Melanesians, who previously had been excluded from the political process. In 1946 the government abolished the *indigénat*, the special system of administration for the native people that had deprived them of legal rights, and ended the requirement that they perform labor service and remain domiciled on their reservations. The General Council election of December 22, 1946, was the first in which Melanesians were allowed to vote, though the number enfranchised—consisting of war veterans and civil servants—was quite small. In May 1951 the French parliament passed a law that enfranchised a much larger number of indigenous adults in all the territories of the French Union, including New Caledonia. Around 9,000 Melanesian men and women were given the vote, comprising almost half the total of 20,000 eligible voters in the colony.

Missionaries had been active in promoting the organization of Melanesian political interests. In 1946 Catholic missionaries established the Union of Caledonian Native Peoples—Friends of Liberty in Order (Union des Indigènes Calédoniens-Amis de la Liberté dans l'Ordre), and the Protestants founded the Association of French Caledonian and Loyalty Island Native Peoples (Association des Indigènes Calédoniens et Loyaltiens Français). These groups requested an increase in the area of native reservations because of a rapidly growing population (though the Melanesians were no longer required to live on them) and the recovery of traditional clan territories, which had social and cultural, as well as economic, significance.

In the July 1951 election for a deputy to the French National Assembly, Maurice Lenormand, campaigning on a platform of multiracial unity, triumphed over conservative opponents with the support of the newly enfranchised Melanesian voters. His party, the New Caledonian Union (Union Calédonienne—UC), advocated a greater measure of autonomy for the territory but continued association with France. Conservatives, including businessmen having interests in the mining sector, particularly in the SLN, wanted closer integration with France. The issue of New Caledonia's relationship with the metropole became especially urgent when a French socialist government passed the *loi cadre* (framework law) in July 1956, designed to afford a greater measure of self-government for overseas territories. (New Caledonia, from that year on, was referred to as an overseas territory rather than as a colony.) A controversy ensued between the UC and conservatives regarding the application of the provisions of the *loi cadre*. Lenormand pressured successfully for the establishment of a Territorial Assembly and a Government Council, an embryonic cabinet whose members would be chosen by majority vote of the Territorial Assembly.

Lenormand and the UC, supported by a coalition of Melanesians and European settlers and businessmen jealous of the privileged position of the metropolitan French, dominated territorial politics until the late 1950s, when conservatives, enjoying the support of Charles de Gaulle's government in Paris, gradually began to gain the upper hand. In January 1964 Lenormand was obliged to resign as deputy to the French National Assembly because of his alleged connection with a bomb plot. His fall marked a serious setback for those Melanesians and Europeans who desired a more liberal political system.

European settlers were beginning to fear that a greater measure of autonomy for the territory meant surrendering political power and economic privileges to the growing Melanesian population. This sentiment was particularly strong among the *pieds-noirs*, French who had lived in Algeria but had left at the time of its independence in 1962 to make a new life in New Caledonia. It was shared by many French who came to the territory to take advantage of the opportunities afforded by the nickel

117

boom in the late 1960s and early 1970s. Moreover, a large number of immigrants from French Polynesia and Wallis and Futuna, who tended to regard France as the protector of their interests, viewed the Melanesians with suspicion and were wary of their growing political assertiveness.

The Social System

The population of New Caledonia was reckoned at 145,368 by the French government in early 1984. The figure for the total population, published after the census of April 23, 1976, was 133,233. Growth rates reflect immigration as well as natural increase. In the 1960–65 period the average annual growth rate was 2.7 percent. It reached a high of 4.3 percent in the 1965–70 period, declining to 3.4 percent in 1970–75 and 0.9 percent in 1975–80. During these periods immigration, largely from metropolitan France and former overseas possessions was affected by the boom and bust of the nickel sector and growing apprehension over Melanesian demands for immediate independence after 1975, which led to significant European repatriation. United States government sources projected an average annual growth rate of 1.5 percent for the population between 1980 and 1985. In 1979 some 49 percent of the population was under 20 years of age.

The population was concentrated in and around Nouméa; its population in early 1984 was 60,112. If outlying areas were included, the population of greater Nouméa was more than half that of the territory as a whole. Other towns of importance included Bourail, Koné, La Foa, Poindimié, Muéo, and Wé. The average population density for the entire territory in 1976 was 7.0 persons per square kilometer, but for the commune of Nouméa it was 1,335.2 per square kilometer. New Caledonia's population density in early 1984 was 7.6 persons per square kilometer.

Eighty-eight percent of the population was located on the main island in early 1984. The largest concentrations off the main island were the communes of Lifou (8,128 persons), Maré (4,610 persons), and Ouvéa (2,772 persons) in the Loyalty Islands, and the Isle of Pines (1,287 persons). The Chesterfield Islands were uninhabited.

Ethnic Groups and Social Structure

Official figures from the 1976 census reveal that at that time 41.7 percent of the population consisted of Melanesians; Europeans made up 38.1 percent; Polynesians 12 percent; and others,

*Session of the Territorial Assembly shows
ethnic diversity of New Caledonian people.
Courtesy Les Nouvelles Calédoniennes*

including Indonesians, 8.2 percent. Comparison with earlier figures shows that the proportion of Melanesians to the general
population had declined since 1951, when it was 51.9 percent. In
the 1976–80 period, however, it increased to 43.3 percent. The
European population grew from 31.1 percent in 1951 to a high of
41 percent in 1969 but declined thereafter to 35.6 percent. The
Polynesians have been the fastest growing group. From a few
hundred in the early 1950s, they had grown to an estimated one-
eighth of New Caledonia's population by 1980. Ethnic breakdowns for that year, the latest available in mid-1984, show 59,800
Melanesians, 49,200 Europeans, 17,400 Polynesians, and 11,600
others.

The different ethnic groups of New Caledonia were spatially,
culturally, and economically segregated, a result of early colonial
policy and the preference of many, if not most, of the territory's
present inhabitants. In contrast to the situation in many other
French overseas possessions, there has been little intermarriage
between Europeans and the indigenous people. A genuine
"creole" culture, a blending of European and indigenous elements, has not developed. The abolition of compulsory Melanesian residence on the reservations in 1946 and the migration of
some Melanesians to Nouméa began to break down the ethnic

119

"compartmentalization" of society. The controversy over the future political status of New Caledonia, however, has sharpened interethnic tensions and rivalries.

The Melanesians. Descendants of the inhabitants of New Caledonia at the time of the coming of the first Europeans are commonly referred to as Melanesians, though a small number, especially the people of the Loyalty Islands, have significant Polynesian admixture. Apart from the indigenous people, there is a small population of Melanesian immigrants from the islands in what is now Vanuatu. The term "Kanaka" (rendered "Canaque," "Kanaque," and "Kanak" in French), originally used by Europeans in a derogatory fashion, has been adopted as a form of self-reference by some Melanesians, including militants demanding "Kanaka Independence."

In the early 1980s only about 18 percent of the population of Nouméa consisted of Melanesians. Most of these had migrated from the Loyalty Islands. The largest concentration of Melanesians on the main island was found in the communes along the east coast—more than three-quarters of the total population. Along the west coast they comprised approximately 47 percent of the total population, excluding Nouméa and its environs. More than 90 percent of the Isle of Pines and 97 to 99 percent of the Loyalty and the Bélep islands consisted of Melanesians. Most Melanesians engaged in subsistence or cash-crop agriculture.

Traditional Melanesian society was based on the clan, or patrilineal descent group. This was small, comprising about 50 people who lived in a small settlement. The center of each clan settlement was the "great house," a ritual place located on a small hill where the totemic images of the clan were kept. Each clan had its own history and legends, and in principle all its members were descended from a common ancestor. The leader of the clan was customarily the senior male of the clan's founding family. Although male heads of families were ranked within the clan (this ranking was expressed through ritual distribution of yams, a staple food), the clan leader was not so much a ruler as a presider over rituals and community consultations. The clans were closely tied to the land and its associated spirits. In places where more than one clan lived, the "original" clan, defined in terms of its relationship to the spirits of the land, had precedence. Leaders of groups larger than clans were limited in power because they were based on constantly shifting alliances of clan heads and their followers. A figure of great importance in the traditional society was the "master of the land," who had extensive knowledge of genealogy and of the claims of each clan in his region to specific tracts of land, which clan members owned communally. Marriage was exogamous, women being brought in from other clans.

During the early colonial period French administrators, partly because of their misunderstanding of Melanesian society and partly out of administrative convenience, ignored the clans and organized the indigenous people in terms of "tribes" led by "chiefs" and "subchiefs." Tribes included large populations and areas of land, and the native reserves were, in essence, their communally owned land. French policies created a political and social vacuum. Clans were separated from their ancient lands and moved into reserves, and the new chiefs set above the people had little prestige or authority.

Asians and Polynesians. The Asian population, consisting principally of Indonesians and Vietnamese but also including Malabaris from the Indian subcontinent and a very small number of Japanese, is concentrated around Nouméa. The repatriation of many Asians after World War II and an influx of new immigrants from Europe and other parts of Oceania have contributed to a decline in their percentage of the total population. In 1963 Indonesians composed 4.1 percent of New Caledonia's people, 4.4 percent in 1969, but only 3.8 percent in 1976.

In contrast the Polynesian component of the population has grown rapidly. In the late 1940s people from Wallis and Futuna began seeking opportunities in New Caledonia, the consequence of the failure of the coconut crop and overcrowded conditions in their home islands. Continued immigration through the decades of the 1950s and 1960s and a high birth rate made the Wallis Islanders the third largest ethnic group (after the Melanesians and Europeans) in New Caledonia by 1969, constituting 6.2 percent of the total population. Immigrants from French Polynesia make up another important Polynesian group. Polynesians, particularly from French Polynesia, have been quick to seize employment opportunities in the modern sectors of the economy and have occupied the uncomfortable position of an intermediate group between dominant Europeans and disadvantaged Melanesians. This has often made them a target of Melanesian resentment.

Among political deportees brought to New Caledonia in the late nineteenth century were about 300 Arabs, rebels against French rule in Algeria. A small Algerian Arab minority remains, although official figures on the number have not been published.

The Europeans. Europeans, predominantly French, are concentrated in and around Nouméa, where they have re-created with considerable success, a distinctly French style of life 20,000 kilometers from home. A significant division existed in the European population between the Caldoches, those born in the territory whose roots often go back several generations, and the metropolitan French, less than 20 percent of the total European population in early 1984. A certain sense of rivalry has developed between the two groups, based in part on the Caldoches' resentment of the transients' higher standard of living and their privileged position within the colonial administration. A minority of Europeans, commonly referred to as *broussards* (from *brousse,* or "bush"), live in the interior and operate farms and cattle stations.

Religion

Traditional Melanesian religion was animistic. The indigenous people conceived of a world inhabited by a myriad of benevolent and malevolent spirits, of which the ancestors of the clan were among the most powerful. The world of humans and that of deities were regarded as closely intertwined. The dead, as ancestors, had an important social role, and the totemic animals of the clans were regarded as possessing great procreative powers, the givers of life through generations.

Traditional religious beliefs have been to a considerable extent supplanted (though not eradicated) by Christianity. According to recent estimates, 90.6 percent of the total population in 1980 consisted of professing Christians, divided between 72.5 percent Catholics and 18.1 percent Protestants. Muslims constituted the largest non-Christian religious group (4 percent of the total population in 1980), found predominantly among Indonesians and Algerian Arabs. Smaller groups included Buddhists, Bahais, adherents of tribal religions, and a "non-religious" category of 4.5 percent. Cargo cults, principally from Vanuatu, have had some influence (see Vanuatu, this ch.).

Missionaries, both Protestant and Catholic, have played a significant role in helping Melanesians adjust to the radical changes following colonization and in promoting their cause to an often indifferent or unsympathetic colonial government. The most important was Maurice Leenhardt, a pastor of the French Protestant Evangelical Mission Society, who headed a mission near Houaïlou on the main island between 1902 and 1926. Making an exhaustive study of Melanesian culture and mythology and training indigenous pastors, Leenhardt sought to fashion a place for the Christian religion within the people's own cultural context. The native peoples' fortunes at the time of his arrival were at a low ebb, and many Europeans expected that they would become virtually extinct within a few years. Leenhardt was successful in gaining Melanesian converts to a great extent because he was the first European to take an active interest in their welfare. Following his example, Catholic missionaries became active on the main island and the number of Christian adherents grew rapidly.

Health and Education

The responsibility for maintaining a system of public health services was borne in the mid-1980s by the French military. Medical facilities—both public and private—were most developed in Nouméa, but there were 17 medical centers, 13 nursing centers, and 25 dispensaries located in outlying areas. Intestinal parasites and gastrointestinal illnesses were relatively common, and there were instances of leprosy and tuberculosis. Although malaria was not found in New Caledonia, the authorities in recent years have taken measures to prevent the spread of mosquito-borne dengue fever. Infant mortality at the time of the 1976 census was 27 deaths per 1,000 live births but by 1982 this had declined to 21.9. In 1976 life expectancy was 64 years.

There were both state- and church-supported primary and secondary schools; two-thirds of students on all levels attended public schools in 1982. The educational system was similar to that found in metropolitan France; five years of elementary education and four years of lower secondary education were followed by a division of upper secondary schools into vocational and academic tracks, the latter leading to the university level. Students had to go overseas, primarily to France, to attend a university, although there has been talk since 1966 of establishing an institution of higher education in the territory.

Official statistics on school attendance suggest that while there were ethnic disparities, Melanesians were taking advantage of educational facilities on all levels. In 1982 a total of 11,381 Europeans, 6,429 Polynesians, 1,838 Asians (Vietnamese and Indonesian ancestry), and 21,979 Melanesians attended public and private elementary schools; on the lower secondary-school level, there were 5,015 Europeans, 1,115 Polynesians, 761 Asians, and 3,900 Melanesians. On the upper secondary-school level, in the vocational and academic tracks, 1,632 Melanesians, 1,915 Europeans, and 1,203 Asians and Polynesians were enrolled. Overall, a smaller percentage of Melanesians enrolled in elementary schools remained in the system through upper secondary school (7.4 percent) than did Europeans (16.8 percent), Polynesians (12.1 percent), or Asians (23.3 percent). Literacy among all adults in 1976, however, was 91 percent.

The Economy

New Caledonia possesses a number of metals of great strategic and industrial importance and has a well-developed mining sector. Among the mineral resources are large deposits of nickel, cobalt, chromium, iron, and manganese. Antimony, mercury, copper, silver, lead, and gold are known to exist in sizable quantities.

Mining has brought a prosperity to the territory unmatched in Oceania (excluding New Zealand and Nauru). Per capita GDP in 1980 was estimated at over US$7,800. The economy, however, has been seriously affected by instability in world demand for nickel, the most important mineral resource. Moreover, the benefits of a modern economy have not been distributed equally. In mid-1984 Nouméa, having a predominantly European population, had a standard of living comparable to that of cities in Western Europe, while the interior, where Melanesians predominate, remained underdeveloped, although the government supplied basic health and educational services. Dependence on the mining sector has resulted in neglect of agriculture and fishing. On numerous occasions the French government has affirmed its commitment to promoting investment in these sectors in order to provide a more stable basis for economic growth in the future.

The economy, measured in terms of GDP, grew almost threefold in the period between 1960 and 1980. Indexed at 100 in 1960, the total value of economic activity in the territory was at a level of 289 in 1980, when measured in constant prices. In 1980 agriculture contributed 3 percent to GDP, the mining sector (extraction and refining), 17.9 percent; public works and construction, 9.1 percent; services and transportation, 18.5 percent; commerce, 21.3 percent; small-scale industries and services, 9.7 percent; and administration—the largest factor—22.5 percent. Inflation in the November 1982-November 1983 period was 11 percent. In October 1982 the government imposed a six-month price freeze.

The census of April 23, 1976, provided detailed information on the territory's labor force. More recent official data had not been published as of mid-1984. In 1976 agriculture, forestry, and

*Mining center of the
Société Le Nickel,
the most important
industrial enterprise
in New Caledonia,
which was the world's
second largest producer
of nickel in 1981
Courtesy
Société Le Nickel*

fishing employed 13,394 persons, of whom 40 percent were Melanesians; mining employed 2,066. Forty percent of these were European, 6 percent were Indonesians, 35 percent were Melanesians, and 19 percent were Polynesians and others. Industries involved in smelting and refining of metals employed 2,891 persons, of whom 44 percent were Europeans, 5 percent were Indonesians, 12 percent were Melanesians, and 34 percent were other groups, mostly Polynesians. Other industries employed 2,578 persons. The labor force totaled 46,689 in 1976. Aside from agriculture and activities connected to the mining sector, important components included transport, 2,632 persons; construction, 4,475 persons; commerce, 6,458 persons; and services (including government employees), 11,338 persons.

The age of the labor force figures makes it difficult to calculate rates of employment for the early 1980s. Government publications reveal that unemployment compensation, provided for salaried workers since 1975, was being dispensed to 1,484 persons in late 1981.

In early 1984 some workers were organized into a labor federation, the Federation of Caledonian Laborers (Confédération des Travailleurs Calédoniens), which included a union for gov-

125

ernment employees, one for industrial workers, and the Union of Exploited Kanaka Laborers (Syndicat des Travailleurs Canaques Exploités). A second labor federation was the Federation of Workers and Employees' Unions of New Caledonia (Union des Syndicats Ouvriers et Employés de Nouvelle-Calédonie).

Currency, Banking, and National Accounts

New Caledonia's currency, the CFP franc (CFPF; for value of the CFP franc—see Glossary), in early 1984 was tied to the French franc at a rate of 1 French franc equal to CFPF18.18. The Institut d'Émission d'Outre-Mer in France issued the territory's banknotes. There were five banks in the territory, two of which were branches of Paris banks and three of which had their headquarters in Nouméa. There were also a number of trust and savings establishments.

The territorial budget in 1983 was CFPF30 billion . The 1984 budget of CFPF31.2 billion included CFPF4 billion for extraordinary expenditure, investment in infrastructure, and the development of the agricultural, fishery, and tourism sectors. A 10-year plan (1980–90) envisioned CFPF130 billion in credits and loans to be invested in the territory's development. Revenues have included personal income taxes since 1980 but have depended primarily on import and export duties and indirect taxes. The French government has also provided direct grants to New Caledonia.

The Mining Sector

In 1981 New Caledonia was the world's second largest producer of nickel ore, the largest being Canada. Its reserves of nickel ore were estimated at 40 million tons, surpassed only by Indonesia's 60 million tons out of an estimated world total of 200 million tons. More than three-fourths of reserves are found in lateritic formations located near Goro at the southern tip of the main island. The principal nickel deposits exploited by the SLN, the territory's largest mining enterprise, are found at Poro, Kouaoua, and Thio, on the east coast of the main island and Népoui on the west coast. The ore is stripped from the mountains and either refined at the SLN's smelter at Doniambo in Nouméa or shipped to facilities overseas. Nickel, in the form of ore, matte, and ferronickel, accounted for an average of 93 percent of exports by value in the 1977–81 period. The principal importers in the mid-1980s were France, Japan, and the United States. Because of nickel's value as a strategic metal, its extraction and export were subject to strict control by the French government.

Excessive dependence on nickel exports has subjected New Caledonia's economy to a series of highly disruptive boom and bust periods. International markets were favorable during the 1969–74 period, ore exports reaching a peak of 4.1 million tons (gross weight) in 1970. The competition of new producers, such as Indonesia, Botswana, and the Philippines, began to have an adverse effect during the mid-1970s. It was estimated that the cost of producing nickel in New Caledonia was as much as four times that of producing it in Indonesia or Canada. Other factors in the occurrence of a nickel bust were the 1975 recession in industrialized countries and new industrial methods that enabled consumers to use less pure grades of the metal. Even France has reduced its dependence on New Caledonia as a source of nickel—75 percent of its requirements were met by the territory in 1975 but declined to 45 percent by 1980. Labor unrest, including a 50-day strike at the SLN's smelter in 1978, has also contributed to a decline in nickel exports.

The irregular fortunes of the territory's nickel industry are reflected in figures for exports of nickel ore in the 1974–82 period. In 1974 some 3.3 million tons (gross weight) of ore were exported, declining to 2.5 million tons the following year. In 1977 the figure was 2.6 million tons but fell sharply to 1.5 million tons in 1978. Although the 1980 figure was 2 million tons, exports in 1982 were down to 1.5 million tons. A similar pattern is revealed in the export of matte and ferronickel. Export revenues, which in 1977 were CFPF26.2 billion, were CFPF15.3 billion in 1978, recovering gradually to CFPF31 billion by 1981. These figures included revenue from the export of ore, matte, and ferronickel, of which the last was the largest component. Although the SLN owned the only smelter in the territory, export operations were also maintained by 15 independent mining enterprises.

The declining quality of the nickel ore mined in the territory is a matter of some concern. During the late nineteenth century, ores averaged 9 percent nickel content. By 1960, however, average nickel content had declined to a little over 3 percent and to 2.7 percent by 1969. By 1982 it averaged 2.5 percent. Although extensive reserves remain, these are primarily in low-grade ores.

In the mid-1980s other metals mined on a significant scale in New Caledonia included cobalt, which is extracted from nickel ore. The mining of chromium, begun in 1897, was abandoned in 1962 because of low world prices. The tripling of the world price for chromium in 1974–75 led to a reopening of the mine at

Tiébaghi in the northern region of the main island, and ore production in the 1977–81 period averaged 7,900 tons a year. The export of iron ore from the territory ceased in 1968.

Agriculture and Other Sectors

Statistics for the 20-year period from 1960 to 1980 revealed a gradual decline in the importance of agriculture's contribution to GDP, from 9.6 percent to 3 percent. Given the difficulty of measuring the productivity of subsistence agriculture and its value, total figures for the sector may be understated. However, the territory was not self-sufficient in food. Imports, including animal and vegetable products, totaled CFPF3.2 billion in 1980 and CFPF4.8 billion in 1982.

Agricultural and fishery exports formed a minute portion of total exports by value, less than one-half of 1 percent in the 1980–82 period. Products included coffee, copra, and *trocas* (a shell used to make buttons).

Principal crops included corn, yams, taro, sorghum, potatoes, vegetables, and fruits. In the 1980–81 period, about 600 cattle ranches covered some 280,000 hectares in the territory. Cattle totaled around 100,000 head; there were smaller numbers of pigs, horses, and sheep. Commercial fishing in early 1984 remained relatively undeveloped, although the territory had tuna fishing agreements with United States and Japanese fishing firms.

In the 1975–80 period the volume of wood extracted from the territory's forests averaged 13,500 cubic meters annually and in 1982 was 16,400 cubic meters. The government's Forestry Commission was in charge of reforestation projects, and the Center for Tropical Forest Technology carried out research projects.

In early 1984 tourism was a sector of some importance and was included in government investment plans. However, New Caledonia's isolation and the cost of living, high for the region, have impeded its development.

The main island was encircled by a system of coastal roads. Total road length in the territory in 1980 was 5,496 kilometers. Bitumen-surfaced highways amounted to 766 kilometers, and 2,523 kilometers consisted of dirt country roads. The major seaport, accommodating frequent cargo service to Asia, Australia, and Europe, was Nouméa. There were 12 commercial airfields in the territory; the international facility at Tontouta served Nouméa. Air Caledonia, the principal domestic airline, was scheduled to begin international service in the Pacific region in 1984.

The Land Issue

Land tenure and land reform were central issues in New Caledonia, having cultural, social, and political, as well as economic, implications. Although colonial policy left to the Melanesian people the lands they occupied, the definition of "occupation" was narrow, excluding hunting, gathering, and even some gardening land. Reserves were whittled away owing to the pressure of European settlers, particularly cattle ranchers, on the government; thus, by 1907 only about 112,000 hectares were reserve land on the main island—less than 10 percent of its area. Melanesian nationalism has evolved to a considerable extent along with the demand for the restoration of ancestral lands. The return of expropriated land has been regarded as essential for the restoration of an authentic Melanesian culture and way of life.

Land in New Caledonia is divided into three legal categories: the public domain, controlled mostly by the territorial government, amounting in 1980 to 1,101,710 hectares; privately owned land, primarily in the hands of Europeans, comprising 443,795 hectares (about 10,000 hectares of which were owned by Melanesians); and reserve lands, inalienably and communally owned by the 234 Melanesian "tribes," amounting to 376,659 hectares in 1980. More than half of total reserve lands was located in the Loyalty Islands.

During the 1907–79 period the government, in piecemeal fashion, added 44,866 hectares to the reserves. However, a more determined policy of land reform, aimed at restoring in large measure the ancestral lands of the Melanesian clans, was proposed by Paul Dijoud, France's secretary of state for overseas departments and territories, in 1978. Dijoud's plan involved government purchase of more than 150,000 hectares of land to be returned to the Melanesians. Distribution of the land was to be carried out on the basis of a comprehensive survey of precolonial clan holdings. A new category of land tenure, "clan properties," was recognized. In October 1982 the Land Administration of New Caledonia and Dependencies was established, and by early 1983 the administration had purchased 43,929 hectares, of which about 35,000 hectares were redistributed. It was estimated that a further 100,000 hectares would be returned to the Melanesians at a rate of about 20,000 hectares a year between 1983 and 1988. In 1983 the government reserved CFPF545 million for the purpose of purchasing land.

Although land reform affected only a very small number of

Europeans (as low as 1.6 percent of the European population, according to one account in the Paris newspaper *Le Monde*), the French government's determination to press ahead with restitution of clan lands remained a complex and emotional issue in early 1984. An important problem was whether Melanesian properties would include improvements, such as buildings, made on the land by Europeans and how the latter would be compensated for their losses. In some cases, disputes arose between clans regarding land claims and had to be arbitrated. Europeans and some Melanesian leaders criticized the official recognition of traditional clan rights as "feudal" and as promoting inequality between clan and tribal leaders and the majority of Melanesians. However, the new arrangements included the right of the clans to lease their land to Europeans and other outsiders.

The Political System

The people of New Caledonia are French citizens. Adults of both sexes have the right to vote for two deputies to the French National Assembly and one member of the Senate. New Caledonia also has a representative serving on the metropolitan government's Economic and Social Council.

New Caledonia's government institutions are defined in accordance with a revised territorial statute enacted by the French government on December 28, 1976. Although it was designed to give New Caledonia a greater measure of autonomy, the metropolitan government retains extensive powers exercised by the high commissioner of the republic. This official, formerly known as the governor, is France's representative and executor in the territory and head of the national civil service. He also plays an executive role in the territorial administration.

The legislature, the Territorial Assembly, is elected by popular vote for a five-year term. Citizens over 23 years of age and in full possession of their civil rights were eligible to run. In early 1984 the Territorial Assembly had 36 members. It was responsible for selecting the seven-member Government Council (not including the high commissioner, who served as president of the council but did not have a vote in its deliberations). The council could be dissolved by a vote of censure of the Territorial Assembly. However, the Council of Ministers in Paris retained the power to dissolve the Territorial Assembly.

The metropolitan government appointed the high commissioner and the highest ranks of the civil service and retained responsibility for foreign affairs and defense, finance, secondary and college education, international communications, and justice. The territorial government was granted authority over such matters as primary education, health, transport, land policy, and agriculture. However, even in these areas it lacked the manpower and financial resources to act without the support of the metropole.

In the early 1980s the territory was divided into four administrative subdivisions: Western New Caledonia, including the Bélep and Huon islands; Eastern New Caledonia; Southern New Caledonia, including Nouméa and the Isle of Pines; and the Loyalty Islands. There were 32 communes, or townships, equivalent to those found in France. Each township had a mayor, a township council, and a local administration.

The administration of justice followed standard French practice and procedures. The principal officers of the courts, appointed by the secretary of state for overseas departments and territories, are the president of the Court of Appeal, the president of the Civil Court, the president of the Court of First Instance, the attorney general, and the magistrates.

The Evolution of Political Forces

Beginning in the late 1960s, a more militant type of political movement became apparent among Melanesians. College-educated youths, some of whom had experienced the student and labor activism of May 1968 in Paris, formed the Red Neckerchiefs (Foulards Rouges), an organization espousing liberation from colonial domination and the revival of Melanesian culture. Another association, the 1878 Group, named for the year of the Melanesian revolt, demanded the recovery of clan lands taken by Europeans. In 1970 Yann Célène Uregei, a Melanesian leader, broke with the New Caledonian Union (Union Calédonienne—UC), the party that had advocated autonomy, to form a group that came to be known as the United Front for the Liberation of the Kanakas (Front Uni pour le Libération des Kanaks—FULK), which by 1977 was demanding full independence from France. Other associations that supported independence at this time were the Marxist-oriented Kanaka Liberation Party (Parti pour la Libération des Kanaques—PALIKA) and the more moderate Progressive Melanesian Union (Union Progressiste Melanésienne—UPM).

During the period between 1970 and 1980, support for independence among Melanesians grew. This was attributable not only to their sense of grievance against the colonial government but also to the fact that other territories in the western Pacific, such as Papua New Guinea, Solomon Islands, and, most significantly, the Anglo-French Condominium of the New Hebrides, were achieving self-rule.

In 1979 a coalition of parties, the Independence Front (Front Indépendantiste—FI), was established and included the UC—which had dropped its autonomy platform and supported full independence—FULK, UPM, and a number of other groups, including a faction of PALIKA. PALIKA's more radical supporters remained outside the FI.

Among the constituents of the FI, a basic consensus on the nature of an independent New Caledonia remained elusive. The majority sought to establish the special status and privileges of the Melanesians as the indigenous population of the country, but some FI supporters advocated a "Caledonian Caledonia" in which all ethnic groups would have an equal role. They opposed land reforms that sought to reestablish the traditional clan holdings.

An anti-independence coalition, the Rally for New Caledonia in the Republic (Rassemblement pour Calédonie dans la République—RPCR), was organized in 1978 and advocated the territory's integration with France as an overseas department. It had close affinities with the Gaullist Rally for the Republic (Rassemblement pour la République—RPR) in France. Centrist forces, organized in 1979 into the Federation for a New Society in New Caledonia (Fédération pour une Nouvelle Société Calédonienne—FNSC), supported, in greater or lesser measure, autonomy for the territory. The Union for French Democracy in New Caledonia (Union pour la Démocratie Française en Calédonie), a group outside the three main coalitions, opposed independence.

In 1978 Dijoud outlined a long-term development plan designed to reduce New Caledonian dependence on nickel exports. This was to be accomplished through greater investment in the agricultural, tourism, and fishing sectors. France would provide financing in the amount of CFPF130 billion. The importance of improving the economic position of the Melanesians, largely through the implementation of land reform, was also stressed. The plan proposed establishing the Melanesian Cultural Institute and teaching Melanesian languages in the schools. The plan was based on the assumption that New Caledonia would remain in association with France, for it was believed that immediate independence was a "vain hope," given the potential for violent confrontation between ethnic groups. It was claimed that "only

France could support real reforms" and that the issue of eventual independence ought to be postponed for a period of 10 years while reforms were put in place.

In February 1979 the plan was approved by the Territorial Assembly with the support of the conservatives and centrists, then in the majority. Leaders of the UC, however, asserted that New Caledonia would sever its connections with France in the early 1980s. The ensuing crisis between pro- and anti-independence forces within the territorial government led Dijoud to dissolve the legislature. In elections for the Territorial Assembly held in July 1979 and regarded as virtually a referendum on the independence issue, the two parties favoring some form of continued association with France, the RPCR and the FNSC, won a total of 22 seats, while the FI won 14 seats. The RPCR and the FNSC formed a ruling coalition. The balloting, however, had been held after the French National Assembly had passed a new election law for New Caledonia that altered the constituencies in a way, it alleged, that favored the anti-independence groups.

There were demonstrations in Nouméa by supporters of the FI in August and September 1979 and forcible occupations of land by Melanesians in various localities on the main island. On September 19, 1981, Pierre Declerq, secretary general of the UC and a major pro-independence figure, was assassinated. This caused an escalation of tensions between activist Melanesians and members of other ethnic groups who were lining up on opposite sides of the independence issue. The situation was exacerbated by the territorial government's inability or unwillingness to find and convict the perpetrator. One man, a European, was charged, but rightist Europeans campaigned actively for his release. According to some observers, the political situation in New Caledonia was beginning to resemble that of Algeria, where a determined group of French settlers had opposed Arab Algerian demands for independence and there had been a bloody civil war.

The Autonomy Statute

The government of Socialist Party leader François Mitterrand, who assumed the presidency of France in May 1981, was more receptive to appeals for the independence of New Caledonia than its conservative predecessor, whose spokesmen had stressed the dangers allegedly inherent in premature self-rule. The position of supporters of independence was also strengthened by the breakdown of the RPCR-FNSC conservative-centrist coalition in the Territorial Assembly and the formation of a new coalition government by the FI and the FNSC in June 1982. However, the political situation was becoming extremely volatile. In July 1982 anti-independence demonstrators, numbering as many as 25,000, turned out in the center of Nouméa. A group of about 250 persons broke into a session of the Territorial Assembly and assaulted assembly members while they were deliberating on a bill that would turn a quarter of the territory's land over to a Melanesian land trust. The bill was eventually turned down by the legislature.

Sources inside the territory estimated that as many as 25,000 illegal arms were in circulation and that anti-independence groups, such as the New Caledonia Front (Front Calédonien—FC), were preparing forcibly to resist separation from France. In the early 1980s there were a number of allegedly political murders in which most of the victims were independence activists or sympathizers. In January 1983 two French police officers were killed in a confrontation with Melanesians at Koindé, a village in the interior north of Nouméa.

In the face of growing violence, the French government sought to negotiate a working relationship between moderate pro- and anti-independence groups and lay the foundations for a peaceful transition to a permanent political status. In July 1983, Georges Lemoine, France's secretary of state for overseas departments and territories, invited 20 political leaders from the territory, including representatives from the FI, to a "round table conference" at Nainville-les-Roches, outside Paris. The conference was successful in building a fragile consensus. The FI leaders declared their satisfaction that new proposals by France, granting a substantially larger measure of self-government, could serve as an instrument of transition to full independence. The RPCR supported certain democratic provisions drawn up at the conference on the grounds that they forestalled a unilateral declaration of independence by Melanesians. Apparently they also believed that a majority of New Caledonians would oppose independence in a future referendum, Melanesians forming less than half the population.

In November 1983 Lemoine presented a detailed proposal for a new territorial statute before the legislature in Nouméa. In his address the minister noted that the preamble of the draft statute affirmed the "equality of Melanesian civilization" and the importance of traditional institutions and practices. The statute was described as initiating a period of "decolonization." Specific provisions included transfer of all executive authority to a popularly elected government. The high commissioner, appointed by

Paris, would, in Lemoine's words, serve as "guardian of the legality of the functioning of the territorial institutions" and would ensure respect for civil rights through recourse to an administrative tribunal. However, the territory would have extensive powers to determine its international relations in the Pacific region "within the framework of France's international commitments." In the economic sphere, New Caledonia would have control over the exploitation of its natural resources and the right to withhold approval from any development project involving less than CFPF1 billion. The government's commitment to land reform was reaffirmed.

Proposed internal reforms included the division of the territory into six regions, each having a regional council. A fixed proportion of the council members would be nominated by the College of Clans and the Council of Grand Chiefs, representing customary Melanesian interests. On the territorial level a regional assembly, containing "customary representatives," would serve alongside the Territorial Assembly, in a new bicameral legislative system. The purpose of the proposed arrangement—a blend of traditional Melanesian authority, the "corporatist" representation of occupational and functional groups, and the conventional democratic representation of individual electors—was to maintain a delicate balance of ethnic and social interests. Elections for the Territorial Assembly were scheduled for July 1984. After the five-year period during which the statute would be in operation, a referendum would be held on the issue of independence.

By early 1984, however, the consensus achieved at Nainville-les-Roches had fallen apart. Elements in the FI demanded a vote on independence as early as 1985, describing the autonomy statute and its five-year transition period as a "treaty of occupation." An issue of great importance was determining who would be allowed to vote in any referendum on self-rule. Some FI leaders declared that only Melanesians and non-Melanesians having a parent born in the territory should be given the right to participate in the referendum. The French government has insisted that more recent settlers ought not to be excluded from any determination of New Caledonia's final political status.

Territorial Security

In early 1982 France maintained about 2,800 military personnel in New Caledonia. Ground forces, including paratroopers and marines, were based in Nouméa, Plum, and Bourail. The French Pacific Fleet maintained an installation at Pointe Chaleix in Nouméa. An air force facility at Tontouta, the site of the international airport, serviced a unit of helicopters used for the rapid transport of troops.

The major police unit in New Caledonia was a single division of the French National Gendarmerie, comprising about 450 men. The gendarmerie was organized along military lines, strictly disciplined, highly mobile, and armed and equipped for security patrols and other police duties in non-urban areas. Its basic personnel, including all officers and noncommissioned officers and a large portion of the lower ranks, were recruited and trained in France before being deployed to the territory. However, vacancies in the gendarmerie may have been filled by inducting local personnel. In mid-1984 it was unclear whether, and in what number, Melanesians served in this national police force. In periods of civil unrest, reinforcements of gendarmerie were flown in from France or French Polynesia

In addition to the gendarmerie, local subdivisions organized police forces. Most of the police officers, called guardians of the peace, were recruited and trained locally.

PAPUA NEW GUINEA

Official Name	Independent State of Papua New Guinea
Political Status	Independent state (1975)
Capital	Port Moresby
Population	3,350,000 (1984 midyear estimate)
Land Area	461,690 square kilometers
Currency	Kina (K)
Major Islands and Island Groups	Eastern half of New Guinea; Bismarck Archipelago; Bougainville; D'Entrecasteaux Islands; Louisiade Archipelago

Flag: Yellow bird of paradise on red field and white constellation of Southern Cross on black field

Physical Environment

Papua New Guinea lies in the southwest Pacific. Its nearest neighbors are Australia, some 160 kilometers to the south, the Federated States of Micronesia (FSM) to the north, and Solomon Islands to the east (see fig. 5). The country includes the eastern half of the island of New Guinea—the second largest island in the world—where it shares a land border some 730 kilometers long with Indonesia. The territory on the main island accounts for approximately 85 percent of the total land area; the remainder is accounted for by several hundred contiguous islands. The largest of these are New Britain, New Ireland, and Manus in the Bismarck Archipelago and Bougainville, which together with Buka are the two northernmost Solomon Islands. The entire country stretches some 2,100 kilometers from east to west and about 1,300 kilometers from north to south.

The main island is distinguished by a central mountain core that is not a single chain but a complex of ranges interspersed with broad, grassy valleys at elevations ranging between 1,500 and 3,000 meters. The mountains include the Star, Hindenburg, Muller, Kubor, Schrader, Bismarck, and Owen Stanley ranges, which peak at more than 4,000 meters. Mount Wilhelm, at more than 4,500 meters, is the nation's highest. The mountain system forms a drainage divide between rivers that flow south to the Gulf of Papua or north and east to the Bismarck and Solomon seas. The nation's largest river, the Fly, flows almost 1,100 kilometers and can be navigated for nearly 800 kilometers; most of the nation's

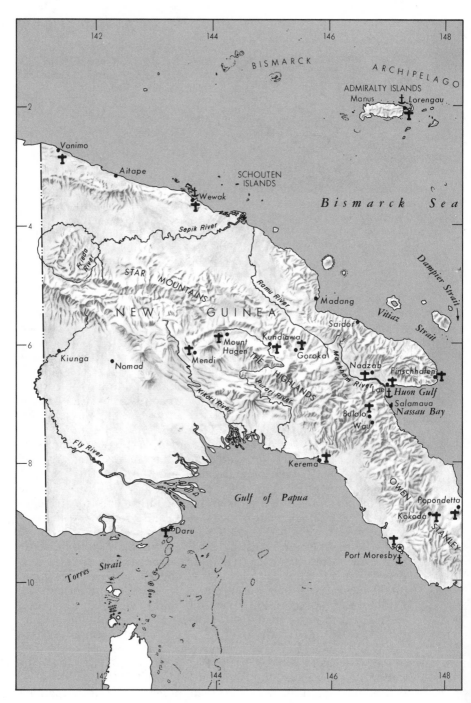

Figure 5. Papua New Guinea. Topography and Drainage, 1984

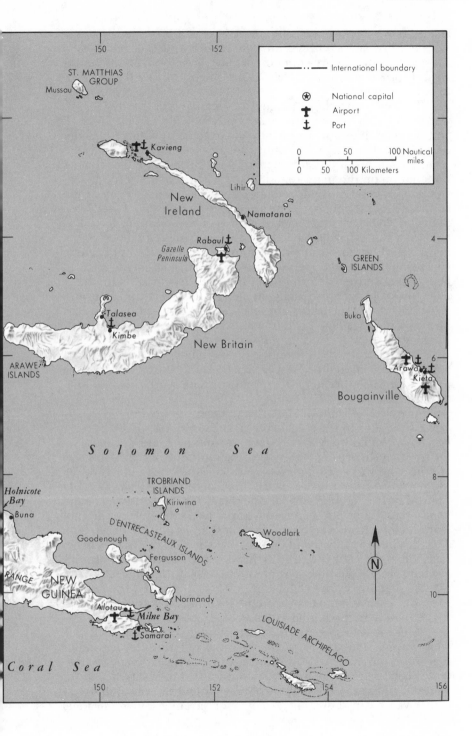

150   152

ST. MATTHIAS
GROUP
Mussau

Kavieng

New
Ireland

Lihir

Namatanai

International boundary

National capital

Airport

Port

0   50   100 Nautical
                          miles
0   50   100 Kilometers

Rabaul

Gazelle
Peninsula

GREEN
ISLANDS

4

Talasea

Kimbe

New Britain

Buka

ARAWE
ISLANDS

Arawa
Kieta

6

Bougainville

Solomon   Sea

8

*Holnicote
Bay*

Buna

TROBRIAND
ISLANDS

Kiriwina

D'ENTRECASTEAUX ISLANDS

Woodlark

Goodenough

Fergusson

N

RANGE   NEW
GUINEA

Normandy

Allotau

Milne Bay

Samarai

LOUISIADE ARCHIPELAGO

10

Coral   Sea

150   152   154   156

139

rivers, however, are navigable only by small boats in the lower reaches. Lowlands and foothills of varying widths cover most of the coasts. Swamps are common in many areas, and on the southwest littoral a great delta plain forms one of the world's most extensive swamps.

The line of northern ranges on the main island extends eastward to form the core of the islands of New Britain, New Ireland, and Bougainville. Severe earthquakes often occur along this line, causing much damage. Volcanoes are also located here, and there were serious eruptions at Rabaul on New Britain in 1937 and near Popondetta on the main island in 1951. The islands of the D'Entrecasteaux and Louisiade archipelagoes are also of volcanic origin and represent the peaks of the submerged extension of the Owen Stanley Range. The three large islands of New Britain, New Ireland, and Bougainville have no rivers comparable to those on the main island but are drained by innumerable small, rapid rivers. Coral reefs fringe all three as well as the north coast of the main island. Because the eastern end of the main island is rising, however, these formations disappear along the eastern and southern coast. Good, deep harbors are relatively few; exceptions are Port Moresby and Madang on the main island, Lorengau on Manus, Kavieng on New Ireland, and Rabaul.

Administratively, the nation is divided into 20 provinces, including the National Capital District around Port Moresby (see fig. 6). Up until the mid-1970s the provinces were referred to as districts.

The climate is humid and rainy, except in the Port Moresby area, which lies in the so-called rain shadow of the Owen Stanley Range. Although many zones have distinct wet and dry seasons, the dry months are characterized by a minimum of 50 millimeters of rain. The wet season generally runs from December through March during the northwesterly monsoon; the dry season lasts from May to October and is influenced by the southeast trade winds. The intervening period is variable. Temperatures are not extreme for a tropical climate, and most areas outside of the high altitudes have a daily mean temperature of 27°C that varies little. At 1,800 meters above sea level, however, the mean temperature is about 16°C; daytime temperatures rise to about 32°C, and nighttime temperatures fall to around 7°C. Similarly, the humidity in the lowland areas varies slightly around 80 percent but fluctuates widely in the highland areas.

Because it lies between Australia and mainland Asia, Papua New Guinea's vegetation cover is similar to both. Dense jungles of tropical rain forests grow profusely in most areas below 80 meters. Plant life in these forests resembles that of Malaysia and Indonesia. In the dry areas of Port Moresby and the Fly and Strickland river basins, the mixed cover of savanna and monsoonal

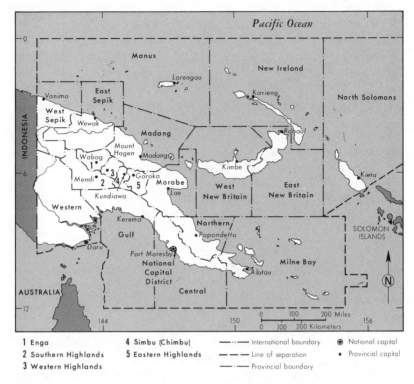

Figure 6. Papua New Guinea. Administrative Divisions, 1984

forests is similar to that of the northern Australian coast. The vegetation of the high, central cordillera resembles that of Tasmania and New Zealand.

Tropical rain forests cover about 85 percent of the main island. The top branches of these trees reach some 37 meters in height and shelter smaller trees, vines, and ferns. Nearer to the ground grow creepers, orchids, and other plants in profusion. The coastal areas contain dense mangrove swamps and forests of a distinctly different kind. Inland swamps feature huge areas overgrown with sago palm, which supplies the people there with their staple diet. In the Markham and Ramu river valleys, there are also grassy areas suitable for crop cultivation and grazing. At around 800 meters above sea level, the forests decrease in height but contain the most valuable species, such as red cedars, oaks, beeches, nutmeg trees, and local mahoganies. Above 3,000 meters alpine forests of conifers, shrubs, and ferns appear, and above

3,600 meters equatorial alpine grasslands emerge. Mount Wilhelm has only rocky crevices and sparse vegetation above 4,250 meters and receives occasional snowfall.

Although the jungles closely resemble those of Southeast Asia, the animal life found there is predominantly Australian. The main island has more than 100 species of marsupials, some of which have become extinct on the Australian continent. The largest is the tree kangaroo; others include opossums, wallabies, and bandicoots. Reptiles are abundant, including crocodiles, large lizards, and more than 70 species of snakes, many of which are poisonous. The myriad varieties of insects include the malarial mosquito. Birds are also abundant. The largest is the cassowary, which resembles the Australian emu. Parrots, cockatoos, kingfishers, thrushes, and magnificent birds of paradise abound. The latter were much prized by the courts of the Indo-Malay world, which frequently sent trading missions to New Guinea to barter for them.

Historical Setting

The archaeological record is limited, but it is believed that man first arrived in what is now Papua New Guinea about 40,000 years ago in the first of a number of waves of immigration from Southeast Asia via Indonesia. Archaeologists believe people may have begun to hunt and gather food in parts of the Highlands as early as 26,000 years ago and may have been among the world's first agriculturists, growing bananas and vegetables some 9,000 years ago.

New immigrants speaking Austronesian languages arrived some 5,000 years ago, occupying the coasts and introducing the craft of potterymaking. They developed elaborate seaborne trading systems, such as the *hiri*, which linked areas of the southern coast, and the *kula* ring, which linked the east peninsula of the main island with the Trobriand (Kiriwina) Islands and the Louisiade Archipelago. Another trading system, the *te* of the Western Highlands, joined interior areas and eventually the coast. Trade goods, such as pottery, food, canoes, stone adz blades, pigs, and prized shell ornaments, were exchanged. Elaborate ceremonies were developed to commemorate such significant events as planting, marriage, war, and death. The absence of a written language documenting the evolution of this rich and varied culture should not obscure its importance.

The main island was first sighted by the Portuguese expeditions of Antonio d'Abreau and Francisco Serrão in 1511. Jorge de

Meneses, who accidently happened upon the main island in 1526–27, is said to have named it "Papua," or Ilhos dos Papua, probably derived from a Malayan word alluding to the frizzled quality of the hair of its inhabitants. The name "New Guinea" was given to the island in 1545 by a Spaniard, Ynigo Ortis de Retez, because of a supposed resemblance between the local inhabitants and those found on the Guinea coast of Africa. Two other Spaniards, Luis Váez de Torres and Diego de Prado, landed on Mainu Island in 1606 and fought with the islanders. They also took 14 girls and boys to Manila for instruction in the Catholic faith. The next two centuries were marked by sightings and landings by Dutch, British, French, and other Portuguese and Spanish navigators.

During the mid-1800s European vessels made frequent short visits to the area, exchanging metal, cloth, and trinkets for food, fish, and coconuts in canoe-to-ship trading. By the 1870s longer visits and semipermanent settlements were attempted by scientists, traders, missionaries, and gold miners. Blackbirders also arrived to lure men to work on plantations in Australia, Fiji, and the Samoa Islands. By the 1880s a small group of coastal villagers had become well acquainted with the Westerners.

The missionary effort in particular had a major effect on everyday life. British missionaries of the London Missionary Society established a few teachers from the Loyalty Islands on islands in the Torres Strait area in 1871, and by 1884 Polynesian pastors had arrived in the Gulf of Papua. Other missionaries, supported by the Methodists, arrived on New Britain. The missionaries' impact was profound in the areas where they worked; European clothes and living styles, steel tools, and new crops were introduced. The pattern of village leadership was altered by the designation of deacons, who often had influence over secular as well as church affairs. In 1884 the first indigenous pastors were graduated from the London Missionary Society School in Port Moresby.

From British New Guinea to the Territory of Papua

Initially, Britain demonstrated little interest in the region, as evidenced in its refusal to recognize attempts by Charles Yule (in 1845) and Captain John Moresby (in 1873) to claim the eastern part of the main island. German commercial activity in the area and the fear of German annexation of the eastern half of the main island, however, triggered fears among the Australians. Eventually, a reluctant Britain acceded to Australian demands to enter into negotiations with Germany, which resulted in the division of the area. The southeastern quadrant of the main island became a British protectorate; the northeastern quadrant became a German possession. The British flag was raised at Port Moresby on November 6, 1884—only three days after the German flag had been raised on New Britain (see fig. 7).

Authorities in Britain and Australia were interested primarily in preventing other nations from gaining influence in southeastern New Guinea but did not develop the area for themselves. Until 1942 the Australian administration was essentially funded by a small grant averaging £15,000 to £20,000 per year and by internally generated revenues.

General Sir Peter Scratchley was appointed special commissioner to establish the administration of British New Guinea in 1885. He and his successors were hampered by a lack of adequate funding and personnel to make and enforce laws. The fragmentation of the indigenous political structure and the absence of strong rulers made it impossible to rule indirectly, as was done in other British colonies. A large number of expatriate officials, therefore, were eventually needed to administer the area, and their intrusion into village life was pervasive.

In 1888 Britain annexed the territory as a crown colony, appointing William MacGregor the first lieutenant governor. Trained as a doctor and possessing extraordinary energy, he was able to accomplish much, despite the lack of outside support. He established a paternalistic administration that prohibited the sale of native land to anyone but government officers and prevented the indigenous inhabitants from being employed outside their home districts—practices that were abusive in German New Guinea. Using foot patrols, he explored the deep interior, and he mapped the coast and navigable rivers by boat. As MacGregor himself put it after 10 years of his administration, he "practically had to subdue by force almost every district." By 1898 more than 100 Papuans had served in the Armed Native Constabulary—an effective police force—and numerous others had acted as village constables. These positions carried much prestige for the Papuans.

Gold was discovered in 1888 on Tagula (Sudest) Island and later on the Misima and Woodlark islands; it soon became the colony's principal export. Despite the low level of permanent white settlement, hundreds of miners sought their fortunes in British New Guinea. Many indigenous inhabitants also worked in the goldfields, staying long after the initial boom had subsided.

In 1906, after an eight-year period of administrative stagna-

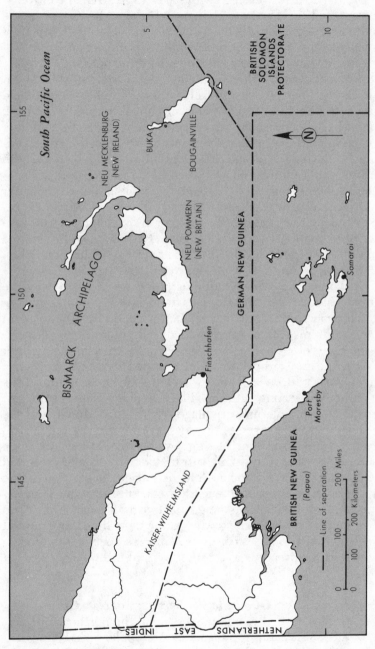

Figure 7. British and German New Guinea, 1895

tion during which Australia and Britain debated the future of the colony, the British transferred the area to Australian control. It was renamed the Territory of Papua. Hubert Murray was made lieutenant governor in 1908—a post he held until 1940. Murray's personality and policies made an enormous impact on Papua, influencing its development over the next three decades.

From the outset the Australian administration was fraught with conflicting aims; its so-called forward policy encouraged white settlement and exploitation of Papua's natural resources, while other policies sought to enhance the welfare of the indigenous peoples. For the first five years of his tenure, Murray encouraged the leasing of land to settlers and sought to increase both the area under cultivation and the number of crops produced—coconuts, hemp, and rubber. He enjoyed initial success, but after 1911 the area planted declined largely because of hardships experienced by the settlers. By 1918 appproximately 24,000 hectares of plantations were under cultivation; this level remained basically unchanged until World War II. The white population stabilized at around 1,200 persons during this period.

Although the Murray administration was criticized by the settlers—and later by the Papuans themselves—for not developing the economic infrastructure, it was generally a benevolent colonial administration. Murray spent most of his career defending the rights of the native Papuans. He favored maintaining their status as peasant-proprietors and opposed demands to recruit women and children as laborers. In large part he renounced the use of force in dealing with the villagers. There were insufficient funds to set up government village schools, but Murray did see that subsidies were given to the mission-run primary and technical schools and made efforts to improve health services. Although the funds invested were small, substantial social changes resulted as larger numbers of Papuans left the villages to earn money to pay a head tax assessed by the territory's administration. They became laborers, noncommissioned officers in the constabulary and police, or tradesmen in the towns. At the same time, government officers and missionaries continued to press deeper into the isolated interior, spreading Western ideas and technology.

From German New Guinea to the Territory of New Guinea

Germany formally took possession of the northeastern portion of the main island, the Bismarck Archipelago, and New Britain in 1884. Buka and Bougainville in the northern Solomon Islands were added in 1886. At the time of the initial annexation, the territory on the main island was named Kaiser-Wilhelmsland. A private business firm was chartered to administer the colony and occupy so-called ownerless land. The firm, called the New Guinea Company, hoped to develop a German colony on the main island, obtaining land for a pittance from the villagers and selling it to the German settlers.

When the company representatives reached Finschhafen on the Huon Peninsula in 1885, they signed an agreement with the illiterate and probably unwitting villagers, transferring large tracts of land to the newcomers. At first the villagers were willing to clear the land in return for iron implements and other goods. Once their immediate needs were satisfied, however, they were uninterested in making long-term labor commitments. When it became evident that no more than a handful of German settlers would come to the colony, the company gave up land speculation in favor of developing large plantations in the Madang area, recruiting thousands of laborers from Sumatra in the Netherlands East Indies, Singapore, and elsewhere. This effort was also doomed; the plantation workers were decimated by disease, and by the end of the century most of the plantations were closed.

Germany's colonization of the Gazelle Peninsula of New Britain proceeded with greater success through the efforts of a mixture of expatriates, who formed a community around the Samoan-American planter, Queen Emma. By the end of the 1890s this community was exporting thousands of tons of copra each year. The Tolai people of eastern New Britain, whose land was systematically alienated for the development of the plantations, nonetheless fought back, and a series of raids between the two groups occurred during the 1890s. It has been estimated that by 1914 some 283,000 hectares of land had been alienated on New Britain. Although this represented less than 1 percent of the total land area, it was by and large the best land and constituted about 40 percent of the former landholdings of the Tolai. Land alienation remained a festering grievance among the Tolai and was not resolved until the nation's independence.

In 1899 German New Guinea was made an imperial colony, administered by German government officials. In sharp contrast to developments in Papua, Germany sought to create a colony for whites and devoted little, if any, attention to the welfare of the indigenous peoples. Over the next decade German power was extended to the islands of New Britain, New Ireland, Bougainville, and Manus, and district officers were aggressive in making the

areas safe and profitable. District officers used force against villagers who objected to their policies, which included the use of cor-
vée labor to build roads. District officers also assisted labor recruiters in getting all the workers they needed. In 1907 Germany
initiated a head tax, which forced the villagers to seek wage employment in order to pay the tax. Subsidies from the German government, moreover, were twice those given to the Papuan government by Australia. German naval vessels and a mobile ex-
peditionary force stationed in Rabaul could be sent anywhere in
the colony on short notice, and in 1913 German New Guinea had
twice the number of police as did Australian Papua.

Within 15 years coastal German New Guinea was changed
from a wilderness to a plantation colony. At least 40,000 contract
laborers were pressed into service from 1908 to 1913, by which
date few of the indigenous men in the controlled area had not
worked for whites. An estimated 100,000 people were recruited
as contract workers, and perhaps one-quarter of those died on the
job. Even so, government authority remained limited to only 20
percent of the territory and rarely extended more than 25
kilometers inland. By and large, Christian missionaries, not the
government, brought the outside world to most inhabitants of
German New Guinea. A complex process of enculturation too difficult to document, religious conversion may well have been the
most significant event in the lives of many inhabitants before
World War I.

German rule ended in September 1914, after Australian
troops seized Rabaul. Australia's interest lay in the area's strategic
position and its potential economic contribution to the war. German missionaries and planters were not deported but continued
their activities until after the war. Labor recruiters were given a
free hand, and many of the techniques used by the German imperial administration were continued.

In 1920 the British government, on behalf of the Commonwealth of Australia, assumed a mandate from the League of Nations to govern the former German area as the Territory of New
Guinea. Australia decided to administer the area separately from
Papua and rejected the recommendaitons of Murray in Papua to
promote the interests of the villagers. Instead, it was decided to
continue the economic exploitation of the territory's resources
and, when possible, to improve village life. It was Australian policy to have the former German territory pay for its own administration, which meant leaving development to European private
enterprise. German private property was expropriated and sold

to ex-servicemen from Australia.

Dreams of riches faded rapidly, however, as the worldwide depression of the 1930s reduced copra prices to about one-fifth of their earlier values. The small-scale farmers fell deeply into debt to Burns Philip or W.R. Carpenters, large shipping and trading firms that completely dominated the economy. The expansion of plantation agriculture continued nevertheless, and copra production in 1940 was almost double that of 1920.

A gold rush started in 1926 at Bulolo near Lae on the main island, resulting in a enormous demand for village labor. Within a few years more than 3,000 inhabitants of the Territory of New Guinea were working in the goldfields; by 1938 this number had risen to 7,000—one-third as many as worked on plantations. Gold made the government of the Territory of New Guinea comparatively richer than the government of the Territory of Papua. Nevertheless, fearing the possible revolutionary consequences of too much modern education, the government spent less money on village schooling in the 1930s than it had in the previous decade. Instead money was allocated for the purposes of opening up new areas where gold might be found and improving the health of the work force. In 1934 Australia even went so far as to suggest to the League of Nations that the responsibility for education be turned over entirely to the missionaries.

Outside of the major population centers, however, some Australians with egalitarian instincts were uncomfortable with the rigid rules established in Rabaul. The wilderness areas, or the bush, as it was called, inspired a respect for ability. Patrol officers were conscious of the skills of their indigenous subordinates, and missionaries lived among converts in conditions of near equality. Some planters in isolated areas developed a sense of community with "their" laborers. A wide variety of experiences resulted depending on local conditions and personalities.

World War II

On the eve of World War II, about one-half of the people in both territories were thought to be registered in village census books—200,000 in the Territory of Papua and 580,000 in the Territory of New Guinea—but no one really knows for sure. Of these, about 1,500 Australians and Europeans were in the former and approximately 4,500 in the latter. There were also about 2,000 Asians in the Territory of New Guinea, mostly Chinese. More villagers were employed in the cash economy than at the turn of the century, but most continued to work as indentured laborers. A handful were educated and were traders or missionaries. About 1,200 were in the force. Others were employed as servants, cooks, waiters, or workers in sanitation crews.

By 1940 approximately two-thirds of the people of both territories were governed by "patrol." Depending on their proximity to administrative centers, they might be visited twice yearly by officials traveling on foot, although some might not see a patrol for years. In other areas, such as the Gazelle Peninsula on New Britain, the people had become deeply involved in cash cropping. Many had received an elementary education, possessed some relatively expensive European goods, and had begun to live in Western-style housing. Vast areas remained virtually unknown, however. This was most dramatically demonstrated in 1933, when it was discovered that an estimated 800,000 near-stone-age people were living in the Wahgi River valley of the Highlands, which theretofore had been considered uninhabited.

Following the attacks in December 1941 on Malaya, Pearl Harbor, and other areas of the Pacific, the Japanese bombed Rabaul on January 4, 1942, and Port Moresby one month later. The Territory of New Guinea had been allowed no fixed defenses under the mandate agreement, and the small Australian garrison of 1,400 at Rabaul was overrun on January 23. The Japanese then moved rapidly to occupy the islands of New Britain, New Ireland, Manus, and Bougainville and landed forces at Lae on the main island. The attacks caused the Australian government to bring the two territories under the control of a single military administration at Port Moresby—the Australian New Guinea Administrative Unit—for the duration of the war.

In May 1942 the Japanese set out from Rabaul to attack and occupy Port Moresby by sea. The force was turned back in the Coral Sea, however, by a combination of land-based air strikes from Australia and Papua and carrier-based air strikes from a United States naval task force. Blocked from an attack on Port Moresby by sea, Japanese forces in July attempted an overland advance on Port Moresby via the Kokoda trail. In August they also attempted to outflank Port Moresby by landing forces at Milne Bay. The ensuing battles on the Kokoda trail and at Milne Bay marked the farthest point of Japanese advance. Allied defenders forced the evacuation of Japanese forces from Milne Bay in early September, and within two weeks fierce opposition and supply difficulties had caused the Japanese to begin withdrawing along the Kokoda trail.

There then followed a long and difficult process in which the Allies slowly reestablished their control over the main island and outlying islands as well, either by isolating Japanese forces or by dislodging them from reinforced positions. In many areas the Japanese refused to surrender. On Bougainville and New Britain, Allied forces, aided by people from the territories of Papua and New Guinea, fought lengthy campaigns. When the battles ended in mid-1945, some 23,000 Japanese soldiers remained on Bougainville, and almost 90,000 Japanese soldiers, sailors, and civilians remained on New Britain. Only 13,500 were still fighting the Australians south of Wewak on the main island. Over one-half of the approximatley 300,000 Japanese sent to the territories of Papua and New Guinea during the war had died there.

Although the war probably had almost no immediate impact on at least one-third of the population of the combined territories, in many areas its effect was profound. Wherever large numbers of Allied or Japanese forces were present, almost all able-bodied men had become laborers. Other islanders entered into cash cropping to provide for the military forces in their areas. Battalions from both territories fought in every major campaign of the war, except Milne Bay. The Pacific Islands Regiment, in which Australians filled all officer and most noncommissioned officer slots, was formed in 1944; it was a tough and respected force, credited with having killed 2,200 Japanese and losing only 63 of its own men. Those islanders who lived in combat zones experienced the massive, uncontrollable, and almost incomprehensible violence of modern war. Communities on Bougainville, New Ireland, and New Britain, in particular, suffered greatly from bombings.

The war also brought local inhabitants into contact with other peoples to a degree not experienced before or after the conflict. More than 1 million United States servicemen passed through Manus Island, the location of the largest base in the southwest Pacific. By virtue of their sheer numbers, the coordinated use of land, sea, and air power, and the application of modern technology the Americans demonstrated a power not previously seen in the area. The conduct of the war had required that islands and their waters be charted, usually for the first time. Tropical medicine was studied, and new methods of administration for the territories were considered.

Australians had traditionally viewed the territories of Papua and New Guinea as a last barrier to invasion, and the war confirmed this perception. Only a few, however, had any detailed knowledge of the territories before 1942. In contrast, by the end of the war some 500,000 Australians had been under arms, many in the island. The population of Australia was only some 7 million, and almost every family had members or friends in the battles that unfolded. Place-names from the territories became well-known and emotionally charged. The press, films, and letters brought home a new image of the territories. In the terrible agony along the Kokoda trail, native bearers had saved innumerable sick or wounded Australians by carrying them to safety through nearly impassable bush and over razor-backed mountains. After islanders fought and died with Australians in dozens of campaigns, the old attitudes could not be maintained nor could the old order be restored.

The New Postwar Order

In July 1945 the Australian minister for external affairs announced that the new Labour Party government believed that his country owed a "debt of gratitude" to the territories of Papua and New Guinea. It was in this spirit that Australia raised its direct subsidy from £212,500 for Papua alone during the 1936–41 period to £16 million for both territories during the 1945–50 period. In 1946 Australia received a mandate from the United Nations (UN) to administer the Territory of New Guinea as a trust territory, an agreement that provided for UN missions to visit every three years to determine how well Australia was promoting social, economic, and political development. Between 1946 and 1949 Australia established a joint administration over both the Trust Territory of New Guinea and the Territory of Papua under the leadership of J.K. Murray. Separate statistics, however, were kept for both halves of the jointly administered area. It became increasingly common thereafter—especially as the country moved toward independence—for the two territories to be called Papua New Guinea and its people Papua New Guineans.

The task of postwar reconstruction was enormous. Little remained of the towns in the Territory of New Guinea, and many plantations were in ruins. The revival of agriculture was one of the most critical needs in both areas. Copra exports in the territory had fallen from 71,000 tons in 1939 to 4,500 tons in 1946, and in Papua, copra exports had decreased by one-half and rubber exports by one-quarter. The government built four main agricultural research stations and 10 smaller extension centers by 1949 and attempted to develop agricultural cooperatives. Some suc-

*Mekeo people from Central Province performing
a traditional ceremony and Highlanders
visiting a government-run cattle farm—two
of many Papua New Guinean peoples
Courtesy Government of Papua New Guinea*

153

cess was achieved in increasing cacao production on the Gazelle Peninsula and coffee production in the Highlands. Many other projects failed. Compensation for war damages was paid to the villagers in hopes that such funds would be invested in cash cropping or other economic activities, but much was consumed rather than saved.

Initiatives in the area of social welfare proved difficult to implement. To ensure that adequate staff would be available, Australia established the Australian School of Pacific Administration, which offered training in colonial administration, tropical agriculture and medicine, anthropology, and a variety of other subjects relevant to working in the territories. A comprehensive program for training indigenous healthworkers was also started, and the government took steps to establish a public school system. The "new deal" offered by the Australian government was only a start, and a limited one at that, but it did signal a new set of attitudes in the administration. Although initiated by the Australian Labour Party government, it soon enjoyed bipartisan support.

The Development of the Highlands. Perhaps the most dramatic events of the immediate postwar period concerned the exploration and development of the Highlands. Until 1930, when two prospectors entered the area, the Highlands were thought to be a series of uninhabitable mountain peaks. Systematic exploration, which had been interrupted by the war, recommenced thereafter and led to the discovery that the Highlands housed the largest population cluster in all of the Pacific islands. Between 800,000 and 1 million people were estimated to live there; they shared essentially the same social institutions and spoke some 60 dialects— 42 of which were related.

The Goroka Valley, where missionaries had been active before the war and where some army units had been stationed during the war, became the center of development in the Highlands; Goroka proper became the administrative center of the vast Central Highlands District in 1950. The first step of the new administration was to bring the "uncontrolled areas" under its fiat. By 1956 contact had been made with about 400,000 people in the "new" areas, which covered about 26,300 square kilometers.

The opening of the Highlands met a very real need for a labor force to expand the economy. The government instituted the Highlands Labour Scheme in 1950, which encouraged workers from the Highlands to contract their labor on the coastal plantations. The number of such laborers rose from 2,300 in 1953 to over 15,000 in 1968—laborers typically agreeing to work for 18 months. The laborers received better rations than their prewar counterparts, protection from unwarranted fines, immunization from tuberculosis, suppressants for malaria, and generally increasing wages throughout the period. In other respects, however, they followed long-established patterns by which young villagers moved out of their districts to earn cash and learn modern ways. By 1970 Highlanders made up almost one-half of the work force employed in lowland areas.

The Highlanders also moved into the cash cropping of coffee in their home district. The boom in coffee prices during the Korean War and the fertile valleys of the Highlands attracted white settlers to the area. They made substantial profits growing coffee, showing villagers how to do so, and processing and marketing the villagers' coffee output. From 1954 onward villagers' production exceeded that of the settlers in the main districts. By 1967 the villagers sold twice as much coffee as foreign-owned plantations. A number of successful villagers expanded into other areas, such as peanut and passion fruit cultivation, cattle raising, and the running of trade stores. Although not all such ventures were successful, many Highlanders in Goroka and other areas learned the nature of *bisnis*, even financing most of their ventures with their own capital.

Profound changes had taken place in many areas by 1960. Goroka was the territory's largest inland town and boasted a population of more than 450 Europeans and three times that number of Papua New Guineans. It had the inevitable golf course, club, and school for expatriates, as well as schools for Highlanders through form (grade) nine, a technical school, and a teachers college that provided new opportunities.

The first local village council had been established in the Highlands in 1958. It was empowered to impose head taxes and raised £9,000 in 1959. It built medical aid posts, schools, and roads; elected councilors; and disposed of considerable sums of money.

During the 1950s the Highlanders developed a sense of common identity and a recognition that their past isolation, state of development, and common cultural and physical characteristics made them separate from others—a sense that was reinforced by their experiences in the coastal areas. Many had passed through revolutionary economic and social change within a generation, advancing their standard of living while retaining their sense of personal dignity. At the same time, they were acutely aware that even the most developed areas of the Highlands were sadly behind the developed areas of coastal Papua New Guinea. Highlanders were thus less anxious than others in the decades ahead to move rapidly toward independence.

Health, Education, and Social Legislation. At the same time, developments that were little short of revolutionary were taking place throughout the territories. To improve health care some 40 European refugee doctors—barred from practicing in Australia by laws favoring Australians—were recruited for local service. Papua New Guineans were also trained as orderlies and were taught to recognize and treat diseases in the villages; by 1962 there were 1,200 aid posts operating throughout the country. Indigenous peoples were also sent to Fiji for higher medical training, and in 1959 students began training at the Papuan Medical College, the first tertiary institution in the territory. Expenditures on health increased from £605,000 in 1948 to £2 million in 1955. In 1954 a hospital building program was initiated. The missions, having considerable medical staffs, contributed greatly to the overall standards of health, and the administration introduced a scheme to subsidize drugs and provide a small grant for each mission medical practitioner.

Education had been the orphan of Australian colonial policy, and following World War II no government primary schools existed except for the Sogeri School near Port Moresby. Despite the considerable efforts of the missions, about 95 percent of Papua New Guineans remained illiterate. In 1951 there were about 100,000 children in mission schools and some 3,000 in government schools. Real development in education proceeded slowly and did not occur until the mid-1960s. By 1965 there were 65,000 students in government schools, but the missions continued to provide more school places than the government. Even so, over one-half of the children still could not be offered an education.

The postwar period also gradually eroded some blatantly discriminatory legislation against the Papua New Guineans. After a period of intense debate, for example, the government decided in November 1962 to lift the prohibition on the consumption of liquor by the indigenous peoples.

Political Developments. In 1951 the Legislative Council, composed of three indigenous nominated members and 26 whites, was established for the combined territories. Sixteen of the whites served in an official capacity as members of the public service. Nonofficial members included John Guise, who undertook to be a spokesman for the common people but was handicapped by the fact that he was of mixed descent. Some Australian critics regarded him as a radical. As disproportionate as the first Legislative Council appears, it well reflected the political balance of forces within the territories.

By 1952 local government councils having largely advisory powers had been established to develop responsibility at the grass-roots level for local affairs and ultimately prepare the villagers for a more advanced political system. Some 150 councils spread over the territories. Although most failed to become autonomous decisionmaking bodies because of interference from the central administration, limited authority, and dominance by white council clerks, they did serve to educate many people who would later become politically active.

The 1960s saw a quickening of political development brought about by the pressure of domestic and overseas influence. These included the emergence of increasing numbers of independent states, pressures from the UN, changing Australian attitudes, and local economic and social change. The enlarged Legislative Council of 1961 had a majority of nonofficial members, and the indigenous membership grew to seven. On the sensitive issue of land matters, the administration for the first time withdrew legislation that the Papua New Guinean members did not support.

During 1961 Australia indicated its intention to take other steps toward self-government within the next five years. Concerned that the form and timing of change be decided within the territory, an Australian planter moved that a select committee be found to make recommendations for constitutional change. In 1962 the committee recommended the formation of a legislature consisting of 64 members, 10 appointed by the administration, 10 from special electorates (for nonindigenous members), and 44 from open electorates. Simultaneously, a UN visiting mission chaired by Sir Hugh Foot recommended a 100-member legislature having no special electorates for nonindigenous groups and only five official representatives. The Foot Report was viewed by some as unworkable UN meddling; however, it probably made the specific recommendations of the select committee more palatable to many expatriates.

The territories' first legislature, the House of Assembly, was established in 1964. The elections—the first under universal adult suffrage—demonstrated that political power continued to rest largely on the strength of traditional indigenous forces. Owing to the newness of formal elections, the weakness of political parties, and the lack of "national issues," voting focused on individuals representing local clan and other interests. The persistence of this local focus became a cause for concern. Few of the Papua New Guinean members were educated beyond the primary level, some were illiterate, and many were not fluent in English, the language used in the administration. Most felt their responsibility was essentially to seek additional roads, schools, clinics, and development projects for their constituencies; they were largely unprepared to address national issues.

Despite their minority status, the 10 official members appointed by the administration were still able to dominate the House of Assembly. Ironically, their primary opposition most often came from expatriate elected members. On the significant issue of compensation for alienated land, however, the indigenous majority was successful in partially influencing government policy. For instance, the representative from Bougainville, Paul (later Sir Paul) Lapun, succeeded in 1966 in amending the mining laws to give Bougainville landowners token royalties from the giant copper mine on the island.

Perhaps the most significant development preceding the 1968 elections to the House of Assembly was the emergence of the Pangu Party (Pangu Pati) in 1967. Australia had not encouraged the development of political parties, and earlier attempts to do so had faltered. The Pangu Party, however, was successful in drawing younger and better educated candidates into the elections. It was formed by two Australians, seven indigenous members, and a group of educated Papua New Guinean public servants. It ran on a platform demanding immediate home rule and greater local power. Michael Somare, a party founder who resigned the public service to contest and win the East Sepik regional electorate seat, stated in an impassioned speech before the 1968 UN visiting mission that it was essential for local people to take higher positions in the public service and control more of the cash economy as well as for the House of Assembly to have the power to dispose of its own revenues. These themes set the tone of the debate over the territory's future in the ensuing years.

The second House of Assembly, elected in 1968, was composed of 94 members—69 members from electorates, 15 members elected at large from regional electorates, each of which combined several open electorates, and 10 official members. Expatriates held only eight of the open electorates but held 11 of the 15 regional seats because they were often more widely known and better financed than were indigenous candidates. More than one-half of the indigenous representatives had some formal education, and nearly one-half spoke English. Somare, Guise, Lapun, Ebia Olewale, Oscar Tammur, Matthais Toliman, Sinake Giregire, and Tei Abel were able to provide a strong indigenous viewpoint. Guise was elected as the first nonwhite Speaker of the House of Assembly.

The Growth and Localization of the Public Service. The public service became the principal vehicle for social change and administrative control throughout the land, its growth paralleling Australia's efforts to develop the territories. Totaling an estimated 1,174 officers and staff in 1951—all of whom were expatriates— the staff then rose in number by 1965 to 9,336, of whom some 4,000 were indigenous employees. Although Australia had established a division of the public service for lower-level officers in 1955 in order to bring in more indigenous personnel, some 99 percent of Papua New Guineans serving in the public service in the mid-1960s held staff rather than officer positions.

The government at first provided the indigenous employees with salaries, status, and working conditions equivalent to those of expatriates, except in the matter of home leave and territorial allowances. It soon concluded, however, that the public service would eventually become localized at salaries too high for the territories to bear. Consequently, in 1964 the Australian government determined that different salaries would be paid, depending on whether an employee was indigenous or expatriate. Local salaries were set at 40 percent of those for overseas personnel. What followed was a chorus of protest but no avenue of redress. In the eyes of many Papua New Guineans, the event symbolized the worst kind of discrimination and reinforced their desire to gain control of the public service at the earliest practicable time.

The Development of Regional Secessionist Movements

The Australian administration had developed few institutionalized political links between the capital at Port Moresby and the indigenous population in the various regions. In the 1960s the administration had established various advisory committees on a provincial basis, but in many areas villagers rejected these as unresponsive to their needs and formed their own movements to press their interests. Movements in the Gazelle Peninsula, Papua, and Bougainville resulted in a new and wider legitimacy within these locales than had existed in any previous political entities and led to the development of regional secessionist tendencies.

The Gazelle. Although the Tolai people of the Gazelle Peninsula had several advantages not found in most of Papua New Guinea— a good education, relative affluence, and a well-defined sense of community—these achievements had been made at great cost and did not offset the fact that more than 40 percent of the best Tolai land had been alienated by outsiders. Population pressures had begun to strain the customary social system in the 1960s, and there was growing impatience among the Tolai for control over their own affairs. They had already displayed sufficient sophistication to refuse to accept new forms of administration or white control over their affairs.

Tolai antagonism with government policies intensified in the late 1960s. Many farmers were upset when management consultants suggested that a Tolai cocoa cooperative be turned into a corporation, seeing this as an attempt to change the cooperative's status as their agent and remove it from their control. A group of farmers, led by Oscar Tammur, who later became a leading Tolai politician, occupied a large plantation in a densely populated part of the peninsula to protest the continued alienation of their land.

The immediate cause of the Gazelle crisis, however, was the formation of a multiracial local council for the area. The proposal made sense in terms of financial policy. As in the past, the local councils were tied to a particular clan or village and had no power to tax white or Chinese residents because neither were part of village or clan life. The plan nonetheless displayed an insensitivity to Tolai fears, and when the multiracial council was announced in February 1969, Tolai residents organized the Mataungan ("Be Vigilant") Association to oppose it. Protests and a boycott of the local elections failed to deter the central government, and on September 1, 1969, a crowd of Mataungan-led Tolai locked the new council out of its meeting hall in Rabaul. The national government responded by sending an additional 800 police, making a total force of 1,000 in Rabaul. They were unable to cope with a systematic wave of Mataungan violence, however, and needed further reinforcements to quell the unrest.

The leading theoretician of the Mataungan Association was university-trained John Kaputin. A brillian orator, he became one of the most controversial figures in Papua New Guinea politics. He broadened the aims of the association, formulating proposals for it to take over most of the local administration. Unable to win much support outside of the Gazelle Peninsula, the association engaged the government in a standoff for the next two years. Most of the violence had subsided by late 1969, but continued activism on the part of the association kept the area on the edge of violent outbreaks. The association disavowed, however, any participation in the murder of the government-appointed district commissioner in August 1971. The participation of the Mataungan Association in national politics after 1971 changed matters much for the better, and the disagreements between the Tolai and the central government became increasingly an internal family affair.

Papua. In the 1970s Papuans began to organize in protest against their absorption into the broader territory. Their leader, Josephine Abaijah, a popular member of the House of Assembly, repeatedly called for a referendum in the Papuan side of the territory to decide the issue. Papuan separatism drew its strength from a belief that people in the southeast had ethnic and cultural patterns separate from those of the northeast. The critical flaw in this argument, however, was that Papua included part of the Highlands, and Highlanders made up 200,000 of Papua's 700,000 people. Nevertheless, Abaijah and the Papua Besena Party promoted an image of the Papuans as civilized and nonviolent, while categorizing the inhabitants of the former Territory of New Guinea as the opposite. The presence of large numbers of immigrant Highlands males in Port Moresby caused social antagonisms, resulting in citywide riots in 1968 and 1972 after rugby matches between teams representing the two groups. The Papua Besena Party also represented Papuan fears that their area was being neglected by the central government.

The party declared its intention to achieve its goals peacefully, focusing its political activities in the Port Moresby area and in Gulf, Northern, and Milne Bay provinces. Some Papuan leaders, civil servants, and university students supported the movement in order to protect themselves from being victimized by the northeastern New Guineans, but the primary purpose of the party was to surface community grievances and resolve community conflicts.

Bougainville. It is difficult to determine precisely when the Bougainville crisis began, but certainly it came into full maturation as a result of the development on the island of one of the world's largest copper mines. Bougainville had long been perceived as being unique in many ways. Its people had kinship and long-established trading ties with the British Solomon Islands rather than with the main island of New Guinea and its adjacent islands. Bougainville had been attached to German New Guinea almost as an afterthought in the colonial division of spoils, Britain renouncing its claims in return for the withdrawal of German claims in other areas of the Pacific. The Australian administration of the island neglected its development, and education had been almost totally left to the missions, most of which were Roman Catholic. Bougainville's leadership, particularly in the late 1960s and early 1970s, was drawn largely from those trained for the clergy; thus, the leaders had a much higher level of education than most politicians on the main island. Last, outside interaction with the world had rarely been beneficial to Bougainville's inhabitants. There were savage punitive expeditions during the period of German rule, and the Japanese occupation brought much cruelty.

It was against this background that an Australian company that later became Bougainville Copper began taking samples of low-grade copper ore in 1964, determining in 1968 that deposits of some 750 million tons should be exploited. From the vantage point of the Australian and Papua New Guinea governments, the scheme had obvious benefits. It was estimated that royalties and taxes flowing to the administration would amount to from $A30 to $A50 million (for value of the Australian dollar—see Glossary) annually, depending on international prices. The Papua New Guinea government decided to purchase a 20-percent equity interest in the mine and planned for jobs to be created for Papua New Guinean workers.

The Bougainville islanders, however, viewed the project from a different perspective. Land to most Papua New Guineans is not only an economic asset but also the ancient source of well-being. For many, the spirits of ancestors and of those not yet born have as much of a claim to the land as the living. Although persons have the right to use the land, it is normally "owned" by the clan or group in general, which must consent to its use. The treasures of any one piece of land, moreover, are considered to belong to the group as a whole.

The administration's insistence that mineral rights were vested in the state and that all royalties accrued to it, therefore, had serious political repercussions. In order to bridge these divergent views, Paul Lapun, Bougainville's leading politician, succeeded in amending mining laws in 1966 in order to pay token royalties to various Bougainville groups. His efforts, however, did not greatly reduce local resentment against the government, resentment that grew as the mine spurred rapid growth in the urban population from 750 people in 1966 to more than 14,000 five years later. Most of the newcomers were single men from the Highlands or the Sepik River area whom the locals accused of lawlessness, drunkenness, and unwanted involvement with the local women.

As early as September 1968 Paul Lapun and 23 other local leaders had requested a referendum on whether Bougainville should remain in the territory. In April of the next year some 1,700 villagers met at Kieta, threatening secession unless the administration revised its land laws. A few months later a political group entitled Napidakoe Navitu was formed to promote the referendum and other Bougainville interests.

Internal Self-Government and Independence

Although independence for Papua New Guinea had been a long-term goal in both Australia and the two territories at least since the end of World War II, progress toward that end was very slow during the 1950s and 1960s. In December 1969, however, the leader of the Australian political opposition, Gough Whitlam, suggested during a trip to Port Moresby that the territories should aim for self-government in 1972 and independence in 1976. The idea was initially viewed with hostility in many circles in Papua New Guinea, particularly in the Highlands, and the specified dates were widely believed to be unrealistically premature. Nonetheless, although Whitlam did not speak for the Australian government, indigenous participation in the administration increased dramatically after his visit, and the agenda for local autonomy and independence became a central issue in the political dynamics of Papua New Guinea. The composition of the 1972 House of Assembly was altered to eliminate all appointed positions, and after elections in early 1972 a coalition of parties formed a national government under Somare. The House of Assembly, calling for immediate self-government, then established a committee to determine what form independent Papua New Guinea should take. In early 1973 Australia, under the leadership of Prime Minister Whitlam since December 1972, endorsed the idea of self-government at the end of 1973 and independence in 1974.

The 1972 Election and the Formation of the National Government. The 1972 election should be viewed as two events: the election itself and the subsequent negotiations between the parties to form a governing coalition. Initially, it was assumed that the largest and most conservative of the organized political parties, the United Party, would win an absolute majority and be able to form a government without outside help. The United Party emphasized private enterprise, overseas investment, and a partnership of the races. Its primary base was in the Highlands, and it urged delay in the move toward independence. It also received strong expatriate support and financing.

The United Party's major rival was the Pangu Party, which advocated immediate self-government, demanded more local control over the economy and the bureaucracy, and emphasized the sanctity of land. Its stronghold was in the Morobe district of the Sepik area, but it campaigned widely.

Several other parties also contested the election. The People's Progress Party was supportive of private enterprise but was nondoctrinaire about many other issues, including the timing of independence. It was based in the offshore islands and the coastal regions of the former Territory of New Guinea. The National Party campaigned in the Highlands, and personal agreements linked it to the Pangu Party. Three parties campaigned on regional interests: the Papua Besena Party from Papua, the Mataungan Association from the Gazelle Peninsula, and Napidakoe Navitu from Bougainville. There was also a host of independents.

The vote for the 102-member House of Assembly resulted in 42 seats for the United Party and 24 for the Pangu Party; the remainder were split among the National Party, the People's Progress Party, the three regional parties, and independents, including former Pangu Party member Guise. Both the United Party and the Pangu Party attempted to win uncommitted members and smaller parties to form a coalition. The Pangu Party had the disadvantage of attempting to assemble a disparate group, but the United Party faced an even tougher task, having been paralyzed by the defeat of many of its strongest members. Two days before the opening of the new House of Assembly, Somare, as Pangu Party leader, announced the formation of a coalition of his own party, the National Party (which had co-opted eight independent Highlanders), the regional parties from Bougainville and the Gazelle, as well as Guise and a handful of other independents. This placed the People's Progress Party, led by Julius Chan, in a kingmaker role, able to determine whether the United Party or Somare's coalition would govern. It chose to join Somare's coalition, and on April 20, 1972, the first national government of Papua New Guinea came into being; Somare served as chief minister.

The United Party was forced to become the opposition. In contrast to the ruling coalition, its members were mainly Highlanders, knew little English, and were resistant to rapid change. It generally had a less detailed platform for dealing with important national issues in Bougainville, the Gazelle, and the Highlands and the rest of Papua.

Throughout the period, Somare faced the difficult task of keeping disparate groups together and placing individuals of varying abilities in positions of power. The desire for self-aggrandizement, patronage, and pressures from constituent groups made it difficult to rely on consistent loyalty from members of the House of Assembly. When pressured, they resorted to the threat of abandoning the government. In addition, members of the committee established to create a constitution for independence were drawn from all parties and tended to vote as a bloc in support of committee proposals.

The first Somare cabinet was carefully balanced in terms of both party and geographic representation. Six Pangu Party members received portfolios, the People's Progress Party and the National Party were each allotted four, and the remaining two ministries went to independents, one of whom was Guise. Geographically, six ministries were allocated to Papuans, four to northeastern New Guinea coastals, three to New Guinea islanders, and four to Highlanders. This delicate balancing of geographical and party interests was to remain a hallmark and a necessity of the Papua New Guinea parliamentary system. Although it had obvious advantages, it also resulted in some extremely weak ministers holding power in order to maintain a proper balance.

Because the coalition had only eight Highlander members, Somare toured the Highlands shortly after taking office and expressed his concern for the interests of that region. He also ensured that the leader of the opposition, Toliman, was accorded the full dignities of his position. These efforts were not in vain. As Somare faced increasing difficulties in the ensuing years, Toliman and his successor, Tei Abel, came to believe that the Somare government, as Papua New Guinea's first "national government," had a right to survive, and the opposition crossed the aisle to support Somare on numerous occasions.

By December 1972 Somare had issued a program of eight pragmatic goals that in large part served as the basis of political debate during his administration. These concerned localization of the administrative apparatus, self-reliance in the raising of revenue, equal distribution of income and services throughout the territories, decentralization, development of small-scale industry, self-reliance in production, equality for women, and, when necessary, government control of the economy.

To accomplish the first of these goals, Somare ordered that

the number of expatriates in the public service be reduced by 3,000 by 1975 and that training programs for Papua New Guineans be accelerated. Somare's initial injunction caused considerable disruption, but by independence all department heads and provincial commissioners and most heads of statutory bodies were Papua New Guineans. Bureaucratic efficiency diminished temporarily, but Papua New Guineans at long last felt they were gaining control of their future.

Self-reliance was a more problematic goal. Australia, which still provided over 60 percent of the Papua New Guinea budget in the early 1970s, had promised to continue to grant $A500 million annually for the 1974–77 period. In 1975 Somare secured a further commitment of $A930 million over the next five years.

Efforts to increase local revenues centered on enlarging Papua New Guinea's share of the profits of the huge copper mine on Bougainville, where regionalism continued to be a potent force. The initial agreement concerning the mine had never been acceptable to the Bougainville leadership. Father John Momis and Paul Lapun—who held portfolios in the Somare government—and regional politicians elected to local governing bodies on Bougainville had campaigned on a platform that opposed the government's activities in their area. Although the inclusion of the Bougainville-based party, Napidakoe Navitu, in the ruling coalition had suggested that the Bougainville secession issue was moot, the "payback" killing in December 1972 of two Bougainvilleans after they had accidentally run over a child in the Highlands shattered this sense of accord. News of the incident incensed Bougainvilleans throughout the country and convinced many that there was no future for them in a united and independent Papua New Guinea.

When Somare visited Bougainville in January 1973, he heard a clamor for secession from all sides. The tenacious Somare, however, once again was able to co-opt the most vocal advocates of secessionism, temporarily appeasing them by establishing a strengthened local government in November 1973. Throughout the next two years the local leaders in charge of the Bougainville administration demonstrated both their efficiency and their sense of autonomy in handling local development projects. Flush with their successes, they demanded a great share of the central government's capital budget and larger royalties from the copper mine, threatening at one point to cut off the water supply to the mine.

Meanwhile, the mine's first full year of production had yielded a profit of $A158 million—far exceeding expectations—

and the pressure to renegotiate the agreement with the mining company became irresistible. The company at first balked but eventually agreed to new terms in October 1974 that resulted in $A93 million going to Papua New Guinea in that fiscal year. This amounted to nearly 30 percent of its total revenues. The national government's lack of responsiveness to demands that Bougainville's share of revenue be increased and that the island be allowed greater autonomy, however, provoked another crisis: the Bougainville provincial assembly voted on May 30, 1975, to secede from Papua New Guinea. Somare declined to arrest the proponents of secession, wishing to let the issue work itself out Melanesian style, and continued to proceed toward independence.

During the same 1972–75 period the Somare government had met the challenge of Papuan regionalism in a similar manner, successfully co-opting Papuan leaders into the government. Somare's first foreign minister was a Papuan, and at the time of independence Papuans held the four top army positions and a majority of the top civil service positions. Nevertheless, on March 16, 1975, the Papua Besena Party unilaterally declared that Papua was an independent state. Because the party's proclamation was not accompanied by violence, however, the central government felt no need to respond strongly, and eventually the Papua Besena Party began to press for a better deal for Papua within the system of an independent Papua New Guinea.

Preparations for Independence. Before Somare had formed his government in 1972, Australia had established a position on the administrator's staff to handle the transfer of power. By June 1972 Somare had announced the establishment of an all-party Constitutional Planning Committee (CPC) to make recommendations on Papua New Guinea's system of government, central-regional-local relations, control of the public service, relations with Australia, a bill of rights, minority protection, and citizenship. Somare was ex officio chairman, and Father Momis of Bougainville served as deputy. Because of Somare's preoccupation with the running of the government, Father Momis came to be identified as the leader of the CPC.

A wide debate over the future of Papua New Guinea resulted as the CPC addressed more than 2,000 meetings in more than 100 centers across the country. By May 1973 it was decided that all powers over domestic affairs would be transferred from Australia to Papua New Guinea by December, that the CPC's final report would be tabled in the House of Assembly for adoption in April

1974, and that the stage would be set for independence in September 1974. The date of self-government was met, but the debate over the constitution consumed one more year than expected, and independence was delayed until September 1975.

The main causes of contention in drafting the constitution were provisions relating to citizenship, the head of state, and the structure of provincial government. The issue of citizenship provoked the most intense debate, the CPC arguing that citizenship would be automatically granted only to those persons having at least three indigenous grandparents. This clearly excluded children of mixed Australian-Papua New Guinea heritage. Somare was able, however, to arrange a compromise requiring only two indigenous grandparents. The CPC report also provided that residents who had accepted a foreign citizenship and even mixed-race people who had accepted a foreigner's salary and status were to wait eight years before naturalization. This was intended to give those who had not benefited from preferential treatment under the colonial government a chance to gain sufficient experience to compete on a more equal basis with those who had been given such opportunities. Somare was able to have this altered to offer provisional citizenship for those having eight years of continuous residence.

The debate over the head of state was difficult and prolonged and was bound up in the attempt to decentralize the government apparatus. Essentially, the CPC called for the prime minister, the Speaker of the national legislature, and the chief justice to share the functions of head of state and for each province to have its own premier and legislature and control its own public service. The government expressed concern over whether the central government could exercise effective control in such a situation and suggested that the head of state be a president elected by the national legislature. The matter was resolved when it was decided that Papua New Guinea would join the Commonwealth of Nations at independence and that the British monarch would become titular head of state. A governor general was to be appointed on the advice of the government, and in July 1974 Guise was elected by the legislature as first governor general of Papua New Guinea.

The debate over decentralization focused almost entirely on the attempt to legislate measures for provincial government in Bougainville. The breakdown of talks with the Bougainville secessionists in mid-July 1975, however, made it futile to continue discussion any further. If a deal could not be struck with Bougainville, a large part of the motivation for establishing provincial gov-

Children holding the national flag
Courtesy Government of Papua New Guinea

ernment was removed. One week after the talks broke down, the House of Assembly moved for Independence Day to be set for September 15, 1975. In the interim the various chapters of the Constitution were passed, and the Constitution was formally adopted.

Postindependence

Perhaps the most significant development during the first year of independence was the settlement of the Bougainville crisis. Bougainville's leaders had set September 1, 1975—two weeks before Papua New Guinea's planned independence—as the date on which Bougainville would secede as the independent state of the North Solomons Republic. They sent Father Momis to present their case to the UN, but he received no encourgement there. In response, just after independence, the Papua New Guinea government abolished the Bougainville provincial government, freezing its assets and trying to isolate its leaders. In late

1975 and early 1976 the Bougainvilleans moved toward violence, and Somare was put under intense pressure to respond in kind with the armed forces. In August 1976, however, Somare and a few trusted advisers flew to Rabaul, where they were able to avoid a final violent confrontation and work out a satisfactory agreement with the Bougainville representatives. This amounted to giving a newly established provincial government local taxing power sufficient to provide for community schools and recreation and local and village government and courts. In addition, the provincial government received a say in the management of major resources. Bougainville, or North Solomons, as was its preferred name, was given a grant of K5 million (for value of the kina—see Glossary) to establish the provincial government, to which Alexis Sarei was elected premier.

This led to high expectations in other provinces that they too could establish local administrative bodies, and the August 1976 budget—the first after independence—included provisions for a number of individual grants to the provinces, at K50,000 each, to initiate planning for their respective provincial governments. An additional K100,000 was provided to each to pay for rural development projects, and in January 1977 the budget allotted to all provinces 1.25 percent of the value of their exports.

Father Momis was given the portfolio for decentralization after the 1977 elections to the legislature—renamed the National Parliament at independence. Organic laws and the necessary amendments to the Constitution to allow for provincial government were passed shortly thereafter. By late 1977 nine of the 20 provinces had interim or fully elected provincial governments in operation, and the Somare government fully supported decentralization. At the same time, Father Momis, who had done so much to promote provincial government, became concerned about allegations of financial mismanagement in certain provinces and prepared legislation giving the National Parliament the right to suspend provincial governments.

The Pangu Party organization had weakened somewhat by the 1977 elections, but Somare himself retained sufficient power to help selected Pangu Party candidates, and he campaigned widely. Of the 82 candidates the party endorsed, 38 won seats in the National Parliament. People's Progress Party leader Julius Chan was able to capitalize on his role in keeping the national currency hard—retaining its value even after Australian devalaution. His party increased its representation in parliament to 20. Guise resigned as governor general to campaign and was succeeded by another Papuan, Tore Lokoloko. The United Party sought an alliance with Guise as its leader, giving rise to rumors of an anti-Somare coalition. Somare prevailed, however, assembling a coalition with the People's Progress Party, nine independents, and two members of a regional party in the Gazelle for a total of 69 supporters.

The contradictions within the opposition were significant. The opposition consisted of secessionists from the Papua Besena Party, regionalists such as John Kaputin, and members of the United Party, which continued to be staunchly committed to national unity. The opposition was also split between radicals and conservatives, and certain of its members had strong personal animosities.

Similar divisions also were apparent to a lesser degree in the ruling coalition. The Pangu Party was more radical than its partner, the People's Progress Party, and within the Pangu Party itself there was a strong division between radical and moderate wings. Lacking the cement of a cohesive ideology, portfolios were again divided by party; the cabinet was then expanded to 22 ministries to allow for the broadest regional basis.

In 1978 tensions within the ruling coalition were heightened when Father Momis and some of the more "radical" members of the Pangu Party convinced Somare to propose restrictions on the financial activities of ministers, senior public servants, and other officials in order to control apparent conflicts of interest. Somare's coalition partner, Chan, criticized the measures as being too severe, and the new opposition leader, Iambakey Okuk, asserted that the measures were contrary to Highlander views of leadership, which required that "big men" (traditional leaders) be wealthy and involved in business. Somare eventually withdrew the proposal but thereafter consulted less with the People's Progress Party and later even downgraded its portfolios. In November 1978 Chan withdrew his party from the coalition. Somare then moved to co-opt part of the United Party, offering to give the faction five portfolios if it would enter the coalition. Once again he was able to defeat a vote of no confidence, although at the price of losing some of his most talented ministers, who were members of the People's Progress Party.

Somare at times had indicated his desire to give up the ceaseless and exhausting task of trying to keep the governing coalition together and to run the country. A number of cabinet ministers habitually defied directives, and politicians from the various parties engaged in continuous scheming to form a new government. His problems grew severe in 1979 and early 1980. The left wing of the Pangu Party sought to see one of its members replace him,

171

and the opposition strove to recruit parliamentarians to form a new coalition while mounting a systematic attack against alleged government inefficiency, corruption, and waste. A breakdown in law and order in the Highlands in 1979 resulted in the government's promulgating emergency decrees that were interpreted as anti-opposition because the opposition had strong Highlander support. In another incident the justice minister, who had challenged the authority of the Supreme Court, was sentenced to eight months in jail for contempt, only to be released by Somare—upon which four of the seven Supreme Court justices resigned.

In January 1980 Somare again reshuffled the coalition, dropping one minister and changing the portfolios of Father Momis and Kaputin. As a result, a majority of United Party members as well as Father Momis and Kaputin left the government, the latter two forming a new party called the Melanesian Alliance. Composed of seven members from North Solomons and East New Britain provinces, the Melanesian Alliance then began negotiations with the opposition to form a new government.

On March 11, 1980, Chan took over as prime minister, defeating Somare by a vote of 57 to 49 in the National Parliament. Okuk became deputy prime minister. The new coalition was largely drawn from groups having regional bases (the Melanesian Alliance, the Papua Besena Party, and the National Party) plus a number of dissidents from the former coalition, including the People's Progress Party and part of the United Party. No attempt was made to designate a minister from each province, but the coalition achieved good regional balance. Party discipline, however, remained weak.

International economic decline undermined the hopes of the new government, which became associated in the public mind with low copper, copra, and cacao prices and slightly declining Australian grants. Chan was unable to control his unruly deputy prime minister, Okuk. The purchase of a ministerial jet for K6 million was a highly unpopular move in the increasingly difficult economic situation. Chan, however, was viewed effective as a consensus leader and was praised as well for fiscal responsibility under pressure. The Chan coalition did badly in the 1982 elections, all coalition partners except the Melanesian Alliance losing strength. A new party, the Papua New Guinea Independent Group, was founded and led by former defense minister Ted Diro. The campaign revolved around Somare, whose better organized and financed Pangu Party won 50 seats. The Melanesian Alliance won eight seats, but two members later defected to the

Pangu Party in the postelection coalition-building process. The Papua Party won three seats; the Papua Besena Party disappeared. The People's Progress Party held 14 seats, the National Party 13, and the Diro-led independent group seven.

On August 2, 1982, Somare was elected prime minister, defeating by a vote of 66 to 40 the outgoing coalition's nominee, Father Momis. The new government was composed of the Pangu Party, independents or independent-Pangu members, and the United Party. The opposition was led by Diro and was composed of Diro's independents and members of the National Party, the Melanesian Alliance, the Papua Party, and the People's Progress Party—the last maintaining an independent position from the formal opposition. The new government received the first unambiguous mandate from the people of Papua New Guinea in a decade—perhaps the first true mandate ever.

The Social System

The 1980 census enumerated a total population of 3,006,799. The rate of increase was estimated at 2.8 percent per year over the 1980–85 period. Although complete population data were not available as of mid-1984, it was estimated that approximately 45 percent of the population was under the age of 15.

Over 98 percent of the population were indigenous Melanesians, the remainder being made up of expatriates—mainly from Australia, Britain, and New Zealand—and small communities of Asians, Polynesians, and Micronesians. The Australian influence was noticeable, especially in urban areas where social clubs and sports teams—rugby and Australian rules football—were common.

The estimated rate of urban growth has ranged from 6 to 10 percent annually since the mid-1970s. Many migrants could not find employment, and shantytowns have grown up around all major urban centers. Services were being extended slowly to these settlements, but urban development has been held up by the refusal of landowners to sell land to the government. Increasing urban crime rates have been blamed on urban overcrowding. For the most advantaged level of society, however, the towns continued to offer the best living conditions, services, and educational facilities. Under these circumstances educated Papua New Guineans were increasingly drawn to them and were fast forming a new urban elite.

Traditional Society

Most scholars believe that the Melanesian population can be divided into two linguistic groups. The first comprises descendants of the original Australoid migration who speak one of a number of languages—grouped into a catchall category called Papuan—that have become so diversified that no relationships to any other past or present-day language can be distinguished. The second group is formed by descendants of later migrants who speak languages belonging to the Austronesian language family. Generally, most Papuan speakers are found in the New Guinea Highlands and most Austronesian speakers in the coastal areas and the islands, but exceptions to this pattern are common. There has been considerable mixing of the groups, and the divisions are often not clear-cut and by no means coincide with clearly defined cultural distinctions. In the minds of most of the nation's residents, the most significant question in dividing the population is not what language one speaks but whether one is a Highlander or a coastal dweller.

Customs and traditions vary from region to region and often from village to village, making it impossible to make generalizations that hold true everywhere. Within the wide variety of traditions, however, repetitive patterns do exist. A vast majority of the population have a tradition of living in settled rather than nomadic communities. In the traditional society most are grouped into small, discrete political units that display little in the way of complex or permanent organization. Although trade, intermarriage, and warfare have created relationships between residents of different communities, most persons feel a common bond only with fellow residents of their own villages, who are usually connected by ties of kinship, language, and right to use settlement land. Suspicion of those outside the community of birth has historically been great and has presented an obstacle to developing a sense of national unity.

Traditional societies tend to be male-dominated and polygamous, women holding low status and often being viewed as a kind of property. Among urban elites, especially in Port Moresby, patterns of male dominance were slowly retiring, however, in the mid-1980s. Several female members of parliament have wielded considerable political influence, and although they were still few in number, women were beginning to enter the professions and middle-management levels of government. The country had an active national council of women, which had functioning chapters in a few of the provinces. The Young Women's Christian Association has been active in Port Moresby and a few

174

other cities. Among a few groups, matrilineages have exercised considerable power, especially over the disposition and use of clan land.

Except for a few very rare exceptions, achievement rather than birth is recognized within the traditional society as the primary qualification for political leadership. Villages and clans are usually dominated by a "big man" or a group of big men, who are sometimes hereditary chiefs but more often individuals who have attained power and influence through ownership of property. Big man status could also be achieved by the traditional clergy or cult leaders and by those having leadership positions in such institutions as agricultural cooperatives, trade unions, local councils, the police, the army, and the public service. Although in practice most societal groupings decide important matters by consensus, big men have usually played a major role in shaping the outcome. Structures such as these have tended to be hidden in Port Moresby and other urban areas but nevertheless exist and are potent elements of the social order.

An important element of traditional culture that continues to permeate the modern sector is the *wantok* system. *Wantok* (meaning one-talk or common speech) by extension refers to a clansman, relative, or friend. The *wantok* system involves people in an intricate network of rights and obligations extending well beyond the family. For a person who has progressed materially, the *wantok* system creates an obligation to assist other members of the group with gifts, money, housing, or jobs. The system is fundamental to the entire social system and provides individuals with important emotional, financial, and physical insurance.

More than 700 languages are spoken in the nation. After World War I the Australians attempted to create a common language form by designating Motu—a Papuan language widely used in the Port Moresby area—as the official language of the Territory of Papua. Usage fell off with the advent of World War II. An earlier attempt in German New Guinea to create a common medium of communication proved more successful. It involved the introduction of pidgin, which is an artifical medium composed of a mixture of English, German, and Malay words using indigenous syntax. Pidgin has tended to supplant Motu in recent years; an estimated 500,000 people used this simplified speech in the early 1980s. English is spoken by the relatively small but growing group of educated Papua New Guineans.

175

Religion

Before Western contact, villagers inhabited a universe in which they formed an integral part of the natural environment and did not distinguish betwen what Westerners would call objective reality and illusion or imagination. Feeling themselves subject to forces they could not control, they sought to use the traditional power of magic to ease their way. In many groups each natural element was seen to have its own creator, and only with the help of the proper deity would crops grow, enemies be avoided or destroyed, or trading expeditions succeed. To tap this power one had to use the correct rituals taught by the deities in ages past. The spirits of ancestors continued to live side by side with the living, bound to the ancestral lands and guiding the affairs of the current generation. Even the proper rituals could be thwarted, however, by others' use of sorcery. Should any harm come to a villager or his kin by sorcery or other means, a "payback" response to either the perpetrator or his kin would be called for to avenge all injuries. This sometimes resulted in a chain of retribution and counter-retribution that could last for generations until a settlement, marked by a ceremonial gift exchange, could be reached.

Conversion to Christianity—over 95 percent of the population was estimated to be made up of professing Christians as of 1980—has had a profound impact on the nation. This was evident not only in religious affairs but also in secular matters. Missionaries—both Catholic and Protestant—were the single most powerful force bringing Western ideas and culture to local inhabitants. In many areas mission schools, clinics, hospitals, and social welfare organizations were the only institutions available well into the 1960s.

Christianity. The London Missionary Society began work in the southern half of the main island in the 1870s, eventually establishing a training school at the mouth of the Fly River. By 1890 Methodist missionaries were active on New Britain, New Ireland, and the main island. Methodists entered the Highlands as they were opened up in the 1930s. Lutheran missionaries began work in German New Guinea in 1886. The initial German effort was later augmented by Lutheran missions from the United States and Australia. A mission of the Missouri Synod Lutheran Church established the Wabag (Good News) Lutheran Church in the Highlands among the Enga peoples in 1948.

During the early 1980s Lutherans made up the largest Protestant denomination in the nation. They were followed by the

Spirit houses in the Sepik River area provide a glimpse at the vividness of indigenous religion. Courtesy Government of Papua New Guinea.

adherents of the United Church of Papua New Guinea and the Solomon Islands, which was formed in 1968 as a union of Presbyterian, Methodist, and other groups. Numerous other denominations and interdenominational faith missions were also present, including the Anglican church and the Seventh-Day Adventists. Protestants accounted for about 56 percent of all professing Christians.

Roman Catholic missionaries first arrived in the Bismarck Archipelago in 1847 but made few inroads until the arrival of the Sacred Heart missionaries in 1881. In 1889 they established the vicarite of British New Guinea. By 1980 there were three archdioceses and 11 dioceses as well as an additional diocese on Bougainville that also served parts of the Solomon Islands. Indigenous vocations were still weak; the first indigenous priest was not ordained until 1937, and he later became the first indigenous bishop. In 1970, the latest date for which figures could be located, there were only 15 indigenous priests but 475 expatriate priests. Catholics accounted for about 32 percent of professing Christians in 1980. A major event for the Roman Catholic population was a papal visit in early 1984.

Cargo Cults. A long series of movements that combine traditional religio-magic elements with Christian and Western secular themes have been collectively refered to as cargo cults because their adherents believed in the imminent arrival of some tangible goods or "cargo." Such movements were first observed in the late nineteenth century in areas experiencing a serious disruption of traditional life, usually caused by the impact of Western culture. They were especially prolific in areas where military campaigns occurred during World War II. More than 115 distinct cults had been identified by the mid-1970s. Cargo-thinking has continued to be endemic in many areas of the nation and promises to remain so until economic development, education, and improved communications expose the villagers to the outside world and help them understand that there are no shortcuts to Western knowledge and possessions.

Cargo cults have as their objective the betterment of traditional groups through the acquisition of Western technology, goods, and wealth through magic means. They are often messianic or millenarian in character, prophesying a future event that must be prepared for in advance. When that event does not take place, the cult usually subsides, sometimes to resurface under new circumstances. Cargo cults are characterized by ecstatic singing, dancing, communal meals, and spirit possession. Adherents may experience auditory and visual hallucinations.

Although Western observers have often regarded cargo cults as a temporary aberration, they are in reality a manifestation of the fundamental sense of deprivation and inadequacy experienced in the face of the superiority of Western possessions. Cargo cults also reflect an incapacity to comprehend how such possessions—or cargo—were obtained or made. Under these circumstances cultists reach the conclusion that they have been deprived of such possessions through either some original sin, accident, a conspiracy by whites, or a combination of all three. Assuming that such gifts come from the deities, cultists conclude that cargo would be forthcoming if one knew and performed the proper rituals. These rituals have taken the form of singing together (in emulation of hymn singing), writing (making out invoices), and a variety of other devices. When these fail, frustration can be extreme, often resulting in violence.

Education and Health

Providing adequate educational opportunity has been a priority of the government since independence. The educational plan of 1976 set a goal of providing all children with six years of primary education and between four and six years of secondary education. The 1983 budget allocated 19 percent of total public expenditures to education—an amount equal to 5.4 percent of the gross national product and 50 percent higher than expenditures in 1979. The preindependence system, however, was a totally inadequate framework on which to build—many areas relied almost entirely on mission schools. Despite having made considerable progress, the government had been unable to meet its goals as of 1984.

The school system was controlled by the government through the Department of Education and embraced government schools and those local and mission schools that met acceptable standards. The government provided salaries for all certified teachers, whether from missions or public schools. It also provided classroom supplies and subsidized approved building programs for high schools, technical colleges, and teachers colleges. In the early 1980s almost 11,500 teachers were employed by the government, including about 1,300 expatriates, most of whom taught in national high schools.

Children began primary education at age seven. In 1982 total enrollment at this level was 319,000, but rates of attendance varied across the nation, averaging 64 percent in 1980. In major cities virtually all eligible children were enrolled in primary schools; in other areas enrollment varied from 7 percent in Eastern Highlands Province to 50 percent in East New Britain Province. Government plans called for 92 percent of seven-year-olds to be enrolled by 1985.

Ideally, primary-school children passed into one of the nation's 94 provincial high schools, but as of 1982 only 13 percent of the eligible age-group attended such schools. Qualified students then attended one of the four national high schools (senior high schools) located at Sogeri, Passam, Aiyura, and Keravat. In 1982 about 1 percent of the eligible group did so.

Tertiary education was available at the University of Papua New Guinea at Port Moresby, which opened in 1966, and at the University of Technology at Lae. The Vudal Agricultural College on New Britain offered a three-year course in which students spent one year at agricultural field stations. Nine teachers colleges, two run by the government and seven run by missions, trained primary-school teachers. Secondary teachers trained at the Goroka Secondary Teachers College—a part of the University of Papua New Guinea. There were also more than 140 technical, vocational, and other specialized training schools. Many Papua New Guineans went abroad to take advantage of advanced and specialized training—most to Australia but some to New Zealand, Fiji, the United States, and Western Europe. The government faced a major challenge in providing sufficient employment opportunities for the educated.

The Ministry for Health administered government hospitals, clinics, and public health facilities. It also coordinated closely with church missions that provided health services and hospital care. Four major hospitals—at Lae, Port Moresby, Goroka, and Rabaul—provided specialized care facilities on a regional basis and also served as centers of routine care for their provinces. Each of the remaining 16 provinces had its own provincial hospital; many of these had been established since the early 1970s. A Lutheran mission hospital provided care for Enga Province, and the Bougainville copper mine established a hospital at Arawa that served North Solomons Province. Hospital charges were based on ability to pay; most persons were treated for free or a nominal fee.

The government has instituted a major malaria eradication program, which entailed the establishment of malaria-free areas and reached approximately 60 percent of the population in the early 1980s. Malaria remained a serious national health problem, however. Other prevalent diseases included tropical ulcers, tuberculosis, and leprosy, but the incidence of the latter two appeared to be dropping. It was estimated that during 1980 life expectancy averaged 50.6 years and that the 1983 infant mortality rate was 95 per 1,000 births.

The Economy

For centuries the people of Papua New Guinea were engaged almost exclusively in subsistence agriculture, fishing, hunting, food gathering, and the production of handicrafts. A few animals, such as pigs and dogs, were domesticated, and some small-scale trading for ornaments, specialized foods, canoes, and other traditional goods took place. In the mid-nineteenth century, Europeans were attracted to the islands for their tropical forest products, especially copra and cacao, and large plantations were developed. Village production was also encouraged to meet growing European needs. The next hundred years saw the development of a plantation economy dependent on copra, cacao, rubber, tea, and coffee. Minerals exploration was also inaugurated, and the country experienced gold rushes in the 1880s and 1930s that presaged the importance minerals were to have in the country's future. Much of the plantation economy was destroyed during World War II but was rebuilt during the 1950s and 1960s. Australia made increasingly large budgetary transfers to pay for the cost of a growing government administration, which was engaged in a major social, economic, and political transformation of the islands in preparation for eventual independence. Small-scale manufacturing and commerce and massive enclave mining were added in the years prior to independence.

These relatively recent developments, however, should not obscure the poor underlying economic base of Papua New Guinea. In 1966, for instance, some 940,000 people were still wholly dependent on subsistence activities for their livelihood. Some 790,000 had moved from total reliance on subsistence agriculture to a mixture of cash cropping of tree crops and subsistence agriculture; 420,000 were entirely or mainly engaged in cash cropping. Fewer than 125,000 Papua New Guineans were in the "wage" work force. Nearly two-thirds of Papua New Guinea's economic activity at the time was sustained by Australian government spending and grants-in-aid that totaled almost $A100 million annually. Most aspects of the modern sector were under expatriate control.

In 1968 the Australian administration published a five-year plan that called for maximizing the economic development of

Papua New Guinea. The emphasis on rapid economic development per se was criticized by several Australian economists as a policy that would inevitably minimize the role of Papua New Guineans and maximize expatriate control over the economy. The policy's critics estimated that at the end of the plan some 52 percent of all commercial agriculture, 90 percent of all commerce and industry, and practically 95 percent of business profits would remain in the hands of foreigners and that by 1980 the situation would not be changed greatly.

Australia, however, was faced with the practical problem of establishing the economic foundation for an independent Papua New Guinea, and time was running short. Consequently, the Australian administration entered into an agreement in 1967 for the establishment of a massive expatriate-managed copper project (Bougainville Copper). Although causing political difficulties, the mine produced considerable income. By 1978 some 20 to 25 percent of GDP came from this one copper mine, an indication of the project's commercial success.

From 1972 to 1976 the first "national government" formed by Somare, with the aid of Australian advisers, established strong economic institutions and policies. These included a planning office, a budget priorities committee, budget controls, the Central Bank in Port Moresby, international accounts, a new national currency, a clear reserve position, exchange regulations, and policies and institutions devoted to development and foreign investment. All this progressed simultaneously with the localization of the public service.

The country was fortunate to receive generally high international prices for its major export commodities from 1975 to 1978. The Australian government agreed as well to provide the equivalent of about US$250 million annually in aid. Decisions taken to keep the currency hard in order to combat inflation, to maintain government expenditures at sustainable levels, and to establish commodity stabilization funds when prices were high later minimized the impact of the worldwide economic recession of the early 1980s.

The recession caused worldwide commodity prices to plummet; copper prices dropped to their lowest levels in 30 years. In the late 1970s copper sales had accounted for about 15 percent of GDP but by 1982 represented only 6.5 percent. Between 1981 and 1982 the revenue to the government from the Bougainville mine fell by K42 million. Meanwhile, the prices of agricultural exports decreased by one-half from their levels of the late 1970s.

In response to these adverse developments, the government

announced in 1981 a number of incentives to stimulate agriculture, including investment incentives, the provision of management services to smallholderes, and regulations to secure land tenure for foreign owners of plantations. The commodity stabilization funds provided a source for price subsidies. In the 1983 budget, expenditures were cut by 3 percent from the previous year, and new sources of revenue were developed. The country was able to limit a scheduled 5-percent reduction in Australian aid to 2 percent through 1985. The government also borrowed moderate sums from overseas and benefited from foreign investment in a major new copper mine at Ok Tedi in the Star Mountains. The economy thus survived the recession of the early 1980s with relative ease.

The economy of Papua New Guinea may be divided into the subsistence sector; the primary sector (commercial agriculture, forestry, and fishing); the government sector; industry (including mining); and finance, commerce, and other services. The subsistence sector, which is extremely difficult to estimate in market terms, probably accounted for 15 percent of GDP in 1982, although it employed some 50 to 60 percent of the labor force. Part of the population, however, was involved in both the subsistence and the primary sectors. The latter accounted for perhaps 20 percent of GDP and about 25 percent of the labor force. The government or public sector amounted to some 25 percent of GDP; mining accounted for 17 percent. Investment at the new Ok Tedi mine alone contributed about 10 percent of GDP in 1982, and production from the mine was expected to add 12 percent of GDP by 1987. A variety of services produced the remainder of GDP.

The real GDP increased at the impressive rate of over 8 percent per year during the 1968–74 period, stagnated until 1976, averaged 7.7 percent growth in the 1977–78 period, dropped sharply in 1979, and stagnated in the early 1980s. The government believed, however, that it could maintain an average growth rate of 6.3 percent through 1987, and already there was some improvement in the preliminary data for 1983.

The country had a population of slightly over 3 million in 1982, and its per capita GDP was equivalent to US$820. This relatively high level of income was deceiving, however, because most of the people still lived at, or just above, the subsistence level. Income from expatriates and foreign-owned enterprises further distorted the picture. Estimates for 1976 suggested that one-half of the population in the subsistence sector had incomes of about US$150 per person. By 1982 the average may have reached US$275. In addition to large regional disparities, national income data suggested that there was little, if any, growth in the per capita income of Papua New Guineans during the 1970s, and the stagnation of the early 1980s may well have resulted in a real decline of 2 to 3 percent.

Between 1972 and 1976 real minimum wages more than doubled because of several generous decisions by the Minimum Wages Board that gave the country the highest wage costs among the developing nations of the Pacific. Subsequently, the rise in public and private wages has been limited to increases in the consumer price index. Annual price levels rose an average of 7.5 percent per year during the 1977–82 period and 6.2 percent in 1982. The devaluation of the kina and the Australian dollar in March 1983 may have caused prices to jump 10 percent. Under the current wage agreement, however, only the first 5-percent change in the price was subject to compensation; real wages may therefore have fallen by 5 percent in 1983.

Formal wage employment grew from about 180,000 people in 1976 to about 218,000 in 1980. Of these, about 53,000 people were employed in agriculture, forestry, and fishing activities; 30,000 in public services; 32,000 in community, business, and social services; 20,000 in commerce; 24,000 in manufacturing; 18,000 in construction; 12,000 in domestic services; 9,000 in transportation; 5,000 in mining; and the rest in other services. Formal employment grew by 1 percent during the 1972–76 period and by 5 percent per year through 1980. Since then, employment has fallen sharply in the primary sector and in construction. In the first nine months of 1982 overall employment fell by 9 percent.

Papua New Guinea will be faced with significant employment problems in the future. It was estimated that no more than 10 percent of the 400,000 potential additions to the labor force in the 1980s could be expected to obtain formal sector employment. An increasing number of high school graduates would be unable to find formal employment, and it was unlikely that they would willingly return to the traditional subsistence economy. Furthermore, urban areas were becoming zones of critical unemployment as youth moved to the towns in hopes of bettering their lives. The 1980 census and other data indicated that the proportion of the urban population earning wages and salaries may have fallen from 54 to 28 percent from 1966 to 1980. If these tentative figures proved accurate, the impact on family life, health, and general living conditions in the cities would be devastating.

Economic Planning and Policy

The government's national development strategy sought to improve the quality of life for Papua New Guinea's predominantly village population and focused on rural development in the less developed areas of the country. A second objective was to reduce the heavy reliance on Australian aid by developing a few large natural resource projects. The first goal recognized that for generations the people would continue to rely on the agricultural sector for their livelihood. Revenues from enclave mining were to provide resources for the financing of development programs. To carry out this dual strategy the government established an annual National Public Expenditure Plan (NPEP), a rolling four-year plan for the public sector to link the planning process with overall economic policy. The first NPEP in 1978 accounted for only 4 percent of budget expenditures, but by 1984 the NPEP covered more than 25 percent of the planned total budget expenditure.

Of particular concern has been the lack of growth in the agricultural sector. Major constraints to developing this important sector have been inadequate extension services, lack of finance, land laws that prevented the consolidation of inefficient smallholdings, the shortage of management talent, and old legislation designed to encourage the transfer of foreign-owned plantations to Papua New Guineans.

In order to attract foreign investment and revitalize the agricultural sector, the government decided in 1980 to suspend the Plantation Distribution Scheme, which had allowed for the compulsory purchase of foreign-owned plantations and their redistribution to Papua New Guineans. Other measures included generous depreciation allowances, permission to introduce piece-rate wages, and allowance for the transfer of estate land titles between expatriate owners under specified conditions. A line of credit was set up through the commercial banks from the Bank of Papua New Guinea to fund foreign-owned estates. The government was also considering developing joint ventures in which it would assume the complicated risks related to land titles from foreign investors. A special ministerial committee was set up in 1980 to develop a comprehensive agricultural policy.

Fiscal and Monetary Policy. Government and Central Bank policies have become increasingly conservative. The devaluation of the kina in 1983, though partially inflationary, was timed to boost export earnings and reduce imports. The decision to restrain wage increases was deflationary and was expected to increase job opportunities. In 1983 the government also decided to cut its staff by 10 percent, restrain the growth of expenditures to 3 percent, and trim the cost of capital projects. Nevertheless, expenditures were projected at K731 million and receipts at only K622 million. Australian aid still composed nearly one-third of all government income. The commodity stabilization funds, moreover, were being depleted. In 1982 the funds paid out K7 million, and K167 million remained. The copra fund was in debt to the government.

Budget forecasts for the 1983–87 period called for expenditures of K3.1 billion, which included the repayment of principal and interest on public loans equivalent to 16.6 percent of total expenditure. Capital expenditures were to be 23 percent of the total. About K1.7 billion of the expenditures were to be paid for from tax and other revenues. Some 62 percent of the forecast resource gap of K1.4 billion was to be met through the Australian budgetary grant, about 24 percent from overseas and domestic commercial loans, and the rest from overseas concessional loans.

The government has mandated several important statutory commercial enterprises, the major enterprise being the Electricity Commission, Air Niugini, the Harbors Board, and the Post and Telecommunications Corporation. Budget expenditures for these four authorities were K209 million in 1981. In 1983 the government expected them to transfer profits of K18 million back to the government. Both the airline and the electricity commission generated profits in 1981, but the profitability of all four depended partly on high tariffs that adversely affected consumer costs.

The government's monetary policy turned restrictive in the 1980s. The narrow money supply decreased in 1981 and 1982, while the broad money supply rose by 8 percent and 5 percent, respectively. Commercial bank lending rose by 12 percent in 1982, but new lending commitments by the Papua New Guinea Development Bank fell sharply. Prime interest rates dropped by 2 percent in 1982 to 12.5 percent but were still high in comparison with inflation. In 1983 the government planned to increase the broad money supply by 7 to 10 percent and bank lending by around 13 percent.

Land Policy. Clan groups held 97 percent of the land of Papua New Guinea under complex customary ownership and usage rights that varied among the country's 700 ethnic groups. Ownership rights were normally acquired through birth, but acquisition of land by purchase had become an established custom in a few areas. Land use must be distinguished from landownership; most land was owned in common by the ethnic group, while usage rights for individuals within groups varied greatly. A further distinction was often made regarding the trees or fruits of the land, which were considered the property of an individual or family and in some instances of the extended group. Under the practice of shifting cultivation (see Glossary), no requirement existed for clear title to land plots. Smallholders, who accounted for about 50 percent of the area under cash cropping, used customary land and still generally did not own their own land. Disputes over usage and ownership were common and hampered agricultural productivity in some areas.

European contact, especially in those areas formerly under German control and in Papua prior to 1906, resulted in considerable alienation of customary land and its transfer to freehold title held by Europeans. Following World War I the Australian administration established the principle that no new freehold land was to be granted to expatriates. In the period prior to independence, some traditional groups insisted on the return to them of lands that had been alienated by foreigners, causing considerable tension and conflict. The Land Commission was established immediately prior to independence to review all land issues in Papua New Guinea. It concluded that freehold titles held by expatriates should be converted statutorily into government guaranteed leaseholds, generally without compensation to the freeholders. Freehold land held by Papua New Guineans was to be converted to group titles. The government was urged to acquire alienated plantations in land-short areas, by compulsory means if necessary, and then to return them to adjacent communities. Legislation was enacted subsequent to 1973 to carry out the recommendations of the Land Commission. Some 70 European plantations (out of some 1,200 plantations in the counmtry) were acquired by the late 1970s. Although individual ownership of land by Papua New Guineans was not encouraged, the government did enact legislation to provide titles to various groups for the customary land they held and to define customary rights for land use. The principal objective of government land policy was to rationalize, strengthen, and revive traditional or customary land usage. The impact of the government's land policies, however, was to discourage long-term capital investment from abroad. Without reversing its basic policy, the government was providing new incentives for foreign investors in agriculture in the mid-1980s.

187

Agriculture, Forestry, and Fishing

Papua New Guinea's agricultural sector consisted of two overlapping components: a traditional sector producing subsistence crops and a relatively modern sector producing commercial crops. Traditional agriculture was based on gardens established on customary clan lands. Clearance of trees (ax work) was traditionally done by men, and women took charge of other agricultural and food preparation tasks. Land use varied greatly, and no firm rule stipulated whether plots were organized by individuals, families, or larger clan elements. Perhaps 80 percent of the people relied on the vegetables they grew for food.

From 4 to 5 million tons of vegetables and fruit were produced annually on some 250,000 hectares of customary land. Sweet potatoes were a staple food in many areas and may represent 40 percent of the total vegetable production. Sago was the staple starch for perhaps 150,000 people living near great rivers and swamps, especially in the southern part of the country. Bananas, taro, yams, sugarcane, and coconuts were also important foods. Tomatoes, maize, citrus fruits, papaw, and peanuts were grown as well. Rice was grown on a small scale, and coastal villagers fished for food. The government has encourged the production of vegetables and in 1976 established the Food Marketing Corporation to handle the distribution of vegetables and fruits throughout major centers of the country. Pigs and poultry were important in village life. In 1980 it was estimated that 20,000 tons of pork, 500 tons of poultry, and 400,000 doezen eggs were produced.

Papua New Guinea was the largest producer of copra and coconut oil in the South Pacific. The most important growing areas were the Gazelle Peninsula, New Ireland, Bougainville, parts of West New Britain, Manus, and the coast of Madang Province, although significant production also came from Milne Bay and Central provinces in the southern part of the country. About 50 percent of all copra was normally produced from village groves, while the remainder came from large plantations—many owned by expatriate interests. Estate production has dropped dramatically in recent years as expatriates have been unwilling to replant and make other capital investments in the face of changing land policies. Copra was marketed through the Copra Marketing Board, which collected a stabilization levy to be deposited with the copra stabilization fund. In the early 1980s the international market for copra was severely depressed. Consequently, there were large drawdowns on the stabilization fund, and by 1982 the government had to provide loan assistance to the fund. In 1982

Papua New Guinea exported copra and copra oil valued at only K25 million. Prices were beginning to revive in 1983, when exports reached K33.7 million.

After the Highlands were opened for settlement in the late 1950s, coffee production increased dramatically. It was the country's most valuable agricultural export in 1983, earning K94.77 million. More than 200,000 smallholders produced some 70 percent of the crop, and most production was in the hands of Papua New Guineans. The main arabica coffee-growing areas were in Eastern Highlands, Western Highlands, Simbu, and Morobe provinces. Robusta was grown widely but was concentrated in Central, Milne Bay, and Northern provinces. The Federal Republic of Germany (West Germany), the Netherlands, Britain, Australia, and South Africa were the principal purchasers.

Cacao was planted as an alternative to copra. Significant plantations were established in East New Britain, North Solomons, New Ireland, and Madang provinces. By the mid-1960s some 64,800 hectares were under cacao, but production declined subsequently because of the age of the trees and reduced production from estates. About 35 percent of cacao-growing areas required replanting, and the government has responded with a replanting program whose benefits will be felt in the mid-1980s. About 50 percent of production came from smallholder plantings. About K41 million worth of cacao was exported in 1983 to West Germany, the Netherlands, the United States, Australia, and Britain.

The government and a private corporation, Harrison and Crossfield, entered into a joint venture in 1967 to develop an oil palm industry in West New Britain Province. The idea was to establish a nucleus estate and to encourage and train adjacent smallholders to produce the palms. By 1974 the company had planted 3,700 hectares; 1,500 smallholders had planted 6,500 hectares. Two palm oil factories have been established for processing, and two other projects have been started—one in Northern Province and one in West New Britain Province. In 1981 exports of palm oil were valued at K14.2 million but in 1982 increased to K21 million.

The Australian administration encouraged the development of rubber plantations near Port Moresby, and the industry was well established by the 1920s. There were about 16,000 hectares in rubber, and production was at a level of 4,000 tons in 1979, valued at about K3 million. By 1981 production reached 4,500 tons, representing an export value of K3.4 million. Some 3,700 smallholders were engaged in production. Australia traditionally pur-

189

chases the entire crop.

Tea was introduced as early as the 1930s in Papua New Guinea. It was not until the establishment of a tea factory in Morobe Province in 1962, however, that the industry grew. The Morobe factory closed in 1973 but not before providing seed for some 10 plantations that had been started in Southern Highlands and Western Highlands provinces. By 1981 tea exports reached K7.1 million.

In the 1960s the Papua New Guinea government adopted a strategy to establish a limited number of large ranches, to be followed by the development of smallholder projects using cattle from the large ranches. The goal of developing a national herd of 300,000 head by 1980, however, had not been met. Ranch cattle stabilized at about 80,000 head and smallholder herds at about 46,000 head. In 1978 local production supplied only about one-third of local consumption, the remainder being provided by imports. Production was estimated to increase only about 20 percent through 1990.

Papua New Guinea was well endowed with forest resources; the area under forest cover was 36 million hectares in the early 1980s—more than 75 percent of total land area. Fifteen million hectares had potential commercial timber assets. Much of the timber was on clan-owned land, which often resulted in disputes over usage rights and ownership. To mitigate these problems the government has purchased timber rights from landowners and then issued timber permits to commercial companies. About 2 million hectares were covered by timber rights owned by the government; some 283,000 hectares were under license to the more than 60 companies operating in the country. Government policy has urged firms to use the entire production of the forest—timber, used chips, and pulp—and then to reforest cut areas to create a permanent industry. It has also encouraged the industry to phase out the export of unprocessed logs and to do more processing within the country. Exports have been growing at about 17 percent per year. By 1982 timber products were Papua New Guinea's fourth ranking export, reaching sales of K62 million.

Papua New Guinea's fisheries resources provided a considerable source of nutrition, income, and export earnings. In 1978 the country was one of the largest skipjack tuna exporters in the world. With the expansion of its fishing waters to the 200-nautical-mile EEZ (see Glossary) limit, the potential catch could reach 100,000 tons per year. However, the industry declined sharply in the 1980s. Fish exports decreased from K32 million in 1980 to K20 million in 1981 and K8.3 million in 1982. This reflected a decline in demand for tuna, especially in the United States, which accounted for half of the world's consumption. A modest shellfish industry exported prawns and lobsters annually.

Industry and Infrastructure

The Bougainville copper mine, which went into production in 1972 after investment of more than US$400 million, remained vital to the well-being of the economy in 1984. In the early 1980s reserves were estimated to be at least 944 million tons of ore having 0.48 copper content, bearing 15.83 grams of gold per ton. Bougainville Copper commissioned two new crushing mills in 1981 and 1982 and was able to increase production by 12.5 percent in the first year and by a further 3 percent in the next. Because of low international prices, however, revenues did not rise correspondingly. Faced with its lowest prices in 30 years, the company earned a profit of only K28.5 million before taxes and K11 million after taxes in 1982. Copper concentrates provided 68 percent of the nation's total export earnings in 1974 but declined to about 50 percent of earnings in 1980; export earnings have been rising since then.

Construction of the Ok Tedi copper and gold mine in the Star Mountains of Western Province under a consortium of the Papua New Guinea government (20 percent of the equity) and Australian, American, and West German private interests was scheduled to reach the first stage of completion in 1984. Production would begin with gold-bearing ores, and gold production could eventually peak at 19 or 20 tons per year. Copper production should begin in the late 1980s. Revenues from the Ok Tedi mine could equal those of the Bougainville mine.

The next major mining project will likely be a nickel-cobalt-chromite mine on the Ramu River in Madang Province; three foreign firms were assaying the area for potential nickel, cobalt, and chromite deposits in 1984. Investment costs for a mine there could exceed US$1 billion. A number of other projects also appeared likely to materialize in the mid-1980s. A consortium of Australian, Japanese, and West German firms were conducting feasibility studies at a copper site on the Freida River that would be similar in scope to Ok Tedi, which is only 80 kilometers to the southwest. Also, gold production could commence by 1989 at a mine in Enga Province. Yet another gold mine was being developed at Lihir Island in New Ireland Province, where initial tests have uncovered 20 million tons of ore averaging 2.1 grams of gold per ton.

For a number of years oil exploration has been proceeding unsuccessfully. The situation brightened in 1983, however, when Niugini Gulf found significant reserves of petroleum and gas at a well in Western Province. Commercial exploitation was likely despite the fact that the find was located in difficult terrain.

The country's potential for hydroelectric power is high, but as of 1984 there was little use for electricity on such a grand scale. Nevertheless, some of the potential has been realized. There were four schemes in development in 1984, and others were planned for Port Moresby, Bougainville, and Ok Tedi. The Ramu River project, which cost K30 million to develop, had an installed capacity of 45 megawatts and would eventually have a capacity of 255 megawatts. Japanese and Australian interests were proceeding with a feasibility study for a 1,500-megawatt station and dam on the Purari River that was estimated to cost K700 million to develop.

Because of Papua New Guinea's difficult topography and poor road network, air and water transportation have played important economic roles. Air Niugini flew scheduled services to 18 airports, and small commercial operators served 133 smaller airports. Operation costs and rates were high. Overseas routes linked the country to Sydney, Brisbane, Cairns, Manila, Kagoshima, Jayapura, Honiara, and Hong Kong. The two main airports were at Port Moresby and near Lae. The country relied on its 18 relatively well-equipped sea and river ports and some 400 minor ports to handle international and coastal trade. In 1980 international cargo amounted to 3.7 million tons and coastal traffic to 800,000 tons. About 15 major companies serviced the larger ports; 170 smaller craft handled the coastal trade. The government's fleet of 61 vessels engaged in maritime transportation.

In 1982 the country's roads covered about 19,000 kilometers, of which 940 kilometers were paved. The national government maintained about 5,000 kilometers; provincial and local governments maintained the rest. Most of the roads were located in or near the major coastal towns and in Central Province, forming unlinked, regional grids. Conditions were poor because of inadequate maintenance and damage from overloaded vehicles. Accidents were common. The government was considering a project to improve the roads and enhance safety in 1984. In 1982 there were about 55,000 vehicles in operation, of which 38 percent were sedans and station wagons, 32 percent were light trucks, 15 percent were heavy trucks, about 6 percent were motorcycles, 5 percent were buses, and the rest were tractors.

*Two views of New Britain economy: market
scene in Rabaul and Tolai farmers cracking cacao nuts
Courtesy Government of Papua New Guinea*

Communications were highly developed in 1984. The country was linked to Guam, Sabah in Malaysia, Hong Kong, and Singapore via the Seacom coaxial cable and to Australia, New Zealand, Canada, and Britain via the Compac cable. Transmission quality was good, and subscribers could dial their own calls to most Australian states. The country was connected to telex services throughout the world. Internal radio communication was provided through a system of centers linked to government or privately owned high frequency stations. The National Broadcasting Commission operated stations at Port Moresby, Rabaul, Madang, Goroka, and Wewak and was generally responsible for programs focusing on the better educated segments of the society. Provincial shortwave stations catered to local areas and tastes. Television was to be introduced in 1985.

Only 24,000 people were employed in the manufacturing sector in 1980. Much of the industry was devoted to producing items to substitute for the nation's many imports—especially food and drink, tobacco products, textiles, wood products, paper, printed matter, fabricated metal products, small ships, and repair services. The small internal market, low purchasing power of the population, and poor transportation network impeded the development of the sector.

Foreign Economic Relations

The modern sectors of Papua New Guinea's economy were based on the export of basic commodities and the import of nearly all capital goods and services. Exports fell in 1980, 1981, and 1982, by which time they were less than 75 percent of their 1979 value. In 1982 exports held their 1981 value following the appreciation of the dollar against the kina in 1982. Exports decreased from 44 percent of GDP in 1979 to 33 percent of GDP in 1982. Imports rose 1.8 percent to K751 million, while exports declined 0.5 percent to K563 million for a net trade deficit of K188 million.

Ranked in value in 1982, Papua New Guinea's major exports were gold (K172 million), copper (K119 million), coffee (K78 million), timber (K60 million), cacao (K32 million), copra and coconut oil (K25 million), and palm oil (K21 million). In 1982 the leading purchasers of Papua New Guinea exports were Japan (K183 million), West Germany (K141 million), Australia (K46 million), Britain (K32 million), and Spain (K25 million).

Imports by sector in 1981 were machinery and equipment (30 percent of the total value), manufactured goods (22 percent), petroleum products (21 percent), and food and beverages (20 percent). Imports in 1982 remained at substantially the same shares. Petroleum products grew to 25 percent. Leading suppliers in 1982 were Australia (K309 million), Singapore (K110 million), Japan (K107 million), the United States (K64 million), and New Zealand (K41 million). The recent downturn in international oil prices benefited Papua New Guinea in 1983.

The deficits in the 1982 trade and current accounts were estimated to be almost US$260 million and US$471 million, respectively, and represented 11 percent and 21.2 percent of the GDP, respectively. Capital flows increased markedly in 1981 and 1982 to finance the Ok Tedi mine construction, but these capital flows did not cover deficits in the current account. Consequently, the overall balance of payments moved to a deficit of US$32 million in 1982.

International reserves were at US$362 million at the end of 1982, representing 4.4 months of imports, down from US$515 million in 1979, or 7.9 months of imports. Outstanding public debt was US$638 million in 1982; it had been US$404 million in 1979. Debt service payments rose from 4.4 percent of total export earnings in 1979 to 10.4 percent in 1982 and were rising further in 1983.

The foreign investment climate in Papua New Guinea remained generally favorable. Investors were obliged, however, to deal with both the national and the provincial governments to have investments approved. In order to ensure rapid localization, investors were also expected to engage in training programs for Papua New Guineans. The National Investment and Development Authority coordinated approval of investment applications. The list of areas where the government encouraged investment was long and included minerals, petroleum, forestry, fishing, shipbuilding, tourism, agriculture and livestock, export-oriented secondary industry, and technical and personal services. Major investment in mining in 1982 more than offset net disinvestment in manufacturing and agriculture. Some K200 milliion was spent on Ok Tedi mine and road construction and K57 million for crushing mills at the Bougainville copper mine.

The Political System

The Constitution provides for a national government having legislative, executive, and judicial branches and names the British monarch as chief of state. The monarch is represented by the governor general, who must be a citizen of Papua New Guinea and whose appointment is made on the advice of the Papua New Guinea cabinet and oconfirmed by the legislature. The governor general acts under the advice of the cabinet.

The legislature is a unicameral body organized on the British model and is known as the National Parliament. Members are elected by universal adult suffrage from open electorates proportioned by population and from provincial electorates, one per province. There were 109 electorates in the early 1980s. A normal term of office is five years. The Constitution provides that an additional three members can be appointed by a two-thirds majority of the legislature, but there were no appointed members as of mid-1984.

Executive power is vested in the cabinet—the National Executive Council. The cabinet is led by the prime minister, who is the leader of the majority party or coalition in the legislature. The cabinet is chosen by the prime minister from among the members of the legislature. The Constitution permits the appointment of up to 27 ministers, including the prime minister.

The Constitution guarantees all citizens a wide range of fundamental rights and freedoms regardless of race, tribe, place of origin, political opinion, color, creed, or sex. The nation's legal system is based largely on that of Australia. The Constitution authorizes the establishment of the Supreme Court, the National Court, and such lower courts as might be necessary. The Supreme Court is the final court of appeals and holds original jurisdiction in constitutional matters. Most major offenses are tried in the National Court, which also hears appeals from lower district courts established at the provincial level. To deal with strife arising out of local disputes, the legislature in 1973 established a system of local courts at the village level to support local peace officers. Village courts are headed by a magistrate—usually a layperson appointed by the government from among the local people. Village courts hold jurisdiction over minor offenses and can levy fines, award compensation, and order up to one month's work for the benefit of the community. They can handle matters of both customary and statutory law. Most land disputes are handled by the Land Titles Commission.

The Constitution was amended in 1977 to provide for a level of provincial government below the national administration in an attempt to devolve administrative and political power to the provincial government. All 20 provinces had established provincial governments by the early 1980s. Most were elected, but some still had an interim status and would eventually become elected bodies.

A system of local government was still developing during the early 1980s. Local government councils having the authority to maintain law and order and to finance, organize, or engage in business for the good of the community were first introduced in 1950. Later legislation provided for multiracial councils having wider power to assess taxes, manage health and education programs, and engage in local commercial projects. City and town councils were formed in 1971, and by the early 1980s there were over 160 local councils of all types. Many were reportedly too small to function efficiently, however, and relied heavily on central government subsidies.

Political Dynamics

The transition to independence was peaceful and stable. On Independence Day 1975, the nation's first governor general, Sir John Guise, declared that all people should note the spirit in which the Australian flag was taken down, commenting: "We are lowering it, not tearing it down." Australia had provided durable administrative and governmental structures and proved willing to continue to assist in managing and funding them. The pragmatic leaders of the new nation were willing to build upon these inherited institutions while localizing and bending them to suit the country's needs. The leaders retained strong ties to the village people, tended toward moderation in their policies, and showed patience by ruling through consensual politics. This permitted the process of national integration to continue, if slowly.

Although Somare had believed that the 1972 elections had given him a mandate to run the government and move the country toward independence, in retrospect this seems to have been an overly optimistic assessment. Except for a small cadre of supporters who were personally loyal to Somare and to his vision of an independent state, indigenous leaders displayed little unified sense of purpose in the ministries, the legislature, or the nation at large. Many members of the legislature were independents, and those who were party members often ignored party directives. Somare was forced to build a consensus on each issue, first within his own Pangu Party, then within the coalition; at times he had to rely on the opposition to garner necessary votes. Even the concept of independence had to be carefully explained and promoted to most of the population. Members of the Constitutional Planning Committee had toured the country for months, soliciting the view of people and at the same time educating them.

While Somare was attempting to build a workable national

government, separate regions—the Gazelle, Bougainville, and the Highlands and the rest of Papua—pressed for the decentralization of political power and for more widespread distribution of development projects and economic opportunity. The regional leadership could not be persuaded to accept postponement by any argument regarding national security, financial, economic, or political concerns, and a compromise had to be reached, "Melanesian style," within the first year of independence. After Bougainville established the first provincial government, others soon followed. Over time decentralization facilitated greater local acceptance of village governments and courts, but the financial resources and staff necessary to manage this secondary tier have been costly. Moreover, some feared that the new generation of local leadership being developed within the framework would have an unduly parochial outlook should they enter the national political arena. Others believed, however, that the entry of younger and better educated politicians who were firmly tied to the wishes of the people could be a very positive development. Although inefficiency, corruption, and shortages of staff and funding have plagued the provincial goverments, they appeared likely to remain in place in the near future.

Having localized and gained control of the public service, the new government was soon faced with the possibility that it had created a new elite who enjoyed salaries and life-styles far beyond the reach of most Papua New Guineans. Expenditures on salaries and wages as a proportion of total expenditures were almost three times the average for Asian, non-oil-exporting, developing countries in 1981 and higher than both Fiji and Solomon Islands, the only two Melanesian states for which figures could be located. A strike by public workers in early 1983 produced a settlement that promised to add to the total. There were an estimated 50,000 government workers during the early 1980s. Although concern over official corruption has been constant since independence, many foreign observers considered the problem to be relatively minor in comparison with other developing and modernized states.

Within the political life of the nation, Somare himself has become a figure of considerable importance. His prestige in the villages has grown over time even though his government was replaced by that of Sir Julius Chan for 30 months in the 1980–82 period. Somare has increasingly come to be seen as a charismatic leader—an element that proved important in the 1982 election. Despite the success of his Pangu Party and the development of a strong coalition in 1982, Somare evidently believed that many of the old constraints continued to exist, and he was careful to account for personal strengths and regional needs when assembling his cabinet. This may have proved to be a wise choice, for in July 1983 former National Party leader Imabakey Okuk won a by-election and returned to the legislature to take over the leadership of the opposition. Okuk attempted to entice Highlands members into leaving the Pangu Party and to get other coalition members to defect. The Somare government was able to win a vote of confidence in the legislature, however, gaining four votes more than it had received after the 1982 elections. It remained to be seen whether this portended a new period of parliamentary stability. It appeared that the Pangu Party was producing younger leaders who might someday be qualified successors to Somare.

Foreign Relations

The nation's foreign minister stated before the UN General Assembly in 1976 that Papua New Guinea's foreign policy would be an active and positive "universalism" that sought no enemies. At the same time, its historical links with Australia have also helped define its postindependence foreign policy, which has generally been moderate, pro-Western, and pragmatic. The nation initially exchanged resident embassies only with those countries with which it had historical ties—Australia, New Zealand, Britain, Japan, Indonesia, and the United States—but later expanded this to include Fiji, the Philippines, the Vatican, Malaysia, and other members of the European Community as well. It has also established relations with over 40 other states that did not have resident missions.

Papua New Guinea was a member of the UN and its principal specialized agencies, as well as the World Bank, the Asian Development Bank, the South Pacific Commission, the South Pacific Forum, the Lomé Convention, and the Commonwealth. It established a liaison with the Association of South East Asian Nations (ASEAN) in 1977 but did not formally join. The nation was also an associate member of the International Council of Copper Exporting Countries and the General Agreement on Tariffs and Trade. It has become a significant regional actor and has sought cooperative relationships with its neighbors.

Bilateral Relations. The country maintained its closest relations with Australia, with which historical links were reinforced by current economic, commercial, and other ties. Australia continued to provide generous financial assistance, aid in 1980 accounting for 30 percent of the total Papua New Guinea budget. The two countries have nevertheless experienced sharp differences on a number of issues. The most significant was the demarcation of the section of the border with Australia that runs through the Torres Strait. In 1879 the original line had run within several hundred meters of Papua New Guinea's shores, giving Australia control over several straits islands having Melanesian populations. In 1969 Ebia Olewale, a member of the Papua New Guinea House of Assembly, called for the border to be moved to five kilometers from Papua New Guinea's shores, but Australia ignored the issue until Olewale again brought it up in the first Somare government in 1972. At that time he called for the border to be placed at the midpoint between the two states. Legal challenges from the Australian state government of Queensland kept the issue in Australian courts until 1975, and it took three years more to arrive at a complex settlement. In addition to establishing a new seabed line, the 1978 agreement set up a protected zone in which Torres Strait islanders on both sides of the border could continue to pursue their traditional economic activities. It also made provision for shared commercial fishing and placed a 10-year embargo on oil-drilling and mining in the area. Determining how to deal with potential oil and other deposits in the area would have to be negotiated in the future.

Relations with Indonesia were also of great importance, a particularly sensitive issue being control of their mutual border in order to preclude members of the anti-Indonesian Free Papua Organization (Organisasi Papua Merdeka—OPM) from finding sanctuary in Papua New Guinea. Australia entered into a boundary agreement with Indonesia in 1974 that demarcated the border, but during the mid-1970s Papua New Guinea became embarrassed by the ease with which OPM rebels crossed the borders. There was also concern that some of the estimated 10,000 refugees from Indonesia who were living in Papua New Guinea might be supporting the rebels despite their pledge not to do so.

In mid-1978 the government decided to demonstrate its displeasure on the matter and closed the border to OPM activity. Troops of both nations conducted operations on their respective sides of the border. This prompted demonstrations within Papua New Guinea, and the issue became embroiled in domestic politics, critics charging that the government was being insensitive to "our Melanesian brothers." The government held firm, however, to its policy of maintaining friendly relations with its powerful neighbor. It appeared determined to continue to do so as of mid-1984, despite several new matters of contention. In 1972 the government announced that a new Indonesian road along the border

*Traditional vessels
of the Papua coast
Courtesy Government
of Papua New Guinea*

had crossed into Papua New Guinea in several places. This prompted an angry debate in Papua New Guinea in spite of an apology from Indonesia. In late 1982 a newspaper in Papua New Guinea published a map allegedly outlining Indonesian plans for moving up to 10 million Indonesians onto its side of the main island. Many people in Papua New Guinea viewed such a plan with alarm, for that figure would represent several times the population of their own nation. In early 1984 Papua New Guinea charged that Indonesian military aircraft had crossed into its territory during a military exercise and made repeated low passes over several villages; Indonesia denied the charge. Tension over this matter was aggravated by a flow of refugees into Papua New Guinea after reports of an Indonesian crackdown on its side of the border.

Indonesia also became displeased when Somare visited China in 1976 as part of his effort to diversify sources of aid, trade, and investment. Hoping to avoid the high cost of Australian imports, he was especially interested in finding sources of consumer goods and hoped as well to obtain new ideas that would promote rural development and diminish urban drift. Shortly thereafter Indonesia indicated that it "would not hesitate" to deal with any communist threat, "within or without," that posed a threat to Indonesian security. Although the statement was directed toward the secessionist movements in Papua New Guinea, it was also interpreted as indicating that caution must be exercised in dealing with communist regimes. It was not until mid-1980 that the government of Sir Julius Chan announced that China would be invited to establish an embassy in Port Moresby.

Papua New Guinea maintained a warm relationship with New Zealand, which has gradually increased its aid since independence, donating fishing vessels and funding agricultural projects. The United States has maintained a cultural exchange program with Papua New Guinea since 1968; it opened a consulate in Port Moresby in 1974, elevating it to an embassy at independence. In 1980 Papua New Guinea and the United States agreed to introduce Peace Corps volunteers into the country.

Japan was not allowed to invest in Papua New Guinea until 1965, but by 1972 Australia had determined that its own commercial interests, which enjoyed substantial advantages and held a near monopoly on the territories' trade, would not be threatened by a Japanese presence and that indeed Japanese involvement might be very useful after independence. Consequently, Japan soon became the major source of automobiles and many electronic goods. It has also regularly purchased large quantities of copper and timber and has invested in fisheries, oil and mineral exploration, and hydroelectric projects.

Pacific Role. Papua New Guinea was an active member of the South Pacific community and considered itself an anchor to the scattered Pacific islands. It pressed the Asian Development Bank to pay greater attention to the islands and was a strong advocate of regionalism, resisting United States membership in a regional fisheries management organization. It also sought to streamline the South Pacific Commission and the South Pacific Forum by consolidating their bureaucracies. Papua New Guinea has joined its neighboring island states in consistently protesting French nuclear testing in the Pacific.

The nation recognizes a special affinity with its Melanesian neighbors, Vanuatu and Solomon Islands. The most striking demonstration of its willingness to aid these neighbors occurred in 1980, when the Papua New Guinea Defense Force intervened to put down a secessionist movement on the island of Espiritu Santo in Vanuatu at that government's request (see Vanuatu, this ch.). On July 22, 1980, a contingent of 150 soldiers, two patrol boats, and three airplanes went to Vanuatu for its Independence Day celebrations. An emergency session of the Papua New Guinea legislature approved a defense treaty between the two countries, and on August 8 another 306 troops were sent there. They remained for seven weeks until the troops quashed the revolt.

The Papua New Guinea action was largely accepted by other

countries in the area because it seemed preferable for Melanesian rather than European troops to put down disturbances in the area. The experience led Chan to suggest publicly that a regional peacekeeping force be established under an agreement among all the island governments. The other governments, however, did not respond to this idea, perhaps wary of its implications for Papua New Guinea's role in the Pacific.

Security

The Papua New Guinea Defense Force, established at independence, traced its origins to the Pacific Islands Regiment (PIR), which was formed in World War II. Australia disbanded the regiment at the end of the war but re-formed it at Port Moresby in 1951 to provide a patrol capability for the main island and the larger outlying islands. A second battalion was raised at Wewak in 1965, when Australia was involved in Indonesia's so-called Confrontation with Malaysia. Creation of a third battalion was announced in 1968, but the idea was abandoned when it became clear that the change in the Indonesian government during the 1965–66 period had made such a move unnecessary. The PIR battalions rarely operated as a whole but were deployed in small units. They had no artillery or other heavy weapons and spent most of their time engaged in civic action projects. Originally, all commissioned and noncommissioned officers were Australians. A small number of indigenous personnel began officer training in Australia in 1963, but in 1971 there were still only 30 indigenous officers. Training accelerated, however, in the mid-1970s.

After independence Australian officers remained on secondment, but in rapidly diminishing numbers, and a Papua New Guinean—Brigadier General Ted Diro—became commander. In addition to the ground component—the PIR—the defense force incorporated the Papua New Guinea Division of the Royal Australian Navy, which had been created at Manus during the 1960s. The defense force also included a small air arm established at independence when Australia transferred four transport aircraft.

The defense force was under the supervision of the National Executive Council through the minister for defense. The commander was a brigadier general, and there was no office of commander in chief. The headquarters of the defense force was located at Port Moresby. The primary mission of the defense force was to defend the nation from external attacks. Since independence it has been heavily involved in the formidable task of patrolling the border with Indonesia—a task made especially difficult by the area's rugged terrain and the defense force's limited mobility and transport capability.

As of mid-1984 the Papua New Guinea Defense Force had a total strength of 3,775. The ground element was the largest, accounting for 3,400 personnel. Equipped primarily with light infantry weapons, the ground force comprised two infantry battalions (headquartered at Port Moresby and Wewak), one signals and one engineer battalion, and miscellaneous logistics units. One forward base was maintained at Vanimo along the northern half of the border with Indonesia. A second was to be established at Kiunga in the southern border area. Kiunga was the river port for the Ok Tedi gold and copper mine. Anti-Indonesian insurgents reportedly established a major base camp in Indonesia directly opposite the mine during the early 1980s.

The air component had one transport squadron based at Lae. Its 300 personnel flew four C-47 transport aircraft and six Nomad marine reconnaissance aircraft. Other air bases were at Port Moresby, Madang, Rabaul, and Wewak. The naval component comprised one patrol squadron on Manus Island and one landing squadron at Port Moresby. It had 75 personnel and four large patrol and three landing craft. Plans released in late 1983 called for the base at Lombrum to be scaled down and the patrol squadron relocated to Port Moresby. Lombrum, along with Wewak and Kieta, would become a forward operating base.

After independence the defense relationship with Australia was informal. The two governments agreed to "consult at the request of either about matters affecting their common security" without accepting further obligations on either side. During the early 1980s Australian defense aid maintained about 120 Australian military personnel in Papua New Guinea; they helped fly aircraft, staff the logistics command, and run the signal battalion. As of 1983 Australia contributed about 43 percent of the $A37 million defense force budget.

All defense service personnel were volunteers and usually served long engagements. Military service offered pay, benefits, and prestige superior to most civilian employment; commissions were issued on merit, and competition for entry into the elite force was keen. Entry into the officer corps required a suitable level of education, which has tended to keep the less developed regions underrepresented. Enlisted personnel, however, were recruited on a nationwide basis, and the force as a whole was generally considered to be a representative one. Esprit de corps was high, and members were believed to have successfully subordinated parochial affiliations to loyalty to the defense force and the state. Officers of all three elements were trained at the Joint Services College at Lae, where many of the instructors were on loan from Australia and New Zealand. Personnel were usually sent to Australia for training in technical specialties and for higher military education.

The Royal Papua New Guinea Constabulary had its origins in the constabulary created for Papua in 1890. King George VI of Britain granted it the prefix "Royal" in 1939. Australia formed the New Guinea Police Force in 1922. After World War II the two were administered jointly, and in 1952 they were officially united. Australia neglected training police except for a paramilitary role, leaving an inadequately prepared urban police force at independence. The constabulary was estimated to have approximately 5,000 members in the early 1980s. They were organized into the Regular Police and the Field Branch. Constabulary personnel were generally paid less than those in the defense forces. The organization continued to experience problems in discipline, training, and administration.

There was a debate in official circles during 1983 over the possibility of combining the defense force with the constabulary. Proponents of such a move claimed that it would be a more cost-effective and efficient allocation of resources. Neither the defense force nor the constabulary expressed any interest in the plan, however, and nothing had been done toward that end as of mid-1984.

The nation has faced significant law and order problems since independence in both urban and rural areas. The increase in urban crime has been especially noteworthy, rising 27 percent in the 1981–82 period. Papua New Guinea had one of the highest prison populations per capita in the Asia and Pacific regions. Liquor sales in Port Moresby were banned on Fridays, Saturdays, and Sundays in an effort to control the crime problem, which has been linked to high levels of unemployment brought on by urban drift and to traditional tolerance of intergroup violence.

In rural areas the most serious threat to law and order was tribal feuding in the Highlands. Such fighting used to be kept in check by tough Australian patrol officers, but after independence most of these were replaced, and fighting became more and more frequent. Clan warfare not only involved considerable destruction of property but also resulted in numerous killings. Although such deaths were not high when compared with traffic fatalities, they were concentrated in area and disastrous to the locales affected. In July 1979 the prime minister declared a state of emergency in the Highlands, giving the police greatly expanded powers in Eastern Highlands, Western Highlands, Southern Highlands, and Chimbu provinces. These measures were relaxed some six months later as order was restored; but the underlying causes for such violence—clan rivalry, disputes over land and livestock, poverty, and unemployment—remained. After another outbreak of clan warfare in the early 1980s the National Parliament enacted legislation in 1983 to stiffen penalties for those convicted. Conviction was difficult, because participants in tribal warfare rarely testified against one another.

SOLOMON ISLANDS

Political Status	Independent state (1978)
Capital	Honiara
Population	251,000 (1984 midyear estimate)
Land Area	28,530 square kilometers
Currency	Solomon Islands dollar (SI$)
Major Islands and Island Groups	Malaita, Guadalcanal, Santa Isabel, Choiseul, Makira, New Georgia, Santa Cruz Islands, Rennell, Bellona, Russell Islands, Florida Islands, Ontong Java

Flag: Five white stars on blue field separated by yellow diagonal line from green field

Physical Environment

The country of Solomon Islands consists of a double chain of islands and island clusters stretching over 1,400 kilometers; the islands of Bougainville and Buta, at the northern end of the geographical chain, belong to Papua New Guinea (see Papua New Guinea, this ch.). The country itself has about 1.3 million square kilometers within its EEZ (see Glossary). The five largest islands make up 73 percent of the territory (see fig. 8).

All the large islands of the main chain and most of the outer islands were formed by volcanic activity, which still occurs in a few areas; the last serious eruption was on Savo Island in 1840. The mountains are generally rugged, except on Makira. Guadalcanal has extensive plains along its northern coast, but the other islands have little flat land. The river systems tend to have straight and swift courses that can flood the coastal areas during heavy rains. Rennell, the largest coral limestone island in the country, is a fine example of a raised atoll.

The climate is almost uniformly hot and wet. The southeast trade winds predominate during the driest season, from April to November, and are strongest and of the longest duration in the southern islands. The northwesterly monsoonal winds can bring stormy weather and gales from January to April. Cyclones pass through the islands but seldom cause serious damage. Rainfall averages 3,000 to 3,500 millimeters per year for the country as a whole and about 2,200 millimeters in Honiara. Temperatures average around 30°C, falling to about 25°C during the night and in the higher elevations.

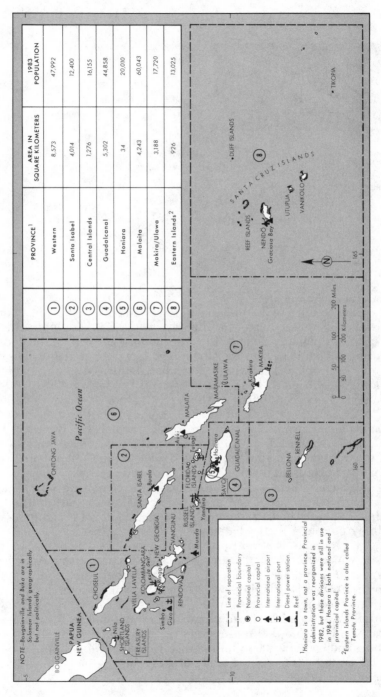

Figure 8.   Solomon Islands, 1984

PROVINCE[1]	AREA IN SQUARE KILOMETERS	1983 POPULATION
① Western	8,573	47,992
② Santa Isabel	4,014	12,400
③ Central Islands	1,276	16,155
④ Guadalcanal	5,302	44,858
⑤ Honiara	34	20,010
⑥ Malaita	4,243	60,043
⑦ Makira/Ulawa	3,188	17,720
⑧ Eastern Islands[2]	926	13,025

NOTE-*Bougainville and Buka are in Solomon Islands geographically but not politically.*

——— Line of separation
——— Provincial boundary
⊛ National capital
○ Provincial capital
✈ International airport
▲ Diesel power station.
≈ Reef

[1]Honiara is a town, not a province. Provincial administration was reorganized in 1982, but these divisions were still in use in 1984. Honiara is both national and provincial capital.

[2]Eastern Islands Province is also called Temotu Province.

Tropical forests, consisting of hardwoods, lianas, orchids, and various other epiphytes cover most of the large islands; the dense cover resembles that found in Indonesia and Papua New Guinea. Some of the forests have been destroyed by slash-and-burn farming and have been covered over with grasses. Many of the river deltas have formed mangrove swamps. The animal life is similar though less varied than that in Papua New Guinea but includes the cuscus, a monkey-like marsupial. There is a distinct break in the fauna between the main chain and the Santa Cruz group, which has fewer of the indigenous species of bats, pigs, and dogs. Insects, including the malarial mosquito, abound.

Historical Setting

Historians conjecture that hunting and gathering Papuan-speaking peoples first came to the islands about 10,300 years ago. Around 2000 B.C. neolithic peoples speaking a variety of Austronesian languages displaced or mingled with the early settlers. These peoples were skilled agriculturists who planted taro on shifting plots and raised chickens, dogs, and pigs. They were able to build sturdy outriggers to cross from Makira to the Santa Cruz group, where the Lapita pottery culture later flourished (see Prehistory, ch. 1). It is unclear when the Polynesian descendants of Lapita culture settled the outlying islands.

In 1568 Spanish explorer Álvaro de Mendaña de Neira became the first European to discover the islands, which in South America were rumored to be the legendary "Islands of Solomon." Some 25 years after his initial exploration, Mendaña returned but was unsuccessful in establishing a permanent settlement in the Santa Cruz group. A second Spanish settlement effort also failed in 1606. Except for some passes by Ontong Java, it was more than a century and a half until other Europeans rediscovered the islands; not until 1838 were they identified as those first explored by Mendaña.

The explorers who passed through the islands in the late eighteenth and early nineteenth centuries had little contact with the indigenous population, but by 1830 whalers and traders had begun to frequent the area. The first Europeans to go ashore for any length of time, however, were a group of Marist Catholic priests, who founded a mission on Makira in 1845. The mission failed after several of the priests were killed by the local population. Cautioned by this experience, the Anglican missionaries who worked out of New Zealand decided to bring some select Solomon Islanders home with them for training. The Anglican recruits returned and set up a successful mission in the Reef Islands. Despite the murder of the first Anglican bishop to the Solomon Islands, the missionary effort expanded steadily and soon incorporated other denominations.

The missionary effort was aided by the importation of Solomon Islanders to work plantations in Australia and elsewhere, a type of trade that was called blackbirding. The Solomon Islanders suffered under the trade but were exposed to European culture and religion in their new environment. Back home, blackbirding caused violent clashes between the islanders and the Europeans, although the missionaries opposed the trade. Violence and lawlessness caused Britain to establish a protectorate over the islands in 1893; Santa Isabel, Choiseul, Ontong Java, and the islands off Bougainville remained in the German sphere of influence. In 1899 an Anglo-German agreement brought these islands into the British protectorate.

The establishment of civil order and the development of a modest plantation economy characterized the efforts of the British administration up to World War II. The task was arduous, being interrupted by World War I and limited by the small number of administrators willing to take up residence in the islands. Head-hunting raids and blood feuding were endemic on New Georgia and Malaita. The last of the main islands, Choiseul, was brought under full administrative control only in 1941. The economy likewise only slowly slipped into the modern era. The government leased 78,000 hectares of land to a British copra processor, and smaller firms and individual planters began to settle the territory, though often at considerable risk.

World War II overwhelmed the Solomon Islands. The Japanese invasion, which moved as far south as Guadalcanal in 1942, destroyed not only the colonial administration but also the myth of British omnipotence (see World War II, ch. 5). Solomon Islanders distinguished themselves in service to the Allied forces—nearly all Americans—as they recaptured the islands in 1943. For many it was the first time they had been treated as equals and with dignity, and a sense of both individual pride and nationalism developed.

In the final years of the war, a populist movement swept the island of Malaita and spread elsewhere. Called the Marching Rule by the British, the movement was much more than a cargo cult (see Glossary). Its leaders organized the indigenous population into paramilitary groups and administrative organizations that simultaneously reconstructed the war-ravaged villages and opposed the reinstatement of British rule. The British acted forcefully to put down the movement when it became violent, virtually smashing it by 1950, but the trend was clear—the Solomon Islanders wanted greater responsibilities for government themselves. In 1952 the government set up local governing councils for the first time.

Political developments intensified during the 1960s, and 1970s. The colonial administration established appointive legislative and executive councils in 1960 to replace the advisory council to the government. Beginning in 1964, elected members joined the councils for the first time. In 1970 a new constitution established a single Governing Council, the majority of which was elected. In 1973 all its members became elected officials, and one year later another constitution created the Legislative Assembly and a cabinet system headed by Chief Minister Solomon Mamaloni. In 1975 the official name of the territory was changed from the British Solomon Islands Protectorate to Solomon Islands. During the next year the responsibility for internal government passed to the Legislative Assembly, and the country set out on a direct course to full independence.

In the decade preceding full independence on July 7, 1978, the pace of economic and social modernization quickened. Commercial agriculture diversified from copra into the production of palm oil, timber, and fish—usually with the aid and guidance of foreign investors. The government began to fill in some of the glaring gaps in the nation's infrastructure, building ports, roads, and telecommunications networks. Enrollment in primary education expanded rapidly; previously isolated groups became more mobile and expanded their contacts with others.

The transition to independence, however, was not altogether smooth; the nation was divided over the issue of local government. The people of the western islands, who were economically better off than the rest of the population, were especially concerned about retaining control over their resources. In fact, when Bougainville attempted to secede from Papua New Guinea in 1975, the Shortland Islands threatened a similar action against the Solomon Islands government (see Papua New Guinea, this ch.). At the constitutional conference held in London in 1977, the western islanders demanded considerable autonomy. Although still expressing some opposition because of ambiguities in the plans for provincial administration, the western islanders eventually acceded to the provisions for independence. The ceremonies proceeded as scheduled, and the country became an independent member of the Commonwealth of Nations, having an indigenous governor general appointed by the British crown.

The Social System

Solomon Islands society has been fragmented into numerous linguistic and cultural groupings since the first influx of peoples millennia ago. According to the 1976 census, about 92 percent of the population of 196,823 remained scattered in some 4,600 villages or settlements averaging about 25 inhabitants each. Melanesians, who made up 93 percent of the population according to the 1976 census, were typically fractured into small cultural and linguistic groupings, the largest of which numbered perhaps only 30,000 people. The lowest estimate suggested that there were 30 mutually unintelligible languages in use around the country; the total number of spoken dialects approached 90. The presence of Polynesian, Micronesian, European (i.e., white), Chinese, and other ethnic minorities added to the complexity of the culture. Notwithstanding this cultural diversity, historical developments have forged larger social identities centered on specific islands or regions. Christianity, education, and the growing dependency of the people on the central government for a variety of social services have also united the divergent groups. The government, moreover, has lent its support to a spontaneous cultural movement that emphasized the value of traditional customs common to the majority of groups in the society.

Social organization among the Melanesian groups varies considerably, although the extended family is the common basis for all groups. Descent lines can be patrilineal, matrilineal, or a combination of the two. The former predominates on Malaita, Guadalcanal, Makira, and Choiseul; matrilineal systems are common on Santa Isabel and in the Santa Cruz Islands. For most groups, however, land and material wealth are the major indicators of social status, which is gained through the ostentatious display of wealth in ritual feast giving. The most successful feast giver, the "big man," becomes the leader of the community or clan group by virtue of his skills rather than by hereditary ascription (see Melanesia, ch. 1). Also common to the Melanesian groups is the careful delineation of taboos and roles for each sex; the separation of the sexes, however, does not imply the subordination of one to the other.

The Polynesians, who made up 4 percent of the population according to the 1976 census, are very different from the Melanesians (see Polynesia, ch. 1). They maintain strictly patrilineal, hierarchical, and hereditary forms of social organization. The

Polynesian islands include, among others, Rennell, Ontong Java, Tikopia, Bellona, and the Reef Islands. In 1976 Micronesians constituted 1.4 percent of the population; they were mostly Gilbertese and lived in or near Honiara (see Micronesia, ch. 1; Kiribati, ch. 3). The Europeans and Chinese, making up 0.7 and 0.2 percent of the population, respectively, also lived in urban Honiara, although a number of European and Part European plantation owners lived in Central Islands Province. Small minorities of indigenous Papuan-speaking people lived in the Russell, Santa Cruz, and New Georgia island groups.

Traditional custom, called *kastom* in the Pidgin English that serves as the lingua franca throughout the islands, has become a rallying cry for many of the indigenous groups and for the government. The ideology of *kastom* first expressed itself coherently during the Marching Rule period but persisted after the nation's independence. As anthropologist Roger M. Keesing has described it, *kastom* is an all-purpose ideology that means different things to different groups or individuals. For some, such as the non-Christianized Kwaio of Malaita, *kastom* has been a potent political symbol in their resistance to the incursions of the Western religious and economic ideologies propagated by the government. For others it has represented a synthesis of traditional and modern systems of thought and behavior. The national political elite—mostly Christian and Western-educated—have used *kastom* as a symbol of national identity and as a way to legitimize themselves to the common epople. Many have justified their preferences for various systems of law, local government, and land tenure on the basis of *kastom*, which retained its popularity precisely because of its nebulousness.

Religion is a unifying force in the society; more than 95 percent of the population was estimated to be Christian in mid-1980. There were, however, inevitable rivalries between the denominations. About a third of the population belonged to the Anglican Diocese of Melanesia, and another 19 pecent were Roman Catholic. The South Sea Evangelical Church, which originated in the community of Solomon Islanders working on plantations in Australia in the nineteenth century, attracted about 17 percent of the population, chiefly in the eastern and southern islands. The United Church, a union of Methodists and Congregationalists, served 11 percent of the population, particularly in Western Province. Seventh-Day Adventists made up one-tenth of the population, while indigenous and marginal Protestant churches, such as the Jehovah's Witnesses, constituted the rest of the Christian community. Only 4 percent of the population might be called tribal religionists, including those affiliated with so-called cargo cults.

Education, a major force behind the modernization and unification of the society, began under the pioneering efforts of the Anglican and Roman Catholic missionaries. In 1980 about 19 percent of the primary schools and 29 percent of the secondary schools were still affiliated with churches. Some 300 primary schools were run by local councils, and in 1983 about 65 percent of the children at primary-school age were enrolled. The World Bank (see Glossary) extended the government a US$10 million loan in 1983 to build 300 rural primary-school classrooms by 1989 in order to raise enrollments to 85 percent of the relevant age-group. One study conducted in the early 1980s showed that about 30 percent of the 1,000 primary-school teachers were untrained and another 20 percent had received minimal training; a teachers college in Honiara trained about 100 teachers in 1977. Eleven provincial schools specializing in practical studies and six national schools having academic curricula served 35 percent of the relevant age-group in 1983. Only two of the academic schools were in rural areas; the rest were in or near Honiara. The small Honiara campus of the University of the South Pacific offered courses in education, culture, finance, administration, industrial development, natural resource management, nursing, paramedical skills, and fishing. The government, which had devoted 11 percent of its budget to education during the 1980–83 period, planned to invest 15 percent of its budgetary resources in this area in 1984. The adult literacy rate in 1976 was only 13 percent.

The development of modern health and other social services has also emanated from the central government and the churches. The Ministry of Health and Welfare ran one major hospital in the capital and five less-developed provincial hospitals in 1980. Provincial authorities operated about 100 clinics. There were some 50 rural health centers and village aid posts; two hospitals and 23 clinics were affiliated with churches. In 1980 there were about 6,250 people per physician, and in 1976 the average life expectancy was 54 years. Endemic diseases included malaria, tuberculosis, and leprosy; in 1981 there were over 61,000 cases of malaria—more than double the number two years earlier. Diseases related to sanitation and hygiene were also common. About 70 percent of all rural households did not have access to safe water in the early 1980s, and three-quarters had unsanitary latrine facilities. In 1978 the government launched a 12-year program to provide safe water to 2,500 villages and build 50,000 sanitary latrines.

Village on Guadalcanal
Courtesy Steven R. Pruett

The improvements in health care and economic development have resulted in changes that have significantly affected the
society. Transportation development has increased the interaction between previously isolated cultural groups. Schools, plantations, and business establishments were replacing the family as
focal points of social interaction. Modern kinds of employment
were replacing traditional arts and handicrafts. Changing social
mores have resulted in some problems, such as alcoholism, violent crime, and pregnancy out of wedlock, that could not be resolved by traditional means. Population growth per se was not a
problem because land was readily available, but migration to
Honiara in particular was overwhelming the capacity of the capital to provide the necessary services. The growing youthfulness of
the population—about 65 percent of the total was between the
ages of six and 16 in 1983—and its rising level of education made it
imperative for the society to generate new employment opportunities.

The Economy

The large subsistence sector, which accounted for over 40 percent of GDP in 1982, complicated macroeconomic analysis of the economy. A rough estimate suggested that the GDP was equivalent to US$560 per person in 1982, but about 90 percent of the population engaged in commercial activities only as sidelines to subsistence agriculture. The economy, however, remained open to foreign trade and investment as a means of spurring commercial development, producing copra, palm oil, cacao, timber and fish for export. Small farmers made significant contributions to the production of copra; foreign companies, acting singly or in joint venture with the government, accounted for the bulk of commercial wealth.

During the 1970s increased exports of timber, fish, and palm oil propelled the economy to grow by about 8 percent per year on average. Food production also increased markedly; domestic supplies rose by nearly 25 percent during the decade—well ahead of the population. In the 1980s, however, growth slowed considerably, and in 1980 and 1982 the real value of GDP actually decreased. The decline resulted from a deterioration in the terms of trade—the ratio of export to import prices—which fell by 40 percent from 1980 to 1982. The nation's current account balance likewise deteriorated from a surplus equivalent to 6 percent of GDP in 1979 to a deficit equivalent to 27 percent of GDP in 1981. Inflation averaged 15 percent per year during the 1980–81 period. The declining profitability of most enterprises caused a drop in private investment that threatened the long-term prospects for economic development.

In response to the economic recession, the government devalued the currency by 10 percent in August 1982, increased duties on imports, and improved its tax collection efforts to promote exports, reduce imports, and raise domestic resources for investment. It concluded an agreement with the IMF in mid-1983 that authorized the withdrawal of US$2.7 million over a 12-month period to support the balance of payments. In return for this loan, the government agreed to keep its overall budget deficit under 10 percent of GDP in 1983, restrain operating expenditures—chiefly civil service wages—while speeding up public investment, maintain a flexible exchange rate, and raise interest rates on bank deposits. The effect of these measures, along with improvements in the international economy, was to reduce the current account deficit to about 6 percent of GDP in 1983 and lower inflation to about 10 percent or less.

The government's economic goals have been to promote growth, improve rural living standards, expand job opportunities for the rapidly increasing labor force, and encourage self-reliance by diversifying the economy. In order to accomplish these objectives, the government increased its capital expenditures from around 8.5 percent of GDP in 1971 to nearly 12 percent of GDP in 1982. Since the mid-1970s more and more public investment has been directed toward developing the agricultural and industrial sectors, although spending on infrastructure remained the largest single category of investment. The government has also tried to localize employment as much as possible, but the shortage of trained labor—perhaps the greatest impediment to the economy's development—has slowed its efforts. In 1982 about 4.7 percent of the commercial labor force of 22,000 were noncitizens, compared with 5.6 percent in 1978. The government's attempts to improve social welfare included establishing minimum wages and safety standards in all commercial enterprises, requiring contributions to a national provident fund, and devoting some 35 percent of its central government expenditures since 1980 to health, social welfare, education, housing, and community development.

The government has also made some important institutional changes, especially in the financial sector. The Solomon Islands Monetary Authority was renamed the Central Bank in 1981, and the bank began to manage the money supply more actively by issuing treasury bills, lending to the three commercial banks, and establishing guidelines for commercial loans. The government also invested in a joint venture with an Australian bank to create the National Bank of the Solomon Islands, which it hoped would expand savings in the rural areas. One year after its establishment, this new venture had nearly doubled its branch offices to 21 and had put into operation four mobile units on ships. Partly as a result of these institutional changes, gross domestic savings rose from a low of 5.5 percent of GDP in 1981 to over 10 percent in 1983.

Overall, however, the economy was dependent on foreign aid and loans to make up the difference between imports and exports and promote investment. Grant assistance from overseas doubled from an average of 8 percent of GDP during the 1978–82 period to 16 percent of established GDP in 1983. The latter figure, however, was based upon commitments rather than actual disbursements, which have often been held up because of administrative delays in Solomon Islands. Bilateral commitments— nearly all from Britain and Australia—reached SI$12.5 million

Table 4. *Solomon Islands. Composition of Trade, 1980–82* (in millions of Solomon Islands dollars)[1]

Commodity	1980	1981	1982
Exports			
Fish[2]	23.2	22.0	14.0
Timber logs	14.9	14.7	21.4
Sawed timber	1.1	1.3	1.5
Copra	10.5	8.1	8.1
Palm oil[3]	7.1	7.5	7.3
Rice	1.5	0.9	0.9
Cacao	0.6	0.9	0.9
Gold	0.6	0.5	0.5
Shells	0.3	0.4	0.3
Tobacco products	0.1	0.1	0.1
Reexports	0.6	0.8	1.2
Other	0.3	0.4	0.5
Total exports[4]	60.8	57.6	56.6
Imports			
Minerals, fuels, and lubricants	9.9	15.2	14.4
Machinery and transport equipment	24.0	19.3	13.3
Manufactured goods	14.9	17.1	14.0
Food	6.6	7.0	8.5
Chemicals	3.2	3.8	3.6
Beverages and tobacco	1.9	2.3	2.1
Crude materials	0.8	0.9	1.2
Other	0.2	0.3	0.2
Total imports[4]	61.5	66.0	57.4

[1]For value of the Solomon Islands dollar—see Glossary; based on free on board (f.o.b.) prices.
[2]Includes fresh, frozen, and canned items.
[3]Includes palm kernels.
[4]Figures may not add to total because of rounding.
Source: Based on information from Solomon Islands, Ministry of Finance, Statistics Office, *Statistical Bulletin*, No. 5/83, Honiara, 1983.

(for value of the Solomon Islands dollar—see Glossary) in 1983. Multilateral assistance—chiefly from the European Development Fund of the European Economic Community (EEC)—rose even more substantially to SI$15.2 million in 1983. At the same time, outstanding foreign loans to the government rose from less than 1 percent of GDP in 1978 to more than 17 percent of GDP by the end of 1982. Because many of the loans were calculated at concessional rates of interest, repayments were estimated to be less than 3 percent of the value of exports in 1983—low by international standards.

The structure of foreign trade basically reflected that of the economy as a whole. Exports of copra, timber, and other crude materials represented over 56 percent of the total value of exports in 1982, palm oil another 13 percent, and edible agricultural products most of the remainder. Imports were chiefly manufac-

Table 5.   *Solomon Islands. Direction of Trade, 1980–82[1]*
(in percentage)

Country	Exports			Imports		
	1980	1981	1982	1980	1981	1982
Oceania						
American Samoa	5.9	1.3	1.1	---	---	---
Australia	2.3	3.1	2.7	30.9	28.0	33.9
New Zealand	1.0	1.6	2.2	7.0	8.6	8.3
Papua New Guinea	0.4	0.8	0.7	5.4	4.1	2.1
Other	3.6	0.9	2.2	0.5	0.6	2.1
Total Oceania	13.2	7.7	8.9	43.8	41.3	46.4
Asia						
Japan	26.3	37.4	58.6	19.7	14.9	14.0
Singapore	1.4	0.7	0.4	14.7	22.1	17.6
China	---	---	---	2.5	2.5	3.3
Hong Kong	0.1	---	---	2.9	2.5	3.1
Other	0.7	1.4	2.8	1.3	1.2	1.8
Total Asia	28.4	39.5	61.8	41.1	43.2	39.8
EEC[2]						
Britain	12.7	11.9	14.4	8.6	8.1	4.4
Netherlands	12.6	11.9	3.6	---	---	0.2
West Germany	5.8	4.9	1.8	1.2	1.0	1.7
France	---	---	---	0.1	0.1	0.1
Other	---	---	2.4	0.4	0.7	0.5
Total EEC	31.1	28.7	22.2	10.3	9.9	6.9
United States	20.5	22.7	0.1	3.2	4.0	5.6
Other	0.7	1.4	7.0	0.6	1.9	1.6
TOTAL[3]	100.0	100.0	100.0	100.0	100.0	100.0

--- means none or negligible.
[1]Based on free on board (f.o.b.) prices.
[2]European Economic Community.
[3]Figures may not add to total because of rounding.
Source: Based on information from Solomon Islands, Ministry of Finance, Statistics Office, *Statistical Bulletin*, No. 5/83, Honiara, 1983.

tured goods and petroleum (see table 4). The major export markets were Japan, and Britain and the rest of the EEC; the principal sources of imports were Australia, Singapore, Japan, and the EEC (see table 5). Government policy toward foreign investment seemed ambivalent, simultaneously encouraging investment and expressing concern about its effect on local development.

Agriculture, Forestry, and Fishing

Reliable statistics on land use were unavailable, but estimates suggested that the smallholder sector had about 7,000 hectares of gardens and 38,000 hectares of coconut trees in 1983. There were more than 19,000 hectares of commercial coconut, cacao, oil palm, and rice plantations. The rest of the land area was under varying degrees of forest cover. The garden plots, which averaged from 0.15 to 0.25 hectares, were managed by means of shifting cultivation. Coconut plots averaged another 1.1 to 2 hectares. Shifting cultivation and permanent agriculture encroached on the forested land at a rate of from 20,000 to 40,000 hectares per year; not all of the newly cultivated lands were in the lowland areas favored by the government for agricultural development.

The system of land tenure made it difficult for the government to regulate the pattern of land development. About 87 percent of the territory in 1980 was so-called customary land under the management of traditional groups. The land could not be sold and could be leased only after being registered with the government. The government has acquired about 9 percent of the land, about one-fifth of which it leased to foreigners for periods of up to 75 years. The remainder consisted of perpetual estates owned by Solomon Islanders. Altogether, foreign residents leased some 2 percent of the land, chiefly in Western, Central Islands, and Guadalcanal provinces. The Constitution stipulates that the compulsory acquisition of customary land can proceed only after negotiations with the traditional owners.

Smallholder farms produced traditional subsistence commodities, such as taro, yams, garden vegetables, and pigs. A survey in the mid-1970s found that only 7 percent of the rural population had received cash income of any kind in the preceding year. Rural household incomes, including subsistence production, were estimated to be one-half of those in the urban areas; their relative size has probably shrunk further in the 1980s. Increasing population pressure and the growing need for cash income have tended to shorten the length of the shifting cultivation cycle from the previous average of 15 to 20 years. In the most populous areas there has been some continuous farming. As the fallow period has shortened and the level of technology remained the same, the soil has been depleted. The government initiated a project in 1983 that would set up one rural development center in each of the seven provinces, improve transportation and marketing in the rural areas, and expand agricultural extension and research. The low level of literacy and dispersed nature of rural communities made this a difficult program to implement.

Cash incomes were derived chiefly from the sale of copra to the government marketing board or private agents. Commercial production from smallholder farms reached a record 24,000 tons in 1981 but fell to 22,000 tons in 1982 and 18,000 tons in 1983. In 1981 about 39 percent of smallholder production came from Western Province, more than 19 percent from Malaita Province, some 18 percent from Guadalcanal Province, and the rest in smaller proportions from the other provinces.

In many areas, young men have left the traditional farm to work, at least temporarily, on plantations. Plantations produced about 10,000 tons of copra yearly; most of the output came from foreign-controlled farms in Central Islands Province. A British plantation company introduced oil palm into the Guadalcanal plains in the 1960s and by 1980 had developed some 3,300 hectares of palms. The affiliated palm oil mill produced almost 19,000 tons of oil in 1982—nearly 80 percent more than in 1980. Most of the increase resulted from the introduction of pollinating weevils from Southeast Asia in 1981. Because many of the palms were past their prime, the company intended to replant many of its holdings in the 1986–87 period, when production was liable to decline. Copra and oil palm products represented about 27 percent of the nation's merchandise exports in 1982.

Rice was also grown commercially; originally it was exported to Fiji, but because of rising costs it was consumed locally in the 1980s. The area harvested decreased from nearly 4,000 hectares in 1980 to about 1,000 hectares in 1983; production was over 14,000 tons in 1980. One commercial crop that has shown rapid expansion was cacao; about 350 tons were produced for export in 1980. Small quantities of tobacco were also produced commercially.

Cattle raising has received much attention from both the commercial and the subsistence sectors. Britain, New Zealand, and Australia have all provided funds to import select varieties, and the total cattle stock was around 24,000 head in 1982. As late as 1980, however, some 10,000 head were located on foreign-owned plantations and church-mission properties.

Forestry has become the leading industry in the country, producing 40 percent of the value of merchandise exports in 1982. About a dozen, mostly foreign-owned, companies have worked the 215,000 hectares of commercial forest owned by the government; in 1981 there were about 160,000 hectares left, having some 9 to 10 million cubic meters of tropical hardwood timber. The logging rate rose from about 300,000 cubic meters in 1980 to 425,000 cubic meters in 1982. Some 16 other foreign companies had placed applications with the government in 1983 to open up another million hectares of primarily customary land. The Forestry Department wanted to confine their activities to the intermediate mountain slopes—permanently reserving the high mountain forests—and keep their activities at levels amenable to reforestation. Because of the lack of staff and adequate legislation, however, the forestry companies have been allowed to extract timber almost at will.

Replanting, which was not required of the logging companies, covered only 800 hectares in 1982, compared with what the government estimated to be the optimal rate of 2,000 to 2,500 hectares yearly. Forestry officials have drawn up management plans but had no control over the management of customary lands. Although detailed surveys of the forests could raise the ecologically sound limits for forestry production—one foreign company estimated that there were 3 million cubic meters of exploitable reserves on Guadalcanal alone—scientists have cautioned that unless reforestation efforts are increased, the nation could become a net importer of timber in 15 to 20 years. The most difficult management problem concerned shifting cultivation and fuelwood gathering, which, some research suggests, has had worse effects than logging operations on forest degradation. Areas of Malaita were already experiencing fuelwood shortages. The government was planting fast-growing softwood species on an experimental basis for fuel and construction material in these areas.

Commercial fishing, which accounted for about 27 percent of the value of merchandise exports in 1982, has developed rapidly since the early 1970s. For more than a decade the government has participated in a successful joint venture with a Japanese company that landed significant quantities of skipjack tuna—about 18,000 tons in 1978. The Asian Development Bank helped the government finance a state-owned fleet in 1978. A modern replacement for the nation's cannery was expected to reach full production by 1985.

Coastal fishing, which was important for the subsistence economy, has not kept pace with the growing population. The use of modern nets, motorized boats, and fiberglass canoes has improved production but has also depleted some of the reef fisheries. Fishery management has therefore become a priority for future development. The country has also needed to improve its storage, transportation, marketing, and processing facilities to serve the inland population.

Industry and Services

The country's mineral resources have yet to be explored adequately. Alluvial deposits of gold totaling perhaps 311 kilograms have been located in north-central Guadalcanal; gold panners extracted from 12 to 22 kilograms of gold and two to three kilograms of associated silver each year. A foreign firm made an agreement with the government in 1983 to explore underground deposits of over 30 square kilometers in the mountains of this area in hopes of establishing a modest open-cut mine by 1987. Low-grade nickel, copper, and manganese deposits have been found on a number of islands, especially on Santa Isabel and in the Florida Islands. The small mines that have been set up in these areas have all failed. Some mining companies, however, believed that copper could be a major resource in the future. The most hopeful prospects were for some 55 million tons of bauxite reserves located on Rennell and a nearby island. The government has acquired rights to the land from the customary owners after lengthy negotiations, but the foreign firms involved have refused to establish a commercial venture until the serious shakeout in the world aluminum industry ended—perhaps in a decade or more.

The nation's energy resources were likewise undeveloped. During the 1969–72 period a few foreign oil companies conducted some 13,000 kilometers of offshore surveys, and during the 1978–82 period two aid teams conducted another 8,000 kilometers of surveys. No deposits have been found, however, although promising formations have been located in the New Georgia Sound and off the northern coast of Guadalcanal. The country's efforts to find oil were hampered by the lack of legislation concerning royalties and joint-venture arrangements; the legislature was considering a draft bill in 1983 that still failed to be explicit in its terms. The nation had excellent potential for geothermal energy at four fields on Vella Lavella, Simbo, Savo, and in western Guadalcanal, but the development costs would probably be prohibitive until the next century. Except for a site on the Lungga River near Honiara, hydroelectric resources were unresearched. The Lungga site was in the early stages of development, but the economical size of the project—about 21 megawatts—would produce more than twice the demand estimated for Honiara in the year 2000. Total energy production was difficult to estimate because some 44 percent came from fuelwood burned in the rural areas and another 25 percent from agricultural waste burned on the plantations. Petroleum imports accounted for the remainder of commercial energy produced, including the 19 million kilowatt-hours of electricity generated by the state-owned electrical authority in 1981.

Transportation services were developed chiefly in the urban areas of Honiara, Auki, and Gizo, which together had about 100 kilometers of asphalt roads. The remaining 370 kilometers of main roads were surfaced with gravel or coral; in 1980 there were some 1,200 kilometers of secondary roads. There were 2,550 registered motor vehicles that year. Near Honiara the principal airport was able to handle aircraft as large as the Boeing 737; Munda could handle turboprop aircraft. There were 18 other airfields around the country serving smaller planes. Solomon Islands Airways operated six small and one large propeller aircraft in 1981, but foreign airlines carried nearly all the international traffic. The two ports of entry were at Honiara and at Yandina on Russell Island. Honiara had two wharves capable of berthing vessels up to 198 meters long and having less than a 9.1-meter draft. International ships sometimes put in at smaller ports. Interisland shipping services, which were probably the most important means of domestic transportation, were provided by 34 government-owned and 106 other vessels in 1981.

Communications services were developing rapidly, but in the early 1980s only the three urban centers had telephone exchanges. There were some 2,500 telephones in service in 1980. Honiara alone ·was connected to the international communications network via satellite. Rural areas were linked only through radio communications. The Solomon Islands Broadcasting Corporation, an autonomous government body, transmitted 118 hours of programs each week from Honiara and Gizo. An Australian aid program was expanding the number of studios and broadcasting range. There were seven general post offices and some 80 postal agencies scattered around the country in 1980; mail normally traveled by air.

Manufacturing was still in its infancy and confined primarily to the processing of commercial agricultural products. In the early 1980s the major manufactures were palm oil, milled rice, canned fish, furniture, processed food, small boats, detergents, tobacco products, and batteries.

Tourist arrivals increased by over 15 percent per year from 1971 to more than 7,000 visitors in 1980. About 38 percent of these were from Australia; Papua New Guinea, the United States, and New Zealand each contributed about 4 percent of the visitors. The government-run Solomon Islands Tourist Authority was actively promoting the attractions of the country's scenery and

Development project outside of Honiara
Courtesy Steven R. Pruett

friendly people.

Local commerce was dominated by cooperatives in the rural areas. In 1979 there were 238 primary and five secondary cooperatives marketing agricultural products and consumer goods and having a membership of some 16,000 households. A few of the cooperatives were credit unions. Many rural households, however, still engaged in barter trade as the primary means of exchange; some even continued to use traditional currencies made of feathers or shells. Private companies were located in the urban areas; in 1978 there were 206 companies, of which 49 were incorporated overseas—the majority in Australia.

The Political System and Security

The Constitution, contained in the independence orders issued in 1978, affirms that the basic rights and freedoms of the individual are inalienable—including life, liberty, and privacy. Articles dealing with these fundamental human rights, the legal system, parliamentary elections, and the positions of auditor general and ombudsman may be amended only with the assent of three-quarters of the Legislative Assembly; other articles may be changed with a two-thirds majority.

The titular head of state is the British sovereign, represented by the governor general, a Solomon Islander who is appointed upon the recommendation of the Legislative Assembly. The head of government is the prime minister, who is elected by a majority of the parliament from among its own members. The prime minister and cabinet may be removed by a vote of no confidence or must stand for reelection after the normal four-year term of parliament ends. Parliament is a legislative body of not fewer than 30 and not more than 50 members elected from single-member constituencies by all individuals over the age of 18. Since 1976 there have been 38 constituencies.

Local government organization has been in a constant state of flux. Seven local assemblies and one town council for Honiara were retained as part of a provincial government structure after independence. The inhabitants of the eight areas had developed loyalty to these institutions. In 1982, however, the Mamaloni government transferred some 500 civil servants and about 23 percent of the central government budget to five provincial administrations that merged Santa Isabel Province into Central Islands Province and consolidated Makira/Ulawa and Eastern Islands provinces into one administration called Makula/Temotu Province. Each provincial government was headed by a cabinet minister. The Honiara town council, after mismanaging some government funds, lost many of its budgetary powers to Guadalcanal Province. As far as could be learned in mid-1984, however, the eight original councils were still in existence.

The legal system is headed by the High Court, which is presided over by a resident chief justice assisted by visiting judges from Papua New Guinea, Australia, and elsewhere as necessary. The chief justice also heads the Court of Appeal. Magistrate's courts, presided over by trained resident magistrates or sometimes lay judges, have limited jurisdiction over criminal and civil cases at the local level. Local courts run by elders of the community hear cases involving petty crime and civil suits, traditional law, and local government. In 1975 the government set up customary and appeal courts to handle appeals from these local courts. The judiciary is independent of the executive government. In 1983 the High Court ruled in favor of a claim by the parliamentary opposition that the pardoning of a former cabinet minister convicted on assault charges had been unconstitutional.

Domestic Politics and Internal Security
 Solomon Islands politicians have been the first to admit that
much of the nation's politics consisted of intense personal infight-
ing over the spoils and perquisites of power. The most critical of
the country's young leaders, however, remained hopeful that responsible and responsive politicians would make up the majority
in time. One influential labor leader noted that Solomon
Islanders tended to vote as individuals, not as party members,
and have voted for independent candidates as often as not. The
freedom that has characterized electoral and parliamentary politics also boded well for the future of the political system.
 In early 1984 the government consisted of a shaky coalition of
two political parties and independent members of parliament
forged in mid-1981. In the 1980 national elections, the first since
the country's independence, Peter Kenilorea's Solomon Islands
United Party (SIUPA) won 16 seats, compared with only 10 seats
won by Solomon Mamaloni's People's Alliance Party (PAP). In
August 1981, however, PAP joined hands with the two parliamentary representatives of the National Democratic Party
(NADEPA) and nine of the remaining independents to form a
new governing coalition under Mamaloni's leadership. The
Mamaloni group presented a so-called program of action promising to create a federated republic, devolve important responsibilities to the provinces, establish an alliance of Melanesian
states, expand the country's defense forces, reorganize the government's holdings in the national airline, create a central bank,
begin a national lottery, and establish diplomatic relations with
China.
 PAP and SIUPA were not ideological parties. The former was
a merger of two parties, one of which was associated with Mamaloni, who had left politics for business in 1976 but returned in
1979 to launch the merger and get himself back into parliament.
SIUPA was formed only in 1979, when Kenilorea who had been
catapulted directly into office by independent members of the
parliament at independence, prepared for reelection. NADEPA
was a more ideological party, formed in 1976 as the political arm of
the nation's largest labor union, which was considered "left-wing"
because of its affiliation with a Moscow-led international labor
federation. The head of NADEPA, Bartholomew Ulufa'alu, has
nonetheless surprised the business community with his pragmatism and integrity as finance minister since 1981. Most of the
parliamentarians, according to one influential labor leader, could
easily be affiliated with any political party. Over 60 percent of the

parliamentarians failed to regain their seats in the 1980 elections.

The year 1983 was a difficult one for the Mamaloni coalition. The prime minister sacked two cabinet ministers in April, ostensibly for refusing to change portfolios but also because they were in trouble with the law. In June he dismissed the minister of police, and Mamaloni's edge in parliament narrowed. He escaped a vote of no confidence in July, however, when one of his former cabinet ministers withdrew the motion for lack of support. A cabinet shake-up in early 1984 was perhaps in preparation for the parliamentary elections required in 1985.

The labor unions were probably the most active political interest groups in the country. The Solomon Islands National Union of Workers (SINUW) was the largest, claiming some 10,000 of the paid work force of only 22,000 or so in 1983. Its leader, Joses Tahanuku, and his associate, Ulufa'alu, founded the organization in 1976, and since then both men have traveled to Moscow to participate in forums held by the communist-affiliated World Federation of Trade Unions. Neither man considered himself to be a communist. During the first two years of its existence, SINUW initiated a number of strikes and job actions to prove that it means business; such actions are perfectly legal under the constitution. It has been particularly active in the plantation sector. SINUW has steadfastly refused to join in a tripartite forum with the government and business leaders to set basic wages and work guidelines. Since 1981, however, three-person panels that included one representative from each of the interested parties have been set up to handle individual disputes. The second largest union in the country was the Public Employees Union, which had about 2,000 members. There were 14 other smaller unions.

Internal security has not been threatened by such actions as strikes or political protests. The most common security problems were individual crimes, such as assault and thievery. The police force was extremely small for a nation as spread out as Solomon Islands. In 1980 there were only 16 senior officers, 19 inspectors, and 388 other ranks; in 1984 the staff was estimated to number around 500. Police headquarters was located in Honiara, and there were 18 other stations around the country.

Foreign Relations and National Security

The primary aim of Solomon Islands foreign policy has been to secure friendly relations with its major trading partners and aid donors, with other Pacific island states—especially its Melanesian neighbors—and with developing countries of the world in general. It has been neutral with respect to the world's superpowers. The government has talked about diversifying its relationships as much as possible, suggesting that it might open relations with communist countries, but its actions have run counter to this purpose. In general, the nation's interests were most closely intertwined with those of the noncommunist countries. As the prime minister said in a speech in 1983, "Solomon Islands people do not accept communism because they wish to enjoy the freedom of democracy and the traditional values they have survived under for many years." Therefore, the government "has established diplomatic relations only with countries who have shared the same democratic relations."

Britain, Australia, New Zealand, and Japan were by far the most important trading partners and aid donors. Britain agreed that it would provide direct budgetary assistance through 1982. Although that has tapered off, Britain committed some 38 percent of the bilateral grants pledged in 1983. In addition, Solomon Islands had accumulated SI$1.3 million of outstanding interest-free loans from Britain by the end of 1982. By virtue of its relationship with Britain, the country received special export arrangements and financial support from the EEC under the terms of the Lomé Convention.

Australia had become the largest bilateral aid donor by 1983, committing 58 percent of the total. In mid-1983 it pledged SI$30 million for a five-year period beginning in July, but the Solomon Islands government was unhappy about the level of assistance, which it felt to be far short of the aid granted to other Oceania countries. Bilateral trade decreased somewhat in the 1970s to about 34 percent of imports and 3 percent of exports in 1982, despite the SPARTECA arrangement. Australia also provided some SI$4 million in defense-cooperation aid in 1983—on a per capita basis, the highest granted by Australia to any country in Oceania.

Japan has been the country's largest export market because of its need for timber and fish. About 2 percent of bilateral assistance came from Japan in 1983. In addition to cooperating in a fishing joint venture, the Solomon Islands government has allowed Japanese tuna boats to work grounds beyond the nation's territorial sea but within its EEZ. In return, the Japanese companies have conducted research on the fishing stock and provided other goods and services.

New Zealand's bilateral aid commitments have been a modest 1 percent of the total, but the nation has also offered to train Solomon Islander medical personnel for free. New Zealand military engineers provided some services to the country in 1981.

Solomon Islands maintained friendly relations with the other areas of Oceania. It supported the initiatives of the South Pacific Forum to establish a nuclear-free zone in the Pacific and to bring independence to New Caledonia. The country did, however, pull out of the Forum Shipping Line in 1983 because of the financial costs and limited benefits for Solomon Islands. Relations with the other Melanesian states were especially close, and the government has called for the creation of a Melanesian alliance—excluding Fiji—that would cooperate in endeavors such as patrolling their combined EEZs. Vanuatu has proposed a similar subregional organization, but Papua New Guinea was apparently not favorably disposed toward the proposal.

Relations with Asian countries were improving, the major exception being China. In 1983 the government established diplomatic relations with Indonesia and recognized that country's control over East Timor, a move that angered the NADEPA members of the ruling coalition. Consular relations were also established with Taiwan, which provided some fisheries and agricultural aid to the country and was a minor trading partner. China was upset at the government's links to Taiwan but has continued plans to aid in the construction of a sports arena in Solomon Islands. It would not, however, agree to open formal relations with Solomon Islands until the open links with Taiwan were severed. Singapore and the Republic of Korea (South Korea) were significant trading partners, and a South Korean company has been active in the forestry industry.

In early 1984 the nation's antinuclear policy marred its generally friendly relations with the United States. After unionized dockworkers refused to service a visiting United States naval vessel in February, the government announced that any ship making port calls or even transiting its extensive territorial seas would have to give a written pledge that it was neither nuclear-powered nor carried nuclear weapons. The United States has refused to do this as a matter of policy. As of mid-1984 it was unclear how firmly the Solomon Islands government would apply its policy.

The Soviet Union did not have diplomatic relations with Solomon Islands. After coming to power in 1981, Mamaloni mentioned diversifying the nation's sources of aid, possibly to the Soviet Union, Cuba, and Libya. As of early 1984, however, the government had not moved to woo such countries as these.

Solomon Islands belonged to a number of international organizations. It set up a permanent mission to the UN in late 1983 in an office provided by Australia to a number of the smaller

Pacific states. In a speech before the General Assembly, Mamaloni requested that the organization should make it easier for poorer nations to maintain permanent representation. Over one-third of the government's outstanding debt at the end of 1982 was borrowed from international organizations of which it was a member—chiefly the Asian Development Bank, but also the IMF and World Bank. Another 8 percent of the debt was from the European Development Fund of the EEC, of which the country was an associate member.

The nation perceived no external threat to its security in 1984 and had no armed forces other than the police. One unit of the police force, however, has been chosen as the nucleus for a specialized external defense force; it consisted of about 50 men and was attached to the Prime Minister's Office. It was unclear whether this new unit would take over the management of the country's only coastal patrol boat. A new boat was being requested from Australia, and the government was moving ahead with plans to purchase two craft from Taiwan and to build one of its own.

VANUATU

Official Name	Republic of Vanuatu
Previous Name	New Hebrides
Political Status	Independent state (1980)
Capital	Port-Vila
Population	132,000 (1984 midyear estimate)
Land Area	12,000 square kilometers
Currency	Vanuatu vatu (VT)
Major Islands and Island Groups	Espiritu Santo, Malakula, Efate, Pentecost, Ambrym, Erromango, Tanna, Aoba, Maewo, Banks Islands, Torres Islands

Flag: Yellow pig tusk curved around crossed palm fronds in black triangle on left with horizontal yellow "Y" bordered in black separating red-brown upper field and green lower field

Physical Environment

Vanuatu consists of some 80 islands and islets located between Solomon Islands in the north and New Caledonia in the south and scattered in the pattern of a broken "Y" (see fig. 9). The two largest islands, Espiritu Santo (or just Santo) and Malakula, account for nearly half of the total land area. They are volcanic islands and have terrain marked by sharp mountain peaks, plateaus, and lowlands. The larger of the other islands are also of volcanic origin but are often overlaid with limestone formations. The smaller islands are coral and limestone, but the only purely coral atoll of significance is Rowa in the Banks Islands. What coastal plains do exist on the volcanic islands are narrow. Volcanism still causes minor earthquakes, and one of the few active volcanoes last erupted in 1945.

Southeast trade winds prevail throughout the year but sometimes give way to short periods of calm, which from November to April can be accompanied by moist northerly or easterly winds. Hurricanes strike during the January to April period. The temperature averages around 26°C on Espiritu Santo, about 24°C on Efate, and 23°C on Tanna. The southernmost islands can cool significantly in winter, which runs from June to September. Rainfall averages about 2,360 millimeters per year but can be as high as 4,000 millimeters in the northern islands.

The flora consists primarily of rain forest, coconut palms, garden plots, and scrub. The indigenous fauna are mostly pigeons,

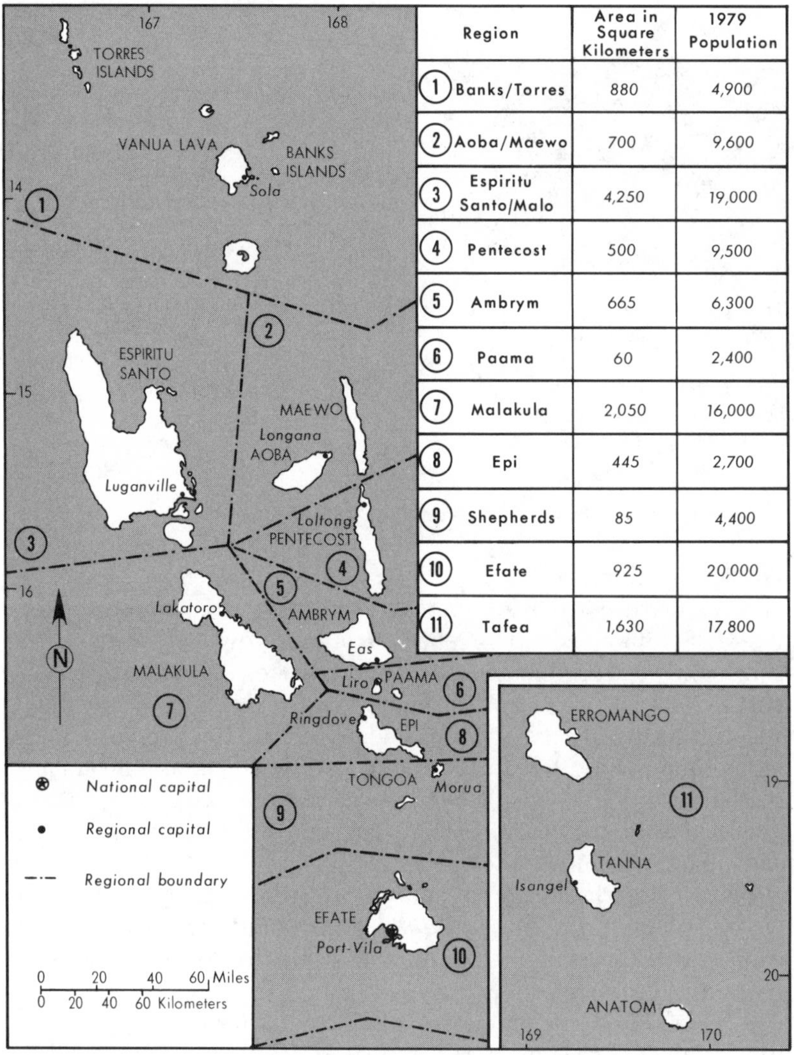

Region		Area in Square Kilometers	1979 Population
(1)	Banks/Torres	880	4,900
(2)	Aoba/Maewo	700	9,600
(3)	Espiritu Santo/Malo	4,250	19,000
(4)	Pentecost	500	9,500
(5)	Ambrym	665	6,300
(6)	Paama	60	2,400
(7)	Malakula	2,050	16,000
(8)	Epi	445	2,700
(9)	Shepherds	85	4,400
(10)	Efate	925	20,000
(11)	Tafea	1,630	17,800

Figure 9.   Vanuatu, 1984.

parrots, lizards, sea life, and insects—among them the malarial mosquito. Livestock and domesticated animals have been imported, although traditionally the farmers have raised small pigs valued for their curled tusks.

According to the January 1979 census, some 85 percent of the population of 112,700 lived in rural areas outside the two urban centers, Port-Vila on Efate and Luganville on Espiritu Santo. Although the average population density was only 10 per square kilometers, there was much variation. The rural population was distributed in some 2,300 settlements having from 25 to 200 people each; the average size was about 40 inhabitants. During the period between the 1967 and 1979 censuses, the population expanded at a rate of 3.1 percent per year; the proportion of people under 15 years of age rose from 35 to 45 percent. During the 1960s and early 1970s immigration to the urban areas was significant, but thereafter the growth rate of the urban population averaged about the same rate as that of the population in general.

Historical Setting

The prehistory of Vanuatu is vague; no archaeological evidence has been found to support the commonly held theory that peoples speaking Austronesian languages first came to the islands some 4,000 years ago. Archaeologists have discovered potsherds from the Lapita culture dating back to 1300–1100 B.C. in the northern islands and to about 350 B.C. on Efate (see Prehistory, ch. 1). A different kind of pottery, bearing incised and applied-relief designs, has been found in the central islands and dates from at least 700 B.C. Around A.D. 1200 a sudden immigration of peoples replaced this culture on Efate, Tongoa, and the smaller central islands. The newcomers, led by a chief known as Roymata, practiced a burial ritual involving the voluntary sacrifice of persons close to a dead chief or other important persons.

The first European to discover the islands was Pedro Fernández de Quirós, who named Espiritu Santo in 1606, but neither he nor the other explorers and navigators who charted the area 150 years later had much effect on the islands. Trader Peter Dillon, however, discovered stands of sandalwood and began an eventual rush to the island of Erromango in 1825. The rush ended in 1830 after a clash between immigrant Polynesian workers and the indigenous Melanesians. The sandalwood trade resumed in 1839 and spread to the other islands, finally centering on Espiritu Santo in the 1860s. Many of the traders were little more than ruffians who introduced firearms and alcohol to the area and often embroiled themselves in the local blood feuds. Their activities and the European diseases they carried tended to disintegrate and depopulate the indigenous cultures.

In 1839 Christian missionaries began what was to be one of the bloodiest and most difficult efforts in the Pacific. The London Missionary Society lost European and Polynesian missionaries alike at the hands of the local Melanesians, who often attacked them in retaliation for atrocities perpetrated by other Europeans. In 1848 a Presbyterian missionary from Canada began a grim episode that turned the tables on the locals; he had visiting naval ships bombard the villages that resisted his efforts. The Anglican bishop of New Zealand had launched a less militant effort in 1847.

In the 1860s the trade moved from sandalwood to human labor. Planters in Australia, Fiji, New Caledonia, and the Samoa Islands were in need of agricultural workers and encouraged the so-called blackbirding of the islands population. At the height of the labor trade, more than half of the adult male population of several of the islands was abroad. The labor trade caused the outbreak of violent conflicts, further extended the influence of European disease and alcohol, and set back the precarious missionary effort.

Actual settlers first entered the islands in the 1870s, looking for land on which to establish cotton plantations. After the collapse of international cotton prices they switched to coffee, cacao, bananas, and, most successfully, coconuts. The earliest European settlements were concentrated on Tanna and Efate but spread gradually northwards. By 1905 there were about 500 European settlers and 240 missionaries in the islands. At the start, British subjects from Australia made up the majority, but the establishment of the Caledonian Company of the New Hebrides in 1882 soon tipped the balance in the favor of French subjects. By 1885 the company claimed it had purchased 80 square kilometers of land. British subjects came to work for the French company, and a few even changed their citizenship. By the turn of the century, French nationals outnumbered the British two to one.

The jumbling of French and British interests in the islands brought petitions for one or the other of the two powers to annex the territory. The issue came to a head in 1886, when the French government in New Caledonia sent troops to Port-Vila to quell disturbances there, prompting Britain to begin earnest negotiations. Anglophone missionaries lobbied strongly for a British administration to counteract what they thought to be atrocious tactics used by the Caledonian Company against the local inhabitants. A convention between the two powers in 1887 set up a joint naval commission to police the area along with the rudiments of an administrative structure. In 1906 further discussions led to the establishment of the Anglo-French Condominium of the New Hebrides—what one historian has called an "elaborate joke." Each power created its own separate administrative structure to serve its nationals and together set up a joint administration over the indigenous Melanesians.

Rivalry between the French and the British continued primarily in the economic sphere. The French, who were allowed to import indentured laborers from French Indochina, quickly demonstrated their superior entrepreneurship. By 1938 the population included 219 British, 687 French, 29 other Europeans (i.e., whites), 2,183 Asians (mostly Vietnamese), and some 47,000 indigenous people who continued to be ravaged by disease.

The Melanesians became increasingly dissatisfied with their lot. As early as 1905 laborers returning from overseas staged political protests on Tanna. It was not until the coming of the Americans during World War II, however, that political activism became significant. The demeanor and apparent wealth of the United States soldiers, who used the New Hebrides as a staging ground, helped expand the influence of an indigenous cargo cult that promised deliverance of the Melanesians by a messianic figure named John Frum. Remnants of the John Frum movement could be found on Tanna 30 years after the war. A different movement, called Nagriamel, arose on Espiritu Santo in the 1960s. Led by Jimmy Stephens (sometimes rendered Stevens), Nagriamel demonstrated for the repossession of undeveloped lands under European ownership and full political control for the Melanesians.

The most important political movement, however, was the National Party, which emerged as a powerful force in the 1970s. Having strong ties to the Presbyterian church and dissociated from cargo cults, the young leaders of this party pressed urgently for greater representation. In 1975 the Representative Assembly was formed along with municipal councils in Port-Vila and Luganville. Although pro-French parties triumphed in the municipal elections, the National Party—which renamed itself the Vanua'aku Pati (VP) in 1974—won all the elected seats in the assembly. The inability of the VP to dislodge appointed Francophone representatives to the assembly, however, caused it to boycott both the assembly and new elections scheduled for 1977. The VP also set up a separate government. The boycott gave the pro-French parties control of the assembly only briefly; a government of national unity was created in 1978 after negotiations had established a timetable for full independence by 1980. The VP won 26 of 39 seats of the fully elected assembly in late 1979.

Opposition groups on Espiritu Santo and Tanna, however, refused to go along with the results of the election and the plans for independence. On July 29, 1980, when Vanuatu became an independent state, Jimmy Stephens' Nagriamel, in alliance with

French interests, maintained that Espiritu Santo was independent of the new government. After negotiations failed, the government requested troops from Papua New Guinea and Australia to help arrest the secessionists. On August 29 Stephens and 70 others were arrested, and in the next two months another 260 supporters were rounded up, many of whom were deported. Two secessionists were killed in the operation—one, a son of Stephens.

After putting down the movement, the government of Prime Minister Walter Lini faced several monumental tasks. The integration of the three separate governments left over from the condominium was difficult for a country short on skilled administrators. More problematic was the implementation of economic and educational policies to link the Anglophone and Francophone, rural and urban, Christian and non-Christian, and traditional and modern communities in a spirit of cooperation and nationhood. Among the most vexing policies was that of land reform, which promised to return to customary ownership all lands acquired by the Europeans under the condominium.

The Social System
The main division in the society is that between the indigenous Melanesians, called ni-Vanuatu, and the small minority of European, Part European (white), Asian, and other Pacific islanders. although the ni-Vanuatu made up 94 percent of the population, according to the 1979 census—about 98 percent of the rural and 73 percent of the urban population—it was extremely fragmented. One official count suggested that there were over 100 indigenous languages in use in 1981. Although the government has ruled that the local pidgin, called Bislama, is to be the national language, English and French are also official languages, separate Francophone and Anglophone ni-Vanuatu communities having emerged during the condominium period. Religious differences between the communities reinforced the linguistic separation, but the most important religious split was probably between Christians and non-Christians. The latter, who made up about 16 percent of the population, followed their customary ways, known as *kastom*. Ironically, the Christian-dominated government has seized upon *kastom* as a syncretic ideology that could join all groups into a common national identity.

The diversity of traditional social organization and behavior and their modern transformations make it almost impossible to define *kastom* (see Solomon Islands, this ch.). Each ni-Vanuatu community had its own *kastom* whereby it legitimized secular and religious patterns of authority, land ownership, and ritual. For most ni-Vanuatu communities, the stereotypical Melanesian "big man" model, tailored to local circumstances, could describe the basis of social interaction (see Melanesia, ch. 1). Graded societies of the classic Melanesian type were especially prevalent in the northern islands, where matrilineal descent groups were common. Hereditary systems of male authority have emerged in parts of the central islands, where church organization has dovetailed nicely with customary structures, providing a vehicle for certain male lines to remain dominant. The customary relationship between the sexes varied from community to community. In the matrilineal societies women generally were treated as equals in all but political interactions. In the societies based on patrilineal descent groups—particularly on Malakula, Ambrym, southern Pentecost, and Tanna—males maintained hegemony over most spheres of social interaction.

The Christian churches have had a profound influence on the ni-Vanuatu societies. About 40 percent of the population was estimated to be Presbyterian in 1980, and most of this denomination was located in the central and southern islands. The Anglican church, which attracted about 16 percent of the population, had its greatest following in the northern islands. About 14 percent of the population was Roman Catholic, and an equal proportion was affiliated with the Church of Christ, French Protestant denominations, the Seventh-Day Adventist church, and others. Each church interacted with *kastom* in different ways. Anthropologist William Rodman observed that in one community on Aoba the Church of Christ had replaced the traditional graded social order with its own strict religious leaders, whereas the Anglican mission had merged its leadership into the traditional order. He noted that the latter was more open to initiatives from the central government during the 1970s. Over time, however, most of the churches have grown more tolerant of *kastom;* there has been less open concern about smoking, drinking, premarital sex, magic, taboos, and superstition left over from the traditional society or emerging from the contact with modern secular culture. This growing tolerance has come about as the missionaries were replaced by ni-Vanuatu priests and ministers, although some were stricter than the foreign missionaries. The dominant Presbyterian church came under independent local control as early as 1948.

Conflicts between Christian and *kastom* villages have occurred. Sometimes, as in land disputes, the conflicts were purely secular; the identification with Christianity or *kastom* was merely a convenient way of rallying political support to one claim or the other. In other cases, however, religious principles were at stake. A story from southern Pentecost by reporter Julie-Ann Ellis showed the practice of *kastom* with an interesting religious twist. In this instance two villages, one converted to the Church of Christ and the other following *kastom*, joined to stage a ritual where males dive from tall towers headfirst with only the protection of two vines attached to their ankles. The issue was not the diving, which everyone found to be good fun, but the scanty, indigenous clothing that the observing tourists had expected to see. The inhabitants of the Church of Christ community wore Western attire for the ceremony but traditional clothes for the diving; afterwards they debated whether they should make concessions for the sake of tourists, though the Christian villagers thought the traditional clothes to be vulgar.

The market system, cash cropping, and demand for modern commercial commodities were also affecting the society. Anthropologist Margaret Rodman has even argued that a class of rich peasants was arising in some rural areas, based on their ownership of large parcels of coconut land. These prosperous ni-Vanuatu were hiring wage laborers to work their lands; others were beginning cooperative enterprises to market produce or manufacture articles for sale in the urban areas. These emerging entrepreneurs, however, legitimized their position by referring to the ideals of *kastom*, which granted status to successful leaders who were able to amass material goods and land. Other anthropologists have noted that the ideology of *kastom* suited quite well the development of innovative roads to personal wealth and status.

Outside of the ni-Vanuatu community, Europeans made up about 2 percent, other Pacific islanders 1 percent, and others—chiefly Vietnamese and Chinese—about 3 percent of the population. Three-quarters of these ethnic minorities lived in the urban centers and dominated urban trade. Some were expatriate civil servants at work only temporarily in Vanuatu, but others had chosen to become citizens.

Education is a major avenue to social advancement for the ni-Vanuatu and other communities alike. In terms of *kastom*, education represents the special knowledge required of those who would be leaders. Vanuatu has, however, inherited two systems of education, one French and one English, which the government has been trying to merge into a single system. In 1980 there were 170 government-assisted and unassisted English-medium primary schools and 115 government-assisted French-medium primary schools that enrolled 11,300 and 12,400 students, respectively—about 75 percent of the relevant age-group. Six English and four French secondary schools accommodated about 2,000 students—some 17 percent of this age-group. The only tertiary institutions were a small teacher's college graduating about 12 instructors per year and a center of the University of the South Pacific that offered correspondence courses leading to study abroad. Schooling was not free at any level, but the French and British governments, as well as church groups, granted substantial amounts of assistance to keep costs low for the ni-Vanuatu. In fact, one of the problems in unifying the school system was the government's fear of upsetting either France or Britain and jeopardizing this important aid.

The provision of health services has been easier to amalgamate into one system than that of education services, and the ni-Vanuatu have seen their health standards improve substantially. Two major hospitals in the urban centers, eight smaller ones, some 39 clinics, and 52 rural dispensaries provided about one physician for every 4,500 people in 1981. Some islands, however, were isolated from the medical centers, and the government hoped to finance a mobile floating clinic. Only five of the 22 physicians in the country were ni-Vanuatu. The major diseases of concern were tuberculosis and malaria, primarily in the rural areas. Because of the low population densities prevailing on most islands, there has been no emphasis on family planning.

Other government programs and projects related to social welfare were also affecting and responding to changes in the society. The Women's Affairs Office, which originally concentrated on the traditional roles of homemaking and child rearing, has allied itself with the increasing number of women's groups advocating enhanced status for women, which went under the banner of the Vanuatu National Council of Women in the early 1980s. The government was in the early stages of forming a social welfare department to address such problems as unemployment, poor living conditions, alcoholism, delinquency, child abuse, and rape—particularly in Port-Vila and Luganville. The Department of Culture has also been established to manage a planned new cultural center for traditional arts.

The Economy

Vanuatu inherited a sharply dualistic economy from the condominium era; about 80 percent of the population was employed in agricultural activities that ranged from pure subsistence farming to smallholder farming of coconuts and other cash crops, while the remaining minority was engaged in the two small urban centers in much more remunerative nonagricultural pursuits. The service sector, including government services in particular, accounted for over half of GDP, which, because of the size of the subsistence sector, was an extremely tentative estimate. Excluding wages paid to expatriate employees, which were as high as 15 times the national average and supported almost exclusively by foreign assistance, per capita GDP was estimated to be the equivalent of around US$600 or less in 1982.

Charting macroeconomic trends was difficult because the statistical capabilities of the National Planning Office (NPO) were so limited. Estimates suggested, however, that real GDP grew by less than 1 percent per year on average during the 1979–82 period. The political disturbances surrounding independence caused a major decline in economic production. Inflation, measured by the Port-Vila consumer price index, was over 18 percent in 1980 and 27 percent in 1981 as import costs rose precipitously. The overall balance of payments remained positive, however, because of the large inflow of foreign assistance.

The macroeconomic picture was obscured also by the existence of an uncontrolled financial sector that catered to the needs of some 1,000 tax-exempt foreign companies—including some 70 banks—that sheltered some of their international transactions in Vanuatu. The Central Bank, which was understaffed and concerned primarily with replacing the old currencies with the new Vanuatu vatu, did not exercise its statutory powers of controlling the monetary system. The five commercial banks—all foreign controlled—could make transactions with the financial agents of the tax-exempt companies and often kept much of their loan portfolios denominated in foreign currencies. Lending inside Vanuatu has therefore been low compared with the high level of monetary liquidity. The government-owned Vanuatu Development Bank and the National Cooperative Savings Bank, however, planned to extend domestic loans equivalent to about 2 percent of GDP in 1982.

Lacking monetary control, the government has used development expenditures and fiscal policy as the principal means of influencing economic development. Public expenditures increased rapidly during the 1970s and probably contributed to inflation. During the 1980–82 period, however, real expenditure decreased, but overall spending was still equivalent to about 36 percent of GDP. Domestic revenues, which came almost exclusively from import duties because there was no income tax, were

Market in Port-Vila
Courtesy Steven R. Pruett

estimated to be less than one-half of total expenditures and about two-thirds of current epxenditures. The so-called fiscal gap was made up by budgetary support from the two former condominium powers, development grants, and loans. In addition, the salaries of some 400 expatriate administrators in the middle and upper levels of the government were heavily subsidized by the former ruling powers outside the normal budget. Some budgetary support was tied to the maintenance of specific programs, such as the French-medium education system. The government, therefore, has been trying to diversify its aid sources and eliminate the deficit in the current budget.

The NPO has consolidated the government's development priorities, projects, and financing strategies into the First National Development Plan, 1982–86. The major goals were balancing regional and rural growth, increasing the use of natural resources, expanding employment opportunities for ni-Vanuatu, fostering indigenous entrepreneurship, preserving the cultural and environmental heritage, and attaining a measure of self-reliance. Development expenditures were expected to average some 20 to 25 percent of GDP over the plan period, about twice the level in 1980 and 1981. Some 59 percent of these expenditures were devoted to productive enterprises, of which almost two-thirds was earmarked for the agricultural sector. Infrastructure development would require 23 percent of development expenditures, social services 15 percent, and general government services another 3 percent of the total.

The success of the development program, however, depended on the availability of funds from the principal aid donors: Australia, Britain, France, Japan, and New Zealand. According to government estimates in late 1982, aid commitments would finance about 55 percent of the development program. The remainder would be gleaned from commercial or concessional lending institutions. The dependency on bilateral assistance has made long-term financial planning difficult and subjected the budget to political exigencies. During the disturbances of 1980, for example, France temporarily suspended its aid payments. Many aid payments were tied to specific projects or to imports from the donor countries.

The persistent trade imbalance, however, made it difficult for the country to finance its expenditure program from the international loan market. In 1982 domestic exports were equivalent to 11 percent of GDP; earnings from reexports pushed this up to 13 percent. Imports were equivalent to 45 percent of GDP, leaving a trade deficit of 32 percent of GDP. Receipts from tourism, travel services, and offshore banking closed this gap to about 9 percent of GDP. Foreign assistance, which totaled 34 percent of GDP, more than offset this gap. Many of the imports, however, were associated with development aid and would also decline if the level of assistance were reduced, as the former condominium powers intended gradually to do. The leading exports were copra, meat products, cacao, timber, and reexported fish, and their principal destinations were the Netherlands, Belgium, New Caledonia, and France. Imports consisted chiefly of consumer items and industrial supplies; the principal suppliers were Australia, Japan, New Zealand, France, and Fiji.

The country's export prices have proved volatile, while import prices have risen steadily with international inflation. The exchange rate has also caused disturbances to the domestic economy. The currency was initially pegged to the French franc, which depreciated greatly in value during the early 1980s, making imported items all the more expensive and pushing inflation to all-time highs. In September 1981 the Central Bank began to peg the currency to the special drawing right, a unit of account used by the IMF and consisting of five major currencies. Because of this switch in valuation and an upswing in foreign capital inflows after the disturbances of 1980, the local currency has appreciated in value, reducing external inflationary pressures.

In mid-1984 the economic prospects for Vanuatu seemed bright. Unemployment was unheard of because most ni-Vanuatu depended on subsistence farming of some sort that could absorb labor onto new lands. As the educational achievements of the ni-Vanuatu progressed, however, the desire for modern forms of employment was likely to increase. Even after rationalizing the provision of public services by eliminating redundancies in the organizations left over from the condominium period, the economy would have to develop productive activities that could finance its expensive government requirements.

Agriculture, Forestry, and Fishing

Although 45 percent of the land area has been estimated to be suitable for agriculture—some 23 percent was thought to be extremely fertile—only 17 percent of the area was under cultivation or cattle grazing in the early 1980s. Coconuts, cacao, and coffee were planted on about 69,000 hectares; subsistence crops and pigs were raised on about 112,000 hectares. Cattle grazed on about 30,000 hectares of pure pastureland and 8,000 hectares of coconut plantations. Customary owners managed about 143,000 hectares and "owned" another 120,000 hectares of undeveloped land. A few ni-Vanuatu individuals or villages operated 250 hectares of plantations; church estates covered 16,000 hectares. Forests of varying density make up some 75 percent of the land.

A major goal of the independence movement was to return the ownership of all land to ni-Vanuatu. The so-called alienators of land sold during the period of condominium government are entitled under the constitution and land legislation passed in 1980 to remain on their farms until they negotiate leases or receive compensation for improvements to the land from the customary owners. Alienators must, however, actively use the land in question, maintain it in good condition, and pay all taxes due on it to the government. Land not meeting these requirements reverts to the government for distribution to the customary owners. During the condominium period foreigners alienated about one-fifth of all land.

Returning the land to the customary owners and registering the vast amounts of untitled land have been problematic. In the

245

two urban areas land corporations were set up in 1981 to negotiate leases with some 2,600 titleholders; by 1982 only 650 titleholders had submitted the necessary applications—many fraught with legal complications. Neither the customary owners nor the government had the funds to compensate the alienators for land improvements, and several politicians have tried to eliminate the provision for repayments. The expatriate director of rural lands resigned in 1982 over what he felt were inadequate provisions for reimbursement. Some 300 titles in the rural areas were on land deemed to be state-owned during the condominium, requiring the government to determine whether they should be returned to customary owners. In areas where land was being registered for the first time, villages and clan groups separated by religious or political differences have often claimed the same parcel. In 1982 the government turned over the adjudication of the mounting number of land disputes to island courts that were in the earliest stages of formation.

About 11,000 out of 34,000 ni-Vanuatu farmers in 1979 were exclusively subsistence growers, and nearly all of the rest depended on subsistence farming for most of their household needs. The basis of the subsistence sector was the raising of taro, yams, sweet potatoes, kava, manioc, and pigs. Each household of approximately five people grew subsistence crops on an average of about eight hectares of land; in the densely populated parts of the Shepherds and Efate regions, however, the area per household was two to three hectares. The crops were easy to cultivate and produced yields of about 18 tons per hectare harvested. Because an agricultural census has not been conducted, actual production was unknown. Subsistence gardens were normally worked for three years and then left to regenerate for 15 to 25 years.

The cash needs of smallholder farmers were met principally from the gathereing of coconuts on about 47,000 hectares of local stands; smallholders accounted for three-quarters of the annual 46,000 tons of copra produced ion the 1976–80 period. About one-quarter of the trees were senescent and declining in productivity, and one-half of the trees were expected to be in this condition by the year 2000. Some 3,750 hectares of cacao plants were also located on smallholder farms, and about 45,000 coffee trees had been planted on 100 smallholder farms on Tanna in a government project. The ni-Vanuatu have also been receptive to the introduction of cattle farming. The government estimated that 35,000 of the total cattle herd of 112,000 head in 1981 were located on smallholder farms; outside observers suggested that this estimate might be twice the actual number. There were a few village piggery projects for commercial production but no such poultry operations among the ni-Vanuatu.

Purely commercial farms or ranches accounted for about 26 percent of coconut production, less than 21 percent of the cacao harvest, and for more than two-thirds of the cattle herd. Average copra yields, however, have fallen to about three-quarters of that on smallholder farms because the planters have not replaced the aging trees, or else they have introduced cattle onto their plantations. Likewise, coffee and cacao production on the plantations has declined. One main reason for the decrease in plantation crop production was the exodus of Vietnamese plantation workers in the 1960s and of Francophone farmers in the period leading up to independence.

Government development projects, usually receiving assistance from bilateral and multilateral aid donors, were concentrating on the development of commercial crops on smallholder farms. These efforts involved replanting some 500 hectres of coconut trees each year and introducing modern copra driers. Assisted by the Food and Agriculture Organization (FAO) of the UN, the government hoped to expand the area under cacao by 800 hectares per year during the 1983–86 period; coffee was being introduced on 50 to 100 hectares per year. Pepper, rice, groundnuts, ginger, chilies, vanilla, and tea were also slated for development. Because the pastureland was overstocked, the government was attempting to add some 3,500 hectares of grazing land each year, primarily on Espiritu Santo but also on Efate and other islands.

Forestry has an important future in the domestic economy, although many of the nation's forest resources are located on lands too steep for logging or are too thin for commercial production. Surveys of 50,000 hectares of the better forest have shown that only 15 to 25 cubic meters of wood per hectare could be extracted. An adequate national inventory of forest resources had not been conducted as of mid-1984, but estimates indicate that they could supply domestic needs until at least the end of the century. During the 1976–80 period the government set up 27 plantations of pine species and planned to add 1,000 additional hectares at 24 sites during the 1982–86 period. Plantation forestry was carried out by casual laborers managed by the nation's few forestry agents. The government also planned to set up 1,000 hectares of industrial plantations that would cater to export markets. In 1982 there were only two sawmills—one in each of the urban centers. About half of the domestic consumption of 3,000 to 5,000 cubic meters of wood consisted of imports of preserved softwoods. Firewood harvested from local forests was the primary source of energy in the rural areas.

Fishing in Vanuatu has not developed as rapidly as in other Pacific countries. Foreign-owned vessels caught some 8,000 to 10,000 tons of fish within the nation's EEZ (see Glossary) each year, storing the catch at a freezing facility on Espiritu Santo for reexport; few ni-Vanuatu were involved in these operations. Even traditional fishing in the coastal areas was a marginal activity. Some commercial boats, however, did catch snapper and lobsters for sale to the hotel and restaurant market. Knowledge of the nation's fish stocks was limited, but a few surveys revealed sizable stocks of skipjack tuna, prawns, and other commercial species. Over the 1982–86 period the government planned to conduct six fishery training courses around the country each year, set up 25 village fishing and freezing facilities, train additional boatbuilders, install some 11 ice plants, and improve marketing channels.

The research, training, and extension services needed to reach the government's many goals for agriculture were the responsibilities of the Ministry of Land and Natural Resources. Although capital spending on agriculture, forestry, and fishing was projected to be more than one-quarter of the total during the 1982–86 period, the level of current spending—about 3 to 4 percent of the total—might be too low to support the ministry's diverse investments.

Industry and Services

Mining and energy production was underdeveloped primarily because of the small resource base but also because of the lack of detailed geological surveys. Exploration has shown that small deposits of manganese exist on Erromango, that magnetite sands are located on a number of beaches, and that Espiritu Santo has extensive limestone formations that may conceal various metals. On Efate and Tanna, pozzolana, which can be used to make a cementlike building material, is abundant. An offshore sedimentary basin running northward from Malakula and Pentecost to the Torres Islands may contain petroleum or natural gas. Geothermal diffusions on Vanua Lava, Efate, and Tanna may also be tapped for electrical energy.

The country remained highly dependent on imported petroleum, however, which accounted for one-third of domestic energy consumption and 57 percent of the value of all exports in

1980. Diesel power generators for Port-Vila and Luganville produced almost all of the electrical energy available and used up about 19 percent of net oil imports. Electricity charges were among the highest in the entire Pacific region, keeping waste at a minimum; a private company had a contract to run the diesel plants until the year 1990. The government was receiving economic assistance from an energy fund of the European Economic Community (EEC) to study the prospects of wood-burning power plants, and another EEC grant was funding a survey of hydroelectric resources near the two urban areas. Pilot solar- and wind-power projects had been installed in four villages as of 1982.

Manufacturing contributed only 4.7 percent of the nation's estimated GDP in 1980 and employed only 6 percent of the wage-earning work force. The lack of government support, foreign investment, skilled labor, and economies of scale severely constrained its development. Besides two meat canneries and the single fish-freezing plant, manufacturing consisted of small-scale, family-run enterprises catering to the two urban markets. The goods produced locally included soft drinks, printed materials, building materials, furniture, and aluminum products—including fishing boats. A UN grant established the office for the Development of Enterprise in 1980, whose small staff developed an industrial policy. Guidelines for foreign investors were critically needed.

Interisland shipping was the most important form of transportation provided for the majority of the population, although the services were best developed for the three most populous islands. The ships picked up copra from rural producers in exchange for imported consumer items, such as canned foods. In 1981 there were 40 privately owned vessels, of which five could carry more than 100 tons of cargo. Four of the five large vessels participated in a government-regulated route system that ensured visits to all parts of the country at least once every three weeks. There were 12 government-owned vessels that provided transportation to various ministries and engaged in research, training, and coastal patrols. There were 11 wharves that could serve interisland ships; the rest of the country had to off-load. Port-Vila and Luganville were the deep-sea ports and served some 13 foreign-registered vessels in 1981. That year the government established its own registry and hoped to attract international lines to document their vessels in Vanuatu. In the 1982–86 period the government planned to set up wharves in all of the regions.

The road network extended for 1,062 kilometers in 1982, of which only 5 percent were paved; about 55 percent were made of coral, and the rest were earthen. The two urban areas accounted for nearly all the pavement and for most of the 5,500 vehicles in use that year. Because of a lack of funds, road maintenance has been insufficient, and the government estimated that it would cost VT1.3 billion (for value of the Vanuatu vatu—see Glossary) per year—equal to the total government budget—to keep them up properly. The government was trying to find labor-intensive methods to maintain the network and add about 400 kilometers a year in the 1982–86 period.

International airports served the two urban centers, but the facility at Port-Vila was most important. This airport was, however, in need of extension and a modern control tower to handle the anticipated increase in air traffic during the 1980s. Air Vanuatu, a government joint venture with an Australian firm, operated one Boeing 737 jet that flew twice weekly on a route to Nouméa and Sydney. The 21 smaller airfields around the country served aircraft carrying a maximum of 18 passengers.

Communications services were developing slowly. Postal services, which were slow, were provided at nine offices around the country, six of which had telegraph facilities in 1981; the two urban offices had telex machines. The urban centers were also connected by telephone and linked to Tanna and three locations on Malakula. Government radio operators provided communication to the other islands. An aid-financed project to construct eight VHF installations around the country and direct-dialing exchanges in Luganville, Norsup (next to Lakatoro), and Isangel was expected to be completed in the early 1980s. By 1986 the government hoped to link all parts of the country by telephone. There was a satellite earth station at Port-Vila that provided adequate international communications.

Marketing and commerce were dominated by cooperatives in the rural areas and by foreign companies in the urban areas. The cooperative movement was unified into a single organizational hierarchy in the 1980s from separate French and English systems that began in the 1960s. In 1979 there were 253 consumer and marketing cooperatives to which some 80 percent of rural households belonged. The cooperative societies marketed some 63 percent of all smallholder copra exports and 43 percent of all the country's exports that year. The Vanuatu Cooperative Federation controlled its own small shipping company and savings bank. The federation was planning to build at least one warehouse in each of the regions during the 1982–86 period. The greatest

problem facing the cooperative movement was the lack of trained personnel at all levels. Foreign-owned companies dominated the import trade; in 1981 less than 5 percent of all registered companies handled 76 percent of all imports. Retail outlets, however, were generally small and run by family members. Individual growers usually sold food at regular markets in the urban areas.

Tourism has only recently developed in Vanuatu, but the government had high hopes for developing this industry. During the 1972–79 period the number of tourists increased by more than 16 percent per year to over 25,000. The political disturbances of 1980 dealt a temporary setback to the industry, but visitors began arriving in increasing numbers in late 1981. The number of Australian, Japanese, and New Zealand tourists increased by more than 30 percent per year during the 1972–79 period and in 1981 made up nearly three-quarters of all tourists; visitors from New Caledonia and France, by contrast, have declined dramatically. The government tourist agency, however, wished to develop markets in New Caledonia and elsewhere to avoid relying too heavily on Australia.

The Political System and Security

Vanuatu politics has been characterized by the dominance of the Vanua'aku Pati (VP) in an open and democratic system guaranteed by the Constitution, which went into effect in 1980. Basic human rights and political freedoms are also provided for in the Constitution and have been upheld. Unresolved questions over the organization and responsibilities of local government and land administration have continued to cause some controversy, however, as have the nation's foreign relations, which opposition groups have found to be too "radical." The government, in turn, has accused outside "conservative" interests of involving themselves in local politics. Foreign policy has generally been concerned with the pragmatic issue of keeping economic aid and trade flowing smoothly.

The Constitution created a republican political system headed by a president who has chiefly ceremonial powers; real power is in the hands of the prime minister. Elected by a two-thirds majority in a college consisting of parliament and the presidents of regional councils, the president serves a five-year term. The only way the president may attempt to veto a parliamentary bill is to submit it to the Supreme Court on the grounds of unconstitutionality. Otherwise, the bill automatically becomes law two weeks after its passage.

Parliament is a unicameral body of representatives elected by all persons over 18 years of age; the elections are managed by an autonomous commission. In the 1983 elections there were 14 constituencies: Port-Vila had four representatives and Luganville two; the remainder of the country was divided into constituencies having from one to five representatives. Parliament normally sits for a four-year term unless dissolved by majority vote of a three-fourths quorum or a directive from the president on advice of the prime minister.

By a similar majority, parliament selects the prime minister, who in turn appoints the Council of Ministers, which is not to exceed one-fourth of the number of parliamentary representatives. Together, the prime minister and the Council of Ministers constitute the executive government. The prime minister, along with the leader of the opposition and specialized commissions, has a hand in appointing judges, an ombudsman, an auditor general, an attorney general, and other executives. The National Council of Chiefs, elected by district councils of chiefs, advises the government on all matters concerning ni-Vanuatu culture and language.

Since the passage of the Decentralization Act of 1980, local government functions have been devolved to 11 elected local government councils. The councils are responsible for charting regional development plans, collecting a per person tax and licensing fees, developing local services and infrastructure, and passing local ordinances.

The Supreme Court, which heads the judicial system, consists of a chief justice and up to three other judges. Two or more members of this court may constitute a court of appeal. In 1981 the chief justice was resident in Vanuatu, but the other justices visited as needed from other Pacific countries. Two senior magistrates were responsible for less important cases than those tried by the Supreme Court in the two urban areas; two others were to be set up in Tanna and Malakula as soon as possible. Under legislation passed in 1980, land courts and land appeal courts were to be established. The constitution provides for the establishment of village or island courts to deal with questions of customary law.

Parliamentary politics has been dominated by the VP, but the primarily Francophone opposition, grouped into the Union of Moderate Parties (UMP), has been effective. Discord within the VP, moreover, caused the dismissal of one cabinet minister and the defection of three others during 1983. The president, also a VP official, has announced his displeasure in a government dominated by churchmen and has indicated a willingness to replace Lini, an Anglican priest, in the top party spot. The VP reunified under the leadership of Lini in time for the November 1983 elections—the first held since independence—but suffered at the polls. The contest gave the VP 24 out of the 39 parliamentary seats and 55 percent of the popular vote, which was down from 26 seats, and 67 percent of the vote in 1979. The UMP won 12 seats, while Nagriamel and two other local parties based in Espiritu Santo and Malakula won the other three. The lesser opposition parties were expected to side with the UMP in parliament. The VP losses meant that the party could no longer count on a two-thirds majority to enact constitutional changes.

The political ideological spectrum was seen as running from the "leftist" government party to the "rightest" UMP. The UMP criticized the Lini government particularly for its overtures to Cuba and close ties to Australia, which it felt was trying to edge France out of the Pacific. The opposition included in its platform for the 1983 elections a proposal to bring back freehold land titles for Vanuatu citizens, regardless of their ethnic background, a position from which the ni-Vanuatu members of the opposition have tried to distance themselves. Just before the elections Lini effectively charged the opposition with receiving funds from the same American business interests that had supported Jimmy Stephens' secessionist movement in 1980. The fragmented nature of the opposition, which was unified only in opposing the VP, also helped keep the government in power, despite its losses. The UMP, however, did gain some surprising Anglophone support in the 1983 elections.

Vanuatu's foreign policy has been more strident than that of the other Pacific island states but in one respect was quite similar—the pattern of foreign relations depended first and foremost on the politics of foreign aid and trade. In early 1984 external trade was added to the portfolio of the minister of foreign affairs, who was also in charge of liaisons with aid-giving organizations. Vanuatu has maintained close relations with France and Britain and, increasingly, with Australia, Japan, and New Zealand. As well as being the largest donor of untied bilateral assistance, Australia was providing some US$1 million of defense-cooperation-assistance each year. Contradictory claims over Île Mathiew and Hunter Island—far to the south on the border with New Caledonia—Vanuatu's strident support for New Caledonia's independence, and opposition to nuclear testing in the Pacific have strained relations with France.

The country participated actively in regional affairs, although it has expressed concern that too many organizations having overlapping interests were being developed. Vanuatu belonged to the organizations of the South Pacific Forum and the South Pacific Commission (see Appendix B). Prime Minister Lini, however, has criticized France's domination of New Caledonia and Indonesia's control of East Timor and Irian Jaya as no other leader in the Pacific has done. The other Pacific states also expressed some concern when Vanuatu opened diplomatic relations with Cuba in 1983 through the latter's embassy in Japan.

Prime Minister Lini has steered what he described as a neutral course between the world's superpowers. Vanuatu has joined the Nonaligned Movement and has not established diplomatic relations with either the United States or the Soviet Union. In 1982 the country turned away two United States naval vessels that wished to make port calls when their commanders, following established American policy, refused to declare whether they carried nuclear weapons or were nuclear-powered. The government stated in 1984, however, that it was considering a United States request to establish formal diplomatic ties. Vanuatu already had opened relations with China.

In keeping with its need for financial assistance, Vanuatu has joined the Asian Development Bank, the IMF, the World Bank, and other international financial organizations. It benefited from its status as a member of the Commonwealth of Nations and as an associate member of the EEC under the terms of the Lomé Convention (see Glossary). In late 1983 the nation opened an office at the UN, supported by a grant from Australia.

The Vanuatu Police Force, which was in charge of all security concerns, consisted of a regular force of 163 people in 1981 and a paramilitary force of 300 people called the Vanuatu Mobile Force (VMF). The former performed general policing, immigration, and prison management tasks, while the latter was primarily in charge of external defense, counterinsurgency, and patrolling the EEZ. Experienced expatriate officers were seconded to the heads of both the police force and the VMF in 1980. About 72 percent of the regular force was stationed in Port-Vila, Espiritu Santo, and Tanna, where members also assisted in development projects. The country had only one patrol boat in 1983.

There were no major internal or external threats to Vanuatu's security in mid-1984. The leader of the 1980 secessionist movement remained in jail, although he had once tried to escape. Some of his supporters, who had been deported or barred from entering the country, were reportedly colluding with outside business interests based in American Samoa that wished to found a libertarian state, but they posed no major threat. A possible threat to security arose from violent conflicts between religious groups—particularly between those advocating *kastom* and those adhering to Christian ways.

Chapter 3.   Micronesia

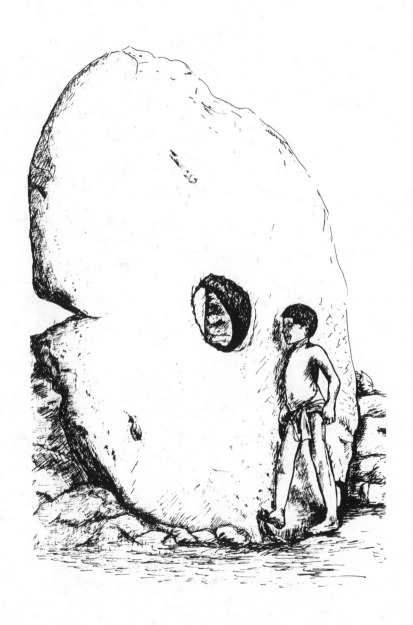

Stone money of Yap in the Federated States of Micronesia

MICRONESIA, OR "LITTLE ISLANDS," refers to a myriad of coral atolls and volcanic islands scattered across the immense expanse of the western Pacific. Its main archipelagic units are the Caroline Islands, including Palau; the Gilbert Islands; the Mariana Islands, including Guam; the Marshall Islands; and the single island of Nauru. Although stretched across an area larger than the continental United States, the more than 2,000 islands of Micronesia have a combined land area of a mere 3,100 square kilometers—roughly the size of Rhode Island. Fewer than 100 of these poorly endowed, economically underdeveloped islands are inhabited. A mid-1984 estimate of the population was 323,000.

Diversity is a distinctive feature of the area—hence very few generalizations are valid for all of the indigenous societies. Major ethnolinguistic groupings include the Chamorros, Gilbertese, Kosraeans, Marshallese, Nauruans, Palauans, Polynesians, Ponapeans, Trukese, and Yapese. The Chamorros are native to Guam and the Northern Marianas, Gilbertese to Kiribati, and Polynesians to outer atolls of Ponape. Other groupings derive their names from their respective island designations.

Politically, Micronesia is complex, but all of its constitutional entities maintain governmental systems that are traceable to the Western democracies. Kiribati and Nauru are fully independent nations. Guam is an integral territory of the United States. The rest of Micronesia—called the Trust Territory of the Pacific Islands—was in 1984 still technically under the administrative authority of the United States, pending the termination of the United Nations mandated trusteeship for the territory. In actuality, however, it comprised four self-governing entities, each having its own constitution. These were the Commonwealth of the Northern Mariana Islands; the Federated States of Micronesia, divided into the states of Kosrae, Ponape, Truk, and Yap; the Republic of the Marshall Islands; and the Republic of Palau. All of these entities, which would survive the termination of the trusteeship, were associated with the United States, which was responsible for their external defense.

GUAM

Official Name	Territory of Guam
Political Status	Unincorporated territory of the United States
Capital	Agana
Population	113,000 (1984 midyear estimate)
Land Area	554 square kilometers
Currency	United States dollar (US$)

Physical Environment

Guam is the westernmost territory of the United States, situated in the western Pacific Ocean approximately 2,400 kilometers east of Manila, 2,600 kilometers south of Tokyo, 4,800 kilometers north of Sydney, 5,900 kilometers southwest of Honolulu, and 9,000 kilometers from San Francisco. The largest, most populous, and southernmost island of the Mariana archipelago, Guam is 48 kilometers long and six to 20 kilometers wide (see fig. 10).

The island was formed through successive upheavals of undersea volcanoes. The northern two-thirds lacks surface streams and consists of a coralline limestone plateau of rolling hills and several volcanic formations set on cliff lines 61 to 183 meters in elevation. The southern one-third is a complex of fertile areas, low volcanic mountains and valleys where small streams and several waterfalls are found. The highest point of the island is Mount Lamlam, 407 meters above sea level. Surrounding the island is a coral reef; swift currents and heavy swells make anchoring extremely hazardous. The only valuable harbor is Apra Harbor on the central western side of the island, one of the largest protected harbors in the Pacific and the site of a major United States naval base.

The climate is tropical year-round, temperatures ranging from about 22°C to 30°C. May and June are the hottest months, and July through October is the wet season, marked by southwesterly monsoons. Rainfall ranges from 1,750 millimeters to 2,250 millimeters per year. Westerly trade winds blow from the northeast during the coolest and driest season, December through February. Earthquakes and destructive typhoons are not uncommon. Tropical storms and typhoons hit the islands at least twice a

261

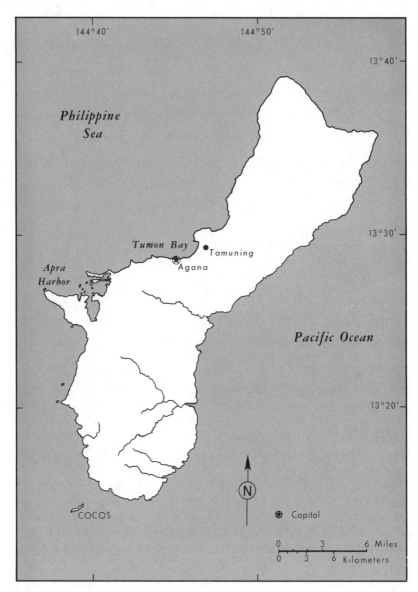

Figure 10.   Guam, 1984

year, accompanied by heavy rainfall and winds gusting in excess
of 130 kilometers per hour. The worst typhoon in the recorded
history of the island struck in 1982, causing substantial environ-

262

mental and property damage.

The tropical climate yields lush vegetation, including vines, savanna grass, various species of palm, and other trees, such as coconut, breadfruit, banyan, ironwood *(ifil)*, bananas, and several flowering species. The ironwood tree is the most valued source of timber and is now protected by law. It is termite resistant, turns black with age, and eventually becomes so hard that holes must be drilled in it before nails or screws can be inserted.

There is a limited range of animal life; the only known native mammals are two species of bats. The bird population suffered, as did most island animals, during World War II and was further reduced by heavy spraying of insecticides after the war. The bird known as the Guam rail, a flightless species native to the island, has been rapidly disappearing, its numbers reduced from about 80,000 in 1968 to about 50 in the early 1980s. The sharp decline is attributed to the predations of the Philippine rat snake, introduced in the 1960s to prey on the island's rats. In early 1984 the United States Department of the Interior tentatively agreed to place the Guam rail on the endangered species list for federal protection. This bird is one of seven species of birds and two of bats for which the government of Guam has sought—unsuccessfully— federal protection since the late 1970s. Two of the birds, the Guam broadbill and the Guam white-eye, are believed to have become extinct.

The only snake on the island until the Philippine rat snake arrived had been a burrowing earthworm-like blind snake. Sea turtles are common visitors in coastal areas. Insect life is minimal except for many species of mosquitoes, none of which are malarial. Stinging ants have been known to kill baby chicks. Nonpoisonous but painful scorpions and centipedes are common. Of the three types of lizards found on the island, the most formidable in appearance is the iguana, which grows 1.2 to 1.8 meters in length. Freshwater fish are not common and are not prized by the islanders. A variety of hermit crabs, along with coconut crabs, sea crabs, and night-feeding crabs, are found in coastal areas. Small, brilliantly colored tropical fish, eels, and small squid live in the bays protected by reefs. Tuna, shark, blue marlin, and other deepwater fish are plentiful along the coast.

Many kinds of domesticated animals found on the island were introduced after the arrival of the Spanish. Mules and horses were brought in for draft purposes, but the water buffalo, introduced from the Philippines, proved the most adaptable to the climate. Most cattle suffered from the heat and provided limited meat and milk. Chickens were an important food item for the islanders, and roosters were highly valued for cockfighting.

Historical Setting

The history of Guam before the sixteenth century is obscure. Early accounts do not record the existence of chronologies or genealogies similar to those found in Polynesia and other parts of the Pacific. Carbon dating of cooking pits shows the presence of man as early as 3000 B.C. Potsherds, stone tools, and weapons found in archaeological diggings indicate that the island was well populated at least 3,000 years ago, emerging as the major population and trade center for all of the Mariana Islands.

The earliest inhabitants of Guam and the Northern Marianas were the Chamorros, largely referred to as Guamanians in current literature. Although their origin is still unknown, on the basis of their language and way of life they are believed to be traceable to Malaysia, the Philippines, and Indonesia. Most anthropologists agree that if the Chamorros did not themselves originate in Southeast Asia, they had prolonged contacts with people who did. The Chamorros depended on fishing and on gathering in the jungle and on the reef and were the only oceanic peoples to cultivate rice. Their religious beliefs centered on the veneration of the spirits of the dead.

The first contact with the West was the arrival of Ferdinand Magellan in 1521, when the Chamorros probably called the island Guahan. After Magellan's landing, however, Guam and the adjacent islands became known by two other names: Ilhas das Velas (Islands of Sails), after the strange triangular sails the natives used on their boats, and Islas de Ladrones (Islands of Thieves), because of the larcenous behavior of the natives. In 1688 the islands were renamed the Marianas by a Jesuit priest in honor of his patroness, Mariana of Austria, widow of Philip IV of Spain.

Except for infrequent visits by European explorers, the major contact with the West during the next 100 years came during the annual layover of Spanish galleons traveling between Mexico and the Philippines. Guam, which was claimed by Spain in 1565, was important to the galleons as a source of food and water, but there was no attempt to influence the indigenous way of life.

Based on the limited and sometimes conflicting accounts of early explorers and Jesuit priests, the Chamaorro society in the sixteenth and seventeenth centuries was broadly divided into three discrete groups of nobles, commoners, and outcasts. Generally, the members of the nobility were associated with high-status occupations, such as village chiefs, navigators, warriors, canoe builders, and traders. Social distance was minimal between nobles and commoners, but it was fairly rigid between the two and the outcasts, whose way of life was governed by restrictions and taboos.

The basic social unit was the family, living in small clusters of villages, each comprising 50 to 150 huts. A large extended, rather than nuclear, family was the dominant aspect of village life. A chief and a council of nobles or elders administered the village, which was the principal political division. The descent system was matrilineal; a man inherited property and titles from his mother's brother. Marriage was monogamous, but concubines were permitted, as was divorce. Marriage within the descent line was forbidden.

Spanish interest in Guam and the adjacent islands grew considerably after 1662, when a Jesuit priest began to Christianize the Chamorros. In 1668 the first permanent Spanish settlement was established on the island. Initially, the work of conversion showed tangible results, even though some natives were perturbed over the Jesuits' insensitivity to their beliefs about ancestral spirits. In 1672 an open revolt broke out, and intermittent hostilities between the Spanish and the Chamorros ensued for more than two decades. Insurrections and Spanish reprisals, coupled with smallpox, syphilis, and other diseases brought by Spanish crews decimated the native population from an estimated 50,000 to 100,000 in the early 1600s to 5,000 by the end of the century.

During the eighteenth century Guam remained an isolated Spanish outpost, administered under a resident governor reporting to the viceroy of Mexico—then a Spanish domain. The process of Hispanicization continued apace, often inseparably from Jesuit influence. The natives began wearing Western-style clothes, adopted Spanish customs, cultivated corn, and learned iron forging, spinning, and weaving. By 1710 nearly all the islanders had become Roman Catholics.

The role of Catholicism as the principal faith of the Chamorros remained unchanged even after the Jesuit order was expelled from Guam in 1769 and its property taken over by the Spanish state. The expulsion was actually ordered two years earlier by Spanish king Charles III, who by that time had come to regard the Jesuit order as a major threat to his authority. Spanish colonization intensified on Guam in the absence of Jesuit interference, but the Jesuits' departure created economic havoc and added to the general deterioration of island conditions. Meanwhile, the decline of the indigenous population continued unchecked, reaching a recorded low of 1,500 by 1783.

Guam was ceded to the United States as a prize of the Spanish-American War of 1898. Administratively controlled by the Department of the Navy, the island was developed as a naval station, and its inhabitants became nationals of the United States. The quality of life on Guam improved gradually, as progress was made in areas such as public health and sanitation, education, roads, and agriculture. Compulsory education was introduced, and land taxation was reformed somewhat to the benefit of small farmers. Other changes included the banning of both religious instruction in public schools and the practice of concubinage.

In December 1941, at the onset of World War II in the Pacific, Guam was seized by the Japanese. The Japanese removed all surrendered American garrison troops from the island. The Guamanians were initially allowed some freedom as a military expediency but came under restricitons as the tide of war began to turn against the Japanese forces. English was replaced by Japanese as the medium of instruction, business and religious freedoms were curtailed, and Guamanians, including women and children, were pressed into labor along with Koreans brought in by the Japanese. Islanders suspected of aiding several Americans hiding in the jungle were shot or beheaded; only one of the Americans survived, many natives having risked their lives to keep him safe. By the summer of 1944 food had become scarce, and conditions of life had become progressively unbearable.

Guam was retaken by the United States in August 1944 at a cost of 7,000 American troops and 17,200 Japanese. It became the headquarters of the United States naval forces in the Pacific in January 1945. Wounds of wartime destruction healed rapidly under extensive reconstruction and rehabilitation. In 1947 the secretary of the navy granted limited home-rule powers to what was then called the Guam Congress, the territorial legislature of the island.

In 1950 the island was placed under a civil administration. The Organic Act of Guam, a law passed by the United States Congress in that year, shifted administrative control to the Department of the Interior. The act defined Guam to be "an unincorporated territory of the United States," provided for three branches of government analogous to those of the United States—executive, legislative, and judicial—and granted citizenship to Guamanians born on and after April 11, 1899, provided that they had not taken steps to retain or acquire foreign nationality.

The Social System

Contacts with foreign cultures and peoples since the sixteenth century have gradually influenced the values, patterns, and structures of Chamorro society. Hispanicization and Catholicism led to a progressive decline of the old way of life. The matrilineal descent system was abandoned, and European concepts of the family were adopted. Spanish clothing styles and adaptations of Manila dress became popular. Towns were laid out on Spanish models. The capital had a cathedral, a central plaza, and stone buildings with red tile roofs. Even the language assimilated many Spanish and Filipino elements. The center of village life for most Guamanians came to be associated with the local church rather than the traditional men's clubs. Instead of observing traditional patterns set around planting and harvest festivals, the islanders followed the church calendar and celebrated its festivals.

Under United States administration since the turn of the century, the pace of change—gradual in the Spanish era—quickened steadily. The secular, public, village school became a popular center of community activity. American concepts of inheritance were introduced, and parental marriage arrangements became less commonplace. A money economy replaced what little remained of traditional dependence on barter. The mestizo (person of mixed blood) upper class lost its elite status as the source of sociopolitical influence shifted to officers of the United States Navy. Increasingly, Guamanian youth abandoned Spanish customs and patterned their lives on American models. Also evident was the growing Guamanian exposure to concepts of equality, freedom, and popular rule. Opportunities to participate in democratic processes remained marginal, however, during the first half of the twentieth century.

The erosion of traditional ways was carried further in the years after World War II. Spanish influence among the old continued, albeit as a marginal aspect of the island life. Most Guamanians came to reflect the basic culture, society, and values of mainland Americans. Except for a small number of older islanders, almost all Guamanians spoke English, the sole official language of Guam until 1974. The use of Chamorro, an Austronesian language, was limited to older islanders. Before the arrival of the Spanish, Chamorro was unwritten; the alphabet was a roman script identical to that used in Spanish. The contemporary form of Chamorro has changed considerably from the original version. Many traditional words and phrases have been dropped from common usage, and new words have evolved. The spellings of words often varied from village to village, depending on the local preference for Spanish and indigenous sounds and forms. As part of the effort to preserve the Chamorro culture, legislation was enacted in 1974 making Chamorro a second official language and the teaching of Chamorro in the elementary schools compulsory.

Guam has a well-developed public and private education system. In 1982 there were two private business colleges, one public community college, and a degree-granting institution of higher learning called the University of Guam. Education was compulsory between the ages of six and 16. Of the total enrollment in the kindergartens and the elementary, middle, and high schools, 84 percent attended the public schools. The University of Guam had originated in 1952 as the two-year, coeducational, and public-supported Territorial College of Guam. In 1963 it received accreditation as a four-year liberal arts college, and a graduate school was added in 1967. The college was made a university the next year, offering a wide range of undergraduate and graduate degrees. The total enrollment in 1982 was 2,395, of which 356 were from the various trust territory islands of the United States (see Trust Territory of the Pacific Islands, this ch.). Two of the strongest academic and research programs in the university were connected with the Marine Laboratory Institute and the Micronesian Area Research Center.

In 1984 there were no persons of pure Chamorro stock remaining on Guam, although a majority of the population traced their ancestry to Chamorros. Modern Guamanians are a mixture of various ethnic and cultural groups. To the original Chamorro traits are added genetic and cultural influences originating in Europe, the Philippines, Hawaii, the Americas, Asia, and Micronesia.

As of mid-1982 the population was estimated to be 108,406, including nearly 15,000 military personnel and their dependents and several thousand nonimmigrant workers and their dependents. About 55 percent of the population was Guamanian or, loosely, Chamorro; 20 percent, Filipino; 19 percent, military personnel and their dependents; and the remainder, alien workers. The annual growth rate of population was 2.2 percent between 1970 and 1980, double that of the mainland United States. The urban population was 40 percent in 1980; it had been 26 percent 10 years earlier. Roughly one-fourth of the island population was concentrated in the capital, Agana, and its four surrounding municipalities in the central, narrowest part of the island.

The Economy

In the early 1980s the economy continued to depend heavily on government activities that made up the public sector. As of March 1981 the territorial and federal government agencies composed 31 and 19 percent, respectively, of the total civilian work force of 33,600. Generally, public sector jobs were more attractive than those in the private sector because of higher pay and better fringe benefits. On Guam the territorial government was responsible for certain federal functions, such as the issuance of passports, customs clearance, environmental protection, marine safety, and tax collection. Moreover, it owned and operated public utilities and hospitals.

Federal spending continued to buttress the island economy. It included loans and grants to the public and private sectors, as well as expenditures for the military and other federal agencies. Income taxes collected from federal employees, including military personnel, reverted to the general fund revenues of the territorial government. In the fiscal year (FY) beginning October 1981, these amounted to 15 percent of such revenues.

The military was by far the most dominant element in the federal government. Government agencies collectively owned 33 percent of the land surface and had 6,400 civilian employees on their payrolls. The military share of the federal landholdings and of the civilian employment was 96 and 93 percent, respectively, in the early 1980s. Two out of every 10 islanders were connected with the military establishment, and at least 20 percent of total island retailing was transacted through military outlets.

Revenues for government operations in FY 1982 totaled US$153.6 million, up 5.9 percent from the previous year. The single largest source of these revenues was the territorial income tax at 48 percent; the second largest, at 25 percent, was the 4-percent gross receipts tax on all sales of goods and services, retail and wholesale. Federal income tax collected from federal employees, including military, accounted for 15 percent. Federal grants-in-aid amounted to 3 percent, and the remaining 9 percent came from miscellaneous sources. Expenditures for FY 1982 were US$158.8 million. The top three operating programs were public education (33 percent), subsidies to autonomous agencies (16 percent), and public safety (14 percent).

Gross receipts for the total market value of all goods and services for FY 1982 were over US$1 billion; gross receipts had reached only US$563 million in 1973. The two leading sectors by value in 1980 were retailing (32 percent) and manufacturing (31 percent), followed by services (12 percent), wholesaling (8 percent), construction (7 percent), financial services (7 percent), and transportation and miscellaneous (3 percent).

Agriculture remained inconsequential to the island economy, seldom exceeding 1 percent of the gross business receipts in any year since the end of World War II. It has suffered from the wartime devastation of cropland and from a steady diversion of labor to services catering to the federal and territorial government activities. In the early 1980s Guam continued to import most of its food, including fruits, vegetables, meat, and fish. The development of agriculture as an import substitution industry was being given serious official attention. Principal agricultural products were fruits, vegetables, and eggs; these three alone accounted for 76 to 86 percent of the value of agricultural production throughout the 1970s and in the early 1980s.

The fastest growing private sector industry was tourism, which had grown spectacularly since the opening of the first scheduled flight between Guam and Japan in 1967. The tourist industry in 1982 was responsible for more than 32 percent of total retail sales, at least 15 percent of the island employment, and some 20 percent of government revenue. Visitor expenditures were US$130 million in 1982, up from US$1.32 million in 1966. About 84 percent of the 326,341 arrivals in 1982 (6,600 in 1967) were from Japan; 8 percent came from North America and Hawaii; and 6 percent came from other areas in Micronesia.

Commercial trade is centered in the highly developed Agana, Tamuning, and Tumon Bay areas, the home of the island's booming and plushest hotel resorts and entertainment facilities. In 1982 trade accounted for 44 percent of gross business sales. A substantial portion of these taxes was generated by the tourist trade, which led to the flourishing of specialty import shops for food, clothing, appliances, and other consumer goods. Guam is a duty-free port; thus a wide range of imported luxury goods can be purchased at a lower cost than in the United States or even in Hong Kong.

Manufacturing has steadily expanded since the 1960s. In 1981 it generated 33 percent of total gross business sales, employing only 3.5 percent of the civilian work force. The single largest manufacturing activity was oil refining, which yielded 90 percent of total manufacturing receipts. Major petroleum products were jet fuel and other special fuels designed for military application and gasoline. Among other manufactured articles were processed foods, soft drinks, rock and concrete products, garments, watches, souvenir items, furniture, and liqueurs and spirits. The lack of raw materials and of a large skilled labor force have presented major impediments to the diversification of manufacturing.

Guam continued to rely on imports for most of its commodity needs. During the 1960s and 1970s imports averaged 91 percent of the total value of trade. Major imports included fuel, machinery, and transport equipment, manufactures, foods, and live animals. In 1980 one-fourth of all imports came from the United States, down from the annual average of 34 percent in the 1975–79 period. Japan was the second major supplier, at 8.3 percent, up from an average of 6.8 percent in the corresponding period.

During the first half of 1981 alone, exports reached US$76.5 million, whereas they had reached US$61 million for the whole of 1980. Many of the exports were reexports and transshipments, largely to the United States and other parts of Micronesia, Guam being a major distribution center for the Marianas and other trust territory islands. In 1981 exports rose sharply because of increases in oil exports to Taiwan, Japan, and the Philippines. Other export items were beverages and tobacco, meats, livestock, fish, watches, jewelry, and garments.

In mid-1984 economic opportunities on Guam were attractive for outside investors and businesses. Among the incentives offered were provisions for a 75-percent rebate on corporate income taxes generated from dividends for up to five years and a 100-percent abatement of real property taxes for up to 10 years. Corporate income taxes were at 25 percent of the federal rates for up to 20 years. Another attraction was Guam's status as a duty-free port, which allowed the tariff-free importation of materials for local manufacturing; finished products could be exported to the United States duty-free, provided that at least 30 percent of the final value was added in Guam. The purpose of these incentives was to offset certain disadvantages, such as Guam's limited market, its isolated location, and its small private sector labor force. On balance, Guam's economic performance has been fairly impressive. In the 1965–75 period business income, personal income, and government revenue tripled in real terms. In 1982 per capita income was US$4,574, nearly double the level of 1972.

Guam is sometimes called the urban center of the western Pacific because of relatively well-developed networks of communications and transportation linking the island to many Pacific islands and to the countries rimming the Pacific Ocean. The island is serviced by Northwest Airlines, Japan Air Lines, Continental Airlines, Continental/Air Micronesia, South Pacific Island Airways, and Air Nauru; in 1984 there were indications that

Hawaiian Airlines and Aloha Airlines might inaugurate flights to Guam to take up the slack of service by Pan American World Airways, which terminated its Guam connection in April of that year.

The Guam International Air Terminal can handle the largest commercial jets. The major harbor and port of entry is Apra Harbor, capable of handling bulk, conventional, and container cargo. The island is serviced also by major cargo carriers, such as United States Lines and American President Lines; augmenting these are several interregional and intraregional cargo carriers.

In the early 1980s Guam had 640 kilometers of excellent all-weather roads, more than double those in 1969. As of 1982 there were 58,207 registered motor vehicles, of which 39,252 were private cars, the principal means of land transportation.

Guam has excellent access to worldwide points via satellite for telephone, telegram, telex, and data communications service. It is served by the domestic postal service of the United States, and rates are equivalent to those for Hawaii and the west coast of the United States. Telephone and other electronic communications rates between Guam and the mainland United States are, however, higher than they would be within the mainland because Guam is treated as a foreign country by the Federal Communications Commission. The island has a daily and a semiweekly newspaper, in addition to several locally published periodicals. There are two commercial radio stations and one commercial television station that also has a radio facility. The television station offered a full schedule of major mainland network programs as well as local live programs. In the early 1980s a public television station began to offer largely educational and cultural programs.

The Political System

The principles underlying the governmental and political processes of Guam are derived from those of the United States. They are essentially consonant, in spirit as well as in practice, with the concepts of checks and balances, popular sovereignty, democratic rule, and popular accountability as ordained in the United States Constitution.

Guam, an unincorporated territory, is under the general administrative supervision of the Department of the Interior, which is one of many federal agencies represented on the island. Its relationship with the United States is defined in the Organic Act of Guam, as amended; this legislation grants the island a home rule that can be exercised within the framework of powers conferred by the United States Congress. Guam is subject to federal laws and regulations and is entitled to one nonvoting delegate in the United States House of Representatives. The Guamanians are United States citizens but cannot participate in the presidential elections of the United States.

The government of Guam, or the territorial government as it is sometimes called, is composed of three branches: the executive, legislative, and judicial. Its chief executive officer is the governor, popularly elected for four-year terms; he can be reelected to a second term but may not stand for a third term unless one full term has intervened. Candidates to the office of governor must have been a United States citizen and a bona fide resident of Guam for five consecutive years preceding the election.

The governor is responsible for the implementation of all federal laws applicable to Guam as well as local laws. He may issue executive orders and regulations and may also recommend bills to the legislature of Guam. Once a year he must submit a report on his administraiton to the secretary of the interior in Washington for transmission to Congress. His accountability is primarily to the electorate of Guam, however; he can be removed for cause by a referendum election initiated by the legislature when such a referendum election is requested either by a two-thirds vote of the lawmakers or by a number of registered voters equivalent to at least 50 percent of the voters who cast ballots in the previous general election. Assisted by a lieutenant governor who is also popularly elected for four-year terms, the governor presides over an administration divided into various line departments, staff offices, and a number of autonomous public bodies.

The legislature of Guam is unicameral, consisting of 21 senators (as these representatives are officially called), who are elected by popular vote every two years in the same year that general elections are held on the mainland. For the purpose of election, Guam's 19 municipalities (also called villages) are divided into four groups, and seats are allocated proportionatey to the number of residents registered in each group.

The legislative power of Guam extends to all local matters. Local legislation must be consistent with all federal laws applicable to the island. As an unincorporated territory, Guam's legislative jurisdiction may not exceed those powers conferred by Congress. All locally enacted bills must be reported by the governor to the Department of the Interior, and Congress is empowered to annul any local legislation.

Judicial authority is vested in the Federal District Court of Guam and other courts established by the laws of Guam. The judge of the district court is appointed by the president of the

United States for an eight-year term, subject to confirmation by the Senate. This court has both original and appellate jurisdiction in all cases arising under the Constitution, treaties, and laws of the United States; it may also handle cases not tried by locally established courts. Appeals from the district court are taken to the Ninth Circuit Court of Appeals of the United States and eventually to the Supreme Court of the United States.

The court of first instance for all cases arising under the laws of Guam is the Superior Court of Guam, formerly known as the Island Court. The judges of the Superior Court are appointed by the governor for renewable terms of eight years, subject to confirmation by the territorial legislature. Justice is also administered by the police court, traffic court, juvenile court, and small-claims courts. Criminal and civil procedures are similar to those on the mainland. The only notable exception is the absence of trial by jury.

Guam does not have county or municipal subdivisions having separate taxing authority. The 19 municipalities (villages) are each headed by an elected commissioner, but this officer has no legal authority. The commissioner presides over varied community matters on a self-help basis.

Political competition is bipartisan. Every two years the Democratic and Republican parties vie for popular support in electing their respective candidates to the office of the nonvoting delegate to the House of Representatives, the governorship, and the 21 seats in the legislature of Guam. In the general election held in November 1982, the Democrats gained control of all three institutions. The voter turnout was 87 percent of the 35,207 registered voters. Since 1950 the voter participation has been consistently high, ranging from a low of 80 percent to a high of 92 percent.

For many years the major interest of most politically aware Guamanians was focused on the political status of Guam. The status issue was voted on in a preliminary plebiscite held in January 1982. Nearly one-half of the 9,929 people taking part favored a commonwealth status with the United States—a status that would give Guam the same semi-independent status as Puerto Rico. Twenty-six percent preferred statehood, and less than 4 percent mentioned independence. In the September 1982 runoff referendum between commonwealth status and statehood, 73 percent opted for commonwealth against 21 percent for statehood.

Apart from the status issue, the Guamanian leaders continued to lobby for the right to vote in the United States presidential elections and for exemption from certain federal laws whose application to Guam would adversely affect the island's interest. From Guam's point of view, certain federal laws were regarded as unrealistic. Exemptions would allow Guam, for example, the use of cheaper imported vessels for shipping between American ports; current regulations require the use of more expensive American-built ships. Another effort concerned the liberalization of visa requirements for Japanese tourists visiting Guam; visa waivers would allow greater access for tourists to Guam, resulting in a substantial boost to the island's tourist industry. For years exemption was also sought from environmental regulations requiring Guam to adopt the same stringent emission controls imposed on mainland industries. In December 1983 a law was passed by the United States Congress, evidently because the application of strict clean air standards to Guam was without merit. The risk of environmental pollution was considered unlikely because trade winds would blow over the island year-round, taking emissions out to the ocean.

Security
The maintenance of public order, safety, and civil defense is the responsibility of the territorial government, whereas external security and foreign affairs fall under the appropriate departments in Washington. Public safety is the responsibility of several functional agencies. The Department of Public Safety operates the police force and supervises motor vehicle registration. Other agencies are the Department of Corrections; the Department of Law, whose head is the attorney general; the Department of Youth Affairs; Public Defender Services Corporation; the Criminal Justice Planning Agency; the Office of Civil Defense; and the Department of Commerce, which is responsible for port security.

Guam continues to play a major role in the national security system of the United States. Units of the air force, navy, and coast guard are stationed on the island. Anderson Air Force Base, located on the northern tip of the island, is the most important Pacific base of the Strategic Air Command (SAC); this base is responsible for SAC operations west of the international date line and in Asia. Its airstrip provides services for the 24-hour inflight air alert of SAC. Another important service provided by facilities on the island is the aerial weather reconnaissance of tropical cyclones throughout the western Pacific.

Apra Harbor provides the navy with major repair and maintenance facilities for the Seventh Fleet and is the major Pacific facility servicing nuclear Polaris submarines. The Naval

Air Station has a joint-use agreement with the territorial government in operating the island's commercial airport. All the military services have provided major aid in the development of island infrastructure and in the support and expansion of local business and service operations. Although there is concern over the amount of land currently under military control, relations between the Guamanians and military personnel have been for the most part cordial and cooperative. In 1984 efforts were under way to release more military-controlled landholdings to the civilian sector.

KIRIBATI

Flag: Yellow rising sun and frigate bird above blue and white waves on red field

Official Name	Republic of Kiribati
Political Status	Independent state (1979)
Capital	Tarawa (Bairiki is administrative center)
Population	61,400 (1984 midyear estimate)
Land Area	690 square kilometers
Currency	Australian dollar ($A)
Main Islands and Island Groups	Banaba, Gilbert Islands, Line Islands Phoenix Islands

Kiribati has an exceptionally large ocean area. Its phosphate resources, formerly the backbone of the economy, were exhausted by 1979, and its hopes for an economically independent future lay largely in the promise of the marine resources within its immense ocean boundaries. Internal regional development has been highly uneven, favoring the Gilbert Islands and its principal atoll, Tarawa, the political and economic center of the country.

Physical Environment

Kiribati (pronounced Kiri-bas) consists of 33 tiny islands; all but one, Banaba (formerly Ocean Island), are clustered in three principal groups separated by immense stretches of water. Their combined total land area is only about 10 times the size of the District of Columbia; but the total ocean area over which the islands are distributed measures, by various estimates, from 3.5 to 5 million square kilometers. The predominant Gilbert Islands group straddles the equator on the western side of the international date line, northeast of Tuvalu and southeast of the Marshall Islands. Banaba lies approximately 440 kilometers farther west. At the other extreme end of the country, the eight Line Islands are located far east of the date line; the main island of the group, Kiritimati (Christmas), is situated some 2,100 kilometers southeast of Honolulu. Between these extremes are the eight Phoenix Islands, which lack permanent populations.

All the islands are low-lying coral atolls, the single exception being the raised limestone island of Banaba, which rises to a height of 81 meters. Kiritimati, covering 363.4 square kilometers, is one of the largest coral formations in the world, but most of the others are patches of sandy, rubbled coral. Many islands enclose a lagoon. Extensive reef areas, nearly dry at low tide, surround the atolls, severely limiting access by boat. Foreign vessels calling at the main overseas port on Tarawa must be served by tugs and barges from offshore anchorages.

The difficulty of approaching many atolls by sea, as well as Kiribati's remoteness and far-flung geography, makes air transport an important means of communication. Overseas and domestic airlines connected Tarawa's Bonriki Airport with Nauru, Fiji, and Hawaii during the early 1980s. Expansion of domestic airline service to the outer islands has been aided by government support for the construction of airstrips. As of mid-1984 there were approximately 17 airstrips in the outer islands, most receiving regularly scheduled domestic flight service.

The Gilberts are covered with coconut palms and smaller numbers of pandanus (screw pine) trees that provide construction materials for traditional buildings. The soil is poor, and organic materials must be added so that taro and other subsistence crops can grow.

Northeast and southeast trade winds flowing toward the equator converge in the area of the Gilberts to form a belt of low-pressure tropical air that moves across the islands in a regular pattern, dominating the climate. The mean annual temperature is 27°C. Rainfall is heaviest from December to February, when the doldrums bring disturbed, showery weather. Rainfall in general is uncertain, however, showing considerable variation not only seasonally but also within short distances.

Drought is a problem, especially in the central and southern Gilberts and in the Phoenix Islands, where a British attempt at re-settling some Gilbertese in the late 1930s had to be abandoned because of water shortages. Other environmental hazards include occasional storms that can create severe wave surges. The absence of high ground—only Banaba rises higher than four meters at any spot—renders freshwater reserves liable to inundation by salt water.

Historical Setting

Although archaeological artifacts indicate that certain of the Line and Phoenix islands were at one time inhabited—probably by Polynesian peoples—at the time of the arrival of the Europeans, only the Gilberts and Banaba were settled. The origins of the I-Kiribati, as the Gilbertese people are called locally, remain obscure. Their own oral tradition associates the evolution of contemporary society with the arrival of Polynesian peoples from the Samoa Islands centuries ago and their interfusion with indigenous inhabitants. Based on their present-day physical and cultural attributes, however, both the Gilbertese and the Banabans are generally classified as Micronesian, having some degree of Polynesian admixture. It is assumed that they reached the islands as migrants from the west, possibly from Indonesia.

Before the arrival of the Europeans, rivalry between various kingdoms and family alliances created a climate of uncertainty and intermittent warfare. Invaders attacked from the north, and Gilbertese themselves raided the Ellice Islands (present-day Tuvalu) to the south. (On the island of Nui, in that group, a Gilbertese dialect became the lingua franca.) On most islands authority rested with a group of kin elders, but on two atolls dominant chieftains held a firm grip on the populace. Struggles for power and control over land among the various groups were frequent, and continuing rivalry between the northern and southern sets of islands carried into the late twentieth century.

Kiritimati was the first island to be encountered by European explorers. The Gilberts were first sighted in 1823, the last of the Phoenix group in 1825. After their discovery the islands were regularly visited by whaling and trading ships. Protestant and Roman Catholic missionaries converted most of the population to Christianity during the mid- and late nineteenth century, leaving the Gilbertese about equally divided between the two major branches of the faith. The islands themselves offered little of value to any colonial power, given the paucity of their resources, apart from coconut palms. From about 1850 to 1875, however, blackbirders raided local settlements to kidnap islanders for use as laborers in Fiji, Tahiti, Hawaii, Australia, and Latin America. Gilbertese offered fierce, but usually vain, resistance.

In 1892 Britain established a protectorate over the Gilbert Islands and the nine nearby Ellice Islands, placing them under the jurisdiction of its high commissioner for the western Pacific, then based in Fiji (see Fiji, ch. 2). In the Gilberts themselves there was only a small British staff; therefore the local headmen and magistrates retained considerable authority over their own affairs. Banaba was annexed in 1900 on evidence of its rich phosphate resources. In 1916 Britain announced the formation of the Gilbert and Ellice Islands Colony (GEIC). Banaba and two of the northern Line Islands were included almost at once, Kiritimati was added in 1919, and the Phoenix Islands in 1939. A joint British-United States administration of two islands of the Phoenix

279

group was agreed on in 1939 in partial settlement of conflicting British and United States claims to the Line and Phoenix groups.

Apart from copra production, the colonial economy was based almost exclusively on exploitation of Banaba's phosphate resources. The British Phosphate Commission, a consortium of the British, Australian, and New Zealand governments, mined the phosphate, which was exported to Australia and New Zealand for use as fertilizer. Britain bought the land from the Banabans— compelling the sale where it was not volunteered—but paid what it saw as a fair price and, after 1913, invested the money on behalf of the population against the day when deposits would be exhausted.

Japanese reconnaissance units landed briefly on Tarawa and Butaritari in the Gilberts in early December 1941, returning in force in 1942 to occupy the GEIC. Temporary headquarters for those parts of the GEIC not in enemy hands were established initially in Australia and later in Funafuti in the Ellice group. In November 1943 Tarawa and other Gilbert atolls were the scene of some of the fiercest fighting in the Pacific theater between Japanese and United States forces.

Banaba remained under Japanese control until 1945. The Japanese had deported its inhabitants to the Caroline Islands, and in 1946, because the traditional living areas on the island had been so ravaged by mine operations, the British resettled them on Rabi Island in Fiji, where most remained permanently.

Steps to self-rule and eventual independence began in 1963, when advisory and executive councils were established, continuing through 1977, by which time the GEIC had achieved total internal self-government. In 1976 the Ellice Islands separated from the GEIC, eventually to become the independent nation of Tuvalu, and on July 12, 1979, the Republic of Kiribati, composed of Banaba and the Gilbert, Phoenix, and Line islands, achieved independence. In a treaty of friendship signed in September 1979, the United States relinquished its claim to the eight Phoenix Islands and five central and southern Line Islands. The two northernmost Line Islands—Kingman Reef and Palmyra Atoll—as well as Jarvis, Baker, and Howland islands, which lay between the Gilbert and Line islands, remained United States territory, however.

In the meantime, the British Phosphate Commission had reestablished its operations on Banaba in 1946, and phosphate mining reemerged as the dominant industry. Export tonnage increased almost fivefold during the 1947–69 period. Royalties were set aside but were paid largely to the GEIC treasury; the

Banaban landowners received proportionately very little. Opposition to these arrangements among the Banabans from 1965 onward brought various concessions, including increases in the royalties, increases in the Banaban share of such royalties (to 50 percent), and ultimately, after Banabans brought suit in the British High Court for back royalties and damages in 1977, an offer of an ex gratia payment of $A million (for value of the Australian dollar—see Glossary). The Banaban community on Rabi Island in Fiji at first rejected the offer, but it was later accepted in 1981, together with the interest accrued. The Banabans were unsuccessful, however, in their bid to prevent their island from being incorported into Kiribati.

The Social System

The most recent census, taken in December 1978, showed 56,213 persons in Kiribati and indicated an annual growth rate over the previous five years of 1.6 percent. On that basis, a population of 62,400 was projected for 1985. Persons under age 15 made up 41 percent of the population. The 1978 census indicated that 90 percent of Kiribati's population was concentrated in the Gilbert Islands, 32 percent of the total found on Tarawa—the nation's only urbanized area. Kiritimati, Teraina (Washington), and Tabuaeran (Fanning) in the Line Islands and Banaba together accounted for slightly over 7 percent. Before World War II Banaba's population had consisted of indigenous Banabans, Gilbertese temporarily employed in its phosphate mines, and descendants of indentured Chinese laborers; at the time of the census it was composed almost exclusively of temporary contract laborers.

Urban growth on Tarawa was a major problem, its ramifications evident in poverty, overcrowding, labor unrest, and youth alienation. Persons from the outer islands—tantamount to the country's rural sector—continued to settle on Tarawa in increasing numbers during the early 1980s, however, drawn by its perceived economic opportunities, Westernized pace of life, and comparatively modernized infrastructure. Tarawa had doubled in size since 1963, and if its explosive growth continued at the same pace, it was estimated that by 1993 Tarawa would contain 4,700 persons per square kilometer, about the same as Hong Kong in the mid-1970s.

Most residents of Kiribati are native speakers of Gilbertese, a Micronesian language having various mutually intelligible dialects—Banaban being one. English is widely used for official purposes, is taught in primary schools, and is used as a language of instruction in secondary schools. Whether any residual use of Chinese lingered from the era of indentured Chinese phosphate workers on Banaba is uncertain. A few Polynesians from Tuvalu add minimally to the ethnolinguistic mixture.

Religion has been a source of major social division. An estimated 95 percent of the population of the Gilbertese in mid-1980 were professing Christians, including more than 31,000 Protestants and 33,000 Roman Catholics. The latter are concentrated predominantly in the five northern Gilberts. A single diocese encompasses the Gilberts, the neighboring countries of Nauru and Tuvalu, and two of the Phoenix Islands. Anti-Catholic sentiment has prevented the building of Catholic churches on the two southernmost Gilbert islands. Indigenous religious leaders work together with a number of foreign Protestant missionaries and Roman Catholic priests and brothers.

The Christian religion plays a major role in the national life. The Catholic bishop of Tarawa has been outspoken in his concern over increasing population pressure, hoping that New Zealand or Australia might be encouraged to accept Gilbertese immigrants. Both Protestants and Catholics support important education programs. They also focus on public information projects, issuing periodical publications and broadcasting radio programs.

Kiribati is proud of its 100-percent literacy rate and large numbers of primary and secondary educational institutions. Yet in Betio, Bairiki, and Bikenibeu on Tarawa, there is evidence that the country shares a problem common with other developing countries, that of large numbers of educated school-leavers who are unable to find suitable employment.

The Economy

Under British rule, phosphate was the main source of foreign exchange, although copra provided some revenue. So too did remittances from Gilbertese employed on phosphate-rich Nauru or by foreign shipping lines. Phosphate mining had ceased altogether by 1980. Kiribati's balance of trade declined from the equivalent of US$7 million in 1979 to a negative balance of US$20 million in 1982 (by provisional estimate). Accordingly, the nation was faced with a critical economic problem despite the interest income earned from overseas deposits of previous phosphate revenues. Britain agreed to provide capital and development aid through 1993, but Kiribati's leaders were determined to achieve economic independence as soon as possible, hoping to tap wealth from the ocean.

Although fishing was an important local activity, the major significance of the sector lay in potential fees from fisheries agreements, particularly related to yellowfin and skipjack tuna fishing around the Phoenix Islands. Kiribati declared a 200-nautical-mile Exclusive Economic Zone (EEZ—see Glossary) in 1978, giving the country potential control at that time of a 1 million-square-kilometer area around the Gilberts alone. In 1982 Japan paid more than the equivalent of US$1 million for fishing rights, and it had cooperated with Kiribati in various fisheries projects. Taiwanese and American tuna vessels also provided revenues. Kiribati had developed its own government-owned fishing company in 1981, using a grant from Britain. The catch was sold to the Star Kist cannery at Pago Pago, American Samoa. Some I-Kiribati have established lagoon fish farms for raising shrimp and fish.

Copra was by far the principal cash crop. In 1978, the most recent year for which production figures were available, smallholders produced 8,200 tons, plantations 1,900 tons. Most came from the Gilberts, but sizable coconut plantations were found on Kiritimati. Coconut products were consumed locally, along with vegetable crops, some poultry, and eggs. New plantings of copra in the Line Islands were expected to increase production.

In 1982 total government expenditures were $A16.9 million; revenues provided $A15.8 million. Foreign aid contributed heavily to economic development. In the 1979–82 period Britain provided about $A8 million per year for capital expenditures, in addition to aid in the form of training programs and development projects. Other major donors included the United Nations Development Programme (UNDP) and the European Development Fund, which contributed $A700,000 and $A4.15 million, respectively, between 1980 and 1982. Australia, New Zealand, and Japan gave aid for various projects in water supply, sanitation, machinery, transport, fisheries, technical training, and other areas. The United States Peace Corps had an active program in the country.

The economy was essentially characterized by free enterprise, but numerous government-owned and -controlled ventures provided employment to large numbers of workers, especially in transportation, communications, and trading. Government-run cooperative societies dominated the retail trade sector.

The dichotomy between urbanized Tarawa and the outer islands was a major aspect of the economic scene. The outer islands were significantly less developed than Tarawa, their inhabitants participating little or not at all in the expanding cash econony. Fishing, cultivating copra, repairing houses, sailing canoes, car-

ing for children, and producing handicrafts were the essential occupations in the outer islands.

Tarawa had received the major share of public allocations for
infrastructure development. Housing, road, causeway, and other
improvements had been focused on the capital area. Explosive
growth had led to overcrowding and inadequate public services.
In most Tarawa households at least one member was employed by
the government; in many households there were two government
employees. In the mid-1980s there was concern over the declining purchasing power of wages. Lower echelon employees in particular complained of dwindling local supplies of food, firewood,
and housing construction materials.

The Political System and Security

Kiribati is a sovereign democratic republic within the Commonwealth of Nations. Its government is based on the Constitution promulgated at independence on July 12, 1979. The document provides for a form of government in which a popularly
elected president *(beretitenti)* is responsible to a parliament,
which may dismiss him. The governor general, representing the
British monarch, has only titular authority; the president is head
of state and head of the government. Executive authority is
vested collectively in the cabinet, which is composed of the president, the vice president, the attorney general, and no more than
eight ministers selected by the president from the House of Assembly. The cabinet is directly responsible to the parliament.

Legislative authority resides in the House of Assembly,
which is composed of 35 elected members, a representative of the
Banabans nominated by the Rabi Island Council in Fiji, and the
attorney general as an ex officio member. Members are elected
for a four-year term. The House of Assembly is presided over by
the Speaker, elected by its members from a slate of nonmembers.
The Constitution provides for a public service and an independent judiciary. The judicial system consists of the High Court, the
Court of Appeal for Kiribati, and subordinate magistrate's courts.

Constitutional provisions with respect to the Banaban community could be seen as an attempt to defuse a potentially explosive issue. In late 1978 the Banaban delegation had walked out of
the preindependence constitutional convention in London after
Britain announced that contrary to the delegation's wishes,
Banaba would be included within Kiribati. In early 1979 members of the Rabi Island Banaban community and locally resident
Banabans staged demonstrations on Banaba, and phosphate in-

stallations were targets of bomb attacks. The Constitution returns to the Banaban community ownership of land that had been forcibly acquired by the government phosphate company. The Constitution also guarantees the right of all Banabans to return to their island to live, if they so choose.

The president is popularly elected, on the basis of universal, free, adult franchise, from a slate of no more than four candidates nominated by the House of Assembly from its members. In the event that the president has to vacate his office after a motion of no confidence, the House of Assembly is dissolved, and a new general election must be held. In the interim the Council of State, composed of the chairman of the Public Service Commission, the chief justice, and the Speaker of the House of Assembly, carries out the executive function.

Local government authority rests in the hands of elected local councils that have been established on all permanently inhabited islands. For administrative purposes the islands are divided into six districts, each having a district officer in charge. These are Tarawa, Northern, Central, Southern—covering the Gilberts other than Tarawa—Banaba, and Line Islands.

Political awareness and participation developed rapidly after 1967, when voters participated in national elections for the first time, choosing representatives to the colonial legislature. Although organized political competition was only beginning to emerge in the early 1980s, partisan struggles for leadership were waged vigorously on the basis of factions and personal alliances.

In the 1974–78 preindependence years, the dominant group had been led by Naboua Ratieta, a representative from the largely Roman Catholic northern Gilbert island of Marakei. He became the country's first chief minister following the general elections of 1974.

Transition was peaceful under a new leadership group headed by a former opposition member of parliament, Ieremia Tabai, who took over after the general elections of 1978. By contrast with the former chief minister, Tabai was a Protestant from the central Gilbert island of Nonouti. Although he did not win an outright majority in any of the five predominantly Catholic northern Gilberts, he received almost one-third of all votes cast. The new president pledged to build trust in government which he said lacked credibility in the eyes of most people. He indicated that he would go no further with the notion of establishing a defense force, which the previous administration had proposed and which many voters had vigorously opposed. He promised to work for development of the outer islands, blaming government neglect for the dramatic urban drift and its related problems. After independence Tabai became the first president; he was reelected for a second term in May 1982.

Tabai himself came under attack in December 1982 on the issue of proposed salary adjustments for six key government officials and costly government subsidies to Air Tungaru and the Kiribati Shipping Corporation. His government was defeated and parliament dissolved, but in new elections in February 1983 he was returned to office, continuing to hold that position in mid-1984.

As of mid-1984 Kiribati belonged to the South Pacific Commission and the South Pacific Forum (see Appendix B). It was a member of the United Nations and the Commonwealth of Nations and was one of the Asian, Caribbean, and Pacific states of the European Economic Community. It maintained diplomatic relations with Britain, the United States, and several Pacific Ocean countries.

NAURU

Official Name	Republic of Nauru
Political Status	Independent state (1968)
Capital	Yaren
Population	8,600 (1984 midyear estimate)
Land Area	20.9 square kilometers
Currency	Australian dollar ($A)

Flag: White star beneath horizontal yellow stripe on blue field

Among the developing countries of Oceania, Nauru is an exceptional case. Valuable commercial mineral deposits make the tiny island-nation one of the richest in the world. Its per capita 1982 gross national product (GNP—see Glossary) puts it in the same category as the United States, the Federal Republic of Germany (West Germany), and other industrial giants as well as the small, oil-rich states of Qatar and Brunei. Its phosphate wealth has been a mixed blessing, however. In mid-1984 Nauruans enjoyed a wide variety of educational, medical, and welfare benefits. Their future was being protected through a careful national investment program, but government leaders were becoming concerned about a number of social issues.

Physical Environment

The solitary island of Nauru (pronounced NAH-oo-roo) is a raised coral limestone atoll, one of the three great rock phosphate islands of the world—the others being Banaba in Kiribati and Christmas Island in the Indian Ocean. The island's narrow coastal fringe is banded by an outlying coral reef. Inland, behind a bank of coral cliffs, lies a barren plateau rich in phosphate, which has been leached from guano, or bird droppings. The rock phosphate occupies the space between pinnacles of limestone, which jut irregularly from the ground once the phosphate has been dug.

Nauru is situated in the central Pacific Ocean, about 4,000 kilometers off the northeastern coast of Australia and 4,160 kilometers southwest of Hawaii. It claims a sea area of 320,000 square kilometers. The climate is tropical, and monsoon season begins in November and ends in February. Rainfall averages 450 millimeters annually but varies considerably. Severe drought can occur.

Historical Setting

The origins of the Nauruans are purely speculative. Some or all of their forebears may have come from the eastern Melanesian area of the Solomon Islands. Or they may have set off from any of the eastern Micronesian island groups—the Marshalls, the Carolines or, carried off course by the strong South Equatorial Current, the Gilberts. Their quite distinctive language offers few clues. Whatever the case, their subsequent contact with other islands was slight. The isolation of the solitary island was reinforced by dangerous ocean currents and the living coral reef that girdled the small raised atoll.

The early Nauruans settled the fertile coastal ring where coconuts flourished but drought intermittently menaced cultivation efforts. For seafood they ventured beyond the reef and built fish-pond reservoirs inland. When continuous European contact began in the mid-nineteenth century, the newcomers found a well-developed culture in which kin relations provided the basis for social life. Nauruans were organized into 12 kinship groups, tracing descent through females and giving political allegiance to a lineage chief. Members married outside the group, and property, mainly in the form of land, was individually held and passed down through the lineage.

Whalers, traders, and beachcombers disrupted traditional social and political patterns. Firearms, knives, alcohol, and disease sparked disorder. Sporadic aggression between lineages developed into almost continuous armed struggle between 1878 and 1888, at which time the German protectorate over the Marshall Islands was extended to cover Nauru.

Phosphate mining, begun in 1907, produced even more dramatic change. The unveiling of the island's extravagant phosphate resources and those of neighboring Banaba had been accomplished by Albert F. Ellis, an associate of the British-owned Pacific Islands Company, based in Sydney, Australia. Informed of his discovery, Britain annexed Banaba and signed a 999-year treaty with the chiefs on Nauru to mine deposits there. In 1905, however, the German government gave permission for the transfer of mining rights to the trading company, by then renamed the Pacific Phosphate Company, in exchange for certain rights and privileges.

The phosphate company employed a number of Nauruans as miners, but its preference was for expatriate labor, especially indentured Chinese. Large numbers of Chinese workers were brought in from Hong Kong and quartered, along with islanders from the Gilbert group and elsewhere, in all-male barracks near the phosphate works. An elite stratum of British administrators and managers ran the company.

Early in World War I a small Australian force seized Nauru from its German administrators, and German shares in the phosphate company were sold in London. After the war ended, the League of Nations granted Britain a mandate over Nauru. The British, Australian, and New Zealand governments then bought the phosphate company and established a joint enterprise known as the British Phosphate Commission (BPC) to manage, mine, and market the mineral deposits of Nauru and Banaba. Britain and Australia each paid 42 percent of the price, and New Zealand paid 16 percent. Profits were shared at the same ratio.

Under the BPC, health and sanitation improvements, educational expansion, and political reforms were undertaken on Nauru. Villagers were encouraged to elect representatives to the Council of Chiefs, rather than simply assigning them that role on the basis of heredity. Traditional beliefs and practices, including polygamy, retreated in the path of vigorous proselytization of Christianity by Western missionaries. A number of Nauruans were given access to secondary and higher education abroad.

Despite the increasing level of educational attainment, however, Nauruan men were not encouraged to seek management or supervisory appointments with the BPC, and the economy provided few other outlets besides teaching. Nauruans who owned land could enjoy a relatively enviable standard of affluence in any case. Company stores whetted the local appetite for imported goods, and within a very short period the indigenous population became highly dependent on the mining community and integrated with the developing cash economy.

Nauru was occupied by the Japanese during World War II, and most of its population was deported to the Truk group in the Caroline Islands. American bombing attacks in 1943 ended Japanese exploitation of the island altogether. Those Nauruans who had survived were returned to their home island after the war, and a United Nations (UN) trusteeship under Australian administration was placed over the island on behalf of Australia, Britain, and New Zealand. The BPC reorganized its activities, and mining resumed.

In the new political climate of the post-World War II period, Nauruans became vocal about a desire for independence and control of their island's resources, annual exports of phosphate averaging 1.5 to 2 million tons a year. The Nauru Local Government Council, replacing the Council of Chiefs, played a more significant role in the political arena than had its predecessor. New career politicians emerged, motivated to seek support abroad for Nauruan political and economic interests.

Nationalist sentiment was further aroused by failure to reach a favorable resolution of the resettlement issue. In the early 1960s Australia, New Zealand, and Britain had all offered to resettle Nauruans in their countries and to give them full citizenship rights over the next three decades as the island's phosphate resources became exhausted. In 1961, when Australia refused to consider their demand for complete sovereignty over the island, they ruled out resettlement entirely and began instead to press rigorously for the right to buy the phosphate industry and for independence for their home island.

Progress toward these goals was rapid. With the help of foreign economic advisers, they were able to increase greatly their phosphate royalties, beginning in 1965. In early 1966 Nauru was permitted a considerable measure of internal self-rule. On January 31, 1968, the independent Republic of Nauru was established as an associate member of the Commonwealth of Nations.

The Social System

A census taken in January 1977 showed a total of 6,966 persons, indicating a 1.3-percent annual growth rate for the preceding decade. Besides the indigenous population, there were substantial numbers of temporary laborers from the Gilberts, as well as some Chinese, Filipinos, and Westerners. Most of the indigenous people are Christian, Protestants outnumbering others. The national language is Nauruan, although English is widely spoken.

The very high level of material consumption has resulted in a modicum of social breakdown and widespread personal health problems. Motorized transportation and imported foods have contributed to an increase in cases of obesity, high blood pressure, and diabetes. This led in early 1983 to an effort by the president to interest people in greater physical activity and exercise.

In mid-1984 all essential services in education and health were provided free to the citizenry. The country had two modern hospitals and a variety of other clinics. Patients requiring specialized care were flown to Australia. Education was free and compulsory to age 16 in government-run schools. In 1979 there were five kindergartens, one primary school, and one secondary school. A Roman Catholic mission operated other schools. Qualifying students were educated at government expense at secondary schools and universities in Australia, Papua New Guinea, Fiji, and New

Zealand.

The Economy

Nauru phosphate, valued as commercial fertilizer, is of the highest quality in the world. Although it has been mined almost continuously since 1907, reserves in the early 1980s still amounted to about 38.8 million tons. The supply was expected to last until 1995 or slightly beyond.

The country's phosphate wealth accumulated rapidly after the mid-1960s. The hard-fought struggle for an increase in royalties resulted in price increases beginning in 1967. Revenues paid to Nauruans by the BPC increased from about US$0.37 per ton in 1965 to US$11 in 1967, subject to fluctuations in world market prices. Later the Nauruan government bought the capital assets of the company, taking control from the BPC in 1970. The government held title to a small portion of the land on which the mining was done, but the vast majority of phosphate-containing land was held by private Nauruan landowners.

Effective management and booming world prices worked in favor of the new Nauru Phosphate Company. To the traditional markets in Australia, New Zealand, and Japan, new markets were added: Taiwan, the Republic of Korea (South Korea), the Philippines, and Indonesia. Import and trade statistics for Nauru were not a matter of public record, but press reports provided unofficial estimates indicating that export revenues from processed phosphate in 1982 were equivalent to US$123 million.

As in the past, the proportion of foreigners in the labor force was high. Britons, Australians, and New Zealanders were numerous among the country's supervisors, government workers, managers, and technicians. Islanders from Kiribati and Tuvalu, Filipinos, and Hong Kong Chinese accounted for much of the unskilled and semiskilled labor force in the phosphate industry.

The government took about one-half of the phosphate revenues; the remainder went to the Nauru Phosphate Royalties Trust and to the Nauru Local Government Council. The long-term trust fund invested its resources in other countries, notably Australia, to ensure a continuing income for Nauruans when the phosphate deposits were exhausted. In early 1983 the value of the trust, according to an official spokesperson, exceeded $A200 million (for value of the Australian dollar—see Glossary). Among its holdings were a commercial building in Texas and an office building in Hong Kong. A hotel in Guam was planned, and phosphate processing plants were being built in India and the Philippines.

Phosphate revenues were expended on the extensive welfare system and on subsidies to the national airline and other enterprises.

A narrow coastal belt around the island and the fringe of a lagoon provided suitable soils for the cultivation of coconuts, bananas, pineapples, and vegetables, but food and water were largely imported along with manufactured commodities. Fishing, manufacturing, and tourism were insignificant economic sectors, although a number of phosphate workers caught fish for their own consumption or sold them to Nauruans.

In the fiscal year beginning in July 1978 (FY 1979), the latest year for which figures were available, total government expenditures were $A40.6 million. Revenues amounted to $A35 million, not including a $A5.7 million surplus from the previous year. Proposed expenditures for the FY 1981 budget included a planned outlay of $A29.4 million for Air Nauru (out of an expected total expenditure of $A59 million). Fuel costs accounted for a substantial portion of the cost of running the airline, which as of early 1982 owned and operated five Boeing 737 aircraft.

Interisland communication was facilitated by the government-owned Radio Nauru, founded in 1968. There were several limited circulation periodicals, published in Nauruan and English, including the weekly *Nauru Post*. The island has enjoyed global telephone communications since the construction of an earth satellite receiving station in 1975. Videotape television sets and videotape recorders were commonplace.

The Nauru Local Government Council provided various social and public services. It operated the several retail stores of the Nauru Cooperative Society, managed the Nauru Insurance Corporation, and provided hotel accommodations and a car rental service on the island. The council also ran the Nauru Pacific Line, a national shipping company. In 1977 a 53-story office complex opened under its auspices in Melbourne, Australia. Other foreign enterprises included several fertilizer-processing plants.

The Political System and Security

Government organization is based on the Constitution of January 1968, as amended in May 1968. Framed by Nauruans themselves through the process of a constitutional convention, the document calls for broadly phrased fundamental rights and freedoms for the individual, including those of legal protection, freedom of conscience, and respect for private and family life. It provides for a form of government combining features of a presidential and a parliamentary system. The chief executive of the republic is both head of state and head of the government. He is elected by parliament from among its members. There is no prime minister. Executive authority is vested in a cabinet over which the president presides; the four or five members of the cabinet are appointed by the president from the membership of parliament. The president himself holds several cabinet portfolios.

Legislative authority is vested in parliament, and its enactments are not subject to review or assent by any other body or person. Unless dissolved in the interim, it serves for three years. Its 18 members are popularly chosen by the Nauruan citizenry by direct election. Voting is compulsory for all citizens over 20 years of age. One of the eight constituencies into which the country is divided for electoral purposes returns four members, and the other seven return two each.

A system of checks and balances operates according to the Constitution. The president may at any time request the Speaker of the House to dissolve parliament. For its part, parliament, on a resolution approved by a majority of its members, may remove the president and the cabinet from office. A new president must be elected within seven days.

The judicial system consists of the Supreme Court, the District Court, and the Family Court. Presided over by a chief justice, the Supreme Court exercises both original and appellate jurisdiction; further appeals may be taken to the High Court of Australia. A minister of justice, appointed by the president, serves in the cabinet.

In mid-1984 Hammer DeRoburt, a onetime schoolteacher and head chief of the Nauru Local Government Council in the preindependence period, was the most powerful political figure in the country. Except for an interval in the late 1970s, when an opposition group formed the Nauru Party and temporarily ousted him from high office, DeRoburt has been president of the country continuously since 1968. His wide-ranging authority was undisputed, and his skill as a practical politician was unquestioned. In addition to the presidency, in mid-1984 he held the portfolios of civil aviation, external and internal affairs, public service, and island development and industry. After general elections in December 1983, DeRoburt co-opted three members of the opposition into his cabinet, including former president and Nauru Party leader Bernard Dowiyogo.

Nauru was an associate member of the Commonwealth of Nations, enjoying all benefits of membership other than the right to attend the Conference of Prime Ministers. It was not a signatory to any defense pact or treaty with any external power. Reports in 1984 indicated, however, that in the event of internal or external threats to its political stability, Nauru might expect assistance from Britain or Australia. A small local police force staffed by Nauruans maintained public order.

Micronesia

TRUST TERRITORY OF THE PACIFIC ISLANDS

Political Status	Four separate self-governing political entities in transition from United States administration under 1947 United Nations trusteeship arrangement
Capital	Saipan
Population	140,000 (1984 midyear estimate)
Land Area	1,836 square kilometers
Currency	United States dollar (US$)
Major Islands and Island Groups	Caroline Islands— Palau, Yap, Truk, Ponape, Kosrae; Mariana Islands— Saipan, Tinian, Rota; Marshall Islands—Majuro, Kwajalein

Physical Environment

The Trust Territory of the Pacific Islands (TTPI) is located in the western Pacific and covers an estimated 7.8 million square kilometers of sea area—roughly equivalent to the size of the continental United States. Scattered across this vast expanse of ocean surface are 2,200 islands and islets, the total land area of which is less than one-half that of the state of Rhode Island. Fewer than 100 of the larger and more productive islands are populated.

The three major archipelagoes of the TTPI are the Mariana Islands, the Caroline Islands, and the Marshall Islands (see fig. 11). All of the islands and island units are small, ranging downward in size from Babelthuap in the Palau cluster, which has a total land area of 396 square kilometers. Countless others are mere specks of coral and sand.

The islands may be classified broadly as high volcanic islands or low coral islands, and as continental or oceanic, according to their geological substructure. The Mariana chain, the Palau cluster, and the island of Yap in the Carolines are classified as high types of varying elevations. They are of continental structure, being exposed peaks of a submerged mountain range that extends from Japan to New Guinea and represents the easternmost limits

295

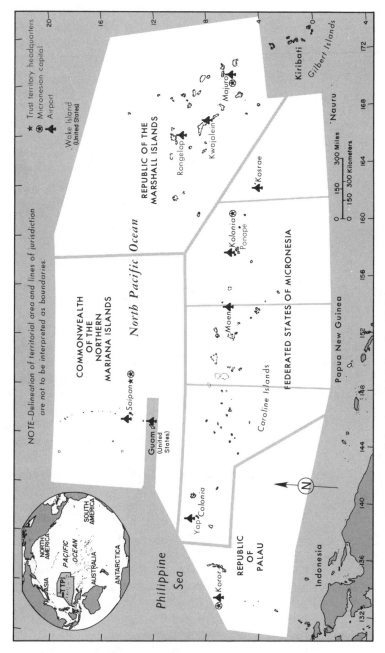

Figure 11. Trust Territory of the Pacific Islands, 1984

of the Asian continental shelf. The outermost reaches of this seaward shelf are delineated by deep ocean trenches. Truk, Ponape, and Kosrae islands in the eastern Carolines are also high islands, having maximum elevations of 457, 762, and 610 meters, respectively. They are classified as oceanic, however, because their substructure is associated with lava extruded from fissures in the ocean floor itself.

All other islands of the TTPI, regardless of the archipelago in which they are located, are low types that rise less than three meters above sea level. These islands are formed by coral growths capping still-submerged peaks of the continental shelf or oceanic lava piles that do not quite reach the surface. Most of these coralline formations are atolls; that is, they consist of a barrier or a fringing reef, or both, enclosing a number of tiny islets around an interior lagoon. Some, however, such as Lib in the Marshall group, are single islands that have neither reefs nor lagoons. Still others, such as Fais near Ulithi in the Carolines, are raised atolls that have been thrust upward by upheavals in the ocean floor so that their lagoons as well as their encircling reefs are fully exposed. In the elevating process their lagoons are often drained away, leaving a shallow, saucerlike, and usually marshy depression.

The TTPI is so large and complex that it is discussed in terms of seven component areas. The relatively compact Marshall and Mariana archipelagoes each constitute separate areas. The larger and more dispersed Caroline group, however, is subdivided into five areas, each centered on and named after the most significant land in its area.

The climate of the TTPI is tropical and maritime, generally marked by high temperatures, high humidity, and heavy rainfall. Seasonal variations are slight and inconsequential. From May through October the temperature rises. The annual mean temperature of the TTPI is about 26°C, and temperatures increase slightly as one travels south. The humidity usually ranges between 77 and 86 percent. Annual rainfall is consistently high but shows some variation among the island groups. The northern portions of the Marianas and Marshalls average 1,500 millimeters and 2,050 millimeters, respectively. All other sections of the TTPI have 2,500 millimeters or more, Ponape averaging as much as 4,625 millimeters annually.

Weather conditions are generally pleasant and healthful but are subject to frequent and rapid changes. From August to December storms are common. The middle part of the TTPI is subject to typhoons, especially between July and November. Islands in the eastern section lie outside the normal track of typhoons, but in the summer they are visited by occasional storms of typhoon proportions or by tropical cyclones.

Virtually all islands of the TTPI have lush and diverse vegetation. The types of plant life vary between the high and the low island forms, although coconut and breadfruit trees and two varieties of bamboo are common everywhere. Hibiscus trees can also be found throughout the territory, except on the driest atolls.

Vegetation on the low islands is limited to coconut palms, breadfruit, casuarina, pandani (screw pines), creeping vines, sedges, and associated strand growth. The high islands are marked by three distinct types of growth. The coastal flats have dense coverings of broadleaf forest in which mangroves predominate, interspersed with nipa palm and other salt-resistant vegetation. Inland from the tidal flats, coconut trees abound but give way on the lower slopes to dense rain forests of exceedingly varied composition in limestone areas or to scrubby growth and grassland in volcanic soil regions. The upper slopes of high volcanic islands usually have thin, leached soils that do not permit the growth of tall trees and are covered with wet, mossy scrub forests and an undergrowth of ferns.

Three main groups of land animals are found in the TTPI: indigenous kinds, those introduced by the migrating Micronesians before European contact, and species brought in subsequently. The only native mammal is the bat, two species of which are fruit eaters and two insect eaters. They are prevalent in both the high and the low islands. Among the introduced animals are dogs, pigs, several species of rats, horses, cattle, water buffalo, goats, cats, and deer.

The TTPI is generally free from harmful reptiles, but two species of crocodiles and two types of venomous sea snakes are occasionally found in the Palau cluster. Palau also has a few non-venomous snakes, including a tree snake, a mangrove snake, and a rare golden burrowing snake. Several species of lizard, including the large monitor variety that reaches lengths of almost two meters, are abundant on many high and low islands alike.

Land birds are relatively few, but marine and shore birds are abundant. These include the tern, albatross, booby, frigate, plover, cormorant, and several kinds of heron. The Palau cluster is noted for one species of rare freshwater duck. Many other varieties of migratory birds, both land and marine, can sometimes be seen in the TTPI.

Marine life is rich in both number and variety. The reefs, lagoons, and shore areas, as well as the open sea, teem with fish and

"Rock islands" scattered throughout Palau harbor
Courtesy Patricia Luce Chapman

other forms of marine life. All kinds characteristic of tropical Pacific waters are represented, including bonito, tuna, albacore, barracuda, shark, eel, snapper, flounder, and sea bass. Many highly colored small fish inhabit the reefs, as do the octopus, squid, jellyfish, and sea cucumber (bêche-de-mer). There are also many kinds of mollusks and crustaceans, such as crabs, lobsters, langoustines, shrimp, oysters, and clams. Of special interest is the giant Tridacna clam, whose heavy, fluted shell is prized by decorators. Marine mammals include the porpoise and the sea cow, or dugong, which once was plentiful in the Palau cluster but now is becoming quite scarce.

The TTPI has limited mineral resources. Except for phosphate, which is found on several of the raised limestone islands, mineral deposits occur only in some of the high islands. Rock phosphate appears and has been mined on several islands, but high extraction costs, coupled with the destruction of much arable land as a result of mining, makes exploitation economically unfeasible. Other known mineral deposits are present in insufficient quantities to warrant commercial exploitation.

Historical Setting

Very little is known of the history of what is now the area of the TTPI before the sixteenth century because the early inhabitants left few records of their life and times. Genealogies and tales of exploits were transmitted orally from generation to generation within the family or village, but over centuries of retelling they have become so embellished and romanticized that it has become impossible to distinguish fact from fiction.

The contributions of modern scientific research and study are scarcely more definitive, not because data are lacking or inaccurate but because scholars have been unable to agree on the interpretation of their findings. About the only point of common agreement is that the original habitation of the area resulted from the successive migratory waves of peoples from Southeast Asia that began around 1000 B.C.

The first European to explore the area was Ferdinand Magellan, who landed on Guam in 1521 during the course of his epic voyage of discovery around the world. In 1525 other Portuguese navigators searching for the Spice Islands (now the Maluku Islands of Indonesia) came upon Yap and Ulithi in the Carolines.

Within a few years the accounts of these first voyages prompted the dispatch of other, mainly Spanish, expeditions to the Pacific, resulting in the discovery of the Marshalls and the rest of the Caroline and Mariana groups. Thereafter, innumerable explorers, missionaries, traders, whalers, and buccaneers from many nations roamed freely but evinced little desire to establish effective political control over any of the area. The poorly endowed islands were considered unimportant and useful only as convenient havens to provision and repair ships, afford rest and recreation for their crews, and provide fertile ground for spreading the gospel. The one exception to this pattern came with Spain's activities in the Marianas.

Spain claimed the Marianas in 1565 and the next year established a port on Guam to serve as a supply station on the burgeoning trade route between Mexico and the Philippines. No attempt was made, however, to enforce Spanish authority or to impose European culture and institutions on the native society, and life for the Chamorros of Guam and the Marianas remained relatively undisturbed until a band of Jesuit priests established a mission on Guam in 1668. This missionary effort was well received initially, but in time the growing power of the priests, supported by harsh punitive action of the troops, created much local opposition. Open rebellion resulted, and Spain was forced to send strong mil-

Gravestone of German soldier killed during local uprising in 1911 in present-day Ponape State, Federated States of Micronesia Courtesy Patricia Luce Chapman

itary expeditions. When the pacification campaigns were over, Spanish secular and religious authority was absolute throughout the Mariana group. The native population declined sharply as a result of the warfare and diseases introduced by European soldiers and colonists.

The Spanish then took steps to extend their influence southward and eastward into the Carolines and the Marshalls. Although no formal declaration of annexation was made and political control over the two island groups was weak, it gradually became understood that these areas fell within the sphere of Spanish influence.

The situation persisted, without significant change, until copra became a major commodity in the world market during the late nineteenth century. Spain's tenuous and unofficial domination of the area began to be challenged in the European rivalry for trade. Fearing political encroachment by German, British, and other European powers, Spain in 1874 reasserted old claims to the Carolines that since the seventeenth century had been shown on European maps as Spanish territory. Meanwhile, German traders had become firmly entrenched on Jaluit in the Marshalls and in 1878 signed agreements with native chieftains giving them preferred commercial rights.

International rivalry came to a head in August 1885, when a German naval contingent seized Yap, provoking a violent Spanish reaction. The threat of an impending war was averted the next month, however, when the issue was submitted to Pope Leo XIII for arbitration. At the end of the year the pontiff sustained the Spanish claim to the Carolines, contingent on Germany's being granted freedom of trade and the right to establish coaling stations there. Spain thereupon took steps to establish an administrative presence in the Carolines. The Marshalls were declared a German protectorate, and for several years thereafter the two countries shared control of the area.

Spain's defeat in the Spanish-American War of 1898 resulted in new political alignments. In addition to losing the Philippines, Spain ceded Guam to the United States. The government in Madrid, weakened by the war, accepted a German offer equivalent to US$4.5 million to buy its remaining possessions in Micronesia. By adding the Carolines and the rest of the Marianas to the Marshalls, Germany became the dominant power in Micronesia; its main interest was in developing a lucrative copra trade, using laborers from the Carolines.

The German presence was brief, lasting only until the outbreak of World War I in 1914. In that year Japan, which had long coveted the islands, took advantage of Germany's total involvement in Europe and occupied all German-held islands until the end of the war. At the Paris peace conference in 1919, Japan, supported by Britain, France, and Russia, sought to gain full sovereignty over the territory. Australia and the United States opposed the move, and, though their objections were not completely effective, they did succeed in changing the final action from a grant of full sovereignty to an award of a mandate under the League of Nations. The government in Tokyo exercised this mandate as though it were a grant of total hegemony, colonizing and exploiting the area as part of its long-range imperialistic objectives. For all intents and purposes, the islands became an integral part of the Japanese Empire after Japan walked out of the League of Nations in 1933. Increasingly thereafter the territory became a closed military area in which existing installations were strengthened and a series of fortified island bases was interposed between Japan and the Western Hemisphere.

The full significance of this action was revealed when World War II spread to the Pacific theater. The islands first became bases for Japanese aggression to the south and east and later were used to blunt Allied counteroffensives in the drive across the ocean to Japan proper (see World War II, ch. 5). Saipan and

Tinian in the Marianas became huge military bases for these assaults against Japan. It was from Tinian, at the site of what was then the longest runway in the world, that a B-29 bomber took off on August 6, 1945, to drop an atomic bomb on Hiroshima and a second one, three days later, on Nagasaki.

The war left the Micronesian economy almost completely destroyed and the living conditions of the islanders chaotic and deteriorating. A 1946 study found that the economy and the quality of life in the area had been set back at least a quarter of a century.

Formation of the TTPI

After a delay of two years because of interdepartmental differences in Washington over the future status of the conquered islands, the United States in 1947 formally notified the United Nations (UN) of its readiness to place the islands under a UN trusteeship and to administer the territory as executive agent of the world organization. An agreement was signed between them, designating the TTPI, as it came to be officially known, "a strategic area" and naming the United States "the administering authority." For accountability the United States reported directly to the UN Security Council, the agency principally concerned with international peace and security.

The other 10 nonstrategic trust territories set up immediately after World War II reported to the UN General Assembly. All 10, incidentally, had become independent or self-governing by 1984. Initially under the stewardship of the United States Navy, the TTPI was turned over to the Department of the Interior in 1951, but the Marianas remained under military control until 1962.

The term *strategic area* has no international precedent under either the League of Nations mandate system or the UN trusteeship setup. It was added to the vocabulary of the UN at the insistence of the United States, which had argued that, given the TTPI's military importance, the area should be treated separately from nonstrategic or ordinary trust territories. In a strategic area the defense and security considerations were deemed paramount and overriding. Thus, the United States was authorized to establish military bases, erect fortifications, and employ troops in the TTPI as necessary to prevent the disruption of peace and security in the area. It was also permitted "to make use of volunteer forces, facilities, and assistance from the trust territory" in carrying out its obligations for peace and security, as well as for the local defense and maintenance of law and order. Because of the special nature of the strategic trust, the United States was additionally empowered to declare the whole or any part of Micronesia to be a closed area for security reasons. As of 1984 only Kwajalein had been declared a closed area.

Under the broad mandate of the trust agreement, the United States established what was commonly known as the Trust Territory Government. Democratic in form, it consisted of separate and independent executive, legislative, and judicial branches. The headquarters of this government was located successively in Hawaii and Guam, then in 1962 was transferred to Saipan. It was charged with the administration of six district components; the Mariana Islands, the Marshall Islands, Ponape, Palau, Truk, and Yap.

The executive and administrative authority of the Trust Territory Government and the responsibility for carrying out international obligations were vested in a United States citizen known as the high commissioner, who was appointed by the president after confirmation by the United States Senate. The Office of the High Commissioner was responsible directly to the secretary of the interior for overall affairs of the TTPI.

Legislative authority was exercised by the Congress of Micronesia, a bicameral body that held its inaugural session in 1965 after three years of joint preparations by the Trust Territory Government officials and Micronesian leaders. Judicial authority was exercised by a single high court, a district court for each of the six districts, and a community court for each municipality.

At the district level each jurisdiction was headed by a district administrator, who was both the direct representative of the high commissioner and the chief executive officer of the district. Each district had a legislature whose members were popularly elected, except for a few legislators in the Marshall and Palau districts who occupied their seats by virtue of their status as hereditary chiefs. At the lowest level of local government were the municipalities. These were usually based on the customary geographic and political divisions of society, whose boundaries might include an island, a group of islands, an atoll, or a locally recognized portion of a large island. In the Marshalls, however, municipalities were formed of islands or atolls without reference to the traditional jurisdiction of hereditary chiefs. In the early 1970s there were 126 municipalities in the territory, of which 22 had a traditional form of administration whereby chiefs ruled without elections. When a chief died and a successor was needed in these traditional subdivisions, a council of elders determined a new leader using ancient methods of discussion and consensus building.

Under the trusteeship agreement the United States was obligated to foster the development of political institutions; promote economic, social, and educational advancement; and further the development of self-government or independence as was appropriate to the particular needs of the territory and its peoples. Another responsibility was to encourage respect for human rights and for fundamental freedoms for all inhabitants. During the 1950s there was little social, economic, and political change in the TTPI because of the relative official inattention in the United States to the territory and the paucity of funds available to the civil administration. In the early 1960s, however, United States economic policy changed, according to Dirk A. Ballendorf, a leading authority on Micronesia, from "one of rather benign neglect to one of rapid development leading to the goal of self-sustaining economic growth." In the 1962–72 period the United States subsidy to the TTPI increased almost tenfold from US$6.3 million to US$60 million annually. Included in the change was the extension in the late 1960s of a variety of federal programs.

The TTPI in Transition

The early 1960s were notable also for a major exploratory step taken toward eventual self-government for the TTPI. In 1962 the Department of the Interior began drafting a charter for a TTPI legislature to be known as the Congress of Micronesia. First convened in 1965, the congress exercised legislative power on all local subjects except for those falling under the federal jurisdiction of the Department of the Interior. One of its initial acts was to establish the Future Political Status Commission, which was designed to study various alternatives for the TTPI's ultimate political status. The commission was composed of six members—one from each of the six administrative districts of the TTPI.

The commission, renamed the Political Status Commission in 1969 and the Micronesian Joint Committee on Future Status in 1970, recommended the option of self-government in "free association" with the United States. The four principles proposed in 1969 to act as a basis for exploratory talks with the United States were as follows:

    1. That sovereignty in Micronesia [TTPI] resides in the people of Micronesia and their duly constituted government;

    2. That the people of Micronesia possess the

right of self-determination and may, therefore, choose independence or self-government in free association with any nation or organization of nations;

3. That the people of Micronesia have the right to adopt their own constitution and to amend, change or revoke any constitution or governmental plan at any time; and

4. That free association should be in the form of a free compact, terminable unilaterally by either party.

The first two rounds of status negotiations were held between the TTPI and the Department of the Interior in 1969 and 1970. The TTPI delegation rejected a United States offer of "territorial" status, which it viewed as being tantammount to annexation, and which raised the fear of concomitant United States eminent domain authority and control over TTPI internal affairs. Similarly, the suggested status of commonwealth was turned down outright by all delegates except those from the Marianas.

In retrospect the third round of negotiations in early 1971 proved to be, in the words of Carl Heine, a Micronesian who served as staff director for the Micronesian Joint Committee on Future Status from 1971 to 1973, "the crucial and significant turning point in the U.S.-Micronesia negotiations." The United States, newly represented at the talks by President Richard M. Nixon's personal envoy, agreed in principle to the first three of the four negotiatory principles proposed by Micronesia in 1969, although the fourth principle on unilateral termination remained contentious. More important, however, the third round produced a broad accord on a framework for free association, envisioning a self-governed TTPI in which the United States would retain authority over foreign affairs and defense. The application of United States domestic laws to the area was to be by mutual accord only.

The concept of free association was not universally shared by Micronesians, however. This point surfaced as a major divisive issue in 1971, when the Mariana District delegation expressed a desire for a much closer relationship with the United States than did the other parts of the TTPI. At the fourth round in 1972, therefore, the United States decided not to press for political unity in Micronesia and in December of that year opened separate status negotiations with the Marianas. These talks led to the signing in 1975 of the Covenant to Establish a Commonwealth of the Northern Mariana Islands in Political Union with the United States. The people of what thenceforth came to be called the

Commonwealth of the Northern Mariana Islands approved the Covenant by a 79-percent margin in a United Nations-observed plebiscite in 1975, and the Covenant was formally endorsed by the United States Congress in 1976. In 1984 most of the provisions of the Covenant had come into effect. The Northern Mariana Islands remained part of the TTPI, however, although administered separately from the rest of the territory. The 1947 trusteeship agreement would continue to apply until its termination.

Meanwhile, the negotiations with the rest of the TTPI over the mechanics of free association continued, progressing to the point where a compact of free association began to be drafted at the fifth round of talks in mid-1972. The work was derailed, however, by an impasse at the sixth round later that year. The deadlock resulted when the Micronesians suggested that independence should be considered as an option—in addition to the free association arrangement as originally proposed. For pragmatic reasons the independence issue was muted thereafter. A new problem arose, however, by the time of round seven in late 1973 over the question of United States land requirements in Palau—a highly sensitive issue in view of the scarcity of land there. At the time, the United States still legally possessed unlimited control over land by virtue of its broad power of eminent domain, owning as much as 63 percent of total land area in the TTPI. The issue was resolved in November 1973, when the United States announced a major concession that public lands would be transferred to local control and that the eminent domain authority would lapse at the termination of the trusteeship.

A rough draft compact was prepared in 1974 through informal talks and initialed in 1976. This occurred, however, against the backdrop of fragile political unity in the TTPI, accentuated by Marshallese and Palauan sentiments favoring a new political status separate and apart from the majority of the Caroline Islands. Such sentiments were largely economic, stemming as they did from the apprehension that an acquiescence in any unified political arrangement would drain the Palauan and Marshallese resources to the more populous and less well-endowed districts of Yap, Truk, Ponape, and Kosrae—the last carved out of Ponape in 1976 as a separate district.

In 1977 Jimmy Carter's administration announced its goal of terminating the trusteeship by 1981 as part of an effort to hasten the status talks, but philosophical differences among negotiators remained unreconciled, resulting in the collapse of the 1976 draft compact. A major breakthrough occurred, however, in April

1978, when the negotiators meeting in Hawaii produced a new agreement under which islanders would have full internal self-government, as well as responsibility for foreign affairs, while the United States would retain for 15 years "full authority and responsibility for security and defense matters in and relating to Micronesia, including the establishment of necessary military facilities and the exercise of appropriate operating rights."

Meanwhile, in January 1978 the Northern Mariana Islands had formally assumed commonwealth status. In July of the same year a United Nations-observed referendum had been held in the other areas of the TTPI on the proposed constitution of what was envisaged as a single unified nation called the Federated States of Micronesia in "free association" with the United States. The draft constitution was rejected in Palau and in the Marshall Islands but approved in the Caroline districts of Yap, Truk, Ponape, and Kosrae. This development resulted in the emergence of three separate political jurisdictions. Marshall Islands District became the first of the three entities to draft and approve its own constitution, declaring self-government on May 1, 1979, under the name of the Republic of the Marshall Islands. The four Caroline districts became self-governing on May 10, 1979, as the Federated States of Micronesia (FSM), and the Constitution of the Republic of Palau was inaugurated on January 1, 1981.

In the years after 1978 the character of the Trust Territory Government underwent substantial changes as executive, legislative, and judicial powers of the high commissioner's government were transferred to the new constitutional governments. During the early 1980s the Trust Territory Government, still based in Saipan, continued to oversee the capital improvement program, the expenditure of funds appropriated by the United States Congress, foreign affairs, and responsibilities incumbent on it through the 1947 trusteeship agreement. The high commissioner's staff remained responsible for technical direction of program operations throughout the TTPI and for the provision of advisory professional and technical services that were not yet provided by the new governments. The former veto power of the high commissioner for general legislation had been relinquished to the executive authorities of the new governments. The high commissioner retained, however, the authority to suspend, in whole or in part, laws that were in conflict with the trusteeship agreement, a secretary of the interior's order, or the treaties and laws of the United States.

Although the high commissioner retained ultimate authority for the conduct of foreign affairs in the TTPI, the United States

*Polling place for 1983 plebiscite in Ponape
State, Federated States of Micronesia
Courtesy Patricia Luce Chapman*

government continued to encourage the new governments to broaden and intensify their international contacts during the transition before the trusteeship was terminated. The United States was prepared to assist these governments in establishing appropriate contacts with third countries and regional organizations.

Despite its earlier intention of creating a single political entity for the TTPI, the United States nevertheless agreed to respect the islanders' right of self-determination and undertook to negotiate separately with each of the four. A draft compact based on the 1978 agreement was initialed, but not signed, by the United States in January 1980, by the Marshall Islands and Palau in October 1980, and by the FSM in the following month.

The initialed document was reaffirmed by the Ronald Reagan administration in October 1981. After 13 years of status negotiations, the United States formally signed the Compact of Free Association and its related documents separately and bilaterally with the Republic of Palau on August 26, 1982, with the FSM on October 1, 1982, and with the Republic of the Marshall Islands on June 25, 1983. The Compact provided that it was to

309

have been ratified by the governments of the three new states in accordance with their constitutional processes, which included approval by their legislatures and by their voters in plebiscites. In December 1982 the United States, with the full concurrence of the governments of the three island states, requested the UN Trusteeship Council to dispatch observer missions to all three political entities.

Under the observance of three special visiting missions, the first referendum was conducted in Palau on February 10, 1983, and 62 percent voted for the Compact. In the FSM the document was endorsed by 79 percent on June 21, 1983, and in the Marshall Islands by 58 percent in the September 7, 1983, plebiscite. In each case the political status of free association was favored over independence or any other kind of relationship with the United States. The Compact has since been formally ratified by the governments of the Marshall Islands and the FSM.

The Palauan case was complex, however. The Constitution of Palau contains provisions requiring approval by three-fourths of the votes cast in a referendum on any issue involving the use, testing, storage, or disposal in Palau of "nuclear, chemical, gas or biological weapons intended for use in warfare." According to a judicial ruling, the defense authority of the United States under the Compact therefore must be approved by a three-fourths margin. The 62-percent endorsement of the Compact in 1983 was short of that margin necessary to settle the question of compatibility between the two documents, and Palau could not formally ratify the Compact.

After July 1983 the United States and Palau continued their efforts to reconcile the question of contradiction between the two documents and its implications for the defense aspect of the free association arrangement between the two countries. At the end of May 1984 a revised Compact was tentatively signed between Palau and the United States. Although the new version retained essentially the same elements as in the original text, it also required the endorsement by Palau's legislature and by popular referendum. Throughout the continuing negotiations since mid-1983, the United States has confirmed its intention not to use, test, store, or dispose of nuclear or toxic weapons in Palau.

To be approved by the United States, the Compact had to be endorsed by a majority in both houses of Congress and signed by the president. When approved, the Compact would have the force and effect of a United States law and an international agreement. The Compact would also incorporate a multiyear authorization for the appropriation of funds to be provided as grants and assistance, a departure from normal annual congressional budget approval procedures. In mid-1984 the Compact, from which all references to Palau were deleted, was awaiting approval in the form of a joint congressional resolution to be applicable only to the Marshall Islands and the FSM.

The Compact of Free Association

The free association arrangement is an innovative concept without precedent in United States constitutional history and has few precedents in international law. As originally written, it sets forth the basic political, economic, and defense aspects of the relationship betwen the three states and the United States. Politically, it recognizes their emergence from the trust territory through the free exercise of their right of self-determination consistent with the principles of the UN trusteeship. These states would each have full responsibility for their internal affairs and substantial responsibility for their foreign affairs. The relationship of free association would be indefinite in duration but could be terminated at any time by mutual agreement or by the unilateral action of any of the governments if so mandated by plebiscite results. The economic and security provisions would be subject to renegotiation and renewal at the end of their specified minimum periods.

Under the terms of the compacts, the three states will be provided with an agreed amount of unrestricted grant funds and "program assistance" (federal government services and assistance) for 15 years in the Marshall Islands and the FSM and for 50 years in Palau. Forty percent of the grant funding would be earmarked for economic development, including new infrastructure programs, major maintenance activities, and revenue generating projects. The United States and the three governments are to consult regularly or on request regarding the recipients' economic development.

The funding procedures provide for a graduated reduction after the fifth and tenth years. In the initial 15-year period the United States grant assistance would amount to US$2.2 billion before adjustment for inflation. The grant funding for Palau during the sixteenth through fiftieth years is estimated to average US$23.5 million annually, generated entirely out of a US$60 million investment made during the first year after the effective date of the Compact.

The Compact and its subsidiary agreements also commit the United States to continue to provide, at no cost to the Micronesian governments, airline and airport safety services, economic regulation of commercial air services, weather prediction, and assistance in the event of natural disasters. The United States Postal Service would continue its international postal service, but each of the three Micronesian governments would handle its domestic postal operations. The United States "program assistance" can be modified or terminated in whole or in part at the request of any recipient government.

The United States would have authority and exercise responsibility for defense and security for a minimum of 15 years in the Marshall Islands and the FSM and 50 years in Palau. The security role is augmented by three separate bilateral agreements covering United States military operational rights (see The United States, ch. 5). In the compact, as well as in the bilateral pacts, the United States agrees to defend the freely associated states from attack or threats to the same degree that the United States and its citizens are defended and to exercise "the option to foreclose access or use" of the states "by military personnel or for the military purposes of any third country." For their part, the freely associated states promise to refrain from actions that the United States would determine to be incompatible with its obligations to defend the areas. The mutual security relationship under the bilateral accords can be changed or terminated only by mutual agreement.

Subsidiary to the Compact are other agreements covering such matters as telecommunications, extradition, the turnover of federal property, federal "program assistance," fiscal procedures, the status of such United States forces as may be stationed in the freely associated states (including personnel at Kwajalein and military civic action teams), and nuclear claims settlement. The last of these is for the comprehensive settlement of all claims arising from the United States nuclear testing program in the Marshall Islands between 1946 and 1958 (see The Nuclear Issue, ch. 5). To this end the agreement signed between the United States and the Marshall Islands in June 1983 would establish a US$150 million endowment for payment of claims against the program. The proceeds of the endowment would be used for the benefit of those persons in the Marshall Islands, specifically the inhabitants of Bikini, Eniwetok, Rongelap, and Utirik atolls, who were adversely affected by the nuclear testing program, and for the financing of Marshall Islands programs aimed at mitigating the lasting effects of these tests. In exchange for establishment of this settlement fund, the government of the Marshall Islands agreed to terminate all pending lawsuits arising out of the nuclear tests and to bar any

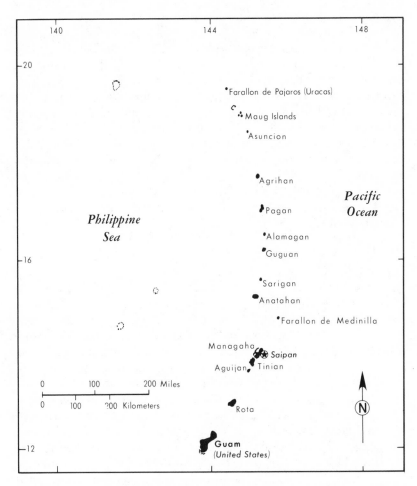

Figure 12. *Commonwealth of the Northern Mariana Islands,*
1984

future claims. As of mid-1984 Bikini Atoll and Runit Island remained closed to human habitation because of hazards stemming
from radioactive by-products. A recent independent scientific
study concluded that a cleanup of the soil of Bikini would cost
US$60 million to US$180, depending on the methods used;
otherwise, a natural disintegration of the harmful substances
would take as long as 100 years.

Commonwealth of the Northern Mariana Islands

The Mariana Islands, which include Guam, are ethnically and culturally separate from the rest of Micronesia. This factor has been responsible for the long-standing desire of the Mariana Islanders to establish a close relationship with Guam and the United States. The Northern Mariana Islands chose commonwealth status through its right to free choice and according to constitutional processes of the island group and the United States. A constitution for the commonwealth was adopted in March 1977 upon approval by 93 percent of the voters. It was formally approved by the United States in October 1977 and became effective on January 9, 1978, when the former Mariana Islands District inaugurated its commonwealth government under a governor and a bicameral legislature that had been elected in December 1977.

Physical Environment

The Northern Mariana Islands is a chain of 15 island units with a combined land area of 471 square kilometers (see fig. 12). Associated with the great Mariana Trench, which reaches a depth of more than 9,000 meters, the Mariana Islands chain is composed of high volcanic, coral, and limestone outcroppings. It is often discussed in terms of a southern section and a northern section.

The southern section contains six islands—Saipan, Tinian, Rota, Aguijan, Farallon de Medinilla, and Managaha—which together form a land area twice as large as that of the northern section. Saipan has a land area of 120 square kilometers and is the largest island in the chain. Saipan, Tinian, and Rota together accounted for nearly all of the commonwealth's inhabitants, economic activity, and energy supply and demand. Guam is only 96 kilometers away from the southernmost island of Rota.

The islands in the southern section of the chain are generally lower than those in the northern section. One peak on Rota rises to 459 meters, but for the most part the land is gently rolling rather than mountainous. Although the southern islands are volcanic in origin, there has been no such activity for a long time, and the islands' volcanic cores are largely covered with limestone terraces. The erosion of this limestone has produced a covering of excellent topsoil, and the well-watered islands have a good growth of vegetation.

The northern section, except for the Maug Islands, a cluster of three minuscule islets connected by a common base beneath the water, is composed of single islands that rise precipitously as mountain peaks of rocky, volcanic materials. All are quite high, and Agrihan's peak of 959 meters is the highest in the entire trust territory. Some of the peaks are active volcanoes; in the twentieth century eruptions have occurred on Farallon de Pajaros (Uracas), Asuncion, Pagan, and Guguan islands. An eruption on Pagan in May 1981 forced the evacuation of the island's small population. The rugged terrain, lack of easily eroded materials to provide soil cover, and insufficient rain make the northern section dry, barren, and generally unsuitable for habitation, although Alamagan, Agrihan, and Anatahan had very small settlements.

Historical Setting
  Little is known of the people who populated these islands before the discovery of Guam and its adjacent islands by Magellan in 1521. For over 300 years thereafter, the islands were ruled by Spain, which used Guam as the administrative, commercial, and religious center for the area until the termination of Spanish presence in the closing years of the nineteenth century. In 1898 Spain relinquished Guam to the United States and the next year sold the rest of the Marianas to Germany. The Marianas were ruled by Germany during the 1898-1914 period and by Japan during the 1914-44 period. The United States wrested control of the Marianas from Japan during World War II. Since 1947 these islands have been included in the Trust Territory of the Pacific Islands.
  The historical background of the Marianas is virtually synonymous with that of Guam, at least until the turn of the twentieth century (see Guam, this ch.). In ancient times the indigenous people—the Chamorros—lived in small villages, usually located near the beaches. Social organization was based on matrilineal clans and families in which children became part of the mother's clan, and inheritance was established through the female line. Marriage was monogamous, but concubines were permitted, as was divorce. The Chamorros had a fairly rigid class system, taboos governing the occupations of nobles, commoners, and outcasts.
  Under the Spaniards, however, the old life patterns changed gradually. The natives became Christianized, the dominant Roman Catholic church replacing the indigenous system of beliefs centered on ancestral spirit worship. The Chamorro language itself changed, absorbing many words of Spanish origin. As Carl Heine comments, "in the Mariana Islands, the impact of Spanish life and culture was so great that it almost wiped out the original culture of the Chamorro people." This impact was also

evident in the disappearance of the original Chamorros by the early decades of the nineteenth century—the victims of ruthless Spanish colonization and diseases brought by Europeans. In their place came "a new race of Chamorro hybrids," as author Robert Wenkam called it, "the product of Chamorro intermarriage with the Spanish, Mexican, and Filipino soldiers and colonists that came to the islands as the Chamorros were dying out."

The German and Japanese occupation together lasted less than half a century. The German presence was too brief to be economically rewarding but nevertheless left a lasting imprint of sorts by transplanting to Saipan a number of Caroline Islanders from Truk in order to make up for a shortage of workers.

The Japanese built harbors and roads, expanded schools, improved health and sanitation, and developed sugar as the dominant industry. They brought a measure of prosperity never before attained. In contrast, Chamorros and other Micronesians were treated as second-class citizens who were useful mainly as common workers for Japanese enterprises and were denied opportunities to advance educationally and economically. The Japanese colonization, stepped up after 1931, also included an increasing acquisition of land; this action became a source of major opposition during the Japanese occupation. The acquisition was designed to relieve population pressures in Japan and resulted in a rapid influx of Japanese settlers. By 1935 Japanese nationals, including Okinawans and Koreans, had outnumbered the 24,345 natives. Two years later there were more than 42,000 Japanese settlers and residents. After World War II these settlers were repatriated to Japan and elsewhere.

The Social System

Between 1970 and 1980 the population increased by an average of 2.5 percent annually, growing to 16,862 in 1981. Over 99 percent lived in the three southern islands of Saipan, Rota, and Tinian—Saipan alone accounting for 86 percent of the islanders. In addition, there were 2,000 alien residents and workers—mainly Filipinos and Koreans engaged in the service and construction industries—as well as several hundred American citizens. The people of the Northern Mariana Islands were scheduled to become citizens of the United States upon termination of the trusteeship, possibly as early as 1985. In the meantime, for purposes of entry to the United States, the inhabitants of the islands were treated administratively as though they were American citizens and were allowed unrestricted entry into schools, businesses, and other institutions. For international travel, the people of the islands would continue to use a trust territory passport until the trusteeship was abolished.

In contrast to traditional times, the present-day Chamorros are patrilineally organized in extended families that are composed of all those who are related by birth, marriage, or adoption. The families operate as a single, tightly knit social and economic unit. The extended family collectively owns its ancestral land, alloting the use thereof to all members on the basis of common agreement. The senior male member is the family's headman; he directs the group's internal social and economic activities and represents the family in councils and in relations with other families. Generally, the social class structure is open, exhibiting no residue of the traditional pattern of nobles, commoners, and outcasts. Within the Saipan area, the Carolinian communities still retain a more typically Micronesian matrilineal social organization.

Reflecting the centuries-long Spanish influence, about 90 percent of the people are Catholic. Saipan had seven Roman Catholic churches and one Protestant mission in the early 1980s. The Catholic missions were within the Diocese of Agana, Guam. Traditional religious beliefs persisted, however, and a devout Christian could still cling firmly to beliefs in ghosts and in the spirits of the dead.

The basic structure of elementary and secondary schools was patterned after that of the United States. Instructional materials and courses offered were also modeled after those in the United States but were modified to meet the unique needs and characteristics of the islands. In the early 1980s education was improving steadily. Total school enrollment in kindergarten through grade seven was 5,502, increasing by an annual average of slightly over 2 percent in the 1973–82 period. About 18 percent were enrolled in private schools, and females constituted about 48 percent of the total enrollment. In 1982 there was one teacher for every 24 students.

As of mid-1981 about 510 students were known to be studying abroad in postsecondary institutions and colleges; half were enrolled in the University of Guam and the remainder in various institutions in Hawaii or the continental United States. Over 90 percent of the students were receiving some form of federal student aid, in addition to grants from the government of the Northern Mariana Islands; these ranged from US$100 to US$5,000.

Teacher education was provided by the Northern Mariana College, established in August 1976 as a two-year institution. In 1980 the college had its first graduation; 22 teachers received their degrees, which were offered through the University of Guam, in elementary, secondary, and special education. In-service teacher education was offered by the Northern Mariana Department of Education in conjunction with the University of Guam, San Jose State University, the University of Hawaii, and the Community College of Micronesia.

Bilingual and cultural programs have been in place since the early 1970s in an effort to preserve and restore the long-ignored Chamorro and Carolinian languages and cultural heritages. Both Chamorro/English and Carolinian/English programs were available in grades one through seven, depending on the needs of the students and desires of their parents. When entering first grade, most students did not speak any English, which was taught as a second language until ninth grade. English was the medium of instruction in all secondary schools.

Literacy was relatively high. Freedom of information was strictly upheld. In the early 1980s one English-language daily newspaper and two weeklies, published in English and Chamorro, were circulated. There were two private radio stations, broadcasting in Chamorro and Carolinian. One commercial television station in Saipan had about 2,300 subscribers. Programming was primarily from the United States commercial networks, but one of the 12 channels was reserved for local programming.

The standard of health and sanitation has been upgraded since 1978. Despite the government policy of encouraging private medical practice whenever it became economically feasible, health care was primarily a public responsibility. The commonwealth government maintained offices dealing with hospital, public health and community services, medical and professional services, dental health, vocational rehabilitation, medicaid assistance, and nursing services. In addition, there were three medical field service programs for the islands of Tinian, Rota, and the northern islands. The bulk of patient care was provided at an antiquated and understaffed 84-bed hospital in Saipan. This hospital had adequate facilities for primary care but was inadequate for specialty treatment at the secondary level. As a result, patients were referred to off-island medical care providers for further evaluation, diagnosis, and treatment.

The commonwealth benefited from a variety of federally and locally funded services and programs designed to meet the needs of youths, veterans, the elderly, and the handicapped under a social security act passed in 1978. The Northern Mariana Social Security System was administered by the United States Social Security Administration.

The Economy

Traditionally, agriculture consisted mainly of subsistence. gardening adjacent to settlements and homes and was the mainstay of economic life. Most families lived on their own land as self-sustaining economic units, producing taro, corn, sweet potatoes, and other staple crops, as well as sugarcane, breadfruit, bananas, cacao, mangoes, and coffee. In the Japanese period agriculture was intensified and greatly improved, and there was a considerable increase in livestock and poultry production. By 1937 over one-third (approximately 15,000 hectares) of total land area was under cultivation. During World War II, however, the formerly productive areas were virtually destroyed by bombing and shelling, the cutting of trees for airfields, and the ravages of insect pests. In the early 1980s fewer than 250 hectares were under cultivation; about 9,100 hectares were used for grazing.

Subsistence farming has become a thing of the past, and the economy was essentially a cash economy in which there were two key components—the government and tourism. In 1978 the government accounted for 43 percent of the total work force of 7,317 (including 1,912 non-Mariana workers). More important, the public sector accounted for 59 percent of the US$28.6 million total wage earnings. This was a slight decrease from the 1977 level of 62 percent.

In 1977 (the latest year for which information was available) employment in the private sector, by business, was in general merchanding, 21 percent; hotels and entertainment, 20 percent; construction, 20 percent; transportation and stevedoring, 9 percent; banks, insurance, financial, and professional services, 5 percent; manufacturing, processing, and handicrafts, 2 percent; private schools, 2 percent; and other miscellaneous businesses, the remaining 21 percent. Agriculture and fisheries employed only five persons. In terms of private sector wage earnings, construction accounted for 25 percent of the US$9.7 million; general merchandising, 21 percent; hotels and entertainment, 13 percent; private schools, 2 percent; and manufacturing, processing, and handicrafts, 2 percent. Agriculture and fisheries claimed 0.2 percent, and miscellaneous business accounted for the balance.

In 1978 incomes of public and private sector employees showed considerable disparity. On a per capita basis the public sector workers—including some United States military personnel—were paid an average of US$5,353; the average private sec-

319

tor salary was US$2,834. In the private sector the Mariana workers earned an average of US$2,363 and the non-Mariana workers, US$3,672. The contrast was much more striking in the public sector, where the non-Mariana workers on average earned three times the wages of the islanders—US$13,871 to US$4,054. As of 1979 the minimum wage in the Northern Marianas was US$1.35 an hour.

In the 1961–77 period tourist-related industries grew by 9.3 percent annually. Tourism was for years the largest private sector industry; in 1980 there were 110,370 visitors, who were estimated to have spent a total of US$60.9 million. In 1982 the tourist arrivals totaled over 120,000, some 68 percent of them from Japan and 29 percent from the United States. There were 802 hotel rooms, 710 of which were on Saipan.

The commonwealth continued to depend on United States grants-in-aid for government operations, capital improvements, and economic development. The grant funding was obligated under an agreement between the United States and the Northern Marianas and equaled the sum of US$14 million annually based on 1975 constant dollars. The agreement also made available all federal programs that were extended to the 50 states of the United States; these programs came to an additional US$10.6 million and were administered directly by the sponsoring federal agencies. For fiscal year 1982 nearly 62 percent of budgetary appropriations came from the United States grants, a decrease of 5 percent from the previous fiscal year. As of 1979 personal income and business gross receipts taxes generated 35 percent of the total internal financial resources; cash reimbursements for job orders, 31 percent; excise taxes, 22 percent; and miscellaneous sources, the remainder.

The commonwealth's external trade consisted almost entirely of imports, which in FY 1981 amounted to US$25 million. Among the key import items were foodstuffs, petroleum and oil products, construction materials and equipment, passenger vehicles, and alcoholic beverages. The Northern Marianas' only export market was Guam, where the military facilities and retail stores sold milk and meat produced on Tinian. Its annual exports totaled US$650,000.

The Political System and Security

The political framework for the Northern Mariana Islands and for its relationship with the United States is set forth in the Covenant signed in February 1975 and enacted by the United

States Congress in March 1976 as Public Law 94–241. Upon the termination of the UN trusteeship, the Covenant would become fully effective. It establishes a self-governing commonwealth "within the American political system" under the sovereignty of the United States. The document, together with those provisions of the United States Constitution and treaties and laws of the United States applicable to the Northern Marianas, is mentioned as "the supreme law of the Northern Mariana Islands." The Covenant gave the Northern Marianas the mandate to enact a constitution and also required its submission to the United States to ensure consistency with the laws of the United States.

The Covenant stipulates that "The [Northern Mariana Islands] Constitution will provide for a republican form of government with separate executive, legislative, and judicial branches, and will contain a bill of rights." The right of local self-government is vested in the Northern Mariana Islands with respect to all internal matters, and the United States will have full responsibility and authority over foreign affairs and defense.

The Covenant defines matters affecting citizenship and nationality, judicial authority, the applicability of federal laws with respect to federal services and financial assistance programs and banking, coastal shipments, the conditions of employment, and revenue and taxation. Of particular interest to the Northern Mariana Islands are provisions dealing with United States financial assistance for local government operations, capital improvement programs, and economic development. The initial period of the multiyear financial support will be seven fiscal years. At the end of guaranteed annual direct grant assistance, the yearly level of payments is to continue "until Congress appropriates a different amount or otherwise provides by law." Additionally, the United States is committed to provide "the full range of federal programs and services" available to its territories or possessions, such as the District of Columbia, the Commonwealth of Puerto Rico, the Virgin Islands, Guam, and American Samoa.

Under the Covenant the Northern Mariana Islands agree to lease a total of 18,182 acres on Tinian, Saipan, and Farallon de Medinilla islands to the United States for 50 years in order for the latter to carry out its defense responsibilities. The lease can be renewed for another 50 years; it will cost a total of US$19,520,600, adjusted for inflation. In view of the scarcity of land and its importance for the culture and traditions of the islanders, the United States signed the Covenant, stating that "it had no present need for or present intention to acquire any greater interest" in leasing property for defense purposes. If the United States should find it necessary to acquire more land under the Covenant, it may acquire "only the minimum area" through "voluntary means"—and then only with congressional authorization. If the power of eminent domain must be exercised, however, this is to be done through due process required by the United States Constitution. The Covenant restricts landownership to persons of Northern Mariana Islands descent for 25 years following the termination of the trusteeship agreement.

The Covenant stipulates that the United States and the Northern Marianas will consult regularly on all matters affecting their relationship at the request of either side or at least once every 10 years. It also calls on the United States to assist the commonwealth in the promotion of local tourism and other economic or cultural interests of the islanders. The commonwealth is eligible, under the Covenant, to participate in regional and other international organizations concerned with social, economic, educational, scientific, technical, and cultural matters "when similar participation is authorized for any other territory or possession of the United States under comparable circumstances."

The government of the commonwealth is headed by a governor, who is popularly elected for a term of four years, as is his deputy, the lieutenant governor. Each may hold office for a maximum of three terms. The governor is assisted by departmental heads and other senior officials who oversee the functioning of the nonpartisan and independent public service. From 1976 to 1977 the executive affairs of the commonwealth came under a resident commissioner appointed by the United States; this office was abolished in 1978, when the islanders' first popularly elected governor inaugurated full-fledged self-government.

The legislative branch is bicameral—the nine-member Senate and the 14-member House of Representatives. Three senators each are elected at large for a term of four years from the three senatorial districts: Saipan and the islands north of it, Rota, and Tinian and Aguijan. In time a fourth district may be established for all the islands north of Saipan when the population of these islands exceeds 1,000 persons. The members of the House of Representatives are elected for two-year terms from single-member districts of roughly equal population. Twelve members are chosen from the six districts covering Saipan and the northern islands, one from Rota, and one from Tinian and Aguijan.

A bill may be introduced in either house except for appropriation and revenue bills, which are under the exclusive purview of the lower house. A bill is passed by a simple majority of members in each house and must be signed by the governor to become law.

A bill is subject to the governor's veto. The Constitution provides a system of checks and balances whereby the legislature may impeach the governor and lieutenant governor as well as judges. Impeachment proceedings are initiated by the lower house by a vote of two-thirds of its members, and the accused are tried by the Senate; conviction requires the affirmative vote of two-thirds of the senators.

The judiciary, which, like Guam, is part of the Ninth Circuit Court of Appeals of the United States, is composed of the District Court for the Northern Mariana Islands and the Commonwealth Trial Court. The former has the jurisdiction of a federal district court of the United States over all matters not under the local jurisdiction. The trial court has original jurisdiction over matters involving land and other civil actions in which the value of the case in dispute does not exceed US$5,000. The Commonwealth Constitution provides for a Commonwealth Appeals Court, but as of 1984 this court had not been established. In the interim, appeals were submitted to the district court.

Under the Commonwealth Constitution citizens are guaranteed the same fundamental rights and freedoms as are United States citizens under the United States Constitution. The minimum voting age is 18. Education is free and compulsory at the elementary and secondary school levels. The acquisition by sale, lease, gifts, or inheritance of permanent and long-term interests in real property is restricted to persons of Northern Marianas descent. A person of such descent is defined as a citizen or national of the United States who is of at least one-quarter Northern Marianas Chamorro or Northern Marianas Carolinian descent or a combination thereof or an adopted child of Northern Marianas descent if adopted while under the age of 18.

In mid-1984 responsibility for public order and safety was vested in the Department of Public Safety, which administered the police, the penal institutions, and fire prevention and juvenile programs. The police force was divided into separate island detachments for Saipan, Tinian, and Rota. The department functioned in cooperation with the Criminal Justice Planning Agency. Law enforcement personnel were trained by the Criminal Justice Academy. The department purchased six patrol boats in 1982 to facilitate island patrolling.

Federated States of Micronesia

The largest and most populous of the three TTPI political entities, the FSM, came into existence on May 10, 1979. Its capital

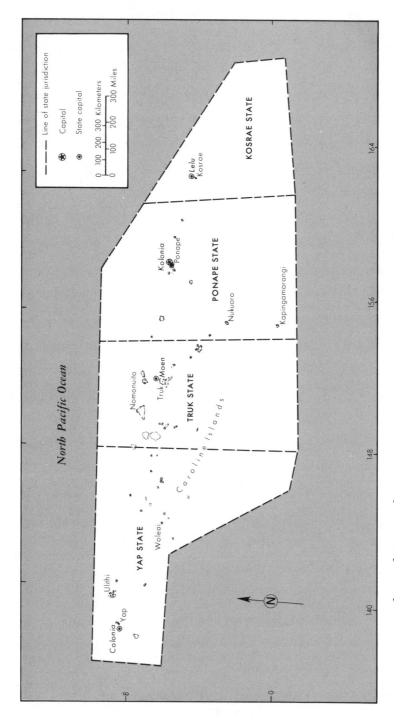

Figure 13.   Federated States of Micronesia, 1984

is located at Kolonia on the island of Ponape. The FSM is divided into four states—Yap, Truk, Ponape, and Kosrae (Kusaie) (see fig. 13). Each is named for the major island or island group and each has its own state government located in Colonia in Yap, Moen in Truk, Kolonia in Ponape, and Lelu in Kosrae. The FSM has a combined land area of 723 square kilometers. It comprises the islands of the Caroline archipelago, except for those in the western extreme of the group, which make up the Republic of Palau.

The state of Kosrae was administered until 1977 as a part of Ponape District. Although commonly described as made up of only a single island—Kosrae—that island actually consists of the island of Ualang, around which Lelu and 14 other minor islets are grouped. The total land area is about 111 square kilometers. There are four natural harbors.

The state of Ponape consists of the volcanic Ponape Island and eight coral atolls; altogether, the state has a combined land area of 373 square kilometers. Ponape Island is among the wettest in the Pacific, and the resultant luxuriant tropical foliage has led some to describe it as the most beautiful spot in the Pacific next to Bora Bora in French Polynesia. Others call it "the garden spot of Micronesia."

The state of Truk comprises 15 island groups containing nearly 300 individual islands that together have a land area of approximately 117 square kilometers. About 40 of the islands are inhabited, and many of the rest are used as "food islands," that is, they are used by inhabitants of nearby islands to grow crops and raise pigs. Truk proper, which accounts for over three-quarters of the area's total land area, is a complex of 11 high volcanic islands enclosed by a coral ring that is broken into 87 tiny, low coral islets. The encircling reef, which in places has a diameter of 64 kilometers, contains several passages into the lagoon, affording excellent anchorage for large ships. This lagoon is the resting place of 67 Japanese naval vessels sunk in 1943–44, many of which still house their cargoes of human remains and war materials.

The state of Yap includes the Yap Islands—having four major, closely grouped islands—as well as nine inhabited outer atolls, two single islands, and four usually uninhabited islands. Nearly 70 percent of the state's population resides in the Yap Islands. The state's total land area is 122 square kilometers.

The FSM has basically the same history of contact with Europeans as does the Marshall Islands group. Portuguese and Spanish navigators chanced on the Caroline Islands in the sixteenth century, but it was after the early 1800s that traders, whalers, and missionaries began frequenting the area. In the 1870s and 1880s Spain and Germany vied for influence in the archipelago, and the attendant questions of claims to sovereignty and freedom of trade had to be resolved through papal arbitration. Pope Leo XIII sustained the Spanish claim to sovereignty over the Carolines, but Germany was allowed to trade, fish, and establish settlements in the area. In 1899, however, Spain sold the Carolines and the Marianas to Germany.

The German presence was brief. At the start of World War I in 1914 Japan occupied the German possessions and proceeded to integrate them administratively and economically into its empire. In December 1941 Japan used the Carolines as bases for its military thrusts into Southeast Asia and into the South Pacific. After World War II the Carolines were mandated to the United States as a strategic trust by the UN.

The Social System

The 1980 census showed a total population of 73,160 persons, all of whom were Micronesians except for 815 Polynesians residing on two atolls in the southern part of Ponape. By individual states, the population of Kosrae was 5,491; Ponape, 22,081; Truk, 37,488; and Yap, 8,100. The Micronesian residents of the FSM are referred to as Carolinians (from Caroline Islands). They are also subdivided into island and linguistic groupings, namely, Kosraeans, Ponapeans, Trukese, and Yapese. Generally, they practice Protestant faiths, the exception being the Yapese, who are mostly Roman Catholics. Social organization is for the most part matrilineal, tracing common descent through the female line—except in Kosrae, where missionary influences since the mid-1800s have helped develop a patrilineal system. Most Carolinians are bilingual, English being the official language, along with their respective vernaculars. The literacy rate in the FSM was over 60 percent in the early 1980s, reflecting both the large percentage of school-age population and the emphasis on education since the mid-1960s.

The Congregational church has played a significant role in the lives of the Kosraeans since the 1850s. In the early 1980s the Kosraeans still practiced observance of the Sabbath. Traditional class distinctions have gradually declined in importance in recent decades owing to missionary influences and contacts with Westerners.

Ponapeans are mostly subsistence farmers and live in scattered hamlets rather than the villages found elsewhere in the TTPI. They comprise both Polynesian and Micronesian com-

Traditional house with stone money in
Yap State, Federated States of Micronesia
Courtesy Patricia Luce Chapman

munities. The Polynesians on the southern atolls of Kapin-gamarangi and Nukuoro are sea oriented, being excellent fishermen and navigators, and their social organization is patrilineal. The Micronesian majority lives mostly on Ponape Island, where there is a duality of leaders. Seven of the 12 municipalities have royal lines headed by paramount chiefs and noble lines led by ministers. In the royal and noble lines, the first 12 senior males hold titles, which carry privileged social status that is still a potent force in local life.

Trukese society and culture reflect the influence of the northeasterly trade winds that facilitate communications between Truk proper and the outer islands to the north and south. The westernmost islands lack this natural advantage; hence their interactions with other islands are infrequent. Kinship ties, barter, and dialectal similarities are more common between Truk proper and the islands to the north and south. Matrilineal descent groups continue to be a significant part of Trukese life, holding ultimate ownership rights over the land and acting as collective economic units. The senior males of the lineages who first settled on a particular island continue to enjoy considerable status and exercise traditional prestige and authority in the local decisionmaking process.

A simplified form of traditonal social stratification still exists among Yapese. In the past the society on the Yap island group was divided into nine social classes, members of the three lowest classes, as well as the Trukese-speaking outer islanders, being relegated to a subordinate status. Traditionally, Yap played an important role as a major center for the exchange of goods and services. Large fleets of outer islander canoes customarily made annual trips to the Yap islands for food and building material needed in the low islands. In return, the low islands provided manpower for major construction. Yap is known as "the land of stone money"—after the huge doughnut-shaped discs made of coral stone that were used as a medium of exchange in the area before European arrivals. Quarried in Palau and ferried to Yap, several thousand pieces of the money remain in Yap and by law may not be removed from it. The value of the stone money depends not so much on size as on age and hardships undertaken to obtain it.

The educational system in the FSM is similar to that of the United States. Public education is free and compulsory. Primary and secondary school enrollment totaled 24,297 as of early 1982, public schools accounting for 91 percent of the total. The Community College of Micronesia, the only institution of higher learning in the TTPI, is located on Ponape; it also serves the needs of Palau and the Marshall Islands. In 1982 there were nearly 1,000 FSM students studying outside the territory. In the early 1980s increasing unemployment among high school graduates was a matter of concern to the authorities at both the national and the state levels.

Courses dealing with indigenous cultures and languages were an important part of school curricula at the primary level, as were bilingual programs. Teacher education was also a significant part of official efforts to upgrade the quality of education through extension programs offered by the Community College of Micronesia, the University of Hawaii, the University of Guam, San Jose State University, East Texas State University, and Eastern Oregon State College.

Human rights and freedom of information are guaranteed by the Constitution of the FSM and are well respected. Newspapers, magazines, and other general periodicals were circulated in the administrative centers of the FSM. Locally produced newsletters were available in Ponape and Truk. Each state government owned and operated its own radio station. There were commercial television stations in Ponape and Truk, and a government-owned cable television station operated in Yap. In mid-1984 efforts were under way to bring television to Kosrae.

The quality of health care and sanitation was slowly improving throughout the FSM. Comprehensive health services were provided by the government, the sole provider of such services, at both the national and the state levels. Hospital facilities were generally inadequate and the hospitals understaffed.

The Economy

The economy was dependent mainly on government spending and augmented by a subsistence economy. Generally, the FSM lacked commercially exploitable natural resources (except for marine resources), skilled labor, and a development infrastructure.

In the early 1980s probably over 70 percent of GDP was derived from wage payments, nearly 80 percent of which were connected with public sector employment. In 1980 the four states could raise only 2 percent of the total budgetary needs, the remainder being provided by United States grants-in-aid and various federal assistance programs.

The majority of the work force was engaged in subsistence farming, copra production, fishing, and handicrafts. Paid jobs were few in most of the outer islands. As of mid-1979 there were 4,785 workers, including 430 nonresident workers in the private sector. In the early 1980s the national government employees in Kosrae numbered 355; Kosrae state-government employees, 535. Information for the other states was not available, presumably because of the embryonic nature of administrative infrastructure building. In early 1981, for example, the state government of Kosrae had only one employee working in its economic development division and two persons in its resources and development department.

At the national level agriculture was given the top priority in the FSM's development plans. Because export earnings were barely enough to pay for the import of foodstuffs—valued at US$3.59 million in 1980—there was a sense of urgency behind these plans. The government felt that the FSM had a great potential to be self-sufficient in food production. Food imports included rice, sugar, flour and wheat, fruits and vegetables, and cereals. The FSM's annual export earnings were about US$3 million in 1980, copra accounting for the bulk of the total. Other major export items included black pepper, handicrafts, and miscellaneous marine products.

In 1982 the FSM received over US$2.5 million in fees from foreign fishing fleets operating in its 200-mile-nautical-mile EEZ (see Glossary); until 1979 these foreign fleets had not provided payment, employment, or other benefits to the FSM. Despite the abundance of marine resources in its fisheries zone, the FSM imported US$700,000 worth of canned fish annually in the early 1980s.

The Political System and Security

In the early 1980s the political structure was based on the Constitution of the FSM, which went into effect on May 10, 1979. Although it was organized according to the principle of federalism and state governments, the political system was built to ensure the primacy of the nation's government over the four component states of the federation. The Constitution mandated a separation of powers into executive, legislative, and judicial categories.

The Constitution incorporates a bill of rights, as well as provisions for "traditional rights." Article V of the document states that "nothing in this Constitution takes away a role or function of a traditional leader as recognized by custom and tradition, or prevents a traditional leader from being recognized, honored, and given formal or functional roles at any level of government as may be prescribed by this Constitution or by statute." The article authorizes the national legislature to establish, when needed, "a Chamber of Chiefs consisting of traditional leaders from each state having such leaders, and of elected representatives from states having no traditional leaders."

The head of state and chief executive officer of the FSM is the president, who is elected by the legislature for a two-year term, renewable for another term only. He must be a member of the legislature elected for a four-year term and is assisted by a vice president, the constitutional heir apparent. In the early 1980s the president presided over the executive branch, which comprised several departments responsible for foreign affairs, resources and development, finance, social services, and the Office of the Attorney General.

The legislature was formally known as the Congress, a unicameral body whose 14 members were divided into two categories; four members elected at large on a nationwide basis to ensure the equality of the states and 10 members elected from congressional districts in each state apportioned by population. Members of the former category served four years and the latter,

Pollution control project on Moen Island, Truk State (above), and Governor Erhart Aten standing before the state power plant Courtesy Patricia Luce Chapman

two years. Apart from its legislative function, the Congress also performed a check-and-balance role vis-à-vis the executive and judicial branches. It was empowered to remove from office the president, vice president, or a justice of the Supreme Court on the grounds of treason, bribery, or conduct involving corruption; action required a two-thirds vote of its members. The removal was subject to judicial review when the president or vice president was involved, and in the case of a Supreme Court justice, a special tribunal composed of one state court judge from each state judiciary was to review the congressional decision.

The judiciary was headed by the Supreme Court, which was divided into trial and appellate divisions. This court was inaugurated in July 1981. There was a trial court subordinate to the highest court. Each state government was authorized to have a state court, Yap being the first to establish one in 1982, replacing the previously existing district court. As of mid-1984 efforts were under way in Ponape, Truk, and Kosrae to establish such courts.

During the early 1980s the executive and legislative organs at the state level were in place and in the process of assuming various functions previously undertaken by the Trust Territory Government. Transition was progressing through active technical and advisory help from the Trust Territory Government.

Information on the public order and internal security of the FSM was highly sketchy. Apparently in the early 1980s there were major efforts on the part of both the FSM and the Trust Territory Government to create a viable law enforcement mechanism. As part of such efforts, 26 police officers from the FSM were reported to have attended in March 1982 a two-week training program on crowd and riot control techniques, assisted by the Federal Bureau of Investigation and the Trust Territory Bureau of Investigation.

Republic of the Marshall Islands
The Marshall Islands became a self-governing republic on May 1, 1979. In June 1983 it formally agreed with the United States to establish a relationship of "free association" under the Compact of Free Association. As of mid-1984 the Compact was awaiting approval by the United States Congress.

Physical Environment
The Marshall Islands archipelago consists of 34 major island units located in the easternmost part of Micronesia between 161°

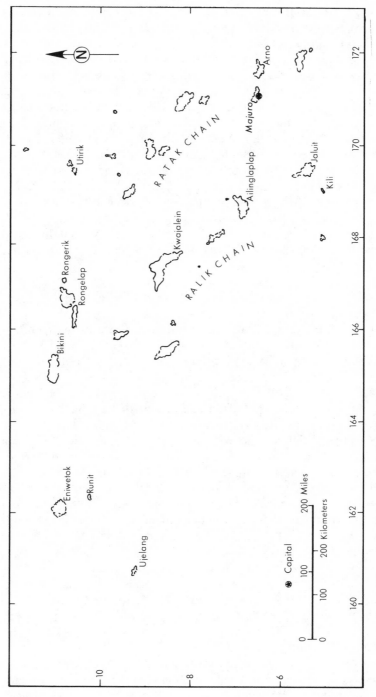

Figure 14. Republic of the Marshall Islands, 1984.

and 173° east longitude (see fig. 14). These island units are arranged in two parallel chains—the Ratak (Sunrise) to the east, having 15 units, and the Ralik (Sunset) to the west, having 17 units. Farther west are the two separate and isolated atolls of Eniwetok and Ujelang. The two chains run some 800 kilometers northwest from the vicinity of the equator between 4° and 12° north latitude. They contain some 1,156 individual islands or islets of low coral limestone and sand formations clustered mostly in groups of atolls; the highest point in the Marshalls is about 10 meters above sea level. The total land area of the islands is about 181 square kilometers. All in all, the territory comprises at least 29 atolls having large lagoons encircled by rings of coral reefs resting on submerged mountaintops and five single coral islands. One atoll, Kwajalein, has the world's largest lagoon, 145 kilometers long at its extreme axis and 32 kilometers across. Kwajalein has 96 associated islets and is the site of a United States missile testing range.

Historical Setting

As with other Micronesian island groups, little is known about the prehistory of the Marshall Islands before they were discovered by a Spanish explorer in 1529. For the next two centuries, however, these islands were virtually lost to the Western world until Captain Samuel Wallis, the discoverer of Tahiti, landed on Rongerik in 1767. In 1788 British captains John Marshall and Thomas Gilbert discovered several more island units in the group, which was later named after Captain Marshall by a Russian hydrographer. An extensive exploration of the island group was undertaken in 1817 by a Russian explorer. From the early decades of the nineteenth century the Marshalls were frequented by American whalers and missionaries and European traders and buccaneers and by blackbirders as well. At that time, however, European and American interest in the Marshalls was minimal.

In 1878 Germany secured the exclusive use of the harbor at Jaluit and special trading privileges in the Ralik chain by concluding a "treaty" with a powerful local chieftain. In 1885 the Marshalls became a German protectorate and were so recognized by Spain and Britain, principal rivals for colonial expansion in the Pacific at the time.

German rule, at first indirect, was efficient. Traditional Marshallese chieftains were left in authority, serving as key local administrative links between the islanders and a small but dedicated

*House and outrigger canoe on Kili in the Marshall Islands,
where Bikinians were resettled, their own island
having been contaminated by radiation from United States
nuclear tests during 1946–58 period
Courtesy Patricia Luce Chapman*

German staff. This helped to minimize the possibility of any friction with the islanders. Copra-related economic exploitation was the main focus of German administration, but this was tempered by a policy of reasonable concern for the welfare of the islanders. Where possible, however, there were discreet efforts to moderate the autocratic political and judicial authority of the chieftains.

German control was terminated by the outbreak of World War I in 1914. Japan, which had cast covetous eyes on these German possessions since 1890, quickly seized Jaluit, as well as other Micronesian islands, and placed them under naval administration. The seizure was unpopular among the major powers, and it was not until three years later that Japanese occupation was recognized by Britain—and then France and Russia—in return for a more active Japanese contribution to Allied war efforts against Germany. In 1920 Japan was formally mandated by the League of Nations to administer Micronesia.

Japan took a much greater interest in the Marshalls than did Germany, and its policy was geared to the attainment of four major objectives: economic development and exploitation, colonization for Japanese emigration, integration with Japan, and militarization. Its initial pattern of indirect rule, like Germany's, was gradually replaced by direct rule. By the mid-1930s it had no fewer than 900 officials present in Micronesia; Germany had never had more than 25 officials at any time. By 1938 Japan had defined the Marshalls, as well as the rest of the TTPI, as "an integral part" of its empire and treated the territory as a closed military area. In December 1941 Japan used some of the islands in the Marshalls from which to launch attacks to the east and to the south. In the Allied counterattacks on Japanese installations closer to the Japanese homeland, the first of the Japanese territories taken were the islands of Kwajalein, Majuro, and Eniwetok in the Marshalls.

After the war the United States controlled the TTPI under an international law of belligerent occupation. In 1946 it began testing atomic bombs on Bikini Atoll in the northern Marshalls, and in late 1947 Eniwetok was declared a closed military area for nuclear testing. The first United States hydrogen bomb was detonated at Eniwetok in 1954; further tests were carried out between 1956 and 1962.

The Social System

The Marshallese are classified as Micronesian. The society is matrilineally organized, descent traced through the female line. As in the past, land continues to be the most precious asset. The custom of land tenure provides for the economic needs of all members of the society.

A rather complex class system still existed in the Marshalls in the early 1980s. At the lower levels were *kajur* (commoners), whose matrilineages were led by *alab* (headmen). Each *alab* directed family affairs and represented lineage interests in larger councils. At the higher levels were the *iroij* (chiefs) of the aristocratic families, of whom the highest were *iroij laplap* (paramount chiefs). Between the royal and commoner leaders were chiefs and families having varying degrees of status.

The language of the islanders is Marshallese, closely related to the Gilbertese of Kiribati and other languages of the Caroline Islands group. It is spoken in separate, mutually comprehensible dialects for the Ratak and Ralik chains.

The 1980 census listed a total of 30,873 Marshallese, an increase of nearly 8,000 since 1970. This represented a rough annual growth rate of 3.5 percent. About 40 percent of the islanders resided in Majuro, the seat of the government and the center of commerce, trade, and communications.

The public school system provided education through grade 12 and, as of early 1982, accounted for 75 percent of the total school enrollment of 9,560 students. This represented a decrease from the 80-percent level maintained in the 1974–79 period. Attendance at public or private school was compulsory for all children from age six through age 14 or until the completion of elementary school. Public elementary and secondary education was free. Elementary schools used a bilingual/bicultural curriculum. English was the language of instruction in all secondary schools. The age span for secondary schools ranged from about 14 to over 20, but in general there was no social stigma attached to attending secondary school at what might be considered in other societies an "over-age." There was no college in the Marshalls. As of 1979 there were 357 students studying abroad, including several at the two-year Community College of Micronesia, located on Ponape in the FSM.

The government was the sole provider of comprehensive health services. In the early 1980s there was one government-operated general hospital on Majuro and a subhospital on Ebeye. Private medicine was not practiced, but the government hospital operated under a management contract with the Seventh-Day Adventists of Micronesia, who were based in Guam.

The dominant faith in the Marshalls is Protestant. Catholics and Seventh-Day Adventists maintain well-established missions, and both operate private schools. Congregations of Jehovah's Witnesses, Assembly of God, Mormons, and Baptists are active. All the missions maintain active outreach programs from Majuro to the outer islands. Church-sponsored functions play a significant role in the social framework of the Marshallese; these include songfests, rallies, youth groups, women's groups, and programs for the elderly.

Freedom of information is guaranteed in the Constitution of the Marshall Islands. In the early 1980s there was one privately owned, independent newspaper published in both English and Marshallese. Newspapers from Guam and Honolulu were readily available. The one radio station in the Marshalls was owned and operated by the government, and its programs were in both English and Marshallese. All sessions of the national legislature were broadcast live by the station and could be heard throughout the Marshall Islands.

The Economy

In the early 1980s the gross domestic product (GDP—see Glossary) of the Marshall Islands continued to be derived largely from United States-funded expenditures, which were made available through the Department of the Interior. These went to cover both government operations and capital improvements—the latter including airports, roads, docks, water, power, and sewage systems. The Interior Department's grants-in-aid were augmented by other federal programs for education, health and food projects, community development, and economic development. In FY 1979 approximately 85 percent of the budgetary resources available to the Marshall Islands came from United States sources, and the remainder was locally generated.

The heavy inflow of United States aid created an essentially cash economy in which taxable salaries for public sector workers accounted for nearly 70 percent of the total wages and at least 50 percent of GDP in 1975 (the latest year for which information was available). The principal source of private sector incomes was copra production. Other sources included an annual United States payment of US$9 million for the use of the Kwajalein missile range facility. The payment provided compensation for the landowners and community leaders of Kwajalein Atoll and also helped fund social welfare projects for all islanders of the Marshalls.

Economic development continued to be hampered, as elsewhere in the TTPI, by limited natural and human resources. A partial solution to the problem has been the promotion of foreign investment. The government was fully supportive of free enterprise and set up an investment board as well as an economic development loan office to encourage ventures in agriculture, fisheries, tourism, light industry and manufacturing, construction, and other businesses. As a result, in February 1981 a loan package was executed with the Midland Bank of London to assist in financing the construction of a 12-megawatt power plant and a fuel storage tank farm.

Much of the land in the Marshalls was unproductive, and foodstuffs and most consumer goods were imported, paid for with the meager earnings from the export of copra, coconut oil, and *trocas* shells. Agriculture and marine resource development ranked first and second among the development priorities to reduce the need for imports. Tourism placed third, but its growth was expected to be slow in view of the inadequacy of hotel and tourist infrastructure. Nevertheless, in FY 1982 there were 3,809 tourist arrivals, over three times the total in FY 1981, when it was

*Delivery of food and other supplies to Kili
in the Marshall Islands, which like most other islands depends
on air transport and ships for necessary supplies
and contact with the outside world
Courtesy Patricia Luce Chapman*

estimated that tourists spent US$323,456 in the Marshalls.

As of mid-1981 the government was the largest employer, having a total of 1,959 workers. The private sector had over 200 workers, including 70 employed in the tourist industry. Additionally, there were over 200 alien workers, mostly in construction. Evidently, the remainder of the working population was in the subsistence economy. Government employees were paid a minimum wage of US$1.00 an hour; the average minimum wage for private sector workers was US$0.85. All skilled alien employees were paid the minimum rate of US$1.25 an hour.

The Political System and Security

The process of transition to the status of a full-fledged self-government was still under way in 1984 under the Constitution of May 1, 1979. The political system was to be based on the principles of democracy but at the same time was to recognize the importance of protecting the rights and responsibilities of traditional

339

leadership. The Constitution created the Council of Iroij, consisting of five *iroij laplap* (paramount chiefs) from the Ralik chain and seven counterparts from the Ratak chain. The allocation of seats was based on the traditional system of hereditary rights and ranks. The Constitution is silent on the extent of *iroij* rights and powers, but the Marshallese know by custom that the *alab* is responsible for harvesting the food on the lands of the *iroij* and, at the beginning of a season, offers part of his harvest to his *iroij*, who is also entitled to collect his share of copra produced on his tribe's lands. Many other traditional *iroij* rights and powers remain valid today, even though they are not expressly recognized in the Constitution.

The council's formal functions are to "consider any matter of concern to the Marshall Islands and to express its opinion to the cabinet." It may request the reconsideration of any action by the legislature affecting customary law, traditional practice, or land tenure. Among the possible actions entertained by the council in the early 1980s were the introduction of a bill in the legislature to prepare a complete genealogy of all *iroij* in the Marshall Islands and a request to the government for strengthening studies of Marshallese culture and customs in the schools.

The Constitution provides for three branches of government. The executive branch is led by the president, who is the head of state and is elected by the legislature, called the Nitijela (Fountain of Knowledge). The president and cabinet ministers are drawn from the legislature and are collectively responsible to it. They must resign en bloc if a motion of no confidence against the cabinet, initiated by four or more members of the legislature, is carried by a majority of the lawmakers.

In mid-1984 the legislature exercised its authority in consultation with the advisory Council of Iroij. Its 33 members were popularly elected by secret ballot to a four-year term from 25 districts. The more populous districts were Majuro, having five seats; Kwajalein, three; and Ailinglaplap, Arno, and Jaluit, two each. The remaining districts accounted for one seat each. The election was conducted under a system of universal suffrage, the minimum voting age set at 18.

Justice was administered by the Supreme Court, the High Court, district and community courts, and the Traditional Rights Court. Trial was by jury. The jurisdiction of the Traditional Rights Court was limited to cases involving titles or land rights and other disputes arising from customary law and traditional practice.

The concept of local government is incorporated in the Constitution which declares that the people of every populated atoll

or island not part of an atoll should have the right to self-government. As elaborated in the Local Government Act of 1980, each of
the 25 municipalities is to have its own constitution and make ordinances to deal with such matters as alcoholic beverages, litter,
pigpens, zoning, or the protection of fish and marine resources.

Law and order was the responsibility of the Department of
Public Safety, which was headed by the chief of police, who reported to the minister of internal security through his immediate
supervisor, the attorney general. The department's five main
functions were patrol, investigation, licensing and registration,
jail services, and fire fighting.

Republic of Palau

The Republic of Palau is located in the westernmost extreme
of the Caroline archipelago, 800 kilometers east of the Philippines. It became a self-governing republic on January 1, 1981,
under a constitution that had been ratified in the July 1979 referendum. Geographically and culturally it shares the same historical experience with the FSM—initial contact with European
navigators in the sixteenth century followed by a short period of
European rivalry in the closing decades of the nineteenth century
that culminated in successive German and then Japanese control.
In 1947 Palau, along with other TTPI island groups, was placed
under the UN's strategic trusteeship to be administereed by the
United States.

Physical Environment

Palau consists of six island units that are arranged along a
northeast-southeast axis at the outer edge of the Asian continental
shelf (see fig. 6). Altogether they stretch nearly 700 kilometers
and have a total land area of 461 square kilometers. Much of the
territory, however, consists of uninhabited volcanic and coral
limestone islands, mangrove swamp, and rocky land. The major
island unit is known as the Palau cluster; it contains about 200 individual islands, the major ones being Kayangel, Babelthuap,
Koror, Urukthapel, Eilmalk, Peleliu, and Angaur. Kayangel is
the nation's only low coral atoll and has a number of islets encircling its well-protected interior lagoon. All of the islands of the
Palau cluster, except Angaur and Kayangel, are enclosed within a
single barrier reef, making for cultural homogeneity and relative
ease of natural communication.

Babelthuap, about 40 kilometers long, is the largest single

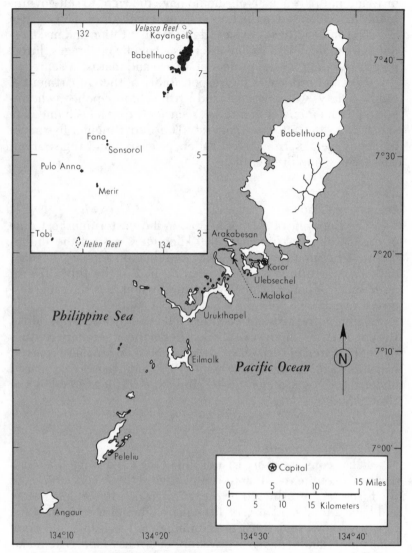

Figure 15.   Republic of Palau, 1984

landmass in the TTPI. Although classified as a high island, Babel-thuap is actually composed of gently rolling hills reaching a maximum height of 213 meters. The island has one of the few real lakes in the TTPI, Lake Ngardok. All the islands of the Palau cluster are covered with a dense growth of trees and bushes in great

342

variety.

The Social System

According to the 1980 census, Palau had 12,116 inhabitants, whose ancestors had undergone a long history of racial admixture. Present-day Palauans are a composite of Polynesian, Malayan, and Melanesian races. Since the turn of the twentieth century, Germans, Americans, and Japanese have also contributed to the racial admixture of the islanders. The people of Palau speak Palauan, the major and official language of the state. About 170 inhabitants in the southwestern islands of Sonsorol, Tobi, and Pulo Anna, however, speak a dialect of Trukese.

Palauan society is organized matrilineally into villages that were traditionally ruled by councils of 10 titled male chiefs and parallel councils of 10 titled female elders, each representing one of the ranking clans of the village clusters. The male council addressed matters relating to the local economy, warfare, and law and order, whereas the female council was concerned mainly with matters of inheritance and interlineage or interclan peace. The traditional village clusters are grouped into today's 16 states of Palau.

In the early 1980s, as in the past, land and money were regarded as the communal property of an individual's clan group, which remained a central part of life. Every Palauan was obligated to contribute money to the clan as an expression of loyalty, especially on occasions such as birth, marriage, divorce, or death. The contribution could be in currency or in an aboriginal system of payment consisting of beadlike money valuables, which, according to the findings of United States Peace Corps volunteers, was still actively used.

In 1982 the public and private school enrollment of both primary and secondary grades totaled 4,114. The public school share was 80 percent. Schooling was free and compulsory through twelfth grade. Most young people who had attended the public and mission schools spoke English. Many persons over the age of 50 spoke Japanese. Teacher education was being upgraded through extension courses offered by the Community College of Micronesia, the University of Guam, and San Jose State University. As of 1979 there were 524 Palauan college students studying abroad; this figure was 4.3 percent of the Palauan population—a relatively high level for the TTPI.

In the early 1980s the government operated a radio station to provide the islanders with local and world news, general information, political and educational programs, and entertainment. The station also served as a direct communications link between Koror and outlying villages and islands. In addition, there was one commercial television station and one independent, biweekly newspaper.

Palau is the home of the only indigenous religious movement still active in the TTPI—the United Sect (Ngara Modekngei). This cult appears to be a modern revival of traditiional Palauan beliefs combining a mixed totem-clan-ancestral worship with belief in an assortment of nature-spirits, female demigods, and protective village deities. About one-third of the population is thought to embrace this movement, and the remainder identified with one or another Christian denomination.

The government was the principal provider of health care in Palau. In the early 1980s it subscribed to the goal of "Health for All by the Year 2000." Emphasis was on primary health care. Because of the lack of adequate secondary care facilities and medical specialists in Palau, about 30 patients were referred to off-island facilities annually, most going to Guam and Honolulu.

The Economy

Palau has been blessed with rich marine resources, but these, like its agricultural potential, were largely untapped in 1984. The extraordinary beauty of the "rock islands" to the south of Koror could in time become a tourist attraction, pending substantial improvements in infrastructure.

Most of the resources available for government spending were derived from United States capital and payroll transfers. In FY 1982 at least 77 percent of the total budgetary resources for government operations, capital improvements, and economic development were made up of inputs from the United States. The remainder of the US$19.7 million was locally generated from taxes and fees and from reimbursements for public services. Top items in the government expenditures were education, health services, public works, and public safety.

In 1979, before Palau became self-governing under its own administrative structure, the total work force was 3,425 persons—2,057 in the public sector and 1,368 in the private sector. On a per capita basis wage earnings averaged US$1,600 in the private sector. As of mid-1981, several months after the inauguration of Palau as a republic, the total work force was officially listed as 2,807 persons—1,127 in the government and 1,668 (including 622 alien workers) in the private sector. Although fewer in

*Traditional chief's house,
called a bai in Palau
Courtesy
Patricia Luce Chapman*

number, the government employees in 1981 earned a per capita average of US$5,874, whereas the private sector workers earned an average of US$3,494. In 1982 (the latest year for which information was available) private sector employment by business was fishers, domestics, and laborers, 41 percent of the total work force; trades, 37 percent; administrative and professional, 12 percent; and clerical, 10 percent. In the first private sector business category, 388 workers out of the 394 were listed as nonresident or alien fishers.

The sketchy information available reveals that in 1981 Palau had a total of 30 vegetable and root crop farmers and four poultry farmers. Van Camp tuna boats from the port of Malakal landed 16,000 tons of tuna, valued at US$3 million. The tourist industry was modest but was a major source of local income. In 1980 a total of 5,145 arrivals was reported, Japan accounting for 53 percent and the United States 39 percent. Palau was serviced by Air Micronesia, a subsidiary of Los Angeles-based Continental Airlines, which flew from Guam, and by Air Nauru through Manila. Aero Belau (Palau), a local airline, made several flights a day between Koror, Peleliu, and Angaur.

The Political System and Security

The Constitution provides for a bicameral legislature, an executive branch, a judiciary, and state governments below the national level. On the matter of sovereignty, it stipulates that "major governmental powers including but not limited to defense, security, or foreign affairs may be delegated by treaty, compact, or other agreement" between Palau and a foreign power or organization. Such treaty, compact, or agreement must be approved, however, by at least two-thirds of the members of each house of the national legislature—called Olbiil Era Kelulau (National Congress)—and by a majority of the votes cast in a popular referendum. Another proviso states that popular approval by at least a three-fourths margin in a referendum is needed in case such agreement concerns the use, testing, storage, or disposal of nuclear, toxic chemical, gas, or biological weapons intended for use in warfare within the Republic of Palau.

The Constitution incorporates a bill of rights and an article designed to protect "traditional rights." The government is enjoined from taking any action "to prohibit or revoke the role or function of a traditional leader as recognized by custom and tradition" that is not consistent with the Constitution. As a result, a traditional leader may play formal or functional roles at any level of government. Statutes and "traditional law" are declared to be "equally authoritative," but in case of conflict, the statute is to prevail "only to the extent it is not in conflict with the underlying principles of the traditional law."

The president is the chief executive of the national government and the head of state. His constitutional successor is the vice president. Both offices are filled by popular election for a term of four years. The president may serve only two terms. The members of the cabinet are appointed by the president with the advice and consent of the Senate of the legislature. Aiding the president in an advisory capacity is the Council of Chiefs, composed of traditional chiefs from the 16 states of the republic. The council's functions are to advise the chief executive on matters of traditional laws, customs, and their relationship to the Constitution and laws of the nation. A member of the council may not concurrently hold a seat in the national legislature.

The National Congress consists of two houses, the House of Delegates and the Senate. The members of the two chambers are elected for a term of four years. In mid-1984 the House of Delegates had 16 members, one delegate popularly elected from each of the 16 states. The Senate was composed of 18 popularly elected members.

The judicial authority is vested in the Supreme Court, which has trial and appellate divisions. All justices of the court, like the president, are subject to impeachment by the national legislature for treason, bribery, other high crimes, or improper behavior. The Constitution states that a national court and other inferior courts of limited jurisdiction may be established by law. The appellate division of the Supreme Court may review decisions of the trial division and all decisions of lower courts, but no justice may hear or decide an appeal of a case heard by him in the trial division.

State governments are to be organized in accordance with the "democratic principles and traditions of Palau." In 1982 all 16 states had a recognized traditional chief and an elected executive officer variously known as the governor, magistrate, or secretary of state. The state governments are authorized to have their own elected legislatures.

In mid-1984 law and order was the responsibility of the Public Safety Bureau of the National Ministry of Justice. The bureau maintained a national police force and was also responsible for fire protection. Total personnel of the bureau was listed as 59 as of October 1981. The prison population in 1981 was 40.

Chapter 4.   Polynesia

*Tahitian tiki, typical of traditional Polynesian
sacred images in human form*

THE REGION KNOWN as Polynesia (from the Greek, meaning "many islands") is vast in terms of sea area, covering approximately 39 million square kilometers—excluding New Zealand and Hawaii, territories originally settled by Polynesians but containing predominantly non-Polynesian populations. In contrast, the total land area of the region is only about 8,260 square kilometers, the largest island being Tahiti at 1,042 square kilometers. The total population of the region in the early 1980s was approximately 500,000. Only Tonga, Western Samoa, and French Polynesia had populations of over 100,000, and tiny Pitcairn Island's population was only 45 in 1983. Scarcity of arable land—in fact, any land at all—and the stagnation of subsistence economies in which copra represented the only significant export stimulated large-scale out-migration to other regions of the Pacific, including Australia, New Zealand, New Caledonia, and the United States. Tourism, fishing, and the exploitation of the resources of the ocean floor, however, presented potential sources of future economic growth.

Polynesia contained an impressive diversity of political entities in the early 1980s. Tonga was an independent kingdom that had been under British protection between 1901 and 1970. Western Samoa and Tuvalu were states that had gained their independence in 1962 and 1978, respectively. Cook Islands and Niue were self-governing but in free association with New Zealand, which assumed responsibility for their defense. Tokelau was a territory of New Zealand administered by that nation from Apia, Western Samoa. French Polynesia and Wallis and Futuna were two overseas territories of France; evolution toward internal self-government was under way in the former in the early 1980s. Pitcairn Islands was a British colony and American Samoa an unorganized, unincorporated territory of the United States. Easter Island was a province of Chile.

Polynesia

AMERICAN SAMOA

Political Status	Unorganized, unincorporated Territory of the United States
Capital	Pago Pago
Population	36,400 (1984 midyear estimate)
Land Area	189 square kilometers
Currency	United States dollar (US$)
Main Island and Island Groups	Tutuila, Manua Islands

Lying in the heart of Polynesia, American Samoa comprises the six eastern islands of the Samoa archipelago and tiny Swains. Throughout the twentieth century it has been politically separated from the larger and more heavily populated Western Samoa, which was administered first by Germany, then by New Zealand before becoming independent in 1962 (see Western Samoa, this ch.). American Samoa's continuing close ties to a major world power in mid-1984 contrasted sharply with the vigorously pursued nationalist aims of many neighboring island states, including Western Samoa. Having few resources and a burgeoning population, American Samoa's greatest challenge in the mid-1980s was probably the strengthening of its economic capabilities.

Physical Environment
American Samoa extends some 300 kilometers from west to east between 11° to 14° south latitude, about two-thirds of the way down from Hawaii to New Zealand (see fig. 16). All of the islands except for the tiny coral atolls, Rose and Swains, are volcanic, their rugged mountains rising abruptly over the surrounding waters of the Pacific Ocean. The largest and most important of these is Tutuila. In addition there are, besides the two coral atolls, Aunuu Island and the three islands of the Manua group—Ta'u, Ofu, and Olosega. Dense forests made up of typical South Pacific

353

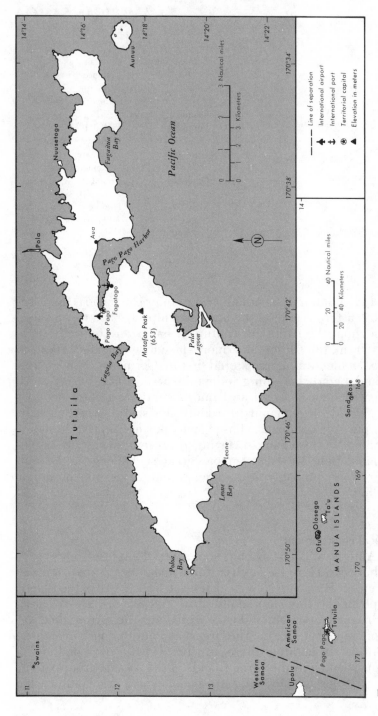

Figure 16.   American Samoa, 1984

trees, such as coconut palms, breadfruit, and mango, cover these islands. Grasses and tropical vegetables flourish on open fields, watered by ample rainfall. The climate is tropical, the average temperature ranging from 21°C to 32°C; average humidity is 80 percent.

The country's closest neighbor, apart from Western Samoa, is Tokelau; other nearby islands include Tonga, Niue, and the Cook Islands. The sea area contained within American Samoa's 200-nautical-mile Exclusive Economic Zone (EEZ—see Glossary) is estimated at 390,000 square kilometers.

Its favorable location astride air and sea routes is one of the few natural resources the territory possesses, apart from its equable climate. The capital, Pago Pago, which boasts one of the finest natural harbors in the world, is a regional center of business and commerce. The port affords protection from adverse weather and oceanic conditions and is accessible to deep-draft vessels. Well-developed port facilities are indicative of its use as a major port of call for over more than a century. Domestic and regional air carriers using Pago Pago International Airport provide regularly scheduled, connecting flight service to the United States and to New Zealand, Fiji, and other parts of the South Pacific.

Most of the population lives on Tutuila, which covers a land area of 115 square kilometers. Tutuila and the Manua Islands are supplied with electric power; total capacity of the power system in 1980 was 14 megawatts, and expansion beyond that was planned. Rainfall and other sources provided a generally reliable water supply, but age-related breakdowns often occurred in the village-owned distribution systems.

Historical Setting

Archaeological research on the origins of the first inhabitants of the Samoa Islands (including present-day Western Samoa) is subject to dispute and contradictory interpretation. Possibly they came by sea from eastern Melanesia by way of Vanuatu, Fiji, or Tonga, arriving as early as 1000 B.C. Considerable contact with Fiji and Tonga preceded the first sighting of the islands by Dutch admiral Jacob Roggeveen in 1722. After 1768 whaling, fishing, and trading boats visited in increasing number, while official contacts through British, German, and United States expeditions in 1791, 1824, and 1838, respectively, expanded Western influence. As agreements were concluded with local chiefs, Europeans and Americans came to dominate the economic life of the islands. At the same time, Christian missionary groups were converting the

Samoans to Christianity. Foremost among their leaders was John Williams of the London Missionary Society, remembered in particular for developing a Samoan-language script that permitted the society to achieve a remarkably high level of literacy within two generations.

Sociopolitical organization was based on extended family groups under the authority of a number of chiefs holding various hierarchically ranked titles. For centuries competition for political power and chiefly titles had kept the islands in ferment. During the nineteenth century the situation was compounded by the struggle of foreign powers for trade, commercial, and strategic advantage and by their efforts to play on local rivalries for their own gain. In 1872 the United States naval commander in the area succeeded in making a treaty with a local chief permitting the fleet to use the harbor at Pago Pago for a coaling station. Despite this setback, Britain and Germany continued to press their own interests, and in March 1889 ships of all three nations confronted one another in the harbor at Apia. It is widely believed that open warfare was averted only because a hurricane struck, destroying all but one British vessel and causing great loss of life. In the aftermath the three powers established a system of joint rule in the Samoa Islands, but this too broke down. In 1899 Britain and Germany settled their rival claims, and Britain renounced its interest in the islands in return for recognition of exclusive claims elsewhere. The next year the islands were partitioned between Germany and the United States. Germany was given paramount interest in those islands of the Samoa archipelago west of 171° west longitude and the United States equivalent interest in all those east of that line.

In 1900 Samoan chiefs formally consented to the arrangement of the 1899 agreement, ceding Tutuila to the United States. In 1904 a separate deed was signed for the Manua group. The United States Congress formally ratified the deed of cession retroactively in 1929. Meanwhile Swains, not part of the Samoa archipelago, was made part of American, or Eastern, Samoa in 1925.

During World War II the Samoa Islands were made an advance training and staging area for United States forces. Tutuila was used as a base for strikes against Japanese forces. Its physical infrastructure was greatly improved by the construction of roads, airstrips, docks, and medical facilities. A number of Samoans volunteered for military service.

Political evolution progressed slowly. During the 1930s a small political group, Mau a Pule (commonly referred to as the

Mau movement), based in the western Samoa Islands, had made little headway in American Samoa. The climate for democratization was more favorable after World War II, progressive reforms beginning with the formation of a bicameral legislature that replaced an advisory board of local leaders.

The naval station was closed in 1951, a severe blow to the local economy, and administrative responsibility for the islands was transferred from the United States Navy to the United States Department of the Interior. Economic development was modest during the 1950s, but political evolution continued. By 1956 American Samoa had its first native-born Samoan governor, Peter Tali Coleman, and the bicameral legislature had called for a constitutional convention. In 1960, after six years of debate, the convention approved the Constitution, which was ratified in 1966 and approved by the United States secretary of the interior in 1967. It continued to serve as the territory's basic law in 1984. In 1977 Coleman became the first governor of the territory to be popularly elected.

The Social System

The census taken in April 1980 enumerated a population of 32,397. By mid-1984 the total population had probably reached 36,400, based on an estimated annual growth rate of 1.7 percent. Population pressure was not the issue that it was in many small island states because American Samoans were free to resettle in any part of the United States, and significant numbers did so. In the early 1980s it was estimated that there were nearly twice as many American Samoans on the west coast of the United States as there were in American Samoa itself, an additional 20,000 or so being resident in Hawaii.

English is the official language, taught in the schools and spoken by most inhabitants. Samoan, a language closely akin to Hawaiian, Tahitian, and Tongan, is the lingua franca.

The intricate pattern of family relationships underlying Samoan society has been widely studied by anthropologists, including the redoubtable Margaret Mead, whose descriptions of sexual mores in the islands have come under strong challenge from anthropologist Derek Freeman. The basic social and economic unit is the *aiga* (extended family), in which all kinsmen related by birth or adoption are considered to be members. Each *aiga* is headed by a *matai* (chief), responsible for directing the use of family land and other assets, for assessing contributions of food and material possessions, for the performance of traditional rites and ceremonies, and for rendering family honors at births, deaths, weddings, and other landmark occasions. These activities and levies are considered family obligations to be performed willingly and without question. In large communities the *matai* appoints other family household heads to serve as lesser officers in conducting community affairs.

In modern times Samoan chieftains have appeared in two types: the *ali'i* (high chief), who exercises primarily ceremonial functions, and the *tutafale* (orator), the new leader and the real source of authority in a community. Although heredity is a determining factor in choosing *matai* of both kinds, accession to status as a *tutafale* is achieved through election by the extended family as a whole. A candidate's general competence, popularity, and ability to make a good speech are governing factors.

Patterns of living on Tutuila have generally remained unaffected by the pace of modern life, except in or near the major settlements around Pago Pago Harbor. In recent years much construction has taken place in this area so that in 1984 its appearance was a far cry from the picturesque shabbiness that Somerset Maugham described in "Rain," his famous short story about Sadie Thompson and the missionary.

The Economy

The economy was tied closely to that of the United States. More than 70 percent of the budget of the territorial government—US$69 million—was provided by the Department of the Interior and other federal agencies. Most United States social programs were normally extended to American Samoa. Although subsistence agriculture and fishing traditionally provided the lifeblood of the economy, Samoans have increasingly abandoned such pursuits, and by the mid-1980s the government employed about 4,000 persons, or about one-half of the labor force. Attempts to trim the payroll, exercise other cost-cutting measures, and develop alternative employment opportunities in industry and agriculture were being stressed amid rumors of government financial mismanagement and corruption. American Samoa's exports, chiefly tuna, went almost exclusively to the United States, and its imports also came primarily from that source. The export industry relied on two major American-owned tuna canneries, Star Kist Samoa and Van Camp Samoa, which in 1981 together accounted for well over one-half of the private sector payroll and furnished exports valued at US$198 million. American Samoa enjoyed duty-free access to the American market.

Apart from its location, which made it a convenient regional center of commerce in the South Pacific, and its equable climate and physical beauty, the territory had few natural resources. The soil was rich and productive in some areas, but arable land was scarce. Tourism was being developed but was subject to a number of constraints, including scarcities of facilities to serve airline and cruise ship passengers.

Land tenure was loosely intertwined with social organization. In the early 1980s about 70 percent of land was communally owned; rights were passed on from generation to generation. About 25 percent was individually owned, while the remainder belonged to the government. Legislation restricting ownership to Samoans was strictly enforced, but 55-year leases and other trusteeships provided loopholes for foreigners interested in investment and retirement sites.

The Political System and Security

In mid-1984 the political status of American Samoa remained, as it had been for most of the century, that of an unincorported and unorganized territory of the United States. The term *unincorporated* signified that American Samoa, like Guam, was not incorporated into the United States as were the 50 states; *unorganized* meant that the United States Congress had not enacted organic legislation for American Samoa that would provide for congressionally mandated powers of self-government. Instead, the Constitution of American Samoa formed the basic law of the territory. This unique arrangement ensured that certain aspects of Samoan culture that were inconsistent with provisions of the United States Constitution and United States law could be preserved, including the customary pattern of landownership and the holding of titles. Under this arrangement United States law did not automatically apply to the territory, and American Samoa with rare exceptions did not have access to the United States court system. The people of the territory were United States nationals but not United States citizens—a status unique to American Samoans. They could, however, quite easily become United States citizens by establishing residence in the United States and complying with relatively streamlined citizenship procedures, and many have done so.

Since 1951, when responsibility for the territory was transferred from the Department of the Navy, American Samoa has been administered by the United States Department of the Interior. Based on legislation passed in 1980, the territory has been represented in the United States Congress by a nonvoting delegate since 1981.

As of mid-1984 any move to alter the territory's political status appeared unlikely. Pursuing a closer relationship with the United States would require abandonment of highly valued customary practices. Movement toward a looser arrangement would result in a substantial loss of United States revenue and would mean sacrificing easy access to United States citizenship. Although very strong ties of culture and consanguinity continued to bind the territory to Western Samoa, any merger with that state would return most American Samoan *matai* to the relatively junior status they occupied in the Samoan hierarchy of titles. Except for one title in the Manua group, the most senior titles in that system pertained to areas in Western Samoa.

The Constitution of American Samoa, as amended or revised in 1967, 1971, and 1977, bears the imprint of American democratic political principles, providing for executive, legislative, and judicial branches of government. It guarantees freedom of religion, speech, and press; rights of assembly and petition; free and nonsectarian public education; and other rights and freedoms. It also stipulates a governmental legislative policy protecting persons of Samoan ancestry against alienation of their lands and guarding against the destruction of the Samoan way of life and language. No change in the law respecting the alienation or transfer of land or any interest therein was permitted without a two-thirds majority vote by two successive legislatures and the governor.

In February 1984 elected delegates to a second constitutional convention held in Pago Pago drafted and adopted a revised basic law for the territory. Envisioning a number of important reforms, the document stressed the collective responsibility of the people of Tutuila and the Manua Islands as an island society of "true Polynesians" to protect against the alienation of their lands or the destruction of the Samoan way of life or culture. The future of the proposed constitution was uncertain, however, for a United States Congress ruling in December 1983 stated that amendments or modifications to the Constitution of American Samoa could be made only by an act of that Congress. The Government of American Samoa submitted the draft constitution to Congress but later withdrew it from consideration.

According to the 1966 Constitution, the governor is the administrative head of the executive branch, responsible for all executive departments, agencies, and instrumentalities. In early 1983 these included departments of administrative services, agriculture, the community college, education, health, legal affairs, port administration, public safety, public works, and Samoan affairs. Special executive agencies included the offices of economic development and planning, marine resources, planning and budget, and territorial energy.

Until 1977 the United States secretary of the interior had appointed the American Samoan governor and lieutenant governor. For three years in succession, annual referenda had rejected the notion of popular election of the governor. According to a number of observers, the reluctance was rooted in the strength of Samoan customs and the extent of rivalry among family groups and *matai*. In 1976, however, the majority of voters opted in favor of popularly elected governors. The first governor, Peter T. Coleman, was elected for a renewable three-year term, beginning in January 1978. In 1980 the term was changed to four years, coinciding with the United States presidential election. Governor Coleman and Lieutenant Governor Li'a Tufele were reelected and began their second terms in January 1981. Under the Constitution governors are not permitted to serve more than two full terms.

The bicameral legislature, known as the Fono, consists of the Senate and a House of Representatives. The Constitution stipulates that the county councils shall choose the 18 members of the Senate according to Samoan custom and from among registered *matai*. Twenty members of the House of Representatives are popularly elected from representative districts. Candidates must be United States nationals. Additionally, adult permanent residents of Swains elect a nonvoting delegate to the House. Senators hold office for a four-year term and representatives for a two-year term, the legislature convening for 45-day sessions twice each year.

In the mid-1980s the judicial branch of government consisted of a single high court that had trial, appellate, and probate jurisdiction throughout the islands; five district courts; a small-claims court; a traffic court; and *matai* courts. As a general rule, a suit filed in an American Samoan court was not appealable to any United States federal court. The secretary of the interior appointed the chief justice, who was an American jurist; the governor, on the recommendation of the chief justice, appointed the associate judges. The United States civil and criminal codes, augmented by such local laws and regulations as enacted by the Samoan legislature, constitute the body of law adjudicated in the courts.

Responsible to the Department of Public Safety were police and fire units and a corrections agency. Members of the uniformed force, numbering 117 in early 1983, were organized in a rank structure based on the United States Army. They were not armed.

COOK ISLANDS

Political Status	Self-governing, in free association with New Zealand
Capital	Avarua
Population	16,000 (1984 midyear estimate)
Land Area	240 square kilometers
Currency	New Zealand dollar ($NZ)
Major Islands and Island Groups	Northern Cook Islands; Southern Cook Islands, including Rarotonga, Mangaia, Atiu, and Mauke

Cook Islands, a self-governing state in free association with New Zealand as defined in its 1965 Constitution, is located west of French Polynesia. Kiribati lies to the north and northeast, American Samoa and Western Samoa to the northwest, and Niue and Tonga to the west. The island of Rarotonga, where the capital, Avarua, is located, is approximately 3,700 kilometers distant from Wellington, New Zealand.

Physical Environment

Having a total land area of 240 square kilometers, the 15 Cook Islands are dispersed over a wide area of the South Pacific. The distance from Penrhyn in the north to Mangaia in the south is 1,400 kilometers. The total sea area, defined by the 200-nautical-mile EEZ (see Glossary) is estimated at 1.8 million square kilometers. Cook Islands claims territorial waters of 12 nautical miles. There are two island groups; the Northern Cook Islands, composed mainly of coral atolls, and the Southern Cook Islands, containing the largest islands, of volcanic origin. The largest are Rarotonga, at 70 square kilometers the most extensive in area; Mangaia, 57 square kilometers; and Atiu, Mitiaro, Mauke, and Aitutaki, all between 20 and 30 square kilometers. The coral atolls of the Northern Cooks rarely exceed a few square kilometers in area, Rakahanga being the largest at 11 square kilometers. Penrhyn, only six square kilometers in size, encloses a lagoon of 280

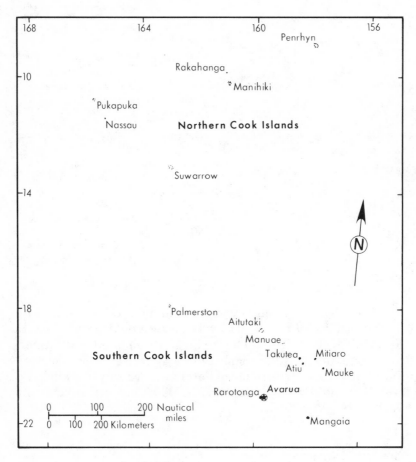

168   164   160   156

Penrhyn

-10

Rakahanga

° Manihiki

° Pukapuka

° Nassau   **Northern Cook Islands**

Suwarrow

-14

(N)

-18   ° Palmerston

Aitutaki

Manuae

Southern Cook Islands   Takutea   ,Mitiaro

Atiu   °Mauke

Rarotonga ,Avarua

0   100   200 Nautical miles

-22   0   100   200 Kilometers   °Mangaia

Figure 17. Cook Islands, 1984

square kilometers, one of the largest in the Pacific (see fig. 17).

On June 11, 1980, Cook Islands and the United States governments signed the Treaty of Friendship and Delimitation of the Maritime Boundary Between the United States and the Cook Islands. The agreement, ratified by the United States Senate in 1983, provided for the relinquishment of United States claims to the Penrhyn, Manihiki, Rakahanga, and Pukapuka (Danger) atolls in the Northern Cook Islands group.

The differences between the volcanic "high islands" and coral "low islands" are quite apparent. Rarotonga, a circular high island described by many observers as one of the most beautiful in the Pacific, has a large number of well-defined peaks and pinnacles, including Te Manga, the highest, at 653 meters. The topography is characterized by steep mountain valleys cut by rapid streams running to the sea. A fringing reef around Rarotonga forms a shallow lagoon close to the shore. Rich, volcanic soils nourish a profusion of vegetation, and even the mountainsides are covered with green. Other volcanic islands are similar in appearance. By contrast the coral atolls have low elevations and fewer varieties of vegetation—primarily coconut trees—as a result of the inability of the limestone-based soils to hold water or provide nutrients.

The islands have a humid, tropical climate, though this is less pronounced in the Southern Cooks, farther from the equator than the Northern Cooks. The prevailing winds are the trades, blowing from the southeast in the Southern Cooks and from the east in the Northern Cooks. Rarotonga's average annual temperature is 24°C and the average yearly rainfall 2,000 millimeters. Tropical storms occur durring the humid months from November to March.

Historical Setting

The indigenous people of the Cook Islands trace their origins to the Society Islands and the Marquesas Islands in what is now French Polynesia, as well as to the Samoa Islands. Migration occurred over an extended period of time, beginning apparently in the eighth century A.D. Local tradition tells of the departure of Polynesian fleets from the islands to New Zealand around the fourteenth century. Although the inhabitants of each of the 15 islands developed their own cultural attributes, a general pattern of social structure could be perceived. The land was divided into small states that on the volcanic islands were often defined by the steep walls of mountain valleys. Society was hierarchical, having a class of *ariki* (chiefs), who occupied the highest positions. Wars between the small states, led by the *ariki*, were a prominent feature of life before the period of European influence.

The first Europeans to reach the Cook Islands were the Spanish navigator Álvaro de Mendaña de Neira in 1595 and his Portuguese associate, Pedro Fernández de Quirós, in 1606. The British captain James Cook, after whom the islands are named, discovered five of the islands of the southern group during his voyages of exploration in the 1770s. Some of the islands were visited by the mutineers on the H.M.S. *Bounty* in 1789.

Polynesian and European preachers of the London Missionary Society were successful in converting the people of many of the islands, especially Rarotonga, to Christianity during the 1820s. This was usually accomplished by converting the *ariki*, who then obliged their subjects to follow their example. The society and culture were deeply transformed in the process. The people were persuaded not only to abandon their old gods but also to adopt Western styles of dress, housing, and legal codes. The missionaries enacted a host of blue laws that prohibited dancing, drinking the traditional beverage, kava, and wearing flowers. *Ariki* occupied high church offices, and what one historian calls a "theocratic" political system evolved.

Protestant missionary dominance and proximity to New Zealand drew the Cook Islands economically, and eventually politically, into the British sphere of influence. In 1888 a British protectorate was established, first over Rarotonga and then over all the islands of the Southern Cooks to prevent French intrusion from their base in the Society Islands. In 1896 the British Colonial Office agreed that New Zealand should annex the islands, and this was accomplished with the consent of the *ariki* in 1901. Annexation included the Northern Cooks.

Although the Cook Islands were not involved in fighting between Allied and Japanese forces during World War II, United States forces were based on the island of Aitutaki in the Southern Cooks, and several hundred young men and women went to New Zealand to work or enlist in the armed forces. After the war, demands for self-government were voiced by members of the Cook Islands Progressive Association, whose most eloquent spokesman was Albert R. Henry, son of an Aitutaki chief.

Parliamentary institutions evolved under New Zealand auspices beginning with the establishment in 1946 of the Legislative Council, which had limited control over internal affairs. This became the Legislative Assembly of 22 elected and five ex officio members in 1957. In November 1964 the New Zealand parliament passed an act providing a constitution for full self-government in domestic matters, although an association was retained in which New Zealand would be responsible for the Cook Islands' defense and would be available for consultation regarding Cook Islands' foreign affairs. The act was promulgated in 1965, when the first elections under the new system were held. Albert Henry's Cook Islands Party won 14 of the 22 seats in the assembly and retained control of the government until Henry was obliged to step down as prime minister in July 1979.

The Social System

According to the census of December 1, 1981, the population of Cook Islands was 17,695 and was estimated at 16,000 in mid-1984. The average annual growth for the years 1981–82 was a negative 2.9 percent, the decrease being attributed to continued migration of young people to New Zealand. Positive rates of growth, averaging 1.8 percent per year, had been recorded in the two decades between 1950 and 1970, but a period of negative growth began after 1970 (when the population was 21,323), reflecting the stagnation of the local economy. Almost 90 percent of the population lived on the volcanic islands of the Southern Cooks, according to the 1981 census. This was owing in part to continued migration from the outer islands to Rarotonga, which had 9,530 people in 1981. In late 1970 more than 20,000 Cook Islanders lived and worked in New Zealand, a number larger than the home population.

The people speak a dialect of the Polynesian language that has very close affinities with those of the people of the Society Islands and the New Zealand Maori. These languages are mutually intelligible and vary chiefly in the matter of the pronunciation of certain sounds. English is also used extensively, especially on Rarotonga.

Almost all Cook Islanders professed belief in the Christian religion in the early 1980s. A majority were affiliated with the Cook Islands Christian Church (CICC), a Protestant group tracing its origins to the first conversions made by the London Missionary Society preachers in the 1820s. There are smaller groups of Roman Catholics, Seventh-Day Adventists, Anglicans, Mormons, and others. During the twentieth century there has been a gradual decline in the power and prestige of the CICC and its pastors because of the inflow of secular influences, particularly from New Zealand. The postwar development of parliamentary politics and the migration of thousands of persons overseas have also eroded the traditional powers and prestige of the *ariki*. For geographic and economic reasons, the Southern Cook Islands have been more open to modern influence than the more isolated Northern Cook Islands.

Education in mid-1984 was compulsory for children between the ages of six and 15 (6,424 students in 1982). There were 38 schools on the islands, providing primary-, secondary-, and college-level (junior college and teacher's college) education. These were operated by the state, the Roman Catholic church, and the Seventh-Day Adventists. The New Zealand government provided scholarships for university-level education in that country.

A system of health services was maintained by the Cook Islands government and was available without charge to all citizens. In general, the population in the early 1980s was healthy. Tropical diseases such as malaria were not endemic to the islands, although there have been outbreaks of filariasis, a parasitic disease.

The Economy

The islands' economic stagnation has been exacerbated by the movement of the most active, ambitious, and best educated members of the population to New Zealand. Tourism, however, has been a sector of growing importance. In 1982 the 17,464 foreign tourist arrivals exceeded the total population. The southern islands of Rarotonga and Aitutaki accommodated the majority. A 1979 study of the labor force revealed that 54 percent of the total was engaged in services, including tourism; 23 percent in agriculture and fishing; 16 percent in manufacturing and construction; and the remainder in other occupations.

The production of crops such as citrus fruits, bananas, pineapples, taro, and copra (the last principally in the northern islands) constituted the agricultural sector. Citrus fruit and juices, papaya, copra, bananas, mother-of-pearl shell, and handicrafts were the principal exports, approximately 80 percent of those being sent to New Zealand. Sale of Cook Islands postage stamps to world philatelists was another important source of revenue. Exports by value have customarily been only a small percentage of imports. In 1981 they were $NZ5 million or less than 20 percent of imports, which were valued at $NZ26.6 million (for value of the New Zealand dollar—see Glossary). Imports included foodstuffs, textiles, and petroleum products. The processing and canning of fruit and fruit juices formed an important component of the local industry. Fishing, in both lagoons and deep waters, had considerable potential for growth but in mid-1984 remained largely unexploited except for subsistence.

The per capita gross domestic product (GDP—see Glossary) was US$1,060 in 1981. However, the economy remained dependent on subsidies from New Zealand, which averaged around US$7 million annually, and on remittances from Cook Islanders living in that country. Improvement in living standards has been impeded by high inflation, which has been associated with the increased cost of imports and has averaged 20 percent per year.

In the early 1980s infrastructure was most fully developed on Rarotonga. West of Avarua was an international airport capable of serving wide-bodied aircraft, and the island was encircled by a 33-

kilometer road sealed with low-grade asphalt. Cook Islands Airways and Air Rarotonga provided domestic service, using propeller-driven aircraft. International shipping was served by port facilities at Avarua and the nearby harbor at Avatiu.

The New Zealand dollar was the currency in circulation in mid-1984, although Cook Islands also minted its own coins in various denominations. There was a post office savings system, and the National Bank of New Zealand operated a branch in the islands. The Cook Islands Development Bank, set up in 1978, had assets of US$2 million in 1983.

The Political System

Cook Islanders are citizens of New Zealand. The 1965 Constitution grants Cook Islands complete control over internal affairs and provides that New Zealand exercise responsibility for defense and provide consultation in foreign affairs. The document allows for a unilateral declaration of full independence by the islands' government. The head of state is the British monarch, who appoints a representative to the islands. Government institutions as defined in the Constitution are similar to the British parliamentary system. The six-member cabinet, headed by a premier, is responsible to a 24-member parliament. Members of parliament serve for a four-year term and are elected by universal adult suffrage. One member is elected by Cook Islanders living overseas. An upper house, known as the House of Ariki, was created by a constitutional amendment in 1965 and is composed of up to 15 members, all *ariki*. It serves solely a consultative function, particularly on issues related to custom or land tenure. Local government is the responsibility of island councils and village committees.

Cook Islands politics was lively in the early 1980s. There were three political parties: the Cook Islands Party (CIP), led in mid-1984 by Geoffrey Arama Henry, the Democratic Party (DP) of Thomas Davis, and the Unity Party (UP) of Joseph Williams. There was a high level of political awareness among the population, and intense personal rivalries between leaders played a prominent role in political dynamics.

The CIP was in power from the time the first parliamentary elections were held in 1965 until 1979, Albert Henry serving as premier. During the campaign preceding the general elections of March 1978, the DP, the opposition party, accused Henry of corruption and other abuses of power, and an acrimonious controversy developed over the issue of the right of expatriate Cook

Islanders to participate in the election. Although the results of the March 30, 1978, balloting gave the DP a larger number of constituencies than the CIP, the inclusion of 1,000 votes by overseas Cook Islanders gave the CIP a majority. Both parties had chartered flights to bring electors from New Zealand, the DP responsible for 200 and the CIP for 800. The DP accused Premier Henry of misusing public money to charter the aircraft, and an investigation carried out by the chief justice revealed that proceeds from the sale of postage stamps had been diverted to that purpose after undergoing an elaborate laundering process involving companies in the islands and in New Zealand, as well as a United States businessman. The DP had paid for its flights out of its own funds. Henry was charged with criminal violations and removed from office. The chief justice ordered the reinstatement to parliament of eight DP candidates who had been elected without the participation of overseas Cook Islanders, and in July 1979 a new government was formed, DP head Thomas Davis serving as premier.

A general election was held on March 30, 1983. The voters returned 13 CIP candidates to parliament, and the DP seated 11 members. No UP candidate was elected. Geoffrey Arama Henry, cousin of Albert Henry and leader of the CIP (Albert Henry had died in January 1981), became premier. However, the death of one CIP member of parliament and the crossover of a second to the DP left parliament evenly divided and forced a change in government. Henry resigned in August 1983 but was appointed caretaker premier by the queen's representative. A second general election was scheduled for November 2, 1983. The DP won 13 seats and the CIP 11, and Thomas Davis resumed the premiership on November 16, 1983.

The judicial system of the Cook Islands was based on the British model. The High Court had jurisdiction over civil, criminal, and land-title cases, and the Court of Appeal heard appeals against its decisions. The final appellate court was the Privy Council, sitting in London.

EASTER ISLAND

Official Name	Easter Island (Isla de Pascua)
Previous Names	Rapa Nui; Pito-O-Te Henua (The Navel of the World)
Political Status	Province of Chile
Capital	Hanga Roa
Population	1,867 (1981 year-end estimate)
Land Area	180 square kilometers
Currency	Chilean peso (Ch$)

One of the most isolated islands in Oceania, Easter Island lies almost 2,000 kilometers from the Pitcairn Islands, its nearest Polynesian neighbor, and nearly 4,200 kilometers from Chile. It is triangular in shape and contains three extinct volcanoes and several parasitic cones, all joined by a lava plain. The largest of the volcanoes, Mount Terevaka, rises 507 meters above sea level. Lava flows have created numerous underground caves and sprinkled the island's rather thin soil with volcanic stones. Fresh-water lakes in three of the volcanic craters provide the only surface water. Droughts have occurred on occasion, rainfall in the semitropical climate averaging about 1,250 millimeters annually but subject to great variation.

The island has no protected harbors or coral reefs, and its shores are precipitous in many areas. Weather permitting, most landings are made at one of four small, sandy beaches. A very small island off the southwestern tip, Motu Nui, was the scene of a "bird-man" ceremony recorded in the mid-nineteenth century. At that time servants of leading islanders would swim out to Motu Nui to await the arrival of a migratory bird, the sooty tern. The master of the first to find an egg would then be placed in seclusion for several months, presumably as the representative of the god Makemake.

Easter Island once supported large stands of forest, but these had been badly depleted by the time the Europeans first arrived in the eighteenth century; by the turn of the twentieth century, the island was grass covered and virtually treeless. There has been some effort to replant trees in recent years, particularly eucalyptus, pine, and fruit trees.

The prehistoric society of Easter Island had been completely destroyed by the time detailed records were first made in the mid-1800s. The unreliability of what evidence is available and its incomplete, confusing, and sometimes contradictory nature have given rise to wide-ranging speculation over the island's prehistory, some of the most extreme theories centering on mythical sunken continents or extraterrestrial astronauts. The great body of responsible scholarship appears to indicate, however, that the island could have been peopled as early as A.D. 400 by Polynesian migrants who were then almost completely isolated from outside contact until the coming of the Europeans. The original settlers are believed to have increased their numbers to as many as 10,000, for several years building impressive statues and monuments until internal conflict and serious environmental degradation associated with the decimation of the original forest forced a decline in both population and culture.

One other school of thought, chiefly represented by Norwegian anthropologist Thor Heyerdahl, posits a major influence of South American migrants on prehistoric Easter Island culture. Although skeletal evidence and most artifacts are clearly Polynesian, there is insufficient evidence to refute this theory altogether or to exclude the possibility of some contact with South America. New World plants, including the Andean sweet potato, among others, were found on Easter Island and could have been introduced either by migrants or by natural methods. A minority of artifacts not of clear Polynesian type and sharing similarities to South American artifacts can also be explained either as products of spontaneous development during long isolation or as evidence of direct South American influence.

Whatever their origin, Easter Islanders left behind an impressive collection of artifacts for which the island has become famous. These include some 600 carved stone statues, a few over 20 meters high, but most between six and nine meters high. Of these, approximately 150 are still unfinished in their quarry. These statues were originally mounted on stone platforms called *ahu,* of which the remains of about 300 are still to be found. The archaeological record also includes numerous stone petroglyphs as well as the remains of stone-walled houses, some boat-shaped in form, which are grouped in large clustered settlements. The significance of the statues and the *ahu* remains uncertain, but there are some indications that they are stylized portraits of important ancestors or chiefs.

One final subject of mystery is presented by several inscribed wooden boards that were kept in some houses. These were first noted in 1864, at which time no islander could read the script in which they were written. Known as *rongorongo,* that script consists of about 120 elements, many based on human or bird-man symbols. Some elements have also been found in petroglyphs or in signatures by island representatives to a treaty with Spain in 1770. As of the early 1980s *rongorongo* had not been satisfactorily translated. Theories explaining the inscribed boards posit variously that they are unique prehistoric examples of a written Polynesian language, were used as pictographs or mnemonic devices, or were essentially ornamental. It has also been suggested that the script was developed in emulation of European writing after the arrival of the Spanish.

By the time the island was first discovered by Europeans, on Easter Day in April 1722 by Admiral Roggeveen, a major cultural decline was already under way, and the population stood at an estimated 3,000. Observers from later French, Spanish, British, and other expeditions noted evidence of an egalitarian society, dominated by warring groups that competed for scarce resources. By 1774 all statues had been toppled, presumably during internal upheavals. These visitors rarely stopped for long or had any grasp of the local language, however, and their observations are lacking in detail and are of questionable reliability.

The first close—and for the islanders, disastrous—contact with the Western world came during 1862–63, when about 1,000 islanders were captured and taken to Peru as slaves. Protests by missionaries and others soon forced their repatriation, but by that time most had died. The 15 who actually survived to return in 1863 carried smallpox and tuberculosis, which then ravaged the remaining population.

During these times of trouble Roman Catholic missionaries settled on the island, by 1868 baptizing the remaining islanders. That same year a French adventurer arrived on the island and began buying up land to establish a sheep ranch. Conflict over the ranch led some islanders and the missionaries to leave Easter Island for Mangareva Island in French Polynesia. Other islanders went to work in Tahiti. By the time the adventurer was killed in 1877, the population stood at 115. Of these, 15 couples, as well as a few outsiders who arrived later, were to be the ancestors of modern-day Easter Islanders.

After Easter Island was annexed in 1888 by Chile, life on the island was very quiet. The sheep ranch was taken over by a Chilean firm, some 18,000 sheep were given the run of the island,

and the few islanders lived in a small fenced-off area near Hanga Roa. During World War I the German navy used the island as a supply base, but otherwise during the first half of the twentieth century it was visited only occasionally by scientific expeditions, yachts, and liners. The island was under the administration of the Chilean navy, which also paid it an annual visit.

In 1965 island leaders wrote an open letter of protest to the Chilean government complaining about the naval administration and their own conditons of life, whereupon the island was placed under a civil administration and islanders were accorded the rights of Chilean citizenship. During the same period a rough airstrip first built in the early 1950s was lengthened and in 1967 regular air service to Easter Island was inaugurated. The airstrip was further upgraded in 1970 to permit jet service.

Ethnic Easter Islanders constituted approximately two-thirds of the total population during the early 1980s, the remaining one-third being made up of temporary residents from Chile who were employed by the government, the airlines, the Chilean air force or navy, or in various service occupations. An unknown number of Easter Islanders resided in Chile and elsewhere in the Pacific basin. The informal life-style on the island reflected a strong Chilean influence in dress, architecture, and certain customs, although local customs also remained in evidence.

Islanders speak a local Polynesian language called Rapa Nui or Pascuense, as well as Spanish, the official languge. They are overwhelmingly adherents of Roman Catholicism. In mid-1984 the school system was run by the Chilean government through a regional department located in Valparaíso, Chile. There was one kindergarten on the island, in addition to one school that provided eight years of primary education and four of secondary. Some children attended secondary schools in Chile, where opportunities for advanced education were also available. A hospital on the island provided medical and dental services.

Most islanders worked in agriculture, fishing, the tourist industry—which handled some 4,000 tourists in 1980—and a few very small businesses. The government also provided employment. Agriculture consisted mainly of small-scale production of food crops for local consumption. The Chilean government also maintained a farm on the island, which was intended to help make Easter Island self-sufficient in food production. Many farmers kept cattle, pigs, and chickens. An estimated 2,000 horses ran wild. Locally caught fish, including tuna, supplemented the local diet. In recent years the government has imposed a season on lobster catching to ensure continued supply. Wool from some

10,000 sheep provided the island's only significant export, but earnings were insufficient to balance the amount Chile spent on providing local services.

The road network on the island was entirely unpaved. Four-wheeled and other vehicles, as well as horses and foot power, were used for transportation. Cargo ships of the Chilean government brought nonperishable supplies to Easter Island, and reports in the international press in early 1984 indicated that the government intended to build a port there. The national airline, LAN-Chile also called regularly, bringing tourists and necessary supplies. A branch of the Chilean post office and state bank were present as well. Telephone service facilitated intraisland communication in addition to contact with Chile and the rest of the world. The amenities of electricity, radio, and televison were also available. Pumped water was supplied to Hanga Roa, but water was also collected in cisterns.

As a province of Chile, Easter Island was administered by an appointed Chilean military governor. A corps of Chilean officials provided most public services, which, along with the legal system, were the same as those in Chile. A branch of the Chilean national police provided law enforcement and maintained a small jail, and the Chilean air force and navy each had a small base on Easter Island. There was only limited local input in island government, mainly through an appointed local mayor. Reports in the international press that some elements of the population harbored pro-independence sentiments could not be confirmed as of mid-1984.

FRENCH POLYNESIA

Formal Name	Territory of French Polynesia
Political Status	Overseas territory of France
Capital	Papeete
Population	159,000 (1984 midyear estimate)
Land Area	4,000 square kilometers
Currency	Cours du Franc Pacifique franc (CFPF)
Major Islands and Island Groups	Society Islands, including Tahiti, Moorea, and Raiatea; Marquesas Islands; Austral Islands; Mangareva Islands (Îles Gambier); Tuamotu Archipelago

French Polynesia, an overseas territory of France since 1958, is located in the south-central Pacific Ocean. The territorial capital, Papeete, on the island of Tahiti, is about 6,600 kilometers northeast of Sydney, Australia, and 4,400 kilometers southeast of Honolulu. The Pitcairn Islands lie to the southeast, the Cook Islands to the west, and Kiribati to the northwest. Although the territory is in the eastern Polynesian cultural area, its population also includes Europeans, Asians, and people of mixed blood. Land is scarce, and agriculture is poorly developed; principal export crops are copra and coconut products. Tourism is an important component of the local economy. France's Pacific Test Center (Centre d'Expérimentation du Pacifique) continued to maintain a nuclear testing site at Mururoa Atoll in the Tuamotu Archipelago in 1984. A reform of French Polynesia's territorial statute, under discussion in mid-1984, was designed to provide a greater measure of self-government while still maintaining a link with France.

Physical Environment

French Polynesia comprises some 130 widely dispersed islands and islets, of which the largest, Tahiti, has an area of 1,042

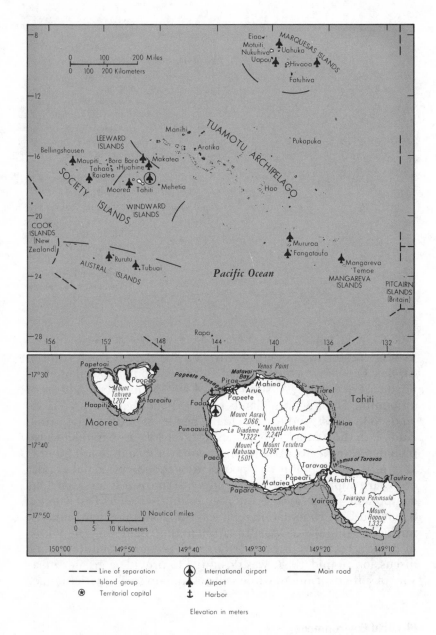

Figure 18. French Polynesia, 1984

square kilometers (see fig. 18). The distance from Rapa in the south to Eiao in the Marquesas Islands in the north is 2,400 kilometers; that from Bellingshausen Island in the west to Temoe Island in the east is 2,440 kilometers.

The French government enforces a territorial limit of 12 nautical miles in its territories, including French Polynesia. Enabling legislation passed in 1976 provided for an EEZ (see Glossary) of 200 nautical miles, which by an unofficial reckoning would make French Polynesia's sea area 5.03 million square kilometers.

French Polynesia is composed of five distinct island groups that include most of its islands. The Society Islands, numbering 14, are divided into the Windward group and the Leeward group. The principal islands are Tahiti and Moorea in the Windwards and Raiatea, Bora Bora, and Huahine in the Leewards. To the northeast of the Society group, about 1,500 kilometers from Tahiti, are the Marquesas, having 10 major islands, including Nukuhiva, Hivaoa, and Uapou. The Austral Islands group, consisting of five major islands, is located to the south of the Society group, while the Mangareva Islands, numbering four principal islands, are found to the southeast. The extensive Tuamotu Archipelago, located between the Society and Marquesas groups, contains 76 islands, most of which are very small.

Geologically and topographically, the islands of French Polynesia can be classified as either "high islands"—volcanic formations—or "low islands"—coral formations, most of which are atolls. The Society, Marquesas, Austral, and Mangareva groups are high islands, interspersed with a small number of atolls. The Tuamotu Archipelago consists of coral low islands, all but one of which are atolls.

The contrast between the volcanic and coral formations is striking. The high islands have steep relief. Their sharp peaks, precipitous cliffs, and deep valleys, usually green with vegetation, struck early European explorers and modern tourists alike as a fitting landscape for an earthly paradise. The soils, particularly in the coastal areas, are comparatively rich, and the islands are generally well watered with streams, small rivers, and waterfalls of great beauty. Tahiti derives its form, reminiscent of a gourd turned on its side, from the juncture of two ancient and much eroded volcanic cones. Its highest peak is Mount Orohena (2,241 meters). Other important peaks are Aorai (2,066 meters) and La Diadème (1,322 meters). One side of La Diadème is a steep cliff more than 300 meters high. Mount Tohivea, on Moorea (also an ancient volcanic cone), is 1,207 meters high, and the most elevated point on Raiatea is 1,038 meters above sea level. On

Nukuhiva in the Marquesas group, the Ahui waterfall, the highest in French Polynesia, drops 350 meters. There are no active volcanoes in the territory.

Because of the abundance of water and the suitability of the volcanic soils, the vegetation is lush. On Tahiti coconut trees, pandani (screw pines), banyans, and flame trees are found along the coasts, while vegetation on the mountain slopes consists of brush and thickets. Rain forests are found in the valleys and the more humid windward slopes of the island. Fruit-bearing trees grow in abundance, providing traditional dietary staples, such as breadfruit, bananas, and Tahitian chestnuts. Tahiti's vegetation pattern is common to most of the volcanic islands, although periodic drought makes the Marquesas less bountiful.

Except for the Marquesas, most of the high islands, including Tahiti, Moorea, Raiatea, Huahine, and Bora Bora, are surrounded by coral reefs. The reefs contain colorful and abundant marine life, but ships approaching the islands must navigate with care through passes in the coral barriers.

The low islands are small and have little relief. During high tides or in violent storms, considerable portions of their area may be submerged. Vegetation is scanty, owing to poor limestone soils and lack of water.

French Polynesia has a humid, tropical climate. The average yearly temperature at Papeete is 27°C and the hottest, in January and February, is 32°C. The prevailing southeastern trade winds serve to moderate temperatures. Most precipitation occurs during the rainy season between November and March. The average annual rainfall in Papeete is 1,750 millimeters. Severe cyclones sometimes occur during the early months of the year.

There is significant variation in climate because of latitude, elevation, and position relative to prevailing winds. The Marquesas, lying closer to the equator, have a warmer climate than the Society group, which in turn is more tropical than the Austral and Mangareva islands. The mountain regions are cool and wet, and on Tahiti the *hupe*, a breeze that blows down from the mountains, cools the coastal areas. The southeastward-facing windward sides of the island are wetter and have denser vegetation than the leeward sides.

French Polynesia has no native land mammals because of its isolation from continental landmasses, but there are 90 species of birds. The Polynesians brought dogs and fowl to the islands, and the Europeans introduced horses, sheep, goats, and cattle. There are freshwater fish in the inland waters of the high islands.

Historical Setting

The Polynesians did not have their own written language, which makes it difficult to trace the evolution of their society and culture before the coming of discerning European observers in the late eighteenth century. Archaeological ethnographic evidence indicates that the indigenous people of what is now French Polynesia came from Tonga or Samoa. Archaeologist Peter Bellwood suggests that a distinct eastern Polynesian culture developed first in the Marquesas Islands beginning around A.D. 300 and was later diffused to the Society, Tuamotu, Mangareva, and Austral islands. For geographic and economic reasons, the center of this cultural region gradually shifted to the Society Islands, particularly Raiatea and Tahiti, though the Marquesas group had a flourishing culture of its own and a population as high as 30,000 as late as the beginning of the nineteenth century.

In eighteenth-century European eyes, traditional Polynesian society affirmed philosopher Jean-Jacques Rousseau's notion of the "noble savage" untainted by the artifices of modern civilization. The beauty, generosity, and good nature of the people were real enough, but below idyllic appearances lay a complex society having a strong sense of hierarchy and its own characteristic tensions. In the Society Islands the population was divided into three strata: the *arii* (ruling chief), the lesser chiefs, and the commoners, who formed the great majority. These categories were strictly hereditary, and any infringement by the lower orders on the privileges of their superiors was severely punished. All chiefs, particularly the *arii*, were believed to possess a superior measure of mana (supernatural power). Prohibitions prevented contact between persons having different degrees of mana, perpetuating social distinctions. Because sexual intercourse between chiefs and commoners was forbidden, children who were products of such unions were usually killed. The power of the *arii* extended over an entire territory while that of the lesser chiefs was confined to well-defined subdivisions. Although chiefs of both kinds had control over the land, resources, and goods produced by commoners, their rule in most cases was not oppressive. There were abundant resources, particularly on Tahiti, and well-established customs of redistributing wealth. Workers and craftsmen, however, could be organized in large numbers for the building of temple enclosures, elaborate war canoes, and extensive offshore fishing traps.

The islands were divided into a number of states, often wedge-shaped territories defined by steep-walled valleys, which were ruled by an *arii* and his family. Warfare between these chiefdoms was constant but not particularly bloody. A balance of power was maintained, no single *arii* gaining permanent hegemony.

Polynesians traced the descent of their chiefs from the gods in myths that established claims of superior mana transferred through the generations. By the eighteenth century, Oro, the god of war, was the most venerated deity in the Society Islands. Oro's cult had its birthplace and center on the island of Raiatea, and its priests enjoyed a special status. A striking feature of Polynesian religion was the *arioi* society, groups of actors and singers dedicated to Oro that traveled through the islands giving performances and receiving tribute from the local populations. In the temples—open-air structures that commonly contained a raised stone platform in a truncated pyramid shape—priests conducted ceremonies that occasionally involved human sacrifice. The most sacred temple was found on Raiatea.

The society of the Marquesas Islands was less complex and hierarchical than that of the Society Islands, having only two ranks: chiefs and commoners. The power of the former was relatively limited, and there were a number of small chiefdoms cut off from each other by steep valley walls. Like the states of the Society Islands, the chiefdoms were constantly at war. Frequent droughts, lack of arable land, and limited opportunities for fishing led to periodic food shortages, and cannibalism was widely practiced.

European Intrusions

The first Europeans to visit Polynesia were members of the expedition of Ferdinand Magellan, who landed on Pukapuka in the northeastern Tuamotu group in 1521. In 1595 Spanish navigator Álvaro de Mendaña de Neira reached the Marquesas Islands, which he named in honor of the Spanish viceroy of Peru. His men treated the local inhabitants with great cruelty, killing several hundred. Fortunately for the Polynesians, the remoteness of their islands precluded frequent visits by Europeans until the late eighteenth century.

Improved shipbuilding and navigational methods, the search for an elusive southern continent, and the scientific curiosity of the "Age of Reason" brought European voyagers in significant numbers to the islands in the eighteenth century. The first Europeans to see Tahiti were the men of the H.M.S. *Dolphin*, a British ship on an expedition around the world commanded by Captain Samuel Wallis. On June 18, 1767, the *Dolphin*, finding

Harbor of Papeete
Courtesy Tahiti Tourist Promotion Board/Tini Colombel

anchorage in Matavai Bay in the island's northwest coast, was surrounded by hundreds of canoes whose occupants sought to drive away the intruder by showering it with stones. After Wallis ordered his crew to sink the canoes with cannon-shot, causing a large number of casualties, the Polynesians changed their tactics and began a lively trade, giving the British much needed food in exchange for iron tools and trinkets. The islanders valued iron nails because they could be bent into fishhooks, and lonely British sailors were happy to discover that the companionship of young ladies could be won by offering them these inexpensive items. A commerce sprang up that was discourged only when the officers of the *Dolphin* found to their distress that the ship's structure was being weakened by eager sailors in search of nails. Tahiti and the other islands of the region soon gained a perhaps undeserved reputation for sexual license. Louis Antoine de Bougainville, the French navigator who landed in eastern Tahiti in 1768, named the island Nouveau Cythère after the island near Greece where the love goddess Venus was supposed to have risen from the sea.

Of the British, French, and Spanish navigators who landed at Tahiti and the other Polynesian islands in the eighteenth century, the most important was Captain Cook, who visited three times, in 1769, 1773, and 1777. Cook's voyages had scientific objectives. The first was to map the transit of the planet Venus across the sun in order to gauge the distance of the sun from the earth. For this purpose, he established an observatory at "Point Venus" off Matavai Bay but failed to get a precise measurement. Cook's second and third visits to Tahiti took place during voyages of exploration that included a search for a southern continent and a northwest passage connecting the Atlantic and the Pacific oceans. He stopped not only at Tahiti but also at Moorea and the Leeward, Austral, and Marquesas islands.

Cook established friendly relations with Tahitian rulers, especially Tu, ruler of the state of Pare in the northwestern part of the island, where modern Papeete is located. The states were, as always, at war. Tu was able to take advantage of his relationship with Cook and other Europeans, who mistakenly regarded him as the "king" of Tahiti, to obtain tools and weapons. This upset the delicate balance of power between the states. Hatchets and chisels could be used to make war canoes more quickly and efficiently than the old method of using fire to hollow out logs. Although Cook opposed such trade, later European arrivals were willing to supply firearms. By the turn of the century, a ragged assortment of beachcombers and deserters from ships' crews, including some from the H. M. S. *Bounty* who had mutinied in 1789, were serving Tahitian rulers as mercenaries. Tu, who now called himself Pomare, benefited most from their services. He was able to defeat his rival chiefs in campaigns more brutal than traditional island combat.

Eighteen members of the London Missionary Society and their wives landed at Matavai Bay in 1797. Although they had enjoyed Pomare's hospitality, the ruler and his subjects were unmoved by their preaching and continued to venerate Oro, the god of war. Long sermons on Calvinist themes of sin and salvation were evidently less attractive than the lively song and dance of the *arioi*. The missionaries failed to persuade the Tahitians to end the practices of human sacrifice and infanticide. By 1800 all but five had left Tahiti. One missionary who had landed in the Marquesas had also left without making any converts.

When Pomare died in 1803, his name passed to his son, who was referred to by Europeans as Pomare II. A drunken despot whose depredations earned him the hostility of chiefs and commoners alike, Pomare II sought to conquer all Tahiti in 1807. He was at first successful, but in 1808 the other chiefs combined against him and forced him to flee to the neighboring island of

Moorea. By this time the fortunes of the remaining missionaries were also at a low ebb, and they were obliged to leave Tahiti. By 1809 practically all had quit the islands in deep discouragement.

Pomare II's misfortunes had apparently induced in him . something of a theological crisis. Despite his sacrifices to Oro, his enemies had been able to defeat him, and the ruler began to think that the Christian God might make a more effective supernatural patron. In 1812 he suddenly announced his intention to become a Christian and asked one of the remaining missionaries to baptize him. Most of his subjects on Moorea followed his example. Three years later Pomare II, now a Christian "king," sent his troops back to Tahiti, where they defeated his pagan adversaries, rendering him ruler of all Tahiti and some of the outlying islands.

Under Pomare II's rule, the missionaries brought about a kind of cultural revolution. The Ten Commandments were made the legal basis of the government, and the Sabbath was strictly observed. Supernatural images (tiki) and other objects sacred to the old religion were burned, and the temple enclosures were forsaken. Except for hymn singing, the missionaries banned all singing, a pastime that had been dear to the old Tahitians. Men wore castoff European clothes and women "Mother Hubbards"—long garments that reached from the neck to the ankles and combined modesty with discomfort. The missionaries established a kind of "morality police," which surveyed the population to root out instances of drunkenness, game playing, dancing, or sex outside the bounds of Christian marriage, an institution the Tahitians only imperfectly understood.

Although the missionaries are accused of having ruined an earthly Eden with their stern Calvinist moralism, the old society was dying even before the first Protestant missionaries arrived in the islands in 1797. The best estimate of Tahiti's population before the coming of the Europeans is 40,000. By the end of the eighteenth century, it had declined to around 16,000 and by the mid-nineteenth century had reached a low of 8,000 (excluding Europeans). The Polynesians had developed few immunities to the diseases carried by European sailors, and the population was ravaged by smallpox, scarlet fever, measles, dysentery, influenza, and venereal infections. Rum and other strong drink contributed to rapid social disintegration. The Marquesas were a popular stopping-over place for whaling ships—which had notoriously undisciplined crews—and the population there had declined from 30,000 to around 4,000 by the end of the nineteenth century.

The islands were gradually drawn into the world economy

during the first half of the nineteenth century. Salt pork was exported to the newly established British penal colony in Australia; other products included coconut oil, pearls, mother-of-pearl, sandalwood, and arrowroot flour. Local chiefs became involved in this trade. Fortunately for the Polynesians, no serious attempt was made by outsiders to set up a large-scale plantation economy such as that which developed in Hawaii and led to the large-scale expropriation of native lands. Decimation of the population left the survivors with ample land on which they could carry out subsistence farming and grow cash crops, such as citrus fruit, vanilla, and coconuts, on small plots.

Pomare II died in 1821, and his infant son, Pomare III, lived only until 1824. The next ruler was Pomare II's sister, who assumed the throne as Queen Pomare IV. During this period the missionaries remained in a dominant position, one of them, George Pritchard, serving not only as adviser to the queen but also as British consul. A royal palace was built at Papeete west of Matavai Bay, and that settlement soon developed into a modern seaport complete with brothels and bars for transient sailors and churches for local believers.

French Catholic missionaries came to the islands in 1836, and Pritchard, sensing a challenge to Protestant—and British— influence, persuaded the queen to have them expelled. France at this time saw itself as the patron of Catholic missionary activities abroad and sent a warship to Papeete harbor in 1838 to demand reparations. Pritchard in turn made urgent requests that Britain annex Tahiti. In 1842 French rear admiral Abel Aubert Dupetit-Thouars, on orders from the French government, took possession of the Marquesas and then sailed to Papeete, where he forced Queen Pomare to sign an agreement making her country a protectorate of France. At Pritchard's urging she renounced the agreement a year later, whereupon French troops occupied Papeete, and she fled to the safety of a British warship. The British government, however, did not wish to go to war over such a remote and economically unpromisiing group of islands and accepted the French annexation. A determined resistance by Tahitian chiefs and their subjects continued until 1847, when the queen finally accepted the status of a ruler "protected" by the French.

French Colonial Rule

Queen Pomare died in 1877. Three years later her son, Pomare V, abdicated, and his kingdom became a colony ruled directly by France. Through the protectorate and early colonial periods, French power was extended from Tahiti and the Marquesas, which served as a naval station, to the other island groups that form present-day French Polynesia. One consequence of French rule was the decline, but not the disappearance, of British Protestant influence as Catholic missionaries came in increasing numbers.

During and after the imposition of French influence and control, a number of Western authors were inspired to write of the beauties of the islands and romanticize the traditional way of life. These included Herman Melville, whose semifictional work *Typee* describes his adventures among the Marquesas Islanders of Nukuhiva; in *Omoo* he related his experiences on Tahiti at the time of the French takeover. Others included Scottish novelist Robert Louis Stevenson, French writer Julien Viaud (Pierre Loti), and British poet Rupert Brooke. Paul Gauguin, who had abandoned the staid life of a Paris stockbroker to become a painter, came to Tahiti in 1891. Although best known for his remarkable depictions on canvas of the Polynesian people, he also wrote a book about Polynesia, *Noa Noa*, and wrote weekly articles for a Papeete newspaper criticizing the hypocrisy of French rule and the government's lack of interest in the people's welfare.

A new society was developing, principally in Papeete but also in the rural districts of Tahiti and in the other islands. Chinese immigrants had been brought to Tahiti in the 1860s to work as laborers on cotton plantations that were set up to exploit world cotton shortages during the American Civil War, but these enterprises went bankrupt after 1865. Some of the Chinese workers stayed on and, joined by later groups of compatriots, came to occupy an important role in the island economy as shopkeepers and moneylenders. By World War II they numbered more than 5,000. Although Chinese intermarried with Polynesians, their community remained quite distinct and supported Chinese schools and associations that preserved close ties with the home country.

The old system of local chiefs had largely disappeared by the late nineteenth century. Colonial society consisted of a small group of French officials, military officers, and businessmen at the apex. Below that were other Europeans, the Chinese, a population of persons of mixed European and Tahitian parentage, and the indigenous people.

The islands, known as French Oceania, remained outside the mainstream of world events through the first decades of the twentieth century. However, a contingent of Polynesian soldiers served in the Pacific Battalion of the French army in France and the Balkans during World War I, and Papeete was damaged by shelling from German cruisers in 1914.

Although the colonial administration was subordinate to the collaborationist regime of Marshal Henri-Philippe Pétain following the fall of France in June 1940, the local population supported the Free French movement of General Charles de Gaulle and forced the resignation of the pro-Vichy governor. A new Pacific Battalion was organized to fight on the Allied side. The Japanese, in their attempt to seize control of the South Pacific, never threatened Tahiti and the other islands of what is now French Polynesia, but the island of Bora Bora in the Leeward group of the Society Islands was used as a base for United States military forces and as a staging area to send men and equipment westward to the front.

The Postwar Period

French colonial domination of the political system and the general breakdown of traditional Polynesian institutions precluded the development of strong political movements among Polynesians before World War II. Popular affection for the memory of the independent Tahitian kingdom under the Pomares and discontent with French rule, however, were strong. In 1947 Marcel Pouvanaa a Oopa, a World War I veteran who had led national revival movements between the wars, established the Pouvanaa Committee, later known as the Tahitian People's Democratic Party, to demand a greater measure of self-government for the indigenous people. In April 1958, on the eve of elections held in all French overseas possessions to determine whether they would remain in association with France, Pouvanaa a Oopa campaigned for full independence. Sixty-four percent of the electorate, however, chose to retain the islands' status as a French overseas territory in which a measure of local power was vested in a popularly elected legislature. Shortly after the referendum Pouvanaa a Oopa and some of his followers were arrested on charges of attempted murder and arson, and he was exiled to France.

Pouvanaa a Oopa's associates, Francis Sanford and John Teariki, carried on the struggle for greater political rights, and in 1977 the French government granted a new statute giving the overseas territory a larger measure of autonomy. Pouvanaa a Oopa had returned to the islands in 1968 and served as French Polynesia's representative to the French Senate between 1971 and his death in 1977.

One development of importance for society in French

Polynesia in the postwar period was the promotion of tourism. In 1960 an international airport capable of handling jet airliners was built at Faaa, near Papeete, and during the following two decades a system of international hotels and resorts was established. By the late 1970s more than 90,000 tourists a year on average were visiting Tahiti and the outer islands, providing considerable employment in the service sector of the local economy.

A development of even greater significance was the French government's decision to establish the Pacific Test Center on the atolls of Mururoa and Fangataufa in the Tuamotu group. In the period between 1966, when the facility was opened, and 1974, when atmospheric testing was halted, France exploded 41 nuclear bombs at the site. Because of strong protests from countries in the Pacific region, such as New Zealand, Fiji, and Australia, nuclear tests were limited to underground explosions after 1974. Critics have charged that nuclear fallout and seepage from the underground test site have contaminated the environment and caused an increased incidence of cancer and other illnesses among French Polnyesia's inhabitants (see The Nuclear Issue, ch. 5). For most Polynesians, however, the most visible effects of the test center have been economic, stimulating further rapid expansion of the service sector—largely at the expense of agriculture—and leading to increased salaries and changed living standards.

The Social System

The population of French Polynesia experienced an average annual growth rate of 2.1 percent in the 1975–80 period. The rate of growth has been slowing since the 1965–70 period, when it attained a post-World War II high of 4.1 percent average annual increase. The 1977 census revealed that 53 percent of the population was below 20 years of age.

The population is concentrated in and around the territorial capital of Papeete on the island of Tahiti. Papeete and environs (including the townships of Faaa and Pirae) had a population of approximately 85,000 in 1983, or 54 percent of the total. In 1981 the population of the Windward group, including Tahiti, was 101,401 (68.1 percent of the total). The Leeward group had 25,042 (16.8 percent of the total), the Marquesas 6,116 (4.1 percent), the Austral Islands 5,628 (3.8 percent), and the Tuamotu Archipelago and the Mangareva Islands 10,768 (7.2 percent). At that time the average number of persons per square kilometer in the territory was 37, ranging from 84 per square kilometer in the Windwards to eight persons per square kilometer in the Marquesas.

Ethnic Differentiation and Social Structure

At the time of the 1977 census, there were 15,338 Europeans resident in French Polynesia, or 11.2 percent of the total population. Estimates for 1983 place the number at approximately 25,000. Europeans lived primarily in urban areas, although a small number could be found in almost every outlying community. Many were men married to Polynesian women. A substantial number of the Europeans were French civil servants or military personnel sent to the territory for specified tours of duty. Others were permanent residents, including families who have lived in the islands for two or more generations. Most Europeans, however, came to the islands during the 1960s and 1970s.

The Asian community, practically all Chinese, numbered 7,356 in 1977, or 5.4 percent of the total population. They were estimated to number 12,000 in 1983. The Chinese have retained a virtual monopoly on retail trade. Although the large majority lived in Papeete, most rural communities had a general store run by a Chinese family. A few Chinese continued to cultivate cash crops, such as vanilla or garden vegetables, owning as much as 15 percent of the territory's arable land. Often they leased plots to other cultivators.

The degree of Westernization of the indigenous Polynesians of the territory varied, a phenomenon that was explicitly recognized by the people themselves and was reflected in census statistics. In 1977 about 23,700 people (17.2 percent of the population) classified themselves as *demis*, meaning persons of half-European extraction. The remainder of the indigenous population regarded themselves as *maohi*, or traditional Polynesians. In 1977 they numbered 90,160 persons (65.6 percent of the population).

The distinction between *demis* and *maohi* is to some extent an ethnic classification in that the *demis* are assumed to be of part European descent. Multiethnic ancestry, however, has been highly prevalent in French Polynesia for almost two centuries, and many persons regarded by themselves and others as unambiguously Polynesian have some European ancestry. Differentiation between *demi* and *maohi* categories is not clear-cut, and French government officials in charge of compiling the 1977 census confessed that in many cases the people themselves could not make a clear distinction. In general, however, compared with *maohi*, *demis* have more modern skills, more years of schooling, and higher incomes. They are also more comfortable speaking French and have pursued a standard of living that more closely approximates that of Europeans.

The cutoff point along the scale of Westernization that determines whether a person is *demi* or *maohi* is a matter of individual judgment, and the criteria keep changing as the entire indigenous population becomes progressively Westernized. As of mid-1984 the *demis* filled the lesser administration posts, were well represented in the Territorial Assembly, operated business enterprises and plantations, and filled some professional and many clerical and skilled labor jobs. The *maohis* were characteristically wage earners or cash croppers who supplemented their livelihood by subsistence farming or fishing. They formed the great majority of the rural and the outlying island population.

Few traces remained of traditional Polynesian social organization and its hierarchical distinctions between chiefs, lesser chiefs, and commoners. Within some indigenous communities where the London Missionary Society had been active, village social organization patterns derived from mission institutions have survived. In particular, the *pupu*, a subdivision of the mission parish for purposes of Bible reading and carrying out church activities, has developed into a meaningful unit for community organization in secular areas as well.

The children of Polynesian and Chinese parents formed a group distinct from the *demis*. There were also small numbers of people whose origins can be traced to other parts of the Pacific, including Wallis and Futuna, Fiji, and Western Samoa, as well as Africans and people from French possessions in the Indian Ocean and the Caribbean.

Political and economic power and the social position that derived from it tended to correlate with ethnic and cultural identification. The Europeans, the most Westernized Chinese, and the *demis* were generally in the higher echelons of a modernized, urban society, and the least Westernized Polynesians formed the base of the society. There was some reluctance on the part of tradition-minded Polynesians to emulate the others, whom they regarded as rich and powerful but lacking in the highly valued qualities of generosity and conscientious reciprocity. The infusion of tourist and French government money into the island economy, however, has tended to make these values less important to the younger generation.

French is the official language of the territory, used in administration and taught in the school system. The mutually intelligible indigenous languages of the different island groups are dialects of Polynesian. The dialect of Tahiti reflects that island's past association with British sea captains, missionaries, and mercenaries. Many words, such as the greeting *ia orana* (your honor) and the term for a local leader, *tavana* (governor), are derived from English.

Religion, Health, and Education

Although traditional religious beliefs largely died out during the nineteenth century, they have retained a certain minimal influence in contemporary Polynesian culture. From 1823 to 1835 the Mamaia sect, combining traditional religious themes with those borrowed from Christianity, gained adherents on Tahiti because its leader promised the expulsion of Europeans. Since then, however, indigenous religious movements have had very limited influence. The two largest religious communities in the territory were the Evangelical church of French Polynesia, having 45,000 members in 1980, and the Roman Catholic church, having 36,000 members. The Evangelical church traced its origins to the London Missionary Society. After the imposition of French colonial rule, however, its congregations were taken over by French Protestant missionaries. Smaller religious groups included Pentecostalists, Seventh-Day Adventists, Jehovah's Witnesses, and Mormons. Folk religions combining Taoist, Confucianist, and Buddhist themes were practiced by some Chinese people.

The French government maintained a system of hospitals and clinics throughout the territory, and military physicians attached to the Pacific Test Center assisted in medical emergencies. In 1947 the Louis Malarde Institute for Medical Research was established in Papeete to conduct research into endemic diseases and such health hazards as toxicity in certain species of fish found in local waters. Tuberculosis, dengue fever, and elephantiasis remained problems but have been largely brought under control. Life expectancy, according to the 1977 census, was 60 years for males and 63 years for females.

The French government has published reports asserting that the nuclear tests carried out by the Pacific Test Center posed no health hazard to the inhabitants of French Polynesia or the neighboring islands. Critics both inside and outside the territory, however, have alleged that the incidence of certain varieties of cancer can be linked to the tests and have recommended that they be halted before the fracturing of the geological structure of Mururoa and Fangataufa atolls causes large quantities of radioactive material to contaminate the ocean and the fish that form an important part of the local food supply.

There was both a state- and a church-run system of primary and secondary education. Primary schools received support from the territory, while secondary schools were financed by the French government. In the early 1980s education was compulsory to age 14 and free in government schools. The school system was organized in a manner similar to that of metropolitan France, having five years of elementary education, four years of lower secondary school, and a division of upper secondary school into academic and vocational or technical tracks. More than 200 scholarship students pursued university courses in France in 1984, there being no university in French Polynesia as of mid-1984. The proportion of literate persons above age 15, according to the 1977 census, was 98 percent.

The Economy

Beginning in the early 1960s French Polynesia's economy was transformed from one in which agriculture accounted for the major portion of GDP and employment to one in which services have become the most important area of economic activity. In 1962 agriculture and fishing employed 46 percent of the labor force, and services, including public administration, employed 35 percent. By 1977 the proportion was 18 percent and 64 percent, respectively, industrial activities employing 19 percent. By 1976 agriculture and fishing contributed only 4 percent to total GDP. Nonadministrative services contributed 47 percent of GDP, industrial activity 17 percent, and public administration 32 percent.

The islands' status as an overseas territory of France has been a primary factor in economic development. The metropolitan French government has provided French Polynesia with social services, including support for the territory's secondary schools, grants for capital investment, and direct subsidies to the territorial budget. The presence of substantial numbers of French civil servants and military personnel and the requirements of the Pacific Test Center have stimulated considerable economic growth. The most spectacular growth was during the 1960–70 period, when GDP quadrupled and average wages increased twelvefold. In 1980 per capita income for the territory was US$6,780, significantly higher than that of neighboring island groups.

Although the urban areas of the territory in and around Papeete have been most deeply affected, changes in living standards could also be perceived in rural and outlying areas. Traditional outrigger canoes have been replaced by motor launches, thatched dwellings by houses made of imported materials such as tin for roofing, and customary staples such as breadfruit, bananas, and fish by a Western-style diet. The rapid depletion of fish in the lagoons and inland bodies of water led one local leader to suggest during the 1960s that it would not be long before people would have to subsist primarily on imported canned goods. By the early 1980s about 85 percent of all food consumed in the territory was imported. Trucks that had been converted into buses continued to provide cheap public transport, but the demand for imported oil increased as ownership of private vehicles, both motorcycles and automobiles, grew sharply.

Critics have charged the French government with fostering the growth of a superficially modern economy that was excessively dependent on imports, subsidies from France, and the uncertainties of international tourism. The French government, in turn, has stressed the importance of developing the productive sectors of the economy in its economic planning. Huge trade deficits have been common. In 1980 imports totaled CFPF42 billion and exports CFPF2.3 billion (for value of the CFP franc—see Glossary). Two years later imports had grown to CFPF62.3 billion, while exports were only CFPF3.3 billion. Principal exports were copra, oil, and cultured pearls. Dependence on imports and the difficulty of transporting goods to far-flung islands have contributed to high inflation. Observers believed in mid-1983 that the official figure of 15 percent a year was greatly understated.

The Service Economy

Government establishments, particularly the Pacific Test Center, and tourism were the most important components of the economy in terms of revenues generated. According to official statistics, the test center accounted for CFPF2.7 billion in customs duties and employed over 3,000 local workers in 1981 at its installations on Tahiti and in the Tuamotus. The metropolitan government also paid a sum, equivalent to around US$30 million annually, to the territory for the use of the test facilities. Employees of the test center from metropolitan France, customarily paid high salaries and allowances, have stimulated the local economy, although some observers have pointed out that many of the newly created jobs in the territorial economy were taken by immigrants from metropolitan France.

French Polynesia's natural beauty and reputation for hospitality have made it a prime tourist destination. A number of large hotels have been built in and around Papeete, as have resorts in more unspoiled parts of the territory. The number of tourists, averaging between 90,000 and 100,000 a year between 1977 and 1981, grew to 114,000 in 1982, and income from the tourist sector in that year was US$66 million. The hotels and resorts employed an unspecified number of local workers, although most of the operations serving tourists were managed by expatriate French or foreigners.

Agriculture and Manufacturing

The most important commercial crop was coconuts. Although a portion was consumed domestically as food or made into soap, oil, or cattle feed, the major part was exported as copra or oil. Large areas on the islands and, in some instances, entire atolls were planted in coconut trees. Production was mostly on smallholdings; few large-scale plantations were in operation in the early 1980s. Some 50,000 hectares, however, or more than 13 percent of the total land area, were planted in coconut trees in 1982. The devastating series of tropical storms that struck the islands in the first months of 1983 destroyed a large number of trees.

Prices for copra and copra oil exported from the islands have been unstable, dependent in large part on the output of the world's largest producers—Indonesia and the Philippines—and on uncertain markets in importer countries such as the United States and the Soviet Union. Between 1977 and 1981 the price for a kilogram of copra varied from CFPF1.66 to CFPF3.35 and for a kilogram of copra oil produced at local refineries, between CFPF2.40 and CFPF5.27.

Vanilla was grown on numerous islands by families, many of whom were Chinese. Because of the careful and time-consuming effort required to grow the plant and process beans for shipment, vanilla did not lend itself to large-scale planting. Between 1977 and 1981 total vanilla production declined from 29 to 13 tons of green, unprocessed vanilla and from nine to one ton of black, prepared vanilla beans. In 1982 the totals were 13 tons and 3.8 tons, respectively.

Other primary products included coffee, vegetables, and fruits for domestic consumption. Livestock were also raised, particularly in the Marquesas, where there was adequate pasturage.

Fishing by indigenous Polynesians has remained a domestic enterprise carried on for the local market or as a supplement to individual food supplies. Aquaculture projects, particularly the raising of freshwater prawns, have been carried out on an experimental basis. Japanese, South Korean, and Taiwanese fishing fleets were authorized in the early 1980s to operate in the territorial waters of French Polynesia, extracting 2,153 tons of fish in 1982. Black cultured pearls were raised in beds around the islands of Bora Bora and Manihi; more than 32,000 grams were exported in 1982, worth CFPF98.7 million.

Phosphates, mined on Makatea Island, were the only significant mineral resource in French Polynesia, but the deposits were exhausted in 1966, and the mine was closed down. Over the long term the government's National Marine Research Center and private firms have drawn up plans to recover mineral resources from the seabed, including nickel, cobalt, managanese, and copper nodules located at a depth of over 4,000 meters.

All manufacturing was for local consumption or for the satisfaction of tourists. Industries included textiles, food processing, breweries, and handicrafts, all on a small scale. The construction sector has grown with the building of installations for the Pacific Test Center and other government facilities and tourist hotels.

There were in the early 1980s about 750 kilometers of surfaced roads in the territory, principally located along the coastlines of islands. The principal port was Papeete, which had a harbor protected by a 1,500-meter seawall built on the adjacent

Marketplace in Papeete
Courtesy Tahiti Tourist Promotion Board

coral reef. The international airport at Faaa, five kilometers from Papeete, had a runway of 3,900 meters and was capable of handling wide-bodied jets. There were 26 other commercial airports handling domestic air traffic in the territory.

The Political System and Security

In early 1984 the people of French Polynesia were French citizens. Adults of both sexes had the right to vote for two deputies to the French National Assembly and a member of the Senate. French Polynesia also sent a representative to serve on the metropolitan government's Economic and Social Council, a consultative body that gave its opinion on government bills from the perspective of its members' occupational expertise.

French Polynesia's government institutions in early 1984 were defined in accordance with a revised territorial statute enacted by the French metropolitan government in 1977. Designed to give the territory enhanced autonomy, the statute granted augmented powers to the locally elected Territorial Assembly and the seven-member Council of Government, which was similar in function to a cabinet.

In 1984 the Territorial Assembly had 30 members, who were elected by popular vote in 1982 to serve a five-year term. Citizens over 23 years of age and in full possession of their civil rights were eligible to run. The Territorial Assembly was responsible for selecting the Council of Government, except for that body's non-voting president, who was appointed by the metropolitan government. The Council of Government could be dissolved by a vote of censure in the Territorial Assembly, but the Council of Ministers in Paris retained the power to dissolve the Territorial Assembly.

The metropolitan government retained responsibility in such areas as foreign affairs, defense, monetary policy, and justice. Local matters, such as primary education, public works, and land policy, fell within the jurisdiction of the Territorial Assembly, which was also consulted by the high commissioner on budgetary matters. A consultative body, the Economic and Social Committee (analogous to the French government's Economic and Social Council), provided additional advice on matters relating to the occupational groups its members represented.

The territory was divided into five administrative subdivisions that corresponded to the major island groups. District officers, appointed by the high commissioner, were in charge of administration in all subdivisions, which were further subdivided into townships (communes). In the late 1970s there were 48 townships, each having a mayor, a township or municipal council, and a local administration. Census figures for 1977 revealed that the townships varied in size from Papeete, having 22,967 inhabitants, to Pukapuka, having 95 inhabitants.

The administration of justice followed standard French practice and procedures. The secretary of state for overseas departments and territories of the metropolitan government appointed the principal officers of the courts and the presidents of the Court of Appeal, the Court of First Instance, and the Civil Court. The secretary also appointed the chief of the Judiciary Service (the attorney general) and the magistrates.

Political Groups

In contrast to New Caledonia, France's other major Pacific territory, strong sentiments for full independence were lacking in French Polynesia during the early 1980s. The call for self-rule voiced by Pouvanaa a Oopa in the late 1950s did not sustain a popularly based political movement through the following decades.

Various historical factors contributed to a relative lack of political activism. Despite the cultural and demographic calamities that accompanied the establishment of European influence and control in the late eighteenth and nineteenth centuries, relations between Polynesians and Europeans were generally peaceful. The *demi* population served as a social and cultural bridge between the two communities, and the *maohi* were not deprived of their lands by aggressive European settlers as had been the case in New Caledonia. Moreover, economic dependence on France, particuarly the income derived from the Pacific Test Center, persuaded many that full independence would result in a drastic decline in the standard of living. A local observer suggested that out of a population of 156,000 only around 500 persons were politically active in late 1983. Although apprehensions over the threat of radioactive degradation of the environment were widespread, this was a less urgent issue for most of the islands' inhabitants than was the Pacific Test Center's contribution to the economy. At public ceremonies the red and white flag of the Pomares' independent Tahitian kingdom flew alongside, rather than in place of, the French tricolor.

Political parties were largely personal followings, although the Tahoeraa Huiratira party of Gaston Flosse had ideological affinities with the Gaullist Rally for the Republic (Rassemblement pour la République) in France. The party has modified its platform of continued close associaton with France and in mid-1984 favored limited autonomy. In the Territorial Assembly election held in May 1982, it won 13 out of the 30 seats contested and 30 percent of the popular vote. In mid-1984 the party maintained a ruling coalition within the Territorial Assembly with the Pupu Here Aia Te Nunaa Ia Ora party of John Teariki, which had six seats in the legislature. Teariki had proposed in 1978 an orderly transition to independence but in September 1982 joined Flosse in issuing a joint statement declaring that an "evolution of the territory's status" and a "programme of economic and social development" were necessary, implying a continued association with France. The coalition chose Flosse to serve as vice president of the Council of Government.

The May 1982 elections represented a victory for political figures advocating continued association with France. The previous ruling coalition, the United Front for Internal Autonomy (Front Uni pour l'Autonomie Interne), including the Pupu Here Aia Te Nunaa Ia Ora party, the Te E'a Api (United Front) party of Francis Sanford, and the Social Democratic Movement (Mouvement Social-Démocrate—MSD), had proposed substantial internal self-government approaching full independence. Sanford's party won only one seat and the MSD, none. Other parties represented in the Territorial Assembly included the Ai'a Api (New Land) party, having three seats; the Marxist, pro-independence Ia Mana Te Nunaa party, three seats; and the Taatiraa Polynesia party, one seat.

In the early 1980s extremist groups remained on the periphery of political life and had committed only sporadic acts of violence against the French administration or persons perceived to be associated with continuing French rule. A terrorist group, Te Toto Tupana (The Ancestors' Blood), was implicated in the murder of a French business leader and the bombing of a post office in Papeete in 1977. Two years later seven alleged members of this group were given prison sentences, although these were overturned by the Court of Appeal because of procedural irregularities. One of the suspects, Charlie Ching, headed Te Taata Tahiti Tiama, a radical party committed to immediate independence. In August 1982 Mai Tetua established himself as president of a "Maohi Republic Provisional Government" but was arrested by the authorities along with 40 of his followers after they had abducted and briefly held two local police officers.

A New Autonomy Statute

In December 1982 the French government proposed a new statute for French Polynesia that would give local elected officials a greater measure of control over territorial affairs. The plan was submitted to the Territorial Assembly for advice on how it could be best modified to suit local conditions. A basic institutional change would be the establishment of a "territorial government" headed by a president who would be elected by the Territorial Assembly and have the power to appoint and dismiss members of the Council of Government. The high commissioner's responsibilities would be reduced to serving as head of the national civil service in the territory and overseer of the legality of government enactments. Other proposals associated with the new autonomy statute included granting the territorial government the power to authorize foreign investments up to a sum of CFPF1 billion, exploit the territory's 200-nautical-mile EEZ (though the French state would retain ultimate ownership), take a part in new negotiations for air and sea links to French Polynesia, and set up a territorial lending authority. Another measure would empower the territory to enter into cultural, technical, and economic agreements with neighboring countries in the Pacific region, subject to approval by the metropolitan government. The territory would also assume control of secondary education within a five-year period.

In September 1983 the Territorial Assembly voted to approve the autonomy statute but posed a number of serious reservations pending further negotiation. These were related to issues such as control of the EEZ, foreign affairs, and the territory's right to impose restrictions on immigration from France. Serious crimes involving persons having criminal records in France had brought the immigration issue to public attention.

Critics pointed out that the autonomy statute was still restrictive when compared, for instance, with the free association agreement worked out between Cook Islands and New Zealand or those being negotiated between the United States and the island polities of the Trust Territory of the Pacific Islands. The statute left extensive powers in the hands of the high commissioner as representative of the French republic and its interests. Some observers suggested that France's determination to maintain the nuclear testing facility necessitated, in its view, substantial limits on territorial self-government.

In early 1982 France maintained about 5,000 military personnel in French Polynesia, chiefly connected with the nuclear testing facilities. An interservice command comprised army, navy, and air force contingents.

The French National Gendarmerie maintained a single division in the territory. It was composed of 22 units, each comprising between four and 15 men. The gendarmerie was organized along military lines, strictly disciplined, and highly mobile. Most of its personnel, including all officers and noncommissioned officers and most of the lower ranks, were recruited and trained in France. However, vacancies may have been filled by inducting local personnel. In addition to the gendarmerie, the townships organized local police forces.

NIUE

Previous Name	Nieue, Savage Island
Political Status	Self-governing, in free association with New Zealand
Capital	Alofi
Population	Under 3,000 (1984 midyear estimate)
Land Area	258 square kilometers
Currency	New Zealand dollar ($NZ)

Niue (pronounced Nee-u-ay) is one of the world's largest coral islands, having a circumference of 58 kilometers. The topography has been likened to an inverted soup plate. In the interior lies a plateau, slightly depressed in the center, giving way rather abruptly to a slope running to the coast. The coast is formed by steep limestone cliffs that make landing difficult. A fringing coral reef surrounds the island. Primary forests, including stands of banyan, Tahitian chestnut, and *kafika* trees, cover approximately one-fifth of the land area, while much of the remaining area is covered by secondary growth. There are no rivers or streams, owing to the porous nature of the predominantly limestone soil, but fresh water is obtained from artesian wells. Caves and blowholes are found in abundance.

Niue, a solitary island, is located due west of the Cook Islands and east of Tonga. Its sea area, defined by a 200-nautical-mile EEZ (see Glossary), is 390,000 square kilometers. The indigenous people are Polynesians, who arrived on the island from the Samoa Islands as early as the ninth or tenth centuries A.D. and from Tonga around the sixteenth century. The Niuean language has affinities to both Tongan and Samoan. Captain Cook landed on Niue in 1774, naming it Savage Island in recognition of the people's fierce behavior. After unsuccessful attempts to land preachers on the island in 1830 and 1842, the London Missionary Society succeeded in establishing a mission headed by a Niuean convert in 1846. By the mid-nineteenth century several hundred people had been converted to Christianity, and traditional beliefs were waning.

During the 1860s blackbirders and Peruvian slave traders seeking laborers for plantations on other islands kidnapped a number of Niuean men and women. In 1876 Mataio Tuitonga was chosen king of the island. His successor, Fataaiki, requested the establishment of a British protectorate, which was granted in 1900. The next year Niue was annexed to New Zealand and became administratively a part of the Cook Islands. In 1960 an island assembly was established. In October 1974 New Zealand granted the island self-government.

The population at the time of the 1979 "mini-census" was 3,578—1,823 males and 1,755 females. By 1984 it was estimated to have declined to under 3,000, largely as a result of migration to New Zealand, where approximately 5,600 Niueans lived in the early 1980s. The main center of population was the island administrative complex of Alofi, having 960 persons in 1979. The nonindigenous population at that time, comprising Europeans and Polynesians from other islands, was 244.

Most Niueans were Congregationalists belonging to the Church of Niue founded by the London Missionary Society, although there were smaller communities of Roman Catholics, Seventh-Day Adventists, and members of the Church of God in Jerusalem. Primary- and secondary-level education was provided by the government and was compulsory between the ages of five and 14.

The economy has remained stagnant in large part owing to the lack of land and resources and to the migration of the most active members of the population to New Zealand. About 200 square kilometers of the island were considered arable, and principal crops in mid-1984 were fruits (especially limes, papaw, and passion fruit) and copra. Other primary products included honey and reconstituted milk. Exports went to New Zealand but on average earned only one-tenth the amount spent on imports during the late 1970s and early 1980s. More than four-fifths of the labor force was employed in government jobs and paid from subsidies made by the New Zealand government. An important source of revenue for the government was the sale of postage stamps.

There were approximately 128 kilometers of all-weather roads on Niue and 106 kilometers of supplementary roads in the mid-1980s. Port facilities were at Alofi. Hanan International Airport, having a runway of 1,650 meters, was located three kilometers to the south.

The 1974 Constitution granted Niue self-government, though New Zealand remained responsible for foreign relations and defense, and a special New Zealand representative was posted in the territory. Niueans are New Zealand citizens. The Legislative Assembly in mid-1984 contained 20 members. Fourteen of these were elected from each of the island's 14 villages and six from a common roll. The assembly chose the government, consisting of a premier and three other cabinet ministers. Local government was the responsibility of the 14 village councils. The judiciary system was integrated with that of New Zealand and the chief justice, who established the High Court when he arrived, and the Land Court judge visited Niue once every three months. In their absence, judicial authority was vested in a commissioner and justices of the peace.

PITCAIRN ISLANDS

Official Name	Pitcairn, Henderson, Ducie, and Oeno Islands
Political Status	Colony of Britain
Capital	Adamstown
Population	45 (1983)
Land Area	36.5 square kilometers

Pitcairn Islands, in mid-1984 the only British colony remaining in the Pacific, is located to the east of the Mangareva Islands in French Polynesia. Pitcairn Island, the only inhabited island in 1984, is a volcanic formation having steep elevations, a rocky and cliff-formed coastline, and no fringing coral reef. Its area is five square kilometers. The volcanic soil is poorly formed, allowing only subsistence cultivation for a small population. Henderson Island (Elizabeth), 30 square kilometers in area, is an uplifted coral formation, while Ducie and Oeno islands are very small, low, coral atolls. The three uninhabited islands are arrayed along a roughly east-west axis approximately 600 kilometers in length, while Pitcairn is located about 150 kilometers southeast of Oeno, the westernmost island.

There are traces of pre-European human habitation on Pitcairn Island, including tombs, rock drawings, stone tools, and breadfruit and coconut trees that earlier residents brought to provide food. However, the island was uninhabited when it was first discovered by the British in 1767. Except for a handful of latecomers, the people of Pitcairn are descended from the crew members of the H.M.S. *Bounty* who mutinied against its master, Lieutenant William Bligh in April 1789, as well as from Polynesians brought by the mutineers from Tahiti. Bligh had come to Tahiti to gather breadfruit trees, part of an ultimately unsuccessful plan to make this the staple food of African slaves on British plantations in the West Indies. The *Bounty* laid over several months at that island, and the mutiny, depicted numerous times in narrative and on film, was apparently the result of Bligh's attempts to impose a minimum of discipline on sailors besotted with Tahiti's earthy delights once the *Bounty* returned to sea. Fletcher Christian, Bligh's first mate, and 17 crew members seized the ship, set Bligh and loyal crew members adrift, and returned to Tahiti. Bligh and the others eventually reached the island of Timor in what is now Indonesia after crossing 5,820 kilometers in an open boat. Christian and eight other mutineers, accompanied by 19 Polynesians, then departed Tahiti in search of a permanent home. After visiting several other islands, they chose Pitcairn, hoping that its isolation, the fact that it was mismarked on navigation charts of the period, and the inaccessibility of its high-cliff coasts would provide protection against the British navy, which was sure to pursue them.

Although the mutineers longed for an easygoing Polynesian style of life, the early years of the settlement were marked by demoralization, jealousy, and murderous violence. By 1800 only one of the original mutineers was still alive. There were, however, nine Polynesian women and 19 children. By the mid-nineteenth century, their descendants had grown to around 200, and the British government proposed moving the entire population to the larger and more fertile Norfolk Island, lying to the northwest of New Zealand. This was accomplished in 1856. By 1864, however, 43 persons, homesick for Pitcairn, had returned to that island. In 1883 the entire population on Pitcairn became Seventh-Day Adventists, forswearing alcohol and pork and celebrating their Sabbath on Saturdays.

Although the twentieth century has witnessed the introduction of conveniences such as electricity and radio communication to the island, life for its people in the early 1980s remained simple. Rough seas and jagged coasts, as much as geographic distance, isolate Pitcairn. During 1983 severe storms made it almost impossible for ships to unload supplies upon which the people were dependent. There was no airfield, although equipment had been dropped by parachute to the island by the Royal New Zealand Air Force.

The population has been slowly declining as families departed for Norfolk Island, a territory of Australia, or New Zealand, falling from 65 persons in 1976 to 45 in 1983. The only settlement was Adamstown, located on the cliff tops above Bounty Bay. Subsistence agriculture and fishing were practiced, although the settlement could not survive without supplies brought in by ship. Social life revolved around families and the Seventh-Day Adventist church. The people speak English as well as their own special dialect, which is a blend of English and Tahitian. Most carried the surnames of the original mutineers, such as Christian and Young. Barter, rather than the exchange of currency, was prevalent.

As a British colony, Pitcairn Islands in mid-1984 was under the authority of the British high commissioner in New Zealand, who acted as the colony's governor. Internal affairs were the responsibility of an island council consisting of an island magistrate and nine other members.

TOKELAU

Previous Name	Union Islands; Tokelau Islands
Political Status	Territory of New Zealand
Capital	None, but is administered from the Office of Tokelau Affairs based in Apia, Western Samoa
Population	1,572 (1981)
Land Area	10 square kilometers
Currency	New Zealand dollar ($NZ); Western Samoan tala also circulated
Major Islands	Atafu, Nukunonu, Fakaofo

Tokelau, a territory of New Zealand, is located north of the Samoa Islands and east of Tuvalu. It consists of three coral atolls strung along a northwest-southeast axis lying across approximately 200 kilometers of ocean. Nukunonu, the largest atoll, has an area of 5.4 square kilometers, while Fakaofo and Atafu have 2.9 and 2 square kilometers, respectively. On December 2, 1980, the governments of the United States and New Zealand signed the Delimitation of the Maritime Boundary Between Tokelau and the United States. One provision of this treaty was the United States renunciation of any claim to the three atolls. The sea area, defined by the EEZ (see Glossary) of 200 nautical miles, is 290,000 square kilometers.

Little is known of the origins of the indigenous Polynesian people, although local traditions point to migration from the Samoa Islands, Rarotonga in the Cook Islands, and Nanumanga in Tuvalu. European navigators first encountered the atolls in the late eighteenth century. In 1841 the atolls were described in some detail by ethnologist Horatio Hale, who was taking part in United States naval exploration of the Pacific. At that time there were only some 700 inhabitants on the atolls. Disease and raids by Peruvian slave traders reduced this number to some 200 by the

411

late 1860s, though the population had been augmented by the arrival of European beachcombers and Polynesians from other islands. In 1889 a British protectorate was formally established over the atolls. In 1916 they were incorporated into the Gilberts and Ellice Islands Colony. Administrative responsibility was transferred by Britain to New Zealand in 1925, and New Zealand assumed full sovereignty in 1948. In 1974 the New Zealand Ministry of Foreign Affairs assumed control over Tokelau's administration.

The census of 1981 revealed a total population of 1,572. The most populous island was Fakaofo, having 650 persons, followed by Atafu and Nukunonu, having 554 and 368, respectively. The total population in 1976 had been 1,575. In the early 1980s about 2,000 Tokelauans lived in New Zealand. Protestant adherents of the Congregational Christian Church in Samoa were located in the early 1980s on Atafu, Roman Catholics on Nukunonu, and adherents of both churches on Fakaofo. The New Zealand government provided primary education in the islands, and scholarships for secondary and higher education were offered for attendance at institutions elsewhere. Health services were provided by local medical officers and those visiting the atolls on a regular basis from Western Samoa. English and the Tokelau dialect of Polynesian are the languages spoken.

The economy consisted primarily of subsistence agriculture and fishing. In addition, a small amount of copra was exported. The economy was heavily dependent on subsidies from the New Zealand government, although the sale of postage stamps to world philatelists provided some revenue. The currency was the New Zealand dollar, but the Western Samoan tala was also used. In 1978 Tokelau minted its first coin.

The Office of Tokelau Affairs, since 1974 under the New Zealand foreign ministry, was based in Apia, Western Samoa, in the early 1980s. Its establishment there in 1925 was the result of considerations of the large distances involved, and the office remained in Western Samoa even after that country obtained its independence in 1962. This arrangement has strengthened economic and cultural ties between the two island groups. There was limited self-government, headmen *(faipule)* and village mayors *(pulenuku)* being elected by the people for three-year terms. The High Court of Niue in mid-1984 had jurisdiction over criminal and civil cases. The territory did not have any prisons, and only about seven police officers were on duty. The people of Tokelau are New Zealand citizens.

TONGA

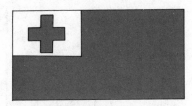

Flag: Red cross in white square on red field

Official Name	Kingdom of Tonga
Political Status	Independent state (1970)
Capital	Nuku'alofa
Population	104,000 (1984 midyear estimate)
Land Area	670 square kilometers
Currency	Tongan pa'anga (PT)
Major Islands and Island Groups	Tongatapu Group, including Tongatapu and 'Eua; Ha'apai Group; Vava'u Group, including Vava'u; Niuatoputapu, Niuafo'ou

Physical Environment

Polynesia's oldest and last surviving kingdom consists of some 170 islands, of which 45 are inhabited (see fig. 19). Tonga is divided into three main regions: Tongatapu ("sacred Tonga") and its nearby islands in the south; the Ha'apai Group, some 100 kilometers to the north; and the Vava'u Group, yet another 100 kilometers farther northward. Niuatoputapu, Niuafo'ou, and their surrounding islands (called the Niuas for short) lie some 600 kilometers to the northeast of Tongatapu, which alone accounts for 35 percent of the land area and is the major population center. Except for a chain of smaller islands along the western edge of the country, which are of recent volcanic formation, the islands are raised limestone or coral limestone structures that have few, if any, hills or valleys. They spread over an expanse of ocean that gives the country a potential EEZ (see Glossary) of about 700,000 square kilometers.

The temperature ranges from highs of around 26°C in February to lows of 21°C in July and August, but the southern islands may have cooler weather. Rainfall averages about 2,600 millimeters per year in the north and 1,700 millimeters in the south; more than one-half of the rain falls during the wet season from January to April. Southeast trade winds predominante from May to November and easterlies for the remainder of the year. During February and March, however, moist winds from the north may

413

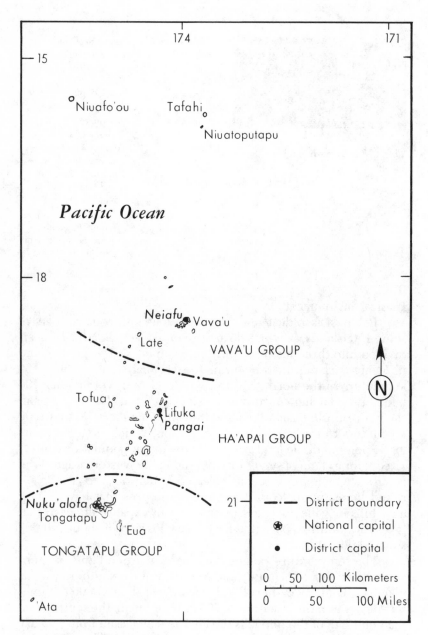

Figure 19.   Tonga, 1984

bring hot weather and violent squalls. In March 1982 a major hurricane devastated the islands.

The indigenous animal life consists chiefly of birds and insects, although there is one native species of bat. Tongan waters are renowned for their abundance of fish. Pigs, fowls, and rats were introduced before the coming of the Europeans. Small pines and low-lying plants make up most of the plant life. The good quality of the soil and the dense population have led to the cultivation of most of the arable land with coconut trees, bananas, and other crops.

Tonga is one of the most densely populated countries in Oceania; nearly all of the population live on about 432 square kilometers of territory. According to estimates for 1983, about 65 percent of the people lived on Tongatapu (one-half this number in the capital), some 5 percent on nearby 'Eua, another 16 percent in the Vava'u Group, about 12 percent in the Ha'apai Group, and the rest in the Niuas.

Historical Setting

Archaeological evidence suggests that the first people settled the islands some 3,000 years ago, probably arriving from the Samoa group or Fiji. Tongan legend, however, preserves no tale of these migrations, claiming rather a special creation of the islands and its peoples. The early settlers were members of the Lapita culture, characterized by its beautifully incised pottery (see Prehistory, ch. 1). Over the centuries their pottery skills disappeared.

The origins of the Tongan nobility are shrouded in myth. The first king, called the Tu'i Tonga, was supposed to have descended from a Polynesian god of the sun or sky some time in the tenth century A.D. Some 500 years later the twenty-fourth king, who feared the fate of assassination that befell many of his predecessors, had his brother take over political power, creating a new line of Tu'i Ha'atakalaua. The seventh king in this line, likewise transferred temporal responsibility to his brother, setting up the Tu'i Kanokupolu title. Some conventional histories suggest that the transitions in leadership were natural and smooth and that responsibilities were clearly delineated among the three lines. Others have pointed out the political and military rivalry that persisted throughout this royal history. These rivalries resulted in a civil war that lasted from 1799 to 1852.

The war doomed the efforts of the first Christian missionaries sent from the London Missionary Society in 1797. In the 1820s, however, Wesleyan missionaries had more success, although many of the Tongan chiefs resisted their efforts. Onè chief in particular proved to be an important convert. In 1831 Taufa'ahau, a brilliant soldier and leader, was christened King George, after the British monarch. Consolidating his power over the Ha'apai and Vava'u groups by establishing strategic alliances and converting the local rulers to his new-found faith, King George succeeded his uncle as the holder of the Tu'i Kanokupolu title in 1845. Overwhelming his opponents, he eventually made himself undisputed king of all Tonga and became known as King George Tupou I. In 1862 he instituted a legal code that freed the commoners from forced labor to the nobility and gave them some control over the land they farmed, including the right to own designated parcels. In 1875 the king promulgated the Constitution (still in effect), which not only backed up these laws but also gave him extensive powers.

The king's principal adviser, Wesleyan missionary Shirley Baker, had drafted the Constitution, but in 1880 he resigned from his ministry and became virtual dictator of the country, ruling in the king's name. Angered by the requirement to send a large proportion of the weekly church offerings to the Wesleyan headquarters in Australia, Baker persuaded the king to establish the Free Wesleyan church, which became the official church of Tonga. Baker's alleged persecution of those who remained faithful to the old Wesleyan church and his inefficient and heavy-handed rule caused the British high commissioner resident in Fiji to demand his deportation in 1890. A Tongan took over Baker's position as premier, and a British administrator was appointed to aid him. In 1893 the king died and was succeeded by his great-grandson.

The reign of King George Tupou II (1893–1918) was marred by his inattentiveness to state affairs and by his reneging on a pledge to marry a particular nobleman's daughter. Complaints from Tongans and foreign residents alike prompted the British to declare a protectorate over the kingdom in 1901. In 1905 Britain obtained the power to review all official appointments and dismissals. Nonetheless, the king retained his basic autonomy.

Queen Salote Tupou III, the only child of the previous king, ruled from 1918 to 1965, ascending the throne when she was only 18 years old. Her marriage to a direct descendant of one of the competing royal lines ensured that her issue would have unquestioned legitimacy in the eyes of the nobility. Greatly adored for her unabashed love of the Tongan people and for her devout religiousness, she was able to achieve the reunion of the Free Wes-

*Former Queen Salote High School,
in the form of a traditional Tongan house,
on Nuku'alofa; destroyed by a hurricane
and scheduled to be rebuilt as a monument
Courtesy Cathleen Curtin*

leyan church and its predecessor. Under her direction public health and education services expanded greatly, and the economy diversified. Her government made primary education mandatory in 1927, provided scholarships for overseas study beginning in 1929, and established a teachers college in 1944. During World War II Tonga established, with Australian assistance, a defense force of some 2,000 men, and some of these troops fought in the Solomon Islands.

Salote's son, King Taufa'ahua Tupou IV, was prime minister during much of her reign and ascended the throne after her death he remained king in mid-1984 at 66 years of age. King Tupou IV was the first Tongan to earn a college degree and has established himself as a scholar of the traditional Tongan calendar and Tongan music. He continued the social development programs begun while he was premier and moved to make the country completely independent of Britain, a milestone achieved in 1970, when the protectorate was ended. The country remained dependent on Britain and other countries, however, for economic aid.

Some social problems emerged during this reign. As Tonga's population grew, more and more people migrated to Tongatapu in search of modern employment, and many emigrated or went overseas as guestworkers to improve their incomes. The government was unable to stop the breakdown of the traditional family-oriented system, the growing restlessness of its youth, alcoholism, and other concomitants of modernization. Most importantly, there were signs of growing resentment over the rights of the monarchy and the nobility, who, despite their general benevolence, retained the ownership of much land.

The Social System

Over 98 percent of the population, according to the 1976 census, were indigenous Polynesians who spoke a common language and had a shared cultural heritage for many centuries; the remainder included Europeans (a census category referring to all whites), part Europeans, other Pacific islanders, and Chinese minorities. About 40,000 Tongans resided overseas in mid-1984. Tongan culture has absorbed many elements of European and American culture, but because the kingdom has been ruled by the same royal family for so long, it has preserved many traditional elements as well.

The basis of social organization remained the extended family, although the nuclear family was typically the basis for the organization of single households. Although males dominated political and economic affairs, they deferred to their sisters on most important social occasions, and social ranking was based on complex bilateral kinship relationships. The eldest sister presided at family functions; she and sometimes her children were called *fahu*, a term connoting special status. Children, especially sons, received favors from their maternal uncles that proved invaluable in their quest for status. Before the establishment of the current royal line, it was generally the case that the three separate royal lines would intermarry to establish intertwining *fahu* relationships.

Tongan society was highly stratified. At the top were the royal family and the nobility, in the middle a group of *matapule* (titled servants to the nobility), and at the bottom the commoners. There were 33 noble families that traced their origins to the first Tu'i Tonga or to ancient Fijian chiefs. Their relationship to the royal family was not always clear, and several of the chiefs first titled by King Tupou I were chosen for political reasons. The highest ranking male in each noble line usually held the title and managed the family's hereditary estates. Often, however, succession to the title was a matter of intricate legal debate, and lawyers who specialized in this type of case formed an elite group of commoners. There were six titled *matapule* lines that also owned hereditary estates. The commoners, who under the Constitution are entitled to allotments of land and are free of the servitude to the nobles practiced in ancient Tonga, nonetheless retained their identification with individual nobles and *matapule*. The leader of a commoner family was usually the male having the closest kinship relationship to a noble family.

Economic modernization has changed the roles of Tongan women. More and more women were becoming involved in marketing activities and even formal employment away from home. Some, however, deplored the fact that money rather than genealogical ranking determined the management and control of family affairs.

Tongans have been devout Christians almost since the conversion of King Tupou I. The Constitution declares it unlawful to work, play, or trade on Sunday, and the Sabbath has become a day of relaxed strolling, visiting friends and neighbors, and feasting. The Free Wesleyan church, of which the monarch is the official head, claimed the allegiance of about 30 percent of the population in 1983. This church, however, has been losing affiliates to the fast-growing Seventh-Day Adventist, Assembly of God, and Mormon churches.

Most of the schools in Tonga were originally set up by the churches, but the government has taken over the provision of primary education to about 92 percent of the students. Primary education from age six to age 14 was compulsory and free of charge. The three government secondary schools taught only about 11 percent of the student body; some 44 church-related and one private school educated the remainder in 1981. Attendance was virtually universal. Government assistance was not available to the private schools as of early 1984, but the government was considering changing this policy. Some 90 to 95 percent of all adults were literate in Tonga, a Polynesian language, and many secondary-school students spoke English, which was the principal second language.

About 85 percent of the government teachers and 72 percent of the private instructors in the primary-school system had received what the government considered adequate training in 1980; only 31 percent of secondary-school teachers were in this category. There were government-run training schools for teachers, nurses, police officers, and public works officers, as well as a private business school and an extension center of the University of the South Pacific; together these were capable of handling 500 to 600 students each year. In the 1980s the government hoped to establish a center for community development training, a maritime school, a rural development center, an administrative training center, a cultural center, and community centers in the outer islands.

Government health services, provided free to those able to get to the centers, have greatly improved living conditions, and the country has one of the lowest death rates in the world. The government operated one hospital on each of the three major islands and numerous dispensaries and rural clinics. Only seven of the 35 medical officers employed in 1983, however, had full medical degrees, and plans for their further training overseas would cause the number of people per physician to rise to about 3,800 in the mid-1980s. The health service had to cope with cases of influenza, pneumonia, typhoid, and gastrointestinal infections caused by improper hygiene and sanitation. The government was implementing a program to rebuild latrines after the destruction caused by the 1982 hurricane. Another program to promote rural water supplies aimed to provide access to safe water by 1985 to all but the 9 percent of the population located in the most remote areas.

The major problems associated with the modernization of the economy and social services were the effects of internal and external migration, the breakdown of the extended family, landlessness, and unemployment. According to the 1976 census, about one out of every five people living on Tongatapu had migrated there from other parts of the country, attracted by better opportunities for education, health services, and employment. The low wages available in the capital area, however, were often below what would constitute a subsistence level in the outer areas. Others have migrated overseas, stretching their kinship ties to the limit, although the high volume of remittances back into Tonga showed extreme loyalty to those remaining at home. The skewed distribution of land has been closely linked with income inequalities, and the rising number of landless people created social as well as economic stresses.

The Economy

Agriculture, forestry, and fishing activities accounted for

*New Mormon church on Nuku'alofa demonstrates
the popularity of one of the fastest growing churches in Tonga.
Courtesy Cathleen Curtin*

some 41 percent of GDP in fiscal year (FY) 1980—the fiscal year
beginning July 1, 1980—and for about 44 percent of the labor
force in 1976. Agriculture's role in the economy diminished significantly in the 1970s, however, as manufacturing, construction,
wholesale and retail trade, and other urban industries expanded.
Behind this upswing in industrial development lay a major shift in
government policy to invest in industries that reduced the country's dependence on imports and remittances. The per capita
GDP in FY 1980 was equivalent to about US$560. Government
calculations two years earlier showed that the per capita GDP in
the Tongatapu Group was 68 percent higher than in the Ha'apai
Group, some 39 percent higher than in the Niuas, and 32 percent
higher than in the Vava'u Group.

Foreign remittances were equivalent to 20 percent of GDP
in FY 1978 and had more than doubled by 1983 to PT7 million (for
value of the Tongan pa'anga—see Glossary). This massive inflow,
along with the income from tourism and travel services, has more
than offset the persistent trade deficit. Tonga's economic
policymakers, however, have been concerned that merchandise
exports were unable to keep pace with imports. From 1981 to
1982 imports jumped in value from PT31 million to PT41 million,
while the adverse effects of the hurricane halved the export earnings from tourism and coconut products—the two major items.

421

Other exports included root crops, fruit, and fish. The principal markets were Australia—whose share jumped from 6 percent in 1970 to 35 percent in 1980—New Zealand, the United States, and the European Economic Community (EEC). Imports were mostly of consumer goods and raw materials, although capital goods were rising in importance. New Zealand was the principal supplier, followed closely by Australia, Japan, the United States, Fiji, and Britain.

The inability of Tongans to earn and save as much at home as abroad was owing in part to the poor domestic resource base and in part to the low level of productive investment in the past. It was also likely that the government's labor policies have caused the expatriation of many skilled workers. A maximum-wage law, having sharply progressive taxation rates, has been in effect for government workers and influenced wage negotiations in the private sector. The wage legislation has discouraged the formation of unions, of which there were none as of mid-1984. Other stumbling blocks to increasing domestic productivity included the traditional abundance of land and the ease of cultivating root crops for subsistence. Both conditions, however, were fast being overwhelmed by the growing population. Even with the maximum-wage law, unemployment, for which there were no official estimates, was a major concern.

Seeking to turn around these adverse economic trends, the government increased its development spending from about 7 percent of GDP in FY 1972 to nearly 14 percent of GDP in FY 1980, raising the level of investment for the economy as a whole from 19 to 31 percent of GDP. If quasi-governmental bodies such as the public utilities were included, the public sector's share of total investment rose from 25 percent in FY 1973 to 52 percent in FY 1979. About 27 percent of public sector investment went to agriculture, forestry, and fishing; some 25 percent to social and community services; another 19 percent to transportation, communications, and storage; about 12 percent to electric and water utilities; some 10 percent to nonresidential construction; and the rest to other sectors. Spending priorities as outlined in the Fourth Five-Year Development Plan, 1980–85, suggested a marked increase in the share devoted to agriculture—especially fisheries—as well as to transportation and communications.

Government current spending increased from 17 to 23 percent of GDP from FY 1973 to FY 1980, bringing total government spending up to 37 percent of GDP. Revenues—chiefly from import duties—rose only to 27 percent of GDP. The deficit had to be financed by foreign capital inflows. During the period from FY

1975 to FY 1979, development assistance both in cash and in kind was equivalent to about 30 percent of GDP, or PT47.7 million. One-quarter of the assistance came from the Federal Republic of Germany (West Germany), about 21 percent from Australia, 18 percent from New Zealand, and 8 percent form Britain. Multilateral donors, such as the Asian Development Bank, the EEC, and the United Nations, made up the rest. The loan component of this aid amounted to about PT17.1 million by June of 1981, but the country's debt-service payments were low. Only PT1.9 million of debt had been contracted locally. Projections for the FY 1980–84 period suggested that foreign aid would remain at about 30 percent of GDP. Committed development aid for FY 1983 was equivalent to US$9.4 million, excluding aid in kind.

In order to increase the revenue base, the minister of finance considered levying a tax on remittances to Tonga in 1983 but put that option aside for fear of curtailing the much needed inflow. Instead, the government was trying to rebuild from the devastation of the 1982 hurricane and a drought in 1983, promote tourism by introducing duty-free stores for visitors, and diversify the export base as much as possible. The government also planned to raise the wages of civil servants sharply in FY 1983 to entice skilled workers to remain at home. The key to the economic revival of Tonga, however, lay in the nation's rich soil and abundant waters.

Agriculture, Fishing, and Forestry

At the end of 1979 the government estimated that 70 percent of the population depended on agriculture for their livelihood and that about 87 percent of all households cultivated at least some of their subsistence needs. In addition, most smallholders harvested some coconut to meet their cash requirements. Despite the good quality of Tonga's resources and long experience in agricultural production, however, agricultural imports have increased more rapidly than domestic production. In 1980 food imports alone cost more than the country's entire merchandise exports.

In 1980 about 53,000 hectares of land were used for crop cultivation, of which coconut palms covered some 40,000 hectares. There were about 4,000 hectares of permanent pastures and meadows; forests covered only 8,000 hectares. Banana trees were planted on some 810 hectares, vanilla on over 200 hectares, and kava, yams, taro, watermelons, tomatoes and other food crops on the remaining area and between coconut trees. Except for the tree crops, however, shifting cultivation (see Glossary) predominated, and much of the agricultural land area was left fallow each year. Government estimates suggested that if intensive farming methods were used, about 7 percent of the agricultural area could produce the country's needs.

The land tenure system was a major impediment to farming modernization. According to the Constitution, every male Tongan is entitled to an allotment of up to 3.34 hectares of agricultural land and from 0.08 to 0.16 hectare of town property when he reaches the taxable age of 16 years. However, the population had grown so fast that the proportion of eligible males actually receiving an allotment decreased from 42 percent in the 1966 census to 35 percent in the 1976 census and was probably less than one-third in mid-1984. Land could not be sold but could be leased with government approval.

In 1979 commoners owned about 47 percent of registered allotments and some 26 percent of unregistered allotments. Estates owned by hereditary nobles made up 8 percent of the area; land leased to the government, churches, foreigners, and private citizens constituted about 7 percent of the area. The government held the remainder, which was made up of the uninhabited islands, forest reserves, and other public areas. Only 1 percent of the land area was officially leased to Tongans, but illegal tenancy arrangements were common. Many of the Tongans who have gone overseas to work owned land at home that either went fallow or was used under an informal rental agreement.

The king has so far refused to take over these lands for reapportionment. As a result, only lands owned by the government or released with the consent of the hereditary nobles could be allotted to the commoners, and these areas were both scarce and of marginal productivity. Advocates of land reform have suggested that the government take over the hereditary nobility's lands. In 1984 the public was awaiting the results of a royal commission of inquiry, made up of three noblemen in the cabinet and two legal specialists, which was investigating this delicate issue. The Free Wesleyan church had proposed such a commission some 16 years earlier.

The coconut palm was the mainstay of the agricultural sector. A survey conducted in 1979 showed that 48 percent of the nearly 5 million coconut palms were located on Tongatapu, 25 percent were in the Vava'u Group, about 19 percent in the Ha'apai Group, and the rest on 'Eua. About 12 percent of the trees were senescent, and another 14 percent were approaching senility; by contrast, 29 percent were young or immature trees that had been planted since the beginning of a special program in 1967. All but 5 percent of the trees were on allotments smaller than 20 hectares. During the FY 1975–79 period, the government spent about PT80,000 per year to replant some 4,700 hectares of palms overall. The government hoped to maintain this momentum in the 1980s, cutting down all the senile trees and replanting them with new, improved plants. Tonga produced over 100,000 tons of coconuts in 1980 and 1981, but production declined in 1982 and 1983 because of the adverse weather.

The banana industry, which catered almost exclusively to the New Zealand market and boomed in the 1960s, seriously declined during most of the next decade. Locally funded investment in agricultural chemicals and fertiliers had halted the deterioration by the late 1970s, and the government planned to expand the rehabilitation program to areas outside of Tongatapu in the 1980s. In 1983 New Zealand assisted Tonga in setting up containerized delivery of quality bananas, a move that was expected to boost exports significantly beyond the 2,700 tons shipped in 1981.

Vanilla was first planted in the 1950s, but it was not until the 1970s that the crop began to expand rapidly. Most of the plantings were on smallholder farms in the hilly areas of the Vav'u Group— often intercropped on coconut farms. In 1982 vanilla accounted for about 15 percent of the value of all exports in spite of the bad weather. The high financial return per hectare of planting would probably make it easy for the government to reach its target of adding more than 100 hectares a year in the FY 1980–84 period. Other commercial crops included kava, fruits, and vegetables. About 94,000 tons of root crops were produced in 1981 for the staple diet.

The livestock population grew rapidly in the second half of the 1970s, but the country still had to import about 74 percent of its meat requirements and 70 percent of its dairy needs in 1980. Pig raising was a traditional farming activity, and there were over 100,000 head scavenging on subsistence farms. Cattle raising has been accepted as a part of smallholder farming; some 10,000 head were distributed on 600 to 700 farms in 1980. Plans to establish a large-scale ranch on 'Eua have been delayed. Most of the dairy industry was set up by church organizations.

Agricultural research and extension took place at one research farm, several demonstration farms, and agricultural advisory centers. In addition, the Ministry of Agriculture maintained machinery pools around the country that offered the services of 38 tractors—20 of them on Tongatapu. The lack of qualified staff and the need for a detailed agricultural census were two major problems that the government hoped to address in the 1980s.

Fishing has received special attention in the 1980s. The inner-reef areas supported a local catch of about 1,600 tons of bottom fish in 1981; estimates suggested that the catch could be increased by at least 1,000 tons per year by exploiting pelagic species, such as tuna, sardines, and mackerel. The outer-reef areas—at depths of from 75 to 365 meters—were believed able to produce an annual catch of about 1,000 tons of bottom fish and 2,000 tons of other fish, but local fishing vessels caught only 300 tons in 1981. Foreign vessels caught about 4,500 tons of fish in the deep-sea areas, and the use of purse seine vessels could probably boost the sustainable yield to some 10,000 tons per year. There were about 250 motorized dinghies, 50 sailboats, 450 outrigger canoes, and 20 inboard motorboats in the private fishing fleet. The latter had just begun to work the outer-reef grounds in 1981. The government operated a number of small open boats and a 200-ton longline tuna boat that suffered low catches and financial losses. The government opened a boat yard in 1979 to build vessels up to 8.5 meters long. The government and the cooperative federation were setting up ice plants around the country and were investigating the establishment of a fish-freezing plant; the development of a cannery was a more distant goal.

Forestry production has been minimal, and Tonga imported about 81 percent of its timber needs. A new government sawmill on 'Eua cut about 720 cubic meters of native hardwood species in 1980, but the government has had trouble establishing a forest reserve there to prevent the ruin of the island's dwindling native resources. The government was establishing a pine forest plantation on the island, but at rates well behind schedule because of the poor performance of the seedlings. The strategy for the FY 1980–84 period was to utilize the coconut timber resources; only 690 cubic meters were cut in 1980.

Industry and Services

Industry was concentrated around the capital and depended almost exclusively on the domestic agricultural sector or imported materials. In 1980 there were six government-owned, seven quasi-government, 30 incorporated, and 29 unincorporated manufacturing companies producing commodities such as coconut oil, paper and paper products, rubber products, wood products, and food and beverages.

Mining was limited to the quarrying of sand and coral for use in roadbuilding and construction; offshore oil prospecting since 1976 has uncovered no exploitable deposits. Liquid fuel imports increased by over 13 percent per year from 1975 to 14.9 million liters in 1980. The only domestic sources of energy were wood and coconut husks burned for cooking and copra drying. Electric power was available through the government utility only on Tongatapu and Vava'u, where 4,125 kilowatts and 110 kilowatts of installed capacity were located, respectively, in FY 1979; the main island had an emergency capacity of 300 kilowatts. The government established small generators in the Ha'apai Group and on 'Eua in the early 1980s.

The increased level of investment in the 1970s brought about a boom in the construction industry. However, there was an undersupply of skilled workers, equipment, and material to accomplish the projects begun. Residential housing had the largest share in construction activity. The 1976 census showed that the nation had some 13,900 houses, and about 600 houses a year were added through 1980. In 1976 some 61 percent of the houses were of the European style, made with concrete block and wood; 10 percent were Tongan style, having metal roofs and wooden walls. The rest were thatched or made of a mixture of materials, and these have been most susceptible to storm damage.

Transportation services improved only slowly during the 1970s and have been beset by the effects of bad weather. The road network extended about as far as was practical—973 kilometers in 1980—but poor drainage and surface conditions caused them to deteriorate; there were only 54 kilometers of sealed (surfaced with low-grade asphalt) roads in 1980. There were some 2,500 vehicles in use in 1979, mostly on Tongatapu. Shipping transportation was hurt when two of the three wharves at Nuku'alofa were incapacitated first by an earthquake in 1977 and then by the 1982 hurricane. In mid-1984 both had been reconstructed, and the third wharf was being extended to triple the capital's berthing capacity by 1985. Two large ferries dominated most of the interisland trade; an average of 176 international ships, excluding warships and yachts, put in at the main port each year during the 1975–80 period. The major airport, on Tongatapu, was capable of handling small jets, and the government planned to extend the runway and the terminal in the 1980s. Tonga Air, a privately owned airline that ran six flights each week to the nation's other three airports, suffered a setback in 1983, when it lost one of its two small planes in a landing accident.

Communications services were most developed in Nuku'alofa, where an automatic telephone exchange came into operation in 1979; there were 1,500 telephone lines. Interisland communications were by radio or telegraph. In 1978 an international firm installed an earth satellite station that greatly improved international communications. The Tonga Broadcasting Commission operated the single AM radio station, broadcasting in English and Tongan some 10 hours each day; the station's equipment was obsolete. In 1983 an enterprising Tongan set up an informal television station that broadcast irregularly to the 100 or so sets located in the capital. Two years earlier another private company had begun distributing videotapes and video tape recorders.

Tourism in Tonga was less developed than in the other Pacific islands; about 52,000 cruise ship passengers and 12,500 airline passengers visited the country in 1980, the latter including nontourists. There were only 400 hotel rooms in 1983, yet the annual occupancy rate was only 50 percent. Cruise ship passengers, however, made a large number of purchases from the handicraft industry. The government hoped that the opening of duty-free centers would attract greater numbers of visitors in the 1980s.

Commercial services were well developed. Wholesale and retail trade of imported items was in the hands of private traders—in particular, two firms based in Fiji. Commercial banking took place at the Bank of Tonga, which was 40 percent owned by the government and 60 percent owned by three foreign banks. The Tonga Development Bank, a government-run institution, lent long-term development funds to private and official agencies alike. Cooperatives were important in the rural areas and often acted as the purchasing agents for agricultural commodities; there were 81 registered cooperatives in 1980, having a membership of 2,600. The government controlled the purchase price of coconuts, vanilla, and bananas.

The Political System and Security

A constitutional monarchy in name, Tonga's political system barely circumscribes the monarch's powers. The Constitution was promulgated in 1875 and has been amended little. It creates a government headed by the monarch and, in decreasing order of power, the Privy Council, the cabinet, and the Legislative Assembly. The cabinet is appointed directly by the monarch, and its members, including the premier and the govenors of Ha'apai and Vava'u, keep their positions until they retire or are shifted by the monarch. When the monarch and the cabinet sit together, they constitute the Privy Council. The premier heads the government and makes all appointments at the district and town levels. In mid-1984 the king's younger brother was premier, and his eldest son and heir apparent was minister of foreign affairs and defense. The rest of the cabinet consisted of two barons and a European minister of finance.

Members of the cabinet also belong to the Legislative Assembly, while the monarch appoints the Speaker to lead the legislature. The nation's 33 nobles and commoners elect seven representatives each to the Legislative Assembly, which is elected every three years. All tax-paying and literate male citizens and all literate female citizens over the age of 21 are eligible to vote for the commoner representatives.

As of mid-1984 local government was accomplished through appointed town and district officers. Town officers were in charge of the larger villages and district officers of agglomerations of smaller villages. In addition, Ha'apai and Vava'u each had a governor of cabinet rank. The crown ruled directly over the capital city.

The Supreme Court is the premier legal institution in the country, having original jurisdiction over all major cases. The chief justice and the Privy Council, however, sit together as the Court of Appeal when needed. Eight magistrate's courts—four on Tongatapu—and the Land Court are responsible for lesser crimes, civil proceedings, and land cases.

Tonga had no political parties as of mid-1984, there being little utility in organizing to win the seven commoner election seats in parliament. Church organizaions, however, have become increasingly political and have been the only institutions having the confidence to criticize the government. Church leaders have most commonly spoken out against the government's neglect of land reform and the use of capital punishment. Private access to the local media was difficult; the royal family set up and owned both the *Tonga Chronicle* and the radio station.

The need for economic aid, the long association with Britain, and the conservatism of the monarchy have influenced Tonga's foreign policy. Tonga has tended to work quietly behind the scenes in its support for the initiatives of the South Pacific Forum (see Appendix B). The country has tried to steer a neutral course between the world's superpowers, although it shocked the Western countries in 1976 when it established diplomatic relations with the Soviet Union. Spurious rumors circulated at the time that the nation had agreed to let the Soviets establish a permanent mission and a fishing base in return for the construction of an international airport. Tonga's high commissioner in Britain—equivalent to an ambassador—was accredited to the EEC and was pehaps the only ambassador accredited to both the United States and the Soviet Union as of mid-1984. Ships of both nations were allowed to dock in Tongan ports. Tonga was, however, one of the few nations of the world that had yet to rcognize China and continued formal relations with Taiwan.

Having a noncontroversial foreign policy and few valuable economic resources, Tonga faced no real external threat in mid-1984. The Tongan Defense Services were small—17 officers and 208 other ranks in 1979. There were three branches: infantry, royal guard, and maritime. The first two branches had responsibility for internal security matters, including the protection of the sovereign. The maritime force was charged with patrolling Tongan waters, which as of mid-1984 extended 12 nautical miles. The nation had yet to declare an EEZ (see Glossary), although the government stated that it would not hesitate to do so should significant underwater mineral resources be discovered. Tonga was a signatory to the United Nations (UN) Convention on the Law of the Sea. As of 1983 the maritime force had two small patrol craft, one transport craft, and a yacht. In addition to the armed forces, Tonga maintained a police force of around 300 personnel. The minister of police had cabinet ranking and was also the chief immigration officer and chief warden of the nation's five prisons.

TUVALU

Flag: British flag and nine yellow stars on blue field

Previous Name	Ellice Islands
Political Status	Independent state (1978)
Capital	Funafuti
Population	8,200 (1984 midyear estimate)
Area	26 square kilometers
Currency	Australian dollar ($A)
Major Islands	Funafuti, Vaitupu

Tuvalu is among the newest, smallest, and poorest nations of the world. In mid-1984 its sixth anniversary of independence was yet to come. Although a 200-nautical-mile EEZ (see Glossary) around its nine coral islands and atolls incorporated some 900,000 square kilometers of ocean area, its land area totaled only 26 square kilometers. Labor skilled in traditional agricultural, handicraft, and maritime occupations and extensive stands of coconut palms were its significant resources.

Weak external transportation and communications links left it even more geographically isolated than many countries in Oceania. Among its closest neighbors were Kiribati to the north and northeast, Western Samoa to the southeast, and Fiji to the south. It had shared a colonial experience under British rule with the Gilbert Islands, which later became part of Kiribati, and it shared close cultural links with Western Samoa. A majority of its people are Polynesians, and their language, Tuvalu, has many Samoan loanwords.

Physical Environment

Tuvalu, meaning "eight standing together," takes its name from its eight inhabited coral islands and atolls, the ninth being uninhabited. Formerly called the Ellice Islands, the group extends in a winding line from about 5° to 10° south latitude and from 176° east longitude to the international dateline (see fig. 20). Few land areas are more than four meters above sea level. Vaitupu is the largest island; Funafuti, the site of government, is the most densely populated.

431

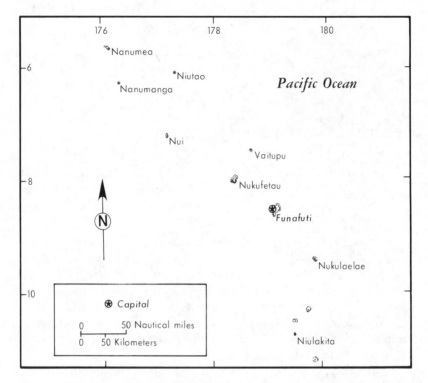

Figure 20. Tuvalu, 1984

Life can be sustained on these physically unfavored coral formations—if only by the exercise of consummate skill in conserv-
ing resources—because of the presence of small patches of arable
soil and shoreline vegetation. Rainfall must be collected for drinking water. Before the coming of the Europeans, 4,000 or more islanders may once have lived in the archipelago; nevertheless,
overpopulation was a constant threat, and emigration provided a
safety net. At times, however, the inhabitants probably resorted
to infanticide.

The climate is hot, but prevailing easterly trade winds moderate the high temperatures between March and October.
November through February bring westerly gales and considerable rain. The sandy, rubbled coral soils are particularly suited to
coconut palms, and some pandani (screw pine) are found; other
vegetation, however is limited. Vaitupu has a closed-off, fish-
filled lagoon.

Estimates since the mid-twentieth century show a steady rise in the population, from 4,700 in 1950 to 5,800 in 1970. A census taken in May 1979, soon after independence, indicated a total population of 7,300. Official sources report an average annual growth rate for three five-year intervals beginning with 1965–70 of 0.9, 1.3, and 3.9 percent, respectively. A growth rate for 1980–85 of 1.6 percent is projected, based on the recent census and average annual growth rate.

Historical Setting

Island tradition has it that the inhabitants emigrated from the Samoa Islands in the sixteenth century. Based on the physical and cultural characteristics of Tuvaluans today, there is some reasons for subscribing to this belief. Over the centuries the islands came in contact with traders and navigators from other parts of the world.

Europeans discovered some of the Gilbert and Ellice islands in 1568 and had come across all of them by 1824. Other than a few copra traders, however, Europeans did not become involved in local affairs as heavily as others were to become on more richly endowed Pacific islands. Blackbirders, who rounded up scores of islanders to work in mines and on plantations in Latin America, and whalers, who visited the islands for rest and recreation, provided the most significant contact with the outside world. The population was decimated by the new diseases introduced by the visitors and by the depredations of the blackbirders.

In the final quarter of the eighteenth century, the Ellice Islands became linked to Britain. In 1877 they were placed with other groups under the British-administered Western Pacific High Commission. In 1892 a British protectorate was declared over the Gilbert and Ellice islands, and in 1916 the protectorate was reorganized as the Gilbert and Ellice Islands Colony (GEIC).

The Gilberts were occupied by the Japanese in 1942, but the Ellice Islands escaped occupation. The capital of the GEIC was moved temporarily to Funafuti. Thousands of Americans were stationed on Funafuti and elsewhere in the Ellice Islands during the war, and islanders working for them gained new skills and earned valuable revenues. After World War II the colony was slowly prepared for eventual self-rule through the evolution of a series of advisory and legislative bodies. In October 1975 a popular referendum brought about the severance of the Ellice Islands from the GEIC, and they emerged as a separate dependency, renamed Tuvalu. Three years later Tuvalu became an independent country. As such, it continued relations with Britain as a "special member" of the Commonwealth of Nations, without representation at the heads of government sessions of that body.

The Social System

Traditionally, social organization was based on a system of clans, whose chiefs held the positions of leadership in island society. The system was supported by sanctions based on customary belief and practice. Much of this changed rapidly in the second half of the nineteenth century, however, owing to the influence of Congregationalist pastors from the Samoa Islands aided after 1870 by the London Missionary Society. By 1900 the overwhelming majority of the population had become Protestant. Within a short time the Samoan missionaries fully usurped the authority of the clan elders and undermined the traditional social order and belief system on which it was based.

In mid-1980 about 95 percent of the population professed Christianity; the leading institution was the Tuvalu Church, founded in 1861. There were about 200 Roman Catholic believers, but anti-Catholic sentiment prevented the building of Catholic churches on some islands.

In other aspects of education and culture, Tuvaluans showed a marked degree of uniformity and homogeneity as well. The Micronesian inhabitants of Nui speak a dialect of Gilbertese, which is a Micronesian language spoken in Kiribati. On each of the other islands, however, the inhabitants speak one or another of seven mutually intelligible Tuvalu dialects. Among the various dialects, Vaitupu is the most widely spoken and most prestigious, more widely disseminated than the others because of its use in the local press and radiobroadcasts. English is also used throughout the islands. Most Tuvaluans were literate, and by the early 1980s primary schools existed on all the islands. Motufoua School on Vaitupu provided secondary education to several hundred students. A few islanders attended secondary schools, colleges, and universities outside the country. Vocational education was offered at a maritime training school, established with aid from Australia.

The Economy

Tuvalu ranked among the low-income countries fo the globe. According to a report published in *Business America* in late 1982, its gross national product (GNP—see Glossary) was the equivalent of US$1 million; its exports were about US$67,000, and its imports US$2 million.

Not surprisingly, agriculture was the predominant sector of the economy, and within agriculture the harvesting of coconuts and the production of copra for export were the paramount activities. The Tuvalu Copra Cooperative Society took responsibility for its production and marketing. Coconut production varied significantly from year to year owing to fluctuating weather and world market conditions. Hurricanes posed a major threat to crop cultivation. Vegetables, pigs, and poultry were also raised by subsistence farmers. Fishing was only moderately developed, although its potential for the economy was increasingly recognized.

Although most of the population was engaged in subsistence agriculture, there were several hundred members of the labor force involved in the cash economy at home and perhaps double that number working abroad as wage earners in phosphate mining or abroad foreign ships. Remittances from these migrants provided needed foreign exchange for import purchases. One issue of concern to some islanders was the growing group of foreign technicians, economists, and advisers employed in the public and private sectors. In particular, civil servants were reportedly uneasy about foreigners in senior government posts who occupied positions that a number of Tuvaluans felt could be handled by islanders themselves.

Fiji, Australia, New Zealand, and Britain were important trading partners. Exports of copra, the main export commodity, were valued at $A29,200 in 1981; imports in the same year totaled $A2.5 million (for value of the Australian dollar—see Glossary).

Commonwealth countries were also important aid sources. In 1983 proposed current expenditures amounted to $A3.5 million, of which $A950,000 was British grant-in-aid. Development funds furnished—among others—by Britain, New Zealand, Australia, Canada, Japan, West Germany, and the United Nations Development Programme for the same year amounted to an additional $A7.1 million.

The Political System and Security

The 1978 Constitution, the supreme law of the country, guarantees the protection of all fundamental rights and freedoms and provides the basis for government organization. It establishes a parliamentary democracy under the titular sovereignty of the British monarch, who is represented by a governor general. The governor general, whose powers are largely ceremonial, must be a Tuvaluan and is appointed on the advice of the prime minister, with whom, as head of the government, the major portion of everyday responsibilities rests.

The unicameral legislature, the parliament for Tuvalu, is popularly chosen on the basis of universal, free, adult franchise to serve a normal four-year term. The islands of Funafuti, Vaitupu, Nanumean, and Niutao elect two members each and the other four inhabited islands one each, for a total of 12. Members select the prime minister from among themselves, and he in turn is assisted by a cabinet of four whose members are drawn from parliament and serve at his pleasure.

The legal and court system bears the imprint of British legal philosophy and experience. The court hierarchy in the early 1980s included the High Court, magistrate's courts, and island courts; a system of appeals operated upward through courts in Fiji and Britain. The eight island courts had limited jurisdiction in civil and criminal matters, but the level of public order and internal security was high on the islands, and most offenses were minor infringements of the law.

Although Tuvalu had no organized political parties in the Western sense, there was political competition. Elections were held in August 1977 and, in the first postindependence experience, again in September 1981, after which Tomasi Puapua succeeded Toalipi Lauti as prime minister.

Tuvalu had diplomatic relations with more than 15 countries, including Australia, Britain, Fiji, New Zealand, and the United States. The governments of Tuvalu and the United States signed a treaty of friendship in February 1979, under which the latter relinquished its claims to Funafuti and three other Tuvaluan islands.

WALLIS AND FUTUNA

Official Name	Territory of the Wallis and Futuna Islands
Political Status	Overseas territory of France
Capital	Mata Utu
Population	11,800 (1983 estimate)
Land Area	255 square kilometers
Currency	Cours du Franc Pacifique franc (CFPF)
Major Islands	Wallis Island (Uvea), Futuna Island, Alofi Island

The French overseas territory of Wallis and Futuna consists of two island groups: Wallis Island, which is surrounded by 22 small islets, and the islands of Futuna and Alofi, which lie 160 kilometers to the southwest and are separated from each other by the narrow, about three-kilometer-wide, Sain Channel. The territory is found in the western region of Polynesia. Western Samoa lies to the east, Tonga to the southeast, Fiji to the south and west, and Tuvalu to the north and west. Futuna should not be confused with an island of the same name in Vanuatu.

Wallis, which has an area of 96 square kilometers, is surrounded by a barrier reef that is broken only in places by passes through which ships can navigate. The resulting lagoon is full of rocky patches, coral formations, and islets large enough to support coconut plantations. Although Wallis is of volcanic origin, its highest elevation is only 143 meters above sea level.

The combined area of the two islands of Futuna and Alofi is 159 square kilometers. Both are volcanic islands, elevations reaching 760 meters above sea level on Futuna and 365 meters above sea level on Alofi. Along the west coast of Futuna and the northwest coast of Alofi lie fringing reefs.

In mid-1984 the French government enforced a territorial limit of 12 nautical miles in its dependencies. The recognition of a 200-nautical-mile EEZ (see Glossary) gave the territory an estimated sea area of 300,000 square kilometers.

The climate of the island is warm and humid. There are two

437

well-defined seasons: a hot, rainy season from November to April, during which tropical storms sometimes occur, and a drier, cooler season from May to October, when the trade winds blow from the southeast. Cultivated plants, such as coconut trees, breadfruit, and bananas, are found in the coastal areas. Upland areas, quite steep in some parts of Futuna and Alofi, often contain forests, while relatively arid interior regions, known locally as *toafa*, have sparse vegetation.

Historical Setting

The two island groups of Wallis and Futuna and Alofi had largely separate histories before the imposition of French colonial rule, although the people of both are Polynesian and trace their origins to Tonga or the Samoa islands. According to local tradition, Wallis was settled by Tongans around 1500. The first European to encounter the island, in 1767, was the British captain Samuel Wallis, after whom it was named. Europeans did not return again until 1825 but subsequently often behaved violently toward the local population. In 1837 a French Catholic missionary of the society of Mary, Father Pierre Bataillon, arrived. Although competing with Protestant missionaries from Tonga, Bataillon succeeded in converting the most powerful of the native chiefs to Catholicism and arranged for the island to become a French protectorate in 1842.

Local traditions in Futuna and Alofi tell of the arrival of a "Chinese" ship whose crew left numerous descendants. Scholars believe it may actually have come from the Marshall Islands. European discovery of the islands was accomplished by the Dutch navigators Jacob Lemaire and Willem Cornelius van Schouten in 1616. A Marist missionary, Father Pierre Chanel, came to the islands in 1837. He was killed by a local chief on Futuna in 1841, but the conversion of the people to Catholicism had to be carried out by his successors. (Chanel was later canonized, and in 1976 his remains were brought back to Futuna.) In 1984 the rulers of Futuna and Alofi agreed to a French protectorate.

The two island groups were administered under a single budget by France, beginning in 1909. In 1913 Wallis was made a colony of France, although its ruler was allowed to retain his traditional status, as remained the case in mid-1984. The French also recognized the status of the rulers of Alo and Sigave on Futuna. although outside the zone of battle between Allied and Japanese forces, Wallis served as a military base for United States forces during World War II, and two airfields were built. In 1959 Wallis and Futuna became an overseas territory of France as a result of a referendum in which the inhabitants voted on whether to maintain the connection with that country.

The Social System

There are no significant urban settlements. The town of Mata Utu, the territorial capital, had around 600 inhabitants in the early 1980s. About two-thirds of the total population lived on Wallis in mid-1984 and the remaining one-third on Futuna, while the other large island, Alofi, was uninhabited. About 11,000 persons from the territory, mostly from Wallis, lived in New Caledonia and another 1,000 in Vanuatu. The territory's population grew by 3.8 percent per year during the 1978–80 period.

Despite the migration of the youngest and economically most active members of the population to New Caledonia, which had greater economic opportunities, it was estimated in 1977 that 57 percent of the total population was less than 20 years of age. Life expectancy in the 1974–78 period was 63 years for men and women.

Except for a small minority of Europeans, many of whom are French government officials, the people are Polynesian, speaking Wallisian and Futunan dialects of the Polynesian language. French was used as the official language in mid-1984. Practically the entire population, 99 percent, was Roman Catholic. Church schools, consisting of seven primary institutions in the early 1980s, provided the only educational opportunities in the islands, although there was a state junior secondary school at Lano on Wallis Island. The adult population was estimated to be 95 percent literate.

During the French colonial period, the influence and power of the Catholic clergy in many cases exceeded that of the civil authorities. Until 1970 the Catholic bishop of the territory bore, along with the traditional rulers, the title of "co-prince" and could punish persons for failing to attend mass. Since then, however, the temporal power of the church has declined, and the influence of European clergy has diminished with the growth of an indigenous Catholic clergy.

The Economy

Wallis and Futuna's economy in the early 1980s was essentially one of subsistence, exports being of negligible value. Some

4,000 hectares of coconut trees were grown on the islands, but the copra of only about one-half of these was collected for domestic use as food, forage for animals, soap, or oil. Other crops included taro, yams, breadfruit, and bananas. Some fishing was carried out in the lagoon around Wallis Island, the coastal waters of Futuna, and in deep waters.

The ravages of the rhinoceros beetle on stands of coconut trees caused copra production to fall, stimulating the first migration of the territory's inhabitants to New Caledonia during the late 1940s. Emigration continued through the 1970s, though it slowed singificantly when the nickel "boom" in New Caledonia ended in 1974–75 (see New Caledonia, ch. 2). Wallisians and Futunans in New Caledonia sent back to their relatives in the territory a stream of remittances that sustained the local economy. By the early 1980s, however, poor economic conditions in New Caledonia and the attenuation of ties between islanders developing new roots abroad and those still in the territory resulted in a significant diminution of the payments.

Outside Mata Utu there were no paved roads in the early 1980s. The airport on the northwest coast of Wallis served flights to and from Nouméa in New Caledonia, Nauru, and Apia in Western Samoa. Limited port facilities were located at Mata Utu and Halalo on Wallis and Sigave on Futuna.

The Political System

In early 1984 the people of Wallis and Futuna were French citizens. Adults of both sexes had the right to vote for a deputy to the French National Assembly and a member of the French Senate. They also voted for the 20-member Territorial Assembly. Executive authority was vested in a high administrator (administrateur supérieur) appointed by the French state, who ruled with the assistance of the traditional ruler of Wallis, the two traditonal rulers of Futuna, and the Territorial Assembly. In the March 1982 Territorial Assembly election, a majority of seats were won by candidates led by Benjamin Brial, a member of the Gaullist Rally for the Republic (Rassemblement pour la République).

WESTERN SAMOA

Official Name	Independent State of Western Samoa
Political Status	Independent state (1962)
Capital	Apia
Population	159,000 (1983 estimate)
Land Area	2,394 square kilometers
Currency	Western Samoa tala (WS$)
Major Islands	Upolu, Savai'i

Flag: White constellation of Southern Cross in blue rectangle on red field

Although the Samoa Islands have been divided into two separate political entities since colonial rivalries resulted in their partition in 1900, residents of Western Samoa and its neighbor to the east, American Samoa, have continued to share close kinships ties and a common culture known as *faa Samoa* (the Samoan way). Although it is therefore possible to differentiate Western Samoa from American Samoa in political and geographic terms, *faa Samoa* pertains in both, making ethnic, social, cultural, and linguistic matters all indivisibly Samoan.

Physical Environment

Western Samoa lies in the tropics between 171° and 173° west longitude and 13° and 15° south latitude, about two-thirds the distance from Honolulu to Auckland, New Zealand. Its eight islands are of volcanic origin. Of the four that are inhabited, the second largest, Upolu (1,100 square kilometers), is home to 75 percent of the population; the capital and only town, Apia, is also located there (see fig. 21). Most of the rest of the population live on Savai'i (1,820 square kilometers). Between the two large islands lie Manono, within the reef system of Upolu, and Apolima, outside the reefs in the strait of the same name. Savai'i rises to a height of 1,858 meters and experienced its most recent volcanic eruption in 1911. Upolu is less rugged and more fertile, its central ridge peaking at 1,100 meters. On Upolu's north-central coast, where the Vaisigano River has created an opening in the reef, lies the town of Apia (population 35,000), which developed as the country's port and became its capital.

The climate is tropical, having wet and dry seasons. The

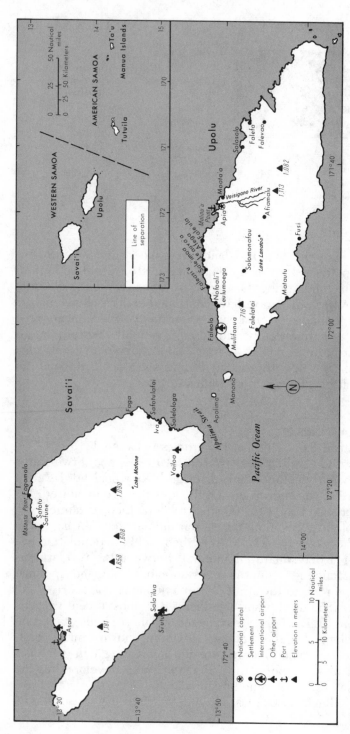

Figure 21. Western Samoa, 1984

mean daily temperature is 27°C. Average annual rainfall is about 287 centimeters, of which 190 centimeters fall between October and March. The islands lie on a slightly inclined northwest/southeast axis, which causes the prevailing trade winds to drop proportionally heavier rains on the eastern ends of the main islands. The Samoa Islands lie outside the usual track of hurricanes, but severe storms do occasionally strike.

These rocky, volcanic islands have only a thin covering of moderately fertile soil, and there is little level land except for a thin band along the coast. The country nonetheless produces taro, bananas, cocoa, breadfruit, and coconuts for internal consumption and some exports. One is seldom out of sight of the sea, which was in the past and must be in the future a major source of food.

Because of the traditional orientation toward the sea and the hot, humid environment of the interior—which is either thickly vegetated or rocky—almost all Western Samoan villages were built along the coast. An extensive system of fringing reefs provides protection from storms and a safe fishing ground. Beyond the reef, larger species of fish are available, although Western Samoa's fisheries zone is not particularly rich.

In recent years the influence of the urban economy of Apia has caused a drift of population to the town in search of jobs. Over one-half the population resided along the northwestern coast of Upolu in the area bounded by the town and the airport at Faleolo, where the interisland terminal was also located. This was the first area of the country to receive electricity and paved roads. The ability of Samoans to move to another village where they have relatives makes significant shifts of population relatively easy.

Historical Setting

It is generally accepted that the Samoa Islands were among the first in Polynesia to be populated. A legend in Polynesia has it that all of its people originated from a common homeland, Hawaiki, quite similar to the name of Western Samoa's largest islands, Savai'i. The Samoa Islands maintained contact with the relatively nearby island of Fiji and with Tonga, which had a language similar to Samoan. Lacking a written language, Samoans developed an extensive oral history that extended back to about A.D. 1250. The enthusiastic embrace of Christianity, however, caused a repression of previous beliefs and loss of information about the islands before the arrival of the Europeans. A noted anthropologist, Peter Buck, who presumed the origin of the Polynesians to be Southeast Asia, was dismissed by a Samoan orator, who informed Buck that the Samoans originated in the Samoa Islands. Some clue of the Samoan world view is revealed by the meaning of the term *palaga*, first applied to the European discoverers, who were believed to have "burst" through the "sky."

After Roggeveen's sighting of Manua in 1722, the islands were next visited by Bougainville in 1768, by French navigator Jean-François de Galaup, Compte de la Pérouse (who was the first to land) in 1787, and by the H.M.S. *Pandora* in 1791 while searching for the *Bounty* mutineers. In the wake of these early explorers came whalers (mostly American, but some British, French, and German), traders, and missionaries. In July 1830 John Williams of the London Missionary Society arrived in the Samoa Islands, and within a few years the islanders had converted to Christianity. Roman Catholic missionaries arrived in 1845.

Williams' arrival on Savai'i occurred just as a violent internal struggle was ending. The victorious chief, Malietoa Vai'inupo, welcomed the missionaries, there being no organized priesthood to oppose Christianity. In any case, the new religion fitted in well with the Samoan taste for ceremony. The Malietoa title held by the chief had originated during earlier wars with Tonga and is regarded by Samoans as one of four highest titles of Samoan rank, the others being Tupua Tamasese, Mata'afa, and Tuimalealiifano. The church developed in the context of each village. *Matai* (chiefs) would have their families join and then would become church elders. Because there were not enough missionaries to go around, Samoan teachers had to be employed, causing the church to become Samoanized rapidly. Church support for education— Malau College was established in the 1840s—and commerce brought into being an educated class that provided the staffs of clerks and secretaries for the developing economy.

Throughout the mid-century, trading contact with the Europeans increased, the son of Williams becoming one of the biggest traders. German involvement in the islands began before that nation's own unification upon establishment in 1856 of the firm of Johann Cesar Godeffroy and Son for the purpose of trading coconut oil. By 1860 over 100 Europeans had settled at Apia and were engaged in various businesses. Cash incomes enabled islanders to obtain Western goods, breaking down the country's self-sufficiency.

As the Europeans settled around the harbor and islanders from outer villages were attracted to the town area, an urban center developed on Beach Road, where a system of administration evolved in which the Europeans were increasingly drawn into mediation of local conflicts. Western influence was also evident as the islands' government began to evolve toward centralization. In 1868 the *matai* of a number of districts established the first central government at Mulinu'u, near Apia.

During the 1870s Western trading companies began to acquire land to establish large-scale plantation agriculture. Islanders were eager to sell, often without permission of the rest of the family or village and often to acquire firearms for use in the intermittent warfare of the era. The outrage over the sale of so much land has continued into recent times, resulting in a prohibition—still in force as of mid-1984—on alienation of land held according to custom. Landholding brought the foreign settlers and their governments increasingly into internal politics.

The United States, Britain, and Germany were most active in the islands. In 1873 a United States Department of State official, Albert Steinberger, arrived and quickly established a reputation as a trusted adviser to the islanders. Through Steinberger, who, in addition to his official duties, became involved in a number of conflicting business enterprises, the islanders sent a request to Washington for United States protection in regional power rivalries. An informal agreement with the United States had already been reached in 1872, which the islanders, but not the United States, considered to have constituted a treaty. Both the United States and Britain, however, favored maintaining the independence of the Samoa Islands.

Germany had different ideas, and while Steinberger was away in Washington in 1874, a German warship intervened in a local dispute to support a land claim of the Godeffroy company. When Steinberger returned the next year without official backing and began to associate himself with Samoan interests, he became involved in a number of intrigues, including one in which he successfully sought support from the Godeffroy firm for a Samoan government he was attempting to put together. Steinberger's lack of real support from the United States and involvement in conflicting areas of interest eventually led to his downfall, however. By connivance of the United States and British consuls, Steinberger, who had become the premier of the Samoa Islands government, was deported on trumped up charges and taken to Fiji, never to return to the islands again.

Internal instability and external involvement in island affairs continued as Britain, Germany, and the United States established treaties with the islands' Samoan government to protect trade and military rights in 1878–79. An agreement in 1879 establishing a municipal authority in Apia gave control to the consuls and foreign residents, undermining an already weak government. By the 1880s German influence was mounting. In 1887 an official of the Deutsche Handels-und Plantagen-Gesellschaft (successor firm to Godeffroy) was appointed premier of a government that the Germans had established, which was led by the holder of the Tamasese title. The Germans had replaced the former government and exiled its leader, Malietoa Laupepa.

The move was designed to weaken United States and British influence but sparked a revolt within the islands, and all three powers ended up sending warships to Apia harbor. There, on March 15, 1889, three German, three American, and one British vessel lay at anchor, unwilling to surrender position even as the barometer dropped steadily. War was probably averted by the arrival of a violent hurricane. All the ships were wrecked except the British *Calliope*, which barely escaped to the open sea. To save his crew the captain of the German ship *Adler* cut the anchor cable just as a huge wave was lifting the ship toward the reef. The *Adler* was thrown on top of the reef, where it lay on its beam for many years as a reminder of the storm. When the *Calliope* was broken up some 60 years later, the British Admiralty presented its steering wheel to Western Samoa.

The natural disaster calmed the political situation, and the three powers agreed to a partition of the country at the Berlin Conference, which began on April 29, 1889. Any thought of independence for the Samoa Islands had vanished. Although order and harmony had been restored to the rival factions, leadership of the government again came into dispute when Malietoa Laupepa, whom the Germans had returned from exile, died in 1898. To solve the matter, in April 1899 the three external powers assumed joint responsibility for government. A German, Wilhelm Heinrich Solf, was assigned as executive officer of the new government; but attempts to maintain it soon ended, and a German proposal to partition the country was accepted. The United States took the large island, Tutuila, in the eastern Samoa Islands which had a fine harbor at Pago Pago, as well as the isolated Manua group. Britain withdrew in return for recognition of claims elsewhere in the Pacific and Africa, leaving Germany in control of the western Samoa Islands. On March 1, 1900, the German flag was raised at Mulinu'u, and the Samoa Islands were divided, a split that continued in the mid-1980s.

German administration brought stability and prosperity, but at the cost of undermining island institutions. Under Governor Solf economic development projects were implemented and Chinese workers imported to augment Solomon Islanders previously brought in to bolster the labor force. The power of indigenous institutions, which were more highly developed than elsewhere in Oceania, was reduced. Solf abolished traditional royal offices and reduced to an advisory status the traditional consultative body, the Fono a Faipule. This motivated a monarchist restoration movement, the Mau a Pule (Mau movement). Solf broke up the Mau movement by exiling its leaders to Saipan in the Mariana Islands and other German possessions, but the movement was to reemerge after World War I. German attempts to establish the complete authority of the kaiser eventually provoked a reaction, and by 1910 the business community was pressing for greater control of local affairs. In the villages locally selected figures were contesting the authority of the government agents assigned to each village.

Meanwhile, in December 1889 Robert Louis Stevenson had arrived in the Samoa Islands, where he lived and wrote for several years before his death on December 3, 1894. He was buried on the summit of Mount Vaea overlooking Apia. His house, Vailima, where such works as *A Footnote to History* were written, was later made the official residence of the head of state.

The German period left a contradictory legacy. Although bent on a policy of breaking cultural barriers to their authority, the Germans nonetheless studied that culture thoroughly. Erich Schultz, who succeeded Solf, had been chairman of the Land and Titles commission and compiled a thorough study of Samoan customary law. Both men were skilled at exploiting the islanders' political differences. Under the Germans, islanders were involved in the European economy chiefly as producers of copra on village land. The large plantations were worked by Melanesians (some from the Solomons) and Chinese from Hong Kong. By 1909 there were enough Chinese to warrant a Chinese consul, and by 1914 the number had risen to 2,200. Most Chinese were eventually repatriated, but some married local women, and their descendants were prominent members of the professional merchant class in the mid-1980s.

At the outbreak of World War I in 1914, New Zealand forces landed, taking over the country on behalf of Britain. New Zealand had maintained some ambitions toward the Samoa Islands during the latter part of the nineteenth century. During the occupation years of World War I, there was little that war-pressed New Zealand could do except act as a caretaker. Confusion caused by expropriation of German property and repatriation of the Chinese, which hampered the planters, were among the problems confronted.

447

On November 7, 1918, a major tragedy commenced upon the arrival of the ship *Talune* from Auckland, which carried influenza on board. In the next few months over one-fifth of the population died. Especially hard hit were the older members of the population. Seventeen of 24 members of the Samoan advisory council perished. The disaster reflected badly on the competence of the New Zealand administration. The ship had not been quarantined as it had been in Fiji, even though the medical officer at Apia was aware of the influenza. American Samoa avoided the epidemic by strict quarantine measures; offers of medical assistance from American Samoa were ignored, however, and efforts to treat the sick were poorly handled. The disaster provoked long-lasting bitterness toward New Zealand. By eliminating so many older, traditional leaders, the epidemic also had the side effect of increasing the power of part-Samoans and Samoans who had a knowledge of European society.

Although New Zealand's administration was benevolent, that nation was on the whole unprepared for its responsibilities, despite its experience with the Maori at home. Its administrative style clashed with the growing assertiveness of the part-Samoan merchants and impinged on traditional custom. New Zealand officials had little appreciation for the islands and their people and reported to superiors in Wellington who had no background in the area.

By this time the Mau movement had reemerged, its members including many titleholders as well as part-Samoans who for various reasons objected to the policies of the New Zealand administration. Among its leaders was a part-Samoan, O.F. Nelson, the most successful merchant in Western Samoa, who also had accepted an important Samoan title. New Zealand exiled Nelson and other leaders for their activities. Tension reached a critical point on December 28, 1929, when New Zealand police attempted to arrest several members of the Mau movement who had gone to welcome home another exiled leader. Shots were fired, and 11 Samoans, among them holders of several of the highest titles, were fatally hit, including Tupua Tamasese Lealofi III. Poor relations between the two countries continued for some time.

In 1935 the victory of New Zealand's Labour Party brought a change. The Mau was no longer outlawed, Nelson was returned from exile, and much of the paternalism of the previous administrations was eliminated, although many of the same officials remained in office. Pressures for greater autonomy continued, but the distractions of World War II interrupted further political development. The war brought American troops in great number to Upolu, but the Japanese advance was halted short of the islands, which saw no fighting. During their stay the Americans constructed the air field at Faleolo.

In 1946 the western Samoa Islands became a United Nations trust territory under New Zealand administration, its request for self-government being denied. The presumption was for eventual self-rule, however, and the New Zealand government was more sympathetic than previously toward the islanders' aspirations, although that attitude was not completely shared by seconded officers in Apia. In 1947 a legislative assembly, the Fono, was established, and other changes gave greater local control over most legislative matters and finance. The New Zealand administrator became the high commissioner, and the term "Government of Western Samoa" came into use.

In 1954 a convention began work on a national constitution. The task was completed by another convention in 1960. Cabinet government was inaugurated in October 1959, the Mataafa titleholder becoming prime minister. In May 1961 a plebiscite overwhelmingly approved independence, which the UN General Assembly confirmed in November. Independence was attained on January 1, 1962, to be celebrated—with considerable pragmatism—in June to avoid the congestion of holidays around the New Year.

The Social System

During the 1839–1930 period the population fluctuated between 40,000 and 46,600. According to the 1976 census the Western Samoan population was 151,983, of which 48 percent were under the age of 15. The crude birth rate of 3.7 percent was partially offset by a death rate of 0.7 percent and net out-migration of 1.3 percent. About 25 percent of the population lived in the urban areas. The latest estimate available for 1983 put the population at around 159,000—71 percent living on Upolu and 28 percent on Savai'i. On Upolu about 34,000 lived in Apia and another 38,000 in the area west of the town. The population was divided into 27,150 households having approximately 5.8 persons each. About 89 percent of the people were categorized as Samoan and another 10 percent as part-Samoan.

Samoan culture was similar to that of other Polynesian peoples. Traditional authority was vested in the *matai,*who were selected by a process of consensus by each extended family. They exercised control over customary land, which by law may not be alienated. *Matai* belonged to one of two categories, *ali'i* (high chief) or *tulafale* (orator). The *ali'i* was the titular leader and ultimate repository of decisionmaking. The *tulafale* was the executive agent who performed a variety of duties for the *ali'i*. *Matai* of both categories held chiefly titles, of which there was a complex hierarchy in Samoan culture. Titles were conferred in elaborate ceremonies and did not necessarily pass along hereditary lines. Most *matai* were males, but a substantial number were females, including holders of some of the most high-ranking titles.

There were 362 villages and 12,600 *matai* in the early 1980s. Within each village the women's committee was active both in protecting health and in certain other village development matters. The pastor of the church, of which there was at least one per village, was also very important in the village social life. Villages were largely autonomous but were grouped with other villages to form administrative districts or subdistricts. The culture was one of collective communalism in which family welfare took precedence over individual rights. Individuals were obligated to assist a family member whenever assistance was requested. Samoans as a rule tried to avoid direct conflict, and disputes were usually discussed in an indirect fashion.

Although the system had inherent rigidity, certain practices worked for flexibility. Titles could be split, new ones created, and old ones subside in importance. Adoption is common. Respect for age is tempered by a recognition of the ability of younger, better educated members to support the family, which has led to a marked number of young and well-educated chiefs. The ability of a *matai* to discipline is moderated by the ability of a family member to move in with another branch of the family in a different location, including overseas.

Population and language are virtually homogeneous within the nation. There is a minority of part-Samoans, who are mixed Europeans, Chinese, Fijians, and Tongans, but this distinction is not of social importance. There are also some people living in Samoa from nearby Tuvalu and Tokelau, closely related Polynesian groups.

Samoans are very religious. The motto "Faavae i le Atua" (founded on God) appears on the national emblem. The largest denomination in mid-1984 was the Congregational Christian Church in Samoa, which was begun by the London Missionary Society and accounted for half the population. Another 25 percent were Roman Catholic, while the rest were Methodist, Mormon, and Seventh-Day Adventist.

Christian institutions have fused with indigenous culture.

Children performing the service at a Congregational church in southeastern Upolu as a part of White Sunday, or Children's Sunday, festivities held each October
Courtesy Steven R. Pruett

Church ritual has accorded well with the formalism of Samoan culture, but concepts of individual responsibility and private prayer and study have not been well accepted. Many aspects of Samoan culture, such as beliefs in the supernatural causes of disease and standards of sexual behavior, have not been affected. As an element of social control, shame is more important than guilt among Samoans living in the traditional culture.

Education was administered through the Department of Education in mid-1984. Paralleling the New Zealand system, there were primary, intermediate, and secondary levels. A teacher's training college and technical training center also existed. The School of Tropical Agriculture at Alafua became affiliated with the University of the South Pacific in 1977. There were also a number of church-run schools. In 1979 about 51,800 pupils were in the school system. The Congregational church established the University of Samoa in 1979, but it had not yet received much recognition. The churches operated theological seminaries that have produced a surplus of pastors, some of whom have been sent to serve as missisonaries in Papua New Guinea. Education, although not costly, was neither free nor compulsory. The great effort that families exerted to pay school fees, however, was indicative of the value placed on education.

The Economy

In the traditional culture, land was allocated by the *matai,* who distributed the fruits of agricultural production to the family. The arrival of the Europeans, however, broke the self-sufficiency of the islands by initiating production for export and creating a desire for Western goods. Improved health measures resulted in an increasing population and a high percentage of dependent children. Lack of sufficient employment opportunities caused many islanders to migrate, principally to New Zealand in search of jobs, where for many years the labor market was characterized by a shortage of workers. Slow overall economic growth in recent years, however, has limited the amount of labor New Zealand could absorb from Western Samoa and other Pacific islands.

Some 80 percent of the land was held in accordance with Samoan custom. Village land was usually fragmented into small plots and produced little surplus above local subsistence. Approximately 70 percent of the total was suitable for cultivation, but only 32 percent, or some 65,000 hectares, was under production. The Western Samoan Trust Estates Corporation (WSTEC), which had its origin in the reparation estates seized from Germany during World War I, farmed 7,000 hectares.

Coconuts were the most important cash crop, and copra historically was Samoa's main export. In 1982 a crushing mill was established to increase local value added. Copra production has stagnated in recent years, export volume in 1981 barely equaling that of 1973. Low world prices and bad weather have discouraged production. Problems were compounded by the trees being of high average age and requiring extensive replanting. Moreover, the rhinoceros beetle has destroyed some 20 to 30 percent of the crop.

Cocoa exports, of which 34 percent came from the WSTEC, have also been stagnant, reaching only 70 percent of 1973 levels in 1983. Here also disease and low prices have discouraged production. Taro exports have increased over threefold during the 1973–81 period, amounting to over one-half of the value of copra exports. Taro was reportedly shipped to Polynesian communities abroad. Bananas were a major export crop in the 1960s, but pests and bad weather affected the trees. Export markets were lost, although bananas continued to be an important domestic staple. Recent improvement in export volume has resulted from the establishment of a government-owned 80-hectare plantation.

There has been success in improving fishing through the use of modern equipment and facilities. Enough fresh fish was being landed during the mid-1980s to meet local demand, but even during a glut on the tuna market the price was still too high to replace imported canned fish of lower quality species. Increased storage facilities and local production of fishing boats able to operate in the deep water beyond the reef promised a larger catch. Western Samoa's maritime zone was more limited than most Pacific island countries, being constrained by the EEZs (see Glossary) of neighboring islands.

Some success has been achieved in establishing a livestock industry, often on coconut lands, but production has not kept pace with population growth, and low-quality meat must be imported. Chicken and pig production has not been commercialized, and the animals produced by village agriculture were allowed to roam free.

A major problem has been the inefficient operation of the WSTEC, which had some of the country's most productive land and should function as a model of modern agricultural practice. Efforts were under way, financed by the Asian Development Bank, to streamline the WSTEC operations.

The industrial sector was small, accounting for around 5 percent of GDP. The 1980–84 development plan called for increased light manufacturing and food processing. Local manufacturing in the early 1980s provided clothing, food processing, beer and soft drinks, paint, cigarettes, and matches. Dependence on imported materials and lack of foreign exchange has caused shortages of some of these products. The Development Bank of Western Samoa was established in 1965 to promote industry, but industrial development has been constrained by lack of raw materials and the necessity to import both raw materials and plant equipment. In common with many developing countries, the services sector, including government, was very large, accounting for 70 percent of the paid work force.

Tourism has long been looked upon as a promising industry, although there has been concern about possibly disruptive effects on the culture. Hotel facilities have nonetheless been expanded, and the airport was being improved to accommodate larger aircraft. In 1981 some 42,000 foreign visitors arrived by air and cruise ship, of which 44 percent came for business or pleasure. The local airline, Polynesian, has formed a joint venture with an Australian firm to improve the operations. During the early 1980s the airline flew to Tonga, New Zealand, Fiji, Vanuatu, American Samoa, Cook Islands, and Tahiti, and rights had been requested to operate to Honolulu. In addition, Air Pacific, which was based in Fiji, flew to Faleolo from Suva, Air New Zealand from Auckland and Tonga, and Air Nauru from that country.

Western Samoa was hard hit by the rise in energy costs in the 1970s. The nation did not have any deposits of fossil fuel, but in 1981 some 80 percent of electricity was diesel generated. Some development of hydroelectric power was taking place, however, and two hydro plants had been completed; another was set for completion in 1985. To discourge fuel consumption, a high price was being set on energy. In 1981 fuel absorbed 22 percent of the import bill.

New Zealand remained Western Samoa's most important trading partner, taking 34 percent of its exports in 1981. The Netherlands was next at 17 percent and American Samoa third at 15 percent. West Germany accounted for 9 percent and Japan and the United States for about 6 percent each. Samoa benefited from the South Pacific Regional Trade and Economic Cooperation Agreement (SPARTECA—see Glossary). It also benefited from the Lomé Convention (see Glossary). New Zealand provided between one-fourth and one-third of Western Samoa's imports over the 1975–81 period. Australia, Singapore, and Japan were also important sources of supply. In 1981 some 22.6 percent of import spending went to food, 21.5 percent for minerals, 21.3 percent for manufactured goods, and 20.1 percent for machinery and transport.

The trade balance has continued to worsen, climbing from WS$6.4 million (for value of the Western Samoa tala—see Glossary) in 1970 to WS$47.3 million in 1981 as exports stagnated and imports continued to rise. This deficit has in the past been somewhat offset by earnings from tourism and by remittances from Samoans working abroad, but in 1981–82 severe balance of payments difficulties required the imposition of austerity measures. In June 1982 an International Monetary Fund (IMF—see Glossary) mission recommended a number of steps, and another mission arrived in October. Changes in the cabinet prevented action until the new government of Tofilau Eti Alesana came to power in December 1982, whereupon the currency was devalued and restrictive budgetary measures were introduced. Dependence on external assistance was unlikely to change for some time to come, however. Action taken to limit public service employment and compensation and devaluation have not been popular but were necessary to restructure the economy.

New Zealand remained the most important source of foreign aid, providing WS$4.2 million of the WS$16 million received in 1982. Australia actually provided more that year—some WS$5.2 million—but has not provided as steady assistance as has New Zealand, Australian aid being only WS$1.9 million in 1981. Other important aid sources were Japan (WS$2.8 million), the United Nations Development Programme (WS$1.5 million), and the EEC (WS$1.4 million). The United States provided US$358,000 of assistance through private and voluntary agencies in 1983.

The Political System

The government is modeled on the parliamentary system and has specific modifications incorporating the Samoan culture. The highest office is that of head of state. At independence it was decided that the office would be held jointly for life by holders of two of the four highest titles, the *tama aiga* (royal sons): Tupua Tamasese Mea'ole and Malietoa Tanumafili II. The former died in 1963, leaving Malietoa as sole head of state. On his death the head of state will be elected by the Fona (parliament), most likely for a five-year term—though there is no formal requirement—from among the four *tama aiga* titleholders. The Council of Deputies, having not more than three members elected by the Fono, would act as head of state in the event of the head of state's absence or incapacity.

Governing power is vested in a prime minister, who is formally appointed by the head of state after selection by the newly elected Fono. The prime minister selects his own cabinet of eight ministers. The Fono is composed of 45 *matai* of each district. Two members are selected by individual voters who live outside the traditional culture. There have been proposals for universal suffrage, but thus far the only election in which all Samoan adults voted has been the plebiscite approving independence.

The Executive Council is composed of the head of state and the cabinet meeting jointly. The council is not a decisionmaking body, nor does it take any part in the formulation of policy. Its power is limited to discussion of particular cabinet decisions if the head of state or the prime minister so requests. It acts as a formal body for the issuance of regulations and the making of important apppointments. Decisions of the cabinet are subject to review by the council, but the cabinet retains power of decision.

Although in mid-1984 the prime minister headed a loose alliance called the Human Rights Protection Party, politics in Western Samoa has not developed along party lines. The first prime minister was Fiame Mata'afa, who died in office in 1975. His tenure had been interrupted once in 1970, when he was unseated by Tupua Tamasese Lealofi II, who later became health minister when Fiame Mata'afa regained the prime ministership in 1973. Tupua Tamasese Lealofi II became prime minister again on Fiame Mata'afa's death but was defeated by his cousin Tupuola Taisi Efi in 1976, whereupon he retired from politics and was appointed deputy head of state. Tupua Tamasese Lealofi IV died in 1982.

Efi is the son of Tupua Tamasese Mea'ole, who was co-head of state in 1962–63. The Tamasese title had then passed to Efi's cousin, who died in 1982. Efi served in parliament from 1965 to 1967, when he lost his seat, but returned in 1970 and served as minister of works, marine, transport, and aviation. He won the prime ministership in 1976 and was reelected in 1979. His choice was a departure from selecting the prime minister from among the four highest titleholders, although his title at that time, Tupuola, was ranked very high. In 1984 he succeeded to the Tupua Tamasese title. In 1982 Vaai Kolone, a successful planter and businessman, defeated Efi, but Kolone's election was challenged in court, and he lost his seat. The head of state reappointed Efi in September 1982, but his government was replaced in December by that of Tofilau Eti, Kolone's deputy in the Human Rights Protection Party. Eti, a prominent businessman, was a former health minister and was chairman of the Congregational church as of mid-1984.

The Constitution provides for an independent judiciary. The chief justice of the Supreme Court and any other judges deemed necessary are appointed by the head of state acting on the advice of the prime minister. In 1983 the first Western Samoan was named chief justice; previous officeholders had been New Zealanders.

Despite efforts by New Zealand to provide training to Western Samoans, the public service was inadequate when Western Samoa received its independence, and the nation continued to be dependent for administrative staff on seconded personnel from the ordinary ranks of the New Zealand public service. The Constitution established the Public Service Commission, which superseded a similar office abolished by the Samoa Amendment Act of 1959. The Public Service Commission, headed by a chairman who was assisted by two other commissioners, was responsible for the general administration of the public service and issuance of regulations pertaining thereto.

There was no formal system of local government. Apart from the administrative officer on Savai'i, who was a member of the prime minister's department, there were no district or regional officers in Western Samoa. Administrative districts, based mainly on geographical regions, were established at the end of 1965 but were used only in the operation of government services such as health, education, police, and agriculture. Although both the district and village board ordinances passed by the Fono as early as 1953 provided the framework of a local government system, the traditional *matai* system continued to dominate all fields of local government.

In this system the village *(nu'u)* was the basic territorial unit of political organization at the local level. However, there were also several subvillages (or *pitonu'u*) that increasingly have achieved administrative autonomy. The village was governed by its own *fono*, the structure and conventions of which reflected both the general characteristics of Samoan society and the particular characteristics of the individual village. Generally, the village *fono* was concerned with the relationship with other villages, the reception of important visitors, and major offenses against custom.

The political system has been remarkably stable. Although suffrage was limited to *matai*, the number of these has doubled since independence to around 12,000, representing a significant proportion of the adult population. An exception to the pattern of stability was a prolonged strike of public servants in 1981, which could be viewed as a challenge to the traditional attitude of respect for authority. This was the nation's first and only strike.

The treaty of friendship signed with New Zealand in 1962 formed the basis for the continuing close relationship with that country. In mid-1984 Western Samoa was a full member of the Commonwealth of Nations; the UN; the World Health Organization (a UN specialized agency); the UN Economic and Social Commission for Asia and the Pacific (ESCAP); the South Pacific Forum; the South Pacific Commission; and the Asian Development Bank. The nation maintained diplomatic offices in Wellington and Auckland, New Zealand, and in New York. Australia, New Zealand, and China had diplomatic missions in Apia. Britain, France, the Republic of Korea, Nauru, West Germany, and the United States had honorary consuls in Apia.

Chapter 5.   Strategic Perspective

Fijian performing ceremonial war dance

A STRATEGICALLY IMPORTANT part of the world by virtue of the sea-lanes of communication running through its vast maritime expanses, Oceania has remained relatively unmilitarized and peaceful since the end of World War II. As of mid-1984 the armed forces operating there that had the capability to affect the regional security setting belonged to four Western nations: Australia, New Zealand, the United States—all three allied since 1951 under a security treaty—and France, which had territories in the region. Only United States forces in Hawaii and Guam were of strategic significance or could mount sizable operations; by and large they kept to areas above the equator. Below the equator French forces generally formed the largest military element in Oceania, excluding New Zealand.

Oceania was largely ignored by military analysts from the late 1940s until the mid-1970s, its status as a secure area for the Western nations active there being widely taken for granted. Reports in 1976, however, that the Soviet Union had made overtures to Tonga and Western Samoa—and established diplomatic relations with the former—motivated Australia and New Zealand to ask the United States to expand its aid programs and diplomatic contacts in the South Pacific in order to foster stability and preclude the Soviet Union from gaining influence in the region. To the north of the equator, the United States was also very active during the late 1970s in negotiations over changing the political status of the Trust Territory of the Pacific Islands, which it administered under a United Nations trusteeship arrangement. France continued to confine its activity to its own territories and to its nuclear testing program in French Polynesia.

Although the mid-1970s witnessed a reawakening of military interest in Oceania—especially by Australia, New Zealand, and the United States—this fell far short of catapulting the area into a position of prominence in geostrategic calculations. It was generally agreed that the region, particularly that portion below the equator, continued to hold relatively little interest for the Soviet Union. Even above the equator, Soviet naval activity in the Pacific has been centered to the north or to the east of Oceania. Moreover, although during the late 1970s Australia, New Zealand, and the United States began to devote more attention to the security aspect of their relations with Oceania, those nations have continued to eschew exerting a more active military presence in the region, apparently in the belief that their interests could best be secured through nonmilitary means and that raising the military profile of Oceania might itself draw Soviet attention to the area.

As of mid-1984 the independent and self-governing states of Oceania, by virtue of their historic heritage, democratic institutions, and economic ties, were generally oriented toward the West and looked to Australia, Britain, France, Japan, New Zealand, and the United States for guidance and support. Intergovernmental relations among island states have been peaceful, the regional style of problem solving being characterized by cooperation and consensus building. The potential for internal disorder escalating to involve outside actors and disturb regional security was clearly present, however, most notably in the French territory of New Caledonia, where an independence movement has been growing more militant. In addition, although there were few outstanding issues of dispute between island states, relations between Papua New Guinea and Indonesia have repeatedly been strained by incidents on their shared border.

A matter of special strategic significance in Oceania was the widespread distaste for all things nuclear—be it testing, waste, weaponry, or even energy. Much of the antinuclear movement has focused on the French nuclear testing program, which—despite deep-seated and strongly expressed opposition from the island states—the French declare will continue indefinitely as long as it is vital to France's national security. There has been strong support in the island states, sometimes expressed through regional institutions, for declaring a nuclear-free zone in Oceania. Individual states have at times closed their ports and waters to nuclear-powered and nuclear-armed vessels. This has proved troublesome for Australia, New Zealand, and the United States, which wanted to ensure that such a zone would not interfere with the ability to communicate with each other and fulfill the responsibilities of their security alliance.

Historical Background

Although Oceania had long been an area in which Western nations rivaled for economic or political advantage—or, around the turn of the twentieth century, for coaling stations—it was not until after World War I that the area first came to be viewed as having a strategic significance in world affairs. The war itself had little effect on the area. At its outset, however, Japan occupied German possessions in Micronesia, New Zealand took over German Samoa (Western Samoa), and Australia assumed control of Germany's holdings in northeastern New Guinea, the northern Solomon Islands, the Bismarck Archipelago, and the island of Nauru. Conflict associated with these operations and during the rest of the war was minimal, but the elimination of German power in the region and, more importantly, the emergence of Japan as a major actor in Pacific affairs and a potential rival of the United States represented a fundamental realignment in the Pacific Ocean area.

In a nine-power conference held in Washington in 1921–22, Japan, Britain, France, and the United States agreed to respect each other's rights in the Pacific, and the United States, Britain, and Japan—which had the world's three largest navies—agreed to stop their naval arms race by capping battleship and aircraft carrier tonnage at a ratio of five each for Britain and the United States and three for Japan. The rationale for Japan's lower rate was that, unlike the navies of the other two nations, the Japanese navy operated only in the Pacific Ocean. Japan also agreed reluctantly not to expand its bases and fortifications in the Pacific beyond those already in existence.

Despite these measures, however, Japan's determination to increase its influence in Asia and the Pacific remained strong, and the Japanese navy was expanded and modernized at a faster rate than were United States or British naval forces in the Pacific. On withdrawal from the League of Nations in 1933 after that organization condemned the invasion of Manchuria, Japan declared its holdings in Micronesia—up to that time administered under a League of Nations mandate—to be an integral part of the Japanese Empire. The islands were then closed off to non-Japanese and began to be developed into a series of fortified bases. In 1935, after repudiating the Washington naval limitations treaty, Japan began openly to build up its naval forces on a scale unmatched by either the United States or Britain.

World War II

Relations worsened in mid-1941 after the United States took an increasingly stiff line in protest of continuing Japanese expansionism in China and Indochina, and the British, Dutch, and United States governments imposed an embargo on shipments of scrap iron, steel, and, most importantly, rubber and petroleum to Japan. Having virtually no other source for these commodities—all critical to the maintenance of a modern state and to the buildup of their offensive forces—the Japanese decided to seize control of areas rich in these resources and exclude Western nations from the western Pacific. The seized areas, later to become part of the Greater East Asian Co-Prosperity Sphere, were to include most of the East Asian and Southeast Asian mainland, the Philippines, and the Netherlands East Indies. The Japanese planned to protect this territory by establishing a defense perimeter in the Pacific that would extend southward from the Kurile Islands in the northern Pacific, enclose Wake Island and the Mariana, Marshall, and Gilbert islands, then run west to Rabaul on the island of New Britain (see fig. 22).

In the Pacific the first of a string of Japanese attacks designed to attain these goals took place at Pearl Harbor, Hawaii, on December 7, 1941. Within a 24-hour period the Japanese had also struck Malaya, the Philippines, Guam, Hong Kong, Wake Island, and elsewhere (see Appendix A). The Japanese had control of Guam, the Gilberts, and Wake Island by late December. In January they took Rabaul as well as the island of New Ireland to complete the defense perimeter. By the end of March, Malaya, Singapore, and the Netherlands East Indies had fallen, and Burma had been overrun. The fall of the Philippines in early May ended organized resistance by United States, British, Dutch, and Australian forces inside the perimeter.

Plans to extend the perimeter further had already been drawn up. As early as February 1942, Allied forces had begun to strike territory already seized by the Japanese, and on April 18 carrier-based planes were able to make a daring bombing raid on Tokyo and other Japanese cities. Although these attacks did not accomplish much materially, they did force the Japanese to take unanticipated defensive measures. The Japanese were also alarmed by the buildup of Allied forces in Australia and by preparations to set up a protected southern route from the United States to Australia. Accordingly, they decided to cut Allied communications lines to Australia and extend the defense perimeter outward to the western Aleutian Islands, Midway Island, the New Hebrides, New Caledonia, Fiji, and the Samoa group. At the same time, air bases were to be established on the northeastern coast of New Guinea and at Port Moresby on the southeastern coast facing Australia to protect the new perimeter. Japan began occupying positions on the northeastern coast of New Guinea in March 1942 and entered the Admiralty and Solomon islands. Plans called for an invasion of Port Moresby via the Coral Sea in May.

Allied forces, under a command structure set up in March 1942, divided the Pacific into two major theaters. In the west

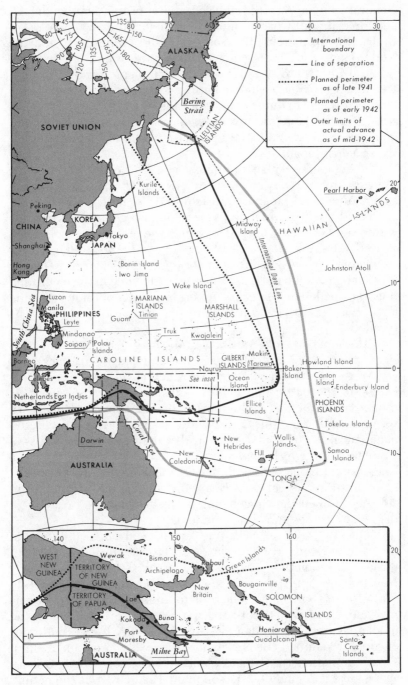

Figure 22. Japanese Advances in the Pacific in World War II, 1941–42

465

General Douglas A. MacArthur became supreme commander Allied forces, Southwest Pacific, which included New Guinea, Australia, the Bismarcks, the Solomons, the Philippines, and the Netherlands East Indies (not including the island of Sumatra). Admiral Chester W. Nimitz was appointed commander in chief, Pacific Ocean areas, which comprised most of the remainder of the western half of the Pacific. Allied forces were charged with resisting further Japanese advances, maintaining open lines of communication to Australia, and preparing for future counteroffensives against Japan.

The Japanese plan to launch a seaborne invasion of Port Moresby in early May had to be called off after a confrontation between Allied and Japanese forces in the Coral Sea. This was the first naval battle in which ships of the opposing forces never came within sight of each other, attacks on the adversary's vessels being carried out entirely by air. Although the battle resulted in a tactical victory for the Japanese, in strategic terms it represented a loss—too many Japanese airplanes were downed in the confrontation to provide adequate air support for the amphibious invasion force headed toward Port Moresby, which then had to be recalled.

The Japanese suffered another and far greater defeat in early June, when forces of the Imperial Navy advancing to attack Midway were met by a much stronger Allied naval force than anticipated. In the battle that followed, the Japanese lost their best trained naval pilots as well as most of their first-line aircraft carrier strength. For the Allies, the Battle of Midway represented a major turning point in the war in that it signaled Japan's loss of strategic initiative; brought Japanese naval strength down to a rough par with that of the Allies; gave the United States breathing space until its new class of Essex aircraft carriers became available; and forced the cancellation of Japan's plans to invade Fiji, the Samoa group, and New Caledonia.

Despite these setbacks, the Japanese advance continued in the southwestern Pacific. Japanese forces pushed southward through the Solomons, landing troops on Guadalcanal in early July 1942. In mid-July they also began an overland advance to Port Moresby via the Kokoda trail, for much of its way a very narrow and treacherous footpath crossing the steep slopes of the jungle-covered Owen Stanley Range. The very tough conditions encountered during the New Guinea campaign provided the first example of what the Japanese and Allied troops were to learn again and again, namely, that on many Pacific islands the natural environment could be at least as deadly as the opposing forces. By mid-September the Japanese had advanced to within 50 kilometers of Port Moresby. There, however, they drew back to regroup and await the outcome of operations on Guadalcanal, where United States forces had landed in early August in the first stage of the Allied counteroffensive.

On Guadalcanal, United States forces, at first poorly supplied and vulnerable to air strikes, were repeatedly attacked by the Japanese, who were successfully reinforced by sea through October. By November, however, after several naval engagements in the area, the United States had been able to reinforce its own troops, who then expanded their hold on the island. After successfully preventing the Japanese from landing further reinforcements, by early February 1943 the Americans were able to compel the evacuation of Japanese troops from Guadalcanal. The campaign, however, had provided a foretaste of the fanatical and determined resistance Japanese forces were to exhibit throughout the war. Meanwhile, in the New Guinea campaign, Australian, in time joined by American, forces, had been able to push the Japanese back along the Kokoda trail. By early 1943 the Japanese had been forced to withdraw from the Buna area to positions farther north on the New Guinea coast.

Encouraged by the successes on Guadalcanal and New Guinea, the Allies launched a two-pronged drive against Japanese positions in which MacArthur's forces advanced northwestward from New Guinea and Nimitz forces moved westward across the central Pacific. Determined to hold territory already seized, the Japanese strengthened the base at Rabaul and tried to maintain positions on New Guinea and in the Solomons. All areas under Japanese control, however, had begun to suffer from ever growing problems of supply caused by Allied air and submarine attacks on Japanese merchant and naval vessels. This severely limited the ability of the Japanese to reinforce positions on New Guinea and elsewhere, and Allied troops were able to fight their way slowly up the New Guinea coast, establishing new air and supply bases as they went. The Allies were also successful in seizing islands off the coast of New Guinea and in the central Solomons, where additional air bases were built to support the continuing advance. By the end of March 1944 the major Japanese stronghold at Rabaul had been effectively isolated.

In the central Pacific the Allies kicked off their offensive in November 1943 in a series of bloody confrontations against heavily fortified Japanese emplacements in the Gilbert Islands. As soon as possible, the Allies established airfields in the Gilberts, from which they launched operations against Japanese positions, first in the Marshalls and then in the Caroline Islands.

Pursuing a strategy of first making air strikes on certain Japanese fortifications and bases—including Rabaul and the Caroline islands of Yap and Truk (the latter a major Japanese naval base)—the Allies then isolated and leapfrogged some of the most heavily fortified Japanese positions. In this manner they advanced from the southeast into the western half of New Guinea and from the east to the northern Marianas, Guam, and the Palau Islands. The two forces joined in an offensive against the Philippines and then fought northward to Japan itself, already weakened by air strikes and supply shortages. Japan surrendered unconditionally on August 14, 1945, after the United States had dropped atomic bombs on the cities of Hiroshima and Nagasaki.

Devastation caused by World War II was obviously most extensive in areas within the combat zones, where assaults, military seizures, and liberation battles had turned settlements into rubble heaps and disrupted or destroyed local industries and communications systems. Thousands of islanders were wounded or killed in the process. Areas outside the combat zones were also greatly affected by the war, however. New Caledonia served as a major Allied naval base. On the Admiralty island of Manus, the Allies constructed a huge naval base, and advance air and naval posts were built on several islands in the New Hebrides. Fiji, Western Samoa, American Samoa, Tonga, the New Hebrides, some of the Cook Islands, and Bora Bora in French Polynesia were used as rest or assembly areas, training grounds, or fuel, service, or communications posts. Four uninhabited central Pacific atolls—Canton, Palmyra, Christmas, and Johnston—became air transport stations. French possessions contributed personnel for the Free French Pacific Battalion, which fought on the Allied side. Jungle scouts from Fiji and Tonga assisted the Allies in the northern Solomons. In both combat and noncombat areas, hundreds of thousands of islanders had been conscripted to serve on military bases or support military operations.

The Postwar Era: 1945–75

The defeat of Japan left six allied nations—Australia, Britain, France, the Netherlands, New Zealand, and the United States—in uncontested control of almost all of Oceania. In the easternmost extension of Oceania, Chile also had the small province of Easter Island. Former Japanese-mandated islands in Micronesia had come under the administration of the United States, which was acting under a United Nations strategic trust

Remains of World War II bunker of Japanese Admiral
Yamamoto Isoroku in Rabaul, Papua New Guinea
Courtesy Steven R. Pruett

agreement after 1947. Each of the six allied Western nations had significant strategic interests in the area, centering mainly on protecting their own territories and maintaining open lines of communications to and through Oceania. These interests, however, were easily secured in the peaceful postwar Pacific setting without resort to military force. Accordingly, almost all military facilities built during the war were rapidly decommissioned or abandoned, and, as the focus of geostrategic rivalry shifted to more volatile parts of the globe, military interest in the islands of Oceania waned.

Two developments in the 1950s helped ensure that Oceania commanded only the most limited attention from strategic and military planners. Primary of these was the 1951 Security Treaty Between Australia, New Zealand, and the United States of America (ANZUS), under which each signatory agreed to take necessary measures consistent with its own constitutional processes should the peace and security of any of the three be endangered by an attack on its territory or forces in the Pacific (see The ANZUS Treaty and Other Security Arrangements, this ch.). The treaty, which was seen by many to turn the Pacific Ocean into an "ANZUS lake," alleviated the concern of the two southern ANZUS partners over nearby islands and ocean areas; the focus of their strategic defense was then identified as lying far forward on the Southeast Asian mainland. In practice, the treaty also allowed the United States to focus attention on its territories lying to the north of the equator, trusting everything south of the equator except for American Samoa to its two ANZUS allies and its North Atlantic Treaty Organization allies, France and the Netherlands. Even in the northern Pacific, however, the Trust Territory of the Pacific Islands (TTPI) and Guam were situated well behind the lines of United States strategic defense, which under the containment policy lay on the Southeast Asian mainland, in Japan, the Philippines, the Republic of Korea (South Korea), and Taiwan.

Technological advances in long-range aircraft and ballistics missiles also helped perpetuate Oceania's low profile in geostrategic affairs. Most of the World War II airfields, even if lengthened as far as topography permitted, were unable to accommodate the new and larger aircraft. Moreover, the extended range of planes and missiles greatly reduced the need for air communications way stations or for mid-range bases to support military operations in Asia.

Although Oceania continued to be perceived as a backwater in geostrategic affairs well into the 1970s, several developments having military relevance nonetheless took place there in the interim. For the most part, however, these were not related to the security or defense of Oceania itself but instead resulted from either the relative isolation of certain islands or the proximity of others to Asian states. The United States base at Guam, for instance, unlike other World War II bases, was kept open after the war. It was used during the Vietnam Conflict as a staging point for manpower and matériel and as a base from which B-52 bombing raids were launched. During the early 1960s the United States also established a facility on Kwajalein in the Marshalls (part of the TTPI) to monitor missile flight tests; unlike the base at Guam, however, Kwajalein had no combat role.

Oceania was also used as a testing area for nuclear weapons (see The Nuclear Issue, this ch.). From 1946 to 1962 the United States conducted numerous aboveground, underground, and undersea test explosions in the central Pacific. Testing resumed in 1966—meeting growing protest from within Oceania—after France transferred its nuclear testing program from the Sahara to French Polynesia in 1963. After 1974 French tests were limited exclusively to underground blasts.

One further event of military significance in Oceania was the 1960–62 confrontation between Indonesia and the Netherlands over the status of the Dutch colony of West New Guinea, now known as Irian Jaya. The conflict ended when the Netherlands agreed to transfer provisional control of the colony to the United Nations to facilitate assumption of control by Indonesia in 1963. This marked the end of the Dutch presence in Oceania. Although military clashes associated with the confrontation were limited in scope and full-scale war was averted, Indonesia's forcible takeover of predominantly Melanesian Irian Jaya proved troublesome for some Pacific islanders. The issue was complicated by the existence of a guerrilla opposition movement there, which Indonesia alleged at times sought support and sanctuary in Papua New Guinea.

Security Setting since 1976

By the mid-1970s developments both within Oceania and outside it had helped transform the regional setting in very fundamental ways. To the south of the equator some of the most important changes were associated with decolonization; to the north they were augured by ongoing negotiations between the United States and the TTPI over modifying the trusteeship arrangement and accommodating greater internal self-rule. Both these developments had the potential to undermine security conditions in Oceania that Western nations previously could take for granted—namely, their ability to ensure strategic denial by preventing any hostile force from gaining access to resources or facilities having a military utility. The security situation had also been affected, at least indirectly, by several extraregional developments, including the winding down of the British presence "east of the Suez"; the enunciation in 1969 of the Guam Doctrine, in which the United States called upon its allies to contribute more to their own self-defense; and the general retrenchment of the United States military presence in Asia.

Until 1976 little attention had been paid to how these developments had affected the strategic setting south of the equator. The movement to independence in the South Pacific had progressed in an orderly and peaceful manner, and the new states shared a community of interests with the West and retained close and friendly ties with their former administrators. As the independent states grew more active in world affairs, however, they began to find common ground with each other. Using vehicles such as the South Pacific Forum, set up in 1971, the island states began to develop common approaches to regional problems and express positions on international issues in a collective voice that often carried more weight than had each acted singly (see Appendix B). This had drawn diplomatic attention to the region but had prompted little in the way of military interest. Nonetheless, the potential impact on regional security was implicit in such developments as the 1975 endorsement by the South Pacific Forum of the concept of instituting a nuclear weapons-free zone in the South Pacific.

Tonga's establishment of diplomatic relations with the Soviet Union in April 1976 and reports that the Soviets had offered Tonga aid in exchange for the rights to build an international airport and set up a permanent fishing base spurred strategic planners to take a new look at the security ramifications of decolonization in the South Pacific. Reports that Western Samoa had received similar overtures soon followed. China's establishment of diplomatic missions in Fiji and Western Samoa in 1976 also helped raise the profile of security issues in the South Pacific, but it was generally agreed that the Chinese would be hard-pressed to project a military presence so far from their shores; thus, their initiatives did not provoke the same degree of alarm as did those of the Soviet Union.

In retrospect, the Tonga incident proved significant mainly as a catalyst that sparked an overdue reappraisal of security in the South Pacific. As it turned out, the Soviet Union was not permitted to open a mission in Tonga. In fact, as of mid-1984 the only Soviet resident mission in Oceania was located in New Zealand; representatives to other states in the South Pacific were accredited through New Zealand and Australia.

The purported Soviet initiatives in the region caused the greatest alarm in Australia and New Zealand. At ANZUS meetings in 1976 and 1977 the two nations undertook to persuade the United States to accept their contention that Soviet activity in the South Pacific was sufficiently threatening to ANZUS interests to warrant more attention to security matters. Neither Britain nor France reemphasized security in their dealings in the area. British responsibilities were being reduced to a minimum by decolonization. Although France still had important territorial, economic, and strategic interests in Oceania, the French showed no signs of considering these to have come under any threat.

The issue of security was also raised in the 1976 decision of the South Pacific Forum to introduce a 200-nautical-mile Exclusive Economic Zone (EEZ—see Glossary) for each nation and the 1977 announcement that the South Pacific Forum would establish a fisheries organization to regulate maritime resources in those zones. For a time, at least, these decisions increased the level of uncertainty over what form the postcolonial regime in Oceania would assume. The announcements predestined changes to nautical charts and maps in which the small land areas of many island states would be dwarfed by their vast ocean areas. They also promised to leave only a few pockets of high seas open to uncontrolled exploitation. The announcements drew world attention to the resources that could come under the control of the new states—resources that over the long term could greatly increase their stratregic importance. For the island states themselves the extension of the EEZs presented challenging and expensive tasks of developing a maritime surveillance and patrol capability.

Having had it brought to their notice that the strategic setting in the South Pacific was changing, the ANZUS allies determined to take active steps to protect their own security interests. According to Australian analyst Richard Herr, the subsequent incremental increase in the level of attention the ANZUS nations paid to the new and emerging states in the South Pacific during the late 1970s can be traced to a commitment, never made explicit, that was undertaken in August 1976 at a meeting of the ANZUS Council of Ministers and reaffirmed the next year. He contends that the three nations agreed that it was totally unnecessary for them to take a direct military response to the situation. Instead, they resolved to increase economic assistance to the South Pacific and upgrade support for regional institutions there. Provision of military aid and development of regional defense cooperation were to form only a minor part of this. Because Australia and New Zealand had the closest bilateral ties to the South Pacific area, it was agreed that they should properly take the leading role in implementing the new policy. Herr asserts that by increasing economic assistance to the South Pacific the ANZUS nations intended to ensure that none of the new states would have to seek aid from any adversary of ANZUS or from sources deemed likely to promote radical ideologies. Additionally, by encouraging regionalism it was hoped that peer pressure and the influence of ANZUS nations themselves—each of which was a member of one or more regional institutions—would constrain individual decisionmakers in the South Pacific from pursuing any "adventurist" policies.

The increased activism by ANZUS members in the South Pacific during the late 1970s represented a break with the past in that the newly perceived need to protect common interests helped prompt Australia, New Zealand, and the United States to upgrade the level of resource commitment to the area; there was no major discontinuity in policy direction. Australia and New

Zealand had initiated a reappraisal of their defense priorities during the early 1970s and had for the most part already retracted their lines of forward defense from the Southeast Asian mainland to concentrate on defending their own national territories and the surrounding maritime environment. The priority Australia assigned to the South Pacific showed the greatest change; aid to the region for the 1977–79 period was four times what it had been for the previous three years. As before, however, most of this went to Melanesia, primarily to Papua New Guinea. New Zealand, already giving about as much as it could afford, continued to build on its already strong diplomatic and economic ties to Polynesia and Fiji and upgraded its defense cooperation in those areas. For the United States the new stress on the South Pacific primarily entailed a gradual enlargement of diplomatic and development assistance contacts in the area.

The United States had long been far more active to the north of the equator than to the south, by virtue of its relationship with Guam and the TTPI. Contrary to the case in the South Pacific, the movement toward political transition in the TTPI and the attempt to address islanders' desires for greater self-rule had generated considerable analysis of related security matters. During the early 1970s the United States initiated a reappraisal of the situation in Asia and the Pacific in order to refine its definition of American needs and interests in the TTPI. Up to that time United States defense policy had been based on the idea that American blood had been spilled to win the islands and that it was necessary to hold them to prevent a repetition of the costly island-hopping campaigns of World War II. This attitude had been reflected in the postwar provisions of the United Nations trusteeship agreement, which had empowered the United States to build or use military facilities in the TTPI or to close off the entire area for security reasons. Despite these provisions, however, the TTPI had not figured significantly in any United States military operations.

The reappraisal of United States strategic needs in the TTPI was affected by the territory's proximity to Guam and by developments outside Oceania itself. Important in this regard was the growing strategic importance of the base at Guam in light of its use during the Vietnam Conflict and its use as a forward base for Polaris submarines. The fall of the Republic of Vietnam (South Vietnam) and the United States decision to retrench its military presence in Asia had greatly upgraded Guam's significance as an element in the broader commitment of United States forces to Japan, the Philippines, and South Korea. Concern that the capability of the facilities at Guam might be overstrained and that they were vulnerable to accident or conflict revived interest in retaining the option to use certain islands in the TTPI as support installations for Guam. Owing to limitations of size, topography, and location, only Tinian and Saipan in the Marianas and Babelthuap in the Palaus were identified as useful in this regard. Other United States defense requirements comprised the continued use of the Kwajalein missile range and the ability to ensure strategic denial in the entire TTPI area.

As negotiations progressed during the mid- and late 1970s and different portions of the TTPI expressed interest in becoming independent from each other, separate arrangements had to be worked out for each. Much of the subject matter of the status negotiations focused on ensuring that defense and security requirements of both parties would be protected under any new arrangement. By the early 1980s provisional agreement had been reached with four separate political entites: The Commonwealth of the Northern Mariana Islands, the Federated States of Micronesia, the Republic of the Marshall Islands, and the Republic of Palau. Ancillary agreements had unique provisions concerning the future defense and security relationship with the United States (see the United States, this ch.). As of mid-1984 there were still matters to be resolved with Palau before the trusteeship agreement could be terminated.

By the early 1980s the initial urgency with which the Soviet threat to the region was viewed had subsided somewhat as observers subjected to sober analysis the capacity of the Soviet Union to expand into the region and its interest in doing so (see The Soviet Union, this ch.). Observers in the ANZUS nations and in island states nonetheless continued to be suspicious of Soviet intentions, especially in light of the rapid and steady expansion of Soviet military forces in Asia. The buildup had not directly affected Oceania as of mid-1984, but insofar as it could potentially threaten the existing military balance in Asia and the Pacific—which favored the ANZUS nations and their friends and allies—growth of Soviet military power was viewed with alarm. Wishing not to present the Soviets with an opportunity to establish a forward base in Oceania, the ANZUS nations as a matter of policy have encouraged island states to deny the Soviets any concessions. When necessary, the ANZUS nations have offered aid or other incentives to counteract or preempt a Soviet initiative. Indeed, it has been suggested that their demonstrated willingness to do so might tempt island states to "play the Soviet card" in order to reap the benefits of refusing a Soviet offer.

Although there did not appear to be an external threat to

Oceania as of mid-1984, several matters internal to the region had the potential to affect the overall strategic setting. The first and most important of these was the widespread support for establishing a nuclear-free zone in the Pacific in which nuclear weapons and nuclear testing would be banned. In some states antinuclear sentiment has prompted efforts to close off the entire region or—with some success—certain portions of it to transit by nuclear-powered or -armed ships and aircraft (see The Nuclear Issue, this ch.). The issue had serious ramifications for the ANZUS alliance, especially as antinuclear sentiment appeared to have great potency in New Zealand and, to a lesser extent, in Australia (see Australia and New Zealand, this ch.).

Interstate relations within Oceania were relatively free of the sort of disputes that might escalate to affect regional security. One exception, however, was the continuing border problems experienced by Papua New Guinea and Indonesia (see Papua New Guinea, ch. 2). At times these have resulted in Melanesian residents of Indonesia fleeing across the border to Papua New Guinea for various reasons. The two nations have settled all disputes peaceably, but there was underlying sympathy in Papua New Guinea for fellow Melanesians who lived across the border and who were perceived as being numerically overwhelmed by Indonesian immigrants. The Papua New Guinea government has been very careful to do nothing to aggravate its powerful neighbor, however, and to avoid any appearance of giving support to the Melanesian insurgent group in Indonesia.

Although there were many sources of tension within various island states that could disrupt internal security, only in one instance—Vanuatu in 1980—has a problem escalated to a degree beyond an island government's capability to handle it. In that case, the situation was quickly brought under control after Vanuatu secured support from Australia and Papua New Guinea to put down a secessionist movement on the island of Espiritu Santo. This example of regional cooperation on security matters prompted the Papua New Guinea government to sound out its neighbors on the possibility of forming a regional peacekeeping force. That suggestion met with little favor, however, for most island governments were uninterested in devoting time and resources to development of a military or internal security capability beyond what they already possessed.

As of mid-1984 one particular source of regional disorder lay in New Caledonia, where the movement for independence has divided the population and received strong support from the South Pacific Forum (see New Caledonia, ch. 2). That support has

*The French military presence in Oceania is
divided between the Territory of French Polynesia
and New Caledonia, where these sailors are stationed.
Courtesy "30 Jours", Nouméa*

so far been confined to rhetoric, but should the movement become radicalized, or the independence process move too slowly, there was a strong possibility that the issue might escalate to involve external actors, either from within Oceania or outside it. At the same time, there was also a danger that forces opposed to independence or to rule by the Melanesian-based independence movement might act in a manner that would disturb regional security. Support for the independence movement among the island governments was grounded in their strong preference for all territories to reach independence as expeditiously as possible. Less directly, it also reflected anti-French sentiments aroused by the nuclear testing program and by the perception that France has only grudgingly acceded to decolonization. As in other parts of Oceania, ethnic tension, landownership, and other issues compounded the problems faced by New Caledonia.

The ANZUS Treaty and Other Security Arrangements

Although there were several bilateral security guarantees and arrangements operative in Oceania during the early 1980s, the most important mechanism underwriting security in the area

477

was the ANZUS treaty, which was signed in San Francisco on September 1, 1951, and became effective on April 29, 1952. In that treaty Australia, New Zealand, and the United States declare their common desire "to strengthen the fabric of peace in the Pacific Area" (see Appendix C). In pursuit of that goal, the treaty commits all three to coordinating efforts for collective defense through consultation and mutual aid and to developing and maintaining their own capacity to resist attack. The treaty provides that the parties will consult with each other should any of their number believe its territorial integrity, political independence, or security to be threatened in the Pacific. Such a threat would encompass "an armed attack on the metropolitan territory of any of the Parties, or on the island territories under its jurisdiction in the Pacific or on its armed forces, public vessels or aircraft in the Pacific." In the event of such an attack, each of the parties agrees to meet the common danger in accordance with its own constitutional processes. The treaty continues in force indefinitely or until one year after any of the signatories gives notice of its intention to withdraw.

The sole organ of the treaty is the ANZUS council, which first met in 1952. The council comprises the foreign ministers of each of the three nations or their deputies. A military representative is designated by each member to assist the minister in an advisory capacity. The council has no permanent secretariat. It has met on an annual basis, the location rotating among the three capitals.

The treaty was originally formed pending the development of a more comprehensive system of regional security for the Pacific area. In the absence of this, the council has evolved into a forum for the discussion of common concerns and regional and international developments. It has also been used to coordinate policy, particularly toward the region. Outside the formal council framework, informal consultation and other forms of practical cooperation among ANZUS members have taken place on a regular basis. Such activities have included information and intelligence exchanges, joint military exercises, and naval visits to each other's ports.

In the years since the ANZUS treaty first went into effect, various newly independent states have expressed interest in ANZUS membership or in securing bilateral defense ties with ANZUS partners. Such guarantees had not been extended as of mid-1984. Most observers of the security setting in Oceania have noted, however, that the island states are to some extent covered by the ANZUS umbrella because the treaty partners would probably consider a direct attack on one of the island states of Oceania a threat to their own national security. Any attack on an ANZUS partner's armed forces or vessels sent to aid a beleaguered state would also trigger the treaty.

In addition to the ANZUS security treaty, there were several bilateral security arrangements in Oceania. France had obvious responsibility for the defense of its overseas territories of New Caledonia, Wallis and Futuna, and French Polynesia, as did Chile for its province of Easter Island, and Indonesia for Irian Jaya. Presumably, Britain continued to hold this responsibility for the Pitcairn Islands. The United States territories of American Samoa and Guam also enjoyed similar protection by virtue of being sovereign United States soil. As of mid-1984 responsibility for the defense of the TTPI continued to devolve to the United States pending the anticipated termination of the United Nations trust agreement. At that time separate arrangements between the United States and each of the four political entities to be created would come into effect (see The United States, this ch.).

New Zealand and Australia also had defense links with various island states. New Zealand exercised responsibility for the defense of the freely associated states of Cook Islands and Niue and for Tokelau, a dependent territory under its administration. New Zealand's treaty of friendship with Western Samoa had no defense aspect, but New Zealand has provided Western Samoa with security support assistance, as it has to Tonga and Fiji. Australia had no formal defense arrangements with any of the island states but retained close ties to the Papua New Guinea Defense Force and has also provided security support assistance to other island states, including Solomon Islands, Nauru, and Vanuatu.

Oceania in Strategic Terms

During the early 1980s the major actors affecting the strategic setting in Oceania were the United States, Australia, New Zealand, and France. The Soviet Union, by virtue of its potential to intervene in the area, was also an important shadow figure in the strategic equation. Britain and Chile retained security ties to the region, as to a greater extent did Indonesia, which also had a security stake in maintaining friendly ties with Papua New Guinea and other Melanesian states in order to preclude their support for Melanesian insurgents in Indonesia. The Chinese presence in Oceania was mainly confined to the diplomatic sphere, although that nation had small trade and aid links to the area. Japan had growing economic interests in much of

Oceania but, like China, showed no prospect of becoming militarily involved in the region or otherwise affecting security there. As of mid-1984 it appeared that Japan's stated interest in undertaking increased responsibility for the defense of sea-lanes in the Pacific would encompass areas "up to 1,000 miles" from Japan but not impinge on the waters of Oceania.

The United States

From the end of World War II until the mid-1970s the United States in effect treated Oceania as two separate regions: one lying below the equator and, excepting American Samoa, under the control of allies and needing no particular United States attention, and another lying above the equator and comprising Guam, the TTPI, and Hawaii, all areas in which the United States had substantial interests. This distinction between the two regions began to be undermined during the early 1970s, however, as the United States began to meet the increased opportunities for involvement in the South Pacific and to move away from its former policy of benign neglect toward that area. The process got a noticeable boost after Australia and New Zealand importuned the United States to take more active steps to offset potential Soviet interest in the South Pacific, and security considerations became one of a number of factors influencing United States action below as well as above the equator.

In 1978 the United States outlined a framework for future activity in the South Pacific, within which it proceeded to work throughout the early 1980s. That framework called for "understanding and sympathy for the political and economic aspirations of the South Pacific peoples" [and support for] regional cooperation; particularly close and cooperative ties with Australia and New Zealand; and continued cooperation with France and the United Kingdom in support of progress of the South Pacific peoples." Guided by these principles, the United States expanded its diplomatic and economic contacts with the region, at the same time insisting that there would be no attempt to usurp the dominant position of Australia and New Zealand in the area. It also began providing certain states, including Tonga, Papua New Guinea, Solomon Islands, and Fiji, with very modest amounts of defense aid, much of which came under the International Military Education and Training (IMET) Program during the early 1980s.

Part of the United States effort to pursue closer relations with the South Pacific states entailed relinquishment of claims to certain islands also claimed by other states. This was accomplished through four treaties, signed during the 1978–80 period and ratified by the United States Senate in 1983. Two of those four treaties—those with Tuvalu and Kiribati—had a defense aspect, containing clauses that provided for consultations with the United States in the event of a perceived threat to those states or prior to permitting any third party to use local bases.

At the same time that the United States outlined the policy dimensions of its increased attentiveness toward the South Pacific in 1978, it also announced its intentions to pursue above the equator "the Micronesian status negotiations with the goal of achieving a free association agreement between the United States and Micronesia and termination of the Trusteeship by 1981." The linkage of what theretofore had been treated as unrelated matters appeared to grant recognition to pervasive sentiments in the South Pacific—as well as the TTPI—that all territories in Oceania should proceed as quickly as possible toward some form of independence. Although difficulties surrounding the negotiations still had not been resolved entirely as of mid-1984, by the early 1980s the United States had increasingly come to treat Micronesia as part of an emerging "Pacific Islands Community." It was envisaged that the Micronesian states would in due time integrate more closely with those of the South Pacific, possibily through membership in regional institutions already in place.

United States policy toward Oceania as of mid-1984 continued to be based on the framework enunciated in 1978, emphasizing United States participation in the region on a partnership basis. The defense aspect of United States policy called for "maintaining, in conjunction with friends and allies in the region, military forces adequate to deter any acts hostile to our independence and integrity." To this end the United States has expressed its interest in retaining contingency access to portions of the TTPI. Beyond that, however, it was stated that existing bases on Guam and Hawaii and access to facilities at American Samoa were sufficient to accomplish its goals. Access to other ports for reprovisioning and shore leave would be beneficial but not essential. The United States emphasized, however, that to fulfill its obligations under the ANZUS alliance, its naval forces must be free to move through the entire Pacific. It strongly contended that closure of any waters to nuclear-armed or nuclear-powered vessels or aircraft would severely hamper its ability to respond to contingencies in the Pacific or to engage in military exercises with or support its ANZUS allies.

United States strategic interests in Oceania have long derived from several sources and have been territorial, political, economic, cultural, and military in nature. The United States had a direct territorial interest in Hawaii, American Samoa, and Guam. Guam itself was an especially valuable asset because it was politically secure and ideally located for supporting allies and friends in Asia and the Pacific and acting as a forward defense base for Hawaii. An element of the United States Air Force Strategic Air Command was stationed on Guam. United States naval facilities located there provided repair and reprovisioning for United States naval craft, including strategic nuclear submarines. Guam was no longer a base for strategic nuclear submarines, however.

The United States had territorial interest in Wake and Midway islands, the latter being under the control of the United States Navy. Several other isolated islands in Oceania, some uninhabited, were also under United States jurisdiction, including Howland, Baker, and Jarvis islands, Kingman Reef, and Palmyra and Johnston atolls.

As of mid-1984 the United States remained responsible for the defense of the TTPI and was anticipated to continue to do so, although under different and varying terms, after termination of the trusteeship agreement. At that time, the United States was scheduled to incur an indefinite defense responsibility for the Commonwealth of the Northern Mariana Islands. The United States had leased land on Tinian and Saipan for possible future use by its armed forces.

United States defense requirements in the other three entities in the TTPI were contingent upon approval of the Compact of Free Association, a framework for future multifaceted relationships with the United States. The Federates States of Micronesia (FSM) and the Republic of the Marshall Islands had both approved the relationship in their acts of self-determination, and their agreements were awaiting approval of the United States Congress as of mid-1984. The agreement with the Republic of Palau was more problematic. In a plebiscite held in February 1983, the compact was endorsed by 62 percent of Palau's population, but this was short of the 75 percent necessary under Palau's Constitution, which stipulates that margin of approval to contravene provisions on the Constitution that essentially establish a nuclear-free Palau in which access by nuclear-powered ships and the transit and overflight of nuclear weapons would be forbidden. These provisions were inconsistent with the defense responsibility and authority of the United States under the free association arrangement.

Under the free association agreements, the United States

*United States missile-tracking and -testing facility
at Kwajalein in the Marshall Islands
Courtesy Patricia Luce Chapman*

would assume responsibility for the defense of the Marshall Islands and the FSM for a minimum of 15 years and of Palau for 50 years. During those periods the United States would retain the right to disapprove any act, after consultation with the relevant government, that would, in the United States view, compromise United States security. For the same periods the United States could also foreclose any third-party use of local territory for military purposes.

The United States also had separate agreements with each of the three covering military requirements. The agreement with the Republic of the Marshall Islands provided for the continued use of the Kwajalein missile range for up to 30 years. That with the FSM provided for transit rights and for the continued presence of a United States Coast Guard station on Yap but did not seek bas-ing arrangements. Under the first Military Use and Operations Rights Agreement with the Republic of Palau, the United States, after consultation with the government of Palau, could make contingency use of various parts of the nation. This contingency right ran for 50 years and encompassed access to anchorage rights in Palau's main harbor, use of nearby land areas for support facilities, joint use of Palau's airfield, use of a further tract of land for logistics installations, and periodic access to other parts of Palau for training exercises. As of mid-1984 the United States apparently foresaw no need to exercise these contingency rights, however. As of mid-1984 a somewhat revised Compact and Military Use and Operations Rights Agreement had been negotiated with Palau, but neither government had formally approved it.

In addition to these territorial and other defense interests, the United States also had an important economic, political, and military interest in maintaining open sea-lanes of communication in Oceania. United States trade with its Asian and Pacific neighbors was estimated to constitute nearly 30 percent of the nation's total foreign trade in 1983, more than United States trade with Europe. A significant proportion of United States naval traffic was also borne over waters of the Pacific. In this regard Micronesia's critical geographic location has rendered it an especially vital strategic area for the United States. Although in peacetime the most heavily traveled sea-lanes in the Pacific run to the north of Oceania, connecting the west coast of the United States with Japan and East Asia, in the event of conflict those sea-lanes would move south, as they did during World War II, to pass through Micronesia. In peacetime Micronesia lies astride major trade routes connecting the United States with the Indian Ocean and Southeast Asia. Naval traffic between the United States and the Philippines and the Indian Ocean also regularly transits Micronesian waters. Other sea-lanes in which the United States has an interest include routes used by friends and allies that run north-south through Melanesian states in the western Pacific and others that cross the South Pacific to connect Australia and New Zealand with the United States, the Panama Canal, and Latin America.

Beyond seeing to the well-being of its territories and maintaining open sea-lanes of communication, United States economic interest in Oceania primarily concerned securing nondiscriminatory access to resources in the region. The only major problem it has experienced in this regard arose out of a jurisdictional dispute over the control of migratory species of fish, primarily tuna. United States law does not recognize the right of individual states to control such species, arguing that by virtue of their migratory habits they live in the ocean at large and not in the waters of any one state and that a regional rather than a national approach was therefore the best way to manage and conserve these species. In contrast the Pacific island states have contended that tuna is one of the few resources available for their exploitation and that each state can exert control over any fish while in its EEZ. Although the issue has caused contention in Oceania, as of mid-1984 it had not disrupted regional security and appeared unlikely to do so.

Australia and New Zealand

Southern Oceania was first viewed as strategically vital to Australia and New Zealand during the nineteenth century, when groups in the British colonies located there urged Britain, with varying degrees of success, to annex several nearby islands as a security shield against non-British influence. Interest in the security of neighboring islands was also demonstrated by the prompt moves of both Australia and New Zealand to take over German possessions at the onset of World War I.

Events of World War II strongly reinforced the perception in both states that a direct relationship existed between their own security and that of maritime regions to the north. Partly in recognition of this, the two concluded the 1944 Australian-New Zealand Agreement, which, aside from providing a formal basis for defense cooperation with each other, called for the establishment of a welfare organization to promote the social and economic development of people living in the Pacific islands and a military alliance to oversee regional security. The former of these aspirations was realized in 1947, when the six Western nations having territorial interests in Oceania agreed to participate in the South Pacific Commission (SPC), an advisory body providing economic and other assistance to the island territories (see Appendix B).

It proved more difficult to develop an effective military alliance. The 1944 agreement had initially been drawn up to proclaim that any postwar policing role in non-Japanese island territories in the Pacific should be reserved for Australia and New Zealand. It very quickly became apparent, however, that this task was far beyond the capability of the two states, and any fear that the United States might usurp the two states' position in the South Pacific was rapidly replaced by a desire to involve the United States more closely in underwriting security there. Much of the turnaround was attributable to changes in the governments of both states and to fears of a resurgence of Japanese militarism.

During the late 1940s Australia led an effort to persuade the United States to involve itself in a regional security arrangement for the Pacific island area. That effort met with success in 1951 when the United States agreed to enter into the ANZUS alliance, at the same time securing the signatures of Australia and New Zealand to the peace treaty with Japan.

Confident that the security of Oceania was adequately protected by the ANZUS treaty, both states devoted limited attention to the defense aspect of their relations with the island states until the purported Soviet overtures to Tonga and Western Samoa in 1976. That motivated them to elicit an ANZUS commitment to increase emphasis on attending to security matters in Oceania as well as to upgrade bilateral efforts to promote a stable environment in Oceania that would serve their own security interests. There were important differences, however, between Australia's and New Zealand's strategic vantage point on Oceania and their defense postures toward the region.

Australia's strategic outlook on Oceania reflected the fact that its pivotal geographic location renders it vulnerable to a widely defined strategic environment in which historical circumstance has demonstrated it could not stand alone. Australia came under direct attack from the Pacific during World War II—a threat it was quite conscious could not have been turned back without United States assistance. That experience motivated Australia to place a higher emphasis on defense than was the case for New Zealand, which had not been directly threatened. That attitude was reinforced during the 1950s and 1960s as the nation perceived threats to its national security emanating from Southeast Asia. More recently, Australia has also expressed concern over its third flank, the Indian Ocean, and over long-term intentions of the Soviet Union, especially in the wake of its invasion of Afghanistan. In all these cases, Australian security interests were seen as broadly coinciding with those of the United States. These experiences have helped sustain in Australia a bipartisan commitment to the ANZUS alliance.

There has nonetheless been some controversy within Australia over reconciling antinuclear sentiments in certain elements of the population with requirements for supporting the ANZUS alliance. This has been expressed at times in reluctance to permit vessels to pay port calls unless they guarantee they are not carrying nuclear weapons. In one instance in early 1984, the British aircraft carrier H.M.S *Invincible* was refused access to dry-dock facilities in Sydney because Britain—like the United States—refuses as a matter of policy to confirm or deny whether any of its ships carry nuclear weapons. Shortly after that incident, however, the Australian government approved a policy stating that friendly warships would not be required to make such assurances before entering Australian ports and that access to dry-dock facilities would be made on a case-by-case basis to ensure adequate safety standards.

Australia was the biggest aid donor to the South Pacific. Most of that assistance was targeted on nearby Melanesian states, particularly on Papua New Guinea, which was under Australian administration before becoming independent in 1975. Although it had no defense treaty with Papua New Guinea, or with any island state for that matter, Australia was responsible for the development of the Papua New Guinea Defense Force and has continued to provide training and support assistance to meet the nation's modest security requirements. Most of this support has been made available through a defense aid program initiated in mid-1977. Under that program Australia has also provided security support assistance to other island states, including Fiji, Solomon Islands, and Vanuatu.

Australian defense assistance has taken many forms. In 1980 Australia played an important support role for the Papua New Guinea forces deployed to restore central government control of the island of Espiritu Santo in Vanuatu. Australian military forces, albeit in decreasing numbers, continued to be stationed in Papua New Guinea to advise and support the Papua New Guinea Defence Force. Australia provided support and training to Fiji troops that were dispatched under United Nations (UN) auspices to Lebanon in 1978 and Zimbabwe in 1980. It also helped meet the costs for training the Vanuatu Mobile Force in Papua New Guinea (see Vanuatu, ch. 2). Military personnel from Papua New Guinea and other island states have also been offered training in Australia. One component of the defense aid package for the early 1980s funded a project to assess the maritime surveillance needs of the island states. There were suggestions in late 1983 that Australia might cooperate with certain island states to make regular trimonthly overflights of their extensive EEZs. Data collected under such a program would have a clear utility for keeping track of fishing craft as well as other vessels, including submarines.

Defense aid has generally constituted well under 10 percent of total Australian aid to the region. The combined civil and defense aid package, however, has been rationalized as a vehicle by which Australia can serve its own security interests through encouraging stability in its neighborhood. Some civil assistance has therefore been targeted on projects having a clear utility for security maintenance, including development of local police forces, coastal survey, and channel clearance.

In contrast to Australia, the South Pacific was the sole area of the world in which New Zealand considered itself to have a direct strategic interest. Official defense policy was predicated on the fact that New Zealand was a Pacific country having many citizens of Polynesian origin and that as such its national security depended on maintaining the goodwill and cooperation of neighboring states. Since the late 1970s that defense policy has been based on supporting the ANZUS alliance while pursing individual initiatives designed to advance regional security.

To this end, the nation provided aid to several South Pacific island states, one component of which focused on security assistance, primarily to Fiji and the Polynesian states. Defense relations with Fiji were particularly close. New Zealand helped develop the Royal Fiji Military Forces, and until December 1980 a New Zealand officer served on secondment as its chief of staff. New Zealand provided training in both Fiji and New Zealand for Fiji forces assigned to UN peacekeeping forces in the Middle East as well as to other Fiji troops. New Zealand army troops regularly conducted jungle-training exercises in Fiji.

New Zealand has also provided training for defense forces personnel from Tonga and Papua New Guinea, both in those states and at home. Military engineers and other support personnel have regularly provided disaster relief assistance and miscellaneous civil support, such as reef blasting, surveying, and bridge building, to these as well as other states. In late 1983 the New Zealand minister of defense announced plans to establish a battalion-sized unit—to be called the Ready Reaction Force—that would be deployed to South Pacific island countries to offer assistance where New Zealand's interests accorded with those of its neighbors.

As of mid-1984 New Zealand was the only nation in Oceania where the Soviet fishing fleet was permitted to pay port calls and maintain shore facilities. The Soviets were granted access in the late 1970s in part because it was believed that this would defuse Soviet efforts to secure similar facilities in smaller island states that had less ability to absorb a Soviet presence without cultural, political, and economic dislocation. In part, the decision also reflected New Zealand's dependence on foreign trade and its need to maintain good relations with an important trading partner.

Although the South Pacific promised to retain its strategic significance for New Zealand, it should be noted that public controversy during the early 1980s over how best to provide for national defense had cast uncertainty over the nation's future defense posture. An official call in 1982 for public debate on this topic brought forth several suggestions, including withdrawal from the ANZUS alliance, opting for armed or unarmed neutrality, or becoming nonaligned. Opponents of current defense policy expressed fear that membership in the ANZUS alliance might make New Zealand a target for nuclear attack. Many noted that the nation has never faced a direct threat, and none was foreseen developing. The defense debate was closely related to very strong antinuclear sentiments in the nation and to associated public support for the proposal to establish a nuclear-free zone in the South Pacific. These were not new issues. During the 1972–75 period it was official government policy to close the nation's ports to nuclear-armed or nuclear-powered vessels. Ship visits were again permitted after a change in government, but support for reinstituting the ban was very strong in the early 1980s. In 1982 and 1984 bills to do just that were defeated by only one vote in parliament. The outcome of this debate was indeterminate as of mid-1984 but could have serious implications for the ANZUS alliance and for the South Pacific security setting.

France

Unlike the ANZUS allies, France was not a Pacific nation and considered the region neither vital to French national security interests nor related to its global strategy except indirectly through the nuclear testing facility in French Polynesia. Aside from that program, the strategic significance of the island territories arose from France's economic stake in New Caledonia and support for French language and culture in all three of its dependencies.

The French military presence in Oceania was divided between New Caledonia and French Polynesia. French forces were deployed in the Pacific to protect French territories from external aggression, act as a backup to internal security forces should the need arise, provide auxiliary logistics and disaster relief assistance to local governments, and maintain and protect the nuclear Pacific Test Center (Centre d'Expérimentation du Pacifique), which was located in French Polynesia.

French forces in New Caledonia operated under an interservice command structure. Personnel numbered approximately 2,800 as of early 1982. Formations included one marine infantry regiment of the French army as well as air force, naval air, and other support units. The French navy had a separate naval command for the Pacific, the air and communication center of which was located at Nouméa. The French Pacific Fleet as a rule comprised four surface combatants and five amphibious ships. These operated out of both New Caledonia and French Polynesia. Routine maintenance for the fleet was performed at Nouméa. Near Nouméa, at Tontouta, was an airfield where naval air detachments flew supply and liaison missions and a small air force unit was equipped with Puma helicopters used in a transport capacity.

Most French forces in French Polynesia were assigned to the nuclear test facility. Total military strength was approximately 5,000 as of early 1982. Personnel served under an interservice command, which comprised one marine and one infantry regiment of the French army as well as air force and naval air units. The headquarters of the nuclear test facility and a support base were located at Papeete on Tahiti. The air force also maintained a small number of light aircraft and helicopters there. A small naval air unit flew P-2H maritime patrol aircraft out of Papeete. A forward support base for the nuclear testing facility was located at Hao in the Tuamotu Archipelago, which had a deep-water port and an air strip equipped with a few helicopters. The nuclear test sites themselves were at Mururoa and Fangataufa atolls. These were chosen because they were uninhabited, located in an area crossed by few shipping lanes, easiily accessible, sizable enough to accommodate requisite scientific equipment, and believed to be geologically stable (see The Nuclear Issue, this ch.).

The Soviet Union

Oceania has never been an area of primary strategic interest for the Soviet Union and as of mid-1984 appeared ullikely to become so in the foreseeable future. Most Soviet strategic interest in the Pacific has been focused on areas to the north and east of Oceania, and the closest Soviet bases to the area were located some 3,000 kilometers west of the Palaus in Vietnam and over 5,000 kilometers northwest of the Northern Marianas in Vladivostok. There have been occasional and, it appears, isolated sightings of Soviet submarines in various parts of the region, but Oceania has remained essentially outside the normal deployment area of the Soviet navy and other military forces.

The Soviet Union is, however, a global power, and as such no area of the world is completely void of strategic significance to it. It was generally assumed that the Soviet Union had subsidiary strategic interests in Oceania that related to the sea-lanes of communication running through it and to the United States military presence in Guam and Hawaii. There has also been speculation that the Soviets might be interested in Oceania as a place where strategic submarines could be deployed to escape detection. This has been subject to debate, however, it being difficult to determine whether such action would be necessary or efficacious given the highly classified ratings assigned to state-of-the-art submarine technology. It has also been suggested, again not without dispute, that over the long term the Soviet Union might be interested in developing mid-range bases in Oceania to support operations in Antarctica.

The Soviet Union had very limited political and economic interests in Oceania, and there was little indication that these could grow sufficiently over the short or medium term to assume strategic significance. Soviet diplomatic influence among island states was very shallow; relations with Tonga and Western Samoa were conducted through resident missions in New Zealand and relations with Fiji and Papua New Guinea through resident missions in Australia. Vanuatu, which did not maintain relations with the Soviet Union, established diplomatic relations with Cuba in July 1983, but as of mid-1984 this had not appeared to have resulted in any increase in local Soviet influence.

There have been several reasons for the Soviets' lack of political influence in the area. The island states were basically pro-Western, and Marxist-oriented movements had little support. What diplomatic contacts the Soviets have had with the island states have at times been conducted in a style that provoked resentment among senior officials and diplomats in Oceania. Decisionmaking, both within and among island states, has been characterized by slow consensus building and courteous and careful attention to each party's viewpoint. The Soviets were seen as heavy-handed and unwilling or unable to conform to this "Pacific Way" of doing business. At the same time, the Chinese and the ANZUS nations have been adept at making a case for their own anti-Soviet outlook.

Soviet economic interests in Oceania were limited to fishing, merchant shipping, and cruise line operations. Only the first of these appeared capable of much expansion. Even there, however, most Soviet fishing in Oceania was done in the cold waters off New Zealand. The Soviets gave no military or economic aid to Oceania. Even including trade with Australia, trade with the region has at most accounted for under 2 percent of total Soviet foreign trade.

Notwithstanding the fact that it had few developed interests in the area, the Soviet Union's demonstrated willingness to attempt low-risk advances in other parts of the globe has kept the

ANZUS nations and several island states alert to the possibility of a Soviet probe in the area. Analysis of Soviet actions and intentions was open to subjective assessment, but there was little doubt that the buildup of Soviet military forces in the Pacific, which had been under way since the mid-1970s, has greatly enhanced the Soviet capability to operate in Oceania. A major factor in the buildup has been the explosive growth of the Soviet Pacific Fleet. Under Soviet military doctrine the navy functions not only as a defensive instrument in wartime but also as an agent of peacetime state policy. In the latter role it was to be used to pursue international objectives and project political influence. Access to port facilities and airfields in Vietnam, although still far distant from Oceania, has enhanced the Soviet capacity to project a presence in the area.

During the early 1980s there was a noticeable increase in the local operation of Soviet hydrographic research vessels, increasing numbers of which have been alleged to carry naval rather than civilian personnel. The research effort, sometimes conducted by aging submarines or disguised fishing vessels, formed part of a worldwide Soviet drive to advance knowledge of maritime conditions in general. The Soviets are recognized experts in the field. Because such knowledge had a clear military utility, however, especially regarding submarine operations, the ANZUS and island governments have tended to take a dim view of Soviet reseach in Oceania.

Soviet diplomatic behavior has contributed to their cool reception. In late 1980 the Soviet research vessel *Kalisto* offered its services to a committee associated with the UN Economic and Social Commission for Asia and the Pacific (ESCAP) at a meeting on Tarawa in Kiribati. The proposal that *Kalisto* would carry out a survey of the EEZs of Papua New Guinea, Solomon Islands, and Vanuatu on behalf of ESCAP was initially greeted favorably by the scientists and development officers attending the meeting. The three nations in question, however, were convinced by the ANZUS nations that security complications favored acceptance of a counteroffer under which a United States vessel would undertake the research. That decision was then endorsed by the South Pacific Forum in 1981. The *Kalisto* nonetheless began operations, to the displeasure of local states. Representatives of these states were also displeased by the efforts of the Soviet delegate to an ESCAP meeting in 1983 to have inserted into the ESCAP minutes a note saying that the Soviet government had offered data to ESCAP collected by the *Kalisto* in South Pacific island areas. Papua New Guinea and Solomon Islands protested the move, inserting in the minutes an additional note saying that the Soviet Union had "persisted in pressing its offer of marine research on [the ESCAP committee] members though these offers were clearly unwelcome."

The Nuclear Issue

Most of the strong antinuclear sentiment exhibited in the region has been focused on the French nuclear testing program. It was rooted in opposition to nuclear weapons per se and in fears of radiation contamination spreading from French Polynesia to the rest of Oceania. It was believed that no matter how isolated the test site, the movement of ocean currents made the Pacific the backyard of all islands, rendering distance no guarantee of safety. Opposition to testing has been intensified by resentment that the Pacific was being used by an extraregional state for purposes deemed too dangerous for its own home territory. The general perception that the French were insensitive to local opposition and intransigent or even arrogant in their dealings on the issue has also helped deepen antinuclear sentiment.

Nuclear testing in the area dates back to the initial United States testing program in the Marshall Islands, which began in 1946 with an explosion on Bikini Atoll and after 1947 used Eniwetok Atoll as well. By 1962, when the program was ended, tests had also been conducted on the uninhabited Johnston Atoll, a United States dependency in the central Pacific. In addition, both Britain and the United States had conducted tests on Kiritimati (formerly Christmas) Island in Kiribati. The United States has provided compensation to the Marshall Islanders for damage to their health and property. The terms of part of this compensation were incorporated into the text of the Compact of Free Association Between the Republic of the Marshall Islands and the United States (see Trust Territory of the Pacific Islands, ch. 3). The long-term effect of the tests on islanders' health has not been determined. Bikinians were permitted to resettle on their atoll in 1971 after it was cleared and declared safe, but tests in 1977 revealed that the atoll was still dangerously contaminated, and Bikinians were again forced to move. Residents of Eniwetok returned to their homes in 1976, but a nuclear waste dump on the atoll was projected to remain contaminated for several thousand years. There were reports in the early 1980s that residents of two atolls over 120 kilometers distant from the test sites were developing an unusually high incidence of thyroid tumors, a condition commonly associated with exposure to radiation.

France announced in 1963 that it was moving its testing program to French Polynesia. During the 1966–83 period it was estimated to have conducted over 100 individual test blasts there, the large majority on Mururoa Atoll and the remainder on nearby Fangataufa Atoll. Atmospheric testing was halted in 1975, but the switch to underground blasts did not defuse opposition to the program. In fact, several incidents in the interim have helped keep concern alive. Among these was an accident in 1979 in which two French workers were killed in an explosion in an underground laboratory. Less than three weeks later, part of Mururoa collapsed in the wake of a nuclear test explosion, causing a tidal wave. In March 1981 a hurricane was reported to have swept nuclear waste stored on Mururoa into the lagoon of the atoll and then out into the Pacific. Stories in the international press, denied by France, claimed that the atoll had been rendered geologically unstable by the repeated blasts. Hurricanes again hit the islands in 1982 and 1983, raising fears of similar accidents.

As of mid-1984 there was every indication that France would continue to use French Polynesia as a nuclear testing site. According to a statement in 1983 by the French ambassador to Fiji, France decided in 1962 that French independence and security required the nation to maintain nuclear armament sufficient to dissuade any aggressor. The only way this would be effective, however, was if the national nuclear capacity remained current, and that required continuous testing. Under these circumstances the French stated it was impossible to set a fixed date for ending the program. Official French statements have emphasized that there was constant and detailed monitoring of all test sites. France has flatly denied reports in the international press that there has been an increased incidence of cancer in the local population. In 1983 it released figures indicating that the cancer rate in French Polynesia was lower than that in Australia, New Zealand, or metropolitan France.

By the early 1970s the hostile reaction in the region to nuclear testing had led the island states to place greater scrutiny on the related issue of nuclear weaponry. This culminated in suggestions that a nuclear weapons-free zone be established in the Pacific in which nuclear weapons and nuclear testing would be banned. The idea was first officially put forward in the election policy of the New Zealand Labour Party government in 1972 but achieved prominence in 1975 when Fiji endorsed the idea. The proposition was then considered favorably by the South Pacific Forum, which agreed that the matter should be raised in the UN.

Later in 1975 Fiji, Papua New Guinea, and other island states urged support for the issue in the UN General Assembly. By 1976, however, the governments in Australia and New Zealand had both changed, and representatives of the new governments were able to lobby successfully for the forum to attach qualifications to the nuclear weapons-free proposal. These greatly watered down its terms and ensured that the United States could continue to operate in the area and that there would be no interference with the ability of the ANZUS partners to exchange port calls and conduct military exercises together. Under the new arrangement the forum declared that the proposed zone would not interfere with the principle of freedom of navigation on the high seas nor would it be developed in any way that would make it incompatible with "existing security arrangements."

That position was still officially in effect as of mid-1984, but the issue has been far from dormant in the intervening years. Reports in 1979 that Japan and the United States had considered using uninhabited islands in the Pacific as temporary storage sites for nuclear waste provoked widespread opposition and drew the condemnation of the South Pacific Forum. The United States and Japan insisted that they had no intentions of using any Pacific island for such purposes. Nonetheless, in 1980 Fiji protested the matter in the UN General Assembly and again called for a nuclear-free zone to be established in the Pacific. The same year Fiji also declared that, lacking the capacity to monitor radiation, it would have to close its ports to nuclear vessels. Fiji reversed that ban in 1983, however, stating that although it was still strongly opposed to nuclear weapons and to nuclear testing, the UN Convention on the Law of the Sea required that ports and sea passages be open to free maritime transit. The decision was also officiallly linked to Australian and New Zealand suggestions that the use of Fiji's ports by ANZUS vessels would enhance the ability of the alliance "to meet the security needs of the region in times of conflict"—a goal Fiji's government also shared.

Other states have also taken concrete measures to demonstrate their antinuclear sentiments. In 1982 Vanuatu refused entry to two United States ships that, following United States policy, refused to confirm or deny whether they were carrying nuclear weapons. The United States and certain of its allies considered such a move tantamount to identifying targets for potential adversaries. In early 1984 it was reported that Solomon Islands declared it would no longer permit vessels to enter its ports or transit its waters unless it received a commitment in writing that the vessel was neither nuclear-armed nor nuclear-powered. Provisions in the Constitution of Palau that bar use, testing, storage, or disposal of nuclear weapons in its territory helped create an impasse over how to end the trusteeship arrangement over the TTPI.

Appendix A

Selected Events of World War II Involving the Pacific Ocean

Date	Event
1941	
December 7–10	Japanese forces land on the east coast of Malaya; attack Pearl Harbor, Hong Kong, Guam, and Wake and Midway islands; conduct air strikes on the Philippines; bomb Nauru and Ocean Island (present-day Banaba); land on the north coast of Luzon in the Philippines; capture Guam
December 16	Japanese forces land on Borneo
December 18	Japanese forces land on Mindanao in the Philippines
December 19	Japanese forces move into Burma in strength
December 24	Japanese forces occupy Wake Island
December 25	Hong Kong falls
1942	
January-March	American forces begin arriving in Australia
January 2	Japanese forces occupy Manila
January 11	Japanese forces take Kuala Lumpur; land on Celebes in the Netherlands East Indies
January 23	Japanese forces land at Rabaul on the island of New Britain and on the island of New Ireland; begin building a major base at Rabaul
February 1	American naval forces shell Gilbert and Marshall islands
February 3	Japanese aircraft bomb Port Moresby on the island of New Guinea
February 15	Singapore falls
February 19	Japanese aircraft bomb Darwin, Australia
February 23	President Franklin D. Roosevelt orders General Douglas A. MacArthur to leave the Philippines for Australia
February 24	American naval air strike on Wake Island

497

February 27–28 . . . . .   Battle of the Java Sea; Japanese
                           forces invade Java in the Netherlands
                           East Indies

March 3 . . . .   Australian air strike on New Britain;
                           Japanese air strike on Port Moresby and sites
                           in northern Australia

March 8 . . . .   Japanese forces land at Lae and
                           Salamaua on New Guinea

March 9 . . . .   Dutch and other Allied forces in Java
                           surrender

March 10 . . . .   Japanese forces land on Buka in the
                           Solomon Islands

March 17 . . . .   MacArthur appointed supreme commander,
                           Allied forces, Southwest Pacific;
                           Admiral Chester W. Nimitz appointed commander
                           in chief, Pacific Ocean areas

April 18 . . . .   Air raid on Tokyo and other Japanese cities

May 3–8 . . . .   Japanese forces occupy Tulagi in the
                           Solomons; Battle of the Coral Sea ends Japanese
                           attempt at a seaborne invasion of Port Moresby

May 6–9 . . . .   Filipino and American resistance in
                           the Philippines ends

June 4 . . . .   Battle of Midway; Japanese fleet heavily
                           damaged by Allied fleet

July 6 . . . .   Japanese forces land on Guadalcanal
                           in the Solomons

July 21–29 . . . .   Japanese forces land at Gona on
                           New Guinea and advance to capture Buna and
                           then Kokoda

August 7–9 . . . .   American forces land on Guadalcanal
                           and Tulagi; capture Tulagi; naval battle of Savo
                           Island isolates American forces on Guadalcanal

August 11 . . . .   Japanese Combined Fleet relocates
                           eastward from Japan to Truk Island in the
                           Caroline group

August 23–25 . . . . . .   Naval battle in the eastern Solomons
                           prevents reinforcement of Japanese on Guadalcanal

August 23 . . . .   Japanese forces occupy Nauru and
                           Ocean Island

August 26 . . . .   Japanese forces land at Milne Bay in
                           New Guinea in an attempt to outflank Port Moresby,
                           but American and Australian defenders force
                           their withdrawal

September 5 . . . .   Japanese troops begin night landings
                           of reinforcements on Guadalcanal

September 11 . . . . . .   Japanese advance halts 50 kilometers
                           north of Port Moresby

September 13 . . . . . .   Battle of Bloody Ridge, Guadalcanal

September 23 . . . . . .   Australian forces counterattack
                           against Japanese forces north of Port Moresby

October 11–
   November 30 . . . . .   Series of naval battles for control

	of waters around Guadalcanal; Japanese eventually repulsed
October 13–16	Japanese heavy artillery and bombers pound American positions on Guadalcanal
November 1	American counteroffensive on Guadalcanal begins
December 2	First controlled nuclear chain reaction initiated at the University of Chicago
December 14	Japanese reinforcements land at Buna

1943

January 2	Australian and American forces capture Buna
February 1	Japanese evacuate Guadalcanal; withdraw from Wau on New Guinea
March 2–5	Battle of the Bismarck Sea thwarts Japanese attempt to reinforce New Guinea from Rabaul
March 25	American forces bomb Japanese airfield on Nauru
April 18	Admiral Yamamoto Isoroku, commander in chief, Japanese Combined Fleet, killed
May 18	Australian forces capture Mubo on New Guinea
June 22–30	American forces take Woodlark and Trobriand (Kiriwina) islands to set up airfields
June 29–30	American forces land at Nassau Bay on New Guinea to set up supply bases; land on Rendova and New Georgia, both in the Solomon Islands, to begin assault on Munda airfield on New Georgia
July 5–16	Japanese reinforce New Georgia from New Britain; naval battles of Kula Gulf and Kolombangara Island
August 5	Munda airfield captured
August 13–18	American air raids on Balikpapan on Borneo and Wewak on New Guinea
August 15	American and New Zealand forces land on Vella Lavella in the Solomons to set up airfields
September 4–16	Australian and American forces land at Lae and Nadzab on New Guinea; advance to capture Salamaua
September 18	American naval air strike on Tarawa in the Gilberts
September 22– October 2	Australian forces attack

	and take Finschhafen on New Guinea
October 5	American air strikes on Wake Island
October 6–7	American forces land on Kolombangara in the Solomons; naval battle during Japanese evacuation of Vella Lavella
October 20	Japanese forces begin reinforcement of Rabaul
October 27– November 6	New Zealand forces take Treasury Islands in preparation for assault on Bougainville in the Solomons
November 1	American forces land on Bougainville to establish airfields
November 5–11	Air strikes on Rabaul
November 12	Surviving Japanese carrier planes and warships withdrawn from Rabaul to Truk
November 20–23	American forces take Tarawa and Makin in the Gilberts; heavy losses on both sides; begin to build airfields
December 4	American air strikes on Kwajalein in the Marshalls
December 8	American battleships shell Nauru
December 15–30	American forces land on New Britain, capture Cape Gloucester airstrip, and establish control over Vitiaz and Dampier straits

1944

January 2	American forces land at Saidor on New Guinea to establish airfields
January 31– February 1	American forces land at Kwajalein and Majuro atolls in the Marshalls
February 10	Japanese Combined Fleet relocates westward from Truk to the Palau Islands
February 15	Australian and New Zealand forces take Green Islands near New Ireland
February 17–22	American forces attack and secure Eniwetok Atoll in the Marshalls
February 29– March 9	American forces land in the Admiralty Islands north of New Guinea and begin construction of a major naval base on Manus
March 20	American forces land in the Bismarck Archipelago to complete the ring of airfields around Rabaul
March 30	American naval air strikes against the Palau Islands

April 22–26 . . . . Preceded by weeks of air strikes,
American forces land at Hollandia in
West New Guinea and Aitape in
northeastern New Guinea; secure
airfields at Hollandia; Australian
forces build airfields at Aitape

May 17–18 . . . . American forces land
at Arare in West New Guinea
and on offshore island of Wakde

May 27 . . . . American forces invade Biak in the
Netherlands East Indies, where
Japanese forces are deeply dug in

June 11–15 . . . . American forces bomb,
then invade Saipan in the Marianas

June 19–21 . . . . Battle of the Philippine Sea
deals severe blow to the
Japanese Combined Fleet

July 2 . . . . American forces land on
Noemfoor off New Guinea
to seize airfields

July 7–9 . . . . American forces secure Saipan
after suicide assault by Japanese

July 10–13 . . . . Japanese counteroffensive
at Aitape on New Guinea met
by Australian and American forces

July 21 . . . . American forces land on Guam
after extensive naval
bombardment of the island

July 24 . . . . American forces land on Tinian
in the Marianas

July 28 . . . . Organized Japanese resistance on
Biak ends

July 30–31 . . . . American forces land at Sansapor
to complete the occupation
of the northern coast of New Guinea
and to set up airfields to strike
the northern Philippines and the
Netherlands East Indies

July 31 . . . . American forces secure Tinian

August 10 . . . . Japanese forces withdraw from
Aitape toward Wewak on New Guinea;
American forces begin bombardment
on Iwo Jima

August 12 . . . . Guam secured

September 15–20 American forces land on
Peleliu and Angaur islands in the
Palau group; meet fierce resistance

September 23 . . . . . . American forces occupy
Ulithi Atoll in the Carolines
to build naval base

October 10–21 . . . . . . Regular naval air strikes
commence on Philippines,

	Formosa, and Ryukyus
October 17–25	American forces land on
	Philippine island of Leyte
	to begin work on airfields;
	Battle of Leyte Gulf demolishes
	core of the Japanese fleet despite
	the first organized use
	of kamikaze attacks
November 24	American forces begin first B-29
	raids on Tokyo and other
	Japanese cities
November 25	Organized Japanese resistance
	on Peleliu ends
December 25	American forces secure Leyte

1945

January 9	American forces land on Luzon
February 19	American forces land on Iwo Jima
	after prolonged air and naval
	bombardment; meet stiff resistance
March 3	Japanese resistance in Manila ends
March 15	American forces secure Iwo Jima
April 1	American forces land on Okinawa
April 2	President Roosevelt dies;
	President Harry S Truman
	assumes office
May 11	Battle of Wewak, the last Japanese
	stronghold on the northern coast
	of New Guinea
June 22	Organized resistance on Okinawa ends
July 4	MacArthur announces the liberation
	of the Philippines
July 16	First atomic bomb tested
	in New Mexico
August 6	United States drops atomic bomb
	on Hiroshima
August 9	United States drops atomic bomb
	on Nagasaki
August 14	Japan surrenders unconditionally
September 2	Surrender formally signed

Note—Accepted dates may vary according to observer's location relative to the international date line. See figures 1, 5, 7, 8, 14, and 22 for locations of place-names.

Appendix B

Regional Organizations

South Pacific Commission

Headquarters and Secretariat: Nouméa, New Caledonia

Origin: The South Pacific Commission was established by Australia, Britain, France, the Netherlands (which withdrew in 1962), New Zealand, and the United States under an agreement signed in Canberra, Australia, on February 6, 1947, effective July 29, 1948. The purpose of the commission is to advise and assist the participating governments and territorial administrations in promoting the economic, medical, and social development of the peoples of Oceania. The commission's work program includes such fields as agricultural development, conservation, cultural exchanges and preservation, development of marine resources and research, English-language teaching, environmental health, epidemiology, fisheries, nutrition, plant diseases and protection, prevention of fish poisoning, regional communications, statistical training, sanitation, and youth and community work. In recent years rural development and regional integration and planning received increasing attention.

Membership:

American Samoa	Niue
Australia	Northern Mariana
Britain	Islands
Cook Islands	Palau
Federated States	Papua New Guinea
of Micronesia	Pitcairn Islands
Fiji	Solomon Islands
France	Tokelau
French Polynesia	Tonga
Guam	Tuvalu
Kiribati	United States
Marshall Islands	Vanuatu
Nauru	Wallis and Futuna

New Caledonia   Western Samoa
New Zealand

Organization: The principal decisionmaking body of the commission is the South Pacific Conference, which meets annually in different locations and is attended by delegates from the member countries and territories. The conference adopts the rules of procedure, approves the agenda for each annual session, discusses matters of common interest, and makes recommendations to the commission on such matters. Decisionmaking is by consensus; unless all efforts at consensus building have been exhausted, voting on substantive issues is forbidden. Should consensus building fail, a decision would require the affirmative vote of two-thirds of all commission members present and voting.

The commission's annual budget is financed by contributions assessed according to per capita income in the case of the insular governments and territorial administrations. Australia, Britain, France, New Zealand, and the United States contribute according to the prospective national interest and benefit from the work of the commission and the administrative responsibilities of the respective states. About 93 percent of the 1984 budget of US$3.4 million was borne by the five remaining original members: Australia, 34 percent; the United States, 17 percent; New Zealand, 16 percent; France, 14 percent; and Britain, 12 percent. The remainder came from contributions by other members.

The chief executive officer of the commission is the secretary general, who is elected by members of the commission. Since 1969 this post has been held by islanders, testament to the growing participation by the insular countries of Oceania.

South Pacific Forum

Secretariat: Suva, Fiji.

Origin: The South Pacific Forum was inaugurated on August 15, 1971, in Wellington, New Zealand, as a conference of the heads of government of the independent and self-governing states of the South Pacific. Founding members had grown disenchanted with the nonpolitical South Pacific Commission. The forum meets annually in the capitals of the member states for informal discussions on political, economic, and other common issues. It is unique in that it has operated without a written constitution or agreement and without any formal rules governing its activities and membership. All decisions have been made by consensus rather than by formal vote. In the early 1980s the organization's work program included such matters as trade promotion, transport, telecommunications, tourism, agriculture, industrial development, fisheries and seabed resources, the environment, and energy.

Membership:

Australia	New Zealand
Cook Islands	Niue
Federated States of	Papua New Guinea
Micronesia	Solomon Islands
(observer)	Tonga
Fiji	Tuvalu
Kiribati	Vanuatu
Nauru	Western Samoa

Organization: In 1972 the forum established the South Pacific Bureau for Economic Cooperation (SPEC) to promote regional cooperation and consultation on trade, economic development, transport, tourism, and other related matters within the South Pacific. In 1975 SPEC became the official secretariat of the forum. In 1977 SPEC established the Pacific Forum Line as a joint-venture regional shipping line. Two years later the South Pacific Forum Fisheries Agency was set up to facilitate mutual cooperation and assistance in fisheries and in policing the 200-nautical-mile Exclusive Economic Zone (see Glossary) of each of the member states. Other affiliated organizations are the Association of South Pacific Airlines (for cooperation among the member airlines) and the South Pacific Trade Commission (for development of export markets in Australia), both established in 1979, and the Tourism Council, set up in 1983. Two-thirds of the forum's annual budget comes from Australia and New Zealand—each contributing one-third—and the balance is shared equally by the other forum members.

Appendix C

Security Treaty Between Australia, New Zealand and the United States of America

Signed at San Francisco September 1, 1951; Ratification advised by the Senate of the United States of America March 20, 1952; Ratified by the President of the United States of America April 15, 1952; Ratification of the United States of America deposited with the Government of Australia at Canberra April 29, 1952; Proclaimed by the President of the United States of America May 9, 1952; Entered into force April 29, 1952.

Ratified by Australia, New Zealand, and the United States of America

The Parties to this Treaty,

Reaffirming their faith in the purposes and principles of the Charter of the United Nations and their desire to live in peace with all peoples and all Governments, and desiring to strengthen the fabric of peace in the Pacific Area,

Noting that the United States already has arrangements pursuant to which its armed forces are stationed in the Philippines, and has armed forces and administrative responsibilities in the Ryukyus, and upon the coming into force of the Japanese Peace Treaty may also station armed forces in and about Japan to assist in the preservation of peace and security in the Japan Area,

Recognizing that Australia and New Zealand as members of the British Commonwealth of Nations have military obligations outside as well as within the Pacific Area,

Desiring to declare publicly and formally their sense of unity, so that no potential aggressor could be under the illusion that any of them stand alone in the Pacific Area, and

Desiring further to coordinate their efforts for collective defense for the preservation of peace and security pending the development of a more comprehensive system of regional security in the Pacific Area,

Therefore declare and agree as follows:

Article I

The Parties undertake, as set forth in the Charter of the United Nations, to settle any international disputes in which they may be involved by peaceful means in such a manner that international peace and security and justice are not endangered and to refrain in their international relations from the threat or use of force in any manner inconsistent with the purposes of the United Nations.

Article II

In order more effectively to achieve the objective of this Treaty the Parties separately and jointly by means of continuous and effective self-help and mutual aid will maintain and develop their individual and collective capacity to resist armed attack.

Article III

The Parties will consult together whenever in the opinion of any of them the territorial integrity, political independence or security of any of the Parties is threatened in the Pacific.

Article IV

Each Party recognizes that an armed attack in the Pacific Area on any of the Parties would be dangerous to its own peace and safety and declares that it would act to meet the common danger in accordance with its constitutional processes.

Any such armed attack and all measures taken as a result thereof shall be immediately reported to the Security Council of the United Nations. Such measures shall be terminated when the Security Council has taken the measures necessary to restore and maintain international peace and security.

Article V

For the purpose of Article IV, an armed attack on any of the Parties is deemed to include an armed attack on the metropolitan territory of any of the Parties, or on the island territories under its jurisdiction in the Pacific or on its armed forces, public vessels or aircraft in the Pacific.

Article VI

This Treaty does not affect and shall not be interpreted as affecting in any way the rights and obligations of the Parties under the Charter of the United Nations or the responsibility of the United Nations for the maintenance of international peace and security.

Article VII

The Parties hereby establish a Council, consisting of their Foreign Ministers or their Deputies, to consider matters concerning the implementation of this Treaty. The Council should be so organized as to be able to meet at any time.

Article VIII

Pending the development of a more comprehensive system of regional security in the Pacific Area and the development by the United Nations of more effective means to maintain international peace and security, the Council, established by Article VII, is authorized to maintain a consultative relationship with States, Regional Organizations, Associations of States or other authorities in the Pacific Area in a position to further the purposes of this Treaty and to contribute to the security of that Area.

Article IX

This Treaty shall be ratified by the Parties in accordance with their respective constitutional processes. The instruments of ratification shall be deposited as soon as possible with the Government of Australia, which will notify each of the other signatories of such deposit. The Treaty shall enter into force as soon as the ratifications of the signatories have been deposited.

Article X

This Treaty shall remain in force indefinitely. Any Party may cease to be a member of the Council established by Article VII one year after notice has been given to the Government of Australia, which will inform the Governments of the other Parties of the deposit of such notice.

Article XI

This Treaty in the English language shall be deposited in the archives of the Government of Australia. Duly certified copies thereof will be transmitted by that Government to the Governments of each of the other signatories.

Bibliography

Chapter 1

Alkire, William H. *An Introduction to the Peoples and Cultures of Micronesia*. Menlo Park, California: Cummings, 1977.

Bellwood, Peter S. "The Peopling of the Pacific," *Scientific American*, 243, No. 5, November 1980, 174–85.

————. *The Polynesians: Prehistory of an Island People*. London: Thames and Hudson, 1978.

Berndt, Ronald M. *Excess and Restraint: Social Control among a New Guinea Mountain People*. Chicago: University of Chicago Press, 1962.

Biggs, Bruce. "The History of Polynesian Languages." Pages 691–716 in S.A. Wurm and Louis Carrington (eds.), *Second International Conference of Austronesian Linguistics: Proceedings, 2*. Canberra: Department of Linguistics, Australian National University, 1978.

Buck, Peter. *Explorers of the Pacific: European and American Discoveries in Polynesia*. Honolulu: Bishop Museum Press, 1953.

Chowning, Anne. *An Introduction to the Peoples and Cultures of Melanesia*. Menlo Park, California: Cummings, 1977.

Craig, Robert D., and Frank P. King (eds.). *Historical Dictionary of Oceania*. Westport, Connecticut: Greenwood Press, 1981.

Daws, Gavan. *Shoal of Time: A History of the Hawaiian Islands*. Honolulu: University Press of Hawaii, 1968.

Finney, Ben R. *Polynesian Peasants and Proletarians*. Cambridge, Massachusetts: Schenkman, 1973.

Firth, Stewart. *New Guinea under the Germans*. Melbourne: Melbourne University Press, 1982.

Fortune, Reo F. *Sorcerers of Dobu*. New York: Dutton, 1937.

Freeman, Otis Willard (ed.). *Geography of the Pacific*. New York: Wiley, 1951.

Furnas, J.C. *Anatomy of Paradise: Hawaii and the Islands of the South Seas*. New York: Sloane Associates, 1948.

Garrett, John. *To Live among the Stars: Christian Origins in Oceania*. Suva: Oceania Printers, 1982.

Goldman, Irving. *Ancient Polynesian Society*. Chicago: University of Chicago Press, 1970.

————. "Polynesia." Pages 227–30 in Louis Shores (ed.), *Collier's Encyclopedia*, 19. London: Collier, 1979.

Goodenough, Ward. "A Problem in Malayo-Polynesian Social Organization," *American Anthropologist*, 57, No. 1, 1955, 71–83.

Grace, George W. "Classification of the Languages of the Pacific." Pages 63–80 in Andrew P. Vayda (ed.), *Peoples and Cultures of the Pacific: An Anthropological Reader*. Garden City, New York: Natural History Press, 1968.

Grattan, C. Hartley. *The Southwest Pacific to 1900*. Ann Arbor: University of Michigan Press, 1963.

Handy, E.S. Craighill, et al. *Ancient Hawaiian Civilizations*. Rutland, Vermont: Tuttle, 1965.

Hogbin, Ian. "Melanesia." Pages 668–70 in Louis Shores (ed.), *Collier's Encyclopedia*, 15. London: Collier, 1979.

Holmes, Lowell. *Samoan Village*. New York: Holt, Rinehart and Winston, 1974.

Howard, Alan. "Polynesian Social Stratification Revisited: Reflections on Castles Built of Sand (and a Few Bits of Coral)," *American Anthropologist*, 74, No. 4, August 1972, 811–23.

Howard, Alan (ed.). *Polynesia: Readings on a Culture Area*. New York: Chandler, 1971.

Keesing, Roger M. *Cultural Anthropology: A Contemporary Perspective*. New York: Holt, Rinehart and Winston, 1976.

Lawrence, P., and M.J. Meggitt (eds.). *Gods, Ghosts, and Men in Melanesia*. London: Oxford University Press, 1965.

Linton, Ralph. *The Tree of Culture*. New York: Knopf, 1959.

Malinowski, Bronislaw. *Argonauts of the Western Pacific*. New York: Dutton, 1961.

———. *Coral Gardens and Their Magic*, 1 and 2. New York: American Book, 1935.

Malo, David. *Hawaiian Antiquities*. Honolulu: Bishop Museum Press, 1951.

Mason, Leonard. "The Ethnology of Micronesia." Pages 275–98 in Andrew P. Vayda (ed.), *Peoples and Cultures of the Pacific*. Garden City, New York: Natural History Press, 1968.

O'Connell, James F. *A Residence of Eleven Years in New Holland and the Caroline Islands*. Honolulu: University Press of Hawaii, 1972.

Oliver, Douglas L. *The Pacific Islands*. (rev. ed.) Garden City, New York: Anchor Books, Doubleday, in cooperation with the American Musuem of Natural History, 1961.

Pacific Islands Yearbook, 1978. (13th ed.) (Ed., Stuart Inder.) Sydney: Pacific, 1978.

Pacific Islands Yearbook, 1981. (14th ed.) (Ed., John Carter.) Sydney: Pacific, 1981.

Price, Willard. *Japan's Islands of Mystery*. New York: Day, 1944.

Sahlins, Marshall D. "Poor Man, Rich Man, Big-Man, Chief: Political Types in Melanesia and Polynesia." Pages 203–15 in Thomas G. Harding and Ben J. Wallace (eds.), *Cultures of the Pacific*. New York: Free Press, 1970.

South Pacific Commission. *The South Pacific Commission: History, Aims, and Activities*. (pamphlet.) Nouméa: 1983.

Thomas, William L. "The Pacific Basin: An Introduction." Pages 3–26 in Andrew P. Vayda (ed.), *Peoples and Cultures of the Pacific*. Garden City, New York: Natural History Press, 1968.

Trumbull, Robert. *Tin Roofs and Palm Trees: A Report on the New South Seas*. Seattle: University of Washington Press, 1977.

Tupouniua, Sione, Ron Crocombe, and Claire Slatter (eds.). *The Pacific Way*. Suva: Fiji Times and Herald, 1975.

Chapter 2

Ahmed Ali. "Economic Problems of Muslim Minorities: A Case of Fiji Muslims," *Institute of Muslim Minority Affairs Journal* [Jiddah], 6, Nos. 1–2, 1982, 82–103.

———. "Muslims in Fiji: A Brief Survey," *Institute of Muslim Minority Affairs Journal* [Jiddah], 2–3, No. 2, 1980, 174–82.

Allen, Michael. "Elders, Chiefs, and Big Men: Authority, Legitimation, and Political Evolution in Melanesia," *American Ethnologist*, 12, No. 1, February 1984, 20–41.

———. "Innovation, Inversion, and Revolution as Political Tactics in West Aoba." Pages 105–34 in Michael Allen (ed.), *Vanuatu: Politics, Economics, and Ritual in Island Melanesia*. Sydney: Academic Press, 1981.

———. "Introduction." Pages 1–8 in Michael Allen (ed.), *Vanuatu: Politics, Economics, and Ritual in Island Melanesia*. Sydney: Academic Press, 1981.

Amarshi, Azeem, Kenneth Good, and Rex Mortimer. *Development and Dependency*. Melbourne: Oxford University Press, 1979.

Asia Yearbook, 1977. (Ed., Donald Wise.) Hong Kong: Far Eastern Economic Review, 1977.

Asia Yearbook, 1978. (Ed., Hiro Punwani.) Hong Kong: Far Eastern Economic Review, 1978.

Asia Yearbook, 1980. (Ed., Donald Wise.) Hong Kong: Far Eastern Economic Review, 1980.

Asia Yearbook, 1981. (Ed., Donald Wise.) Hong Kong: Far Eastern Economic Review, 1981.

Asia Yearbook, 1983. (Ed., Donald Wise.) Hong Kong: Far Eastern Economic Review, 1983.

Asia Yearbook, 1984. (Ed., Donald Wise.) Hong Kong: Far Eastern Economic Review, 1984.

Baldwin, George B. *Papua New Guinea: Its Economic Situation and Prospects for Development.* Washington: World Bank, 1978.

Barrett, David B. (ed.). *World Christian Encyclopedia: A Comparative Study of Churches and Religions in the Modern World, A.D. 1900–2000.* Nairobi: Oxford University Press, 1982.

Bastin, Ron. "Economic Enterprise in a Tannese Village." Pages 337–55 in Michael Allen (ed.), *Vanuatu: Politics, Economics, and Ritual in Island Melanesia.* Sydney: Academic Press, 1981.

Baxter, Michael W.P. *Food in Fiji: The Produce and Processed Foods Distribution Systems.* (Development Studies Monograph, No. 22.) Canberra: Australian National University, 1980.

de Beer, Patrice. "Tonga and Fiji: Racial Tensions and a Generation Gap," *Manchester Guardian Weekly* [London], September 25, 1983, 12–14.

Bellwood, Peter. *Man's Conquest of the Pacific: The Prehistory of Southeast Asia and Oceania.* Auckland: Collins, 1978.

Belshaw, Cyril S. *Island Administration in the South West Pacific: Government and Reconstruction in New Caledonia, the New Hebrides, and the British Solomon Islands.* London: Royal Institute of International Affairs, 1950.

Blackwood, Peter. "Rank, Exchange, and Leadership in Four Vanuatu Societies." Pages 35–84 in Michael Allen (ed.), *Vanuatu: Politics, Economics, and Ritual in Island Melanesia.* Sydney: Academic Press, 1981.

Blaustein, Albert P., and Gisbert H. Flanz (eds.). *Solomon Islands.* (Constitutions of the Countries of the World series.) Dobbs Ferry, New York: Oceana, 1978.

————. *Vanuatu.* (Constitutions of the Countries of the World series.) Dobbs Ferry, New York: Oceana, 1981.

Britain. Admiralty. Naval Intelligence Division. *Pacific Islands, Vol. III: Western Pacific (Tonga to the Solomon Islands).* (Geographical Handbook series, B.R. 519B.) London: 1944.

Brown, Carolyn Henning. "Demographic Constraints on Caste: A Fiji Indian Example," *American Ethnologist,* 8, No. 2, May

1981.

──────. "Ethnic Politics in Fiji: Fijian-Indian Relations," *Journal of Ethnic Studies*, 5, No. 3, Spring 1978, 1–17.

Brunton, Ron. "The Origins of the John Frum Movement: A Sociological Explanation." Pages 357–77 in Michael Allen (ed.), *Vanuatu: Politics, Economics, and Ritual in Island Melanesia*. Sydney: Academic Press, 1981.

Bullivant, Brian M. "Cultural Reproduction in Fiji: Who Controls Knowledge/Power?" *Comparative Education Review*, 27, No. 2, June 1983, 227–45.

Callick, Rowan. "France Out, Australia In," *Far Eastern Economic Review* [Hong Kong], February 13, 1981, 22.

Carstairs, R.T., and R. Deo Prasad. *Impact of Foreign Direct Private Investment on the Fiji Economy*. Suva: Center for Applied Studies in Development, 1981.

Central Bank of Vanuatu. *Annual Report and Statement of Accounts for 1982*. Port-Vila: 1983.

Chandra, Satish. *Energetics and Subsistence Affluence in Traditional Culture*. (Development Studies Center Occasional Paper, No. 24.) Canberra: Australian National University, 1981.

──────. "Food Production and Consumption on Fijian and Indian Farms in the Sigatoka Valley, Fiji," *Fiji Agricultural Journal* [Suva], 43, No. 1, January–June 1981, 33–42.

Chapelle, Tony. "Customary Land Tenure in Fiji: Old Truths and Middle-Aged Myths," *Journal of the Polynesian Society* [Auckland], 87, No. 2, June 1978, 71–88.

Clifford, James. "The Translation of Cultures: Maurice Leenhardt's Evangelism, New Caledonia, 1902–1926," *Journal of Pacific History* [Canberra], 15, Nos. 1–2, January–April 1980, 2–20.

Cochrane, Glynn. *Big Men and Cargo Cults*. Oxford: Clarendon Press, 1970.

Coombe, Christine. "Turmoil at the Top in Vanuatu," *Pacific Islands Monthly* [Sydney], 54, No. 3, March 1983, 35–37.

──────. "Uproar in Vanuatu," *Islands Business* [Suva], 9, No. 3, March 1983, 19–20.

Craig, Robert D, and Frank P. King (eds.). *Historical Dictionary of Oceania*. Westport, Connecticut: Greenwood Press, 1981.

Crocombe, Ron. "Wantok Rules—OK?" *Islands Business* [Suva], 9, No. 7, July 1983, 51–56.

"Current Developments in the Pacific—PNG: The First General Elections after Independence," *Journal of Pacific History* [Canberra], 13, No. 2, 1978, 77–90.

"Current Developments in the Pacific—The Achievement of Independence: The Legal Aspect," *Journal of Pacific History* [Canberra], 15, No. 3, July 1980, 175–93.

Davis, Rex. "'Folk Churches' of the Pacific Face Challenge of Ecumenism," *Pacific Islands Monthly* [Sydney], 53, No. 11, November 1982, 23–26.

Deschamps, Hubert, and Jean Guiart. *Tahiti, Nouvelle-Calédonie, Nouvelles-Hébrides*. Paris: Éditions Berger-Levrault, 1957.

Dousset-Leenhardt, Roselène. *Colonialisme et contradictions: Nouvelle-Calédonie 1878–1978, les causes de l'insurrection de 1878*. Paris: Éditions L'Harmattan, 1978.

———. *Terre natale, terre d'exil*. Paris: Maisonneuve et Larose, 1976.

Ellis, Julie-Ann. "Culture Clash on Pentecost," *Pacific Islands Monthly* [Sydney], 54, No. 7, July 1983, 19–21.

———. "Land, Foreign Policy, Set to Dominate Vanuatu Election Campaign," *Pacific Islands Monthly* [Sydney], 54, No. 9, September 1983, 51.

Facey, Ellen E. "Hereditary Chiefship in Nguna." Pages 295–313 in Michael Allen (ed.), *Vanuatu: Politics, Economics, and Ritual in Island Melanesia*. Sydney: Academic Press, 1981.

The Far East and Australasia, 1983–1984. (15th ed.) London: Europa, 1983.

Fiji. Bureau of Statistics. *Current Economic Statistics* [Suva], July 1983 (entire issue).

———. *Facts and Figures, 1983*. Suva: Government Printer, 1983.

———. *Overseas Trade Fiji, 1982*. (Parliamentary Paper, No. 48.) Suva: Government Printer, 1983.

Fiji. Census Office. *Report on the Census of the Population, 1976*, 1. (Parliamentary Paper, No. 13.) Suva: Parliament of Fiji, 1977.

———. *Report on the Census of the Population, 1976*, 2. (Parliamentary Paper, No. 43.) Suva: Parliament of Fiji, 1979.

Fiji. Central Monetary Authorty. *Annual Report, 1983*. Suva: 1984.

Fiji. Economic Development Board. *Fiji Investment Guide*. Suva: 1982.

Fiji. Ministry of Agriculture and Fisheries. *Annual Report for the Year 1982*. (Parliamentary Paper, No. 66.) Suva: Government Printer, 1983.

Fiji. Ministry of Finance. *Budget Speech, 1983*. Suva: Government Printer, 1982.

Fiji. Ministry of Information. *Fiji Today, 1982–83*. Suva: 1983

Fiji Handbook and Travel Guide. (Ed., John Carter.) Sydney: Pacific, 1980.

Fischer, Edward. *Fiji Revisited: A Columban Father's Memories of Twenty-eight Years in the Islands*. New York: Crossroad, 1981.

Fisk, E.K. *New Guinea on the Threshold: Aspects of Social, Political, and Economic Development*. Pittsburgh: University of Pittsburgh Press, 1968.

Fitzpatrick, Peter. *Law and State in Papua New Guinea*. London: Academic Press, 1980.

Fox, Charles F. *The Story of the Solomons* (rev. ed.) Sydney: Pacific, 1975.

France. Embassy in New York. Press and Information Service. *New Caledonia*. (Documents from France series, No. 82/50.) New York: 1982.

France. Institut d'Émission d'Outre-Mer. *Exercice 1981, rapport d'activité: Nouvelle-Calédonie*. Paris: 1981.

Glanville, Ian. "The Changing Face of PNG's Defence Force," *Pacific Defence Reporter* [Sydney], 11, No. 4, April 1984, 14–15.

Government Finance Statistics Yearbook, 1983. Washington: International Monetary Fund, 1983.

Griffin, James, Hank Nelson, and Stewart Firth. *Papua New Guinea: A Political History*. Exeter, New Hampshire: Heinemann Educational, 1980.

Groussard, René, and Gérard Vladyslav. "Nouvelle-Calédonie: la réforme foncière," *Regards sur l'actualité* [Paris], 96, December 1983, 33–45.

Hasluck, Paul. *A Time for Building: Australian Administration in Papua New Guinea, 1951–1963*. Melbourne: Melbourne University Press, 1976.

Hass, Anthony (ed.). *Fiji and Its Peoples*. Wellington: Asia Pacific Research Unit, 1982.

Hastings, Peter. "Defence under Attack," *Far Eastern Economic Review* [Hong Kong], June 23, 1983, 44–45.

————. *New Guinea: Problems and Prospects*. Melbourne: Cheshire, 1969.

Hawkins, Edward K., et al. *The Solomon Islands: An Introductory Economic Report*. Washington: East Asia and Pacific Regional Office, World Bank, 1980.

Hegarty, David, and Peter King. "Papua New Guinea in 1982: The Election Brings Change," *Asian Survey*, 23, No. 2, February 1983, 217–25.

Higgins, Ean. "Letter from Mon Asavu," *Far Eastern Economic Review* [Hong Kong], November 24, 1983, 96.

Hill, Helen. "Mara's Close Race," *Far Eastern Economic Review* [Hong Kong], July 30, 1982, 22.

Howe, K.R. *The Loyalty Islands: A History of Culture Contacts, 1840–1900*. Honolulu: University Press of Hawaii, 1977.

Ingleton, Roy D. *Police of the World*. New York: Scribner's Sons, 1979.

International Financial Statistics Yearbook, 1983. Washington: International Monetary Fund, 1983.

International Monetary Fund. *International Financial Statistics*, 37, No. 6, June 1984 (entire issue).

Jane's Fighting Ships, 1983–84. (Ed., John Moore.) New York: Jane's, 1983.

Joint Publications Research Service—JPRS (Washington).
>The following items are from the JPRS Series;
>*Southeast Asia Report*.
>*Tam Tam*, Port-Vila, February 4, 1984. (JPRS 84037, No. 37, March 7, 1984, 89–92).
>"Vanuatu . . . and the Cuban Connection," *West Australian*, Perth, December 14, 1983. (JPRS 84013, No. 13, January 23, 1984, 102–103).

Jolly, Margaret. "Birds and Banyans of South Pentecost: *Kastom* in Anti-Colonial Struggle," *Mankind* [Sydney], 13, No. 4, August 1982, 338–56.

———. "People and Their Products in South Pentecost." Pages 269–93 in Michael Allen (ed.), *Vanuatu: Politics, Economics, and Ritual in Island Melanesia*. Sydney: Academic Press, 1981.

Jones, D.R.W. "Night Life and Cultural Imperialism in Suva: An Empirical Riposte," *Pacific Viewpoint* [Wellington], 23, No. 1, May 1982, 77–82.

Keegan, John (ed.). *World Armies*. Detroit: Gale Research, 1983.

Keesing, Roger M. *Kwaio Religion: The Living and the Dead in a Solomon Islands Society*. New York: Columbia University Press, 1983.

Keesing, Roger M. (ed.). *'Elota's Story: the Life and Times of a Solomon Islands Big Man*. New York: St. Martin's Press, 1978.

Keith-Reid, Robert. "Fiji's Fishing Fracas," *Islands Business* [Suva], 9, No. 10, October 1983, 30–31.

———. "Fiji's Nuclear Reversal," *Islands Business* [Suva], 9, No. 9, September 1983, 32–33.

———. "Indians Galore, but Can They Be Chiefs?" *Far East-*

ern Economic Review [Hong Kong], 79–80.

————. "Juggling with Power," *Islands Business* [Suva], 9, No. 6, June 1983, 23–24.

————. "Malaria Plague Boom" *Islands Business* [Suva], 9, No. 6, June 1983, 29–30.

————. "The Other Side of Paradise," *Islands Business* [Suva], 9, No. 3, March 1983, 12–16.

————. "State of the Union," *Islands Business* [Suva], 9, No. 7, July 1983, 21–22.

————. "Where to Now for a President?" *Islands Business* [Suva], 9, No. 6, June 1983, 70.

Kent, Janet. *The Solomon Islands.* Harrisburg, Pennsylvania: Stackpole Books, 1972.

King, Peter. "Papua New Guinea in 1983: Pangu Consolidates," *Asian Survey,* 24, No. 2, February 1984, 159–66.

Kling, Georges. *En Nouvelle Calédonie.* Paris: Hachette, 1981.

Knapman, Bruce, and Salvatore Schiavo-Campo. "Growth and Fluctuations of Fiji's Exports, 1875–1978," *Economic Development and Cultural Change,* 32, No. 1, October 1983, 97–119.

Knapman, Bruce, and Michael A.H.B. Walter. "The Way of the Land and the Path of Money: The Generation of Economic Inequality in Eastern Fiji," *The Journal of Developing Areas,* 14, No. 2, January 1980, 201–222.

Lal, Brij V. "The Fiji General Election of 1982: The Tidal Wave That Never Came," *The Journal of Pacific History* [Canberra], 18, No. 1, January 1983, 134–57.

Larcom, Joan. "The Invention of Convention," *Mankind* [Sydney], 13, No. 4, August 1982, 330–37.

Larmour, Peter, Ron Crocombe, and Anna Taungenga (eds.). *Land, People, and Government: Public Lands Policy in the South Pacific.* Suva: Institute of Pacific Studies, University of the South Pacific, 1981.

Latham, Linda. "Revolt Re-examined: the 1878 Insurrection in New Caledonia," *Journal of Pacific History* [Canberra], 10, Nos. 3–4, 1975, 48–63.

Leenhardt, Maurice. *Do Kamo: Person and Myth in the Melanesian World.* Chicago: University of Chicago Press, 1979.

Levine, Hal B., and Marlene Wolfzahn Levine. *Urbanization in Papua New Guinea: A Study of Ambivalent Townsmen.* Cambridge: Cambridge University Press, 1979.

Lindstrom, Lamont. "*Leftkamp Kastom:* The Political History of Tradition on Tanna," *Mankind* [Sydney], 13, No. 4, August 1982, 316–29.

"Lini's Slender Thread," *Islands Business* [Suva], 9, No. 12, December 1983, 17–18.

Macclancy, J.V. "From New Hebrides to Vanuatu, 1979–80," *Journal of Pacific History* [Canberra], 16, No. 1, January 1981, 92–104.

Macnaught, Timothy J. *The Fijian Colonial Experience: A Study of the Neotraditional Order under British Colonial Rule Prior to World War Two*. (Pacific Research Monograph, No. 7.) Canberra, Australia; Miami, Florida: Australian National University, 1982.

Mamak, Alexander, et al. *Bougainvillean Nationalism: Aspects of Unity and Discord*. Christchurch, New Zealand: University of Canterbury, 1974.

Mayer, Adrian C. *Peasants in the Pacific: A Study of Fiji-Indian Rural Society*. (2d ed.) Berkeley and Los Angeles: University of California Press, 1973.

Métais, Éliane. *La Sorcellerie canaque actuelle: les "tueurs d'âmes dans une tribu de la Nouvelle-Calédonie."* (Publications de la Société des Océanistes, 20.) Paris: Société des Océanistes, 1967.

The Military Balance, 1983–1984. London: International Institute for Strategic Studies, 1983.

Milne, R.S. *Politics in Ethnically Bipolar States: Guyana, Malaysia, Fiji*. Vancouver: University of British Columbia Press, 1981.

Minerals Yearbook, 1978–1979, Vol. 3. Area Reports: International. Washington: GPO for United States Department of the Interior, Bureau of Mines, 1981.

Nair, Shashikant. *Rural-born Fijians and Indo-Fijians in Suva: A Study of Movement and Linkages*. (Development Studies Monograph, No. 24.) Canberra: Australian National University, 1980.

Nayacakalou, Rusiate R. *Leadership in Fiji*. New York: Oxford University Press, 1976.

New Caledonia. Direction Territoriale de la Statistique et des Études Économiques. *Annuaire statistique 1983: résultats de l'année 1982*. Nouméa: 1983.

New Zealand. Ministry of Defence. *Report of the Ministry of Defence for the Year Ended 31 March 1981*. Wellington: Government Printer, 1981.

New Zealand. Prime Minister's Department. External Intelligence Bureau. *Atlas of the South Pacific*. Wellington: Department of Lands and Survey, 1978.

Norton, Robert Edward. *Race and Politics in Fiji*. New York: St.

Martin's Press, 1977.

Nyamekye, Kwasi, and Ralph R. Premdas. "Papua New Guinea-Indonesian Relations over Irian Jaya," *Asian Survey*, 19, No. 19, October 1979, 927–45.

"Ok Tedi—Going for Gold," *Papua New Guinea Post-Courier* [Port Moresby], May 30, 1984, 1.

Oliver, Douglas L. *The Pacific Islands*. (rev. ed.) Garden City, New York: Anchor Books, Doubleday, in cooperation with the American Museum of Natural History, 1961.

"Optimism on New Ireland Gold," *Pacific Islands Monthly* [Sydney], 55, No. 4, April 1984, 31.

Pacific Islands Yearbook, 1981. (14th ed.) (Ed., John Carter.) Sydney: Pacific, 1981.

Papua New Guinea. National Statistical Office. *1980 National Population Census, Preliminary Bulletin, No. 1: Field Counts—All Provinces and Districts*. Port Moresby: 1981.

————. *1980 National Population Census, Research Monograph, No. 1: Urban Growth, 1966–80*. Port Moresby: 1982.

Parsons, Mike. "Vanuatu Stakes Claim" *Islands Business* [Suva], 9, No. 4, April 1983, 22–23.

"Par un groupe d'autochtones calédoniens." *Mélanésiens d'aujourd'hui*. (Publications de la Société d'Études Historiques de la Nouvelle-Calédonie, No. 11.) Nouméa: Société d'Études Historiques de la Nouvelle-Calédonie, 1976.

Peet, Richard. "Reply to an 'Empirical Riposte'," *Pacific Viewpoint*, [Wellington], 23, No. 1, May 1982, 82–85.

Philibert, Jean-Marc. "Living under Two Flats: Selective Modernization in Erakor Village, Efate." Pages 315–36 in Michael Allen (ed.), *Vanuatu: Politics, Economics, and Ritual in Island Melanesia*. Sydney: Academic Press, 1981.

Premdas, Ralph R. "Papua New Guinea in 1976: Dangers of a China Connection," *Asian Survey*, 17, No. 1, January 1977, 55–61.

————. "Papua New Guinea in 1977: Elections and Relations with Indonesia," *Asian Survey*, 18, No. 1, January 1978, 58–67.

————. "Papua New Guinea 1979: A Regime under Siege," *Asian Survey*, 20, No. 1, January 1980, 94–99.

————. "Secessionist Politics in Papua New Guinea," *Pacific Affairs* [Vancouver], 50, No. 1, Spring 1977, 64–85.

Premdas, Ralph R., and Kwasi Nyamekye. "Papua New Guinea 1978: Year of the OPM," *Asian Survey*, 19, No. 1, January 1979, 65–71.

Premdas, Ralph R., and Jeffrey S. Steeve. "The Solomon Islands:

First Elections after Independence," *Journal of Pacific History* [Canberra], 16, No. 3, July 1981, 190–202.

Pritchard, Chris. "South Pacific Makes Waves for U.S. Ships," *Christian Science Monitor,* March 29, 1984, 9.

Richardson, John. "How Gold is Fiji's Valley?" *Islands Business* [Suva], 9, No. 6, June 1983, 14–16.

———. "Solving Cuba's Crisis," *Islands Business* [Suva], 9, No. 5, May 1983, 36–39.

The Road Out: Rural Development in the Solomon Islands. Suva: Institute of Pacific Studies, 1981.

Rodman, Margaret. "A Boundary and a Bridge: Women's Pig Killing as a Border-Crossing Between Spheres of Exchange in East Aoba." Pages 85–104 in Michael Allen (ed.), *Vanuatu: Politics, Economics, and Ritual in Island Melanesia.* Sydney: Academic Press, 1981.

———. "Masters of Tradition: Customary Land Tenure and New Forms of Social Inequality in a Vanuatu Peasantry," *American Ethnologist,* 12, No. 1, February 1984, 61–80.

Rodman, William L. "Big Men and Middlemen: The Politics of Law in Longana," *American Ethnologist,* 4, No. 3, August 1977, 525–37.

Rubinstein, Robert L. "Knowledge and Political Process on Malo." Pages 135–72 in Michael Allen (ed.), *Vanuatu: Politics, Economics, and Ritual in Island Melanesia.* Sydney: Academic Press, 1981.

Sacerdoti, Guy. "A Cry from the Pacific," *Far Eastern Economic Review* [Hong Kong], August 18, 1983, 80–81.

Salisbury, R.F. *From Stone to Steel: Economic Consequences of a Technological Change in New Guinea.* Melbourne: Melbourne University Press, 1962.

Salmon, Malcom. "Vanuatu Leadership: President Sokomanu Throws Down the Gauntlet," *Pacific Islands Monthly* [Sydney], 54, No. 6, June 1983, 10–11.

Saussol, Alain. *L'Héritage: essai sur le problème foncier mélanésien en Nouvelle-Calédonie.* (Publications de la Société des Océanistes, No. 40.) Paris: La Société des Océanistes, 1979.

Shineberg, Dorothy. *They Came for Sandalwood: A Study of the Sandalwood Trade in the South-west Pacific, 1830–1865.* Carlton, Victoria: Melbourne University Press, 1967.

Sivan, P. "Review of Taro Research and Production in Fiji," *Fiji Agricultural Journal* [Suva], 43, No. 2, July-December 1981, 59–68.

Société des Océanistes. *Rank and Status in Polynesia and Melanesia: Essays in Honor of Professor Douglas Oliver.*

Paris: Musée de l'Homme, 1978.

Solomon Islands. Government Information Service. *How Government Works*. Honiara: Government Printer, 1982.

———. *An Introduction to Solomon Islands*. Honiara: Government Printer, 1983.

Solomon Islands. Government Information Service and Statistics Office. *Solomon Islands Facts and Figures, 1981*. Honiara: Government Printer, 1982.

Solomon Islands. Ministry of Finance. Statistics Office. *Statistical Bulletin*. (No. 5/83.) Honiara: Government Printer, 1983.

Sundhaussen, Ulf. "Ideology and Nation-Building in Papua New Guinea," *Australian Outlook* [Canberra], 31, No. 2, August 1977, 308–18.

Thompson, Virginia M., and Richard Adloff. *The French Pacific Islands: French Polynesia and New Caledonia*. Berkeley and Los Angeles: University of California Press, 1971.

Tjibaou, J. and Philippe Missotte. *Kanaké: mélanésien de Nouvelle-Calédonie*. Papeete: Les Éditions du Pacifique, 1976.

Tonkinson, Robert. "Church and *Kastom* in Southeast Ambrym." Pages 237–67 in Michael Allen (ed.), *Vanuatu: Politics, Economics, and Ritual in Island Melanesia*. Sydney: Academic Press, 1981.

———. "National Identity and the Problem of *Kastom* in Vanuatu," *Mankind* [Sydney], 13, No. 4, August 1982, 306–15.

———. "Vanuatu Values: A Changing Symbiosis," *Pacific Studies*, 5, No. 2, Spring 1982, 44–63.

United States. Department of Commerce. Bureau of the Census. *World Population: Recent Demographic Estimates for the Countries and Regions of the World*. Washington: GPO, 1983.

United States. Department of State. *Country Reports on Human Rights Practices for 1983*. (Report submitted to United States Congress, 98th, 2d Session, House of Representatives, Committee on Foreign Affairs, and Senate, Committee on Foreign Relations.) Washington: GPO, February 1984.

United States. Department of State. *Papua New Guinea Post Report*. Washington: GPO, July 1981.

United States. Department of State. Bureau of Public Affairs. Office of Media Services. *Background Notes: Papua New Guinea*. (Department of State publication, No. 8824.) Washington: January 1980.

United States. Embassy in Port Moresby. *Foreign Economic Trends and Their Implications for the United States/Papua*

New Guinea. Washington: Department of Commerce, June 1982.

Vanuatu. National Planning Office. *First National Development Plan, 1982–86*. Port-Vila: n. d.

Varley, R.C.G. *Tourism in Fiji: Some Economic and Social Problems*. (Bangor Occasional Papers in Economics, No. 12.) Bangor, Wales: University of Wales Press, 1978.

Walter, Michael A.H.B. "The Conflict of the Traditional and the Traditionalized: An Analysis of Fijian Land Tenure," *Journal of the Polynesian Society* [Auckland], 87, No. 2, June 1978, 89–108.

Ward, Alan W. "The Independence Movement and the Plan Dijoud in New Caledonia," *Journal of Pacific History* [Canberra], 15, Nos. 3–4, July-October 1980, 193–99.

―――. *Land and Politics in New Caledonia*. (Political and Social Change Monograph, No. 2.) Canberra: Research School of Pacific Studies, Australian National University, 1982.

Wolfers, Edward P. "Papua New Guinea and the Southwest Pacific." Pages 167–95 in T.B. Millar (ed.), *International Security in the Southeast Asian and Southwest Pacific Region*. St. Lucia, Australia: University of Queensland, 1983.

―――. "Papua New Guinea in 1980: A Change in Government, Aid, and Foreign Relations," *Asian Survey*, 21, No. 2, February 1981, 274–84.

Woolford, Don. *Papua New Guinea: Initiation and Independence*. St. Lucia, Australia: University of Queensland Press, 1976.

(Various issues of the following publications were used in the preparation of this chapter: *Asian Survey*, January 1974-July 1984; *Asia Yearbook* [Hong Kong], 1974–84; *Christian Science Monitor*, January 1981-July 1984; *Far Eastern Economic Review* [Hong Kong], January 1974-July 1984; *Financial Times* [London], January 1982-July 1984; *Islands Business* [Suva], January 1982-July 1984; Joint Publications Research Service, *South and East Asia Report*, January 1979-December 1982, and *Southeast Asia Report*, January 1979; *Marchés tropicaux et méditerranées* [Paris], January 1982-December 1983; *Le Monde* [Paris], January 1982-May 1984; *Pacific Islands Monthly* [Sydney], January 1982-May 1984; *Pacific Perspective* [Suva], 1977–84; *New York Times*, January 1981-June 1984; and *Washington Post*, January 1979-June 1984.)

Chapter 3

Armstrong, Arthur John. "The Emergence of the Micronesian Mini-States into the International Community: The Strategic Underpinnings of Free Association." n. pl.: n. d.

———. "Strategic Underpinnings of the Legal Regime of Free Association: The Negotiations for the Future Political Status of Micronesia," *Brooklyn Journal of International Law*, 7, No. 2, Summer 1981, 179–233.

———. "Understanding the Legal and Political Environment: Emerging Independence and Regionalism in the Island Nations of the Pacific Basin—The Impact of Investment and Trade." Washington: n. pub., n. d.

Ashby, Gene (ed.). *Some Things of Value: Micronesian Customs as Seen by Micronesians.* Saipan: Education Department, Trust Territory of the Pacific Islands, 1975.

Ballendorf, Dirk Antony. "Post-Colonial Micronesia: A Future for Japan and America," *New Zealand International Review* [Wellington], 7, No. 4, July-August 1982, 2–5.

Barnett, Homer. *Palauan Society: A Study of Contemporary Native Life in the Palau Islands.* Eugene: University of Oregon Press, 1949.

Barrett, David B. (ed.). *World Christian Encyclopedia: A Comparative Study of Churches and Religions in the Modern World, A.D. 1900–2000.* Nairobi: Oxford University Press, 1982.

Bast, Benjamin F. (ed.). *The Political Future of Guam and Micronesia.* (Proceedings of All-University Seminar on Political Status, University of Guam, February 1–2, 1974.) Agana: University of Guam Press, 1974.

Bates, Marston, and Donald Abbott. *Ifaluk: Portrait of a Coral Island.* London: Museum Press, 1959.

Beaglehole, J.C. *The Exploration of the Pacific.* (rev. ed.) Palo Alto: Stanford University, 1968.

Beardsley, Charles. *Guam Past and Present.* Tokyo: Tuttle, 1964.

Bellwood, Peter. *Man's Conquest of the Pacific. The Prehistory of Southeast Asia and Oceania.* Auckland: Collins, 1978.

Bhalla, K.S. "Nauru: A Central Pacific Parliamentary Democracy," *Parliamentarian* [London], 64, No. 3, July 1983, 127–33.

"The Billion Dollar 'No'," *Islands Business* [Suva], 9, No. 3, March 1983, 30–31.

Bouck, Gary D. "The South Pacific Conference," *Business*

America, 5, No. 20, October 4, 1982, 2–10.

Britain. Her Majesty's Stationery Office. *Gilbert and Ellice Islands Colony and the Central and Southern Line Islands: Report for the Year 1968*. London: 1969.

Brookfield, H.C. (ed.). *Population-Environment Relations in Tropical Islands: The Case of Eastern Fiji*. (MAB Technical Notes, No. 13.) Paris: United Nations Educational, Scientific and Cultural Organization, 1980.

Brower, Kenneth. *Micronesia: The Land, the People, the Sea*. n. pl.: Mobile Oil Micronesia, 1982.

Bryan, E.H., Jr., et al. *Land in Micronesia and Its Resources: An Annotated Bibliography*. Honolulu: Pacific Scientific Information Center, 1970.

Chapman, Patricia Luce. "U.S. Territories Wait for Congress: Pacific Islands Prepare to Go it Alone," *Christian Science Monitor, November 28, 1983*, 18–19.

Clune, Frank. *Captain Bully Hayes, Blackbirder and Bigamist*. Sydney: Angus and Robertson, 1970.

Cordy, Ross. "Social Stratification in the Mariana Islands," *Oceania* [Sydney], 53, No. 3, March 1983, 272–76.

Coulter, John Wesley. *The Pacific Dependencies of the United States*. New York: Macmillan, 1957.

Craig, Robert D., and Frank P. King (eds.). *Historical Dictionary of Oceania*. Westport, Connecticut: Greenwood Press, 1981.

Del Valle, Teresa. *Social and Cultural Change in the Community of Umatac, Southern Guam*. Agana: Micronesian Area Resource Center, 1979.

De Smith, Stanley A. *Microstates and Micronesia: Problems of America's Pacific Islands and Other Minute Territories*. New York: New York University Press, 1970.

Driver, Marjorie G. "Notes and Documents: Fray Juan Pobre de Zamora and His Accounts of the Mariana Islands," *Journal of Pacific History* [Canberra], 18, No. 4, October 1983, 198–216.

Eilenberg, Matthew. "Notes and Documents: American Policy in Micronesia," *Journal of Pacific History* [Canberra], 17, No. 1, January 1982, 62–64.

The Far East and Australasia, 1981–82. (13th ed.) London: Europa, 1981.

The Far East and Australasia, 1982–83. (14th ed.) London: Europa, 1982.

The Far East and Australasia, 1983–84. (15th ed.) London: Europa, 1983.

Feeney, Thomas J. *Letters from Likiep*. New York: Pandick

Press, 1962.

Fischer, John L., and Ann M. Fischer. *The Eastern Carolines.* New York: Taplinger, 1957.

Fisk, E.K. "Development and Aid in the South Pacific in the 1980s," *Australian Outlook* [Granville, New South Wales], 36, August 1982, 32–38.

"Focus on the Pacific Islands," *Business America*, 5, No. 20, October 4, 1982, 6–7.

Foster, Charles R. "Kiribati." In *World Encyclopedia of Political Systems and Parties*, 1. (Ed., George E. Delury.) New York: Facts on File, 1983.

————. "Nauru." In *World Encyclopedia of Political Systems and Parties*, 2. (Ed., George E. Delury.) New York: Facts on File, 1983.

Freeman, Otis Willard (ed.). *Geography of the Pacific.* New York: Wiley, 1951.

Gigot, Paul A. "The Smallest Nation Has a Rare Problem: Too Much Wealth," *Wall Street Journal*, September 22, 1983, 1.

"The Gilberts Go Russian," *Commonwealth* [London], October-November 1979, 12–13.

Gilliland, Cora Lee C. *The Stone Money of Yap: A Numismatic Survey.* (Smithsonian Studies in History and Technology, No. 23.) Washington: Smithsonian Institution Press, 1975.

Gladwin, Thomas. *East Is a Big Bird.* Cambridge: Harvard University Press, 1970.

Glasby, G.P. "Pacific Is Favored for Sub-Seabed Radio-Active Waste Disposal," *Pacific Islands Monthly* [Sydney], 54, No. 4, April 1983, 15.

Guam. Criminal Justice Planning Agency. *Comprehensive Criminal Justice Plan, 1979.* Agana: n. d.

Guam. Department of Public Works. *Island of Guam: Official Highway Map.* Agana: 1982.

Hartley, Jean Ayres. "The Wonder Lakes of Palau," *Pacific Islands Monthly* [Sydney], 54, No. 1, January 1983, 21–23.

Heine, Carl. *Micronesia at the Crossroads: A Reappraisal of the Micronesian Political Dilemma.* Honolulu: University Press of Hawaii, 1974.

Hezel, Francis X. "The Beginnings of Foreign Contact with Truk," *Journal of Pacific History* [Canberra], 8, 1973, 51–73.

Holmes, Mike. "Earth's Richest Nation—A Tiny Pacific Islet," *National Geographic*, 150, No. 3, September 1976, 344–53.

Hughes, Daniel T., and Sherwood G. Lingenfelter (eds.). *Political Development in Micronesia.* Columbus: Ohio State University Press, 1974.

Iuta, Taomati, et al. *Politics in Kiribati*. Suva: Kiribati Extension Center and Institute of Pacific Studies, University of the South Pacific, 1980.

Joseph, Alice, and V.F. Murray. *Chamorros and Carolinians of Saipan: Personality Studies*. Cambridge: Harvard University Press, 1951.

Joy, Charles R. *Young People of the Pacific Islands*. Des Moines: Meredith, 1963.

Kahn, E.J., Jr. *A Reporter in Micronesia*. New York: Norton, 1966.

Kanost, Richard F. "Administrative Development in Micronesia: The Senatorial Election in Truk District in 1974," *Journal of Pacific History* [Sydney]. 17, No. 3, July 1982, 158–65.

Keesing's Contemporary Archives, 1980. (Ed., Robert Fraser.) London: Keesing's, 1980.

Keith-Reid, Robert. "Death Knell at the Forum" *Islands Business* [Suva], 9, No. 10, October 1983, 16–19.

Kent, George. "Development Planning for Micronesia," *Political Science* [Wellington], 34, No. 1, July 1982, 1–25.

Kiribati. Ministry of Home Affairs. *Report on the 1978 Census of Population and Housing. Volume 1: Basic Information and Tables*. Bairiki: 1980.

Kiste, Robert C. *Kili Islands: A Study of the Relocation of the Ex-Bikini Marshallese*. Eugene: Department of Anthropology, University of Oregon, 1968.

————. "The Policies That Hid a Non-Policy," *Pacific Islands Monthly* [Sydney], 54, No. 10, October 1983, 37–40.

————. "A View from Honolulu: The Fine Print of the Compacts," *Pacific Islands Monthly* [Sydney], 54, No. 11, November 1983, 22–23.

Lachica, Eduardo. "Guam Delegate Puts His Island on the Map in Congress," *Christian Science Monitor*, November 24, 1983, 1.

Lewis, David. *We, the Navigators: The Ancient Art of Landfinding in the Pacific*. Wellington: Reed, 1972.

Lingenfelter, Sherwood. *Yap: Political Leadership and Culture Change in an Island Society*. Honolulu: University Press of Hawaii, 1975.

Linn, Gene. "The Pacific: No Goodbye Columbus," *Far Eastern Economic Review* [Hong Kong], September 24, 1982, 27–28.

Lynch, C.J. "Three Pacific Island Constitutions: Comparisons," *Parliamentarian* [London], 61, No. 3, July 1980, 133–41.

MacDonald, Barrie. "Current Developments in the Pacific: Self-determination and Self-government," *Journal of Pacific His-*

tory [Canberra], 17, No. 1, January 1982, 51–61.

Macdonald, J. Ross. "Termination of the Strategic Trusteeship: Free Association, the United Nations, and International Law," *Brooklyn Journal of International Law*, 7, No. 2, Summer 1981, 235–82.

MacKenzie, Tenaia. "Kiribati Sets Its Sights," *Islands Business* [Suva], 9, No. 9, September 1983, 45–47.

McHenry, Donald F. *Micronesia: Trust Betrayal. Altruism vs Self Interest in American Foreign Policy*. New York: Carnegie Endowment for International Peace, 1975.

McPhetres, Samuel. "Elections in the Northern Mariana Islands," *Political Science* [Wellington], 35, No. 1, July 1983, 103–16.

Manhard, Philip W. *The United States and Micronesia in Free Association: A Chance to Do Better?* (National Security Affairs Monograph series, No. 79–4.) Washington: Research Directorate, National Defense University, June 1979.

Manning, Robert, and Frank Quimby. "Micronesia: A Sort of Independence," *Far Eastern Economic Review* [Hong Kong], 121, No. 28, July 14, 1983, 19–20.

Marshall, Mac, and James D. Nason. *Micronesia 1944–1974: A Bibliography of Anthropological and Related Source Materials*. New Haven: Human Relations Area Files Press, 1975.

Marshall Islands. *Constitution and Laws of the Marshall Islands*. Majuro: May 1979.

"Marshalls Leaders Cry 'Foul' at U.S. Action on Honolulu Cable Link," *Pacific Islands Monthly* [Sydney], 54, No. 3, March 1983, 29.

Meller, Norman. *The Congress of Micronesia: Development of the Legislative Process in the Trust Territory of the Pacific Islands*. Honolulu: University of Hawaii Press, 1969.

Michener, James A., and A. Grove Day. *Rascals in Paradise*. New York: Random House, 1957.

Micronesia. *Constitution of the Federated States of Micronesia*. Kolonia: n. d.

Nevin, David. *The American Touch in Micronesia*. New York: Norton, 1977.

New Zealand. Prime Minister's Department. External Intelligence Bureau. *Atlas of the South Pacific*. Wellington: Department of Lands and Survey, 1978.

Northern Mariana Islands. *Constitution of the Northern Mariana Islands*. Saipan: 1976.

Nufer, Harold F. *Micronesia under American Rule: An Evaluation of the Strategic Trusteeship (1947–77)*. New York: Exposition Press, 1978.

Oliver, Douglas L. *The Pacific Islands* (rev. ed.) Garden City, New York: Anchor Books, Doubleday, in cooperation with the American Museum of Natural History, 1961.

Pacific Islands Yearbook and Who's Who. (10th ed.) (Ed., Judy Tudor.) Sydney: Pacific, 1968.

Pacific Islands Yearbook, 1981. (14th ed.) (Ed., John Carter.) Sydney: Pacific, 1981.

"Pacific Report: Pacific Nations on London 'Rescue' List," *Pacific Islands Monthly* [Sydney], 55, No. 2, February 1984, 5.

Packett, C. Neville. *Guide to the Republic of Nauru.* Yorkshire, England: Lloyds Bank Chambers, 1972.

Palau. *Constitution of the Republic of Palau.* Koror: 1979.

Price, Willard. *America's Paradise Lost: The Strange Story of the Secret Atolls.* New York: Day, 1966.

Purcell, David C., Jr. "The Economics of Exploitation: the Japanese in the Mariana, Caroline, and Marshall Islands, 1915–1940," *Journal of Pacific History* [Canberra], 11, Pt. 3, 1976, 189–211.

Quimby, Frank. "The Strategic Trusteeship," *Far Eastern Economic Review* [Hong Kong], 121, No. 28, July 14, 1983, 20–21.

Richardson, John. "Who's for the Hot Seat?" *Islands Business* [Suva], 9, No. 10, October 1983, 24–25.

Ronck, Ronn. *Glimpses of Guam.* Agana: n. pub., 1974.

Schutz, Billy. "Airline, Shipping Issues in Fall of Kiribati Government," *Pacific Islands Monthly* [Sydney], 54, No. 2, February 1983, 13.

Shabecoff, Philip. "A Tiny, Flightless Bird Stalls U.S. Strategic Air Command," *New York Times,* April 8, 1984, 1.

Sharp, Andrew. *The Discovery of the Pacific Islands.* New York: Oxford University Press, 1960.

Shuster, Donald R. "Elections in the Republic of Palau," *Political Science* [Wellington], 35, No. 1, July 1983, 117–32.

"The South Pacific," *Australian Foreign Affairs Record* [Canberra], 52, No. 5, May 1981, 198–219.

"The South Pacific," *Australian Foreign Affairs Record* [Canberra], 54, No. 8, August 1983, 379–402.

Takeuchi, Floyd K. "Exile Without End for the Bikinians," *Pacific Islands Monthly* [Sydney], 54, No. 5, May 1983, 19–21.

―――. "The Ghosts That Haunt U.S. Policies in Micronesia," *Pacific Islands Monthly* [Sydney], 54, No. 2, February 1983, 29–30.

————. "Marianas: The 'Other' Micronesia," *Pacific Islands Monthly* [Sydney], 54, No. 7, July 1983, 17–18.

————. "Palau: A Role for Principles," *Pacific Islands Monthly* [Sydney], 55, No. 2, February 1984, 29.

————. "A Piecemeal End for the Trust?" *Pacific Islands Monthly* [Sydney], 54, No. 6, June 1983, 19–21.

————. "The Super Tangle That Is Palau," *Pacific Islands Monthly* [Sydney], 54, No. 4, April 1983, 23–25.

Thompson, Laura. *Guam and Its People*. Princeton: Princeton University Press, 1947.

Tobin, J.A. "Land Tenure in the Marshall Islands." Pages 1–76 in John De Young (ed.), *Land Tenure Patterns, Trust Territory of the Pacific Islands*. Agana: Trust Territory Government, 1958.

"Tradition, Peoples in Yap," *Pacific Islands Monthly* [Sydney], 54, No. 4, April 1983, 31–33.

Trumbull, Robert. "World's Richest Little Isle," *New York Times Magazine*, March 7, 1982, 25.

Trust Territory of the Pacific Islands. *Annual Report to the Secretary of the Interior, 1981*. n. pl.: n. d.

"Unchanged Change in Nauru." *Pacific Islands Monthly* [Sydney], 55, No. 2, February 1984, 49.

United States. Congress. 97th, 1st Session. Senate. Committee on Foreign Relations. *Pacific Island Treaties*. Washington: GPO, 1982.

United States. Congress. 98th, 1st Session. Senate. Committee on Foreign Relations. *Treaty of Friendship with the Republic of Kiribati*. Washington: GPO, 1983.

United States. Department of Commerce. Bureau of the Census. *World Population: Recent Demographic Estimates for the Countries and Regions of the World*. Washington: GPO, 1983.

United States. Department of Commerce. International Trade Administration. Office of the Pacific Basin. *Market Profile for South Pacific Islands*. (Overseas Business Reports, OBR 83–02.) Washington: GPO, April 1983.

United States. Department of State. *Trust Territory of the Pacific Islands, 1972*. (25th annual report by the United States to the United Nations, July 1, 1971, to June 30, 1972.) Washington: GPO, 1973.

————. *Trust Territory of the Pacific Islands, 1974*. (27th annual report to the United Nations, July 1, 1973, to June 30, 1974; Department of State publication, No. 8820.) Washington: June 1975.

————. *Trust Territory of the Pacific Islands, 1979*. (32nd annual report to the United Nations on the administration of the Trust Territory of the Pacific Islands, October 1, 1978, to September 30, 1979; Department of State publication, No. 9121.) Washington: May 1980.

————. *Trust Territory of the Pacific Islands, 1982*. (35th annual report to the United Nations on the administration of the Trust Territory of the Pacific Islands, October 1, 1981, to September 30, 1982; Department of State publication, No. 9336.) Washington: May 1983.

United States. Department of State. Bureau of Intelligence and Research. *Status of the World's Nations, June 1983*. (Department of State publication, No. 8725.) Washington: GPO, 1983.

United States. Department of the Interior. Office for Micronesian Status Negotiations. *Compact of Free Association*. Washington: 1983.

————. "Draft Environmental Impact Statement for the Compact of Free Association." Washington: n. d.

————. "The Negotiations for the Future Political Status of the Trust Territories of the Pacific Islands." Washington: September 1983.

————. "The Political Status Negotiations for the Trust Territory of the Pacific Islands and the Compact of Free Association." Washington: September 1983.

United States. Department of the Interior. Office of Territorial and International Affairs. *General Fact Sheet on U.S. Administration of the Trust Territory of the Pacific Islands*. Washington: February 1983.

————. *Guam*. Washington: February 1983.

————. *The Northern Mariana Islands*. Washington: February 1983.

United States. Department of the Navy. *Handbook on the Trust Territory of the Pacific Islands*. Washington: GPO, 1949.

United States. Peace Corps/Micronesia. *Country Narrative, FY 1982*. n. pl.: n. d.

————. *On Being a Volunteer in Micronesia*. n. pl.: n. d.

————. *An Overview of Micronesia*. n. pl.: n. d.

United States. Peace Corps/Solomon Islands/Kiribati. *Kiribati Country Management Plan and Budget, FY 1985*. n. pl.: n. d.

Viviani, Nancy. *Nauru Phosphate and Political Progress*. Honolulu: University of Hawaii Press, 1970.

Vayda, Andrew P. (ed.). *Peoples and Cultures of the Pacific: An Anthropological Reader*. Garden City, New York: Natural

History Press, 1968.

Walker, Andrew. "Four New States About to be Born Out of 2,000 Pacific Islands," *Commonwealth*, 26, No. 3, December 1983, 100–101.

"'Walk!' PM Tells Nauru," *Islands Business* [Suva], 9, No. 4, April 1983, 25.

Ward, R. Gerard, and A.S. Proctor (eds.). *South Pacific Agricultural Survey, 1979. Pacific Agriculture: Choices and Constraints*. Manila: Asian Development Bank, July 1979.

Webb, James H., Jr. *Micronesia and U.S. Pacific Strategy: A Blueprint for the 1980s*. New York: Praeger, 1974.

Wenkam, Robert. (With text by Bryon Baker.) *Micronesia: The Breadfruit Revolution*. Honolulu: University Press of Hawaii, 1971.

Wilford, John Noble. "Banished Bikinians Sue U.S. for Nuclear Cleanup," *New York Times*, May 2, 1984, A25.

Williams, Maslyn. *Three Islands*. Adelaide: Griffin Press for British Phosphate Commissioners, 1971.

Williamson, Ian. "Island Population, Land Area, and Climate: A Case Study of the Marshall Islands," *Human Ecology*, 10, No. 1, March 1982, 71–84.

Ziehmn, Michael V. "Federal Land Ownership," *Guam Recorder* [Agana], 9, 1979, 42–50.

(Various issues of the following publications were also used in the preparation of this chapter: *Asian Survey*, January 1974-July 1984; *Asia Yearbook* [Hong Kong], 1974–84; *Christian Science Monitor*, January 1981-July 1984; *Far Eastern Economic Review* [Hong Kong], January 1974-July 1984; *Financial Times* [London], January 1982-July 1984; *Islands Business* [Suva], January 1982-July 1984; Joint Publications Research Service, *South and East Asia Report, January 1979-December 1982*, and *Southeast Asia Report*, January 1979; *New York Times*, January 1981-July 1984; *New Zealand International Review* [Wellington], January 1982-July 1984; *Pacific Affairs* [Vancouver], January 1977-July 1983; *Pacific Islands Monthly* [Sydney], January 1982-July 1984; *Pacific Perspective* [Suva], 1977–84; and *Washington Post*, January 1980-July 1984.)

Chapter 4

Barrett, David B. (ed.). *World Christian Encyclopedia: A Com-*

parative Study of Churches and Religions in the Modern World, A.D. 1900–2000. Nairobi: Oxford University Press, 1982.

de Beer, Patrice. "Tonga and Fiji: Racial Tensions and a Generation Gap," *Manchester Guardian Weekly* [London], September 25, 1983, 12–14.

Bellwood, Peter. *Man's Conquest of the Pacific: The Prehistory of Southeast Asia and Oceania.* Auckland: Collins, 1978.

Biersack, Aletta. "Tongan Exchange Structures: Beyond Descent and Alliance," *Journal of the Polynesian Society* [Auckland], 91, No. 2, June 1982, 181–212.

Bott, Elizabeth. "Power and Rank in the Kingdom of Tonga," *Journal of the Polynesian Society* [Auckland], 90, No. 1, March 1981, 7–81.

Bouck, Gary D. "The South Pacific Conference," *Business America,* 5, No. 20, October 4, 1982, 2–10.

de Bovis, Edmond. *Tahitian Society Before the Arrival of the Europeans.* (Monograph series, No. 1.) Laie: Institute for Polynesian Studies, Brigham Young University, Hawaii Campus, 1980.

Britain. Admiralty. Naval Intelligence Division. *Pacific Islands, Vol. II: Eastern Pacific.* (Geographical Handbook series, B.R. 519B.) London: 1943.

———. *Pacific Islands, Vol. III: Western Pacific (Tonga to the Solomon Islands).* (Geographical Handbook series, B.R. 519B.) London: 1944.

Buck, Peter H. *Introduction to Polynesian Anthropology.* (Reprint of 1945 ed. paper.) Millwood, New York: Kraus Reprint, n. d.

Campbell, I.C. "The Tu'i Ha'atakalaua and the Ancient Constitution of Tonga," *Journal of Pacific History* [Canberra], 17, No. 3, July 1982, 178–93.

"Canneries Pollute Bay," *Islands Business* [Suva], 9, No. 8, August 1983, 40–43.

Chilean Cultural Panorama. Washington: Cultural Department, Embassy of Chile, 1978.

Chile. Instituto Nacional de Estadísticos. *Compendio estadístico, 1981.* Santiago: Ministerio de Economía, Fomento, y Reconstrucción, 1981.

"Chile to Build Easter Island Naval Port," *Times of the Americas,* 27, No. 7, March 28, 1984, 1.

Craig, Robert D., and Frank P. King (eds.). *Historical Dictionary of Oceania.* Westport, Connecticut: Greenwood Press, 1981.

Crocombe, Ron G. *Land Tenure in Tonga—The Process of*

Change: Past, Present, and Future. Suva: South Pacific Social Sciences Association, 1975.

Davidson, J.W. *Samoa Mo Samoa*. Melbourne: Oxford University Press, 1967.

Daws, Gavan. *A Dream of Islands*. New York: Norton, 1980.

Deschamps, Hubert, and Jean Guiart. *Tahiti, Nouvelle-Calédonie, Nouvelles-Hébrides*. Paris: Éditions Berger-Levrault, 1957.

Ellem, Elizabeth Wood. "Sālote of Tonga and the Problem of National Unity," *Journal of Pacific History* [Canberra], 18, No. 3, July 1983, 162–82.

Faletau, Meleseini. "Changing Roles for Tonga's Women," *Pacific Perspective* [Suva], 11, No. 2, 1982, 45–55.

The Far East and Australasia, 1981–82. (13th ed.) London: Europa, 1981.

The Far East and Australasia, 1983–84. (15th ed.) London: Europa, 1983.

Finau, S.A., J.M. Stanhope, and I.A.M. Prior. "Kava, Alcohol, and Tobacco Consumption among Tongans with Urbanization," *Social Science and Medicine*, 16, 1982, 35–41.

Finney, Ben R. *Polynesian Peasants and Proletarians*. Cambridge, Massachusetts: Schenkman, 1973.

Fisk, E.K. "The Island of Niue: Development or Dependence for a Very Small Nation." Pages 441–58 in R.T. Shand (ed.), *The Island States of the Pacific and Indian Oceans: Anatomy of Development*. Canberra: Australian National University Press, 1980.

France. Conseil Économique et Social. *Les voies et moyens de l'expansion économique des territoires d'Outre-Mer du Pacifique*. Paris: 1977.

France. Embassy in New York. Press and Information Service. *French Polynesia*. (Documents from France series, No. 82/57.) New York: 1982.

France. Institut d'Émission d'Outre-Mer. *Exercice 1981, rapport d'activité: Polynésie Française*. Paris: 1981.

―――. *Exercice 1981, rapport d'activité: Wallis-et-Futuna*. Paris: 1981.

France. Institut National de la Statistique et des Études Économiques (INSEE). *Resultats du recensement de la population de la Polynésie Française: 29 Avril 1977*. Paris: 1979.

Freeman, Derek. *Margaret Mead and Samoa: The Making and Unmaking of an Anthropological Myth*. Cambridge: Harvard University Press, 1983.

Gray, J.A.C. *Amerika Samoa: A History of American Samoa and*

Its U.S. Naval Administration. Annapolis: United States
Naval Institute, 1960.

Hau'ofa, Epeli. *Our Crowded Islands*. Suva: Institute of Pacific
Studies, University of the South Pacific, 1977.

Henderson, John W., et al. *Area Handbook for Oceania*. (DA
Pam 550–94.) Washington: GPO for Foreign Area Studies,
The American University, 1971.

Howard, Edward. "Pitcairn and Norfolk: The Saga of Bounty's
Children," *National Geographic*, 164, No. 4, October 1983,
510–41.

Howarth, David. *Tahiti: A Paradise Lost*. London: Harvill Press,
1983.

Howells, William. *The Pacific Islanders*. New York: Scribner's
Sons, 1973.

Ingleton, Roy D. *Police of the World*. New York: Scribner's Sons,
1979.

Jane's Fighting Ships, 1983–84. (Ed., John Moore.) New York:
Jane's, 1983.

Keesing, Felix M. *Modern Samoa*. London: George Allen and
Unwin, 1934.

Kutscher, Mario Acha. "The Riddles of Easter Island," *UNESCO
Features* [Paris], No. 794, 1983, 1–4.

Langdon, Robert. *Tahiti: Island of Love*. (3d ed.) Sydney: Pacific,
1968.

Larmour, Peter, Ron Crocombe, and Anna Taugenga (eds.).
*Land, People, and Government: Public Lands Policy in the
South Pacific*. Suva: Institute of Pacific Studies, University of
the South Pacific, 1981.

Levy, Robert I. *Tahitians: Mind and Experience in the Society Islands*. Chicago: University of Chicago Press, 1973.

Lowenstein, Bill. "Land Boom in Samoa," *Islands Business*
[Suva], 9, No. 3, March 1983, 48.

Lynch, C.J. "Three Pacific Island Constitutions: Comparisons,"
Parliamentarian [London], 61, No. 3, July 1980, 133–41.

MacDonald, Barrie. "Tuvalu: The 1981 General Election" *Political Science* [Wellington], 35, No. 1, July 1983, 71–77.

Marcus, George E. "Succession Disputes and the Position of the
Nobility in Modern Tonga," (Pt. 1), *Oceania* [Sydney], 77,
No. 3, March 1977, 220–41.

—————. "Succession Disputes and the Position of the Nobility
in Modern Tonga," (Pt. 2), *Oceania* [Sydney], 77, No. 4, June
1977, 284–99.

Newbury, Colin W. *Tahiti Nui: Change and Survival in French
Polynesia, 1767–1945*. Honolulu: University Press of Hawaii,

1980.

New Zealand. Prime Minister's Department. External Intelligence Bureau. *Atlas of the South Pacific*. Wellington: Department of Lands and Survey, 1978.

————. *The Economy of Western Samoa*. Wellington: 1983.

Noricks, Jay S. *A Tuvalu Dictionary*, 1. New Haven: Human Relations Area Files Press, 1981.

Oliver, Douglas L. *The Pacific Islands*. (rev. ed.) Garden City, New York: Anchor Books, Doubleday, in cooperation with the American Museum of Natural History, 1961.

Pacific Islands Yearbook, 1981. (14th ed.) (Ed., John Carter.) Sydney: Pacific, 1981.

Paeniu, Isakala. "Who Controls Tuvalu?" *Islands Business* [Suva], 9, No. 10, October 1983, 26.

Patton, H. Milton. "The Pacific Basin: Toward a Regional Future," *State Government*, 53, Spring 1980, 68–76.

Richardson, John. "Cash Crisis Hits Samoa," *Islands Business* [Suva], 9, No. 8, August 1983, 12–17.

————. "A Nation on the Brink," *Islands Business* [Suva], 9, No. 7, July 1983, 28–30.

————. "The Not-So-Vocal Voice of Tonga," *Islands Business* [Suva], 9, No. 7, July 1983, 74.

————. "The World of the Sun King," *Islands Business* [Suva], 9, No. 7, July 1983, 32–33.

Rogers, Garth. "'The Father's Sister Is Black': A Consideration of Female Rank and Power in Tonga," *Journal of the Polynesian Society* [Auckland], 86, No. 2, June 1977, 157–82.

Rougié, Michel. *Île de Pâques: Îsla de Pascua; Easter Island*. Paris: Delroisse, 1979.

Roux, J.C. "Migration and Change in Wallisian Society." Pages 167–78 in R.T. Shand (ed.), *The Island States of the Pacific and Indian Oceans: Anatomy of Development*. Canberra: Australian National University Press, 1980.

Rutherford, Noel (ed.). *Friendly Islands: A History of Tonga*. Melbourne: Oxford University Press, 1977.

Sahlins, Marshall D. *Social Stratification in Polynesia*. Seattle: University of Washington Press, 1958.

Schweitzer, Niklaus R. "Tahiti's Long Road to Independence," *Swiss Review of World Affairs* [Zurich], 33, No. 8, November 1983, 21–25.

Siers, James. *Tahiti: Romance and Reality*. Wellington: Millwood Press, 1982.

"The South Pacific," *Australian Foreign Affairs Record* [Canberra], 52, No. 5, May 1981, 198–219.

Statistical Yearbook for Asia and the Pacific, 1981. Bangkok: United Nations, Economic and Social Commission for Asia and the Pacific, 1983.

Suggs, Robert C. *The Island Civilization of Polynesia*. New York: New American Library, n. d.

Thompson, Virginia M., and Richard Adloff. *The French Pacific Islands: French Polynesia and New Caledonia*. Berkeley and Los Angeles: University of California Press, 1971.

Tonga. Central Planning Department. *Fourth Five-Year Development Plan, 1980–85*. Nuku'alofa: 1981.

Topping, Donald M. *The Pacific Islands, Part I: Polynesia*. (American Universities Field Staff. Fieldstaff Reports. Southeast Asia, 25, No. 2.) New York: AUFS, 1977.

Trumbull, Robert. *Tin Roofs and Palm Trees: A Report on the New South Seas*. Seattle: University of Washington Press, 1977.

United States. Department of Commerce. Bureau of the Census. *World Population; Recent Demographic Estimates for the Countries and Regions of the World*. Washington: GPO, 1983.

United States. Department of State. *Country Reports on Human Rights Practices for 1983*. (Report submitted to United States Congress, 98th, 2d Session, House of Representatives, Committee on Foreign Affairs, and Senate, Committee on Foreign Relations.) Washington: GPO, February 1984.

United States. Department of State. Bureau of Intelligence and Research. *Status of the World's Nations, June 1983*. (Department of State publication, No. 8735.) Washington: GPO, 1983.

United States. Department of State. Bureau of Public Affairs. Office of Media Services. *Background Notes: Western Samoa*. (Department of State publication, No. 8334.) Washington: GPO, 1983.

United States. General Accounting Office. Comptroller General. *American Samoa Needs Effective Aid to Improve Operations and Become a Self-supporting Territory*. Washington: September 1978.

Urbanowicz, Charles F. "Drinking in the Polynesian Kingdom of Tonga," *Ethnohistory*, 22, No. 1, January 1975, 51–56.

"Welcome to a Micro-state," *Commonwealth* [London], December-January 1979, 14–15.

Western Samoa. *1984 Budget Statement by the Honourable Prime Minister and Minister of Finance, Hon. Tofilau Eti Alesana*. Apia: November 1983.

Western Samoa. Department of Economic Development. *Invest-ment in Western Samoa*. Apia: December 1982.

————. *A Substantial New Program for the 1980s*. Apia: 1980.

————. *Western Samoa's Fourth Five-Year Development Plan, 1980–84, Vol. II: Project Descriptions*. Apia: 1980.

Western Samoa. Department of Statistics. *Quarterly Statistical Bulletin, 3d Quarter*. [Apia], 45, July-September 1982 (entire issue).

Western Samoa. *Western Samoa: Socio-Economic Situation, Development Strategy, and Assistance Needs, Vol. I: Main Report*. (Prepared for the Asian-Pacific Round Table Meeting Concerning Implementation of the Substantial New Programme of Action for the Least Developed Countries.) Apia: December 1982.

A Yearbook of the Commonwealth, 1983. London: HMSO, 1983.

(Various issues of the following publications were also used in the preparation of this chapter: *Asian Survey*, January 1974-July 1984; *Asia Yearbook* [Hong Kong], 1974–84; *Christian Science Monitor*, January 1981-July 1984; *Far Eastern Economic Review* [Hong Kong], January 1974-July 1984; *Financial Times* [London], January 1982-July 1984; *Islands Business* [Suva], January 1982-July 1984; Joint Publications Research Service, *South and East Asia Report*, January 1979-December 1982, and *Southeast Asia Report*, January 1979; *Marchés tropicaux et méditerranees* [Paris], January 1982-December 1983; *Le Monde* [Paris], January 1982-May 1984; *New York Times*, January 1981-June 1984; *Pacific Islands Monthly* [Sydney], January 1982-May 1984; *Pacific Perspective* [Suva], 1977–1984; and *Washington Post*, January 1979-June 1984.)

Chapter 5

Albinski, Henry S. *The Australian-American Security Relationship*. New York: St. Martin's Press, 1981.

Argyle, Christopher. *Chronology of World War II*. New York: Exeter, 1980.

Australia. Ministry of Defence. *Defence Report, 1982–83*. Canberra: 1983.

Australia. Ministry of Foreign Affairs. *Australia's Overseas Developmental Assistance Program, 1983–84*. (1983–84 Budget Paper, No. 9.) Canberra: 1983.

Bergin, Anthony. "Fisheries and the South Pacific," *Asia Pacific Community* [Tokyo], No. 22, Fall 1983, 20–32.

Bowen, Alva M., Jr. "Pacific Ocean: Where the United States Goes the Limit," *Sea Power*, 26, No. 5, April 15, 1983, 78–83.

Britain. Admiralty. Intelligence Division. *Pacific Islands, Vol. I: General Survey*. (Geographical Handbook series, B.R. 519.) London: 1945.

———. *Pacific Islands, Vol. II: Eastern Pacific*. (Geographical Handbook series, B.R. 519B.) London: 1943.

Cameron, Allan W. "The Strategic Significance of the Pacific Islands: A New Debate Begins," *Orbis*, 19, No. 3, Fall 1975, 1012–36.

Charollais, Francois, and Jean de Ribes. *Stratégique: le défi de l'Outre Mer: l'action extérieure dans la défense de la France*. Paris: Fondation pour les Études de Défense Nationale, 1983.

Collier, Basil. *The Second World War: A Military History*. New York: Morrow, 1967.

Craig, Robert D., and Frank P. King (eds.). *Historical Dictionary of Oceania*. Westport, Connecticut: Greenwood Press, 1981.

Davis, Diane. "Armed Neutrality: An Alternative Defence Policy for New Zealand," *New Zealand International Review* [Wellington], 8, No. 1, January-February 1983, 24–25.

Dols, Richard J. "United States Strategic Interests and Concerns in Oceania." (Conference paper presented at symposium sponsored by the Pacific Islands Association, May 9, 1983.) Washington: May 1983.

Dorrance, John C. "Coping with the Soviet Pacific Threat," *Pacific Defence Reporter*, 10, No. 1, July 1983, 21–29.

———. *Oceania and the United States: An Analysis of U.S. Interests and Policy in the South Pacific*. (Monograph series, Nos. 80–86.) Washington: National Defense University, 1980

The Far East and Australasia, 1983–84. (15th ed.) London: Europa, 1983.

Fry, Gregory E. "Regionalism and International Politics of the South Pacific," *Pacific Affairs* [Vancouver], 54, No. 3, Fall 1981, 455–84.

Hart, B.H. Liddell. *History of the Second World War*. New York: Putnam's Sons, 1970.

Hearn, Terry. "Arms, Disarmament, and New Zealand," *New Zealand International Review* [Wellington], 8, No. 4, July-August 1983, 12–15.

Herr, Richard. "American Policy in the South Pacific: The Transition from Carter to Reagan," *New Zealand International Review* [Wellington], 8, No. 2, March-April 1983, 10–14.

————. "Preventing a South Pacific 'Cuba'," *New Zealand International Review* [Wellington], 7, No. 2, March-April 1982, 13–15.

Hill, Helen. "Stirring of Solidarity," *Far Eastern Economic Review* [Hong Kong], March 19, 1982, 34–36.

————. "A Winter of Discontent," *Far Eastern Economic Review* [Hong Kong], September 22, 1983, 44–45.

Hoyt, Edwin P. *Pacific Destiny: the Story of America in the Western Sea from the Early 1800s to the 1980s*. New York: Norton, 1981.

Huisken, Ron. *Defence Resources of South East Asia and the South West Pacific: A Compendium of Data*. Canberra: Australian National University, 1980.

James, Colin. "Shifts in the Wind," *Far Eastern Economic Review* [Hong Kong], September 8, 1983, 42–44.

Jane's Fighting Ships, 1981–82. (Ed., John Moore.) New York: Jane's, 1981.

Kay, Robin L. (ed.). *The Australian-New Zealand Agreement, 1944*, 1. Wellington: New Zealand Department of Internal Affairs, Historical Publications Branch, 1972.

Keesing's Contemporary Archives, 1963–64. (Eds., Walter Rosenberger and Herbert C. Tobin.) Bristol, England: Keesing's, 1964.

McLean, Denis. "The Case for Defence," *New Zealand International Review* [Wellington], 8, No. 3, May-June 1983, 15–20.

Maiava, Iosefa A. "Australia and the South Pacific: Politics and Defence," *Pacific Perspective* [Suva], 11, No. 1, 1982, 1–22.

Michel, Henri. *The Second World War*. New York: Praeger, 1975.

Mihaly, Eugene B. "Tremors in the Western Pacific: Micronesian Freedom and U.S. Security," *Foreign Affairs*, 52, No. 4, July 1974, 839–49.

Millar, T.B. "From Whitlam to Fraser," *Foreign Affairs*, 55, No. 4, July 1977, 854–72.

————. *International Security in the Southwest Asian and Southwest Pacific Region*. St. Lucia: University of Queensland, 1983.

————. "Weapons Proliferation and Security Problems in the South Pacific Region." Pages 222–35 in Robert O'Neill (ed.), *Insecurity! The Spread of Weapons in the Indian and Pacific Oceans*. Norwalk, Connecticut: Australian National University Press, 1978.

New Zealand. Ministry of Defence. *Report of the Ministry of Defence for the Year Ended 31 March 1976*. Wellington: Government Printer, 1976.

——. *Report of the Ministry of Defence for the Year Ended 31 March 1977*. Wellington: Government Printer, 1977.

——. *Report of the Ministry of Defence for the Year Ended 31 March 1978*. Wellington: Government Printer, 1978.

——. *Report of the Ministry of Defence for the Year Ended 31 March 1979*. Wellington: Government Printer, 1979.

——. *Report of the Ministry of Defence for the Year Ended 31 March 1980*. Wellington: Government Printer, 1980.

——. *Report of the Ministry of Defence for the Year Ended 31 March 1981*. Wellington; Government Printer, 1981.

——. *Report of the Ministry of Defence for the Year Ended 31 March 1982*. Wellington: Government Printer, 1982.

——. *Report of the Ministry of Defence for the Year Ended 31 March 1983*. Wellington: Government Printer, 1983.

Pacific Islands Yearbook, 1977. (12th ed.) (Ed., Stuart Inder.) Sydney: Pacific, 1977.

Pacific Islands Yearbook, 1981. (14th ed.) (Ed., John Carter.) Sydney: Pacific, 1981.

"Security Treaty Between Australia, New Zealand, and the United States of America." *Australian Outlook* [Canberra], 35, No. 2, August 1981, 201–202.

Smith, Thomas Rudman. *South Pacific Commission: An Analysis after Twenty-Five Years*. Wellington: Price Milburn, 1972.

Steinberg, Rafael. *Island Fighting*. Alexandria, Virginia: Time-Life, 1978.

Trumbull, Robert. "South Pacific: Russia Eyes an 'American Lake'," *U.S. News and World Report*, March 22, 1982, 37–39.

Turner, John. "Rethinking New Zealand's Defence Policy," *New Zealand International Review* [Wellington], 8, No. 2, March-April 1983, 15–17.

United States. Congress. 90th, 1st Session. House of Representatives. Committee on Foreign Affairs. *Collective Defense Treaties with Maps, Texts of Treaties, a Chronology, Status of Forces Agreements, and Comparative Chart*. Washington: GPO, 1967.

United States. Congress. 95th, 1st Session. Senate. Committee on Foreign Relations. Subcommittee on East Asian and Pacific Affairs. *The United States and the Emerging Pacific Islands Community*. Washington: GPO, July 1978.

United States. Congress. 97th, 1st Session. Senate. Committee on Foreign Relations. *Pacific Island Treaties*. Washington:

GPO, 1982.
United States. Congress. 98th, 1st Session. Senate. Committee on Foreign Relations. *Treaty of Friendship with the Republic of Kiribati*. Washington: GPO, March 1983.
United States. Department of Defense. Security Assistance Agency. *Congressional Presentation: Security Assistance Programs, FY 1984*. Washington: 1983.
United States. Department of the Interior. Office for Micronesian Status Negotiations. *Compact of Free Association*. Washington: 1983.
———. "The Negotiations for the Future Political Status of the Trust Territories of the Pacific Islands." Washington: September 1983.
———. "The Political Status Negotiations for the Trust Territory of the Pacific Islands and the Compact of Free Association." Washington: September 1983.
World Armaments and Disarmament: SIPRI Yearbook, 1980. London: Taylor and Francis for Stockholm International Peace Research Institute, 1980.
Young, P. Lewis. "Pacific Danger Signals," *Pacific Defense Reporter*, 8, No. 11, May 1982, 18–21.

(Various issues of the following publications were also used in the preparation of this chapter: *Asian Survey*, January 1974-July 1984; *Asia Yearbook* [Hong Kong], 1974–84; *Christian Science Monitor*, January 1981-July 1984; *Far Eastern Economic Review* [Hong Kong], January 1974-July 1984; *Financial Times* [London], January 1982-July 1984; *Islands Business* [Suva], January 1982-July 1984; Joint Publications Research Service, *South and East Asia Report*, January 1979-December 1982, and *Southeast Asia Report*, January 1979; *New York Times*, January 1981-July 1984; *New Zealand International Review* [Wellington], January 1982-July 1984; *Pacific Islands Monthly* [Sydney], January 1982-July 1984; *Pacific Perspective* [Suva], 1977–84; and *Washington Post*, January 1980-July 1984.)

Glossary

Australian dollar ($A)—Australian currency, divided into 100 cents. On average, $A1 was equivalent to US$1.14 in 1980, US$1.15 in 1981, US$1.02 in 1982, US$0.90 in 1983, and US$0.92 in April 1984.

cargo cult—One of a series of movements that have appeared in Melanesia since the late 1800s and that combine traditional religio-magic elements with Christian and Western secular themes. They are often based on the expectation that material goods or other cargo will soon come from the ancestors via some magic ship or airplane or from an ill-defined source. Noncooperation with the government is common among adherents, as is destruction or consumption of all the community's goods while awaiting the millennium.

CFPF—Cours du Franc Pacifique franc. Currency of French Polynesia and New Caledonia, divided into 100 centimes. US$1 equaled CFPF138.7 in June 1983.

Exclusive Economic Zone—A 200-nautical-mile belt of sea and seabed adjacent to a state's 12-nautical-mile territorial sea where the state claims preferential fishing rights and control over the exploitation of mineral and other natural resources.

Fiji dollar (F$)—Fiji currency, divided into 100 cents. On average, F$1 was equivalent to US$1.22 in 1980, US$1.17 in 1981, US$1.07 in 1982, US$0.98 in 1983, and US$0.96 in April 1984.

gross domestic product (GDP)—The value, in market prices, of all final goods and services for consumption and investment (excluding those intermediate to the production process) produced in an economy in a given period, usually a year. GDP is "gross" because it does not deduct depreciation costs and is "domestic" because it excludes income earned abroad and includes that earned by foreigners in the country. GDP is sometimes calculated at "factor cost" by deducting indirect taxes and adding subsidies.

gross national product (GNP)—Gross domestic product (q.v.) plus the income earned by domestic residents abroad (including investment income) less the income earned in the domestic economy by foreigners. These earnings are referred to as factor payments.

International Monetary Fund (IMF)—Established along with the World Bank (q.v.) in 1945, the IMF is a specialized agency affiliated with the United Nations and is responsible for stabilizing international exchange rates and payments. The main business of the IMF is the provision of loans to its members (including industrialized and developing countries) when they experience balance of payments difficulties. These loans frequently carry conditions that require substantial internal economic adjustments by the recipients, most of which are developing countries.

kina (K)—Papua New Guinea currency, divided into 100 toea. On average, K1 was equivalent to US$1.26 in 1977, US$1.41 in 1978 and 1979, US$1.49 in 1980 and 1981, US$1.36 in 1982, US$1.20 in 1983, and US$1.16 in April 1984.

Lomé Convention—The first Lomé Convention (Lomé I) came into force in 1976. Lomé II came into effect in 1981, and Lomé III was scheduled to start in 1985 after negotiations were completed in 1984. The convention covers economic relations between the members of the European Economic Community (EEC) and their former colonies in Africa, the Caribbean, and the Pacific (ACP). The convention allows most ACP exports to enter the EEC duty-free or at special rates and, among other things, provides funds to offset adverse fluctuations in the prices of ACP exports.

New Zealand dollar ($NZ)—New Zealand currency, divided into 100 cents. On average, $NZ1 was equivalent to US$0.97 in 1980, US$0.87 in 1981, US$0.75 in 1982, US$0.67 in 1983, and US$0.66 in April 1984.

shifting cultivation—Farming characterized by the rotation of fields rather than crops, the use of short cropping periods and long fallow periods, and the maintenance of fertility by the regeneration of natural vegetation on fallow land. Clearing of newly or previously cropped land is often accomplished by burning. Also called slash-and-burn, swidden, or land rotation agriculture.

Solomon Islands dollar (SI$)—Currency of Solomon Islands, divided into 100 cents. On average, SI$1 was equivalent to US$1.15 in 1979, US$1.20 in 1980, and US$1.16 in June 1983.

SPARTECA—South Pacific Regional Trade and Economic Cooperation Agreement. A nonreciprocal trade agreement between the members of the South Pacific Forum requiring Australia and New Zealand to offer duty-free, unrestricted, or special access for specified products made by other members of the forum (see Appendix B).

Tongan pa'anga (PT)—Tongan currency, divided into 100 seniti. The Tongan pa'anga is at par with the Australian dollar (*q.v.*).

Vanuatu vatu (VT)—Vanuatu's currency. As of June 1983, US$1 equaled VT99.41.

Western Samoa tala (WS$)—Western Samoan currency, divided into 100 sene. On average, WS$1 was equivalent to US$1.22 in 1979, US$1.09 in 1980, US$0.96 in 1981, US$0.83 in 1982, US$0.65 in 1983, and US$0.62 in April 1984.

World Bank—Informal name used to designate a group of three affiliated international institutions: the International Bank for Reconstruction and Development (IBRD), the International Development Association (IDA), and the International Finance Corporation (IFC). The IBRD, established in 1945, has the primary purpose of providing loans to developing countries for productive projects. The IDA, a legally separate loan fund but administered by the staff of the IBRD, was set up in 1960 to furnish credits to the poorest developing countries on much easier terms than those of conventional IBRD loans. The IFC, founded in 1956, supplements the activities of the IBRD through loans and assistance designed specifically to encourage the growth of productive private enterprises in the less developed countries. The president and certain senior officers of the IBRD hold the same positions in the IFC. The three institutions are owned by the governments of the countries that subscribe their capital. To participate in the World Bank group, member states must first belong to the International Monetary Fund (IMF—*q.v.*).

Index

Published Country Studies

(Area Handbook Series)

550–65	Afghanistan	550–151	Honduras
550–98	Albania	550–165	Hungary
550–44	Algeria	550–21	India
550–50	Angola	550–154	Indian Ocean
550–73	Argentina	550–39	Indonesia
550–169	Australia	550–68	Iran
550–176	Austria	550–31	Iraq
550–175	Bangladesh	550–25	Israel
550–170	Belgium	550–182	Italy
550–66	Bolivia	550–69	Ivory Coast
550–20	Brazil	550–177	Jamaica
550–168	Bulgaria	550–30	Japan
550–61	Burma	550–34	Jordan
550–83	Burundi	550–56	Kenya
550–50	Cambodia	550–81	Korea, North
550–177	Cameroon	550–41	Korea, South
550–159	Chad	550–58	Laos
550–77	Chile	550–24	Lebanon
550–60	China	550–38	Liberia
550–63	China, Republic of	550–85	Libya
550–26	Colombia	550–172	Malawi
550–91	Congo	550–45	Malaysia
550–90	Costa Rica	550–161	Mauritania
550–152	Cuba	550–79	Mexico
550–22	Cyprus	550–76	Mongolia
550–158	Czechoslovakia	550–49	Morocco
550–54	Dominican Republic	550–64	Mozambique
550–52	Ecuador	550–35	Nepal, Bhutan and Sikkim
550–43	Egypt	550–88	Nicaragua
550–150	El Salvador	550–157	Nigeria
550–28	Ethiopia	550–94	Oceania
550–167	Finland	550–48	Pakistan
550–155	Germany, East	550–46	Panama
550–173	Germany, Fed. Rep. of	550–156	Paraguay
550–153	Ghana	550–185	Persian Gulf States
550–87	Greece	550–42	Peru
550–78	Guatemala	550–72	Philippines
550–174	Guinea	550–162	Poland
550–82	Guyana	550–181	Portugal
550–164	Haiti	550–160	Romania